Peoples

of All Nations

TUNIS

See page 4957

Frontispiece—Vol. VII.

PEOPLES OF ALL NATIONS

Their Life Today and the Story of their Past

By Our Foremost Writers of Travel Anthropology & History

Illustrated with upwards of 5000 Photographs, numerous Colour Plates, and 150 Maps

Edited by

J. A. Hammerton

VOLUME VII
Pages 4673-5436

Including General Index

South Africa to Wales

Published at THE FLEETWAY HOUSE London E.C.

TABLE OF CONTENTS

Descriptive, Historical and Other Chapters

List of Colour Plates

Pages in Photogravure

Photographs in the Text

Photographs in the Text (contd.)

List of Maps

List of Colour Maps

South Africa

I. A New Nation in the Making

By Hamilton Fyfe

Author of "South Africa and Rhodesia To-Day"

THE people of South Africa probably present more problems to the square mile than any other part of the earth's surface. The whites are divided, not merely by difference of nationality, but by the memory of past quarrels and by charges of present unfair discrimination. There are many races of native inhabitants, each with its own particular grievance. There are a large number of Indians who are popular neither with black nor with white, yet who prosper and increase exceedingly.

How to evolve out of this human chaos a type of South African citizenship, how to induce all the conflicting elements to settle down and live contentedly together, seem, at first acquaintance with them, to be aims impossible of realization. Yet South Africa is on the way to realize them.

It was the belief that one of the two white nations in South Africa could impose its will on the other that hindered the country's development. To a certain extent, while much of the old rivalry and animosity has been swept away, the idea that the land should belong to one or the other still hampers that full cooperation between them that is essential to progress, and that alone can avert the danger of both of them being submerged by the blacks.

You may very likely get your first insight into what is called the native problem before you leave the docks at Cape Town. You see a train filled with natives : running in, if it be morning ; running out, if the time draw on towards night. Out of every window look out shining black faces, good-humoured, with liquid, often beautiful eyes, with kindly smiling expressions, most of them. They are the faces of dock labourers who live in a native settlement, a "location," not far from the city. They are brought in every morning and taken home every night.

All the hard work is left to them. South Africa is not a white man's country in the same sense as Canada and Australia and New Zealand are. The white man is the skilled worker, the overseer, the foreman. He must not offer the labour of his hands alone, for that would degrade him ; that would bring him into competition with the blacks. The white labourer would want higher wages than the black, the cost of production would rise, it would be hard to put the whole of the

RICKSHAW MAN IN DURBAN

Durban's rickshaw men are mostly Zulus. They wear very little clothing, but are fastidious about their headdress, which includes feathers and quills, and often a pair of cow's horns

DUTCH AFRIKANDER FARMER AND HIS FAMILY

Ten in the family, as here, is a fair average for the Boers or Dutch Afrikanders. The book, the frontispiece of which is being so proudly shown, is the " History of the Voertrekkers," a work held in great esteem by all Boers ; indeed, in many Dutch homesteads in South Africa, it forms with the Bible the whole of the family library.

Photo, Horace W. Nicholls

increase on the consumer, there would be grumbling all round.

The puzzle is complicated by there being many different grades of black intelligence. The Bantu tribes, including the Zulus, are higher in the scale than the Hottentots ; the Bushmen, so far as there are any left, occupy a lower place still. Then there are the half-castes, many in number, filled with ambition to take their places among the whites, ready to learn and capable of reaching the civilized condition.

The Cape boys, as they are called, may not make a very favourable impression as they parade the streets of Cape Town on a Sunday evening in knickerbocker suits, bowler hats, bow-ties of marvellous pattern, shoes with bulbous American toes. But get to know even these young men, who are not the pick of their race, and you cannot help liking them.

Faults they have (in common with all other people !) but these are largely the consequence of neglect. They have not until recent years had any decent chance of education. Go into one of

their schools and see how pathetically eager they are to take advantage of their opportunities. The children are nicely dressed, they are well-mannered. A teacher told me they were cleaner than London children : " I know both," she said.

Many of the " coloured " folk could hardly be distinguished by their appearance from white ; some of them speak with the accent and accuracy of the English population. They have the vote in Cape Colony, and they can sit in the Provincial Parliament. In spite of organized opposition, the coloured artisan has penetrated into most occupations, and even pure blacks have shown cleverness beyond the common in picking up highly skilled trades, such as electric light fitting. What would happen if all children were brought up alike it is hard to say. The influence of home would give many of the white boys and girls the advantage still, but the differences would be greatly diminished.

At present, owing to their lack of early discipline and education, the mass of the natives have to be treated like children. They may not have alcohol sold to them, they may not be out at night after a certain hour without a pass from their employer ; mine-workers are obliged to live in compounds, and are not allowed to have their wives with them. The wives stay at home to look after the family and the crops, while the men make enough to keep

HORSEMEN AND MARKSMEN FROM CHILDHOOD

Though possibly equalled by the Swiss, there are no better marksmen than the Dutch Afrikanders, a fact brought to light during the South African War ; and they are equally expert in horsemanship. At one time it was the custom for the boys to be sent out in the morning with but one cartridge and expected to return with food for the day

Photo, Horace W. Nicholls

BUSY CORNER OF AN OPEN-AIR MARKET AT CAPE TOWN UNDER THE SHADOW OF TABLE MOUNTAIN

The beautiful capital of the Cape Province of the Union of South Africa rises like a vast amphitheatre between the crescent-shaped Table Bay and the imposing mass of Table Mountain, which towers grandly behind it. In its physical features among the most picturesque cities in the world, Cape Town is made additionally attractive by its modern architecture, the Parliament Buildings and City Hall being especially notable, while its parks, gardens, playgrounds, stately avenues of oaks and pines, and pink and purple covered mountain slopes have won for it the name of the City of Flowers

EARLY MORNING ACTIVITY IN THE MARKET SQUARE OF THE CITY OF CONFERENCES

Capital of the Orange Free State and seat of the provincial government, Bloemfontein is situated nearly 5,000 feet above sea-level and commands glorious views over the illimitable veld. Well laid out in broad streets, with a fine market square in the centre, its numerous public buildings are mainly of red brick and white stone. Facing the market square is the historic and colonnaded Raadzaal, once the meeting-place of the Free State Raad and now of the provincial council. An important educational centre, the city possesses a training school for aviators and other units of the Union Defence Force

Photo, South African Government

them in idleness for a good long time. It has always been the custom for the women to do all the work except attending to the cattle. The men do that and they hunt, not for amusement, but for the purpose of stocking their larders; otherwise they do nothing.

STURDINESS AND STOLIDITY
He is a wealthy farmer of the Dutch Afrikander class. In the old days he would have been described as a Boer, but this name is becoming obsolete
Photo, Horace W. Nicholls

Very few who work regard their occupation as anything but temporary. They will submit themselves to unpleasant conditions, adopt regular habits, live in compounds, for a time, in order to be able to buy a wife, or to add to their land, but they look forward to returning home after a certain period of exile. Natal has a separate and distinct coloured difficulty dating back to the importation into the districts which grow sugar and tea of many thousands of Indian coolies. The natives were found to be too careless to cultivate plantations such as these; the Indians were glad to come. Now there is general regret that they were ever sent for. In Cape Colony there are also a number of East Indians, but they are the descendants of the "Malays," as they are called, who came from the Dutch colonies when South Africa was in the possession of Holland.

The street fish-sellers in Cape Town are Malays; they blow a melancholy horn to announce their wares. In their particular quarter of the city the visitor finds himself among an Oriental population. Men in turbans and cotton petticoats hurry by. Women with brightly coloured handkerchiefs round their heads, and gaudy stuffs swathed loosely about their fat bodies, seek to draw passers-by into their shops. Slim veiled women stand in doorways enjoying the spectacle of life. From the tower of a mosque the muezzin sounds the call to prayer, for they have held to the faith of Islam; they are a decent, hardworking race.

If you happen to go on the same day into this slice of the East, and to the country house of one of the Cape English families, in that delightful district which lies close to Cape Town you notice an extraordinary contrast. The English family lives a spacious, comfortable life; it speaks in a slow, masterful way, with an accent of cultivation, such as in England has almost disappeared. These pleasant people have big pleasant houses set among parks and wide meadows; they are interested still in horses; they play cricket; they enjoy themselves with that gusto and that leisurely determination to miss nothing that can give satisfaction or add to their physical well-being, which used to characterise the leisured class in England. Both the climate and the tradition inherited from the early Dutch settlers have contributed to save this small remnant of nineteenth century survivors from infection by the restlessness and hustle of the twentieth.

The Dutch were stolid, and they loved comfort. The sunshine and the soft air make an easy life the most agreeable. Yet the number of those who can take life easily diminishes. Both the old English type and the old Dutch type are dying out. What is arising to take their place is the Afrikander race, which is something quite distinct from either, and a phenomenon that must be studied before one can either understand the present of South Africa, or hazard any forecast of the country's future. That the Dutch strain in the Afrikanders is a little stronger than the English strain may be gathered from these figures. Of the white population in Cape Colony, seventy per cent., twenty years ago, were D u t c h. In the Orange River Colony the proportion was eighty-five per cent.; in the Transvaal, sixty per cent. Only in Natal was there a preponderance of British-born; there the Dutch were only one-quarter of the white inhabitants. Yet the structure of life tends to become more and more British, or perhaps it would be more correct to say Afrikan.

The Afrikander grows up with two languages at his command, English and the Taal. Some philological purists would object that the Taal is not a language. Certainly it varies a good deal in different parts of the country; no a t t e m p t has ever been made to standardise it. As it is taught in schools, as it is spoken in church and in the law courts, as it is written in the newspapers, it is not the Taal which is spoken in everyday life. The more formal speech is a good deal closer to Dutch than the colloquial, which has been simplified as much as possible, and has had numbers of words from other tongues, even native tongues, incorporated in it.

It is thus possible to hear three varieties of Dutch spoken by Afrikanders: true Dutch, as it is used in Holland; the local form of that language which is used for educational and public purposes; and the Taal. This division

TILLERS OF THE MEALIE FIELDS
Except tending the cattle, all the work of a Zulu community is done by the women. Maize is the staple food, and the cultivation of the mealie fields, as of the millet, sweet potatoes, and vegetables, is wholly in female hands
Photo, South African Government

BOER FARMER, WITH HIS FAMILY AND HOUSEHOLD GOODS ON A BULLOCK WAGON, TREKKING TO A NEW HOME

Though South Africa has its great townships possessing all the amenities of modern civilization, the trek by bullock wagon over the veld is not yet a thing of the past. This fine photograph of a Dutch household on its way across the open country makes a strong appeal to the imagination, an essentially human touch being provided by the sight of mother and infant in the lumbering wagon. Meanwhile her sturdy spouse, with long ox-goad over his shoulder, urges on the train of powerful and patient beasts yoked to the vehicle laden with his household goods

Photo, Horace W. Nicholls

LIGHT-HEARTED KAFFIR BOYS INDULGING IN A CONCERTED SONG AND DANCE

It is in their action dances of all kinds that the childish element in the negro character finds its fullest expression among all African tribes. Among the Kaffirs in the south the dance commonly degenerates into an orgy lasting all night and accompanied by the consumption of vast quantities of native beer, and very often entailing considerable trouble next morning for the revellers, who will probably have to appear in a police court to answer charges of being drunk and disorderly and out at night without a pass—this last a serious offence from the white man's point of view

SERGEANT AND CONSTABLES OF SOUTH AFRICA'S NATIVE POLICE

Natives have been employed in police work in South Africa for many years, and have proved so efficient that between two and three thousand of them are now on the strength. At the establishment of the Union centralisation of administration became necessary, and the pre-existing police forces of the constituent provinces were placed under a chief commissioner at Pretoria

Photo, Horace W. Nicholls

makes it easier for English to conquer, as it is conquering steadily and surely, though not very fast.

What has happened in Cape Colony, so far as language is concerned, is bound in time to happen throughout the land. The wealthy Dutch families there have become scarcely distinguishable from the British, except by their names. They have adopted English ways of life, they send their sons to schools and universities in England; they found long ago that it was more convenient to speak English among themselves.

The Afrikanders will be a blend, they will have their own racial characteristics, just as those of the English have been developed from the union of " Norman and Saxon and Dane," with a dash of Celt added.

The Boers (a word which means simply " farmers," and is dropping out of use) looked upon the native as an inferior animal created to work for the white man, and deserving of no consideration at the white man's hands. Their harshness to the blacks helped to create the prejudice against the Boers which persisted in Britain until quite recent years. They were, of course, nothing like the picture formed of them by the popular imagination. They are, in truth, not unlike the Lowland Scots, with one marked difference. Whereas the soil and climate of Scotland have forced habits of hard work upon the population, the Boer has found it easy to make a living and is often inclined to be lazy.

The Boer has much the same Calvinistic religion as the Scot ; he shows the same carefulness where money is concerned, though he often makes a bad bargain just because he tries to be too " slim." He has, too, the same appreciation of pawky humour. He is not

STURDY ZULU CHILDREN IN THEIR KRAAL IN NATAL
Unlike those of America and Australia, the natives of South Africa have thriven in contact with civilization and multiplied exceedingly. Child life in the kraals is care-free under British rule, and boys and girls grow up to vigorous adolescence in conditions familiar for ages to their race, with no clothes to worry about, and happy with the simplest playthings
Photo, Horace W. Nicholls

SOLEMN CONSULTATION WITH A ZULU MEDICAL MAN

Zulu doctors have been shorn of much of their former power to inspire awe. Their " mystery " embraced less of medicine than faculty of " smelling out " criminals, especially poisoners, whose fate after exposure by a witch-doctor was summary. Smelling out was discountenanced by Cetywayo, and was finally suppressed by the British at the beginning of this century

Photo, W. H. Craft

a quick thinker, though at times he can surprise one by a witty retort or a pithy comment. He is far too obstinate and self-opinionated to be driven from any of his beliefs or conceptions, but he can be led by those who take the trouble to understand him.

At one period the Boers were inclined to regard themselves as the successors of the Children of Israel, as a people chosen by the Lord, for whose benefit all other peoples were to be destroyed. The injunction to be hospitable they obey readily, and they entertain strangers with a very pleasant absence of formality or self-consciousness.

The best they have is brought out as a matter of course. Their manners are naturally courteous. Snobbery is a fault from which they are free, until they take to town life ; then it sometimes becomes a very bad fault.

Their large families are, undoubtedly, a help to the Boers in farming, but the practice of dividing up land among a number of children, either voluntarily or legally, if the possessor left no will, has led to the creation of a dispossessed class, a class of poor relations, which adds another to the many problems in South Africa. These " Bywoners," as they are called, cultivate small plots of land, on which they are allowed to put their huts and eke out their livelihood by working for others. They have no incentive to produce more than they need, for they may at any moment be turned off their plots.

Most of them keep their pride of race and a certain dignity, which often strikes a stranger as being absurdly out of place. For example, they will not, however dire their poverty may be, let their children earn money by domestic service. That they hold to be " work for Kaffirs " ; they will not condescend to compete with the blacks.

That the Dutch Afrikanders have tried since the Union of South Africa came into being to get as many jobs as possible out of English and into Dutch hands is undeniable. But it is not the outcome of racial jealousy so much as the desire to secure well-paid places for themselves. In South Africa the Dutch feel that, as they form the majority of white people, they ought to have most of the political advantages, and most of the salaries, too.

It is natural enough that a majority should dislike being governed mainly by officials belonging to the minority, and resent having their language treated as if it did not matter. The Canadians would have just the same grievance if most of their Ministers and a great many of their most responsible officials were men from England. As soon as there is a South African nation this difficulty will disappear. It is the result of long-continued colonial government. Since there have been Dutch Premiers of the Union, Botha and Smuts, it has been diminishing. When all are Afrikanders such jealousies and rivalries will have become evils of the past.

It is in Cape Colony that one is reminded most of the long supremacy of the English, and more than anywhere

SCANTY AND SIMPLE PLENISHING OF A ZULU HOME

Furniture interests the Zulu hardly at all, and presents no practical problem to a young couple setting up housekeeping. A few pots, notably tripod iron pots, some gourd vessels and earthenware jars, including a large one for mealies, one or two low stools, and a few skins represent the sum of their household gear, with perhaps a little matting and cheap printed calico

else, in Cape Town. The policemen remind you of English policemen by their air of calm authority, although their helmets are white instead of blue. The telegraph boys look the same. The names over the shops are mostly English.

Adderley Street, running up from the sea to the cathedral, and then merging into a pleasant shady avenue, has an unmistakably English look. On one side of the avenue are the

not so many anxieties. English, too, are the suburban roads—Newlands Avenue, with its oaks that are well over a century old, the road to Constantia, and its vineyards, the road through Weinberg with the tidy houses set back in their trim gardens. But not at all British the exquisite soft scenery of the Cape Peninsula, the vivid blues and greens of the sea, the brilliant blossoms on the shore, the

PUTTING THE FINISHING TOUCHES TO A COIFFURE IN NATAL
While the Zulus pay comparatively little attention to costume they are very fastidious about their hair, and the women will spend a long time arranging one another's coiffure. Twisted into clay-daubed ringlets, it is worn low down over the eyes and to the nape of the neck, each little rope at the sides and back of the head being finished off with a ring
Photo, South African Government

Houses of Parliament and the gardens of Government House; on the other, a museum and a botanical garden. On the slope of the mountain, higher up than the famous Mount Nelson Hotel, are the houses of the important people, with glorious views across the bay to other mountains dimly visible in the clear air. Except for the sunshine and the views, you might think yourself in England—not the England of to-day, but of thirty years ago, when there was more leisure and self-confidence, and

deep clefts of Table Mountain filled with flowering shrubs, orchids, and ferns.

Such lovely surroundings, such generous sunshine, make for smoothness of temperament; they incline towards taking life easily, though the south-easterly winds, which are not infrequent, give the air a bracing touch at times and keep the city healthy.

One can understand why politics are taken more seriously in Pretoria. In winter the weather there is crisp and clear; in summer the damp heat brings

ZULU BUILDERS AT WORK UPON AN ELIGIBLE FAMILY RESIDENCE

Zulu huts are of the beehive type of architecture. The framework consists of flexible branches or saplings set firmly in the ground and bent over to form hoops, increasing in height to the middle of the hut. These are interlaced with withes horizontally, and the whole is thatched with leaves or grasses. The only aperture is a low archway through which the occupants pass on hands and knees

PUNCTILIOUS RELIGIOUS AVOIDANCE OF A MOTHER-IN-LAW

" Hlonipa " is the name given to a remarkable custom prevailing among the Zulus whereby a man carefully avoids meeting his wife's mother, and if he comes across her unexpectedly hides his face until he has passed her. Similarly a woman shuns both her husband's parents, and, further, must not utter their names. The custom originated in the system of taboo, found all over the world

HANDSOME WOMEN OF THE FORMIDABLE ZULU RACE

The Zulu woman's hair is arranged in fantastic fashions, twisted and plastered into a hard high top-knot or wonderfully waxed into myriad hanging curls, while much bead and bone trumpery adorns her scanty clothing. The Zulus are lively and sociable, gifted with great natural intelligence, and something of the proud bearing of conquerors is still manifest in every member of this intrepid race

Photo, South African Government

DUSKY CITIZENS OF WHITE MAN'S AFRICA

The Zulus have long been distinguished as the most warlike of Bantu tribes, and though slowly assimilating the precepts of Christianity and the white man's civilization they show no disposition to forget their old-time independence, and the peaceful occupations which are theirs to-day have not obliterated memories of the wild war-dances and wilder orgies of their grim past

Photo, South African Government

"BEFORE MAN MADE US CITIZENS GREAT NATURE MADE US MEN"

Proud and haughty, as becomes the descendants of a race of warriors whose military genius secured the ascendancy in South Africa until its conquest by white civilization, the Zulus are a people from whom Europeans might learn a good deal. Physically the men are superb, with intelligent faces and a native dignity that marks them as true aristocrats in their proper state and own environment

Photo, Horace W. Nicholls

out irritability, increases intolerance and political animosity. Lying in a hollow among the low hills, the town is delightfully green. It has ceased to be a glorified village, and has risen to its position as the seat of government for six months in the year.

It was an inconvenient arrangement to divide between Pretoria and Cape Town the honour of being the capital of the Union ; it had to be made in order to propitiate opinion in both places. The one benefit it has brought has been to endow Pretoria with government buildings that display Mr. Herbert Baker's genius for classical architecture touched with modern feeling.

Not until these were well in hand did Bloemfontein give up all hope that some day it might be the capital. It is in a central position, it is healthy, it is well laid out with good roads and water and l i g h t and drainage. But there is another reason now for considering Bloemfontein out of the running. Should Southern Rhodesia enter the Union, then Pretoria will be more like the centre of the Federation. In time it is likely to become the sole centre of government, and quite possibly Parliament may sit there as well.

Near Pretoria is a famous diamond mine, the Premier, but that is an outcrop from the chief diamond-mining district of the Union, which lies around Kimberley. Between Cape Town and Kimberley lies the Karroo, the stony desert which needs only water to make it bring forth plenteously all the fruits of the earth. The farms are irrigated,

and prosper. Here you can see ostriches mincing their way along, two and two, with brainless gaze. You also notice sheep and goats, engaged, as it may well seem to you, in eating stones.

SNAKE-LIKE COIFFURE OF A ZULU BELLE

Zulu women are magnificent creatures physically, muscularly strong, erect in carriage, graceful in movement, and statuesque in pose. A favourite fashion of dressing the hair is to twist the strands into tight curls and fix them with clay

Photo, Horace W. Nicholls

Barren though the light brown soil looks, the scrub which covers it provides feed for these animals ; millions of them flourish upon it. Thus the monotony of the vast expanse of rocky flatness, broken by low hills, is relieved by signs of life. The mimosa hangs golden among its wicked thorns and scents the hot air. Patches of a flower like sea-lavender gladden the eye. At night there is a bracing freshness in the air, for the Karroo lies a good deal higher than Cape Town. As you go north, you rise all the time ; though

CONCERTED MOTION THAT STRIKES TERROR INTO THE HEART: A ZULU IMPI PERFORMING THE WAR DANCE

Of all war dances still performed among native races that of the Zulus is the most impressive. In their war-paint, with nodding plumed headdresses, striped hide shields and short stabbing assegais, they are formidable figures, even taken singly. Drawn up in crescent battle array an impi is a sight to make even a brave enemy anxious. It is in this formation that the war dance is performed, the regiment stamping the feet till the earth shakes with the rhythmical thud, brandishing weapons, uttering cries, and representing all the actions of a fight to the death

you are travelling towards the Equator, the climate becomes less hot.

Hot enough in the day-time is Kimberley, though; but dry, and therefore bearable. The people look as if it agreed with them thoroughly. They live in pretty, creeper-covered houses along wide, green roads. They sit on verandas or " stoeps," as they are called in Dutch; they play lawn tennis. The white workers for the De Beers Company have a village of their own called Kenilworth, prettily-built houses all among a wood, each with its garden, where flowers grow in luxuriance on what used to be bare veld.

It was in 1869 that diamonds were discovered in the blue clay, and since then an enormous amount of money has been put into the ground, with the result that a far larger quantity of wealth has been taken out. When you see the stones in their original state lying on the tables in the sorting office, you wonder how it was that anyone could recognize them for diamonds.

Precious Contents of the Blue Clay

The natives live in compounds, where they are made comfortable and encouraged to be clean in their habits.

All the hard manual labour of the diamond mines is done by them. They fill trucks with the blue clay in which the stones are found. For many months it lies out on the open veld in the sun so that it may become friable and ready to be dealt with. As it comes up at first, it is too stiff to do anything with. The ground on which it lies is called " the floors," and has to be guarded by armed men as well as being surrounded by barbed wire.

When the clay is ready to be crushed it is put into trucks again and disintegrated with water and strong-toothed machinery. Out of a hundred truckloads of clay one load of diamond-bearing gravel is obtained. This one load goes into a machine, which sorts the stones into six different sizes and throws the soil aside. Then an uncanny

contrivance, called the Pulsator, separates the heavy stones, among which are the diamonds, from the light, which are worthless. After this all that remain are turned on to an inclined plane covered with thick grease. The diamonds being the heavier—and a few of the heavier pebbles stick to the grease—the worthless lighter pebbles are carried away by running water. The final choice is made in the office.

A City Founded on a Gold Reef

Not so easy is it to see the process of winning the other precious export of South Africa. When you go down a gold mine, you must put on old clothes and old boots and be prepared for a fatiguing time. There are long walks to be taken through the workings, if you want to see everything; there are slopes down which you must wriggle on your stomach, where the loose shale shifts beneath you and the hard rock above bumps your head.

Here you see the making of the holes into which the dynamite charges are fitted so that the reef may be blasted away. After the explosions have brought down the rock, it is loaded into skips and run up to the surface, where it is crushed and ground, until it has become sand that will go into the stamps.

If Johannesburg Lost Its Gold

After this final treatment, which reduces the sand to an even finer condition, it is carried over a table covered with quicksilver. To this a good deal of the gold sticks. The rest is compelled to yield itself up by the cyanide process, which is carried on with a welcome absence of noise in tanks.

What would happen to Johannesburg if the gold-mining which made it were to be abandoned, who can say? It might decay and cease to be, or it might, with the aid of electric current generated at the Victoria Falls, fifteen hundred miles away, become a manufacturing centre.

SOUTH-WEST AFRICAN NEGROES ENJOYING A REST BY THE WAY

Pristine savage life is just outside the doors of white civilization in South Africa. In the towns the natives may swagger about in knickerbocker suits and bowler hats, but in the country one comes upon them in conditions unchanged from those of their forebears a hundred years ago. These natives, resting from their never very exhausting labours, are of the Bantu race, settled in South-West Africa, now administered by the Union under mandate. The picture of savagery they present could be matched any day within a walk of almost any South African town

Johannesburg is a pleasant place to live in if you can afford one of the houses among the firs on the rocky Parktown ridge. From here you look down on the Wood, which, like the Wood at The Hague, offers the citizens the chance to walk or ride in delightful surroundings quite close to busy streets. It was planted to provide timbers for mine-props thirty years ago; luckily, the tree-cutting was stopped before it had spoiled the beauty of the big plantation. Now it makes a most attractive park.

Beyond, the open country rolls towards distant mountains. No wonder men and women who have lived in this invigorating air with that view before them long for it when they have left it, and call English scenery tame.

Cities of Wealth and Civic Pride

Yet, in general, the Johannesburg people have little thirst for beauty of any kind. There are sets which go in for New Thought—for drama, for interest in painting (which they can satisfy at their distinguished little picture gallery), for the latest in poetry and fiction. But, added all together, these are only a small minority. For the most part the interests of Johannesburg are material.

Even more is this true of Durban than it is of Johannesburg. The Durban people are rich and hospitable, they have a great deal of civic pride which has prompted them to build a magnificent town hall, they have constructed docks, which are models of what docks ought to be, they live in villas smothered by flowering creepers and with gardens round them which make your eyes ache with their vivid colour; yet, somehow, the impression the visitor brings away from Durban is mostly that of a rather dull society, content to be wealthy and not greatly interested in much that lies beyond its own concerns.

There is a keener and fresher intellectual life in Pietermaritzburg, where the provincial council sits; this is little more than a country town, but it has the atmosphere of a place where other things are thought of than making money and adding to the comforts of life.

The Indian Factor in South Africa

In Natal the natives have been treated harshly, even more harshly than they were treated by the Boers, which is saying a good deal. Again, Natal's treatment of Indians has been unfortunate. The colonists wanted labour sixty years ago, and invited some twelve hundred natives of India to cross the ocean and work in their tea and sugar plantations. There are now in Natal close on 150,000 Indians. They add another to the many problems of South Africa. All kinds of efforts have been made to keep any more from immigrating, and to induce or compel some of those who are there already to return to India; but nothing stops their steady increase. They work hard, are quick to scent opportunities for enterprise, and flourish in the hot, damp climate, and can live while they are making a start in trade on a tenth part of what the white man requires.

In the Transvaal the attempts to keep the Indians out have been even more desperate than in Natal. Yet the agitation and the hardships inflicted do not prevent them from keeping pretty well all the small stores in large areas of South Africa.

Indian Merchants and White Mechanics

They are not confined now to small business. They have gone in for commerce on the large scale, and they show so much more enterprise than the white trader that they can often get financial accommodation when the white man seeks it in vain.

Once they have started up the ladder of prosperity they very seldom turn back. Thus you may see in Durban Indian merchants being driven in their motor cars by white mechanics, and even on the Berea, the range of hills behind the city with glorious views over the harbour and the ocean, they have

WEALTH BEYOND THE DREAMS OF AVARICE ON THE "FLOORS" OF THE DE BEERS MINES AT KIMBERLEY

Kimberley is the centre of the diamond-mining district of the Union of South Africa. The diamonds are found in the blue clay, the crystals varying in size from microscopic dust to quite large pebbles. The stiff clay is brought up from the mines in trucks and turned out on to the open veld in the sun so that it may become friable and ready to be dealt with. The ground on which it is dumped is called the "floors," and is surrounded by barbed-wire entanglements and guarded by armed men. A hundred truck-loads of this clay yield one load of diamond-bearing gravel

BLACK WORKERS WHO RETRIEVE THE PRECIOUS PEBBLES FROM THE BLUE CLAY OF KIMBERLEY'S DIAMOND FIELD

About 98 per cent. of the world's diamond supply comes from South Africa, and the great centre of the industry is Kimberley, where diamonds were discovered in 1869. Here we see debris washing being carried on at the St. Augustine mine by black workers under white supervision. Not only the hard manual labour of the mines, but the sorting also is done by blacks, who sit at white tables all day in rooms with large windows and no blinds, and, with a speed surprising to the uninitiated, separate the true stones from the false, under the watchful eye of a trained official;

Photo, South African Government

YOUTHFUL NATIVE SORTERS AT THE OPEN-AIR TABLES OF THE PREMIER DIAMOND MINE NEAR PRETORIA

The largest diamond-bearing "pipe" found so far in South Africa is at the Premier mine, near Pretoria, an outcrop from the principal field around Kimberley. Here, in 1905, was discovered the famous Cullinan diamond, a clear, white-water stone of 3,025¾ carats, or rather less than 1¼ lb. Purchased by the Transvaal Government and presented to King Edward VII., it was cut into nine large stones and a number of small brilliants. The largest of the cut stones, known as "The Star of South Africa," is now in the British sceptre, and the next largest is in the British crown

Photo, South African Government

pushed in among the white "best people." In the tea gardens almost all the work is done by Indians, and the tea planters say the talk about getting rid of them is all rubbish. Neither tea nor sugar could be made to pay without Indian labour. Besides, you cannot clear 150,000 people out of a country. There they are, and there they will go on increasing ; of that there can be no doubt.

Many of them live in conditions which are neither attractive nor sanitary. They are not as clean in their personal habits as the natives, they are not as orderly in their homes. They may at times become a danger to the health of the community by breeding epidemics.

Indian Industry and Versatility

But they are quick at picking up Western ways and at copying Western manners ; they are intelligent as well as industrious ; their children are anxious to learn to be like white people ; wherever they compete with whites, they hold their own, as much as clerks in banks and business offices, as lawyers' clerks or draughtsmen for architects, as in small storekeeping or the Durban tailoring trade. They have taken to playing football and other games.

So far they have not taken any part in politics. They have not got votes and they do not ask for them with any vigour. But in time they must be admitted to full citizenship, and then they are likely to bring forward the project which appeals to many of them, the shipment of more and more Indians to South Africa so that the country may be filled up and the vast spaces which are now uncultivated turned to good account. From such a prospect the white South African recoils in disgust. But there is no likelihood of the country ever being filled up by whites or even of the whites forming the majority of the population.

The black people certainly impress one more favourably when one sees them in their habit as they lived before the coming of the whites than when they wear trousers and bowler hats. The very fact that association does make them want to be like the whites proves that it is useless to try and keep them children, useless to say "They are happier without education."

Educational Ambition of the Blacks

It may be true. One is tempted to believe it when one sees the weedy products of the colleges and notices spectacles over tired eyes, and contrasts the cheerful nakedness of the bush native with the weary, disillusioned air of many native teachers. Yet how can we expect races which are told they are inferior not to aim at resembling those who vaunt themselves upon their superiority ?

The blacks hunger and thirst after education because they think it will make them equal to the whites. They object to any kind of teaching which is different from that provided for white people. "Why should it be different ?" they ask. When it is suggested that it would be better for them to go in for manual training, they say : "The white children and young people do not learn to make chairs and tables. Why should we ?"

Negro Envy of the Indian

The Indians are not so much interested in education. They are born with minds more acute, or else their minds are sharpened in childhood by association with their elders. They are quick at picking up information as they go along. The blacks envy them, feel some resentment against them, call them interlopers, ask why they should have privileges which are denied to the native races (such as buying land anywhere, trading anywhere, procuring drink). In the scale of intellect the Indian is a good deal higher than the negro, which makes many of the former complain when they are compelled to share railway carriages or the cheaper parts of theatres with all kinds of

NATIVE CHARM FREE FROM GLOSS OF ART
Costume, or lack of it, in Africa is a matter of tribal custom only.
Dress means personal adornment, and her beaded necklaces and
earrings and scarified skin are as important to this smiling
girl as her scanty beaded apron
Photo, Horace W. Nicholls

ways. If this is remarked upon, the reply is, "Oh, but what could we do without them ? "

The native girls, oddly enough, do not make nearly such good " helps." One merit they have, however ; they are not so keen as the " boys " upon dances. A native dance is a tremendous affair. It means getting drunk on native beer, staying up all night, being out minus a " pass " very likely (which is an offence for a black man), and turning up in the morning, if there is any turning up at all, sleepy and stupid after the exercise and liquor combined.

Basutoland, with Bechuanaland Protectorate, which is on the other side of the Free State, is outside the Union. Neither the Basutos nor the Bechuanas want to be taken in. Bechuanaland Protectorate is rather an attractive-looking country, not unlike the Harz or the Black Forest,

aborigines. One thing that surprises all visitors is that the whites, although they will not allow natives near them in public, employ them in their homes as a matter of course. They are as a rule good servants. They pad about noiselessly, they are good-tempered, they are fond of children, they are clean. They have a fairly easy time of it. Quite early in the evening they depart to their quarters at some little distance from the house ; they are well paid and for the most part decently treated. No one seems to think it strange that they should slip in and out of rooms, listen to conversation, pick up white people's

and a good pasture land. Here the natives are, as far as they can be, " unspoilt," yet they have just the same desire to adopt the white man's dress on ceremonial occasions and to move up towards an equality with him.

Once it was thought that the blacks had no system of morality, that no training of character was practised among them. Now we know better. We have learnt that there exist strict codes of tribal customs and taboos. We are aware of the nature of native discipline.

It is unfortunate that white influence should have been exerted in the direction of making this discipline less effective. Under the intoxication of the Victorian idea that European civilization was the ideal to be imposed on all sorts and conditions of men, it was thought a duty to uproot any other attempts at civilization to be met with. The religious missions especially undertook this clearing of the ground ; then pioneers who wanted cheap and plentiful labour found it politic to break up native ways of existence.

But you can still find hundreds of native kraals where people live as they have lived for countless ages. In the beehive-shaped huts they have no furniture. Their possessions are a few pots, a big earthenware jar of mealies, a few skins of deer and small tiger-like animals, perhaps a roll or two of gaudily-printed calico. On the ground they sleep, with the rugs under them, maybe. They wear next to no clothes, their wants are very simple in the way of food. Their livelihood is assured to them,

they have no unsatisfied ambitions or desires, they enjoy such perfect health and vigour that they are unconscious of their bodies and their vital processes, and they are magnificent to look at. Both men and women are graceful in their movements, their poses are what we call " statuesque," because among us beauty and dignity have been banished from life to " art."

Look at a man and his wife walking through the bush. He goes a little way ahead, not to show his superiority, but so that he may defend her from any danger. He carries two sticks, she carries whatever load they may happen to have. On her head she will balance it most likely, and what incomparable charm there is in the line of her neck and shoulders, in her firm yet lithe poise! Nor is her man less satisfying to the eye ; it is only his woolly head which prevents him from being accepted as an ideal specimen of the human form.

DIAMOND SEARCHERS IN A SORTING SHED AT KIMBERLEY

For its white employees, some of whom are seen in this photograph of a diamond-sorting shed' of the De Beers Corporation, this company laid out the prettily-wooded Kimberley suburb of Kenilworth, each villa in which has its garden and fruit trees. Kimberley itself has grown since 1871 from a rough mining encampment into a city of which any nation might be proud

CHILDREN OF A LARGER GROWTH
Grown up though they are, these Kaffirs take a childish delight
in playing on the drums they have fashioned from tubs and tins
and barrels, and recalling the sounds that once roused the
martial ardour of their forebears

Photo, Keystone View Co.

scarcely anything to worry about.

The Zulus especially are a people from whom whites might be able to learn a good deal. Even in Durban they make one feel their simple human worth, although they are engaged mostly in the menial occupation of dragging rickshaws. The costume of these rickshaw men consists chiefly of paint. Nearly to the thighs their legs are bare and daubed with patterns in white. Around their bodies, which are also almost bare, they wear strings of beads, roughly made but gaily coloured. All their attention is paid to their heads, which are ornamented with feathers and usually with a pair of cow's horns.

Up and down the Esplanade with its fine buildings they run swiftly with the bulkiest passengers. This is the pleasantest part of Durban. The outlook is glorious across the lagoon, which is called the Bay, to wooded hills drowsing in the sunshine. A slight breeze from the ocean lifts the leaves of the palm trees. Tropical flowers scent the air. Yachts are flashing their white sails.

Over in the harbour work is going on, cranes are swinging cargo, orders are being shouted by perspiring ships' officers. But on the Esplanade you might fancy yourself in the land where it is always afternoon, and where no such necessity as toil is even thought of.

Now tell your rickshaw man to run you along to the Ocean Beach ; or you can pay him off and take a street car. " Coney Island " is what you say to yourself if you have been in America.

Among the many different races of natives there are differences of physique, grades of intelligence, varying codes of social duty. Among groups of labourers or miners or house servants you will find many types, from the handsome and aristocratic to the heavy-browed and thick-featured and uneasy-eyed. But among natives who have scarcely been touched by the changes that white men have introduced it is rare to notice any who do not seem quick, active, and, within the limits imposed by their surroundings and their pursuits, intelligent.

Certainly they are happier than the products of white civilization in the sense of being more contented, having

TAILINGS WHEEL IN OPERATION AT A TRANSVAAL GOLD MINE

Tailings is a term for refuse accumulated during the process of ore-extraction. Mixed with water the tailings flow into the lower part of the wheel and on the revolution of the latter are raised to its upper position and then discharged into the launder situated within the housing at the top of the wheel and above the platform shown in the photograph

COLLECTING WATTLE BARK FROM THE SOUTH AFRICAN VELD

Acacias abound in Africa, and several of the species have considerable commercial value, yielding gum arabic and the astringent medicine catechu, while others make valuable timber. The bark of all the species is very rich in tannin, and in South Africa its collection and preparation for use by tanners is becoming an important industry, as it already is in Australia

CUTTING LUMP SUGAR IN A SOUTH AFRICAN SUGAR REFINERY

Coloured workers are employed in many factories in the coast provinces of South Africa—Natal and the Cape Province. Sober and industrious hands, they can do skilled work of a purely mechanical kind quite efficiently after a course of training, and also skilled work that requires a little simple thought. For work requiring calculation, or artistic instinct, they seem unfitted

Photos, South African Government

NATIVE TROLLEY-MEN AT THE MOUTH OF A COAL MINE, MOLTENO
Natal and the Transvaal are exceedingly rich in coal, which also exists in the Orange Free State and the Cape Province. The total area of the coal-bearing formation in South Africa is about 12,000 square miles, and coal ranks second in the list of the mining activities of the Union. Hitherto only the coal near the outcrop of the beds and near existing railway lines has been worked.
Photo, South African Government

That was the model on which the Durban speculators modelled their beach, but there is beauty here with which the Atlantic coast cannot offer anything to compare. There is surf bathing, too, quite safe in an enclosure, which keeps out both the enormous Indian Ocean rollers and the sharks.

So you find at this other end of South Africa (not really the other end, but that is how one thinks of it) loveliness equal to that which met you in the Cape Peninsula. And yet there are people who say that the country has no charm !

One can understand that some eyes might miss the colour effects of the Karroo, that the monotony of the veld might dull its majesty after long years, that bush and endless low hills might soon lose the interest they have at first for the new-comer. But with such contrasts of sheer beauty as the Cape and Durban have to show, South Africa must rank among the lands which most delight the eye, in addition to being one of the most interesting because one of the most puzzling countries in the world.

FEARSOME BALLET DANCERS AT A KAFFIR COMING OF AGE CELEBRATION

All over Africa the ceremonies attending initiation into manhood are grotesque to the verge of madness, but have a general similarity proving a common originating idea. Among the Kaffirs of the south the officiating celebrants of the rites don ballet skirts of reeds and reed headdresses that mask the face; also plastering their bodies with lime or chalk through which the black skin shows in spots. The general effect is only a variant of that achieved in the initiation and bridal ceremonies of South Kukuruku, Mendiland, and Basutoland, illustrated in pages 686, 687, and 689 respectively

Photo W H Craft

South Africa

II. Anglo-Dutch Rivalry and Final Union

By W. Basil Worsfold

Author of " Sir Bartle Frere," etc.

DISCOVERED in 1486 by the Portuguese navigator Bartholomew Diaz and colonised by the Dutch soon after 1652, the Cape became a British Colony in 1806. Its population then included 26,720 Dutch settlers, 17,657 Hottentots, and 29,256 slaves ; and the annual value of its trade was £160,000. Beyond the borders of the colony there was a vast dark-skinned population—the virile and prolific Basuto.

A hundred years later there were in South Africa 1,250,000 Europeans, of whom nearly one-half were British, with an external trade of the annual value of £75,000,000 ; roads and railways, harbours and public buildings, had been built ; and great industries established. The area under European occupation had been carried beyond the Zambezi, and the native population, still four or five times as numerous as the European, had been brought under civilized governments. All

this was accomplished in the teeth of certain special difficulties, which provide a key to the history of South Africa under British rule.

First, the Dutch and British colonists differed so much in their manner of life that, instead of being blended into a single people, they remained separate nationalities, and ultimately fought with one another for the mastery of South Africa. Second, the natives, unlike those of America and Australia, instead of dwindling, throve and multiplied by contact with civilization, with the result that up to the last quarter of the nineteenth century the numerical inferiority of the whites increased rather than diminished. And third, these natives, by themselves providing manual labourers for the industries founded by the colonists, excluded from South Africa the British immigrants of this class, i.e., the very class from which the white populations of

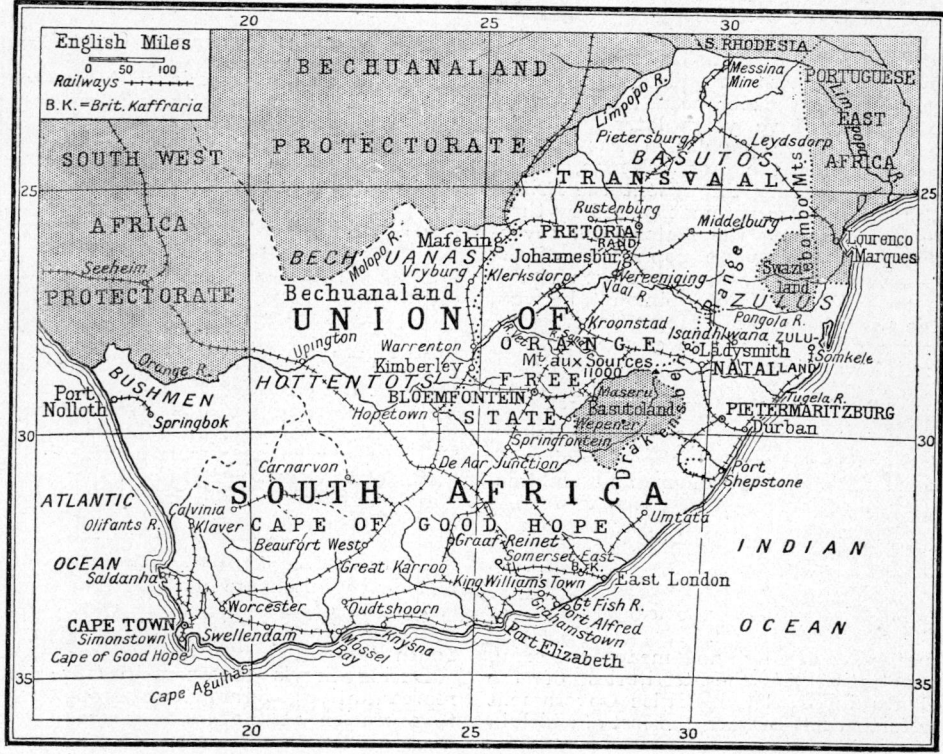

THE UNION OF SOUTH AFRICA AND ITS PEOPLES

Canada and Australasia were chiefly built up during the nineteenth century. This, together with the large capital outlay necessary for successful farming in South Africa, accounts for the fact that, even after the discovery of diamonds and gold had quickened the flow of British emigration, the Dutch continued appreciably to outnumber the British.

Up to 1820, although the Governor and a few high officials and merchants were British, the white population of the Colony remained Dutch ; and during this period, with the exception of an improvement in the conditions of the Hottentots, Dutch institutions were maintained, and administered through the Dutch officials whom the British had found in the Colony.

Divergent Views of Dutch and British

In this year (1820), however, a body of British colonists, 5,000 in all, was established between the Bushmen and Fish rivers. These Albany Settlers, as they were called, founded Grahamstown and Port Elizabeth ; and their descendants formed the predominantly British white population of the Eastern Province of the Colony. This important step was followed by administrative changes, the general effect of which was to recast the Dutch institutions on British lines, and English was made the official language.

At the same time, mainly through the advocacy of the British missionaries, the free Hottentots were placed under the same laws as the Europeans (Ordinance 50 of 1826). Five years later the more numerous slave population was emancipated under the Act of 1833, which abolished slavery throughout the British Empire. The resentment caused by these measures among the Dutch, still seven-eighths of the white population of the Colony, was increased by a most unfortunate " divergence of opinion " between the Governor and the Home Government, which arose out of one of the recurring native wars in 1834.

Results of the Great Boer Trek

During the years 1835-38 the Dutch farmers, or Boers, to the number of some 10,000 men, women, and children, packed their household goods into great ox-wagons and, driving their sheep and cattle before them, made their way across the Orange River northwards into the interior.

The immediate political results of the secession were these : (1) This premature, but by no means peaceful, penetration of the territories of the Bantu involved the British Government in further native wars, the cost of which in life and treasure was borne mainly by the United Kingdom. (2) The " emigrant farmers " (as the Boers were styled officially, since their independence was not recognized) founded settlements between the Orange and Vaal rivers, across the Vaal, and in Natal. The burden of these native wars and the slow material progress of the Cape, as compared with the British Colonies in Australasia and North America, led the Government to endeavour in 1853 to reduce its responsibilities in South Africa. To effect this purpose the original policy of non-intervention was applied in three directions.

(1) The (internal) independence of the Boers both north and south of the Vaal was recognized under the Sand River (1852) and the Bloemfontein (1854) Conventions ; and thus the two Dutch Republics of the Transvaal and Orange Free State were created.

The case of Natal was different. The first settlers here were Englishmen who had established themselves at Durban in 1824 ; and being a maritime territory, and as such accessible to a foreign Power, Natal was retained. In 1848-50 some 4,000 British settlers were introduced. And, as most of the Boer settlers had withdrawn upon the establishment of British authority in 1843, the European population became predominantly British, and representative institutions were conferred upon them in 1856.

Representative Government Granted

(2) The alliances made with certain native chiefs to prevent them from being deprived of their lands by the Boers, were modified or withdrawn. The purpose of this was to leave the Boers and the natives to settle their disputes by themselves, and to give neither party a right to ask for assistance from the British Government.

(3) Representative Government was granted to the Cape Colony in 1853. As the result of this measure it was expected that the colonists would assume a larger share of responsibility for the administration of the natives, and in particular for the defence of the Cape frontiers.

Thus, in 1854, when Sir George Grey was appointed Governor of the Cape, the British Government was left with direct administrative responsibility for the Cape, Natal, and British Kaffraria (the " buffer State " created in 1847). Beyond these possessions its responsibilities were limited to those of the Paramount Power, and for the discharge of the latter recent Governors of the Cape Colony had also held the office of High Commissioner in South Africa.

During Grey's governorship (1854-62) representative government was brought into operation at the Cape ; some 6,000 European settlers (mainly German) were established in British Kaffraria ; and more efficient methods of native administration were put into practice, with the result that peace was maintained on the eastern frontier for fifteen years.

Grey held the "dismemberment" of European South Africa, as he called it, to be a grave political error; and he proposed to remedy it by uniting the Republics with the British Colonies in a federal system. He had begun actually to apply this remedy by accepting the offer of the Free State to enter into a federal union with the Cape Colony, when the Home Government forbade him to proceed.

Eight years after Grey left South Africa the Kimberley diamond mines were discovered (1869). This event subjected the non-intervention policy to a strain to which it succumbed. The establishment of the diamond industry led to the employment of natives drawn from the centres of the Bantu population. These natives, who served in the mines for short periods and then returned to their homes, used their wages in buying guns.

Annexation of the Transvaal

In the year 1875, the signs of a general revolt among the natives were so widespread that the Imperial Government, realizing that it was only by union that the European States could control the natives, determined to adopt Grey's remedy. In a despatch of May, 1875, Lord Carnarvon, Colonial Secretary in Lord Beaconsfield's Government, urged the Colonies and Republics to form a federal union, as the only means of averting a great war between the white and dark-skinned peoples.

In 1876 the defeat of the burgher forces in the Transvaal by Secococni, the consequent breakdown of the Republican Government, and the threat of Cetywayo, Secococni's overlord, to take vengeance on the Boers with the great Zulu army which he had built up, showed how very slender was the plank between the colonists and the great deep of savagery and barbarism in South Africa. In the autumn of this year, therefore, Lord Carvarnon determined to annex the Transvaal, and to entrust the work of confederation to a statesman and administrator of the first order, Sir Bartle Frere.

Frere reached the Cape on March 31, 1877. Twelve days later, Sir Theophilus Shepstone, acting under Lord Carnarvon's instructions, annexed the Transvaal. When this step had been approved by the Home Government, Frere was instructed to visit the Transvaal and Natal directly the Cape Parliamentary Session was over —(the Cape was now under responsible government, granted in 1872)—in order that he might arrange an acceptable form of government for the Boers, and induce Cetywayo to reform his barbarous methods of government and live in peace with his white neighbours.

But Lord Carnarvon's plans, promptly as they had been made, were anticipated by the revolt of the natives in an unexpected quarter. Having started for the Transvaal, Frere was called back to defend the eastern border of the Cape Colony, where he remained in barracks at King William's Town for seven months. Under Frere's supervision this, the last of the Kaffir wars, was fought more quickly and successfully than any of the earlier wars; but peace was not restored until June 1878, and his administrative duties kept him at the Cape until September.

Natal and the Zulu Peril

By this time the outlook was dark with storm-clouds. Cetywayo had transferred his anger from the Boers to the British, and it was felt that at any moment the Zulu army might overrun Natal. The twelve months' delay in giving an acceptable constitution to the Transvaal had embittered the malcontent Boers, and their leaders were preparing to restore the Republic by force of arms. The most immediate danger was in Natal, and Frere went there first, reaching Durban on September 23.

He saw that the few available British troops could not defend this Colony, with its 200 miles of frontier bordering on Zululand, against the Zulu army, 40,000 strong and twenty-four hours' march away, except by a defensive-offensive, i.e., by invading Zululand and pinning down Cetywayo's mobile impis to their own country.

Home Government and Sir Bartle Frere

This was done; and, in spite of the tragic disaster of Isandhlwana, Natal was saved from invasion, and within six months of the advance of the British columns on January 11, 1879, South Africa was freed from the menace of a great native war by Lord Chelmsford's victory at Ulundi on July 4.

When reinforcements from England had made Natal safe, Frere went on to the Transvaal. He arrived just in time to avert a rebellion. At the risk of his life, and by great patience and skill in conference, he induced the Boer leaders to disband the burgher force assembled six miles from Pretoria, and to rely on his promise to do all in his power to obtain the immediate grant of a constitution which they could accept.

Unhappily for South Africa and for England, as with Grey so now with Frere, at the determining crisis of events the Home Government, alarmed by the catastrophe of Isandhlwana, withdrew its confidence and support from its representative " on the spot."

Frere was " rebuked for disobedience " (March 19, 1879) in making war on Cetywayo without waiting to refer home for instructions, and two months later the management of what were at the moment the most important affairs in South Africa, the settlement of Zululand and the Transvaal, was taken out of his hands.

Formation of the Afrikander Bond

Contrary to Frere's advice, the Boer Government of the Transvaal was restored in 1881. The retrocession " reacted dangerously " upon the colonial Dutch, as Frere foretold ; and in this year the Afrikander Bond was founded to bind the Colonial and Republican Dutch alike to work for a United South Africa under its own flag. (For Frere's administration and relations with the Home Government, see "Sir Bartle Frere," by W. Basil Worsfold, 1923.)

The twenty years which followed the recall of Frere (1880) formed a period of rapid economic development. Gold mining began in the eastern districts of the Transvaal in 1882, the year after the retrocession ; and in 1886 the Rand was proclaimed a public goldfield. While this new and potent factor of gold discovery brought a great increase of material prosperity to South Africa, it enhanced the political dangers which Frere had declared would be incurred by the withdrawal of British authority from the Transvaal.

President Kruger Prepares for War

As the seat of the gold industry, the Rand became the chief centre of British population and enterprise, and the great purchasing area of South Africa. But this seat was under a Dutch government. The Boers refused to admit the British " outlanders," who soon became almost as numerous as the burghers, to the rights of citizenship ; but they drew nine-tenths of their revenue from them. The expansion of gold mining made the Transvaal the richest state in South Africa, raising its annual revenue from £400,000 in 1886 to £5,000,000 in 1897 ; and in the five years preceding the great South African War (1899-1902) these revenues were used by President Kruger to buy munitions of war sufficient to arm not only the two Republics, but their Dutch supporters in the British Colonies.

Broadly speaking, from the retrocession (1881) to the Jameson Raid (Dec. 29, 1895—Jan. 2, 1896), the Imperial Government, while extending and improving the administration of the natives by European officials, left the nationality difficulty to be settled by the colonists themselves. In this conflict between Dutch and British there emerged three outstanding personalities : Paul Kruger, who worked for Dutch supremacy ; Cecil Rhodes, who stood for British supremacy ; and Jan Hofmeyr, who believed Dutch supremacy was not incompatible with South Africa's membership of the British Empire.

In securing the extension of British authority northward to the Congo Free State by the agency of the British South Africa Company, and in his effort to unite South Africa in a Customs Union, Rhodes obtained the support of Hofmeyr and the Afrikander Bond ; and in 1890 he became Prime Minister of the Cape Colony. During his five years of office an appreciable advance in native administration (notably through the Glen Grey Act of 1892) was achieved ; and the economic ties between the Free State and the Cape were strengthened by building a railway through the Free State to link the Cape ports with the Rand.

Case for Imperial Intervention

When, however, the catastrophe of the Raid, by ending the Rhodes-Hofmeyr alliance, made local South African statesmanship bankrupt for the time being, the Imperial Government was compelled to resume the full responsibilities of the Paramount Power.

Everything was done to make amends for the injury of the Raid.

But all overtures were received coldly by the Cape Dutch, whose resentment at the " duplicity " of Rhodes was too deep to be removed. Then the whisper " We are losing South Africa " reached England, and Joseph Chamberlain (the Colonial Secretary) determined, like Lord Carnarvon, to send out to South Africa an exceptionally competent administrator. His choice fell on Lord (then Sir Alfred) Milner, who left for the Cape on April 17, 1897.

After nearly two years of careful observation and anxious endeavour, during which the position of the British population in the Transvaal became steadily worse, Milner reported that " the case for intervention was overwhelming." A last effort was made by Hofmeyr to avert war. By his arrangement Milner and Kruger met in conference at Bloemfontein (May 31—June 5). Hofmeyr used all his influence to lead Kruger to grant a reasonable measure of enfranchisement, but the dour old President offered nothing more than a fictitious concession, which Milner refused.

The great South African War, which began with the expiry of the Transvaal ultimatum on October 11, 1899, lasted for nearly three years. For, although the power of the Republican and the Colonial

Dutch to maintain an " organized resistance " to the army of the Empire was broken in less than a year, nearly two years of guerrilla warfare followed before, on May 31, 1902, at Vereeniging, the remnant of the burgher forces agreed to surrender their arms, and acknowledged Edward VII. for their lawful sovereign.

When the army was withdrawn, the moulding of the new South Africa was left to Lord Milner. Some 30,000 Boer prisoners of war were brought back from their camps in India and other parts of the Empire, and they and their families (155,000 in all) were provided with seeds, farming implements, stock, and building materials, repatriated, and supplied with food for periods up to two years.

At the same time the general work of reconstruction was going on, and three years unexampled activity on the part of Lord Milner raised the new Colonies to a far higher plane of civilization than any they had attained previously.

Lord Milner left South Africa, which he, more than any other man, had kept within the Empire, in 1905. Three years later the Cape, Natal, the Transvaal, and the Orange River Colony, by this time all alike under responsible government, were confronted by a ruinous competition in customs tariffs and railway rates for the market of the Rand. The sole remedy lay in placing customs and railways under a common administration, and thus removing the conflict of interests between the separate states.

Under the compelling force of this conviction a National Convention was held. It met in 1908, and in May, 1909, it adopted a draft act of Union, which provided for the constitution of a Central Administration, with subordinate Provincial Administrations for the local affairs of the four Colonies. Southern Rhodesia was represented at the Convention, but did not become a Province of the Union. Provision is made in the Act, however, for the future admission of this Colony to the Union.

The draft Constitution was adopted by the Imperial Parliament, and, upon receiving the royal assent on September 20, became the South Africa Act, 1909. On May 31 following, the Union of South Africa came into being, and General Louis Botha was called upon to form its first Ministry. In the Great War South Africa (in spite of the rebellion of a few Dutch extremists who desired to join hands with the Germans in South-West Africa) threw in its lot with the rest of the British Empire. Since the Peace (German) South-West Africa has been administered by the Union Government under a mandate from the League of Nations.

SOUTH AFRICA : FACTS AND FIGURES

The Country

Occupies southern portion of African continent bounded south-east and east by Indian Ocean, and west and south-west by South Atlantic. North the boundary states are Angola or Portuguese West Africa, Bechuanaland, Southern Rhodesia, and Portuguese East Africa. Coast line mainly low and unindented with ranges of hills behind. Interior is largely occupied by a high grassy plateau called the veld. From this main rivers drain to Atlantic and Indian Ocean. Total area of Union 473,089 square, miles, with an estimated population of about 7,305,000.

Government & Constitution

Under the South Africa Act of 1909 the self-governing states of the Cape of Good Hope, the Transvaal, Natal, and the Orange River Colony, now the Orange Free State, were incorporated in a legislative union called the Union of South Africa and administered by one Government. British Sovereign appoints Governor-General, who exercises executive power with the aid of an Executive Council. Parliament comprises a Senate of forty members and a House of Assembly with 134 elective members, and must meet annually. The former territory of German South-West Africa is now South-West Africa, and is administered by the Union under a Mandate of the League of Nations.

Defence

The South Africa Defence Act Amendment Act of 1922 makes provision for a permanent force both naval and military, of all arms, and also a Coast Garrison Force, a Citizen Force, and the Royal Naval Volunteer and Special Reserves.

Commerce and Industries

Among main products are wheat, maize, oats, barley, potatoes, tobacco, and dairy produce. There are over 8,500,000 head of cattle and 31,700,000 sheep. Wool, mohair, and ostrich feathers are produced, and cotton, sugar, tea, and fruits cultivated. Industries include those of leather, cement, dynamite, matches, boots and shoes, wine, rope, furniture, and firebricks. The Union is very rich in minerals. The most important of these is gold, of which the production was valued at £43,082,162, including premiums, in 1921. For the same year coal production reached a value of £5,072,501, and diamonds £3,103,448. Among other minerals worked are lime, salt, asbestos, silver, tin, copper, and zinc. Imports include apparel, cottons, chemicals, food and drink, hardware and machinery, and totalled £57,800,316 in 1921. Exports, of which gold, wool, diamonds, maize, coal, and angora hair are among the chief, were valued at £65,819,139 for same year.

Communications

There are in the Union over 10,800 miles of state railway, and more than 500 miles of private lines. Post offices number over 2,700, miles of telegraph wire over 44,000, and of telephone wire over 140,000.

Chief Towns

Pretoria, administrative capital (estimated population 74,000), Johannesburg (288,000), Cape Town (207,000), Durban (146,000), Port Elizabeth (46,000), Bloemfontein (39,000), Kimberley (39,700), East London (34,500).

COUNTRY BULL-FIGHT IN FULL SWING ON THE UNPRETENTIOUS PLAZA DE TOROS IN THE PROVINCE OF CÁCERES

The bull-fight is undoubtedly the favourite sport of the Spaniards, though whether it is worthy of the name of "sport," at all is still a disputed question. The business of the Spanish torero is to kill the bull after goading it to a high pitch of fury, and to elude its furious onslaughts with the trained nimbleness essential to all success in the bull-ring. The horses used are chiefly old, worn-out animals, and frequently furnish additional carnage to the play. It is in this satis-faction of the blood lust that the Spanish bull-fight differs essentially from the Portuguese form, in which the bull is baited but not slaughtered

Spain

I. Spanish Life in Town & Country

By Hamilton Fyfe

Author and Traveller

IN Spain there are several distinct races. The Gallegos of Galicia are unlike the Andalusians; the Castilian is quite a different type from the native of Catalonia. Yet in one thing all Spaniards are the same. They all have good manners, and they expect good manners from you.

There is in Spain a real equality and fraternity, a feeling for the dignity of the individual man, whether he be prince or beggar, employer or employed, which tends to put all upon a more nearly even level than can be found in some other lands which pride themselves upon their higher civilization.

It is said sometimes in derogation that the good manners of the Spaniards are surface politeness, and that the "equality" on which they insist in form is no more than a tradition lingering on among a people who live in the past. I do not think that opinion would be supported by anyone who has travelled much in Spain.

There is much more behind Spanish courtesy than superficial observers notice. The people of all classes will go out of their way to help a stranger, and I have very rarely induced a Spaniard who had done me a service to take anything for his trouble. I remember losing my way once, coming down from the Guadarrama Mountains towards Madrid, and being guided for some distance by a young peasant. When I said that I should regard it as an additional favour if he would allow me to offer him some little reward, he smiled and said he had been amply rewarded for the small amount of trouble he had taken by the pleasure of my conversation. This was flattery so gross, since I spoke Spanish badly, that I laughed back at him. But he was not to be moved. That experience I have often had repeated.

The French writer Stendhal once said of the Spaniards that they "knew deeply the great truths," and the English traveller George Borrow wrote of them: " I will say that in their social intercourse no people in the world exhibit a juster feeling of what is due to the dignity of human nature, or better understanding of the behaviour which it behoves a man to adopt towards his fellow-beings." That pleasantness

MARKET QUEEN IN OLD MADRID

Every year the market people of Madrid elect one of themselves as Queen of the Markets. A beautiful mantilla is presented by the city to each newly-elected queen

WHERE A LITTLE LOCAL GOSSIP SELDOM COMES AMISS

Best clothes are gay clothes throughout Spain, and a well-to-do farmer and his lass make a brave show when arrayed for a ceremonial visit. Local colour riots in this sunny corner of Murcia where a bearded friar enjoys his coffee and dessert and entertains a couple of prosperous villagers who have brought him a rabbit for his larder

of intercourse is one of the features which make travel in Spain agreeable. Another is the remoteness of so many parts of the country from what is artificial in modern civilization. There are regions where the cultivation of the soil is effected with implements of the kind that were used when Julius Caesar conquered the Spaniards and put them in the way of becoming Roman citizens.

The ploughs belong to the era of Virgil's "Georgics." The farm-carts are of archaic build. In autumn the threshing of the corn is done in a manner which must have prevailed since Phoenician days. On the floor of the barn the grain lies three or four feet deep. Mules pull at a circular platform made to revolve, and having on its underside jagged teeth. When these teeth have done their work the grain is tossed in the air so as to separate the chaff from the wheat.

Customs in the country districts are often in keeping with the simplicity of the agriculture. In village streets the women can be seen arranging each other's hair. It is only taken down once or twice a week, and they sleep with their heads on a most uncomfortable-looking wooden pillow, with a hollow in it for their necks to rest, so that their coiffures may not be disturbed. Or mothers will be rubbing oil or fat into the heads of children so as to form a hard cake over the skull, and, as they say, to strengthen the growth of hair. In the early morning there is a great washing of small boys and girls at the public fountain. At village fairs the girls go from stall to stall offering their hair for sale ; when the price suits off it comes.

On the hillsides and in the deep, bare valleys the shepherds and goatherds live as nearly as possible the life of man in the pastoral stage of history. They will bake you a bread cake on a griddle, and give you wine from a skin. Sometimes they bring down a bird with an ancient fowling-piece, and make a savoury stew. If you notice their dress, you will very likely see that they are clad entirely in leather. Leather cap with fur on the inside, a shirt of soft leather fastened with leather laces in place of buttons, a tough leather jerkin and breeches, and leather sandals.

Their dogs are sometimes dangerous, as the dogs in Spain are apt to be, seeing they are kept for that purpose, but the herds themselves are mostly ready enough to make friends with a stranger who is " simpatico," and appreciate highly a few cigarettes if you have the kind they smoke. The finest brands are wasted upon them, but produce the mild, sweet tobacco of the Spanish masses wrapped in thick chocolate-coloured cigarette paper and they overwhelm you with gratitude.

Another sight which one comes across carries one straight back to the medieval Spain of Don Quijote (please pronounce Kee-hoe-tay. " Quixote " is a barbarism). This is the cleansing of cloth, fresh from the loom, of the grease which clings in it. The pieces of stuff are thrown into clay-pits where men tread them well with bare feet until they are plastered with the clay. Then they are

MURCIA'S ANCIENT METHODS IN THE MOST ANCIENT HUMAN ART
Bread is baked in Murcia by methods virtually identical with those employed by the Moors in the eighth century and even with those practised in Rome a thousand years earlier. A large dome-shaped oven is built in the open air, with a vaulted opening through which the oven is charged and the batch inserted and withdrawn on a long wooden shovel or peel

STOUT PICADORES WITH THEIR LANCES AND PADDED LEGS

In " la corrida de Toros," the first blood of the victim is drawn by the lance of a picadore whose mount, as often as not, is the initial victim. While in Portugal (see pages 4184-4187) the bull-fighter mounts a horse of the best breed, in Spain his sorry mount usually has the appearance of being half dead with fright when it enters the bull-ring

THE MATADOR, GORGEOUS IN COLOURED SATIN AND GOLD

When the picadores with their lances, and banderilleros with their darts have played their part, there steps forward, alone, the pride of the bull-ring, the matador or espada. With scarlet cloth in left hand and sword in the right, risking his skill against the onrushes of the now infuriated beast, he finally despatches it by a dexterous thrust of his weapon between its shoulders

laid out in the sun to dry, and off comes the clay, bringing the grease with it. After that the cloth is put into long troughs called " batañes," and pounded so as to get it quite clean.

All this seems very backward to an English visitor, and, indeed, the verdict of English people about the Spaniards is generally pretty much what Lord Salisbury said when he spoke of them as "a dying race." But there is another side to the shield. Here is what an Englishman wrote not many years ago : " Is it Spain that is decaying or is it Great Britain ? Surely the nation which makes money its idol and derives no inconsiderable part of its national revenue from the sale of strong and poisonous liquors, must be classed in a lower category than that people which is sensible enough to take life gently and to enjoy each day wisely and temperately." This point of view, provocative of wholesome thought, leaves too much out of account. It overlooks the poverty which prevents large numbers of Spaniards from living " wisely and temperately " ; the heavy taxes which the peasant slaves, year in, year out, have to pay ; and in certain parts, Andalusia for example, the extortions of rich, absentee landlords.

Here is a cry of protest from a Spanish small farmer in Galicia : " We live from hand to mouth. All we earn by our hard work is swallowed up by taxes. We cannot even buy bread for our children. We are kept down by the burdensome and unjust taxation, and there is nothing to encourage us either to work or hope." Exaggerated, no doubt, but with a painfully true substance behind the cry.

Usury, again, weighs heavily upon the Spanish peasant proprietor who gets into debt. The people do work

PATIENT PERSISTENCE IN LIFE'S DAILY ROUND
Dim-eyed, and tottering with age and ailments, this farmer of the province of Murcia still superintends much of the labour expended on his small holding. The question of irrigation is a vital one in most parts of Spain, but many of the rural population have succeeded in overcoming the difficulties and by dint of artificial watering are able to produce fine crops from very unpromising soil

A MOMENT'S RESPITE IN THE LABOURING DAY

Murcia is one of the most especially Moorish places in Spain, and owing to its long stagnation was said to be the only place Adam would recognize if he returned to earth. Modern industry is removing that reproach, but very ancient methods still survive in the adjoining country, such as wooden ploughs and brushwood harrows drawn by large-eyed oxen, their collars hung with jangling bells

hard. Spain is not a country of idlers. Nowhere do cultivators spend longer hours at their toil. Scarcely anywhere are wages so scanty. Three shillings a day for labour from earliest light until nightfall ; that is not unusual even now.

Small wonder that the peasants' cottages have next to no furniture in them. Come into one. It looks like a shed, you think. Well, the lower part is a shed where the pigs and poultry, perhaps a cow and a horse, are kept. Up a stairway is the human dwelling. The smell, as you can imagine, is, until you get used to .it, scarcely bearable. The room in which the family live is very often black and shiny with smoke.

The fireplace is in the middle, a rough construction of mud and stones. There is a way for the smoke to get out, but it often declines to take that way. There are cooking pots of clay, stone platters and bowls, perhaps a metal chocolate pot. In a " cupboard-room " there is a bed. That may be all.

Yet, for all his hard work and for all his poverty, the Spaniard is not bitter or savagely discontented. Is it the sun which prevents him from brooding over his grievances ? I have often thought the golden light and warmth in which Spain is wrapped most days in the year must have something to do with it. But they are a tired people, tired, I mean, of struggle with authority. They have found that political changes make very little difference to their lives. Anything which they are not obliged to do to-day they are quite ready to put off until to-morrow. Too much has been written about their preference for Mañana (to-morrow), but one has to get used to it.

On my first visit to Spain I came up against it very soon. I stayed a

ON THEIR WAY TO CHURCH
Except on rare occasions the mantilla is never worn in the street, but during the Holy Week this charming headdress of black silk lace is part of the regulation costume

night at San Sebastian, the fashionable seaside place close to the frontier. Next day I said I wanted a carriage to take me to the station for an early afternoon train. Very good, the hotel omnibus would be going; I must be ready at a quarter-past two. I waited, ready, until half-past two. Then I made some inquiry. No hurry, I was told; the omnibus would come. I hung about another quarter of an hour. Still no sign of any vehicle.

I began to make the usual British disturbance. The hotel people smiled and shrugged their shoulders. What did it matter, they seemed to ask, whether

I caught one train or another? I thought it mattered a great deal. But I did not catch my early afternoon express. When the omnibus at last drew up at the railway-station it had gone.
" No matter," said the conductor, " there is another train later on."

That is the Spanish temperament. They do not value time as the English do; they are not so set upon carrying out their plans. I am not sure that they may not be the wiser. After all, hurrying seldom gets one more quickly to one's destination, and the importance of saving time can easily be exaggerated. The only act which I have seen performed regularly in a hurry in Spain is eating lunch or dinner in a railway restaurant.

Nowadays the fast long-distance trains have restaurant-cars, but on cross-country journeys the habit still obtains (it was formerly universal) of stopping trains for twenty minutes at midday and in the evening, having a meal all ready in the station buffet, and thus letting the passengers take in sustenance (and indigestion) at a very moderate cost. Several courses are always served, beginning with hot soup, which the wise ones leave to the end, and including at least two dishes of meat, with a salad and a sweet. The rate at which all this is disposed of is alarming. It showed me that Spaniards can do things quickly when they feel inclined.

The food in the station restaurants is, as a rule, excellent. Spanish cooking generally is both appetising and wholesome. For some people it is too rich; others denounce it for its use of garlic. But when one is hungry, few dishes are more welcome than a savoury Spanish stew, an " olla podrida " or a " puchero," or a pie such as they make in and around Valencia of varied and nourishing ingredients, including chicken and snails. In the middle of the day the well-to-do Spaniard eats largely. He will begin with soup, then a stew of vegetables will appear, next mutton or beef; garbanzos (chick-peas), a universal dish,

IN SUNNY SPAIN
Land of Old Romance

Scarlet blossoms and white lace mantilla draped over hair and shoulders display to advantage the southern beauty of the Andalusian

Photo, Photochrom Co.

All Spanish women own a manton de Manila, a silk shawl richly embroidered, but worn only at fiestas or on other special occasions

Photo, Photochrom Co.

*The beauties of Spain seem centred in Granada, where gypsy
girls with blue-black hair dance divinely—for a consideration*

Photo, Neville Hardy

A cloaked figure, a girl's form, iron bars between, dreamy whisperings of guitar and soft laughter complete a summer nocturne of Seville

Photo, Lehnert & Landrock

Oratory is a gift seldom lacking in the Spaniard, but there are moments when he finds silence infinitely more eloquent than words

Photo, Lehnert & Landrock

Clashing castanets and twanging guitars accompany the rhythmic dances of the light-hearted, lithe-limbed young gypsy girls of Granada

While her companion plays the guitar the young girl lightly claps her hands; most Spanish dancers favour this form of accompaniment

Photo, Photochrom Co.

Sunny humour is a very natural thing in Sunny Spain, and bright eyes and enchanting smiles are the prerogative of the señorita

Photo, Lehnert & Landrock

may come next, then chicken, and a very oily salad, fruit, and good Spanish wine and coffee, not so good, to drink.

That sounds a great deal, but when you have breakfasted off a small cup of chocolate and a sweet cake, you are hungry by midday, and the evening meal is usually light, so there is nothing much else to look forward to. This evening meal the Spaniard generally takes at home. In the towns he is apt to eat his principal meal at a restaurant or a club. To his home he very seldom invites guests. That is not entirely true of the cosmopolitan Spaniards who form the diplomatic and political society of Madrid. But these are the exceptions. It is not easy, therefore, to become well acquainted with Spanish women, unless they have broken through tradition and decided to live in the modern French or English way.

One of their own writers has called the Spanish woman a "tame savage." That seems to support the common notion that Carmen is typical of the race. The delusion is widely spread that Spanish women dress in gay costumes, smoke cigarettes, carry fans, wear mantillas, are fierce and passionate and uncomfortably jealous. So it happens that many persons of romantic imagination are disappointed when they see the Spanish woman habitually dressed in black, modest, and with the sense of sex less developed in her than in the women of other countries.

If they had the opportunity to study her, they would find her very interesting. To start with, she is gifted

with a subtle charm. It is hardly beauty in the English sense, though the Italian Professor Mantegazza has declared, after long investigation, that the British and the Spanish women are the most beautiful of all. He would say, no doubt, that beauty expresses itself not less in carriage and walk and in attitude when sitting than in features or complexion or hair. And if the Spanish woman's hair is not in itself beautiful, one can admire entirely the way in which it is piled high on her well-shaped head, with a rose or a carnation fixed in it. If her features and complexion are not striking, her charm of expression is compensation. You very seldom see a discontented

REGULATION DRESS OF RELIGIOUS FESTIVAL
Spanish women have many costumes which are worn only on special occasions, and this remarkable attire, peculiar to the province of Salamanca, is to be seen almost exclusively at Candlemas when the above headdress is likewise the prescribed fashion

UNDER THE TREE OF KNOWLEDGE AT A HUMBLE DOOR

Education is seriously hampered in Spain by a shortage of teachers, and only something like one in twenty of the population attends school. Determined efforts are being made to remedy so grave a national evil, but meantime many of the children have little better schooling than that suggested by this photograph of a peasant woman in Murcia giving some grown girls a reading lesson

looking girl or woman in Spain. In the Spanish home the wife, or it may be the mother-in-law, lays down the household laws and the man takes second place. This has been traced to the ancient custom of matriarchy or government by women, which is said to have prevailed in Spain. In the Middle Ages there was certainly more freedom for women in this country than in its neighbours. Women were more nearly on an equality with men. Sons sometimes took their mother's names instead of their father's.

Nowadays the equality idea has faded. It may have been due in part, though this seems out of keeping with the Moslem treatment of women elsewhere, to the large-mindedness of the Moors in educating their women thoroughly and holding them in honour. After the Moors had gone it persisted for a long time, but gradually lost its power. Catholicism weakened it, and modern Liberalism appears to have killed it. A woman in the last century was obliged to disguise herself as a man in order to attend university classes. The universities have been for many years open to both sexes, but in general Spanish women are less emancipated than most others from the traditions and disabilities forced upon women by men. They still, however, keep up their authority in the home, while the bond between mothers and sons is close and very tender. In many houses the mother remains supreme even after the son's marriage, and many sons remain at home under their mother's influence until they are well on in years. So long as their fathers live, they are treated as dependents. It is only when they inherit the family property that they learn responsibility and to take a line of their own. This helps to account for the lack of initiative in Spain.

It is not a rich country so far as the soil generally is concerned, though there are regions in the south and along the Mediterranean which bring forth grain and fruits and vegetables in profusion. But Spain has many resources which might be profitably developed for the benefit of her people. In Galicia vines grow well, but there is no wine-making industry. Beets grow well, but there are no sugar factories

on a large scale. Sardines are so plentiful that they are used as manure for the fields. Salmon trout abound and are given away. Neither is canned. Cod could be caught in great quantity, yet even this part of the country imports from Norway the dried cod which is eaten everywhere in Spain on fast-days.

In recent years the railways have been pushed farther, and the minerals in which certain regions are rich have been attacked more energetically. The water-power in the north is being used to drive mills. Irrigation is being extended with the result of making waste land prolific. The export of wine, not only of the sherry and malaga still drunk by a great many old-fashioned people in England, but of red and white wines of a lighter character, has been speeded up. Olives and oranges have been produced and sent abroad in slightly larger quantities. But a great deal more could be done. For the

BEAUTY IN EARTHEN POTS AND COMMON THINGS
In many a peasant home in Murcia there are articles in common use that are entirely charming examples of native art and honest craftsmanship. The earthenware plates and jugs are mainly blue, with patterns in darker blue or black, Moorish influence being evident in the designs. Water is precious in Murcia and is stored in huge jars, usually kept on a dais of blue-and-black tiles

PRETTY PEASANT GIRL OF MURCIA IN FÊTE-DAY COSTUME

Murcia, a Moorish city, beautifully situated at the base of the Montaña de Fuensanta, has an interesting though a humble population, many of whom are engaged in the silk industry, including the cultivation of the mulberry tree and the manufacture of many silken articles. Religion is a very real thing to the people of Murcia, and their church festivals and holy days are scrupulously observed

GATHERING MULBERRY LEAVES FOR SILKWORMS IN MURCIA

Sericulture was introduced into Murcia by the Moors in the eighth century, and the silk industry is still a staple one in the capital. Large numbers of the white mulberry tree, whose leaves provide the best food for silkworms, are cultivated around the town. This variety, native of China, was established in Europe in the twelfth century and thrives especially well in the Mediterranean region

TRIPPING A PAS DE DEUX IN SEVILLE

Dancing is a living art in Spain, and in Seville especially is practised to perfection by the Andalusian whose gestures and undulations can express almost every human emotion

Photo, Kadel & Herbert

passed. Then he suggested as the next gift good government. "No, no," said the Queen of Heaven, "I cannot grant you that, for if to all the other advantages of your country were added the boon of good government, we should have Heaven empty. All the angels would go and live in Spain."

That is how the Spaniards talk about their political system. Yet they do not stir themselves up to alter it, so presumably its evils do not press very hardly upon them. They are, in the towns at any rate, eager about political "mitins," as they call them, and ready to listen at any length to speeches.

I recall a huge gathering in the bull-ring of Madrid one Sunday morning. It had to be in the morning, for in the afternoon there was to be the usual bull - fight. It began at ten o'clock, by which hour the place was full. The speaker wanted to make a bid for office. It was easy to detect in his speech frequent truckling to the Clericals who bulked largely among his supporters. There were many priests in the bull-ring. They had come from all parts of Spain, and had brought groups of their parishioners with them. Whenever the speaker said anything against France or England the priests stood up and gave their followers the word to clap their hands vigorously. When the orator said that by traditions of culture and literature Spain was closer to France than to Germany, the priests scowled and their obedient sheep sat motionless. The speech was characteristic of

lack of enterprise many blame the Government. But the politicians are far too busy feathering their own nests and preparing for elections and planning how to turn or keep their opponents out of office, to draw up or encourage schemes for increasing the country's prosperity.

A story is told in Spain—I have generally had it repeated gleefully to me whenever I have talked about Spanish politics with casual acquaintances in trains or clubs or newspaper offices—about the petition which a certain Spanish king made to the Queen of Heaven. He asked for sunshine, and it was granted. He asked for beautiful women and courteous men. That also

Spanish politics. It enunciated no principles. It postulated no beliefs. What the speaker aimed at was to secure as much support as possible by saying things which would please all the groups represented at the meeting. He did not even give the impression of being sincere. Certainly he found it hard to make his voice heard by all the ten thousand people who listened to him, and that may have caused his manner to seem artificial and his phrases lacking in warmth of conviction.

But the record of almost all Spanish politicians is the same. Their efforts are always directed to getting into office and, having got there, to staying there. When they feel that the country is sick and tired of them, they arrange to retire in favour of the other side, knowing that their turn will come round again in due course. For the Spaniard's

FRUIT TRADING IN A PROVINCIAL CORNER OF SEVILLE

The market places of Spain are attractive and interesting chiefly because of the variegated costumes of the peasantry and the diversity of goods offered for sale. The fruit markets of Seville especially present a delightful medley of colour, for the richness of the soil of the south is responsible for an abundance of luscious fruit, beautiful specimens of which are procurable throughout the province.

Photo, Underwood Press Service

ROMANTIC IF INCONVENIENT METHOD OF COURTSHIP

All the lower windows of Andalusian houses are securely barred, but this formidable grille is not without its romantic aspect and the preliminary steps in Andalusian courtship are usually conducted through its iron bars. Window-sill trysting still holds good in the Andalusia of to-day, and a scene such as the above is common to almost every town and to almost every street

Photo, Brown & Dawson

BEGUILING A QUIET HOUR WITH MUSIC AND MEDITATION

An undeniable etiquette hedges in the Spanish woman, be she of the aristocracy or a simple working girl, and it is said that the women of high degree of Spain are kept in more seclusion than those of any other European country. The guitar—Spain's national musical instrument—is popular in all circles and an admirable accompaniment to the melodious syllables of the Castilian tongue

COUNTRY PEOPLE OF MALAGA TAKING THEIR GOODS TO MARKET BY FERRY ACROSS THE RIVER GUADALHORCE

Mules are the chief pack-animals of these peasants, and market-day sees long lines of them winding down the hilly slopes and along the rugged bridle-paths, bearing large panniers heaped with marketable wares. When a river is reached and no bridge available, a ferry-boat will convey master and mule with their varied appurtenances to the opposite bank. The River Guadalhorce flows through very beautiful scenery, including richly-cultivated valleys and wild mountain passes, and its waters are led off in numberless small channels to irrigate the local fruit and vegetable gardens

WRAPPING ORANGES FOR EXPORT TO ENGLAND, AT A FRUIT DEPOT OF ALORA

The orange is grown extensively in many parts of Spain, especially in the southern provinces, where the fruit trade is an important one, for the demand for Spanish fruits in the foreign markets is rapidly increasing. Alora is a centre of the orange trade for the province of Malaga. Women are largely employed in the packing process, and, after carefully assorting the fruit, which varies in size and quality, they wrap each orange up in a piece of tissue paper, usually stamped with the exporter's name, and place it in the specially-prepared packing-cases

LIGHT REFRESHMENT IN A COBBLED COURTYARD OF SOUTHERN SPAIN

Fruit abounds in the neighbourhood of Alora, where vineyards, olive plantations, and some of the finest orange and lemon groves in the world are to be found, and figures conspicuously in the diet of all classes.   After working hours these natives of Alora find it no displeasing occupation to engage in friendly converse, regaling themselves the while with olives and other succulent fruits

BONNIE BASQUE BABIES OF THE MOUNTAINOUS NORTH

When entering Spain at the bend of the Bay of Biscay, near the western extremity of the Pyrenees, one discovers a delightful country, diversified by low wooded hills, rich in a luxuriance of fern and heather, of oak and ash. In this pleasant land dwell the Basques, a vigorous, healthy race, of which two sturdy young representatives are here seen on the threshold of their cottage home

RUGGED FEATURES FROM BISCAY

Entering Spain from France the traveller comes, on passing the Pyrenees, to the coast province of Biscay or Viscaya, a district un-Spanish in people and landscape. This peasant has more Basque than Spanish blood in his veins

they have learned the benefits of peace, and their aim is to keep them.

Long before the Great War this wish was expressed. At the club in Ciudad Real, where so many retired officers are to be found, an old colonel of Engineers many years ago spoke thus to a pair of foreigners, " Do not rob us of our quiet. We ask you for nothing. Leave us with the best thing in the world which we now possess. What is the best thing in the world ? It is peace." So long as their Government keeps them out of war the Spaniards, however much they may abuse it, show no inclination to try any other.

The Church is often blamed along with the Government for the absence of a more vigorous intellectual industrial and commercial life in Spain. The priests have beyond doubt a powerful influence over the mass of the people, and that influence is used to the advantage of the Papal System, which implies hostility, open or veiled, to progressive ideas. The clergy are not, as a rule, men of much education or superior moral worth. Yet they have in many an out-of-the-way parish a hold upon their parishioners which saves the district from relapsing into barbarism.

In the towns the Church has lost a good deal of its grip upon the minds and imaginations of the people. A workman in Alicante, watching a procession of priests, spoke of them with tolerant contempt. They were not a bad lot. They even tried to move with the times as far as they could.

interest in politics does not make him really desirous of seeing changes carried out. There is an immense amount of intriguing and of wirepulling and of electioneering, but there is very little genuine reforming energy outside Catalonia, where the people are altogether different in character from the Castilians and Andalusians. There is not among the latter much belief in any future for Spain brighter than the present. They do not want to bestir themselves. It may be that in the past they have had too much fighting. They were reckoned a people by nature warlike. Now, as they showed during the Great War,

" But now we are going to have Trade Union schools," he added, " and be independent of them and all other religious nonsense."

That is the hope of the intellectuals as well as of the workmen who have drunk at the fount of the New Spirit. One of Spain's foremost writers, who is not personally hostile to Roman Catholicism, has described the religiosity of the Spanish race as " part of our legend." " We are no longer a religious people, even in observance," he asserted. It may be found difficult to square this statement with the survival of religious observances such as the Passion Week processions in Seville. But I think it can be squared all the same.

The King of Spain is still styled " his most Catholic Majesty," and if all these religious observances were the outcome of sincere belief, the Spaniards would certainly be the most Catholic people.

But my Easter experiences in Seville left me with the impression that it was custom and tradition which kept up the processions of the Confraternities, and that faith had very little to do with them. These Confraternities or brotherhoods date back almost to the Middle Ages. Each is connected with some church, and each carries with it on high platforms which are raised to the level of men's shoulders an image or a group of images from its particular church. In its origin the observance is said to have been a penance imposed by the clergy hundreds of years ago, the penitents being obliged to walk barefooted and in sackcloth through the city from their churches to the cathedral.

The processionists wear the costume which we associate with the Inquisition, monkish robes of black, white, or purple, with tall, conical hoods high above their heads and covering their faces. Only their eyes are visible through tiny eyelet

PEASANTS OF BISCAY IN THE TAP-ROOM OF AN INN

Descendants of an ancient Mediterranean people, the Basques still retain many of their racial characteristics. Certain primitive practices exist among them until this day and in their ceremonial dances traces of early animism are found. Their language is said to bear some relation to that of the palaeolithic peoples and to be older than any of our Indo-European tongues

FRESH MILK WHILE YOU WAIT IN A BYWAY OF ANDALUSIA

Spain is a thirsty country and the Spaniards are a thirsty people ; yet they are singularly abstemious where alcoholic drinking is concerned. Water is scarce in many parts, especially during the summer months, when it has its market value. Milk is another precious liquid, but goats' milk may be bought without much difficulty, for the goatherd periodically parades his flock through the town

Photo, Horace W. Nicholls

SUNLIT CORNER OF A COURTYARD IN ROCK-BOUND RONDA

Ronda is a city set on a hill of rock with precipitous sides and accessible only from the west. From its position on this lofty hill the old city looks down on the fertile valley some 600 feet beneath, fringed by rugged mountains. Doorways and windows of Moorish mouldings, carved portals, and graceful arches are among the town's fascinating bits of ancient architecture

Photo, Horace W. Nicholls

MATURED BY HARDSHIP AND TOIL
Though diverse in many main characteristics the men of north and south Spain share some fine qualities; even among the lowest peasantry are found generous and law-abiding natures, intense loyalty to king and creed, and remarkable patience in misfortune
Photo, R. Gorbold

was no sense of solemnity in the demeanour of the people. They chattered and joked. At two o'clock the lights were extinguished and the crowd began to catcall for the procession to appear. In a few minutes the heavy doors swung slowly back and the "penitents," each carrying a lighted candle, came streaming through.

Above the heads of the crowd I could see only their pointed hoods and the yellow patches which their tall candles made against the darkness. But when the platform came forth it could be seen by all. Then for a moment silence fell upon the people. Women bowed their heads before the image of the Saviour bent beneath the burden of the Cross. All hats were taken off. But the silence was quickly torn by a strident voice, singing a hymn in praise of the Christ.

The melody was unmistakably Moorish, a florid yet monotonous Arab chant. It is the custom to "welcome" the images with these traditional airs. Professional singers are engaged to perform them at certain points along the route. At others they are sung by unknown singers in the crowd.

holes. They assemble towards midnight. As I went out to take up my place in the crowd before the doors of the Church of San Lorenzo, I saw numbers of them flitting about. The streets were fuller of people than I had ever seen them in daytime. Wineshops and cafés were open, and kept open all night. They were doing a brisk trade. So were the tobacco sellers.

In the square outside the church there was a dense crowd waiting for two o'clock, the hour at which the most famous of all the images, "Jesus of Great Power," is brought out. There

The singing relieved the tension. Talk and laughter began again. The crowd broke up and a great many of us made for the big square, where stands are put up and seats sold at high prices. All the processions pass through here, beginning at about three o'clock and not finishing until six or so.

Here, again, the whole thing was treated as a show, and for the first hour

MOORISH SURVIVALS IN THE COURTYARD OF A HOUSE IN RONDA

In the southern coast province of Malaga, on the railway from Bobadilla to Algeciras, stands Ronda. The Moors built it on either side of the gorge of the Guadalevin river and many traces of the founders can be seen in the houses to-day. In essentials the structure and ornament of this patio or court differ little from the Moorish house seen in page 3571

Photo, Horace W. Nicholls

or two a very diverting show it was. The famous images of the Virgin were magnificent in robes of gold brocade with jewels all over them. Diamonds glittered on their necks and stomachers. Rings adorned their fingers. Bracelets hung on their wrists. All these jewels had been given in gratitude for prayers answered. Their value must have run into hundreds of thousands of pounds.

That was the night between Maundy Thursday and Good Friday. On Good Friday evening I sat another five hours to watch more processions, " Cofradias " as they are called, pass by. All the seats in the square were full. The mayor and town councillors lounged in a box, not paying much attention, smoking endless cigarettes. The daylight faded as the cloaked and hooded figures moved interminably on. The moon lent Seville's famous tower, the

Giralda, a fairy, far-off loveliness. But it was still a show.

The clergy keep a hold upon the mass of the nation. They do this mainly by using the power of women. Men find it pays them better to have the good word, and not the bad word of the priests. But there is not the old fervour of faith which once distinguished Spain. " The people find it hard to believe in anything," a Spanish acquaintance told me, " we do not even believe in ourselves."

Certainly there has been a complete change since the age of the Inquisition. Voices are raised now and again for the re-establishment of a clerical court to try and to punish those who will not conform to the doctrine and the observances of the Church. But these cause only pitying smiles. Some who have tried to understand the Spanish character have been inclined to think,

TOWARDS THE END OF AN EVENING'S SERENADE IN OLD SEVILLE
When the dazzling sun disappears behind the horizon the city of Seville comes to life. Gardens, almost deserted during the heat of the day, are thronged with people, and there is not a seat vacant under the palms and orange trees. Along the streets cloaked figures with guitars make soft music in the moonlight—friendly greetings which not infrequently end in lovers' meetings

as they saw how firm the hold which bull-fighting still has upon the mass of the people, that it might be possible to revive the most hideous cruelties of the Inquisition.

Those who form this judgement consider the Spanish nature to be cruel. That it is hard and indifferent to pain cannot be gainsaid. That it is inclined to formality is notorious. Spain is the country of the most rigid ceremonial in social affairs. Allied to that is the attachment to ritual in religion which has always marked this nation. System and formality appear in every shoot put out by the tree of the national spirit.

Yet side by side with this there are to be noticed a tenderness and a sympathy which seem to be utterly opposed to it. It seems as if the warm humanity of the Spanish character persisted in peeping out, however inhuman may have been the acts committed and the systems set up by potentates and priests. Sometimes in the same individual has been found the most puzzling contradiction between hardness towards the mass of those who were held to be sinners and kindness, so far as it was possible to show it, towards each separate one.

It was an enlightened humanity which gave poor prisoners in Spain the assistance of counsel hundreds of years before this was thought of in Britain. The mixture of resolve to be pitiless and of inability to turn away from the guiding of humane impulse is illustrated by a story told of a poor Spaniard who decided that, as he could live no other way, he must take to highway robbery. He went out on the road, stopped a cart filled with farm produce, and called upon the driver to hand over all the money he had about him. Thirty dollars was the sum produced. "That is all I have," the driver said ruefully.

"I am very sorry," the highwayman told him, "but I have my wife and children to think of. However, I need not take all you have. Here are

GALA DAY IN GRANADA

Spanish girls, more especially in the south, usually dress in black. The wonderful film of the mantilla and the use of colours are kept exclusively for gala days

Photo, E. R. W. Lincoln

twenty-nine dollars back. I will keep one only."

"I thank your honour," said the grateful carter. "Now is there anything among my store of produce that your honour would like to take home to your family?"

"Some rice and beans would make us a meal of which we are so sorely in need," the robber answered. "But I must pay you for them. Here is your dollar again."

When the carter had given out the rice and beans he was smitten with

PEASANT INDUSTRY AND INGENUITY FASHIONING A PAIR OF SANDALS

He is a native of the modern province of Lugo in Galicia, that north and north-western ancient province of Spain which is washed by the waves of the Atlantic and by the Biscay waters. The people of Galicia are chiefly of Celtic origin, and their honesty, sturdiness, and virile temperaments have assisted not a little in the promotion of the spirit of industrial enterprise in Spain

ANTIQUE FARMHOUSE IN THE COUNTRY OF THE BASQUES

They are conversing in a strange tongue unfamiliar to their neighbours the Spaniards, for though in Spain and belonging to Spain their country is scarcely Spanish at all. For long centuries the Basques have been a distinct community inhabiting the western Pyrenees, and despite Moorish, Roman, and Gothic conquest, they have remained faithful to their language, customs, and institutions

POPULAR PLAYERS OF POPULAR MELODIES: DRUM AND FIFE BAND OF SAN SEBASTIAN

No people could be fonder of music than the Spaniards; they delight in it in all its forms but, undoubtedly, the favourite form of Spanish popular music is that of the guitar, an instrument known but little out of Spain. But though the guitar may be found in nearly every home throughout the land, and guitarists—men and women—are in constant evidence, there are many other musical instruments which enjoy high favour; and this fife and drum band of San Sebastian in the province of Guipuzcoa attracts large numbers of musical devotees

sympathy, and he asked the other to accept five dollars as a gift. "Take them for luck, then," he pleaded, when the robber refused the gift, and so the matter was arranged.

I have not come across anything like that in the folk-lore or the anecdotes of any other nation. It hits off the Spanish character with a nice exactitude as well as with humour.

Some of the contradictions in this character may be due to the mixture of Arab blood in the race. Those marvellously clever Moorish invaders of Spain left much behind them. The Alhambra on its glorious Granada hilltop, the mosque at Córdova, long since turned into a Catholic cathedral, the system of irrigation which is still in use to-day, these and many less evident signs show what a permanent mark was made upon Spain by that episode of the twelfth and thirteenth centuries.

Bad government, the government of kings and ministers and soldiers who sought their own enrichment and their own glory, and gave no thought to improving the conditions under which the people lived, this and the supremacy of the priesthood wiped out nearly all that the Moors had done for the country. Only in recent years has a strong wind of reform been stirring the dry bones of Spanish politics.

Among a small progressive class there are signs of a rebirth of the old Spanish energy which conquered half the world. The change in Madrid, as the city is now, from its gloomy shabbiness of the

WELL-DESERVED REFRESHMENT DURING WORK
The water-seller is a familiar figure in most Spanish towns ; in the country the peasantry cater for themselves, and a similar water-cart, with crudely-fashioned hood, may be seen in almost every field during the torrid days of summer

early years of the century is a symbol of the new spirit. It used to be mean, dirty, undistinguished. Now it is a worthy capital. Whole new quarters have sprung up, airy and attractive. Dilapidated buildings have given place to blocks of shops, offices, and flats. Tree-bordered boulevards make the city gay and green.

The celebrated Prado, which, when I saw it first, disappointed me sorely, is now one of the pleasantest strolling-spots I know. It has a good driving road on either side. The broad walks down the centre are divided by flower-beds, evergreens, and palms; they are shaded by avenues of trees. The Puerta del Sol (Gate of the Sun), which is the principal square of Madrid, has also been improved, though not so much as to rob it of its character. Crowded at all hours of the day and night, for the Spaniard goes very late to bed, it is at once the capital's gossip centre and enlightenment must be carried among the mass of the people.

It has been the law since 1857 in Spain that all boys must be educated, but it has never been properly enforced. The only part of the country where the Spaniard seems to be anxious to march with the times is Catalonia.

This province, lying along the Mediterranean at the top of Spain's eastern

IN THE PRECINCTS OF THE OLD CATHEDRAL AT SALAMANCA

The two cathedrals of the ancient city of Salamanca stand side by side; the smaller and older building, founded by Bishop Geronimo, was erected largely in the twelfth century, but the first Mass was said there in 1100. Though devoid of the over-ornate decoration which distinguishes the more modern church, the old cathedral possesses a rare beauty and dignity all its own

open-air business exchange and idlers' promenade.

Another sign of change is the new liking for open-air exercise among the Spanish young men of the towns. The men have become smarter, well set up, athletic in build. Many of the university students might be American boys. It is rare now to see the bristly cheeks, slovenly dress, and listless manner once common among Spaniards. To this the example of their active, sportsmanlike king must have contributed. But before there can begin a national regeneration,

coast, is the most fertile and energetic and prosperous region in the whole peninsula. It is also the most discontented. Catalonians have been turbulent and rebelliously inclined ever since they were united to Aragon in the twelfth century. They have always resented being yoked with and being ruled over by Castilians, proud and indolent and unskilled in the delicate art of government.

As you travel north-east to Barcelona from Madrid, the journey is for the greater part of the way through stony

YOUNG BASQUE REAPER AMID THE SLOPES OF THE PYRENEES

Nearly nine-tenths of the Basques of North Spain are agriculturists and devoted to the soil, though many intrepid seamen have been numbered among them. Crops of various kinds are grown, mostly on small holdings. The standard of education is high in the Basque provinces, which enjoy a certain measure of home rule and are said to be some of the most progressive districts in Spain

COUNTRY LIFE ON A SMALL HOLDING NEAR DURANGO IN THE BASQUE PROVINCES OF SPAIN

The Basques inhabiting the provinces of Biscay or Vizcaya, Guipuzcoa, and Alava in the north, differ both in race and in language from the rest of the population of Spain. They call themselves Escualdunac, holders of the Escuara speech; more than half of the vocabulary is borrowed and in the remainder there is traceable some affinity with Derber, thus supporting the theory that the earliest Basque-speaking people were of Mediterranean race. The Basques are capable agriculturists, and those who have emigrated to America have shown themselves very successful colonists

steppes, across dusty yellow plains, among ranges of sinister, rocky hills. From time to time you pass a mud-coloured village or small town, all one colour, the same colour as the country, a yellowy, browny grey. Wherever there is water, there are trees gladdening the eye with their leafage, and giving grateful shade to the lean sheep which elsewhere have to stand together in clumps, getting what shelter they can against sun and wind from one another. But these green oases are few and far between. The general character of the landscape is arid. After you have travelled for half a day you seem to have spent half your life in the train.

At each station there is a break in the monotony. Sun-dried peasants are gathered on the platform, their heads wrapped in gaudy kerchiefs, over which they wear broad-brimmed black hats of measureless antiquity.

STURDY STUFF OF THE SPANISH PEASANTRY

He has led a sober, healthy life, dedicated to agriculture and cattle-breeding in the highlands of Guipuzcoa, and now that its prime has come and gone he still retains much of the vigour and freshness of his youthful days

Their legs are cased in leather knee-breeches and their bodies enveloped in voluminous black cloaks. Save for the gleam of their black beady eyes you might take them for mummies, so brown and deeply-furrowed are their faces, so motionless their pose. Impish boys and girls offer the passengers glasses of water, sweets, fruit, live tortoises, fish, or any local speciality. The station-master and the engine-driver exchange views on politics. Then, with an effort, the train gets under way again.

Presently the aspect of the country alters. Instead of deserts you begin to see cultivated fields. Bare hills give place to woods and vineyards. The slopes are terraced and made to yield their increase of grape or olive. Forests of cork-trees enliven the landscape. Stone-pines stand sentinel, dark and dramatic. Groves of evergreen oaks refresh the traveller's wearied gaze.

As the coast is approached there begins tropical vegetation. The palm waves green hands of welcome. The feathery bamboo quivers in the hot air.

You notice also that the type of inhabitant has changed, has become more sturdy and sinewy. Great workers the Catalonians are—their land shows

HURDANO WOMEN WHO LIVE AMONG THE MOUNTAIN RANGES IN THE NORTHERN PART OF THE PROVINCE OF CÁCERES

These women belong to the Hurdanos, a people numbering some 4,000 persons, who inhabit the wild region lying amid the mountain fastnesses of Cáceres. They are left severely alone by their neighbours, the Spaniards and the Portuguese, and are regarded as the least intelligent people in the peninsula. Many members of the tribe are very depraved and degenerate, and, according to various accounts, dwell in a state of squalor and savagery, huddled together in cave-like hovels, contented to lead a semi-bestial existence, depending for sustenance on their ill-fed livestock, wild fruits and roots, and on charity received outside their region

WORKERS IN THE RIPE FIELDS OF A TREELESS COUNTRYSIDE

On the great plains of Castile almost anything could be grown if the secrets of agriculture known to the Moors of yesterday were possessed by the Spaniards of to-day ; for it was the Moors who made fertile these arid stretches and initiated the Spaniards into the mysteries of irrigation, and even now where the land is watered and tended nature is not backward in bestowing rich reward

it ; and great talkers, too. Jolly, vivid people. As you walk about the fine streets of Barcelona, up and down the Rambla, the long promenade which runs through the city, with its tall trees and its delicious flower market, you see proofs enough that the Catalonians are an enterprising, business-like race. They are sufficiently business-like to have made their city a pleasant place to live in as well as a commercial and an industrial hive.

The impressions one brings away from Barcelona are not of gloom, and chimneys filling the air with filth, and narrow, squalid streets, but of limitless

avenues, a bracing, clear atmosphere, dignified buildings, a full and busy, but in no sense a sordid, life. In the evening, when the street cars are filled with home-going workmen, an amusing note of contrast will be struck by a goatherd driving his flock through the bustling streets and milking the nannies at the doors of his customers. Then up at the back of the city are exquisite glimpses of luxuriant hills where nestle villages well worth a climb.

Southern Spain is the more languorous and romantic. Seville in spring is exquisite. Hot, white sunshine, roses and carnations scenting the warm air,

CASTILIAN INDUSTRY IN THE SHADE OF THE VINE

It is in the Castiles, the core of the kingdom, that the true Spain is to be found, and the Castilian speech ranks as its standard language. Here, even in the remote districts where the inhabitants are forced to lead a life of strict frugality, hospitality and courtesy are not lacking, and some of the finest qualities and most attractive characteristics of the Spanish nation are manifest

REAPER FROM ONE OF THE SCATTERED CORNFIELDS OF CASTILE

To one travelling the vast plateau of Castile, cornfields appear as a welcome sight suggestive of life and therefore of water. For the most part the horizon encloses succeeding undulations of tawny soil disintegrated by the sun and strewn with rocks. But near the villages cultivation persists, for beneath the friable surface is good loam that retains the nourishment from the scanty rainfall

FARM BUILDING IN A NOTABLE GROVE OF GIANT DATE PALMS AT ELCHE IN THE PROVINCE OF ALICANTE.

The magnificent palm forest of Elche contains more than 115,000 trees and is a Moorish heritage. The enterprising Moors, so skilled in all that pertained to irrigation, are said to have directed the water to this spot from a distance of nearly three miles that they might create an oasis in the centre of the barren district which was, and is, little more than a desert. Some of these trees, which reach a height of seventy to eighty feet, produce large crops of dates, and supply many of the palm-leaves bought extensively throughout the country by the pious at religious festivals

SHOWY COSTUME IN VOGUE AMONG THE SPANISH PEASANTRY

Embroidery heightens the attractiveness of the costumes of both men and women in Spain, and the short, braided jacket, a favourite style of the Spaniard, is seen in many parts of the country. The white shirt of these young peasants, who live in a district where four provinces, Salamanca, Zamora, Valladolid, and Avila, almost touch, is gathered round the neck and fastened with a button

orange-trees aglow with their golden lanterns, almond and double cherry-blossom, geranium and wistaria covering the houses with pink and mauve delight. Peep into the patios of the houses and you see flowers in every one. On the stalls at the street corners lie heaps of big, fragrant violets and scented stocks.

Granada, with the restrained beauty of its Moorish Alhambra on the hilltop, and its glorious views spreading out to the snowy sierra and the tinkle of water ever in one's ear, is an ineffaceable memory. Cordóva's ancient streets and marvellous Arab mosque call one back with insistent charm. Sunny Valencia and green Alicante, proud Segovia and mysterious Burgos and shining Cadiz, all contribute to the fascination.

But I think that the mind returns most often to Barcelona. The other cities of Spain radiate the glamour of the past. Barcelona is so actually, so vibrantly, alive.

WHERE NATURE MAKES EVEN WASHTUB DRUDGERY GRACIOUS : WOMEN OF ELCHE WASHING THEIR LINEN

Luxuriant tropical vegetation, with coolness and freshness due to many running streams, make Elche a paradise for artists. It is in the province of Alicante on the Mediterranean, about thirteen miles south-west of the town of Alicante, and is strikingly Moorish in the appearance of both its architecture and its people. The women do most of their laundry work in the streams, presenting many a charming picture as they kneel by the swift-flowing water under the shade of lovely palms scouring their linen on flat square slabs, and using water vessels of classical design

Spain

II. Two Thousand Years of Eventful History

By Edward Wright

Writer of "The Story of French Expansion Overseas"

THE huge, bleak tableland which forms about five-sevenths of the total area of Spain was once well-wooded, moist, and fruitful. Its fertile fields served as a Roman granary. For centuries, however, the Castilian plateau has been included in a drought belt running on either side of the Mediterranean through Persia and Central Asia to the dry lands of the United States. This Castilian barrier, while it has affected the character of the people compelled by it to a hard struggle for existence, helped to save Western Europe from becoming part of Islam, whose crusading followers, after their conquest of the country, gradually fell back to the warm valleys of Andalusia

In prehistoric times, of which cave paintings, weapons and other implements, pottery, tombs, skulls, still undeciphered inscriptions, and certain forms of speech are the sole remains,

Spain is believed to have been peopled by tribes belonging to a race, called the Iberian, that spread over Aquitania as well as Spain, occupied the Canary Islands, part of North Africa, Corsica, and even penetrated to Britain. To the Iberians in Spain succeeded, about 500 B.C., the Celts, who, entering by way of the Pyrenees, mingled with the Iberians and are known as Celtiberians, or Celtiberi. Of this mixed race the Basques are regarded as the surviving representatives.

In the third century B.C. the peninsula was invaded by the Carthaginians, who founded Cartagena (Carthago Nova), and whose ancestors, the Phoenicians, had established a trading port at Cadiz (Gades) between eight hundred and nine hundred years earlier.

In the year 205 B.C., the Carthaginians were expelled by Roman legionaries, and the Roman conquest thus begun was not

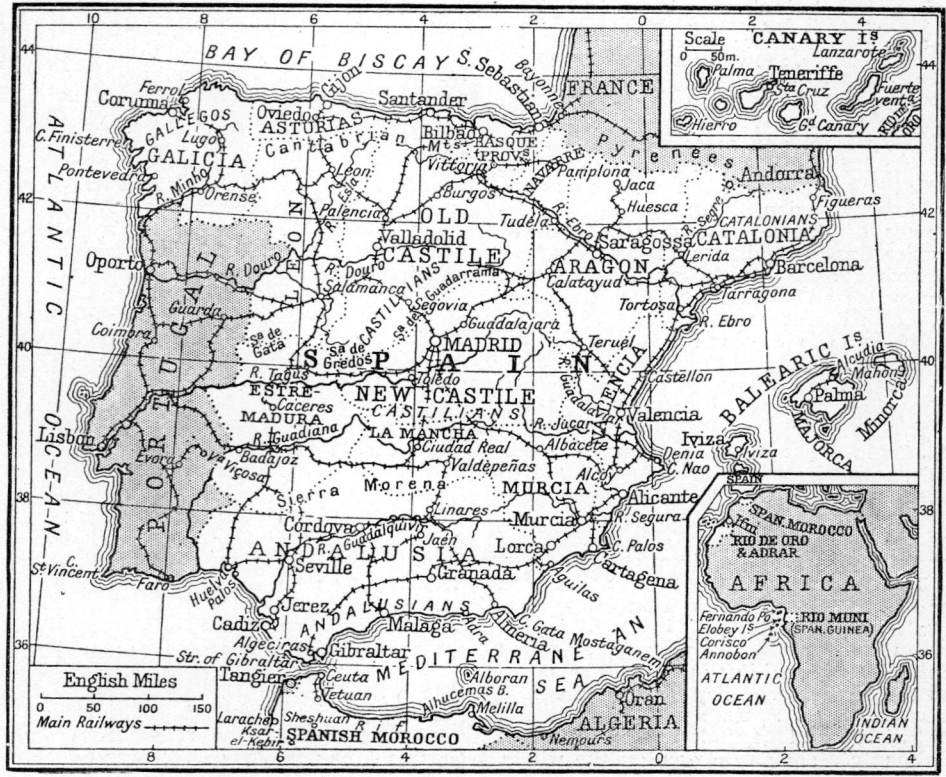

THE KINGDOM OF SPAIN AND ITS PEOPLES

SPLENDID CEREMONIAL COSTUME

The province of Salamanca has an incredible variety of fête-day costumes, each vying with the other in beauty of style, richness of embroidery, and vividness of colouring

completed until A.D. 19. Thenceforward, for some four centuries, Spain formed one of the richest and most influential parts of the Roman Empire. Rome made an indelible impression on the manners, customs, religion, language, and place-names of Spain. Trajan was born at Italica, near Seville, and Spanish-born writers like Seneca, Lucan, Martial, and Quintilian added lustre to the Silver Age of Latin literature.

In A.D. 409 the land was over-run by Vandals, Alans, and Suevi. Rome called to her aid the Visigoths, or West Goths, who since about 250 had occupied the region roughly corresponding to modern Rumania. Thus began the great Visigothic rule, which lasted for some three hundred years, its most notable period being that between the reign of Leovigild (569-586) and that of Roderic, who was defeated and slain by the Moors in 711.

The Moorish conquest of Spain was extraordinarily swift. Within three years the Saracen invaders had settled in the warm southland of Andalusia and had extended their military camps as far north as the Pyrenees. They made themselves masters of all Spain except Galicia and Asturias, and founded the Western Caliphate. Their rule was, on the whole, tolerant, and their influence in art and literature, science, and philosophy lasting. Before the wide sweep of their armies many of the nobles of the conquered peoples retreated to the Asturian hills or the Pyrenees, there to prepare for the revanche which took so long in its consummation, or made their way to France, Italy, and other parts of Europe, including Ireland. But the poorer classes profited by the impetus the Arabs gave to agriculture.

The story of the reconquest of the country is the great romance of chivalry. The conflict between Crescent and Cross which proceeded as the hardier survivors of the Saracen invasion slowly pushed their way southwards was tempered by a spirit that survived in the peninsula until it became an affectation, and its ridiculous ghost was exorcised by the satire of Cervantes in the second half of the sixteenth century.

It took some five centuries to loosen the hold of the Moors and about two centuries and a half to destroy the remains of their power in Spain. Two great battles mark their decline and fall. Driven into armed union, the Moors inflicted a signal defeat on the Spaniards at Alarcos, July 11, 1195. Almost exactly seventeen years later, on July 12, 1212, on the fateful field of Las Nevas de Toloso, in a valley of the Sierra Morena, the Christians having united in their turn, the combined forces of Castile, Navarre, and Aragon routed the army of Mahomed III., killing 100,000 Arab warriors and virtually destroying the Western Caliphate.

Not only is this event important in the history of the Moorish dominion in Spain, it marks the beginning of the dynastic and political union of the country and a distinct weakening of the independent and individual dominance of the nobles.

Riven by racial, tribal, dynastic, and sectarian differences, Spain had grown into a miniature continent of little conflicting nations, a condition of things reflected even in the life of the people to-day.

While descendants of the Iberians, as already indicated, had found refuge in Biscay, survivors of their Celtic conquerors were to be found in the west and south. Defeated Vandals had fled to the tangled heights of Galicia, from which, with Goths who found shelter in Asturias, they had fought southward to Portugal, which became a separate kingdom in 1095.

French invaders of the seventh century made their home in the Catalonian hills. Fragments of Saracen stock are still to be found in Andalusia.

It will thus be seen that, probably because of its highland divisions and fastnesses, few of the races that have occupied the peninsula have been entirely driven out.

By the middle of the fifteenth century Spain was within measurable distance of becoming mistress of the world. The hitherto independent states had been reduced to four—Castile, Aragon, Navarre, and Moorish Granada, the last-named still magnificent as regards its court, but under the suzerainty of Castile.

In 1469 took place the marriage of Ferdinand, son of John II., King of Aragon and Sicily, and Isabella, daughter of John II., King of Castile and Leon. Isabella succeeded to the throne of Castile in 1474 and Ferdinand to that of Aragon in 1479. The greater part of Spain was now united under one monarchy, though the two monarchs both retained special and independent rights of their own.

It was in Castile that the old Gothic monarchy first revived. Castile absorbed Leon, Biscay, Asturias, Galicia, Estramadura, Murcia, and Andalusia, and extended its sway from the Bay of Biscay to the Mediterranean. The history of the Basque provinces of Alava, Biscay, and Guipuzcoa offer remarkable points of interest for the ethnologist and the student of political and social life.

Golden Age of Ferdinand and Isabella

The virility and independence of the Basques, who form to-day almost the whole of the population of Guipuzcoa, secured to them a political freedom that lasted until the third decade of the nineteenth century, a freedom that included the right to make independent treaties with foreign powers.

Aragon had linked itself with Catalonia in the twelfth century and conquered Valencia in the thirteenth. With the aid of the Catalonian navy, it disputed successfully with the fleets of Pisa and Genoa the control of the Mediterranean and conquered Sicily, Sardinia, and the Balearic Islands. As early as the fourteenth century a Catalonian commander who declined to attack a force not exceeding his own by more than one vessel was liable to capital punishment.

Isabella died in 1504, Ferdinand in 1516, and their successor, Charles of Ghent (better known as the Emperor Charles V.), abdicated in 1556 and died in 1558. The years 1479-1556 embrace the great period of Spanish history. In 1492 Granada was captured and the banners of Castile and Aragon flew proudly over the magnificent fortress-palace of the Alhambra, this recovery of Christian Spain balancing the fall of Constantinople to the Turks.

In the same year, under the patronage of Isabella, Columbus started on his momentous first voyage across the Atlantic, queen and navigator being inspired by the idea of reaching the rich Indies by a westward route and with the profits derived from the trade so opened up converting the Orient to Christianity.

Ferdinand refused at first to take any part or interest in the adventure. He preferred that Portugal should exhaust her substance in Africa and the East while Spain held her own best forces in reserve to conquer Europe.

Spanish Expansion Under Charles V.

He married his only son to the daughter of the Emperor Maximilian, and doubled this thread of dynastic intrigue by wedding his elder daughter Joanna to that emperor's only son Philip, heir to all the great possessions of the Hapsburgs. Another daughter was made queen of Portugal, while the younger, Catherine, was married first to Arthur, Prince of Wales, and after his death to Henry VIII.

After Isabella's death, when he succeeded as regent to the throne of Castile, Ferdinand's astuteness degenerated into cunning. Isabella, though sharing with her husband responsibility for the Inquisition, the expulsion of the Jews, and the breach of covenant with the defeated Moors, was, despite her bigotry, a noble-minded woman, whose death was the occasion of general and deep-seated mourning.

Under their gifted grandson, Charles of Ghent, Spain became mistress of the New World, conquering Mexico in 1519-21, and Peru and Chile in 1531-41. At Pavia, in 1525, they broke the chivalry of France and took the French king (Francis I.) prisoner. They trampled in glory through Germany, threatened the Turk on land, smashed the naval power of the Ottomans, and took Tunis. But great as was the genius of Charles and formidable as was his famous infantry, he found Europe too strong for him, and, broken in health and ambition, retired in 1556 to a monastery, where he spent the two remaining years of his life.

Decay of the Hapsburg Dynasty

To his brother Ferdinand he left his imperial rights over Germany. To his son Philip II. he gave Spain and the possessions of Spain in Europe and America, with a good chance of the virtual kingship of England.

Philip II. (1556-98), stupefied by pride in his material power, inflexible in error, and a megalomaniac palliating the grossest ambitions by cruel bigotry, frittered his great inheritance, which included the Netherlands, Sicily, and much of Italy, the southern part of North America, and South America, except Portuguese Brazil. Beaten on land by the Dutch, broken at sea by the English, outplayed in intrigue by the French, he left Spain depleted of riches and pompously decadent.

The process of national decay quickened under the last kings of the Hapsburg dynasty, which ended with Charles II. (1665-1700). Spain was still supposed to be receiving fabulous treasure from the mines of Mexico and Peru ; but only the untaxed grandees waxed fat ; the common people were ground down under the weight of taxation on their food and industry to such an extent that the population dwindled rapidly, the revenues fell into hopeless insufficiency, and the whole country groaned in discontent.

Rule of the French Bourbons

Thoroughly beaten by France, Spain, in 1713, had to accept as ruler the grandson of Louis XIV., after a twelve years' War of Succession, in which Britain, while winning military renown through the victories of Marlborough, suffered political defeat at the hands of the French. Under the French Bourbons, the first of whom was Philip V. (1701-16), Spain lost all her Italian territory, Portugal (which had been annexed in 1580) and the rich Netherlands. She sank into the position of a French vassal, and except under the good administration of Charles III. (1759-88), the people were seething with hatred of their new masters.

When, in 1808, Napoleon seated his brother Joseph Bonaparte upon the Spanish throne, this hatred took the form of a popular rising. The French forces were beaten at Baylen and elsewhere, Joseph Bonaparte had to fly in haste from the country, and a French squadron was captured at Cadiz.

Revolution and Reaction

There followed the great War of Liberation (1808-14), known also as the Peninsular Campaign, which made Wellington famous and resulted in the expulsion of the French and the placing of Ferdinand VII. upon the throne.

The people now looked forward to enjoying the fruits of the constitution of Cadiz, adopted in 1812, a system of free government which restored parliamentary liberties older than those of the English.

Ferdinand, liberated by Napoleon and welcomed back to Madrid in March, 1814, at once abolished all free government, arrested the Liberal leaders, re-established the Inquisition, and re-imposed the old iniquitous taxes. In January, 1820, Ferdinand was made prisoner by a successful revolutionary government ; but Bourbon reactionaries in France came to the aid of Bourbon reactionaries in Spain. In April, 1823, a French army of 100,000 troops crossed the Pyrenees, scattered the Spanish national militia, and restored despotic power to Ferdinand, who died in 1833.

Ferdinand married four times, but had children only by his fourth wife, Maria Christina of Naples. His eldest daughter (born in 1830) was proclaimed queen as Isabella II., and Christina ruled as regent (1833-40). Then came the first Carlist War (1834-39) in favour of Ferdinand's brother, Don Carlos, who was largely supported by the mountaineers of the Basque provinces, and the hillfolk of Upper Aragon, Catalonia, and Valencia. The Carlists had the better fighting men, but suffered defeat largely through the incapacity of their leaders.

A revised constitution was promulgated in 1837, and in 1843 Isabella was declared of age. During 1843-68, when real power was in the hands of an Irishman, General Leopold O'Donnell, there were wars with Peru, Chile, and Morocco. Following another revolution and the flight of Isabella, a provisional government was set up in 1868-70, under a fighting Liberal from Catalonia, General Prim.

Restoration of the Bourbons

As Spain generally, tired of revolution and military despotism, wanted a constitutional monarch, several of the great Powers contended for the opportunity of placing their candidates on the throne. The Prussian advocacy of Leopold of Hohenzollern and the French opposition to it was one of the factors in bringing about the Franco-Prussian War.

Eventually, General Prim conducted to the throne Amadeus, Duke of Aosta, son of Victor Emmanuel of Italy, who, proclaimed as Amadeo I., entered his capital on January 2, 1871. An able man, intrigued against by the nobles, he abdicated in disgust on February 11, 1873.

By the summer of 1873, a second Don Carlos, grandson of the first, was fighting in the north at the head of 50,000 men. A republic was formed, the Carlists were beaten back, and the Bourbon dynasty was once more restored, the son of Isabella II. ascending the throne as Alphonso XII. and reigning from 1874-85.

The young monarch, who was studying at Sandhurst in England, when called to Madrid, proved a good, gallant, prudent man, and, by reconciling the better kind of reactionaries with the more moderate of progressives, directed his care-worn, suffering subjects along the difficult path to social peace. When he died, on November 25, 1885, Spain possessed, in principle, if not in effect, a limited monarchy and parliamentary government.

His son, Alphonso XIII., was born on May 17, 1886, and his Hapsburg mother,

Queen Christina, acted as regent until 1902. She kept the country free from civil war, but could not escape misfortune. In 1895, the Cubans, who had been promised self-government, rose to secure it. So furious were the Spanish reprisals, however, that when, in 1897, autonomy was offered to the islanders, they refused it, and continuing the struggle, now for independence, were in 1898 joined by the forces of the U.S.A.

One Spanish squadron was sunk at Manila, and the main fleet was trapped at Santiago, in Cuba, the town being enveloped on the landward side by an American army corps and blockaded on the other by a powerful American fleet. Once more Spain vanished as a naval power, and had to part with the last remnants of her possessions in the West and the East—Cuba, Porto Rico, and the Philippines.

Free from the burden of colonies she was unable to develop, the mother country began to grow stronger, though more by economic progress of the people than by political development.

When Alphonso XIII. came of age and established a British connexion by marrying Princess Victoria of Battenberg, the attempt on their lives and the courage they displayed won for them a popular esteem which has never wavered. During the Great War, while king and people were strongly on the side of the Allies, Spain, as a whole, declared neutrality.

SPAIN: FACTS AND FIGURES

The Country

Occupies greater part of Iberian peninsula and is bounded north by the Bay of Biscay and the Pyrenees mountains, which latter divide Spain from France; west by Portugal and the Atlantic; south and east by the Mediterranean. Pyrenees form barriers between extreme end of great European plain and the meseta or Spanish table-land which has an average altitude of about 2,500 feet. In the south-east the Sierra Nevada mountains form an almost unbroken chain from Cape de la Nao to Cadiz, while the Cantabrian range backs the north coast. Principal rivers are the Douro, Tagus, and Guadiana whose mouths are in Portugal, and the Minho and the Ebro. The meseta has more continuous sunshine than any other part of Europe. In the inland regions considerable variations from freezing point to 100° F. are not unusual in a year. Many rivers become nearly dry towards the end of summer. Total area of country exclusive of Canary and Balearic Islands about 190,050 square miles, with an estimated population of about 20,000,000.

Government and Constitution

Spain is a constitutional monarchy. The Crown has executive power while legislative authority is shared by the King and the Cortes or Parliament. This consists of a Senate and a Congress. Senators are divided into three classes: those who hold rank in their own right; life senators nominated by the sovereign; and those elected by the corporations of State or communal and provincial states, the universities and the church. Numbers of first two classes of senators are not to exceed 180. Third class has same number. Congress consists of deputies and has a proportional representation basis of one deputy for every 50,000 of population, and is elected for five years. Voting compulsory for men over 25.

Defence

Compulsory military service in force for one year in a depot, eight years in active army and nine years in reserves. Country is divided into eight military districts under Captains-General; six of these provide two divisions, the remainder one. For constabulary purposes there is a Guardia Civil, while military police work and Customs protection are furnished by the Carabineros. Both are recruited from army. Spanish troops in Africa are always on war footing. Navy includes battleships and cruisers, some of which are obsolete, and there are about 40 destroyers besides submarines and coast defence boats.

Commerce and Industries

Agriculture is main occupation of people; 45 per cent. of the soil is naturally unproductive, 10 per cent. bare rock. Among important crops are wheat, of which over 68,200,000 cwts. were obtained in 1921, barley, rye, and maize. In same year 3,286,000 acres were under vines from which were extracted over 506,900,000 gallons of wine. Olives, flax, esparto, oranges, and hazel nuts are also grown, and there are activities in connexion with silk culture and cane and beet sugar. There are great numbers of livestock, including more than 20,500,000 sheep. Mineral resources include copper, coal, iron, zinc, quicksilver, lead, sulphur, and silver. Among main manufactories are woollen, cotton, paper, cork and glass. In 1921 imports totalled £50,455,873 and included machinery, cotton, chemicals and timber. Exports for same year included wine, silk, stone, and wool, and were valued at £32,497,615. Standard coin the silver peseta, nominal value 9½d.

Communications

There are over 9,500 miles of railway all privately owned, though most companies have government subventions or guarantees. Roads and highways total about 46,600 miles, while telegraph lines measure some 73,000 miles, and telephone stations number more than 73,400. There are important wireless stations at Aranjuez and Barcelona.

Religion and Education

Religion of National Church and majority of population is Roman Catholic and there are nine metropolitan sees. Under Spanish constitution State is bound to aid clergy and sacred structures. The establishment of religious houses is regulated by government. There is complete religious freedom for all denominations. Country is divided into eleven educational districts of which the universities are the centres. There are over 25,000 public schools supported by the State. Universities are located at Barcelona, Granada, Madrid, Murcia, Oviedo, Salamanca, Santiago, Seville, Valencia, Valladolid and Zaragoza. These have each at least two faculties for science, medicine, law, pharmacy and philosophy and letters.

Chief Towns

Madrid, capital (estimated population 751,000), Barcelona (710,000), Valencia (243,500), Seville (205,500), Malaga (150,500), Murcia (141,000), Zaragoza (141,000), Bilbao (113,000), Cadiz (76,500), Alicante (64,000), Coruna (62,000), Badajoz (38,000).

PEASANT WOMEN AT A SPRING IN THE VICINITY OF LAS PALMAS

Notable for their perfect climate and luxuriant vegetation, the Canary Isles attract a large number
of foreign visitors. One of the principal health-resorts is Las Palmas, an attractive town situated
on the north-east coast of Grand Canary. The volcanic soil of the islands is very rich, and, where
natural streams or irrigation obtain, abundant crops of cereals, fruit, and vegetables are produced

Spain

III. Rise & Fall of Spain's Colonial Empire

By W. Francis Aitken

Assistant Editor, " Harmsworth's Universal Encyclopedia "

THE Spanish Empire was the first on which it could be said that the sun never set. From the third to the fifteenth century the mother country was swept by successive waves of invasion. Then, in the second half of the fifteenth century, when the greater part of the country was united under Ferdinand of Aragon and Isabella of Castile, the merest accident gave to this land the key to the New World of the West.

The story of the countries which came under Spanish dominion are told in some detail under the headings of the countries themselves.

For eighteen years the Genoese navigator, Christopher Columbus, waited wearily for the opportunity to put to the proof his theory of a western passage to the Indies. His own country failing him, from 1470 to 1484 he pleaded his cause in vain at the Portuguese court. Then, sending his brother to Henry VII. of England— who, had not shipwreck delayed the envoy, might have lent his support to the quest—Columbus went to Spain.

Columbus's First Voyage of Discovery

Spain was then in the throes of her final struggle against the Moors, and it was not until 1492, when he was on his way to the French court, that the interest of Isabella was secured, and Columbus was granted his charter.

With three small vessels of indifferent seaworthiness, and scratch crews, he set sail from the little port of Palos on August 3. He had secured his appointment as perpetual and hereditary admiral and viceroy of any territories discovered, and the promise of one-tenth of the resulting profits.

After touching at the Canary Islands, annexed by Spain in 1495, he reached the Bahamas, landing at Watling Island, and having visited Haiti (Hispaniola) and Cuba, returned to Spain in March, 1493, convinced that he had reached the eastern extremity of Asia. It was now that the Pope, Alexander VI., was called upon to divide the territory outside Europe between Spain and Portugal.

Spanish Dominion in the West

On his third voyage Columbus, who died after his fourth voyage in 1506, for the first time reached the mainland of South America.

In 1513 Vasco Nunez de Balboa sighted the Pacific, and in less than fifty years after Columbus first landed in the West Indies the entire continent from Labrador to Patagonia had been visited, and for the most part annexed to the crown of Castile.

In 1519-21 Mexico was conquered by Hernando Cortés ; in 1520 Magellan threaded the strait that bears his name, and in the following year reached the Philippines. In 1533-34 the Spaniards under Francisco Pizarro added Peru to the Spanish dominions, while Chile was settled by Valdivia in 1541.

Meanwhile, with the accession of the emperor Charles V., the Netherlands were annexed in 1516. Tunis became Spanish in 1535, and the Philippines were absorbed in 1569. Portugal was added in 1580, to be lost again in 1640. Sicily and much of Italy also came under Spanish rule.

With the accession of Philip II. (1556-98) the sun began to set on the great empire, for the annexation of Portugal was more than balanced by

PROSPEROUS PEASANTS OF TENERIFFE

The inhabitants of the Canary Islands are chiefly of Spanish descent with traces of the original natives, the Guanches, who are now extinct. Education is backward, but the islanders are by no means unenterprising and have several flourishing home industries

When the Cubans rose and were supported by the U.S.A. in 1898 Cuba secured her independence, Porto Rico and the Philippines were acquired by the U.S.A., and in the following year Spain's remaining possessions in the Pacific, the Caroline, Pelew, and Ladrone Islands, were ceded to Germany. For the Philippines Spain received the sum of £4,000,000.

The Spanish Council of the Indies, founded in 1511, which became the supreme authority in colonial affairs, and was known later as the Colonial Office, closed its doors in January, 1899.

Spain, from whose soil first sprang political liberty, set her face resolutely against local self-government in her oversea possessions.

Columbus himself was inspired with sound ideas of colonisation; he saw the need of permanent settlement. As governor of Haiti he declared that there should be no permanent grants of land to those who had not cultivated it for three years. He expected all who went out to the new territories to work, and refused to recognize distinctions of rank among them.

But Columbus—referred to as " no Spaniard "—was pushed on one side, and, while the first governors sent out were on the whole good men, the foundations of empire were sacrificed to the reckless pursuit of wealth, which, to the early Spanish adventurers, meant gold, then silver.

Up to the end of the eighteenth century no less than 1,000 millions sterling of gold and silver was exported

loss of prestige (as in the destruction of the Armada) elsewhere.

The Netherlands declared their independence in 1581, and secured it in 1648 ; Chile and Colombia severed allegiance in 1818-19, and Peru and Mexico became independent in 1824-25.

At one time, towards the end of the eighteenth century, it seemed as if Spain was destined to be the dominant power in North America. But Louisiana, ceded by France to Spain in 1762, was sold by Napoleon to the U.S.A. in 1803 for sixty millions of francs. Florida passed from her hands in 1819, as did part of Texas, New Mexico, and California in 1848.

to the mother country from Spanish South America, irrespective of the large quantities spirited through clandestine channels to escape duty. With the grants of land went allotments of Indians to work it (the repartimientos), and when it was found that the Indians were unequal to the demands made upon them, negroes were imported from Africa.

From 1501, when the great commercial inquisition known as the Casa de la Contratación, or board of trade, was instituted, nothing could enter or leave Spain without the supervision of this authority. All civil and religious officials were sent from the homeland; the Inquisition exercised its maleficent sway; the colonists were restricted in their relations with foreign powers, and could import or export nothing except

from and to Spain, a restriction which involved costly reshipments in some Spanish home port. Restrictions were placed also on production.

These are some of the reasons why to-day the once vast colonial empire of Spain is confined to a few undeveloped holdings in Africa. The Balearic Islands and the Canary Islands, where the aboriginal Guanches have been absorbed, form provinces of the kingdom.

Of Spain's African possessions Rio Muni, or Continental Guinea, is a settlement between the Cameroons and the French Congo. Extending about 125 miles inland, a region characterised by low-lying swamps, forests, treeless plateaux, and isolated mountainous areas, it is inhabited by sub-tribes of the Fan or Fang race in the interior, and by Bengas (almost the only natives who can read

MODERN TROGLODYTES AT HOME IN TENERIFFE

Teneriffe is the largest of the Canary Islands, a volcanically-formed archipelago in the Atlantic Ocean. It has a rich, though rugged, surface, crowned by the volcanic Pico de Teyde, over 12,000 feet high. Some of the poorest inhabitants make their homes in strange cavern-like houses bored in the rock-formation—a genial climate making this primitive mode of living far from unpleasant

NATIVE LIFE IN THE MARKET PLACE AT TETUAN, THE CAPITAL OF SPANISH MOROCCO

The Spanish zone in Morocco extends along the Mediterranean for some 200 miles, with an average breadth of 60 miles. Tetuan, situated about six miles from the Bay of Tetuan, and connected with its port by a short railway, is the headquarters of the Moroccan Khalifa who rules under the control of the Spanish High Commissioner. The town's trade is much in the hands of the Jews, who number about one-third of the population estimated at 30,000. Attractive tilework has long been a favourite industry and the manufactures include slippers, flintlocks, and artistic cloths much patronised for wear by Moorish country girls

and write), Kumbes, Balengues, Bapukos, and Bujebas along the coast-line. The population is estimated at about 101,000, and may be much larger, but the Spanish authorities only exercise effective control over a fringe of seaboard and strips of territory along the navigable rivers, the chief settlement being at Bata, and the seat of government at Santa Isabel, on Fernando Po, part of the two groups of islands comprising Insular Guinea.

Fernando Po, which was ceded to Spain by Portugal in 1778, occupied by the British in 1827-34 during the slave trade suppression, and over which Spain formally declared her ascendancy in 1843, has an area, inclusive of adjacent islands, of rather more than 800 square miles, and a population of about 20,000, mainly Bubis, of Bantu stock, and Portos, descendants of negro slaves, the last-named occupying the coastal

RIF WARRIOR OF NORTH MOROCCO

Rif or Er-Rif, a mountainous district in North Morocco, falls within the Spanish zone and is very wild and difficult of access. Here are to be found the retreats of the turbulent Berber tribes who have been in constant insurrection against Spain

districts. Much educational progress has been made, largely as a result of the work of Roman Catholic and Protestant missions, who instruct the natives in handicrafts, and the government has instituted an up-to-date labour bureau.

If its railways were extended and its labour problems solved, Fernando Po should be at least as profitable as Portuguese San Thomé and Principe, in the production of cocoa, coffee, sugar, palm-oil, copra, yams, bananas, tobacco, and quinine ; while the mainland of Rio Muni is said to be rich in minerals. Spanish Morocco is divided into two zones, one in the north, between the Mediterranean coast and its hinterland (the Rif and greater part of the Jebala) ; and the other the south-western enclave on the Atlantic seaboard around the town of Ifni. Much of the country is peopled by wild tribes, and has been only partially explored.

The town of Melilla occupies a rocky promontory situated some fifty miles east of the Bay of Alhucemas ; and there are a number of small islands on the Mediterranean coast which are used to some extent as penal settlements. Melilla, which has been Spanish since 1597, has a population of about 41,000 ; Tetuan, the capital, occupied in 1913, and opposite Gibraltar, 30,000 ; Larache, 15,000 ; Ksar-el-Kebir (Alcazar), 8,500, including many Jews.

The port and territory of Ifni were ceded to Spain in 1860, but are only nominally occupied. The natives are largely of Berber extraction. There are fisheries in the enclave of Ifni and along the coast between Larache and Tangier. The Rif district has possibilities of mineral and agricultural development.

The Spanish Sahara, which includes Rio de Oro and Adrar, is a district of north-west Africa extending north-east and south-west from the Wad Draa, on the southern frontier of Morocco, to Cape Blanco, on the northern confines of Mauritania, and has an area of about 100,000 square miles, bounded on the west by the sea, and on the other sides by the French Sahara and Moroccan territory. The Spanish possessions are divided into three zones—the colony of Rio de Oro and Adrar, the protected area, and " occupied territory " of uncertain delimitation. The population, estimated at about 80,000, consists of Moors, Arabs, and Arabised Berbers, more or less crossed with negro blood, and is almost wholly nomadic.

The territory between Cape Bojador and Cape Blanco was declared a Spanish protectorate in 1885.

Rio de Oro is valuable as a curing station for the fishing fleets of the Canary and Balearic Islands, and has some importance from a strategic point of view. But it has no navigable river (the Rio de Oro being an inlet of the sea), it lacks fresh water, has no harbours, no railways, and the nomadic habits of the population militate against development. Its future prosperity would seem to depend upon the growth of the fishing industry.

MOORISH WATER-SELLERS OF TETUAN REPLENISHING THEIR SUPPLIES

Where cleanliness is concerned Tetuan can compare favourably with most Moorish towns ; many of its streets are wide and fairly straight, while several of the aristocratic Moorish families, whose ancestors were expelled from Spain, own pleasant houses, with courts containing fountains and orange trees. The present town dates from the late fifteenth century and was built by Andalusian Moors

Sweden

I. The Elder Nation of the Hardy North

By A. MacCallum Scott

Author of " Through Finland," etc.

SWEDEN (known in Swedish as Sverige) is the immemorial home and breeding ground of that mighty northern race which has been the dominant strain in the world since the Goths broke up the Roman Empire.

Here in the sacred land of Odin, with the most ancient temple and place of sacrifice of the Gods of the North at Upsala, for unnumbered thousands of years before the birth of Christ, while the Romans and the Greeks were yet barbarians, before the nomad Abraham migrated with his flocks and his herds from Ur of the Chaldees, before the earliest Pharaoh ruled in Egypt, the blue-eyed, flaxen-haired, long-headed Goths had settled.

Century by century, amid the forests, lakes and meadows, they increased their numbers and developed those special traits of character, intellect, and physique which, in the fullness of time, were to give their children's children the world for an inheritance.

Here was the " Northern Hive " from which issued the swarms which settled all over Europe. No written record of their early life

PEASANT GIRL OF GARPENBERG
The people of Sweden are as interesting in character and appearance as the scenery itself, and many lovely faces may be seen in the old land of Goths and Vikings

remains, but the ancient stone and bronze and iron implements and weapons, the skulls and urns and ornaments and coins found in numerous graves and burial mounds, and displayed in wonderful sequence in the Northern Museum, in Stockholm, tell a story which archaeologists are just beginning to learn to decipher.

Most other European races have changed greatly since history first began to be recorded. It would be impossible now to find the pure stock of ancient Greece and Rome. Celtic, Iberian, Teutonic, and Slavonic are mingled in inextricable confusion from the Urals to the Atlantic, and from the Baltic to the Mediterranean. From the cross-breeding new and vigorous races have sprung. The Jews, with marvellous tenacity, though dispersed over the face of the world, have succeeded in retaining their racial purity in a remarkable degree. But in Scandinavia nature alone has preserved the Gothic type undiluted. The Swedes to-day are, in character and physique, very much what their pagan ancestors were, according to the descriptions of

ANTIQUATED FIRE ALARM OF LEKSAND

"Break the glass and blow the horn!" This old-world device, still to be found in some of the more remote villages of Sweden, is gradually being displaced by electrical fire-alarm boxes, which afford instant communication with the fire stations

Photo, Publishers' Photo Service

In the ninth century they were equally at home on their pasture farms in Iceland and in the Emperor's Guard at Constantinople, fighting savage Finns in the northern forests or fanatical Arabs on the edge of the Syrian Desert. This adaptability accounts for the sharp national distinction between Norwegians and Swedes who, nevertheless, spring from the same Gothic stock.

Although they are parts of the same Scandinavian peninsula, and lie alongside each other for 1,000 miles, north and south, the character of the two countries is radically different. It is the difference between the Highlands and the Lowlands, between the deep, far-reaching fjords of the Atlantic seaboard and the broad, fertile plains of Scania projecting into the Baltic.

The narrow strips of arable land at the head of the fjords and in the bottom of the deep, narrow valleys of Norway afforded little scope for increase of population, or for the accumulation of wealth from agriculture. The Norwegians were forced by nature to take to the sea as fishers, or in search of plunder or new homes "West Over Sea." Norway was preeminently the home of the pirate Vikings. War, rather than trade, was the motive that drove them abroad. Their poor country afforded them little to barter, so, with the strong hand, they took what they required.

The same race in Sweden grew rich in flocks and herds and tillage. There

Tacitus and other Roman writers. In Norway, which was colonised at a later period than Sweden, the Goths acquired somewhat different characteristics. One of the qualities which have made this race so powerful a stock is its rapid adaptability to changing conditions. In war, in commerce, and in social culture, they displayed an extraordinary facility for breaking away from old conventions, and for finding the best equipment with which to survive in a new environment.

was a large and prosperous agricultural population with plenty of room for expansion. Round the coast, and on the numerous rivers and inland waters, was bred a hardy race of fishers and sailors. They had not the same imperative need for plunder, but an adventurous and enterprising spirit drove them eastwards in search of trade.

In their own country they had been accustomed to river and lake navigation. They ventured up the great rivers which fall into the southern Baltic until they met the Syrian and Greek traders from the Byzantine Empire, and they bartered with them amber, furs, fish, and slaves, for rich fabrics, gold and silver ornaments, weapons, and wine. They adapted themselves to commerce with the same facility as they adapted themselves to war by sea or land. By-and-by they reached Constantinople itself, ready for any enterprise in trade or war.

This is not the place to tell how the Swedish Viking traders at length established, under Rurik, the Empire of Russia. But it is necessary to point out how this long-continued intercourse along the "Varangian Route" with

BEVY OF SWEDISH YOUNGSTERS IN TRADITIONAL COSTUME

In the Swedes a predilection for handicraft seems to be innate, and the arts and crafts movement inaugurated in 1874 has swept the country. "Sloyd," meaning all forms of handicraft, is part of the school system, and home industries now put large sums into the pockets of the peasantry. The revival of home weaving and home dyeing has led to a readoption of national folk costume

Photo, Publishers' Photo Service

RECRUITS ROUND CAPTURED GUN IN STOCKHOLM'S PALACE YARD
Many years have passed since a Swedish army took the field, but in its existing army Sweden
possesses troops who are worthy heirs of the military genius that once made her a great
Continental power. The total peace establishment numbers 104,000 troops, of whom about 72,500
are infantry, armed with the Mauser rifle and comprising a very high percentage of crack marksmen
Photo, Donald McLeish

the Byzantine Empire in its most glorious days, and with the East, gave the development of the Swedish people a different turn from that of the Norwegians, whose face was towards the Atlantic. Notable traces of that ancient intercourse have been found in the shape of thousands of gold and silver coins and other articles of Byzantine, and even Arabic, manufacture, which have been unearthed in Sweden.

The difference between Norwegians and Swedes is very much the difference between Scots and English. Norway is the poorer country, and her conditions have remained more simple. Sweden is opulent by comparison, maintains a much larger population, in closer community, and has been much more highly industrialised.

The Norwegians are more democratic, less conscious of class distinctions, more inclined to resent the exercise of central authority. Sweden, with greater accumulation of wealth, has acquired an aristocracy. Social distinctions are much more pronounced. Stockholm is not only a larger town than Christiania, it is more cosmopolitan, less provincial. Sweden is the elder brother who has inherited the estates. Norway is the younger brother who has had to go out

STALWART SWEDISH GUARDIANS OF THE KING'S MAJESTY

Swedish soldiers are noted for their height and military bearing, and in parade order present a most spectacular appearance. The lifeguards, who furnish a special guard at the royal palace in Stockholm on state occasions, wear an imposing uniform of the time of Charles XII., recalling the most glorious period of the country's history when Sweden was still at the zenith of her power

Photo, Donald McLeish

HARDY YOUNG DEVOTEES OF SWEDEN'S POPULAR WINTER SPORT

Almost as soon as a Swedish child can walk he puts on the skates, for on the ice the Swede is usually invincible. " Idrott," or sport, is a native word which holds great significance for him ; it is an heirloom from antiquity, and like his ancestors the youth of Sweden delights in every kind of vigorous exercise—especially those which have a spice of danger in them

SWEDISH SCHOOLBOYS SKI-RUNNING OVER THE FROZEN PLAINS

All classes of people in Sweden are greatly addicted to sport. In skating especially the Swedes are adepts, and like their neighbours, the Norwegians, they are devoted to the skis. Much is done by them to encourage ski-ing, which is one of the finest, healthiest, and most invigorating of winter sports, and a well-known society has been formed to arrange matches and supervise competitions

into the world to push his fortune.

Sweden stretches for over 1,000 miles northwards, from the latitude of the south of Scotland to well beyond the Arctic Circle. Malmö, in the extreme south, lies in about the same latitude as Edinburgh. Gothenburg, the second largest town, corresponds to Aberdeen, and Stockholm, the capital, to Kirkwall, in the Orkney Islands. Sundsvall, the centre of the timber trade, is farther north than Cape Farewell, in Greenland; Haparanda, at the head of the Gulf of Bothnia, is on the same parallel as the centre of Iceland; while Gellivare, in Lapland, beyond the Arctic Circle, lies nearer the North Pole than the north-most cape in Iceland.

While Labrador and Greenland, in the same latitude, are wrapped in snow and ice, and properly belong to the Arctic regions, Sweden, which comes within the central heating system of the Gulf Stream, enjoys a temperate climate. The winter cold, though severe, is crisp, dry, and exhilarating, and affords ample opportunity for winter sports. In summer the heat is greater than in the south of England, and the almost continuous sunlight encourages extraordinary development of vegetation.

Sweden is one and a half times as large as Great Britain and Ireland together, and embraces a wonderful variety of scenery. Its coasts on the

SWEDISH GAMES: THROWING THE DISCUS

From Viking times the Swedes have enjoyed a reputation for skill in all sports and manly exercises, and the uniform success of the Swedish athletes in the Olympic games testifies to the physical proficiency of the race

Kattegat and the Baltic are fringed by a wide belt of innumerable islands, ranging from water-worn granite rocks, protruding like the back of some sea-monster, to large agricultural territories like Gothland and Öland. Many of these islands are covered with forests of pine and birch. The world does not offer a more complete rest-cure than a

LAYING IN STORES OF NATURAL ICE AT STOCKHOLM FOR USE IN THE TORRID DAYS OF SUMMER

"Venice of the North," as it is sometimes called from its situation about an island-dotted lake and sea, Stockholm has large water frontages. The capital is free of frosts for about four months and a half in the year, and in anticipation of the hot days that occur in the sunny though short summer stores of ice are laid in by provident ice merchants. The ice is sawn out in large slabs and kept in underground cellars until it can be profitably retailed. As explained in pages 4275 and 4310, a similar custom obtains in Petrograd

yachting cruise in the Skärgard, as this belt of islands is called, over summer seas between shores billowing with foliage, through air fragrant with balsam from nature's own distillery.

The rich plains of southern Sweden have been cultivated for thousands of years. The beech, the oak, and the elm flourish there, and the nightingale sings in the white nights of summer on the shores of Lake Ring. The interior of the country is riddled to an almost incredible extent by lakes great and small, connected by a perfect network of rivers. By lake and river one can sail right across the country. And these lakes again are studded with tree-clad islands. Sea, land, and fresh water, forest, field, and meadow, are mingled in inextricable confusion.

Farther north, in the provinces of Östergötland and Scaraborg, and beyond the great lakes, Wetter and Wener, cultivation begins to yield place to forests of pine and spruce. In the very heart of the country is the wide-spreading valley of Dalarne, or Dalecarlia, with Lake Siljan in the midst of it. Here for centuries the heart of Swedish life beat strongly and deeply. It is inhabited by a race of stalwart and prosperous yeomen, owners of the land they till, intolerant of oppression, independent and self-reliant, who, on more than one occasion, by their resolute action and staying power, have determined the course of Swedish history. They placed Gustavus Vasa on the throne in 1523, and in the following century they supplied the

PRIZE PORKER OF THE LITTER

Most peasant families of Sweden keep a certain number of farmstock. Pigs seem to predominate, perhaps because they are easily reared, thriving on feed which other animals would reject, and because they themselves are eatable from " end to end "

indomitable troops who, under Gustavus Adolphus, placed Sweden among the Great Powers of Europe.

In their valley, remote from the world, the Dalecarlians have preserved the primitive simplicities and traditions of an earlier age. The railway is opening the door to change, but in Dalecarlia may still be seen, on gala days, the picturesque ancient peasant costumes— the men and maids still dance round the maypole in the old-fashioned folkdances—the fires of Baal, under the name of S. John, still burn on midsummer eve, and the great church boats still cross the lakes on Sundays, bringing the congregation from remote

SNUG HOMELINESS OF A COTTAGE INTERIOR IN THE LAND OF THE DALE PEASANTRY

The interior of a peasant house in the Siljansdal presents a delightful, spick-and-span appearance. The Dalecarlian women are good housewives, not afraid of hard work, and bent on having their premises swept and garnished and everything done to make the home surroundings bright and healthy. Articles of furniture are not excessive in these small homes; ofttimes kitchen, dining-room, and bedroom are combined in one room, the beds being constructed on shelves within a kind of cupboard, screened from view by curtains, a short ladder giving access to the higher berth. Electric lighting is common even in remote districts

farms and hamlets to church as they have done for centuries.

Farther north yet lie the vast primeval forests of Norrland, intersected by broad rivers, snow-fed from the mountains on the Norwegian frontiers and

prehistoric monster, and is indeed an aboriginal survival. Bears and wolves are found in the remoter parts.

Farthest north of all lie the bleak and desolate uplands of Lapland, where the pine gives place to birch, and the

IN A CORNER OF A SWEDISH YEOMAN'S DWELLING

The comparative isolation of Sweden has undoubtedly assisted the preservation of national characteristics. On the more remote districts the stamp of antiquity still rests lightly, and in many a peasant house strange, old carved benches and cupboards may be found lined up against walls which are decorated with fantastic modern paintings, often of Biblical subjects

flowing eastward into the Baltic. Such rivers are the Angerman and the Indals, which are navigable for many miles into the interior, and which abound in picturesque scenery. Millions of logs are floated down these rivers every summer to the sawmills round Sundsvall.

Many of the rivers are diversified by magnificent waterfalls and by rapids, where the water boils over rugged shelves of rocks. The river-men, trained from childhood to the task, think nothing of shooting these rapids in their frail boats, and, though accidents are rare, it is a terrifying experience for a stranger. The forests are the haunt of the elk, the greatest of European mammals, which looks like a

birch to dwarf birch and creeping willow, and that again to bare rock and boggy tundra, beyond the limit of trees. These wastes are inhabited by thinly scattered tribes of nomad Lapps, who subsist upon the fish in the rivers and lakes, and the fur-bearing animals which they trap, and their herds of reindeer which, in turn, subsist upon the moss, digging beneath the snow for it in winter.

There are, altogether, about 7,000 Lapps in Sweden, about one-third of the number in Norway, though, as nomads, they pay very little respect to frontiers, and in many cases it is difficult to determine whether their nationality is Swedish, Norwegian, or Russian. They are the dwindling remnants of the

OFF FOR A DAY'S WORK IN THE PLEASANT FIELDS

Their home is near Ockelbo, in Gestrikland, where the lovely Land of Dales is beginning to merge into the sterner Norrland. Only about a tenth of Norrland is under cultivation as yet, but the district, nevertheless, has great agricultural possibilities, and many a young couple make a good living on a small holding of perhaps only five acres, wife helping husband in all the work

SWEDISH PEASANT GIRLS IN THEIR QUAINT LEATHER APRONS

With the advent of machinery which made it no longer necessary for the peasant women to make their own clothes a deterioration in the charms of national dress set in. Happily it was followed by a reaction, and in the country districts vigorous womanhood may still be seen in these leather aprons that defy both wear and tear

WASHING PARTY WITH THEIR PARAPHERNALIA IN A DALE VILLAGE

The linen has been brought to the river in a huge tub of water, but the actual washing or pounding of the clothes is done at the river-bank, chiefly in the manner illustrated in the opposite page. Love of hard work seems to be one of the main qualities of the Dale women who, strong and self-reliant, perform much manual labour which would be expected from men in other countries

Photo, Publishers' Photo Service

aboriginal race, still living in conditions little removed from the Stone Age.

There are also some 25,000 Finns in Sweden. The Finns are a Turanian race, quite distinct from the general Aryan stock of Europe, who possibly occupied the country before the ancestors of the Swedes found their way to it. They are kin to the Hungarians and the Tartars, and probably they have the same remote ancestry as the Lapps, whose language closely resembles theirs. But, as they have proved in Finland proper, they are capable of a high degree of civilization. They are settled on the land in the northern parts, like the Swedes themselves, and they make excellent farmers and woodmen.

For centuries Swedish Lapland has been the resort of those who desire to see that wonderful Arctic phenomenon—the midnight sun. M. Regnard, a French savant, visited it in 1681, and in 1737 M. Maupertuis, of the French Academy, with M. Celsius, Professor of Astronomy at Upsala, led a scientific expedition to measure a degree of the meridian at the Polar Circle.

Since then a constant stream of travellers have made Lapland their goal both in summer and in winter. From their numerous descriptions

OLD AND NEW FASHIONS IN SWEDEN OF TO-DAY

Many characteristics of the Sweden of yesterday are rapidly fading, and the note of modernity is now audible in village as well as in town, but on the conservative population of Dalecarlia industrial revolutions have made little impression, and like many another of her kith and kin this young girl pedals a bicycle about the countryside yet adheres to the costume peculiar to her parish

WASHING DAY IN THE LAND OF DALES

The native dwellers of Dalecarlia have long been renowned for their staunchness to the primitive simplicities of bygone days, and though the bulk of them enjoy a well-earned prosperity, they are as yet unspoiled by modern innovations. In the country districts the linen is laundered at the streams, pounding with a special flail being the method of cleansing most in favour

Photos, Publishers' Photo Service

Lapland became more familiar to English readers than many other parts of Europe, and this early knowledge is reflected in many literary allusions. Wordsworth's famous lines :—

> An old age serene and bright
> And lovely as a Lapland night,

come readily to mind.

Land of the Midnight Sun

The Arctic Circle is the extreme southern limit from which the midnight sun can be seen. Here it is visible on just a single day in the year. On midsummer day the sun never sets, but just touches the northern horizon at midnight and immediately begins to rise again. The farther north we go beyond this circle the greater the number of summer days during which the sun never sets, until at the Pole the sun never sets for six months continuously. Of course, in winter there is a corresponding period during which the sun never rises, a single day at the Arctic Circle, and beyond it an ever-increasing period, until at the Pole the winter night lasts six months.

The long white nights of the north are a wonderful experience. The hard outlines and sharply defined figures of garish noon disappear. Everything is bathed in a soft and tender light. Every object in the landscape appears to be luminous and radiant. A hush that is almost sacred falls on nature. The impression left upon the mind is indelible.

Magic Beauty of the Arctic Night

In winter the atmospheric effects are equally remarkable. The long Arctic night is not a shroud of blank darkness. The Aurora Borealis flashes its flaming streamers far up the sky. The starry vault of heaven seems to tingle and ring like a bell. When the moon is up, and her light reflected by the snow, it is almost as clear as daylight. But it is a witching light.

Bayard Taylor, the American traveller, has given the following vivid description of a winter day in Lapland.

The northern sky was again pure violet, and a pale red tinge from the dawn rested on the tops of the snowy hills. The prevailing colour of the sky slowly brightened into lilac, then into pink, then rose colour, which again gave way to a flood of splendid orange when the sun appeared. Every change of colour affected the tone of the landscape. The woods, so wrapped in snow that not a single green needle was to be seen, took by turns the hues of the sky, and seemed to give out, rather than to reflect, the opalescent lustre of the morning. The sunshine brightened instead of dispelling these effects. At noon the sun's disc was not more than one degree above the horizon, throwing a level golden light on the hills. The north, before us, was as blue as the Mediterranean, and the vaults of heaven, overhead, canopied us with pink. Every object was glorified and transfigured in the magic glow.

Feudalism and Democracy

Agriculture remains the chief occupation of the Swedish people, nearly one-half of the population being engaged in the cultivation of the land, in one form or other. About one-third are engaged in industrial occupations, manufacturing, lumbering, and mining, and about one-fifth in trade and commerce.

Sweden is a land of peasant proprietors who own the land they cultivate. Feudalism was one of those institutions which were the direct outcome of the irruption of the Gothic races into the Roman Empire, and by which Western civilization was rebuilt from the ruins of the old order.

It is remarkable that the farther south one goes the more feudalism tended to become a despotism, while the farther north, and the more purely Gothic the race, the more it tended to be based upon the independent rights of the occupiers under the feudal lords.

The Swedes are given to maintaining that feudalism never obtained hold in Sweden at all, but that is due to a misconception of the part which feudalism played in the historical evolution of democracy. The prosperous yeomen, or peasant proprietors, of Sweden were so numerous as to form a separate estate in the Parliament up to

RURAL SWEDEN
And Its Peasant Folk

Blonde beauty predominates in the women of Sweden, and the Leksand
lassies are true descendants of the flaxen-haired, blue-eyed Goths

In the village school for girls at Leksand in the Dalecarlia district, known as the "Heart of Sweden," the bright-coloured and picturesque local costumes are in daily use both by the teachers and the pupils

Photo, Donald McLeish

These four merry little maids of Leksand are enjoying an open-air tea-party. High days and holidays are not very frequent in Sweden, so when they come they are hailed with the more delight by Swedish childhood

Photo, Donald McLeish

*In old-world dress and dark cloth tasselled cap the fiddler of Helsing-
land Province is an ever welcome figure at all local festivals*

Photo, Donald McLeish

This Dalarne woman is practising the most noted home industry of her district and making the coloured ribbon worn on caps and dresses

Photo, Donald McLeish

*Pointed cap, green jacket and skirt, and coloured striped apron make
this costume of Rättvik one of the quaintest of old Swedish styles*

Photo, Donald McLeish

This attractive costume may always be seen in Leksand village, and is not, as in other parts of Sweden, confined to Sunday and gala days

Photo, Donald McLeish

Lapp women carry their babies about in cradles of reindeer skin that can be suspended from the ceiling when the mother is busy in the home

Photo, F. H. Owen

1866. In spite of the rapid growth of industrialism in recent generations they are still powerful to protect their interests, as when they were menaced by the encroachments of the great lumber corporations and magnates in Norrland.

Little wheat is grown, but much oats, barley and rye. The growing of beet for sugar is an important modern development. In dairying Sweden has been a pioneer in scale of operations, in methods, and in machinery. Vast quantities of butter are exported to England. The invention of milk separators gave the Swedes a long start, not merely in the dairy industry, but also in the manufacture of dairy machinery which has become famous all over the world. Large co-operative dairies in which the manufacture of milk products is carried to the highest state of perfection have been established all over the southern provinces.

But if agriculture occupies a larger number of people, forestry is by far the most important industry, measured in volume and value of exports. The forests which cover half of the total surface of Sweden are an inexhaustible gold reef, for, under a provident system of legislation, the denudation of the country is prevented, and the felling of timber is always balanced by renewals. In Sweden 48 per cent. of the surface of the country is under forest, as compared with 32 per cent. in Austria, 26 per cent. in Germany, and only 4 per cent. in Great Britain.

In terms of population, for every 100 inhabitants, Sweden has 950 acres of forest, Austria 90 acres, Germany 60

acres, while Great Britain has only 7 acres. Nevertheless, it has been estimated that there are millions of acres, in Scotland, about one-quarter of the total surface, which is at present lying

VILLAGERS FROM THE "HEART OF SWEDEN"
The natives of the village of Leksand are exceptionally prepossessing and well-built, and their quaint, decorative attire, including the multi-coloured apron worn by both young and old, presents some of the most attractive "local colour" in Sweden

waste or devoted to poor grazing, which is not only capable of growing timber, but would yield a larger profit from timber than from any other crop, besides giving employment to ten times the number of people required for sheep farming on a similar area.

Nearly two-thirds of the total exports of Sweden consist of timber, or timber products such as wood-pulp or paper. The rivers not only provide an ideal means of transport, but they also supply the power for the mills in which the logs are converted. Far in the interior, 100 miles and more from the coast, the trees are felled in winter and sleighed easily over the snow to the banks of the

BRIDE AND BRIDEGROOM, BEST MAN AND BRIDESMAID, DRESSED FOR THE HAPPY DAY

Considerable freedom is allowed to lovers in Sweden, the amount of paternal acquiescence and blessing expected varying in the different parts of the country, whereas in Norway the patriarchal system is more apparent in matters of parental interference. The bride in these rural districts is expected to work as hard as any serving wench on the farm, nor does the bridegroom take life any easier than his labourers. The somewhat clerical costume worn by the bridegroom is of the style and cut affected by all the Swedish yeomen for Sunday and ceremonial wear. For women the popular wedding colour is blue

CHEERY COMPANY OF DALE FOLK RETURNING HOME AFTER A DAY'S WORK IN THE FIELDS

North-west of Svealand lies Dalecarlia, or Dalarne in Swedish, the "Land of the Dales," inhabited by one of the bravest and most manly races in the peninsula. Good reason have they to sing their song: "Manhood, pluck, and doughty men still are found in old Dal-Land," for it was the Dale folk who in Sweden's hour of need rose time upon time as one man and never rested until they had driven away the enemy and saved the state from destruction. The women of Dalarne are as sturdy and energetic as the men, and much of the land labour is performed by them

Photo, Publishers' Photo Service

4803

PRETTY COSTUMES OF A CONSERVATIVE AND PICTURESQUE DISTRICT

Near Lake Siljan, in the centre of the wide-spreading valley of Dalecarlia, one of the richest and loveliest of Swedish districts, is situated the village of Leksand. It is here that the neighbours gather on Midsummer Eve, all resplendent in the varied gala costumes of their parishes, to dance the old-fashioned folk-dances and to celebrate the festival with sacrificial fires on the hilltops

Photo, Publishers' Photo Service

frozen river. The spring floods carry the logs the rest of the way, either singly or in huge rafts.

Sundsvall, at the mouth of the Indals river, the lumber trade capital, is ringed round by thirty sawmills. Deals, pit-props, sleepers, door and window frames, plywood, are turned out in great quantities. A host of subsidiary and auxiliary industries gathers round, and by domestic handicrafts in wood the peasants add considerable sums to their income. Some of the allied industries assume great proportions, such as the manufacture of safety matches, which centres on Jönköping.

The Swedish matches—Tändstickor—are known all round the world.

Sweden possesses valuable deposits of copper and iron ore, and from time immemorial the smelting of these ores has been an important industry. The smith was a mighty man among the sons of Odin, for he forged, and often wielded, the weapons which gave victory. The earliest worked ores were situated in the central province, round Dalecarlia, where is Falun, long famous as the greatest copper mine in the world. Over £50,000,000 worth of copper have been taken from it. In the central provinces, north of the great lakes, from

LITTLE MAIDS OF MORA IN THEIR COUNTRY COSTUMES

Mora lies on the north shore of Lake Siljan, that lovely lake—the " eye of Dalecarlia "—about which dwell the lusty Dalecarlians whose love of liberty and independence has remained celebrated through the centuries. An old church with a conspicuous spire is a dominant feature of the village, while the costume of the locality of red, orange, and green provides a pleasing touch of colour

Photos, Publishers' Photo Service

primitive times, ore was smelted and iron forged with charcoal from the surrounding forests for fuel, and here have remained the headquarters of the industry. For centuries Sweden dominated the international iron market. The ore was plentiful and rich and free from phosphorus, a very valuable quality for the making of high-grade steel.

The development of the coalfields of other countries has diminished the importance of Sweden as an iron producer. The ore is now shipped to the countries with the coalfields and smelted there. More recently the richer ore fields of Lapland have been developed by the construction of the most northerly railway in the world, from Lulea, on the Gulf of Bothnia, to Narvik, on the coast of Norway, beside the Lofoden Islands. This line crosses the Arctic Circle at a station called Polar Circle (Polcirkeln), and passes between mountains of solid iron ore at Gellivare and Kirunavara. The richness of these deposits is unsurpassed. Although Sweden figures now in the markets of the world as an exporter of ore rather than of iron, another prospect is being opened up by the application of electricity, instead of coal, to the heating of furnaces. The ores of Sweden lie close to the rapids and falls which are inexhaustible sources of electric energy.

Industrially and commercially Sweden is developing rapidly, and the predominance of the agricultural interest is now seriously challenged. More and more timber is being exported in a manufactured, or semi-manufactured, form, rather than as a raw material. In the manufacture of dairy machinery, and in electrical engineering, Sweden has been a pioneer. She is fully conscious of the potential wealth which lies dormant in the great storehouses of electric energy, in innumerable waterfalls and rapids. This is the " white coal," which may yet remove the reproach that industrialism means a black country. Hernösand, on the Gulf of Bothnia, as far north as Greenland,

THREE OF THE HEALTHY, HAPPY COMMUNITY OF RURAL DALECARLIA

No province of Sweden is more full of rural charm and interest than Dalecarlia, and it represents that part of the country which has most uninterruptedly preserved old-time costumes and old-world customs. Peasant handicrafts flourish here apace, peasant lore differs but little from that prevailing in past ages, and the peasant women and girls still wear the brightly-coloured local costumes

YEOMAN FARMER OF RÄTTVIK AND HIS YOUNG HOPEFULS

Swedish peasant farmers, like the English yeomen, are the backbone of their country. Religious without being narrow-minded, and often well educated, they have a native worth of character that secures for them a material independence wholly admirable. At church and market many family groups like this may be seen, well dressed, well nourished, and well mannered

was the first town in Europe to be lighted by electricity. The telephone is installed in practically every house almost as a matter of course, as the water or electric light is laid on. Its cost is about £2 15s. a year. Stockholm holds the European record of one telephone for every five of her population, as compared with one to every thirty-three in London. The farmer in the remotest parts is in touch not merely with his neighbours, but with the markets of the town and of the world.

Stockholm has aptly been called the Venice of the North. It is built upon a number of small islands, and it is intersected in all directions by waterways, opening out into the winding fjord with its labyrinth of islands. The Stockholmers are a gay people, polished in their manners, punctilious in old-fashioned courtesies, and of an abounding hospitality. In summer they delight in the open-air life of the cafés, and in entertaining parties at the numerous restaurants. A Swedish dinner, with its preliminary smörgasbord, its long sequence of toasts, or "skolls," and its gay talk, is a happy memory.

Gothenburg is the great shipping and commercial port, whose wealthy and powerful merchants have a reputation

OUTSIDE A NATIVE KOTA, OR WIGWAM, IN SWEDISH LAPLAND

The Lapps of Swedish Lapland, though now but poor, superstitious nomads, are one of the oldest races in Europe, and were one of the last to embrace Christianity. They are remarkably fine huntsmen, endowed with courage and hardihood, in constant contact with wild nature; yet their numbers are gradually decreasing, and their complete disappearance is only a question of time

for probity and ability established throughout the world. They carry on worthily the tradition of the trading Vikings who were their ancestors. Gothenburg is also the place of origin, and of the successful development, of the well-known system of managing the liquor traffic by means of a company, in which the shareholders are limited to a certain small percentage return on their capital, the surplus profits being expended on purposes of public utility.

Mr. Joseph Chamberlain during a visit to Sweden became an enthusiastic advocate of the " Gothenburg System," which he declared was performing noble and religious work. On his return to England he converted the Birmingham Town Council to his views, but failed to induce the British Parliament to move in the matter.

The total population of Sweden is a little over 6,000,000. How far the Swedish stock has been disseminated over the world during the past 2,000 years it is impossible to estimate. The Gothic strain has permeated all the ruling races of Europe. As the result of emigration during the past half century, there are one and a half million of people of purely Swedish descent in the United States of America.

Now that she has definitely embarked upon a career of industrial development the population of the home country will increase rapidly. The Scandinavian North is beginning to develop its own resources.

Norway, Sweden, Denmark, and Finland are among the most progressive nations of Europe. They are exercising a steadily increasing influence in European politics, and if the efforts to bring about a Scandinavian League are successful its effects upon the balance of power will be immediately felt. And Sweden leads the North.

NATIVES OF THE BLEAK THOUGH BEAUTIFUL LAND OF THE LAPPS

The old national costume of thick blue cloth is still in existence among the Lapps, and fur—as with all the northern races—plays a notable part in their wardrobe. Most of the Swedish Lapps lead a roaming life, tending their herds, for to many the reindeer is the first and only consideration. They are a pacific people and retain a large number of their Mongolian characteristics

Photo, Publishers' Photo Service

Sweden

II. Stirring Chronicles of the Northern Kingdom

By J. A. Brendon, B.A., F.R.Hist.S.

Writer on Modern European History

THE old method of telling history as a chronicle of kings is generally to be deprecated. The historian of Sweden, however, has no option in the matter. He must follow the old method. And for this reason: the history of Sweden is the history of her kings.

Under the rule of a succession of brilliant monarchs the Swedes maintained themselves, in the seventeenth and eighteenth centuries, in the front rank of European nations. The sovereigns of the house of Vasa, almost without exception able administrators with a genius for war, were not self-seeking adventurers. Their aims were essentially national; they made their interests the interests of the people. Their glory is the epitome of Sweden's story.

Links with Russia and Great Britain

The seafaring, heathen Swedes of old came of that same Viking stock which peopled the other Scandinavian territories. To the Vikings the modern world owes much. To the Viking strain in British blood can be traced the maritime and colonising genius of the British race. In France the Vikings became crusaders and builders of cathedrals. Most of the peoples of northern Europe learned from the Vikings the lessons of leadership.

The establishment of Russia as a European country is the outstanding achievement of the Vikings of Sweden. The chieftain Rurik created a Swedish kingdom in Russia towards the end of the ninth century and, upon the foundations he laid, Peter the Great (1672-1725) subsequently built the Russian Empire. Russia preserves in her very name the record of her Swedish origin. The word " rus " is a Slavonic corruption of the Scandinavian " ruotsi " (the rowing men). This was the name given to the first Swedish settlers in the country.

The early kings, or overlords, of Sweden were known as " ynlings." They were so called because they claimed descent from Yngvi, son of Niord, one of the gods of heathen Scandinavia. They made Upsala their seat of government. Stockholm (the islet defended by a palisade, or stock), designed as a stronghold against Danish aggression, was not established until late in the twelfth century.

S. Ansgar first preached Christianity in Sweden—in the ninth century. But the Swedes did not readily accept the Christian faith; they adhered to the worship of Thor, Odin, and Frey, with its attendant human sacrifice, for nearly three hundred years. Their final conversion, in the twelfth century, was largely the work of British missionaries, and in 1152 the Pope sent Nicholas Breakspear, afterwards Pope Adrian IV., the only native of the British Isles who has ever occupied the Papal chair, to organize their Church.

Eric IX., who became King of Sweden in 1150, showed throughout his reign a burning zeal for spreading Christianity. In him missionaries found a stout supporter. One day in 1160 a Danish army beset Eric while he was attending Mass. The king refused to cut short the divine service in order to fight, and so fell a victim to the besieging Danes. Subsequently canonised, he became the patron saint of Sweden.

During the Middle Ages Denmark dominated the other Scandinavian countries and, in 1397, by what is known as the Union of Kalmar, Margaret of Denmark brought Norway and Sweden under the Danish crown. A national union, sealed by a community of national interests, would have been to the advantage of all the Scandinavian kingdoms. The Union of Kalmar, however, rested on a dynastic basis only. Norway and Sweden, though under the sceptre of Danish sovereigns, remained as individual kingdoms, and—particularly in Sweden—the monarchy exercised but little authority. The wealth of the Church and the independence of the nobles stripped it of all save the title to rule.

The Maddest Crime in History

Christian II., who succeeded to the throne in 1513, determined to end this state of affairs. Christian was a man of exceptional ability, but his arbitrary methods robbed him of support which enlightened opinion might otherwise have given him. His proposed measures were well conceived and unquestionably tended to advancement. By headstrong conduct he wrecked them; and in 1523 he found himself an exile even from Denmark.

In Sweden, instead of proclaiming himself as the strong man bent on destroying the power of a selfish nobility and so heading a popular movement, he falsely lured the nobles to an assembly at Stockholm, and there had them slaughtered. For two days the streets of the capital ran with blood. The "Stockholm Bloodbath " of 1520 was the maddest crime recorded in history. It completely defeated the purpose it was intended to serve, and had the effect of evoking for the first time in the country a national spirit. Thus the stage was set for the dramatic entry of Gustavus Vasa, the liberator and creator of Sweden.

Gustavus Vasa came of noble descent. His father and all his brothers perished at Stockholm in 1520. He himself escaped death only by a miracle. Thenceforth he consecrated his life to vengeance. With a price upon his head, he made his way to the wilds of Dalecarlia, in the north of the country. There he lived for a year, sharing the rough life of the peasants and maturing his schemes. Then, having collected a small band of loyal followers, he set out on his great adventure.

A series of striking successes, gained over the forces sent by Christian to oppose his advance, brought him to the gates of Stockholm. But he had neither artillery nor the material necessary for the conduct of a siege ; the Danish garrison easily repulsed his attempts to take the city by storm. Gustavus thus found himself in a perilous position.

Then came the news that Christian had been expelled from Denmark. The Danes at once withdrew from Stockholm, leaving the capital in the hands of the rebel peasants. On June 7, 1523, Gustavus was crowned king. His first move was to introduce the Reformation into the country.

A man with no strong religious convictions, he adopted Lutheranism mainly to serve political ends. The Swedish crown was wretchedly poor. The Church in Sweden was immensely rich. Gustavus saw at once that without money he could never establish a strong monarchy. He resolved, therefore, to

sequester ecclesiastical wealth, and to press it into the service of the state.

Within three years he accomplished his design. This in itself did not solve the problem of regenerating Sweden. Christian of Denmark, by killing off the nobles, cleared the path of Gustavus of several possible rivals. Also, however, he removed all possible colleagues. What was done in Sweden during the reign of Gustavus, the king did himself. He was his own chancellor, his own home secretary, his own

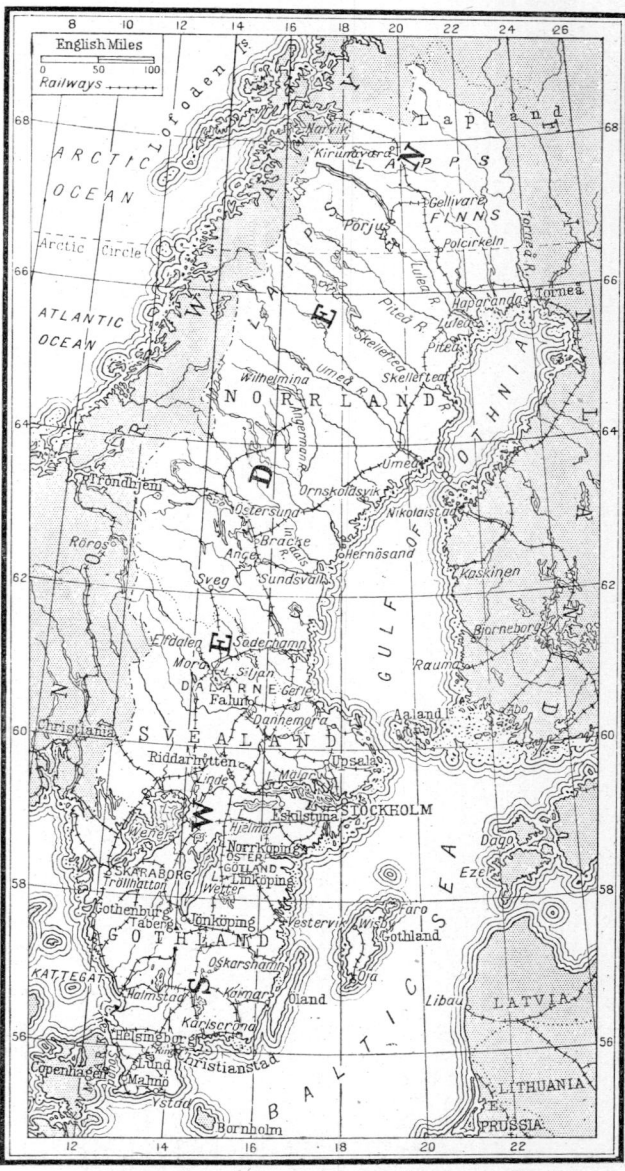

THE KINGDOM OF SWEDEN

foreign minister, his own war minister; he had no one to help him.

His difficulties may be gauged by the fact that, on one occasion, he could not find in all his dominions an ambassador with a knowledge of the German language. Personally he taught his people mining, trade, and agriculture. He acted not as a king, but rather as the benevolent landlord of a large estate. He possessed an infinite capacity for taking pains.

Life-Work of Gustavus Vasa

The rise of Sweden under Gustavus I. is an outstanding feature of the political history of the sixteenth century. At the beginning of the century the country, poor in material resources and thinly populated, without roads or means of communication, and frost bound for half the year, gave no promise of pending greatness. When Gustavus I. vacated the throne in 1560 Sweden was a Power in Europe.

She had a full treasury, a well-trained army, an efficient fleet. And already she had made her first bid for the hegemony of the Baltic and for the spoils which the decline of the commercial supremacy of the Hanseatic League rendered available.

The greatness of the Hansa towns, ranged along the German coast, rested—as did the greatness of Venice—largely on the spice trade, borne overland from the East. In days before men grew green vegetables spices were a prime necessity of life.

In 1453 Constantinople fell into the hands of the Turks, and old trade routes seemed to be endangered. Columbus made his first voyage to America avowedly to open a new way to the East. What Columbus failed to find, Portuguese navigators found by creeping along the African coast and so around the Cape of Good Hope.

Disintegration and Recovery

Early in the sixteenth century merchants from Lisbon appeared in the markets of northern Europe, offering spices at one-tenth of the former price. This spelled ruin to the Hansa towns. But there still remained the valuable carrying trade of the Baltic, a prize to be coveted. The determination to secure this prize is the keynote of the policy of the Vasa kings.

Gustavus I. was succeeded by his son, Eric XIV., the one weak link in the Vasa chain. Eric, an importunate suitor of Queen Elizabeth of England, had a pronounced leaning towards the Roman Catholic Church, and during the eight years (1560-68) that he occupied the throne, he undid much of Gustavus' constructive national work.

His brother, John III. (1568-92), also had papistical tendencies. Under him the process of national disintegration continued. John's son, Sigismund, married a princess of the house of Jagellon, the heiress to the crown of Poland. As her husband, Sigismund, in 1587, became king of that country. Five years later he succeeded to the throne of Sweden. The Swedes were not then such staunch Lutherans as to reject a papist king. Their newly awakened national spirit, however, would not allow them to see their country pass under Polish domination. Charles Vasa, the king's uncle, and the ablest of the sons of Gustavus, took advantage of this and, as the leader of a national revolt against his nephew, usurped the crown (1604).

Charles IX., a brilliant administrator, securely re-established the Swedish monarchy on a Protestant basis, and restored its naval, military, and commercial organization, which had fallen to pieces since the death of his father. As a statesman Charles was unfortunate, and he died leaving the Swedes committed to wars with Denmark, Russia, and Poland. To conduct these wars, however, he left an heir who, though only a lad in his seventeenth year, was soon to prove himself one of the greatest of the captains of all times.

Triumphs of Gustavus Adolphus

Gustavus Adolphus (1611-32) had a natural genius for war. The minor struggles bequeathed to him by his father trained his prentice hand and gave the soldiers of Sweden experience which served them well when the time came for them to decide the fate of Europe. In 1630 the hour struck. On May 19 Gustavus Adolphus, holding in his arms Christina, his three-year-old daughter and only child, took solemn leave of his people. Then, at the head of his army, he set out for Germany, the self-appointed champion of Protestantism, to stem the tide of the Counter-Reformation.

In the Thirty Years War the Swedes and their king won undying fame. Such was their might that it seemed even to the eyes of good Catholics as if " God had suddenly turned Lutheran "; and Gustavus Adolphus, when he fell, in 1632, on the stricken field of Lützen, had already fulfilled his mission. He had saved the Protestant cause in Germany. He had secured Pomerania for Sweden, and so given his country that secure foothold on the German coast which was essential to her if she would be mistress of the Baltic.

Gustavus Adolphus made Sweden a dominating military power. His daughter made Stockholm the centre of European culture. Christina of Sweden (1632-54) ranks with Elizabeth of England and Catherine of Russia among the really notable queens of history. She was only a child when she came to the throne. During her long minority, the affairs of the country remained in the safe hands of Axel Oxenstjerna, her father's trusty chancellor.

Christina personally assumed the government in 1644. By her wit and the brilliance of her intellect, she soon made the Swedish court the most famous in Europe. Thither flocked the foremost thinkers of the age. Grotius, Vossius, and Descartes may be mentioned among them. As time went on her philosophic researches shook Christina's religious beliefs. At last, to escape the torments of doubt, she resolved to adopt the Roman Catholic faith. None saw more clearly than the queen herself that the interests of Sweden demanded a Protestant monarchy. In 1654, therefore, she abdicated her throne and withdrew to Rome, where she died in 1689.

From Christina the Swedish throne passed to her cousin, Charles X. The " Pyrrhus of the North " reigned only six years (1654-60). During this time he astounded Europe by the resource and daring he displayed in his endeavours to turn the Baltic into a Swedish lake.

His successor, Charles XI., was a minor, and a troublous regency ensued. Then Charles XII. (1697-1718) raised Sweden to the apogee of her glory. As a leader of men, Charles stands out conspicuous among a race of great leaders. His long, fierce duel with Peter of Russia merits an epic. That Peter won was enough in itself to justify his sobriquet " the Great."

Alas for Sweden, Charles XII., when he fell, dragged down his country with him. Such was the crash that only the king's death in 1718 saved Sweden from extinction. Even so, she was shorn of much of Pomerania and of other territories south and east of the Baltic, which the house of Vasa had laboured to acquire ; and she sank speedily to the level of a third-rate power.

Under Gustavus III. (1771-92) a marked revival occurred. Since the death of Charles XII., however, Sweden has hardly been a vital factor in European politics. In 1818 on the death of Charles XIII., the last of the old line of kings, the Swedish crown passed to Marshal Bernadotte, who had been elected heir to the throne in 1810. The house of Bernadotte still reigns in Sweden.

As part of the European settlement of 1814, Norway was handed over in an arbitrary manner to Sweden. An uneasy union continued until 1905. Then, in deference to the emphatic wishes of the Norwegian people, Norway again became an independent monarchy.

During the Great War (1914-18), Denmark, Norway, and Sweden were all able to preserve their neutrality.

SWEDEN: FACTS AND FIGURES

The Country

Occupies east and south portions of Scandinavian peninsula. Boundaries are Finland on the north, the Gulf of Bothnia and Baltic Sea to the east and south-east, to the west Norway and a sheet of water called Kattegat, with another, the Skager Rak, on the west. In the north is the region where elevations of over 3,000 feet are found. About half the country is covered by forests of pine, birch and spruce, while in the south are oak and beech forests. The bear, lynx and wolf are still found. Climate varies between extremes though summer is short. Total area about 173,000 square miles, with an estimated population of some 6.000,000.

Government and Constitution

King, who must be a member of the Lutheran Church, wields executive power in conjunction with Council of State of about twelve ministers with and without portfolio at whose head is Prime Minister. Royal assent necessary to all legislation. Parliament or Diet is composed of first and second Chambers. Members of the former number about 150, who are elected by members of the " Landstings " or provincial representations and by electors from six towns outside the " Landstings." The Second Chamber has about 230 members elected by universal suffrage for four years. Both sexes have vote if over 23 and not under legal disability.

Commerce and Industries

Agriculture chief occupation of people, and there were over 428,000 farms in cultivation during 1919. Among chief crops are rye, wheat, barley, oats and hay. Mineral resources include iron, silver, lead, copper and coal. Saw-milling, the making of pig-iron and steel, and the manufacture of lighthouse apparatus, cream-separators, motors and porcelain are among chief industrial activities. Imports for 1922, which included textiles, coal, machinery and live animals, totalled £64,116,823, while exports, among which were metal goods, wood pulp and paper were valued at £63,456,868. Standard coin the silver krona at nominal value of 1s. 1¼d.

Communications

There are over 9,400 miles of railway, of which about a third are owned by the state. Telegraph wires aggregate more than 49,500 miles, state telephone lines over 412,800 miles, and private telephone wire 6,000 miles. Post offices number more than 3,600.

Chief Towns

Stockholm capital (estimated population, 422,000), Gothenburg (227,000), Malmö (113,000), Norrköping (58,000), Helsingborg (47,500), Upsala (29,000).

HISTORIC LANDMARK IN THE CENTRE OF MEDIEVAL BERNE

This Zeitglockenturm, or clock-tower, once formed the west gate of Berne, "youngest and haughtiest of the famous towns of the Swiss." Rebuilt in the fifteenth century, and modernised in the eighteenth, the clock marks each hour by cock-crowing and a procession of bears, mechanical devices rivalling in ingenuity the appearance of the Magi in the clock-tower of S. Mark's Square at Venice

Photo, Georg Haeckel

Switzerland

I. The Peoples of the Mountain Republic

By Dame Katharine Furse, G.B.E.

SWITZERLAND is a Federal Republic, consisting of twenty-five cantons or half cantons, most of which, originally either independent states or under the sovereignty of some other country, have been gradually brought together during the last ten centuries by a common bond of sympathy.

It is a neutral country surrounded by large Powers, and with no outlet to the sea. Geographically it is the watershed of Europe, as the glaciers of the Alps give rise to the rivers Rhine, Rhône, Po and Inn (which flows into the Danube), all these rivers having their outlet into different seas. Were it possible to make these rivers navigable within her borders, and could they be internationalised throughout their course, Switzerland might proudly fly her flag on the ocean, as is her ambition.

The Swiss nation is composed of different nationalities, each of which has retained its language, so that German, French and Italian are not only spoken by the people in different districts

AN IDYLL OF NEUCHÂTEL

Instinctive grace marks her unaffected pose as this girl worker in a Neuchâtel vineyard pauses in her pleasant task of gathering the luscious fruit that shall presently be turned into wine

Photo, Hermann Stauder

but are, also, the official languages. In addition to these there are Romanisch and Ladin, left by the Romans in two valleys of Canton Grisons, as well as Gouverin Walsch, a Romance dialect spoken in Canton Fribourg, which was originally Burgundian.

Every child has the option of learning two or more languages in the schools, and all employees of the state must necessarily know three, all postal, railway, and other official notices being printed in German, French and Italian. Many Swiss learn English also.

The population of Switzerland is about 4,000,000, and the area some 16,000 square miles, of which 4,500 square miles is unproductive, consisting of glaciers, rocks, and lakes, while the greater proportion of what is termed productive land is composed of steep mountain slopes, covered with forests, and almost devoid of human habitation or cultivation.

The only large towns are Geneva, Basel, and Zürich, which are very cosmopolitan, while St. Gall, and Winterthur, are eminently manufacturing centres. Berne

BERNESE GRACE IN BERNESE SETTING
As will be noticed in the dress of this smiling daughter of Berne, Swiss local costumes combine artistry of design with excellence of material, but as a rule they are reserved for wear on festal occasions
Photo, Underwood Press Service

together to form the canton or county, to the governing council of which they send representatives. The cantons in their turn are so far independent of the Federal Government that they have their own laws.

The cantonal government sends delegates to the Council of States, which, together with the National Council, consisting of representatives of the people, in proportion of one to every twenty thousand voters, elects the Federal Council which selects its own president who becomes President of the Swiss Republic.

The people are further protected in their right to self-government by the Initiative and Referendum, which are the machinery by which questions may be referred to all voting citizens for their decision.

The cantons are governed in different ways according, mainly, as to whether their inhabitants were originally German, French or Italian.

Parties are mainly divided into agricultural and labour; the former being the stronger. Patriotism for the fatherland and loyalty to commune and family lie at the root of Swiss character and education.

There is no established Church, but each canton or commune can have the Church of its choice.

The Federal Government is empowered to insist upon religious freedom and upon peace being kept between the different sects. Religion has a strong hold upon the people. Education

having been finally chosen as the capital, contains the Houses of Parliament; but the Federal law courts are at Lausanne and the Politechnicum at Zürich.

The Government is democratic and much decentralised; the Federal or supreme Government only controlling such affairs as foreign policy, national railways, postal services, customs, the coinage of money, and to a certain extent the army and education.

The actual government is mainly carried out locally by the commune, which is the village or district community. The communes combine

COUNTRYMAN OF APPENZELL REVIVES AN ANCIENT PRACTICE

At the prime of its development and the height of its popularity about the middle of the thirteenth century the crossbow, from the shape of its stock, probably provided the idea that adapted the unwieldy bombard to a handy portable weapon. The men of Appenzell—a canton in the north-east near the southern end of Lake Constance—still find that it provides an admirable pastime

Photo, Hermann Stauder

GROUP OF DAIRY WORKERS IN A CANTON WHERE THE "WHEY CURE" IS PRACTISED WITH GOAT'S MILK

They belong to Appenzell, the men of which canton are noted for their skill in wrestling, hurling, and other sports, and the women for their blue eyes, fair hair, and the picturesqueness of their native costume. The canton, once under the dominion of the abbots of S. Gall, hence the name Abtszelle or Abbatis Cella, has been divided since 1597 into Roman Catholic and pastoral Inner Rhoden, where hand-embroidery is a flourishing home industry, and Protestant and industrial Outer Rhoden. The primitive institutions of the canton include the compulsory general deliberative assembly, once a year, of all male citizens over twenty years of age

Photo, Kadet & Herbert

SILENT ORISONS IN AN ALPINE SANCTUARY OF LOCARNO

Some of the more notable of Alpine shrines, like the frescoed church of Madonna del Sasso at Morcote, or this in the wild Val Verzasca, are in the Italian parts of Switzerland. The architecture and inhabitants, as well as the scenery of Locarno, which is situated on Lake Maggiore and is a favourite health resort famous for its flowers, foliage, and genial climate, are characteristically Italian

Photo, Hermann Stauder

is highly developed. The Federal Government has some responsibility for ensuring that it shall be "sufficient, obligatory, gratuitous, and non-sectarian," but the actual control is left to the cantons and communes. Rich and poor send their children to the same schools. Girls and boys are taught in separate classes, except in small village schools, girls being put on exactly the same footing as the boys, Switzerland having been the first country in Europe to admit women to the universities.

In mountain districts, where the parents need the help of the children during the summer to get in the hay and to herd the cows and goats, school terms are confined to autumn and winter; but in the towns they are very much the same as in England. Pauper children, who in most cantons are entrusted to foster parents and not segregated in institutes, attend the same schools as their richer neighbours, and the local educational authorities are obliged to ensure that all children are sufficiently clothed, and that those who have to walk long distances to school, which is often the case in the mountains, are provided with food. Every man who is physically fit,

IN "THE GLACIER VILLAGE" OF PICTURESQUE GRINDELWALD

One of the most popular of summer and winter resorts in the Bernese Oberland, Grindelwald's many attractions include the majestic Wetterhorn (12,150 feet) and Eiger (13,040 feet), the Mettenberg (10,193 feet), with its wonderful glaciers which feed the Black Lütschine, the beautiful walks in the vicinity, and the facilities afforded for ski-ing and other out-of-door winter pastimes

Photo, Georg Haeckel

FAVOURITE STAND FOR STREET TRADERS IN LUCERNE

Entrance to the quaint old roofed wooden bridge which crosses the River Reuss diagonally, dates from the fourteenth century, and contains, suspended from its rafters, many paintings illustrating lives of Lucerne's patron saints and deeds of her brave sons. Near its south end is the Wasserturm, or water tower, from whose lantern (lucerna) the town is doubtfully said to have derived its name

Photo, Georg Haeckel

WELCOME REST BY THE ROADSIDE IN EVOLENA

Eyes of youth and of infancy look towards the camera with calm directness, and the firm lips of girl and child express well the independence of the Swiss character. Evolena is a holiday resort in Canton Valais, its picturesque houses being survivals of ancient Valaisian architecture and the costumes of its womenfolk among the few spared by latter-day developments

Photo, Donald McLeish

except Government employees, is obliged to serve in the army, and recruits are required to sit for a written examination. Those who are unfit are taxed according to their means. The Confederation supplies arms, but equipment and uniform are furnished by the cantons and the men are recruited territorially. After a man has reached the age of seventeen he is liable to be called up for forty-five days' training in the Elite, or first division, after which he joins the first reserve for a period of sixteen days, every other year and, finally, the Landsturm, or second reserve, being called upon every four years for nine days' service. During the whole of this period he keeps his uniform and arms at home, and is obliged to produce them periodically for inspection.

The army is run on the same democratic lines as the schools; the sons of rich and poor serving side by side, so

YOUNG GOATHERD OF THE MOUNTAIN PASTURES

Swiss boys and girls play a serious part in the hard struggle for existence which characterises the life of large numbers of the peasantry, and this fact makes the intellectual progress of the people the more remarkable, and provides a thought-provoking contrast to the blue lakes, glittering pinnacles, beautiful flora, and other physical features that appeal to the eye of the passing tourist

Photo, Donald McLeish

FULL OF YEARS AND ADVENTUROUS EXPERIENCES

This aged Alpine shepherd, standing by the doorway of his rude châlet, pipe in one hand for solace
and in the other the short staff whose support is but seldom needed, looks for all the world like Rip
Van Winkle after his sleep on the Katskills, save that the years have left him calmly contemplative
and apparently content with the simple life of the mountains

Photo, Donald McLeish

AT THE HOSPICE OF THE GREAT ST. BERNARD

At the summit of the pass of the same name, 8,111 feet high, a hospice existed in the ninth century, and was refounded by S. Bernard of Menthon two centuries later. On its steps is seen the prior with one of the famous dogs, Leon, who, when but three years old, had already saved thirty-two lives. The training of the dogs of the St. Bernard hospice takes about two years

Photo, Donald McLeish

SCANTY FOOTHOLD IN THE DEPTHS OF A CREVASSE

Remarkable photograph of a famous Swiss guide, Andreas Hartmann, poised on an icy pinnacle some eighty feet down in a crevasse. Only the most hardy and experienced mountaineer would dare such a venture to see the beautiful effect of the sun's reflection and refraction through the ice, for an involuntary descent would mean death by drowning or freezing if not by the fall itself

Photo, Donald McLeish

CALLING THE CATTLE HOME IN THE BERNESE OBERLAND

As haunting to the memory as the " Ranz des vaches," sung on the departure for the mountain pastures, is the sound of the alpenhorn calling the cattle home at sunset. The sound echoes from alp to alp, and all within hearing uncover their heads and say their evening prayer. The alpenhorn is often eight feet long, but varies in size, shape, and curvature with each locality

THE LEISURE HOUR IN AN ALPINE GASTHOUSE

Games of hazard seem an almost natural form of recreation for men who, in the pursuit of their livelihood, daily stake their stamina and skill against the forces of nature on the perilous, snowclad, crevasse-scarred peaks of their native land. They often possess small pastoral holdings which are carefully tended by their wives, aided by the willing hands of younger members of the family

Photos, Donald McLeish

SURROUNDED BY CRAGGY AND SNOW-CAPPED PEAKS: MOUNTAINEERS ON THE SUMMIT OF THE FAULHORN

Among the many ascents that offer themselves to the climber whose starting-point is Grindelwald, one of the most popular is that of the 8,803 feet of the Faulhorn, because of the ease with which it may be negotiated in about five hours, and because of the grandeur of the panorama that is commanded from the summit, with its "close-up" views of the Schwarzhorn, Wetterhorn, Schreckhorn, Finsteraarhorn, Fiescherhörner, Eiger, Jungfrau, Blümisalp, and other of the Bernese peaks as well as the lakes of Brienz, Thun, Neuchâtel, and Lucerne. The return to Grindelwald can be made in about three hours and a half

that employer and employed live under the same conditions and discipline. Officers are promoted from the ranks, being given the additional training necessary to fit them for their duties.

Labour is well organized and the conditions under which men and women work are controlled by the Government. There is generally sufficient work, of one sort or another, for everybody

PERILS OF PASTORAL LIFE IN THE ALPS
On this steep Alpine slope shepherd and goatherd carry their lives in their hands, having to be as surefooted as the animals in their care. Should a homestead or châlet be built, suddenly and without warning an earth tremor may precipitate it in splintering ruin down the mountain-side. Some such tragic happening is suggested by the broken timber in the foreground cf the photograph

The boys are taught drill in the schools and every Swiss man is usually accustomed to using a rifle—shooting matches for prizes, throughout the cantons, forming one of the chief attractions of local fêtes.

In theory, class distinction does not exist, and all laws tend to prevent it. No one thinks any more of a neighbour because he is rich, or belongs to a family dating back many centuries. The use of titles is not tolerated at home, but members of the old patrician families are sometimes permitted to use them when appointed to foreign courts. There are virtually no poor people, and charity is regarded as a duty, not a right, among all citizens.

and loafers are not tolerated. Farmers and peasants usually own their own land and the accumulation of large properties is prevented by law. The Alps, or pasturages, and the forests are owned by the commune and every member of the commune has a right to graze so many head of stock, according to the size of his property, as well as to a certain amount of wood for fuel or other purposes.

In some cantons almost every village has its cooperative store, while the peasants also combine in the sale of their produce and even in the cultivation of their land, in exceptional circumstances. The communes appoint herdsmen who look after the cows up

LITTLE HANS TELLS AN AMUSING STORY

His face is turned from the camera, but as, hands in pockets, he stands with one knee bent, he appears to be older than his years. The older boy, too, with carrier on back, has taken up the burden of life early, and the young girl keeps her knitting-needles busy while she listens to little Hans. The scene is at Unterschächen in Canton Uri

Photo, Hermann Stauder

WOMEN WORKERS OF CHAMPÉRY IN MOURNING GARB

Normally the women of Champéry, at the head of the Val d'Illiez, in Canton Valais, wear bright scarlet kerchiefs wound round their dark hair. They do the bulk of the field work, and in winter don long trousers of thick locally woven cloth. The people, traditionally of mixed Roman and Saracen descent, speak French, which is, however, combined with a patois of Celtic origin

Photo, Hermann Stauder

HAY HARVESTING IN THE ENGADINE: BRINGING HOME THE GARNERED WEALTH OF THE ALPINE MEADOWS

The scene is bathed in sunlight, the road is dusty, the carter's garb suggests summer's genial warmth, but the climate of the Inn is often described as "nine months winter and three months cold." The Engadine, while famous for its winter sports, attracts swarms of summer visitors seeking the baths and health-giving air of St. Moritz in particular. But apart from this source of income the chief wealth of the natives is in their hay-meadows, which usually yield three crops before October sets in. The use of oxen as draught animals is common throughout the valley

Photo, Donald McLeish

BY FOAMING TORRENT AND SOMBRE MOUNTAIN PINE

Young cowherd and her solitary charge on the boulder-strewn edge of the Visp torrent, the two branches of which are divided by the glacier-clad height of the Balfrin, or Balen-Firn, a projecting peak of the Saasgrat. The Visp, or Viège, gives its name to an old village delightfully situated on a hillock at the entrance to the Visp valley

Photo, Donald McLeish

on the Alps during the summer, milking them and making the cheese, which is divided among the owners of the cows, in proportion to the amount of milk given by each cow, this being periodically tested.

The chief industries are agriculture, including cheese and wine making, machinery, especially electric engines, cotton and silk goods, muslin curtains and embroideries, artificial silk, chocolate, condensed milk, watch making, and, last but by no means least, the "Fremden," or foreign industry. In addition to these, many home industries exist, such as wood and ivory carving, straw plaiting, lace making, flax spinning and weaving.

The home industries are being much developed, as it is recognized that the hard and dull life of the peasants, especially in winter, when they are practically confined to their villages in the higher valleys, is driving many of the younger people into the towns and even further, beyond the borders of their country.

Agricultural Switzerland may be divided into three types—the fertile valley of the Aar, forming a plateau running from south-west to north-east, which is the centre of the milk and cheese country from the export point of view; the valleys of the larger lakes and rivers; and the narrower valleys penetrating to the shadow of the Alpine giants, where the peasants scrape a poor living off the slopes.

Vines are grown mainly on the south slopes of the lakes of Geneva, Neuchâtel, Zürich, and along the Rhône and Rhine, as well as in the Canton of Ticino. These require but little soil, so long as they get plenty of sun, and the vineyards are banked or terraced in order that the vines may always grow on the south side. Swiss wines are seldom met outside Switzerland, but they are pure and wholesome.

The vintage is a time of great gaiety, but it entails hard work and, often, disappointment when a sudden hailstorm has ruined the grapes and, with them, the prospect of the small holder, who was depending upon their yield.

The richest part of agricultural Switzerland lies in the valleys of the Rhine and Aar. Large farm houses are scattered throughout this pasture land, which produces most of the condensed milk, and chocolate factories are also seen. The finest cattle are bred here and the whole aspect of this country is prosperous, the farmers living almost entirely on the produce of their land.

The cows are put to graze the meadows in early spring, after which two or even three crops of hay are mown and, again in the autumn, the cows go into the meadows before being shut in their stables for the winter. The meadows are manured, and the result is hay so rich that no other food is required by the cows during the winter.

On the stable doors near La Gruyère, which is one of the richest of the districts, and the cheese of which is

MIXED SCHOOL IN ONE OF THE FOREST CANTONS
Except in such small schools as this at Unterschächen, Canton Uri, Swiss boys and girls are taught separately, and though climate and scattered homesteads present special difficulties in particular districts the Swiss educational system is admittedly one of the most efficient in the world; the excellence of its primary education being regarded as the corner stone of Swiss democracy
Photo, Hermann Stauder

SMILING GIRLHOOD OF NORTHERN SWITZERLAND

In the pleasing local costume of Hallau, Canton Schaffhausen, these two sisters make a charming picture as the sun lends sheen to their fair hair and brightens their laughing blue eyes

Photo, Hermann Stauder

BY THE FIRESIDE OF A TICINESE COTTAGE

Canton Ticino, so named from the river of that name, is in Italian Switzerland, but its people, while Italian in language and descent, are essentially Swiss in sentiment. Poverty is their normal lot, but should they emigrate, they are ever eager to return to the verdant slopes, smiling valleys, vineclad terraces, and chestnut groves of their homes on the shore of Lakes Maggiore and Lugano

Photo, Hermann Stauder

well known in England—shields are nailed up, showing the prizes obtained by the cattle or cheese of the farmer. Each shield shows the grue or crane, the punning crest of La Gruyère, and in the case of cheese prizes the crane is drawn on a cauldron on the shield.

Labour in these districts is easy, as the meadows are flat or on gentle slopes, but agricultural machinery is seldom seen and both mowing and threshing are still performed by hand.

Orchards of fine pear, apple, and cherry trees surround the farm houses, the fruit being dried and stored for winter use, or sent to the jam factories lately built at Lenzburg near Zürich, or Saxon in the Rhône valley.

Very little snow lies in the country we have been describing, and farm work can be carried on throughout the winter. Conditions are very different

in the mountains. Here the peasant lives a hard life, in some places scraping his living from almost unproductive slopes. Yet, even here, his frugality and industry enable him to live contentedly, as he has but few wants, and he is usually sufficiently prosperous.

While the people of Grisons are different from those of the Bernese Oberland, who, again are totally unlike those of Valais, the soil is much the same, the slopes are as steep, the rocks push through as ruggedly, and the land slips as easily, in all the mountain cantons.

During the winter the men are occupied with cutting, or fetching the hay from the higher slopes, spreading manure on the snow so that it lies ready to melt into the ground when spring comes, and looking after the cattle and goats, which are shut in almost hermetically-sealed stables. How the animals survive, living in the atmosphere necessary if their bodily warmth is to be sufficiently hoarded to prevent their dying of cold, is often a marvel, and their excitement and joy when let

and water power enables the commune to provide electric light which has saved many villages from destruction by fire—a constant menace to the wooden châlets in the days of paraffin lamps. The post penetrates to the highest

WHEN EVENING FALLS IN THE BERNESE OBERLAND

Lovers of the open air from their childhood, the Swiss often take their meals alfresco. Here we see a peasant family seated at supper at Meiringen, a village of the Hasli-Tal, whose people are believed to have descended from Scandinavian immigrants. Meiringen, which was almost entirely destroyed by fire in 1891, and afterwards rebuilt on improved lines, lies in a valley on the Aar

Photo, Hermann Stauder

out in the spring are pleasant to watch. The women stay in their châlets looking after the housework, often spinning and weaving their cloth, or linen, while the children toboggan to school and home again. It is a quiet life, now and then enlivened by a dance, or wedding, or choral festival.

The Swiss peasant is a very frugal person, with but few wants, and an inveterate dislike of waste. Everything he does is of profit to himself, or his land, so that there is a constant incentive to hard work.

Conditions have been much improved by electricity, as even the remotest village is now reached by telephone,

hamlets, and hardly a châlet could be found where some newspaper is not taken in. The Swiss post carries almost anything, from a tourist's trunk to a pair of skis seven feet long. It also facilitates trade, as goods may be sent to be paid for on delivery. Debts may be collected by post, a claim arriving with the postman.

The peasants buy very little, living almost entirely on their own produce, but corn, potatoes, or dry chestnuts must be bought, where the villages lie too high to grow what is required in the way of starch food stuffs. The herdsmen sometimes live entirely on cheese during the weeks they are

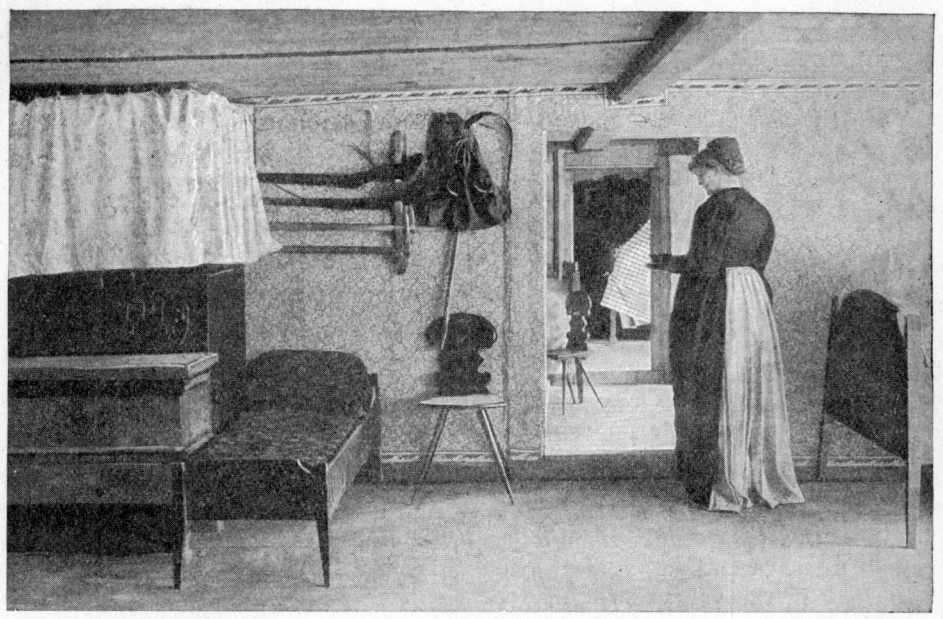

HOME OF A SWISS PEASANT IN THE HASLI-TAL

Alpenstock, ice-axes, knapsack, and rifles, neatly suspended on the wall, serve to indicate the outdoor life of the master of the house, and the carved wooden furniture suggests the skilful work of native handicraftsmen, while the scrupulous cleanliness and tidiness that appeal at once to the eye are eloquent of the love and care bestowed by the housewife upon the little kingdom under her devoted rule

BURGHER'S DAUGHTERS OF THE BERNESE OBERLAND

They are within the porch of one of the decorated wooden houses of Zweisimmen that form so familiar a feature of the Simmer-Tal, and are wearing the pretty costumes peculiar to this valley. With Swiss girlhood the May-day of life is the hey-day of life; they know well how to make the most of it, but few prove better wives or mothers

Photos, Hermann Stauder

away on some very high Alp, but they suffer in health as a result.

The dangers to the mountain habitations are very serious ; storms producing landslides in summer and the snow, falling in huge avalanches in winter, are a constant menace to life and property.

The usual avalanche tracks are well known, and no one would build his house on one, or if he does, he protects it with a triangular wall which will cut the snow like a plough as it rushes down. But sometimes a very heavy fall of snow will enable an avalanche to start in a place which has not known one before. As it gathers strength it carries with it the forest, the trees snapping like twigs in the wind which pushes ahead, and a village lying peacefully in the valley below may be entirely buried.

There are two forms of avalanche— the " Staub Lawine," or dust avalanche, falling in winter when the snow is still light and powdery, and the " Grund Lawine," or solid avalanche, falling in spring, and composed of heavy wet snow. The former is suffocating, as it penetrates everywhere, and a man buried by it has but little chance of living. The latter, being made up of lumps, with air holes between them, gives more chance of life to anyone who is not too much crushed by its weight. The wind which precedes an avalanche will lift a man and hurl him across a valley, sometimes even beyond where the snow rolls, so that if he survives the fall, he may escape.

The ravages of nature are not confined to the mountain valleys. The Rhône, which swirls down to Lake Geneva, and is fed by numbers of streams from very steep valleys on either side, rises and falls with terrible rapidity, and often threatens to break through its high banks. In 1920 it caused a flood which did infinite damage to the property of the Valais peasants, who are among the poorest

GATHERING THE LUSCIOUS FRUIT IN A SWISS VINEYARD

Wine is made in nearly all the Swiss cantons, especially on the southern slopes of the lakes of Geneva, Neuchâtel, Zürich, and along the Rhône and Rhine. Plenty of sun is more essential than depth of soil. The Swiss vintage is a time of great gaiety, but it involves hard work, for a sudden hailstorm may ruin the yield and its promise of winter sustenance for the small holder

Photo, Hermann Stauder

in Switzerland, as, at the best of times, they have difficulty in cultivating sufficient to live upon. Fires are often caused by lightning striking a wooden roof and, before the peasants can collect from the fields, the sparks fly, and the whole village may be on fire.

It is on all these occasions that the best spirit of the Swiss nation is shown. The Federal Government publishes an appeal throughout the country, offering free carriage by railway or post of all goods sent to the stricken area. Local branches of mutual aid societies, of which several exist, immediately open centres where food, clothing, and money, are collected, and whence they are despatched without delay.

The Swiss, both as a nation and as individuals, are always ready to help

YOUNG VINEYARD WORKER OF HALLAU

Hallau is in Schaffhausen, one of the most prosperous of the Swiss cantons, and a few miles from the famous falls of the Rhine. It gives its name to the red wine known as Hallauer

Photo, Hermann Stauder

those who are in trouble, and a good example of their international fore-thought is shown by the Red Cross Society. A citizen of Geneva happened to be present at the battle of Solferino, in Italy, and was so horrified by the suffering of the sick and wounded, that he hurried home, and persuaded his town to call a conference of the Powers. The result of this was the Geneva Convention of 1864, forming the International Red Cross Society, whose central office remains to this day at Geneva. As a compliment to Switzerland, its flag, a white cross on a red ground, was adopted, the colours being merely reversed.

The Swiss take a great pride in their humanitarianism, and cling to their neutrality by the whole will of the

people. They have accepted the League of Nations as an ideal, but had great doubt as to whether, by joining it, they might not be involved in European politics to the extent of losing their position as a neutral state ready to offer its hospitality to all schemes for the greater good of the world, and to citizens of other countries who might be in distress. For Switzerland has always been the home of those driven away by political stress from their own countries, and has, to a certain extent, suffered as a result. In this case a referendum was held, and the people voted for joining the League, but with certain reservations adapted to their position in Europe.

Summer time provides much enjoyment for everyone among the Alps;

these used to be the playgrounds of foreigners, but are now attracting the Swiss themselves. The people from the towns migrate in whole families to the mountain villages for their holidays, and excursions are arranged for the school children, while both boy and girl students go off for two or three days, equipped with ice axes, ropes and rucksacks, for climbs among the glaciers and peaks. No longer is it the tourist who holds the field, except on mountains like the Rigi.

Holiday Making in the Homeland

The mountain trains and lake steamers are crowded with jolly parties of Swiss excursionists, nearly always singing. The songs they sing are invariably patriotic, the words " Thou beloved Fatherland " or " Thou beautiful Switzerland " being heard continually. Sometimes a gay soul will carry an accordion, on which to accompany his friends, or a tuning fork is produced, and the note given by the leader of the party.

The school children are accompanied by their teachers, and the length of their excursions is governed by the prosperity of their parents or commune. It may be only a whole day, on a mountain near their homes, or they may go off for two or three days, carrying their food and spare clothing in rucksacks, tramping to some high Alp, where the military authorities will sometimes lend them blankets and straw in a mountain hut.

Edelweiss and Alpenrose

Certain flowers possess an overwhelming attraction for the Swiss. Every year men and women are killed in their effort to pick edelweiss on some steep grass slope, where a slip means rolling to death over a precipice. This edelweiss is almost a fetish, and the fact that in many places it is so common that it is mown with the hay does not seem to detract from its value. It is difficult to analyse such attraction in a

flower, especially in a flower so like a bit of shrunk, torn, and dirty white flannel as the edelweiss.

It is easier to understand the love of the alpenrose or Alpine rhododendron, which grows in profusion on the slopes of the higher valleys. This is almost the national flower, and wreaths of alpenrose and oak are painted on all the post carriages. People returning from an excursion carry immense bunches of alpenrose tied to sticks and carried over their shoulders. The Narcissus Poeticus, which grows in white sheets in the meadows above Montreux, is another favourite, and an annual fête is arranged in its honour.

Economic Effects of the Great War

Some of these fêtes are organized as an attraction for the tourist, and the Montreux one, though attended by large numbers of Swiss from the surrounding villages, is mainly a battle of flowers, in which the foreigner takes part. A large proportion of Swiss lived mainly by the tourist industry before the Great War. Huge hotels sprang up wherever any special attraction existed. Shops followed the hotels, and the tourist centres were busy for nine months of the year. The Great War has changed this sadly, many of the hotels having to be shut up, while others are hardly able to exist. The whole nation suffered as a result, the men who used to earn good incomes as guides, or the owners of carriages and motor-cars, being all in a very bad way, while, owing to their high exchange, the Swiss found it difficult to dispose of their produce to advantage.

Great singing competitions are held at different centres, the one at Lucerne in 1922 being attended by thousands of singers from all over the country. Every village and town has its choral society, and the children learn to sing in unison in the schools.

An Aelplifest on Sunday in spring is a charming sight, representing the moving of the cattle up to the Alps

SWITZERLAND
Alpine Life & Scenery

Their large-heartedness no less than their mountaineering skill has won for the Swiss Alpine guides the admiration of the world

Photos (except those on pages 4847 and 4848), Donald McLeish

In the foreground, devotion before an Alpine Calvary; beyond the pine line, the silent snowclad majesty of the towering Matterhorn

*Happy Swiss childhood at play by the old chapel-porch of Winkel-
matten, a charming little hamlet in the very heart of the Alps*

Erect despite her age and heavy basket this aged peasant of the Saas Valley leads her goat home from pasture, enjoying her pipe the while

Although there has been a steady increase in Swiss factories, the graceful art of the hand lace-maker survives in Wengen and elsewhere

*Sturdy young Switzer, who promises to prove a worthy son of Zermatt,
the training-ground of some of the most famous of Alpine guides*

Cowherds of Toggenburg, they are on their way to the high pastures
with broad collars and great bells to adorn their wandering kine

Photo, Hermann Stauder

Roman Catholicism has a stronghold in Canton Valais, and this semi-military religious procession at Kippel, in the picturesque little valley of the Lonza, has its occasional supplement in the miracle plays that are performed here

Photo, Hermann Stauder

in summer. The people dress up in their local costumes, and march through the villages with their cattle, goats, sheep and pigs, followed by carts or horses, laden with the great copper cheese-cauldrons, and other paraphernalia. The inhabitants of the district collect to see the show, and men wearing old uniforms, and carrying arms, which have probably been stored for possible use since Napoleon's time, lead the procession. Sometimes the setting is very elaborate, and large haycarts, decked out as châlets, carry men and women engaged on various industries, such as cheesemaking, weaving, or wine-pressing in full swing.

Happiness in Homespun

After the procession round the village, the whole company adjourns to some orchard outside, where wrestling will take place, and here the young gymnasts in their white vests and pants grapple with goatherds and cheesemakers in their homespun suits. The spectators sit round on the grass, or on benches, where wine and beer are served. The fun stops early, as the people all have to get home to look after their cattle, and the roads in every direction are crowded with whole families, who have got just as much joy and interest out of seeing their own daily toil depicted at the fête as townsmen would out of some drama at a cinema.

Climbing used to be mainly indulged in by a certain type of scholarly Englishman, who was greeted with joy by the guides and innkeepers, but watched with tolerance and wonder by the Swiss as a whole. Now, however, the people of the towns and villages are climbing their mountains far more, and without guides, being themselves good mountaineers and with no money to spend. The Swiss Alpine Club has built huts at a great many points where a night's shelter is necessary before the final ascent can be made. These huts are very simple, merely providing shelter, with fuel, and some cooking utensils, hay or mattresses to sleep on, and a first-aid equipment, as well as a selection of different sized clogs lined with wool for the footsore climber who has not weighted his rucksack with luxuries such as slippers.

Universal Use of the Ski

Now that skis or Norwegian snowshoes have been brought to Switzerland, the mountains are open to the climber in winter as well as summer, and ski-ing is already a national pastime. The first pairs of skis were imported from Norway by the monks of the Great St. Bernard Hospice in 1883, as they realized that their life-saving work in the deep snow would be immensely facilitated by their use, and in 1887 skis were introduced to the Canton of Grisons and, gradually, this sport was adopted. Now, in almost every village where the snow lies the children learn to ski, while men and women go off on long excursions in the mountains. Races are held, as well as jumping competitions, in which Norwegians find it hard to hold their own.

Old and New Methods of Transport

Toboggans are used more by the Swiss themselves for practical purposes than for amusement. The postman on his rounds or the children going to school, or the mother of a family who has commissions in the village, slide down much faster than they can walk, and think nothing of dragging the light toboggan uphill.

The winter is the time when most of the hay and wood is carried, as the heavy loads slide easily over the snow. There is a law of the right of way in some cantons by which, when the snow lies on the ground, anyone may travel across any land which is not actually enclosed. This enables the peasants to take the shortest cuts to their goal and no damage can be done to property, as the snow protects it.

Another way by which wood, hay, and even milk are transported, is along

MERRY STAVE IN THE SONG OF THE VINE

Earth has given forth her increase, and the smiling faces of these happy young people reflect the prospect of a good vintage. This autumn scene is in a vine-growing district of Neuchâtel, where the people are mostly French-speaking, and where large quantities of wine of excellent quality are produced, of which most of what is known as the "petit vin blanc" is consumed locally

Photo, Hermann Stauder

wires stretched from some high cliff to the valley below, with a windlass by which the burden is let slowly down. These wires may be seen shining in the light like a spider's thread, travelling miles across the mountains.

Most of the larger streams and rivers are being dammed at intervals to provide electricity. The water is often carried for miles through tunnels in the rock, until it is finally led into huge iron pipes and allowed to rush down to the turbines in a power station, whence wires carry the power away to distant towns and factories.

The mountain railways are nearly all electric, and the main lines through the St. Gotthard, Simplon, and other passes are gradually being electrified. The Great War drove the Swiss to a feverish development of their water power because they suffered terribly from lack of coal, which was originally imported from Germany and Belgium, but which, during the war, had to be brought from America and transported at the convenience of the French or Italian railways to the Swiss frontier. Coal was so scarce that the Swiss were paying £15 a ton, and more, for it and were often unable to procure sufficient, so that wood had to be used for the railway engines.

The Swiss are very chary of cutting too much wood which is growing at high altitudes, and which protects the valleys from avalanches, as the trees bind the snow and tend to prevent it from slipping So important is this fact that the forestry laws are very strict, and foresters, approved by the Federal Government, are appointed to superintend all wood cutting.

An owner of forest land in some cantons is not allowed to cut one of his own trees without the approval of the forester, who marks the tree which can best be spared, choosing it with a view to the purpose to which the owner desires to put the wood. In some districts two young trees have to be planted for every one cut, in order that the forests may be maintained.

The heights of various places may be roughly ascertained by observing the trees. For instance, fruit trees, beech, ash, and other deciduous trees do not grow above 5,000 feet. The larch ands pruce stop at 6,000 feet, while the pinus cembra or arolla pine is only happy at 6,000 feet and grows above that line. Only the juniper can live up to 7,000 feet, where it becomes so scrubby that it is almost a creeping plant. Vegetation of all sorts except,

SWISS INDUSTRY AS WORLD-FAMOUS AS THE SWISS ALPS
More than three hundred years have passed since the art of watchmaking was introduced into Switzerland by a Burgundian who settled in Geneva. A large percentage of the serviceable watches in the world's market still come from Geneva and Neuchâtel. Many of the best workmen ply their calling in their own homes in the manner shown in the above photograph
Photo, Hermann Stauder

FASHIONING ARTISTIC POTTERY IN A BERNESE VILLAGE

In Canton Berne, as elsewhere in Switzerland, are few if any idle burners of the oil of life, and like their fellow-craftsmen in other industries, Swiss potters evince infinite pride in their handiwork. The chief centre of majolica manufacture is Heimberg, but in the adjacent village of Steffisburg, where this photograph was taken, much artistic ware is produced

Photo, Hermann Stauder

perhaps, some lichens, stops at 9,000 feet, while glacier level may be taken roughly as 8,000 feet, though many glaciers roll down to 4,000 feet above sea-level.

Many of the big spruce or larch trees in the forests 5,000 feet above the sea are hundreds of years old and their wood is generally used to build with. The rooms of châlets are usually panelled with these, the larch being of a deep red-brown, but the cembra is much prized as a panelling wood. It shows great knots, and the panels are made of two planks reversed so that these knots make a formal pattern.

Most Swiss peasants are good carpenters and build their own châlets, decorating them with carving and often painting mottoes or prayers under the eaves, together with the initials of the owner and his wife, and the date when the châlet was built. The rooms

are low and the windows small, double windows being fitted for winter use. A huge porcelain stove is often built between two rooms and becomes the centre of home life during the winter months. A wooden bench surrounds it and there may be a seat between part of the stove and the wall where the grandfather or delicate member of the family sits through the winter. These stoves require but little wood to warm them, as, when the flame has burned out, and only charcoal remains, the chimney of the stove is shut and the heat is kept in and lasts for hours.

Wood for fuel is stored on the sunny side of the house from one year to another so that it dries thoroughly. The sun is so strong that on the south side the wood composing the châlets is burnt to a deep brown, while on the north side it is grey where wind and rain beat against it.

The air being so dry, the wood never rots, and these châlets are dry and warm. Where it is necessary to build a house above tree level as well as on the plain, when wood is scarce, stone is usually used, the masonry work being performed by Italians who migrate to Switzerland in summer-time for the purpose. It is curious how the Swiss seldom do any stone work themselves, though the Great War altered this, too, to a certain extent.

In lower Switzerland chestnut and walnut woods are much used for panelling and furniture, and cherry wood may also be found. The wood carving of commerce is mainly done in lime or walnut and comes mainly from the Canton of Berne, Brienz being the great centre. Here nearly every house has its workshop, each producing one type of carving. One family devotes itself to producing eagles, and another

to bears, while another may make nothing but toy châlets. Herr Hugler lately started a new school of carving at Brienz, but, even his disciples tend to limit their work to a repetition of certain patterns, originally cut by himself.

Very little fine art exists in Switzerland, which has not produced one world renowned painter, or poet, or sculptor. At the same time every Swiss citizen takes trouble to make his house attractive, and the " stube," or parlour, invariably contains some beautiful bit of furniture or attractive pottery or linen of which the family is very proud. Home crafts are being encouraged by societies throughout the country, and it is the Swiss themselves who mainly buy their produce, which is invariably good and solid.

The continual fight with the elements which has been the lot of the Swiss in their mountain homes has probably

BEAUTIFUL AND USEFUL BY-INDUSTRY OF THE SWISS PEASANTS

Since the first school of wood carving was founded at Brienz in the Bernese Oberland many years ago this art has spread widely and become an important by-industry of the Swiss people, whose skill has proved a delight to the connoisseur as well as to the child, and served also to relieve the peasantry from the pressure of what formerly was a more or less precarious livelihood

Photo, Hermann Stauder

SUNDAY AFTERNOON IN THE VAL D'HÉRENS
That it is the day of rest is shown by the dress of these old folk of the valley village of Evolena, by the look of peace that has fallen upon their toil-worn faces, and by the costume of the child
Photo, Hermann Stauder

responding, this habit will soon die out. The schoolmasters regret this very much because they do everything in their power to teach the children to be courteous and friendly. "Gott Grüsse" (God greet you) or "Leb' Wohl" (good health to you) are the usual greetings in German Switzerland.

The honesty of the Swiss is proverbial, and if petty pilfering takes place it can usually be traced to people of other nationalities living in the country. Orchards are seldom protected by walls or hedges, and the mass of fruit on the trees hangs safely till picked by its owner. The peasants seldom resent the passer-by helping himself to a handful of cherries or an apple, and no one seems to abuse their generosity. If a traveller loses a bag it almost invariably is recovered, and doors need seldom be locked in Swiss hotels.

tended to produce a very practical character which is well seen in their houses and clothes.

Local costumes are not generally worn, except on festal occasions. They are made of the very best materials such as silk, fine cloth, or fine linen with lace, the men of some districts wearing coloured leather caps and belts, while the women have beautiful silver or gold jewelry which is part of their dowry and which may be handed down from generation to generation.

Swiss children are almost invariably nice-looking and well-mannered. In country districts the inhabitants greet the stranger as they greet each other, but, owing to the foreigner seldom

The Great War was a great test of patriotism, because language can influence sympathy, and there was undoubtedly some feeling between the different cantons, but they refused to allow this to influence them in their foreign policy. They maintained their neutrality at great expense to themselves as the army was mobilised throughout the war, the whole frontier being guarded against attack by any one of the belligerent Powers which might have taken a short cut, as did the Roman armies, as well as the Austrians and, later, Napoleon, when wishing to get at an enemy beyond Switzerland. The maintaining of the army entailed so much expense that the

Federal Government was obliged to appeal by referendum to the people to sanction a national debt which had never been incurred before. The nation responded whole-heartedly, and the poorest peasant bore his part of the burden forced upon him by the warring of great Powers in which he had no interest. Not only did the Swiss suffer financially owing to the war, but many a healthy young citizen gave up his life in the terrible epidemic of grippe, or influenza, which attacked the army. These men, accustomed to the open-air life of the mountains, died in large numbers when crowded together in barracks, living a life to which they were unsuited.

In spite of her own suffering during the war, Switzerland did everything possible to alleviate the suffering of the belligerents. The International Red Cross Society at Geneva worked busily for the betterment of the conditions of prisoners of war in all countries, and Swiss towns and health resorts opened their hotels to those prisoners who could be sent to them.

It is often said that this was merely done to bring money into the country, but those who know how much the Swiss nation suffered from lack of the necessities of life which they could not import, except at the pleasure of the surrounding countries, realize at what a sacrifice the Swiss maintained their best traditions of neutrality and charity.

It is not improbable that some among the readers of these pages will recall in this connexion the good work that was carried on in Chateau d'Oex, a pretty little village of Canton Vaud, famous for the health-giving qualities of its delicious air, which has helped to make it such a favourite summer and winter resort. Chateau d'Oex lies in a green valley rather more than twenty-two miles from Lausanne, and here many British sick and wounded, released from prison camps in Germany, found a haven of rest where their physical and mental recovery was helped forward, not only by medical skill and invigorating climatic conditions, but by the sympathetic reception accorded them by their kind-hearted hosts.

VETERAN COWHERD OF THE MELCHTAL

Melchtal is in Canton Unterwalden, whose menfolk are said to have helped to defend Rome from the Goths, and whose green slopes and rugged summits rival in beauty and grandeur those of any other of the forest cantons

Photo, Hermann Stauder

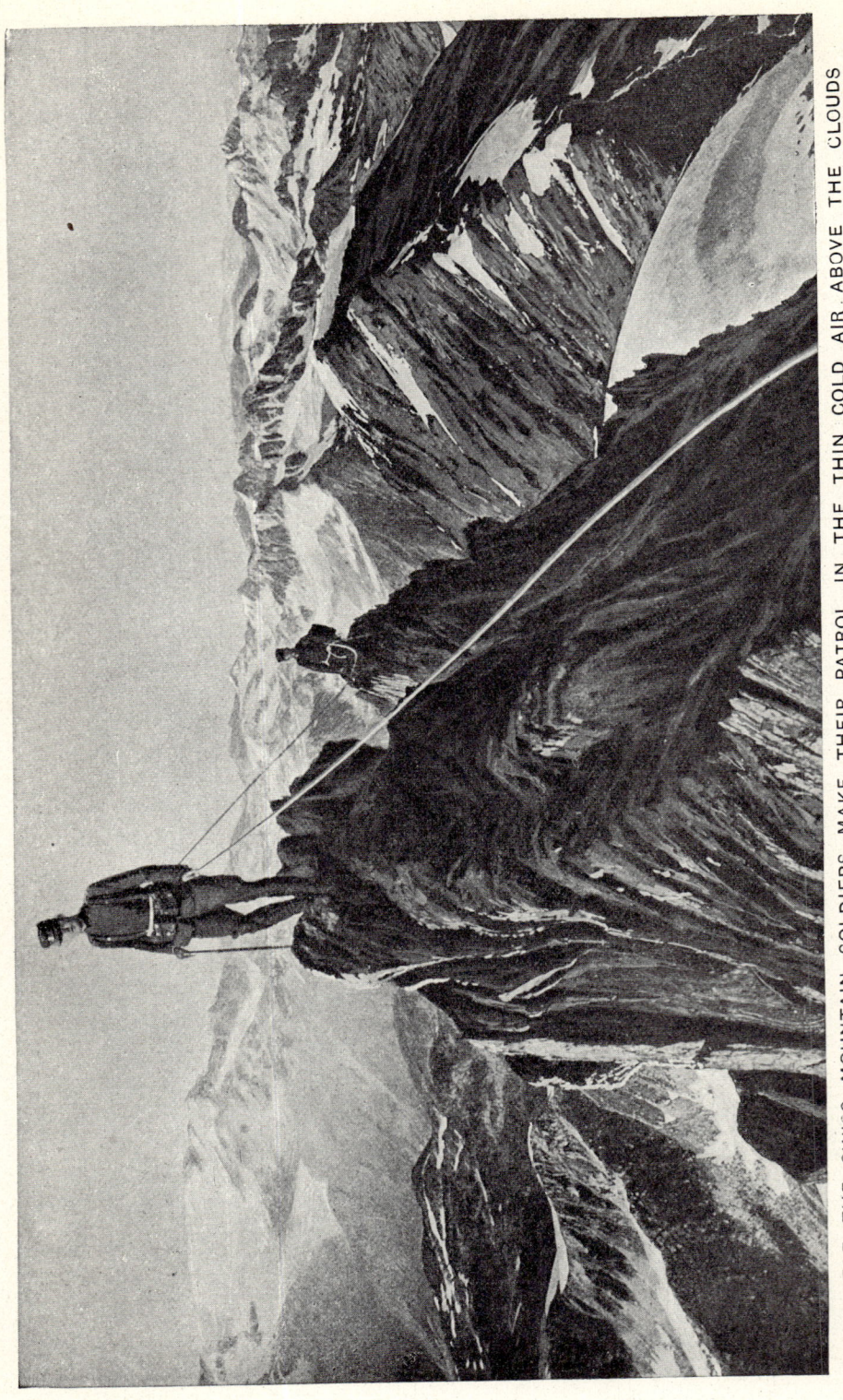

WHERE THE SWISS MOUNTAIN SOLDIERS MAKE THEIR PATROL IN THE THIN COLD AIR ABOVE THE CLOUDS

As in other European countries that include within their borders some portion of the Alps, Switzerland makes a special and very spectacular feature of its mountain troops. Manoeuvres that develop from military evolutions to sheer exhibitions of hazardous rock climbing are common. The Swiss remember that whatever means of destruction may devise, the frozen peaks of the Alps are their surest and ever-ready bulwark against attack. In the photograph two officers of a mountain patrol are seen upon the last height of some weather-split crag

Switzerland

II. Origin and Development of the Confederation

By Francis Gribble

Author of "Lake Geneva and Its Literary Landmarks," etc.

THE territory which eventually became Switzerland first figures in history in Julius Caesar's "Commentaries." It is there related that the Helvetii entered Gaul, as emigrants rather than invaders, through the Jura passes, but were defeated near Lyon, and rolled back into their own country.

The Romans followed them; and Roman rule speedily spread over the land. Broadly speaking, it encircled the country, leaving the centre comparatively independent. Forts were built along the northern frontier, at Basel, Constance, and elsewhere to keep out the Germans.

Under the Foot of the Conqueror

The Roman dominion lasted about 450 years; but the collapse began long before the expiration of that period. Then it came about that Germans and Burgundians divided the country between them—the former establishing themselves in the east and the latter in the west; but they were invaders of widely differing temper and quality. The Germans came as barbarians, sweeping Roman institutions away, and superseding the Latin language with a new jargon. The Burgundians, who had accepted Roman civilization, kept its traditions alive, and spoke the language which evolved into French. They were Christians and had bishops at a time when the German Swiss were still heathens. But these, too, were presently converted.

There followed the confused time of the Middle Age. The country then formed a part of the dominions, first of the Merovingian, and subsequently of the Carlovingian kings. It was also raided by Hungarians and Saracens; and it eventually became a part of what is sometimes called the Holy Roman and sometimes the German Empire, ruled by feudal lords, who owed allegiance to the Emperor.

The first great date is 1291. In that year, the men of the three Forest Cantons—Uri, Schwyz and Unterwalden—formed a Perpetual League against the arbitrary rule of their overlords of the House of Hapsburg. In spite of the League, acts of oppression continued; and then three peasants—Werner Stauffacher, Walter Fürst, and Arnold von Melchtal—met, in 1307, in a meadow, close to Lake Lucerne, and swore the famous oath of Grütli, to the effect that they would free the people and drive out the governors who had been set over them. The familiar story of William Tell belongs to this period; but modern historians declare that there is no word of truth in it.

What is unquestionably true, however, is that, with the League and the Oath, the Swiss Confederation came into being. The Duke of Austria tried to suppress it, but his army came very badly to grief at the battle of Morgarten (1315)—another proud date in Swiss history.

As a result of the victory Lucerne joined the Confederation. Zürich joined it in 1351, Glarus and Zug in 1352, and Berne in 1353. Gradually the Confederation expanded, the last cantons to join being Geneva, the Valais, and Neuchâtel.

Thus the political beginnings of Switzerland were an assertion of the right of small nationalities to self-determination; and the Confederation originated in an alliance to secure and defend that right. Their success in dealing with the hereditary oppressor gave the Swiss the strength and renown of a military power. Foreign potentates were glad to enrol them as mercenaries or to conclude alliances with them. Their most famous victories were those which they achieved, in alliance with Louis XI. of France, over Charles the Bold of Burgundy, at Grandson and Morat, in 1476. In the immediately succeeding years, the Confederation was still further enlarged until, in 1513, the incorporation of Appenzell raised the number of cantons to thirteen. The further additions, which made the number up to twenty-two, were delayed until after the close of the Napoleonic wars.

Influence of the Reformation

Meanwhile the history of Switzerland became in large measure the history of Bernese imperialism.

Berne was the appanage of the Dukes of Zähringen. Berchtold V. of that House founded it in 1191. It became a Free City after his death, and had a long and stern struggle with the jealous nobility before its admission to the Confederation, in 1353. It came into prominence as a State disposed to conquer and annex during the Reformation.

In Switzerland, as elsewhere, that great religious change brought war in

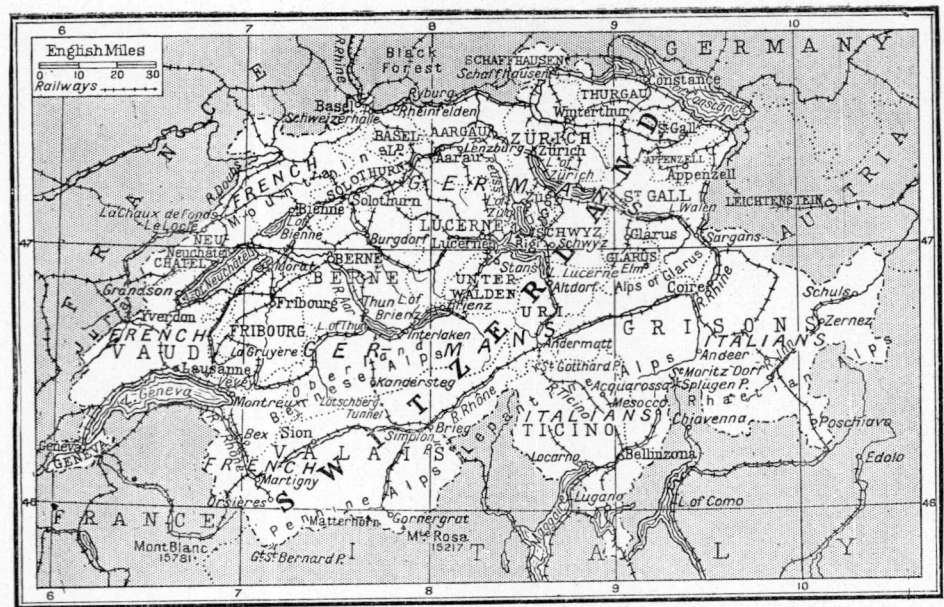

THE SWISS CONFEDERATION AND ITS PEOPLES

its train. Berne adopted its principles soon after Zürich, moved by Zwingli's preaching, had shown the way. The Forest Cantons resisted them, and there was hard fighting, terminated by the Peace of Kappel (1529), which happily guaranteed liberty of conscience to every one. Another war, a little later, launched Berne on her career of aggrandisement.

Vaud belonged, at that time, to the Dukes of Savoy. Geneva was a Republic, which had lately emancipated itself from his rule, but still owed him a vague allegiance. In both territories alike the Reformation was making progress; and the Duke of Savoy, as the champion of the Church, resolved to reassert his authority.

He prepared to lay siege to Geneva. That city appealed for help to the Bernese, who in response marched through Vaud to Geneva, stopping at the famous Castle of Chillon, on their way, to release Bonivard from his captivity, and receiving the submission of Lausanne, Vevey, and Yverdon.

The Canton of Vaud became, in 1536, a Bernese colony. Such liberties as it had acquired under the Dukes of Savoy were swept away. It was divided up into bailiwicks, and governed from Berne pretty much as India was until lately governed from England, but far more dictatorially.

That was the status of the canton in the years in which its leading towns acquired cosmopolitan celebrity and became the resort of fashion, the years in which Ludlow the Regicide fled for

refuge to Vevey, where he is buried, and Gibbon settled at Lausanne to finish the " Decline and Fall."

It was a time of outward prosperity, but of inward discontent. Scions of aristocratic families, excluded from all official careers at home, shook the dust of their birthplace from off their feet, and, in the service of some foreign power —as Governors of Canada, Mayors of Paris, Polish Ambassadors, and honoured Russian functionaries—intrigued against the Bernese tyrants. Those who remained sulked, biding their time. One of them— a certain Major Davel—marched into Lausanne, and proclaimed the independence of the canton, in 1723, but was taken into custody and executed. Liberty was to come to Vaud only as a sequel of the French Revolution.

The liberator was a political exile, Frédéric-César de la Harpe, who had been tutor to the grandsons of Catherine of Russia, had settled in Paris, and had acquired influence with the Directorate. Thanks to him, the rising of January, 1798, was supported by a French invasion which Berne could not resist. A French army entered Berne in March; and, in the confusion which ensued, Switzerland was turned upside down and a Helvetian Republic established under French auspices, with Lucerne for its capital. Internecine strife resulted, and, in 1803, Napoleon imposed his mediation. Then followed the Napoleonic wars. Switzerland was one of the cockpits of that period. Already, in 1799, the French, Austrians and Russians had fought battles on the St. Gotthard and near Zürich; and, later, Napoleon invaded Italy by way of the Great St. Bernard, made the Simplon Road to serve as a line of communication with that country, and annexed the Valais to France, in order to secure it. When, however, his power was broken at Leipzig, in 1813, his Swiss constitution began to crumble. In 1815, a Swiss army took part in the invasion of France ; and a new Federal Pact, approved by the Congress of Vienna, was accepted in August of that year.

That Pact was the beginning of the political Switzerland of our own time ; but, even so, there were to be further tribulations and changes. Three separate problems remained to be settled. The constitutions set up in the cantons were aristocratic, and the democrats were knocking at the door. The religious rivalries of Protestants and Catholics continued to be acute ; and in one canton, Neuchâtel, the King of Prussia retained overlordship and a garrison.

Trouble began to come to a head in the general European turmoil of 1830. From that year onward insurrections, revolutions and civil wars were frequent.

The year 1847 was specially critical. The Catholic cantons, by forming a separate alliance, the Sonderbund, threw down a challenge which the Protestant cantons had to take up.

The situation, in short, was closely analogous to that which brought about the Civil War in the U.S.A. A quarrel which had long smouldered ended in the War of the Sonderbund. The Federal Government declared the Sonderbund dissolved, and sent an army, under Colonel Dufour of Geneva, 100,000 strong, to compel its dissolution. He won a battle at Gislikon, near Lucerne ; and, after a campaign of only twenty-five days, the new Confederation collapsed. In 1857, Switzerland became politically complete, though a final (if it be, indeed, the final) revision of the Constitution was judged necessary in 1874. Its subsequent history has been tranquil.

During the Great War large numbers of wounded or invalided soldiers of the various belligerent armies were, by arrangement, interned in the country in comfortable conditions ; and after the war Geneva became the headquarters of the League of Nations.

SWITZERLAND : FACTS AND FIGURES

The Country

Land-locked state of Europe, bounded north by Germany, south-west and west by France, south-east by Italy, and east by Liechtenstein and Austria. From south-west to north-east, and including the lakes of Geneva and Constance, runs a plain, sloping down to the comparatively moderate heights of the Jura Mountains along the French frontier, while to the south is the central section of the Pennine Alps, comprising some of the greatest heights in Europe. Principal rivers are the Aar, Rhône, Reuss, Ticino, Rhine, and Inn, while the lakes include those of Bienne, Thun, Neuchâtel, Lucerne, and Zürich. Total area about 15,975 square miles, with an estimated population of 3,880,000.

Government and Constitution

Executive and legislative power are in hands of Parliament, which consists of two chambers, the State and National Councils, containing forty-four and about 200 members respectively. Members of the National Council are elected on a basis of proportional representation, there being a deputy for every 20,000 inhabitants. Members of the State Council are chosen by the cantons, each of which returns two members. For purposes of local government Switzerland is divided into cantons and demi-cantons, which have sovereign power in so far as the national Constitution permits, and independent organization. Legislative alteration may be inaugurated by a system known as the popular initiative, it being necessary to submit any law to the national vote if 30,000 citizens or eight cantons present any petition for its modification or annulment.

Commerce and Industries

About 300,000 of the population are peasant proprietors, and over 34 per cent. of the soil is under fruit, crops or gardens. Main agricultural products are condensed milk, cheese, wine, fruit, and tobacco. More than 3,200 square miles or about 29 per cent. of total area, is occupied by forests, which are supervised by police under the Swiss Confederation. Among important industries are watch and clock-making, salt production, and brewing. Mineral deposits are sparse and include iron-ore, asphalt, and coal. Imports for 1922 were valued at 1,914,465,000 francs, and included cereals, cottons, and minerals. Exports, of which silks, clocks, machinery and cotton goods were the chief, totalled 1,761,576,000 francs for same year. Standard coin the silver franc. Par rate of exchange is 25.22½ francs for £1 sterling.

Communications

There are over 3,800 miles of State railway, the principal routes being from Basel to Vienna, via Zürich, and to Milan, via Lucerne and the St. Gotthard Tunnel ; and from the Simplon tunnel, via Martigny, to Paris and via the Lötschberg tunnel to Berne. Main cross line runs from Lausanne to Solothurn, Zürich, and St. Gall, by way of Neuchâtel or Bienne. There are more than 23,800 miles of telegraph and 272,600 miles of telephone wire. There is also a State aerial service.

Religion and Education

Protestants are in majority in twelve cantons and Catholics in ten. No bishopric can be created in Switzerland without sanction from the Confederation. There is complete liberty of conscience. Elementary education is free and compulsory in every canton, and there are more than 4,200 primary schools. There are universities at Basel, Zürich, Berne, Geneva, Lausanne, Fribourg, and Neuchâtel.

Chief Towns

Berne, capital (estimated population 104,600), Zürich (207,000), Basel (136,000), Geneva (135,000) Lausanne (68,500), Winterthur (50,000).

ROMAN GATEWAY IN THE STREET WHICH IS CALLED STRAIGHT

One of the longest thoroughfares in Damascus, the Long Bazaar, is associated by tradition with the "street which is called straight," where the blind Paul lodged at his conversion and received his sight. The archway, above which rises a minaret, is the only remaining one of three which formed the east gate of the city. Near this spot is the Christian quarter, a place of narrow lanes and crumbling houses

Photo, Donald McLeish

Syria

I. Mixed Races of Mountain & Plain

By the Rev. W. Ewing, D.D.

Author of "Arab and Druze at Home," etc.

SYRIA, a land of rich diversity, lies along the east shore of the Mediterranean from the Taurus range in the north, to the desert in the south, bounded on the east by the Euphrates and the wilderness. Arabia Petraea, Palestine, and Lebanon, falling within these limits, are treated in separate articles. Here we deal mainly with the country to the north and east.

The land falls into five clearly-marked divisions of plain and mountain, running roughly parallel to the shore. The streams descending from the mountains to the sea and the desert are rapid and short. True rivers are found only in the central valley. Two rise close together near Baalbek. One, the Orontes—Nahr el 'Asi—flows northward and round the base of Jebel Ansariya past Antioch to the sea. The other, the Leontes—Nahr el Litany—flows southward, then turns abruptly, breaks a passage through the mountain, and issues on the shore north of Tyre. Streams rising at Hasbeya, Dan, and Caesarea Philippi, join to form the Jordan. These rivers are not navigable, but their course fixed the direction of the great highway between the empires of the East and that of Egypt.

Mute Wonders of the Past

The flowers of spring are glorious everywhere. The plains yield rich crops of cereals; there are gardens and orchards, walnut and mulberry trees. On the uplands we have pine and carob, olive, vine, fig, and dwarf oak, cypress and cedar. Higher still are alpine plants. On the spacious pasturelands are herds of cattle, sheep, and goats.

A striking feature of Syria is the multitudes of ancient ruins, the pathetic remains of once splendid cities, the relics of temple and fortress, church and monastery, tomb and monument. On yonder mountain, remote and lonely, lie a few columns and carved stones, mournful witnesses of vanished glories. From this grey crag a crumbling castle frowns over the land which once it held in awe. On many a hill, in many a vale, in bosky shades where, deep in the mountain's heart, the sweet spring waters rise, you will see the broken arch, the prostrate pillar, the carven capital, the delicately-sculptured frieze, the tumbled wreck and confusion of shrine and citadel. Anon we find streets of houses built of massive stones that need only roofs to be habitable again. A date or name may be found on a "written stone," but inscriptions are often illegible, and the secrets of the past are locked in age-long silence.

Improved Means of Communication

The Great War hastened the development of railways, and most of the main centres of population are in touch with Egypt, Arabia as far as Medina, Mesopotamia, and the shores of the Bosporus. The chief cities stand in two almost parallel lines, the first along the edge of the maritime plain, like pearls upon a string of emerald; the second studs the centre of the great inland plain.

Alexandretta, the principal seaport of North Syria, surrounded by green hills, is a fever-haunted place. Antioch, some fifteen miles inland from the ruined Seleucia, is poor and shrunken compared with the once splendid city on the Orontes. Latakia, a squalid town in a picturesque position, fronting the island of Cyprus, boasts of a triumphal arch of the time of Septimius Severus. Tripoli stands astride the

PICTURESQUE DRESS OF SYRIAN ARABS

No people exists which is more proud of its nationality and intolerant of foreigners than the Arabs. Europeans are regarded as heaven-sent sources of wealth, but the rest as mere unbelievers

adorned with graceful silver poplars, are seen to perfection the great wheels lifting water from the Orontes for irrigation.

Homs, the old Emesa, birthplace of Heliogabalus and of Julia Domna, wife of Septimius Severus, is dominated from the south by the castle mound, which may be of Hittite origin. Away southward, in the middle of the valley, stands the remarkable monument, of unknown origin, Kamu'a el Hermil, a lofty tower capped by a pyramid, and decorated with pilasters and hunting scenes sculptured in low relief. Its purpose is quite unknown.

Incomparable in grandeur are the ruins of Baalbek, on the edge of the spacious plain in full view of the snow-capped heights of Lebanon. Resting on massive substructures of high antiquity, and guarded by walls in which are seen the mightiest stones ever cut and placed by the hand of man, the majestic remains of temples, church, and fortress fill the beholder with awe and admiration.

holy river Kadisha, a little way from the shore, on the hill slope under the grim castle of Tancred. The most prosperous city of Syria is Beirut, on the south shore of beautiful St. George's Bay. The mountain behind it rises grandly through terraced slope, fair field, and lofty woodland, away to the snowy summit of Jebel Sannin.

For Aleppo the natives claim a fabulous antiquity. It stands in a wide plain near the desert, traversed by the river Kuweik, which ends in a morass to the south. The citadel, partly in ruins, crowns a gigantic artificial mound in the centre of the city, supported, says Arabian tradition, by 8,000 pillars. In the beautiful gardens at Hama,

Damascus, first and fairest of Syrian cities, holds a place of its own. The Barada, ancient Abana, flows down from Anti Lebanon through a wild gorge, doubles its volume with the stream gushing from 'Ain Fije, and throws itself, fan-like, over the plain, redeeming it from the desert, and creating a veritable earthly paradise. Here stands the city, surrounded by gardens and orchards where, in myriad channels, tinkle the sweet waters of the Abana. Despite the invasion of things Western—e.g., in electric light and tramway cars, Damascus still charmingly preserves its ancient Oriental character.

The Syrians are Semites. A slight admixture of alien blood in ancient and modern times has hardly affected the stock. But within the unity of race there are to be noted many well-marked distinctions, in history and traditions, in social customs, and more particularly in religion.

Among the villagers, alike in mountain and plain, life is reduced to very simple terms. Impecunious, and improvident as sparrows, they yet suffer no real penury. Winter in the uplands can be rigorous, but Syria as a whole is a sunny land, where necessary food, clothing, and shelter are comparatively inexpensive. As in other parts of the world, things are dearer now, but I once knew a man who maintained his wife and family adequately on sixteen shillings a month.

Flesh food is seldom seen, save at festivals, or in honour of a guest. Bread and olives are the staple food, with eggs and vegetables. Olive oil and melted butter are largely used in such cooking as is done. A universal

BEDUIN OF THE SYRIAN DESERT ARMED AGAINST ADVENTURE

Mounted on his fleet Arab and well equipped with rifle and ammunition the nomad Beduin of the vast Syrian sands is supreme in this his native element. Swooping suddenly down upon caravan or village, bands of these wild nomads are away again before, in the shock of surprise, reprisals are even thought of. Yet they can be courteous, too, as many a desert traveller has found

Photo, C. Chichester

IN ONE OF THE NARROW COBBLED LANES OF ANCIENT ANTIOCH

In the lovely and fertile plain of the lower Orontes, on whose left bank it stands, Antioch scarcely suggests its ancient greatness, nor does it occupy more than a tenth of its one time wide area. The streets, each furnished with a pavement and deep gutter, are narrow, and the tiled houses having few windows save on the inside present dull expanses of blank wall

Photo, American Colony in Jerusalem

dish is the deliciously refreshing "leben," slightly acid, curdled milk. With boiled rice it forms an excellent meal. In season much wholesome fruit is eaten.

Men usually wear wide, baggy trousers and long shirt of white calico, the latter confined at the waist by a leather strap. Over this is worn a garment like a dressing-gown of coloured cotton, or, on gala days, of silk striped in bright hues, from the looms of Homs or Damascus, with a belt of elastic cotton webbing. Over all is worn a square-cut cloak of wool and cotton, which serves as a waterproof ; or, supported on sticks, as a shade from the heat, and at night as a blanket. The "furweh," a jacket of lambskin dressed with the

TRAM LINES INFRINGE ON THE LITTLE-CHANGING CUSTOMS OF THE EAST

In Syrian towns it is usual for sellers of a similar "line" of goods to congregate together in one street. Thus among many others in Damascus are the silk bazaar, the bazaar of the joiners, and the cloth bazaar. Basket-work is for sale in these booths, while above, lattice work, daintily contrived, guards the womenfolk against unlawful glances from the street

Photo, Donald McLeish

wool on, is sometimes worn in cold weather. On the head a close-fitting felt cap, red tarbush with tassel, or turban of white or coloured cloth is worn. Often the men go barefoot ; but red leather shoes, and long boots coming half-way up the calf, with tassel in front, and iron-shod heels, are common.

Women's dress resembles that of the men, the coloured upper garment being open to the waist, where it is kept in

animals—sheep, goats, donkeys, mules and hens. Whenever possible they sleep in the open air. The women carry water, gather firewood, wash, bake, cook ; and, of course, the children are their special care. The men till the soil, tend vineyard and orchard, and see to irrigation. The women often dig the parts that cannot be reached with the plough. The younger people look after the flocks and herds. The happiest times are those of harvest, the gathering

SYRIAN GOLDSMITH AND JEWELLER AT WORK IN ALEPPO

Many of the native goldsmiths in Aleppo are extraordinarily clever craftsmen, producing beautiful and intricate work with the crudest implements—a tiny charcoal forge, bellows worked by a handle on the top, and a paraffin lamp and blowpipe for soldering and welding. Much of the gold used to be obtained from English sovereigns, melted down and mixed with a certain amount of copper

Photo, E. F. Blaze

place by a girdle. Round the head is wound a piece of dark cloth, leaving the crown uncovered. Women are usually unveiled. On festive occasions they blossom forth in brilliant colours. They are very fond of jewelry, wearing rings, bracelets, and anklets of such metal as they can afford.

In times of storm and winter cold the one-roomed, flat-roofed houses shelter the family, and also their domestic

of the olives, and the vintage, when men, women, and children lighten the long day's toil with frolic and laughter and song.

Marriages are arranged by parents and guardians, and, as a rule, simply acquiesced in by the parties. It is rare to find a girl of over twenty unmarried. The gay attire worn by the guests typifies the unrestrained rejoicing that marks the marriage day. Children,

EUROPEAN DRESS AND ORIENTAL SPLENDOUR IN A DAMASCUS HOUSE

Among the wealthy of the city the houses usually follow the same ground plan. Living-rooms ascend in storeys around a central court, and this is where most of the decorative artistry is lavished, and where, upon a divan at one end, visitors are received. The custom prevails of the master of the house advancing so many steps towards the guest according to the warmth of his welcome

Photo, Canon Parfit

ON THE DESERT ROAD FROM DAMASCUS TO PALMYRA: A HALT TO WATER THE HORSES

Where once stood the towers and temples of Palmyra—the Tadmor mentioned in the Old Testament, 2 Chron. viii. 4, as having been built by Solomon—is now a miscellany of huts built of and among the fragments of ancient masonry. The journey from Damascus takes about four days with an equipage of this kind. An armed guard is necessary as the country hereabouts is admirably suited to the practice of brigandage. The enterprising traveller is, however, well rewarded for the discomforts and dangers of his journey by the wonders of antiquity, especially the Temple of the Sun, that make marvellous the journey's end

Photo, C. Chichester

especially boys, are regarded as the most precious of God's gifts. They are often pampered and thoroughly spoilt. At birth they are swaddled in cloths dusted with salt. A Syrian once told me, confidentially, that white people had a curious smell about them. He said it was because we had not been salted as babies.

You must never admire a baby without saying first, " In the name of God," or your praise will bring disaster. A blue bead, or a disk of blue glass with a white centre, strung on the hair or attached to its person, is worn to protect the babe against the evil eye. If the little one is weakly, give it the name of a wild beast ; something of the animal's strength and toughness will enter the child and lend it powers of endurance. A sure defence against all pulmonary troubles is a segment from a wolf's backbone worn on a string round the neck.

Forms of Local Superstition

For the Moslems, lack of a beard is of sinister significance. " Meet goblins in the morning rather than a beardless man," so says the proverb. To meet a woman carrying an empty water jar is most unlucky ; for a marriage procession it is a desperate business. Evil consequences, however, may be avoided if the woman smash the jar, or even thrust her hand and arm into it.

Many of the peasantry are shy of the photographer. A man's picture takes something of his essence, and may put him in the power of its possessor. For a like reason they carefully destroy their nail-parings and hair-cuttings. With growing education the blood-feuds that so often darken life in the villages will gradually disappear.

In the cities a few successful merchants and others live in considerable luxury. But the life of the humbler classes resembles that of the peasantry. Many men affect European dress, retaining only the red tarbush. The more religious, especially among the Moslems, cling to the graceful flowing robes and turban. The ladies of the harem, in their secluded life, are beautifully attired in dresses of rich material. When out of doors they wear neat European footgear. The whole person is enveloped in a loose overall—izár—of white or black, which comes over the head and is gathered by a girdle at the waist. The Moslem ladies are closely veiled.

Mingling of Orient and Occident

The bazaars, especially in a cosmopolitan city like Damascus, present a most picturesque appearance ; people from everywhere, in garb of their own cut and colouring, mingle together amid the babel of many tongues. Silks from native looms jostle Manchester and Birmingham goods on the stalls. There is much delicate artistic work in the precious metals and jewelry, in ornamental and inlaid woodwork, with the fine rugs and carpets of the Orient. Good trade is done in tobacco, fruit, and other produce of the country, in native soap, wine, raisins, and grape honey.

In north-east Syria many of the Arabs dwell partly in curious beehive-formed houses of clay, and partly in ancestral tents. The men are generally well-favoured and handsome. The women are graceful, and would be even beautiful but for the disfiguring tattooed under-lip. They marry young, and in their hard life the bloom of youth soon fades. A woman is already old at thirty.

Lingering Customs of the Wilderness

A well-to-do sheik may be clad in coloured silk, with a silken kerchief bound to his head by a coil of thick woollen cord, a sword with a silver handle and scabbard at his side, and jewelled-hilted daggers and pistols in his belt. The rest are content with calico shirt and rough hair cloak. The women wear a single ample garment of blue calico, hanging in loose folds over the girdle that gathers it at the waist.

PATRIARCH OF THE MARONITE CHURCH AND ONE OF HIS BISHOPS

From the eighth century, when they were converted to Christianity by John Maro, the Maronites, referred to in the chapter on Lebanon, have kept themselves a separate sect, more or less in sympathy with the Roman Church. They retain a special liturgy, and have about nine bishops, the figure on the right holding the see of Baalbek. They live mainly near Damascus

Photo, C. Chichester

Round the head is wound the characteristic strip of dark cloth.

The men do something in tilling the soil and tending their sheep and camels, but the women are the great toilers. Among other things they take their produce to the market and carry back their bargains. These people have preserved many customs of the wilderness, notably that of hospitality. But they are held in contempt by the desert Arabs, who would scorn to guide the plough, or trade in chickens, eggs, and milk. For them the freedom of the wild, and the exhilaration of the robber raid.

Religion is a thing of serious import in Syria. It binds a community together in something closer than blood-brotherhood, and as decisively marks it off from all others. Even the different sects of the same faith—Moslem and Christian—dwell apart in their own districts, and in their own quarters in the cities.

The Orthodox Mahomedans—Sunni —are in a majority in all towns except Beirut. The heretical Shiites, followers of 'Ali, known in Syria as Metawileh, live chiefly in the western mountains. Uncleanly in their habits, they are yet great sticklers for ceremonial purity. They pray singly, not in groups like the Orthodox. Their women also pray in the open air. They hold the doctrine of "taqiyah" (guarding oneself), common to all the secret religions in Syria. Originating in the necessity that long existed of professing orthodoxy to escape persecution, this cautious mental reservation was established as a doctrine by the Shiites. If you remain true in heart to your own faith you may feign any other for the sake of safety or personal advantage.

The Nusairiya, living in the mountains bearing their name, are descendants of the Nazarini of Pliny the elder. They

LAYING THE DUST OF A PARCHED HIGHWAY THAT LEADS TO DAMASCUS

By the hot, white surface of the road trickles a grass-bordered ditch, and from this the waterer fills his clumsy ladle. Upon the shady side some Turkish effendi walks his horse, and on either hand cool gardens for which Damascus is famous make the way still more torrid for those who, like the old woman with her basket, have to foot it in the dust

Photo, Donald McLeish

STREET ARABS IN THE EUROPEAN QUARTER OF BEIRUT
Though included within the territory of greater Lebanon, Beirut remains essentially a port of Syria, as it has been since before the Crusades. It lies upon the Mediterranean, and is connected with Damascus by sixty miles of railway. Wool, gums, silk, and oil leave its bustling quaysides, and the annual export trade is valued at £800,000

BRIGHT COLOURS AMONG THE SHADED COBBLES OF A BEIRUT ALLEY
Much of that charm which is, for Europeans, usually associated with towns of the Orient, despite the accompanying squalor, is absent from Beirut, and Western influence is observable in many parts. Nevertheless, the old town, with its fine site upon St. George's Bay, and its usually tolerable climate, makes a strong appeal to the visitor coming from the heat-ridden cities elsewhere in Syria

give divine honours to 'Ali, and practise mysterious rites into which only Nusairi born are initiated. The use of wine is lawful. Women have no reasonable souls, and cannot be entrusted with the secrets of the faith. No soul of man perishes eternally. The good pass swiftly to rank among the stars. But even the worst, purified by much transmigration through beasts and men, enter Paradise at last.

The Ismailiya are seceders from the Shiites. Little is known of their special beliefs. They are sceptical as to God's existence. They think that a man lives only as the receptacle of a partial soul which rejoins the universal soul at death. The Assassins were a section of the Ismailiya. Their name is derived from hashish, an intoxicating extract of hemp with which they were sometimes drugged. They reduced assassination to a fine art, and in Crusading times the Old Man of the Mountain, the chief who controlled them, was a name of dread.

Secret Faith and Ritual

A few thousand of Ismailiya still exist in the neighbourhood of their old Syrian haunts. They send annual tribute to the modern representative of the Old Man of the Mountain, who lives in Bombay, believing him to be possessed of supernatural powers.

The Jews, who since the Dispersion have probably lived continuously in Syria, are, in everything but religion, practically native Syrians, sharing the same customs, superstitions, and language. Here also we have all branches of Oriental Christianity, living alongside each other in what may be called a state of armed neutrality. Something is said of the principal sects in Syria in the chapter describing Lebanon.

While these distinctions are deep and abiding, it is yet true of the Syrian people, as a whole, that a great common inheritance of pagan superstition mingles in their mysteries, and finds expression in secret faith and ritual practice.

Little is known of what goes on at their ancient sanctuaries or "High Places." But pilgrimages are made, gifts are brought, prayers are offered, and vows registered. And these are vows no man is ever known to break. At times sheep and goats are slain, and their blood smeared on wall, doorpost, and lintel, also on horse and camel to protect them. The victims are cooked and eaten by the worshippers, who rise up to play, footing the solemn dance under the greenwood tree.

Salvation by Sacrifice

Important enterprises are begun with sacrifice. The blood of a sheep will be poured into the foundation of a new house, or smeared on part of the rising walls, " for the safety of the workmen." A victim is slain for the health of a new-born child, whose forehead is marked with the blood. The new moon is greeted with outstretched hand, which then is kissed and raised to the forehead with mutterings of " Honour to God. Honour to thee."

During an eclipse of the moon an unholy clamour is made with every available instrument of noise to frighten away the monster that is attempting to swallow the orb of night. " Let go our moon," they cry, " or we will be up at you with a club ! " When my beautiful Arab mare died, Moslems, Jews, and Christians came expressing the fervent hope that it was my " redemption "—that the mare had redeemed my life with hers.

Paganism in Syria's Heart

These are but illustrations of hoary superstitions that have proved singularly tenacious of life. Foreign influence is manifest here, introduced no doubt with the large admixture of immigrant blood in the early history of the country. There is still very much to be learned, but we know enough to show that, by whatever name the people choose to be known, an old-world unconquered paganism still holds dominion in the heart.

MAHOMEDAN BURIAL GROUND OF DAMASCUS WHERE SLEEPS THE DAUGHTER OF THE PROPHET

Under the domes of the three nearest mausoleums are the tombs of two of Mahomet's wives and of his favourite daughter Fatima. From her is descended the line of Fatimate Caliphs of Syria, and she was accounted by her father to be one of the four perfect women in the world. On Thursdays the women of Damascus come to this cemetery to mourn by the graves of their dead. In the photograph are seen an Arab and his boy, who are tending the shrubs left in the pots at the foot of the headstones, which are elaborately carved and engraved with Oriental patterns

Photo, Donald McLeish.

4874

Syria

I. From Hittite Monarchy to French Mandate

By E. S. Bouchier, M.A., F.R.Hist.S.

Author of "Syria as a Roman Province," "A Short History of Antioch," etc.

A POWERFUL Hittite monarchy, with its centre in the east of Asia Minor, extended over northern Syria, where the inhabitants when history begins had attained some skill in arts and manufactures, due chiefly to early relations with Assyria and Egypt. As the Hittite power declined various petty Semitic states grew up, as those of Damascus, where the Aramaean dynasty was engaged in frequent warfare with the kingdom of Israel, of Hamath, and of Zobah.

In the eighth century B.C. the greater part of Syria became tributary to Assyria, then at the height of its power; and when the empire of Nineveh was overthrown by a Medo-Babylonian alliance it was in turn subject to the Babylonian kings. Towards the end of the sixth century the conquests of Cyrus led to the inclusion of most of Syria in the Persian empire, and his son Cambyses, the conqueror of Egypt, extended his dominions along the Phoenician coast. Damascus was the seat of government, but considerable local independence was allowed, both to the rich commercial cities of the coast and to various tribal chiefs and priest-kings.

Alexander, after his victory at Issus, overran Syria with little opposition; and during the next thirty years it was ruled by a succession of Macedonian satraps, under whom there took place a considerable immigration of Greek veterans and other colonists. The ultimate success of Alexander's general, Seleucus, enabled him to establish a powerful military monarchy in northern Syria, with its headquarters at the new capital of Antioch on the Orontes, some sixteen miles from its mouth.

Coele-Syria for a time remained to the Ptolemies of Egypt, and only became incorporated in the Seleucid dominions

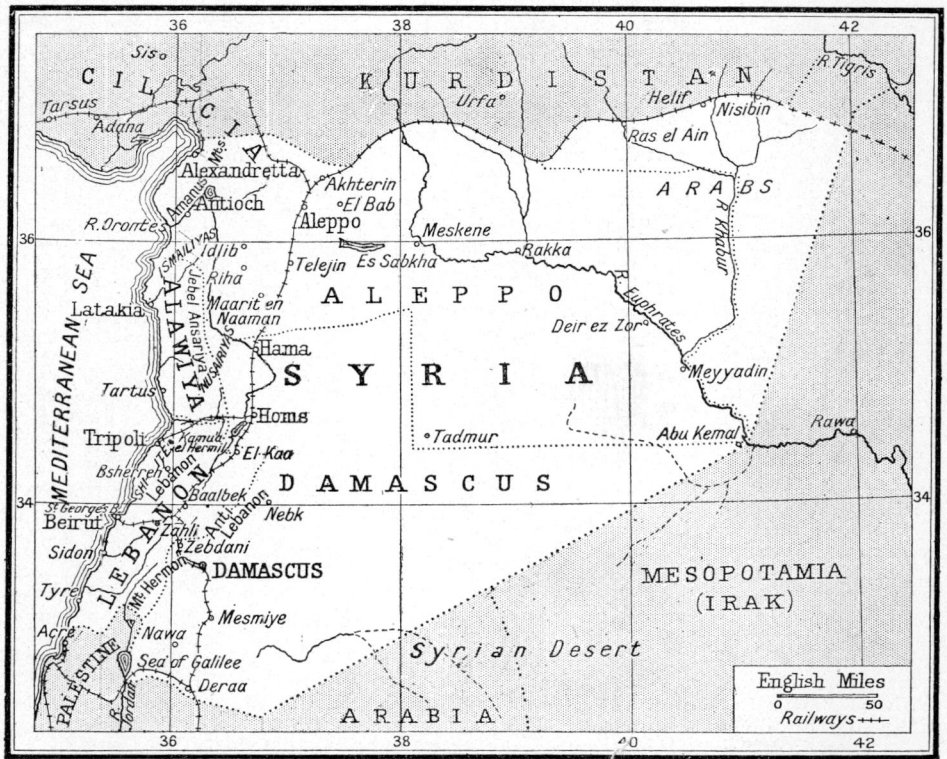

SYRIA AND ITS TERRITORIES

after the victories of Antiochus the Great a century later. The kingdom, however, lacked cohesion. Greek civilization was almost confined to the chief urban centres, and as family divisions and Jewish wars weakened the Seleucid state, Arab and other native peoples overran a large part of Syria. The campaigns of Lucullus and Pompey ultimately led to the formation of the Roman province of Syria (A.D. 64), and a governor with a strong military force was stationed at Antioch.

Prosperity in the Days of Augustus

For thirty years the Roman civil wars kept Syria in a disturbed state, but the accession of Augustus inaugurated a period of great prosperity. The frontiers were successfully defended against Parthians and Arabs, Roman veteran colonies were planted, as at Berytus (Beirut) and Heliopolis (Baalbek), and an extensive export trade grew up, both in the products of the province and in goods brought by eastern caravans for despatch to Europe from the Syrian ports. This prosperity, though interrupted by the Jewish war of Vespasian's time, continued till the growing weakness of the empire in the third century A.D., and the rise of the Sassanian monarchy in Persia, in place of the effete Arsacids, inaugurated a series of troubles.

In the reign of Valerian a great part of Syria was overrun by Persian troops, and the authority of Rome was only re-established by the energy of the royal house of Palmyra, which, at first professing to act as imperial representatives, for some years secured the practical separation of Syria from the rest of the empire. The campaigns of Aurelian, who overthrew the rebel queen Zenobia, and later of Diocletian, strengthened the hold of the empire on these parts.

Ommiad Caliphs at Damascus

Christianity had developed through the same period, and sectarian conflicts, connected chiefly with the Arian, Nestorian, and Monophysite heresies, play a large part in the history of the fourth and fifth centuries.

From the reign of Justinian the decline was rapid. The persecuting policy of the Byzantine government alienated the native heretical sects, which were quite ready to make common cause with invaders. Thus the great Arab invasions of the period 634-38, under the first generation of Mahomet's successors, met with but feeble resistance. The Ommiad Caliphs were able to set up their capital at Damascus, which again became a rich and splendid city.

With the new Abbasside dynasty, the centre of government was moved away to Bagdad (750). Syria was left to the rule of lieutenants, while the affairs of the Christian communities were in part administered by their own bishops.

Towards the end of the tenth century the Byzantine empire had an unlooked-for revival ; and Nicephorus Phocas found himself able to reconquer a large district from the Hamdanides, and establish a Byzantine duke at Antioch (969).

Southern Syria fell into the hands of the new Fatimite dynasty of Egypt, which, taking its origin from heretical Shiite leaders in Barbary, now drew away a great part of Islam from obedience to the Abbasside Caliphate. In the eleventh century the power of the new Seljuk Turkish empire made itself felt in Syria, where Antioch was captured in 1081. The Turkish sultan depended largely on mercenary forces officered by Mamelukes, or slaves of the royal household, raised in central Asia and rewarded by grants of castles, cities, or provinces.

Nur-ed-din and Saladin

Thus most of Syria came to be divided among a number of military fiefs, whose chiefs levied taxes for their own use, but were bound to supply troops when called upon ; and they in turn had vassals similarly bound to supply men in war, and prepared to aid them even against the Seljuk sultan himself. So long as the central government was strong this system was successful ; the Mahomedan faith was revived, education encouraged, roads and bridges laid out or repaired.

By the end of the century, however, the Seljuk kingdom had split up into petty principalities of mixed Turkish and Arab origin, and on the arrival of the first Crusaders (1097) the whole Syrian coast was gradually allowed to pass under Frankish control. Four crusading states, with their capitals at Urfa (Edessa), Antioch, Tripoli, and Jerusalem, were set up, and the port towns received Italian mercantile colonies, which greatly stimulated trade with Europe. Yet the Crusaders only held a coast strip some fifty miles wide ; and theirs was rather an armed occupation than a systematic conquest.

A Moslem revival was not long in coming, led by Zengy, atabeg, or regent, of Mosul, who protected Aleppo against Frankish exactions, won Damascus from a hostile dynasty, and reconquered Edessa. On his death in 1146 his son Nur-ed-din continued the work, and rose to be virtually sultan of Syria, while by means of his famous lieutenant Saladin he overthrew the rival Fatimite power in Egypt.

The Ayyubid dynasty which Saladin founded continued to rule till 1260, with Egypt as the centre of the empire and emirs at Aleppo, Homs (Emesa) Hama, and elsewhere. In 1258 came a destructive inroad of Mongols, who ended the Abbasside Caliphate and overran Syria as far as Gaza. Egypt fell under the rule of a series of usurpers from the Mameluke class, and the ablest of these, Beibars, expelled the barbarians, destroyed Antioch (1268), and carried the Egyptian arms into Asia Minor. Before the end of the century the last possessions of the Franks on the Syrian coast had fallen.

The Circassian line of sultans (1382-1517) allowed the internal administration to become corrupt and oppressive, and proved unable to resist the invasion of Timur the Tartar, who occupied Aleppo and Damascus and devastated northern Syria. This soon fell into a state of anarchy under rival emirs, while the coasts were raided by Frankish pirates.

In the year 1516 the Ottoman sultan Selim I. secured to the Turks the possession of all Syria. Damascus remained the Syrian capital, with pashas also at Acre, Aleppo, and Tripoli.

In the nineteenth century the most noteworthy incidents are the occupation of Syria by the rebel governor of Egypt Mehemet Ali (1833-40), and the despatch of a French expedition to restore order in the Lebanon district (1860). As a result of the Great War the country has been divided between a native Arab state and a French protectorate on the coast.

Cilicia, before the Great War part of the Turkish vilayet of Adana, fell into two distinct halves, the western or Rugged and the eastern or Plain Cilicia, the latter including the trading centre of Tarsus.

The first Roman province, dating from 103 B.C., only included the Plain country, but it was enlarged by Pompey in 64, and the city of Pompeiopolis on the site of Soli was used for settling former pirates. Tarsus was the seat of government.

Various kingly or priestly native dynasties were, however, allowed to subsist till the time of Vespasian (74). Tarsus had a Greek element from very early times, and it received important privileges from Antiochus Epiphanes, and in the early empire was one of the chief seats of learning in the east. Augustus favoured it for its Caesarean sympathies; it became a free state, and the franchise was widely conferred.

Cilicia belonged to the Byzantine empire until the Arab conquests of the seventh century. Nicephorus reconquered it from the Arabs in the tenth century, but in the eleventh the foundation of the Seljuk kingdom of Rûm resulted in the southerly migration of the Christian Armenians, whose settlement eventually grew into the kingdom of Lesser Armenia.

A Latin dynasty was established in 1342, but subsequent internal dissensions led to its conquest by the Egyptian sultans. The western half was occupied by the Ottomans in the fifteenth century, the eastern shortly before the subjection of Syria. Like Syria it was held by Mehemet Ali from 1833-40, and subsequently, as already stated, formed part of the vilayet of Adana.

SYRIA: FACTS AND FIGURES

The Country

Held by France under mandatory of Supreme Council of Allied Powers, with the confirmation of League of Nations. Situated in Asia Minor, it is bounded north by Turkey, south by Palestine, east by Mesopotamia, and west by the Mediterranean. Continuations of the Amanus and Taurus ranges run from north to south, and include the Lebanon and Anti-Lebanon heights. Large part of country is a plateau sloping to Mediterranean on the west and to the desert on the east. Main rivers are the Euphrates, Orontes, and Khabur. Total area about 60,000 square miles, with an estimated population of about 3,000,000.

Commerce and Industries

Agriculture and cattle breeding form principal occupation of bulk of population. About 6,000 square miles are normally under crops, the principal being wheat, barley, sesame, lentils, chick peas, and durra, or Indian millet. Tobacco is an important product, Latakia being one of the chief production centres. Sugar-cane, hemp, and cotton are grown, and among fruits are the vine, orange, olive, mulberry, and lemon. Mineral deposits are largely undeveloped, and include iron, lignite, gypsum, marble, and building stone. Main industries are the production of soap, wine, oil, flour, and silk thread. Imports for 1921 were valued at 600,146,643 francs, while exports for the same year totalled 69,848,500 francs. Monetary unit the Syrian pound of nominal value of 20 French francs.

Communications

Syria is served by portions of the Hejaz and Bagdad railways, and there are branches to the principal ports. Total railway mileage exceeds 1,000, while roads aggregate about 1,500 miles.

Religion and Education

Population includes about 1,500,000 of the Sunni sect of Mahomedans and some 113,000 Shiites. There are at Antioch three Uniat Patriarchs and one Orthodox Patriarch. The French have established about 300 schools, with accommodation for some 50,000 pupils, and there are some 120 elementary schools of British missionary societies. A Jesuit university has been formed at Beirut, and other educational activities are engaged in by American Missions and Roman Catholic agencies.

Chief Towns

Damascus, capital (estimated population 170,000), Aleppo (140,000), Beirut (80,000), Homs (60,000), Hama (35,000), Tripoli (30,000), Antioch (30,000).

FELLING A WOODLAND GIANT IN GEEVESTON FOREST, TASMANIA

Tasmania possesses immense forest regions, eucalyptus, acacia, and pines in particular covering
extensive areas, and timber now represents an appreciable sum in the State's export figures. All
timber on Crown lands comes under the control of the Department of Lands and Surveys, whence
licences are issued for felling, cutting, and removing timber, and saw-milling leases are granted

Photo, Beattie

Tasmania

Farmers & Fruit-Growers of the Antipodes

By Frank Fox

Author of "Australia," "Beneath an Ardent Sun," etc.

TASMANIA, the southern island of the Australian Commonwealth, reproduces curiously both the natural features and the social atmosphere of England. Its fields recall " green and cloudy England " ; it has a noble lakeland district ; its many beautiful rivers, such as the Derwent and the Tamar, are as English in character as they are in name. The crops, too, are markedly English in character. Hop-growing is one of the chief agricultural industries. On the rich river-flats of the river Derwent and its tributaries the vines are planted, and, as in England, the harvest-time is the signal for an exodus of city workers who come with wives and children to make a happy and wholesome living hop-picking for a month or more.

Another characteristic Tasmanian industry is that of apple-farming. Probably the biggest flow of money from abroad comes to Tasmania when the apple harvest cheques arrive from London. Under the stimulus of those cheques there has grown up a fine race of sturdy " mixed farmers " on the Huon river frontages in Tasmania. Their staple crop is the apple, and the average yearly yield from the apple crop sent to London in a good season would be £250 or £300. In addition to growing apples the Huon farmer runs a few sheep on the poor-soil hills at the back of his river meadow, and keeps a few cows and pigs, the latter, fed on skim milk, apples, and oats, producing bacon fit to rank with any in the world. Astonishingly little do these farmers need from outside their farms. The town stores are drawn upon only for clothes and a few groceries. Some of the older-fashioned farmers even grist their own grain, and have their breakfast porridge of home-grown oats.

Of great value to a country is such a class as this, since there is no imaginable blow of fate which can seriously threaten their stability. A war, or some such calamity, may cut them off from their market and make them for a while poor, but it cannot make them hungry. Whatever happens, they can be sure of food and some degree of comfort. It is

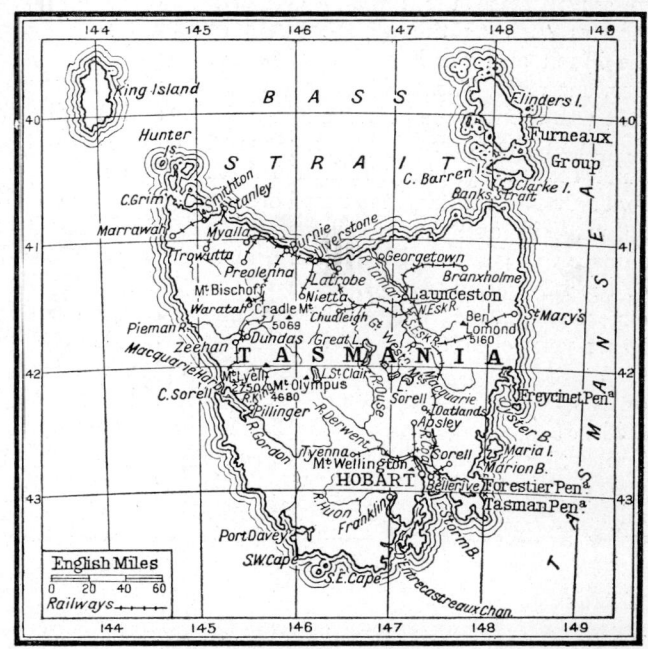

THE ISLAND OF TASMANIA

4879

GATHERING THE HARVEST IN A TASMANIAN APPLE ORCHARD

Orchards that were the glory of Devonshire are rivalled in the fruit-growing districts of Tasmania, where thousands of acres are devoted to apples, pears, plums, cherries, apricots, and peaches, besides strawberries, raspberries, gooseberries, and currants. The largest area is devoted to apples, and this fruit is the staple crop of the mixed farms on the Huon river frontages above Hobart

Photo, Spurling

the ideal of the reformer in many a land to see increase the number of petty farmers such as the apple-growers of the Huon and the hop-growers of the Derwent river, Tasmania.

It was the fortune of Tasmania to be chosen in the early days as a place of quiet retreat by many retired British civil servants, military and naval officers on pension, and Anglo-Indians. The climate was gentle ; the natural beauty of the land great ; the absence of the expensive luxuries of civilization made living very cheap. These colonists set themselves to reproduce English conditions as far as they could. English fields, English gardens, and English houses ; English trout and salmon in the rivers—all helped to make Tasmania an antipodean Home Country. Social life, too, was modelled very closely on that of England of a century ago. Hobart, the capital, had very much the atmosphere of Bath in England. Thus, until recently the social life

of Tasmania was in marked contrast to that of the neighbouring Commonwealth. Before it threw in its lot with the Commonwealth, Tasmania was rather proud of being " old-fashioned and English," as contrasted with the more advanced and modern mainland. She modelled her educational system closely on that of England. The Government endowed with liberal grants of free lands great schools which modelled their systems exactly on those of Eton and Harrow and Rugby. Long before the patriotic genius of Cecil Rhodes founded the Rhodes Scholarships to send young citizens of the overseas Dominions to learn the culture of English Universities, the Tasmanian Government had discovered the value of this plan, and sent yearly to the Home Country Universities two " Tasmanian scholars."

Tasmania was discovered first by the Dutch. Antony Van Diemen, the governor-general of the Dutch East

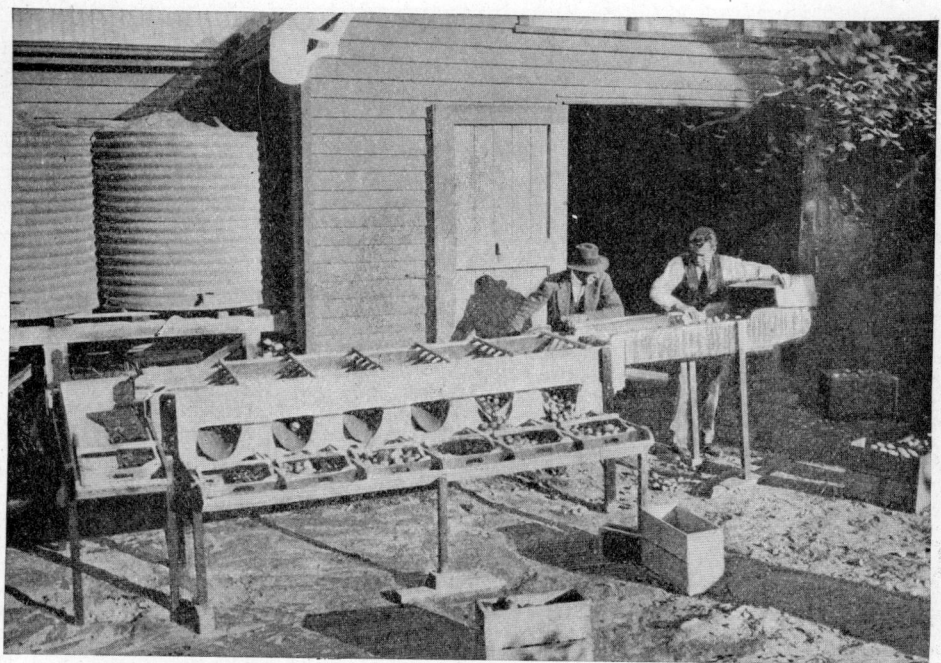

GRADING APPLES IN A SIZING MACHINE NEAR HOBART

As illustrated in the opposite page, apples for the export market are all picked most carefully by hand to avoid bruising. From the orchards they are carried to the sheds where they are graded according to size in a simple but ingenious sizing machine. During this process opportunity is provided for further inspection and the rejection of injured fruit which might spoil a consignment

TASMANIAN APPLES BEING PACKED FOR EXPORT

After being graded according to size the apples are packed in cases which hold an average of 43 lb. apiece. The Tasmanian fruit-grower sends the bulk of his produce to New South Wales and to Great Britain, and in a good season looks to make £250 to £300 from his apples alone. Tasmanian fruit-canning and jam-making industries readily absorb the rest of his crops

Photos, Merl La Voy

ROUNDING UP A LIKELY LOT OF MERINO SHEEP ON A FARM NEAR LAUNCESTON

Tasmania ranks high among the states of the Commonwealth for the quality of its sheep. Sheep-breeders' associations specialise on the improvement and development of particular stock, such as Southdowns and Shropshires, and these crossed with the Merino strain have produced such good results that Tasmanian stud flocks are largely drawn upon by breeders in the other states. There was a somewhat serious shortage of sheep in 1921, but, despite this fact, the number of sheep in Tasmania remains generally steady at something over a million and a half

Indies, sent out an exploring expedition in 1642 under Abel Janz Tasman to explore the seas south and south-east of the Dutch territory. Tasman encountered the coast of Tasmania on November 24 of that year. He named the land Van Diemen's Land, in honour of his governor-general, and followed its coast-line for some time, and then went on to visit New Zealand, the Friendly, and the Fiji Islands.

The Dutch did not attempt to follow up their discovery of Tasmania. In 1787, when Captain Phillip founded the first Australian settlement at Botany Bay, it was thought that Van Diemen's Land (which was not renamed Tasmania until 1856) was part of the Australian continent, and it was included in the annexation of that country. An adventurous voyage by Flinders in a whale-boat gave the first evidence of a strait cutting off Van Diemen's Land from the continent. In the year 1795, Lieutenant Flinders, of the Reliance, started in a small boat, with Surgeon Bass, a series of explorations of the Australian coast.

First White Settlement in Tasmania

In December, 1797, when Flinders was away with his ship, Bass obtained the loan of a whale-boat and a crew of eight men, with the object of following the unknown Australian coast southward. He discovered Twofold Bay on his way, and, proceeding onward, rounded Wilson's Promontory, and reached, in spite of head winds, the inlet that he named Western Port. He took careful note of the evidence this gave regarding the existence of a strait cutting off Van Diemen's Land from the continent; and, towards the close of the next year, Governor Hunter placed a schooner and its crew at the disposal of Flinders, that the question might be cleared up. Bass joined him, and the two set out for the Furneaux Group, and thence sailed along the north of Van Diemen's Land, round Cape Grim, down the west coast of the island, round into Storm Bay, up the Derwent, and then back to Sydney.

The first white settlement in Tasmania was not made until 1803. In 1825 the island was proclaimed as a separate Crown Colony independent of Australia, to be governed by a nominated Legislative Council. From that date until the foundation of the Australian Commonwealth in 1901, Tasmania shaped her independent course, securing responsible government in 1856. In the negotiations for the union of the Australian states into the Commonwealth, Tasmania took a very independent part.

" Braddon's Blot "

It was Sir Edward Braddon who fixed in the first Australian Constitution the clause which was known to its critics as " Braddon's Blot," and which was designed to prevent the small states having their identity obliterated when they joined in the Commonwealth.

Since the foundation of the Commonwealth Tasmania naturally has lost her special characteristics to a great extent ; she is more Australian, less distinctively Tasmanian. But there will always remain some distinction. The Tasmanian climate makes the faces of the people softer and rosier than those of the mainland, and will keep their character a little different from that of the Australian living under his ardent sun.

Who Were the Original Tasmanians ?

The differences between the Tasmanian and the Australian white races of to-day are easily enough explainable by the different character of the colonisation and the different climate. Far more difficult it is to explain the very curious differences to be observed at the time of the first white settlement between the aboriginal population of Tasmania and her fauna and flora, and those of the neighbouring continent. The Tasmanian aborigines (now extinct) were in several respects different from the Australian type. The question of their

EXPERT ASSESSORS VALUING THE YEAR'S CLIP IN THE WOOL SHOWROOM AT HOBART

Unlike New Zealand, where the frozen meat industry has led to the breeding of large sheep with valuable carcasses and mediocre wool, Tasmania has preferred to produce sheep with more useful types of wool, and wool is now Tasmania's principal export, the average quantity being between eight and nine million pounds. The great wool showroom at Hobart provides a remarkable spectacle when filled with the great bags creaming over with fleece, between the long lines of which the valuers pass, assessing the market value of the clip

Photo, Beattie

origin is one of great complexity and difficulty to ethnologists.

Huxley concluded that they were a Negrito modification of the great Negroid type of mankind which had migrated eastwards to New Caledonia, and subsequently southwards to Tasmania. Another authority considers that they were an autochthonous race, or possibly a cross between such a race and invading colonists of the Polynesian family. Yet another authority, Barnard Davis, classes them as a peculiar and distinct race dwelling in their own island. Other ethnologists have classed them as (1) a distinct sub-division of the black races or (2) as wandering members of the Melanesian group modified from the original type.

Yet another scientific opinion is that the physical characters, manners, customs, mental qualities, and the language of the Tasmanians make reasonable a theory that they were the original inhabitants of Australia who were displaced from the continent by the present straight-haired natives, but who survived in the southern island until the advent of white colonisation.

A Race Now Quite Extinct

The Tasmanian aborigine was generally of a more robust and more enterprising type than the Australian, and had the negro characteristic of curly hair. If he occupied the island when it formed continuous land with Australia, and arrived there with the marsupial animals, his history connected with the island must date back to a very remote age, for the continental aboriginal type had departed very far from the Tasmanian when the white men arrived, though there are some characteristics of the South Australian aborigines which link them with the Tasmanian aborigines.

It has to be recorded, unfortunately, that the Tasmanian aboriginal race is now quite extinct. Convicts in the early days, escaping to the bush, by their cruelties inflamed the natives to hatred of the white disturbers. The Tasmanian black was far more courageous and truculent than the Australian black. He retaliated freely and outrages were frequent. The state of affairs got to be so bad that the Government formed the idea of herding together all the black natives and putting them on a special reserve on Tasman Peninsula. The help of the settlers was enlisted, and a cordon was formed round the whole island, as if it were to be beaten for game. The cordon gradually closed in on Tasman Peninsula after some weeks of " beating " the forests. It was found then that one aboriginal woman had been captured ! Such a result might have been foreseen. The cordon did not embrace 2,000 settlers. The idea of these being able to drive before them a whole native race familiar with the bush was absurd.

" Tasmanian Tiger " and " Tasmanian Devil "

After that the old conditions ruled in Tasmania. Blacks and whites were in constant conflict, and the black race quickly perished. To-day there is not a single member of that race alive, Truganini, its last representative, having died in 1876.

The fauna of Tasmania is also in some respects markedly different from that of Australia. Most of the Australian animals are represented, but there exist in addition, as peculiar to Tasmania, the " Tasmanian Tiger " and the " Tasmanian Devil," which are the last representatives of carnivorous marsupials. The " tiger " is about the size of a small Bengal tiger, the " devil " about the size of a large wild-cat. Both are extremely fierce and bloodthirsty, but are now almost extinct.

Fruit Garden of the Antipodes

The " tiger " would ravage a whole flock of sheep in a night. The " devil " would attack any man or beast.

Most European animals thrive in Tasmania. It is a notable place for breeding the highest quality of sheep. Horses and dairy cattle flourish. Deer

HYDRAULIC SLUICING IN A TIN MINE ON THE NORTH-EAST COAST OF TASMANIA

Tasmania is showing most commendable energy in harnessing the inexhaustible resources of water-power that exist, and applying them to the generation of power for industrial purposes. It is estimated that 500,000 h.p. can be obtained, and factories to utilise as much as possible of this are projected and being constructed. Work initiated by the Hydro-electric Power and Metallurgical Company was taken over by the Government in 1914, and a special scale of charges has been established for the employment of water-power in various industries

Photo, Tasmanian Government

WORKING A TIN FACE IN THE FAMOUS MOUNT BISCHOFF MINE IN RUSSELL COUNTY

Tasmania's mineral wealth is considerable, especially in copper and tin, its production of the latter exceeding that of any other state in the Commonwealth. At one time mining was the foremost industry in Tasmania, but the total mineral production is decreasing in quantity, though its total value of about £1,500,000, averaged since the beginning of this century, is approximately maintained by the increase in prices. Mount Bischoff, in Russell county, is the chief source of tin in Tasmania. It is worked as an open quarry, and since it was first tapped has paid very large dividends

Photo, Beattie

TASMANIAN FORESTERS ENGAGING IN A WOOD-CHOPPING MATCH

Expert woodsmen develop a dexterity in the use of the axe positively astonishing to the prentice hand who, with much pain and effort, merely succeeds in butchering a tree. They place each blow with perfect precision, freeing and swinging the axe with rhythmic celerity and beautiful ease. Wood-chopping competitions are a frequent amusement in the timberlands of Tasmania

Photo, Publishers' Photo Service

do well. Some South African and European animals have been acclimatised.

Tasmania has an area of 26,215 square miles. The coast is very wild and picturesque in the south and on the west. In the centre of the island is a great chain of lakes. There are several important mountain systems and some great rivers, such as the Derwent, the Huon, and the Tamar. The climate is far more equable than that of the mainland.

Up till very recently Tasmanian industry depended chiefly on farming, stock-breeding, and the tin, copper, and silver-lead mines. Lately the island has developed ambitions to become a manufacturing State by developing hydro-electrical energy. Vast water power resources exist and they are being harnessed for the generation of power. It is estimated that at least 500,000 h.p. can be obtained. Already works developing 34,000 h.p. are in operation.

But whatever may be the future manufacturing developments, it may be presumed that Tasmania will draw always the greatest part of her wealth from her good, well-watered soil, and a gentle, sunny climate. She is very well suited to be the fruit garden of the Antipodes and the summer resort of the Australian population.

Tibet

I. Manners & Customs in "the Forbidden Land"

By Sir Francis Younghusband, K.C.S.I., K.C.I.E.,

Author of "India and Tibet: Within," etc.

TIBET is a large country—as large as France, Germany, and Italy together—and its people differ considerably, those of the towns and villages being of an almost different race from the pastoral nomads of the steppes, and the inhabitants of the side of Tibet adjoining India differing widely from those of the side adjoining China. Consequently, manners and customs vary greatly. Still, there is much in common between them.

The Tibetans have, for example, a common religion. With the exception of a few Chinese and some Nepalese traders, they are all Buddhists, and Buddhists of a peculiar type. They are all, therefore, dominated by the same fundamental ideas, all the more so because in Tibet religion is the rule. The sovereign ruler is the incarnation or manifestation of a Buddhist saint, and the whole country is dotted over with monasteries, three at Lhasa containing over five thousand monks, and many holding several hundred. Of every family of position at least one member becomes either a priest or a monk.

United thus by a common bond of religious observance the Tibetans are by nature a solid people—a strong, massive people built on big lines. Many of the tribes on the Chinese border are quarrelsome and given to feuds and brigandage. And even in holy Lhasa itself—Lhasa, the residence of the Dalai Lama, the Supreme Pontiff of Tibet—there is much brawling and pillaging. But in the main the people are orderly and unaggressive. No great waves of conquest have issued from Tibet to spread over the plain of either India or China.

Surrounded as the Tibetans are by stupendous mountains, a spirit of seclusion is bred in them; they like to keep themselves to themselves, and are nervous about the ingress of foreigners, who might disturb their habit of thought and introduce new ways of life.

On the whole, they are content in their religious life, in cultivating the land, tending their flocks, and in such petty trading as may be necessary to supply their simple wants. They have a sturdy independence in regard to the foreigner, but to their own authorities they

PATRICIAN LADY OF TIBET
Though the eyes are distinctly narrow, the noses of these women of high rank are often noticeably less flat and Mongoloid than the rest of their features

FOUR CABINET MINISTERS WHO NEGOTIATED WITH GREAT BRITAIN
Assisting in the long-drawn-out negotiations between the representatives of the British military
mission and the Tibetans were these four Shapés or Councillors. Conferences were difficult as,
in Tibet, many strange ideas were prevalent. It was firmly believed that the erection of a holy
wall of loose stones could effectually stop several regiments of British and Indian infantry
Photo, John Claude White

are most amenable. The heads of big monasteries on the Chinese border may acknowledge only a somewhat nominal allegiance to the Dalai Lama at Lhasa, but, as a rule, the Tibetans recognize his authority implicitly. And their reverence for a personage regarded as extremely holy produces in them habits of kindliness and courtesy.

The Tibetans are not a highly intellectual race, and have not the polish of the Chinese, from whom their culture has been mostly received, for their Buddhism did not come direct from India, but from China. But they have imbibed from the Chinese much distinction and politeness of manner. A Tibetan of any position will always comport himself with dignity and composure. And the ordinary Tibetan, while full of deference towards his superiors, will always retain his solid self-respect. As hosts they excel. A host will not receive his guests with that grave and frigid dignity common in other parts of Asia, but with genuine warmth and geniality. Even strangers whom they have to repel from their country they will, as a rule, repel, if firmly, at any rate with courtesy.

His superior in rank and position the Tibetan will always treat with the greatest respect, bowing deeply before him and not presuming to sit unless first invited to do so. And equals are also ceremonious to one another. When paying a visit of ceremony a very graceful custom of exchanging white silk scarves is observed. The host or the guest will place on the outstretched hands of the other a long white or light blue silk scarf and wish him peace.

Tea-drinking is a custom prevalent throughout Tibet. The tea drunk is of a very coarse kind imported from China. It is stewed and mixed with butter and salt, and is then poured into china cups. The host and guest sit on a carpet on either side of a low table on which the teacups are placed. And over their successive cups of tea they carry on a cheerful if not very intellectual conversation, and exchange jokes of a simple, homely kind.

One very remarkable custom the Tibetans have—though it is only practised by men of the lowest degree. It is the custom of putting out the tongue as a form of salutation. The man will bend the knee very low, putting the right hand beside the right cheek and the left hand under the elbow of the right arm, and at the same time stick out his tongue. It is meant to signify that he places himself entirely at the disposal of his superior.

Dancing the Tibetans delight in. And though the dance itself is dull enough, being nothing more than a slow shuffle, the dancers monotonously circling round each other, the Tibetans sing and drink and make merry during the performance, and it seems to satisfy their simple needs. They will also, when

STOLID SONS AND DAUGHTERS OF TIBET'S FAR MOUNTAINS
Solidity and stolidity are the main characteristics of the Tibetan, and these show themselves in the outward appearance of this group. While they resent the intrusion of foreigners into their fastnesses, they will, if necessary, receive them as guests with considerable politeness and even charm of manner. The women hold a singularly advanced position in this otherwise backward land

Photo, Publishers' Photo Service

LADAKHI VISITORS TO TIBET IN THEIR FLEECE-LINED COATS

Near the Kashmir border, where the young Indus flows, live the Ladakhis. For the most part they are Mongoloids, and by religion Buddhists. They live in villages of huts, above which are usually to be seen the walls of some Lama temple. The villagers grow peas and wheat, keep sheep and yaks or Tibetan oxen, and sometimes augment their incomes by serving with caravans

Photo, Georg Haeckel

MONGOL PILGRIMS TO TIBET'S SACRED SHRINES

There is an enormous veneration felt throughout China and Mongolia for the holy places in Tibet. Tradition makes these spots wondrous, and their remoteness adds an awed curiosity. These men, one of whom wears a fox-skin cap, while the other exhibits jewelled charms, a trumpet and prayer-wheel, are on the road from Tashi Lunpo, near Shigatze

Photo, Publishers' Photo Service

possible, turn their work into a dance with song. In stamping down mud on the roofs they will stamp rhythmically and chant as they stamp.

The most weird of their dances, and one which the Tibetans will attend in crowds and never tire of watching, is the devil dance—a religious performance, in which priests wearing masks of the most fantastic description, representing the heads of demons, slowly

They go about unveiled, and in trade and business take an active part.

During the course of the mission to Tibet in 1903-4 crowds of women used to appear outside the camps bringing country produce for sale. They work in the fields, and though they do not follow the religious life to the same extent as the men, there are nunneries as well as monasteries in Tibet, and some of these contain several hundred

FERRY BOAT THAT CARRIES PILGRIMS OVER THE BRAHMAPUTRA

When, during the early days of February, hundreds of pilgrims are making their way to Shigatze for the New Year Festival, numbers of boats of this kind are in use for transport across or down the river. The construction simply involves the making of a light framework of boughs, covered with sewn yak-hide. The blades of the oars are forked, with a leather web between the prongs

Photo, John Claude White

circle about one another to the accompaniment of drums, cymbals, and flutes, while high lamas, drinking tea, look on. The dance is supposed to remind the people of the terrors that await them if they behave ill.

All these dances are performed by men and not by women. But women play a great part in the life of Tibet. They are not secluded as are the women of India and of Mahomedan countries.

nuns. A curious custom which is prevalent among the lower classes is that of the women smearing their faces with a mahogany-coloured dye in order to conceal their good looks. This custom is founded on a law enacted three hundred years ago and designed to reduce the natural attractiveness of women—thereby going straight against the natural and praiseworthy instinct of every human being, whether man or

YAK DRIVERS WELL WRAPPED AGAINST WINTER AND ROUGH WEATHER

Any expedition into Tibet depends to some extent upon these sturdy men. Accustomed, like the shaggy cattle they tend, to great altitudes, they and the beasts form the sole method of transport over a large part of this desolate land. They wear their sheepskin coats fleece inwards, and, equipped with caps of the same material, can defy weather that might daunt the hardiest European

WEAVING THE STRIPS OF CLOTH THAT GO TO MAKE A CLUMSY GARB

Grace and line and new-fangled fashions find no place in the costumes of Tibet. Both sexes wear an outer garment like a dressing-gown. It is made of blanket-shaped pieces of cloth striped in various bright colours and sewn together. The cloth is woven of wool on a simple loom, very similar in principle to the more delicate implement of Celebes illustrated in page 3726

Photos, John Claude White

woman, to beautify and not disfigure himself or herself.

The marriage customs vary considerably according to the locality. But there is one custom for which Tibet is remarkable—the practice of polyandry—that is, of one woman having two or more husbands. This is perhaps not so common in Tibet as has been supposed. Still, it is a recognized custom,

DEPUTY OF THE DALAI LAMA
When the British military mission reached Lhasa in 1904 for the purpose of stabilising both prestige and trade, the Dalai Lama fled, leaving this man with the great seal of office. He it was who signed the treaty
Photo, John Claude White

and it is regarded as perfectly legitimate. The most common form it takes is for two or more brothers to hold a wife in common. For economic reasons not being able each to afford a wife they combine together to have one between them, though it is generally the case that one or other of the brothers is absent from home. There are also cases in which two or more men who are not

brothers marry the same woman; and others where a woman already married gains influence over her husband, and with his consent marries another in addition to him. In case the mother of a family dies either the father or the son takes a new spouse, who becomes at the same time the wife of the other male members of the family. But the marriage of brothers with sisters or of cousins is prohibited by law and censured by public opinion.

When we consider the great number of men who enter the monasteries, and are therefore supposed to be celibates, it seems strange that many of the women should have more than one husband apiece. But a large number of the women of Lhasa and of the big towns form temporary and recognized marriages with Chinese, Nepalese, and other foreigners who come to Tibet without their womenfolk, and perhaps polyandry is not actually very prevalent.

The Tibetan women are capable and masterful, and, according to the Japanese traveller, Kawaguchi, from whose book, "Three Years in Tibet," the following account of the marriage customs is taken, the wife's authority over the husband is surprising. All the money which the husbands have earned has to be handed over to their common wife, and when a husband needs money for a particular purpose he has to beg it of his wife. If she happens to find one of her husbands keeping back his earnings the wife will break out in anger and slap him. She will also order her husbands to go out shopping for her,

WITHIN THE MAGIC PRECINCTS OF NA-CHUNG MONASTERY

Lhasa is famous for its religious houses. Near the De-Bung, illustrated in page 4901, stands the monastery of Na-chung, the seat of the chief wizard of Tibet. The buildings are bright with scarlet and gilding, and in summer the whole place blooms with hollyhocks, stocks, and clumps of feather-topped bamboos. Na-chung is a good example of Buddhism and devil worship side by side

Photo, John Claude White

PRAYER FLAGS THAT FLUTTER THEIR MESSAGE TO HEAVEN IN THE COURTYARD OF A TIBETAN MONASTERY

Upon a thousand lonely sites, among lofty peaks or beauteous woodlands, by ravine and mountain torrent, overlooking unexplored lakes and rivers, the monks of Tibet have built themselves solid and time-resisting structures. The endless, unvarying round of ritual and worship goes its monotonous way, and almost every Tibetan family of position has one member either priest or monk. Among the paraphernalia of these places may be seen strings of flags, upon each of which is inscribed a prayer. As the wind stirs them the prayers are supposed to ascend to heaven

Photo, John Claude White

and the husbands are quite obedient. An agreement to the effect that either husband or wife may divorce the other whenever either he or she has become averse to continuing as the other's partner is acknowledged as a legitimate condition of a matrimonial contract.

The Tibetans generally, whether men or women, marry between the twentieth and twenty-fifth year, and not so extremely young as boys and girls marry in India. Perhaps this is one of the reasons why the Tibetans are of a more robust, sturdier type. If a woman who has several brothers as her husbands gives birth to a child, the eldest husband is called the father and the rest uncles. The woman does not choose her husbands. She is compelled to marry the husbands her parents select. The parents do not even tell their daughter that a proposal has been made. These compulsory marriages, therefore, frequently end in divorce.

Marriages Planned by Parents

The parents of a young man make inquiries for a suitable bride among families of the same social position as his own and, when a girl is found, communicate through a middleman with her parents, and the parents before giving a definite reply will consult a fortune-teller or priest. The whole of these negotiations are kept a secret from both the girl and the young man till the actual wedding-day. There is no custom of exchanging presents or of the bride bringing a dowry or anything like a marriage contract regarding the property of the parties concerned. Only the bride's parents, for the sake of social opinion, furnish the bride with all things needed for her marriage.

On the morning of the wedding the girl's parents casually tell the girl that the weather being fine they intend going to the temple, and that she had better go with them, and as they are going to have a " lingka feast," she had better have her hair done. Her parents then give her new toilet articles, and

when at last the toilet is complete inform her for the first time that an engagement is made, and that she is to be married that very day—or, rather, that the commencement of the marriage festivities is to be made that day, for the rich give a series of pre-nuptial banquets for a fortnight, and even the poor give feasts for two or three days before the actual wedding ceremony takes place.

Pre-Nuptial Festivities

During these festivities the relatives and acquaintances of her parents visit the family with presents of money, food, or clothes to congratulate them on their daughter's happy wedding, and then visitors are cordially entertained, Tibetan tea and cold spirits, which they drink to excess, being provided. While drinking they eat nothing at all, but at the afternoon meal they take some meat and wheat-cakes, and boiled rice mixed with butter, sugar, raisins, and Chinese persimmons.

In the evening again the guests are entertained to a dinner. When the feasts begin to flag the fun is revived by singing and dancing, the dances being regular and systematic, and each dancer keeping step with the music as carefully as soldiers at drill, though their regularity and solemnity do not interfere with the zest and keenness of enjoyment.

Wedding-Day Observances

Towards the close of the festive time the parents of the bridegroom send their representatives with a number of attendants to the bride's home for the bride, taking with them some money as " breast money," or nursing expenses, that is remuneration for the mother's care in bringing up the girl. Then the middleman gives the bride the dress, belt, Chinese shoes, and all the other articles necessary for the bride during the wedding ceremony. A precious gem, such as is usually worn in the middle of the forehead, is also presented. The bride's own parents present her

BRIGHT PAINTED WALLS AND GORGEOUS BANNERS ENLIVEN THE ROCKBOUND EXISTENCE OF THE TIBETAN MONK

In Tibet's Lamaist monasteries the sombreness of the scenery around is relieved by bright colours within. The lamas paint the walls of their houses in bright scarlet and gilt. These little communities have often the appearance of villages, entire streets being built within the sacred precincts. The ornateness of the banner seen here, on which is depicted the Buddha, well shows the need for brightness engendered in the minds of dwellers in this rugged country

Photo, Edmund Candler

MONKS OF DE-BUNG, ONE OF THE WORLD'S LARGEST MONASTERIES

Lhasa, Tibet's sacred city, lies in a great plain girt with hills. At the foot of these and overlooking
the valley of the Kyi-chu river stands the monastery of De-Bung, which contains about eight
thousand monks. Much of the building which overlooks this fine terrace is painted in brilliant
colours. The Dalai Lama, head of the Lamaist creed, visits De-Bung once a year

Photo, John Claude White

with valuable ornaments—a fringe, neck-
rings, ear-rings, finger-rings, ornamental
armlets, and breast jewels.

Early in the morning of the nuptial
day the parents give a farewell banquet
in the house of the bride. At the same
time the Buddhist priests are asked by
the family to hold a festival service in
honour of the village and family gods.
Simultaneously, another festival is held
in the house of the bride by the priest
of the Bon religion—the ancient religion
of Tibet. The banquet over, there
enters the preacher who is to exhort
the bride. He stands in front of her

and instructs her by means of a collection of maxims. She must behave with
kindness, obey her superiors, including
her parents-in-law, wait upon her husband and his brothers and sisters with
equal kindness, and treat her servants
as if they were her own children. The
father and mother with tears repeat
similar exhortations, and then relatives
and friends, bursting into tears, take the
bride by the hands and most tenderly
make their own exhortations.

When the bride leaves her house she
weeps bitterly, and very reluctantly is
placed on horseback and taken to the

COMPETITOR IN THE SHIGATZE SHOOTING COMPETITION

It has been found necessary by the monks, who live entirely upon the credulity and superstition of the people, to provide their supporters with occasional diversion. This must always be of a spectacular nature, and, since even Tibetans might tire of unrelieved devil-dancing and other religious show, an annual shooting competition is held on a plain outside the town of Shigatze

Photo, Percy Brown

house of the bridegroom. Her head and face are covered with a cloth so that no glimpse of her face can be caught. On her way three banquets are given by the bride's relatives and three by the bridegroom's. But when the bride reaches the bridegroom's house she finds the gate bolted and barred till a man with a sword of secret charm tears to pieces such evil spirits or epidemic diseases as may have come with the bride.

Then the mother of the bridegroom comes out with some sour milk and a mixture of baked flour, butter, and sugar, and leads the party to a banquet, when a priest is brought in to inform the gods of the village and of the house that an addition has been made to the members of the family, and they are asked to extend their arms and welcome the bride. These prayers over, the father and mother of the bridegroom give a piece of silk to the couple and to all the people who have come to see the bride off and to receive her. And this ceremony makes the couple husband and wife.

The burial customs of the Tibetans are no less remarkable than the marriage customs. In their funeral ceremonies neither a coffin nor an urn is used in which to deposit the corpse. It is

ARCHER-MUSKETEER READY FOR THE NEW YEAR CELEBRATIONS

So soon as the competitors are assembled, they parade along the racecourse, cavaliers and horses decked in the brightest colours. The course is about seven feet wide, with a mud bank a foot high on either side. Then each horseman takes his turn at riding at full tilt down the course and shooting at two targets, about sixty yards apart, first with the bow, and then with gun and bow alternately

Photo, Percy Brown

simply laid on a wooden frame, a piece of white cloth is thrown over it, and it is carried away by two men. The corpse is then disposed of in one of four different modes, according to the advice of the priest who has been previously consulted, first, as to the auspicious day, then as to the mode of funeral, and, lastly, as to the final disposal of the corpse.

The four modes are distinguished from each other according to the agency brought into the service—water, fire, earth, or birds of the air. Of these four the one generally regarded as best and

most commonly used in Tibet is the mode of leaving the corpse to be devoured by vultures. The other modes are cremation, water-burial, and burial in the earth. This last method is never adopted except when a person dies of smallpox, and when the British troops buried the Tibetan corpses after a fight during the progress of the mission to Lhasa in 1904 the Tibetans surreptitiously in the night dug them up again and exposed them to be devoured in the usual way by vultures.

When the burial is by air the corpse is taken out to some rock, the white sheet

SISTERS OF A REMOTE TIBETAN NUNNERY IN WIGS, BEADS, AND BRACELETS

It is rare indeed for such folk to see a camera. Living in complete isolation in an isolated land, difficult of access, the nuns of Tibet's religious houses have perforce to keep themselves strictly to themselves. The aged women wearing caps are lay sisters, old almost beyond humanity and inhumanly dirty. The rest are full-fledged nuns. These must shave their heads and assume great mop-like wigs. The largest of these matted coverings conceals the bald head of the abbess seated in the centre and wearing at her throat a charm-box studded with turquoises

Photo, John Claude White

4904

is removed, the priest chants texts to the accompaniment of drums and cymbals, and a man with a sword comes forward, cuts open the abdomen, removes the entrails, and severs the various members of the body. Vultures having by this time gathered round they begin to eat the flesh. The bones are pounded to powder, mixed with baked

peaches, and small black persimmons. The head of the house first picks up some of the fruits with his right hand, tosses them up three times, and eats them. Then his wife, guests, and servants follow his example, one after another. Tea is then served with fried cakes of wheat flour for each. The eating is much enjoyed, and the New Year season is very

PILGRIM WHO MEASURES WITH HIS BODY TWO HUNDRED MILES

No more striking example of the stern demands of Eastern faiths could be given than this. The pilgrim has vowed to make the journey from Lhasa to a monastery upon the sacred mountain, Everest. This he does by a series of prostrations, lying down, stretching out his hands, rising and standing on the spot they marked, then lying down again, and so for two hundred miles

flour, and thrown to the vultures. The cloth is the perquisite of the men who cut up the body and pounded the bones.

While the burial ceremony is taking place a religious service is also conducted at the house of the deceased, and when the ceremony is over those who have attended it call at the house of the bereaved family and are feasted by the members of it.

New Year's Day is observed in Tibet with much ceremony. In the morning a piece of coloured silk, or handkerchiefs sewn together in the shape of a flag, is put over a heap of baked flour on which are strewn some dried grapes, dried

festive. But, strangely enough, no words of congratulation are exchanged.

The Tibetans in their personal habits are by no means cleanly. They very seldom wash, and the lower classes are extremely dirty and clad in filthy clothes. Their houses also are very dirty, and, having only very small windows, are very cold and dark. But they are well and solidly built. All the buildings, in fact, whether domestic dwellings, monasteries, or forts, have a solidity and massiveness which are almost Egyptian, and fully in keeping with the character of the people. They have the same simplicity of design and the same

GRIM REMINDER OF THAT WHICH AWAITS THE ERRING TIBETAN IN THE NEXT WORLD

Tibetans never tire of witnessing this eerie spectacle. Lama priests, dressed in weird garments and with their faces encased in masks, jump and sidle this way and that to the hooting and grunts of twelve-foot trumpets and the thumping of drums. A fiendish cleverness reveals itself in the making of these masks, which are inhuman and aloof enough in their fixed expressions to inspire awe, and sufficiently ghastly to affright the most stolid onlooker when, returning home, he recalls this grim horror and his own misdeeds. Similar scenes are illustrated in pages 2832 and 2833

Photo, Georg Haeckel

TANGLED DRAPERIES THAT FORM AN IMAGE OF THE FEARSOME SNAKE-GOD

In all parts of the world superstitions connected with snakes are to be found. The brazen serpent of the Children of Israel, the snake-symbol of the Bacchanalia, and the snake-gods of Mexico and Australia indicate the universality of the awe and cult of mysticism, in its various forms, that have centred in this uncanny reptile. In the photograph a crude representation of a snake has been made, and upon the head rests a crown. The effigy is hauled from place to place, and the populace turn out and bring various offerings, the whole ceremony creating great excitement in the remote Tibetan villages

Photo, Georg Haeckel

method of sloping slightly inwards from the base upwards that the Egyptian buildings show, and they give the same sense of permanence and four-squareness. There is nothing graceful or elegant about any building in Tibet, but there is not one that is not impressive by its strength.

the visitor emerges into spacious rooms with nothing mean about them. An ordinary farmhouse would be of two storeys, with perhaps a courtyard. The roofs are flat, and are used for drying grain. The rooms in each wing of a courtyard would be inhabited by various

RETINUE OF SERVING MAIDS DISPLAY THE FAMILY HEIRLOOMS
Beads and elaborate ornaments for the hair constitute the main features of feminine titivation in Tibet. The wife of some local magnate will see to it that her tire-women are suitably splendid on any public occasion, and delights in showing off her stock of jugs and other utensils, made usually of copper. Of their teapots the Tibetans are specially proud
Photo, Percy Brown

The interior of a Tibetan house is, however, more comfortable than the exterior would lead us to think. It is cold, and it is dirty. But it is full of carpets, clothing, furniture, utensils, ornaments, etc.—all of real beauty. In his own way the Tibetan makes himself very snug.

The entrance to the building, of whatever description, is always very narrow. But once through this narrow entrance

relations, and filled with the usual agricultural implements.

In the main part of the building will nearly always be found a little private chapel filled with figures of Buddha and the Buddhist saints, and kept neat and clean and with flowers constantly renewed. Painted banners with pictures of the saints and representations of heaven above and hell below will be hung from the walls, and texts from the

WONDERFUL HAIRDRESSING THAT IS KEPT INTACT FOR DAYS

Tibetan ladies " do " their hair as seldom as possible, for the creation of such a coiffure is an anxious and tiring affair. The features framed thus in hair have a certain dainty melancholy, and when these women abstain from smearing their faces with a popular concoction whose chief ingredient is soot, they are often not ill-favoured. Similar long sleeves are illustrated in page 3523

Photo, Percy Brown

TIBETAN BUILDERS AT WORK UPON THE ROOF OF A NEW HOUSE

As one of the chief uses to which the Tibetan puts the roof of his house is the drying of grain, a uniform flatness is the rule. The soft material is pounded by a number of workers who use a wooden implement in shape something like a cricket bat. In the photograph two men can be seen with watering-cans who are engaged in softening some uneven spot for re-levelling. The entire roof is made to curve slightly so that the rain will run off readily

Photo, Georg Haeckel

AN AUDIENCE WITH THE TASHI LAMA, SECOND IN IMPORTANCE IN ALL TIBET

Near Shigatze, on the river Nyanchu, is the monastery of Tashi Lunpo. Its abbot is the second dignitary in Tibet. In the photograph he is seated on the right, wearing a hat reserved for persons of the highest rank. As he is travelling, a whole set of paraphernalia for conducting services is placed in his tent. No Buddhist functionary ever travels without them. Among the various articles on the table before him will be noticed a European clock

Photo, John Claude White

LAMAS WHO TRAIN LITTLE TIBETANS IN THE WAY THEY SHOULD GO

Such teaching as children receive in Tibet is in the hands of the lamas, or monks, who successfully
instil into the young minds the fog of superstition and demonology that fills their own imaginings
Still, as all over the world, the children provide a lighter side, and these merry little urchins,
grinning in their rags, find plenty of fun to counteract gloomy folklore

Photo, Georg Haeckel

Buddhist books inscribed on scrolls. The kitchen is big and dark and filled with smoke, but here again the dirtiness is redeemed to some extent by the beauty of the utensils. These kitchens in Tibet are filled with numbers of huge copper vessels which have become family heirlooms, and in which the family takes a real pride. The chief of these are the cooking vats—gigantic vessels of beaten copper, with rounded bottoms, and built into the clay oven-bank. These are kept brightly burnished, and are decorated with birds, fishes, roses, and other objects. They are the special treasures of the family.

Besides, there are hot-water jugs, milk-jugs, and, above all, teapots, these

NUNS AND LAY SISTERS OF A NUNNERY OF TIBET

Many years ago a law was passed in Tibet which aimed at making the women, at no time remarkably attractive outside their own country, still less so in their own. The effects of this still endure, and it is not surprising that, in the few nunneries that exist, the inmates should live in a state of uncleanliness surprising even in Tibet. One of the group holds a prayer-wheel

Photo, John Claude White

last often being of enormous size and impressive from the big simplicity of their design, while the smaller ones are richly ornamented and studded with coral and turquoise.

The house will contain also examples of Chinese porcelain and jade often of great beauty, and, unluckily, in these days, much garish European ware, such as lamps and vases. Piles of valuable clothing will also be found in the better-class houses—rich and exquisite Chinese silks and satins, Chinese shoes, thick blankets and quilts, fur coats, and so on.

Of actual cash the Tibetans possess little. Their wealth consists in their flocks of sheep and herds of yaks, and in the produce of their lands. This is sufficient to make them comfortable and, on the whole, contented. And with the women wearing charm boxes (containing charms, texts, or relics of the saints), ear-rings studded with turquoises, headdresses ornamented with strings of seed-pearls, the people, though dirty, present a well-to-do appearance.

Perhaps the most interesting custom is that associated with the selection of a successor to one of the many incarnations of the Buddhist saints, or Living Buddhas, as they are sometimes called. The best known is the Dalai Lama of

MAGICIAN IN FULL DRESS AND AN ADMIRING BAND OF MONKS

To the Tibetan every river, mountain-top, or waterfall has its particular devil. The houses are infested with them. It is the magician's part to find out which particular demon is causing harm, and to indicate suitable propitiation. A favourite device is the hanging up of miniatures of the home and its occupants carved in wood in order that the devil may vent its wrath upon those instead

Photo, Georg Haeckel

Lhasa—the Grand Lama, as he is often styled. He is not only a personage of high spiritual repute, but has political governance of the country. More important spiritually but less important politically is the Tashi Lama of Shigatze. And, besides these chief incarnations, there are lesser lights such as the Holy Lama living in a monastery at a height of 16,000 feet above sea-level near the foot of Mount Everest and visited by the Mount Everest Expedition in 1922, and the Living Buddha of Nalang in Eastern Tibet visited by Reginald Farrer in 1915.

These sacred persons are regarded with peculiar reverence by the people, who will shade their eyes with their hands, as they would when looking at the sun, in order not to be blinded by the glory radiating from them. They almost invariably sit cross-legged, as in the figures of Buddha, upon a raised dais, and are approached by all with the utmost deference of demeanour. And, having been brought up from their very babyhood in the belief that they are holy above their fellows, and having never known what it is to be treated as anything else but holy, their holiness sits with perfect naturalness upon them.

Sanctity of the Living Buddhas

They are, of course, very ignorant of the world outside Tibet and outside Buddhism, but they spend much of their time in studying their own sacred books, and in learning passages of them by heart. No doubt in the monasteries in which they live there are jealousies and wars of ambition between the inmates, and some of these may touch even the Living Buddhas, but in the main their sanctity is respected and preserved with surprising regularity, and the result is, perhaps, due to the rigidity of the etiquette with which they are hedged about. What they may and what they may not do, when they may stand and when they must sit, and every detail of their comportment, is all laid down with the clearest precision.

When one of these Living Buddhas dies—or, as the Tibetans would express it, wishes to change his existing body— his adherents look about for a new body into which he must have transferred his spirit—or transferred himself. They therefore look about for babies born about the time he died, for one whose body bears the recognized marks of Buddhahood, and, according to Reginald Farrer, before him they lay an assortment of rosaries and thunderbolts and mitres and other ecclesiastical paraphernalia, among which are the trappings of the late Living Buddha. If the child has, indeed, the latter's spirit he will unerringly pick out the property which was formerly his, and thus prove his claim to be, indeed, the new incarnation of the Living Buddha who for a time had passed away.

Manifestations Through the Flesh

But Reginald Farrer insists that the word " incarnation " usually employed when speaking of these Holy Lamas conveys an entirely false idea, and makes the whole conception appear yet more antagonistic to the doctrines of the founder of Buddhism than it really is. These are not, he says, incarnations but manifestations through the flesh of certain aspects of the Supreme Holiness. The idea of these revelations was born in northern Buddhism long after the time of the Buddha, and has never met any favour in the purer school of the south.

These incarnations or manifestations required the ratification of the Emperor of China and the sanction of the Church, and the heads of the Church may declare at will that a certain manifestation has determined and will never reappear.

Enormous Power of the Dalai Lama

They are, however, not necessarily or finally attached to a religious foundation, and are not Church dignitaries in the sense that the priors and abbots are, but stand as it were aside from the ecclesiastical organization, though of

STREET OF HOLY LHASA, CITY OF MYSTERY AND DISILLUSION
For centuries Lhasa, the lone city hid somewhere behind the Himalayas, was known only to a few
Chinese officials and a handful of priests and adventurers. The first view of the place reveals it upon
an eminence in a surrounding plain. On entering, most buildings, fair outside, are filthy within,
and in the streets dogs and pigs munch the garbage from house and booth
Photo, Edmund Candler

superior sanctity and importance. Nevertheless, it usually happens that districts
and abbeys develop their own manifestation, and that on such and such a
community such and such a manifestation sheds the illumination of his
permanent presence. They accept all
the deference shown them with complete assurance but without any air
of arrogant superiority—rather, indeed,
with a touch of truest kindliness.
They have a poise and ease which affect
all beholders and their courtesy and
graciousness are especially attractive.

In the case of the Dalai Lama, who
wields such enormous power, being both
spiritual and political sovereign of Tibet,
it has been found in practice that much
trouble results from a youth of eighteen
—the age at which new incarnation
comes into his full powers—having
such absolute authority in his hands.
In many instances, therefore, the
regent in whose hands has been the
authority during the child's minority
has taken measures to ensure that the
incarnation again changes its body. The
average age of the Dalai Lamas is very
low. The present Dalai Lama is an
exception. He is a man of political
proclivities and was more than a match
for his regent.

LONELY ANCHORITE OF THE MOUNTAINS AND HIS RUDE CELL

Of several classes of hermit recognized in Tibet, the holiest consists of lamas who enter monasteries and are walled up in a small cell vowing never to come out save as a corpse. Others live in grottoes in the mountains and are attended by pilgrims. There are constant relays of the latter, who spend the winter months obtaining free food and shelter for their services

Photo, Georg Haeckel

MONOLITH THAT RECORDS A TREATY WITH THE CHINESE EMPEROR

In the centre of Lhasa city, under a sacred willow tree, stands this monolith, set in a granite frame and called Do-Ring. It is said to date from A.D. 783. The indentations on its surfaces are "cup-markings," a term given to primitive incisions on rock surfaces and made, perhaps, by mothers of old Tibet as votive offerings for the safety of themselves and their babes in time of childbirth

Photo, John Claude White

Tibet

II. The Land of the Lamas and Its Story

By Sir E. Denison Ross, C.I.E.

Director, School of Oriental Studies, London Institution

TIBETAN writers trace their history back to a king who is said to have reigned in the fourth century B.C., but the more or less authentic history of Tibet, apart from mere legend, begins in the seventh century of our era with Srong-Tsan-Gam-Po, who brought the scattered Tibetan tribes under his single rule, and founded an empire which extended from Ssu-chuan to the borders of India and Baltistan, with its capital at Lhasa.

This kingdom was known to the Chinese as T'u-fan or T'u-p'o, from which the name Tibet is derived. Srong-Tsan-Gam-Po was sufficiently powerful to demand and obtain a princess of the royal house of T'ang in marriage. His first wife was a daughter of the King of Nepal. Both his wives were Buddhists, and it was no doubt mainly due to the influence of these two queens that he introduced Buddhism into the country.

It is, however, probable that during the preceding century sporadic efforts had been made by Indian Buddhist missionaries to convert the Tibetans. Hitherto, the Tibetans, though they possessed a local religion known as Bon-Po, had remained illiterate, but the introduction of Buddhism led to the creation of an alphabet—based on that employed in Northern India—for the purpose of translating the Sanskrit canon into Tibetan.

By the end of the ninth century the frontiers of Tibet had been extended over Baltistan, and for one hundred years the Tibetans actually held sway in the Tarim valley. In recent years much documentary evidence of their most northerly conquests has been rescued from under the sands of Central Asia. They even came into contact with the empire of the Caliphs of the West.

During this period of foreign conquest Buddhism had been somewhat neglected, but at the beginning of the tenth century a great revival took place, and Buddhist priests were imported from India, bringing with them all their sacred texts, which were systematically translated into Tibetan, and formed the basis of the two great Tibetan collections known as the Kanjur and the Tanjur.

It was Padma Sambhava, an Indian monk, who laid the foundations of the Lamaist hierarchy by establishing many

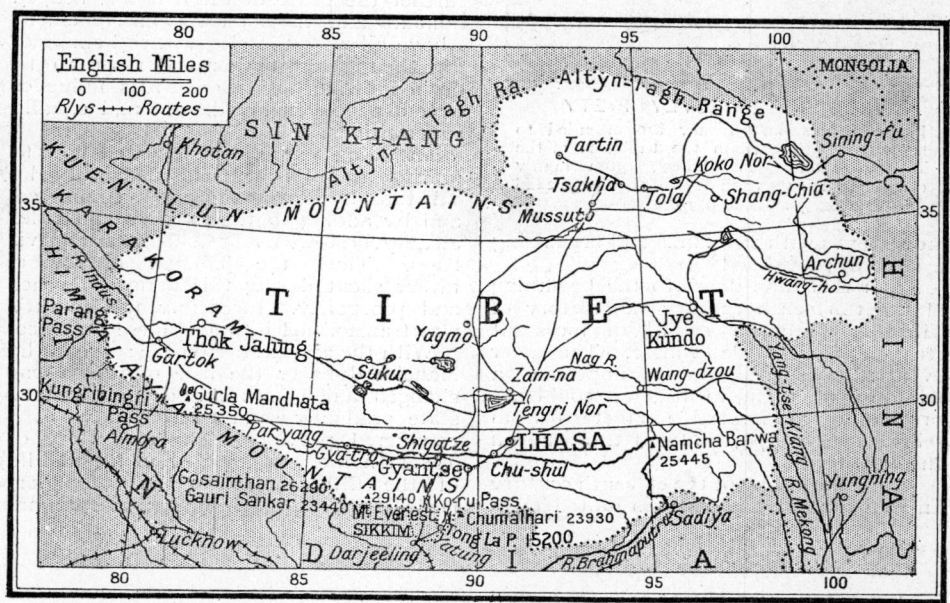

THE SEMI-INDEPENDENT STATE OF TIBET

AIDS TO PRIESTLY PIETY

Praying-wheel and rosary are intended to keep the faith ever in the thoughts of the Tibetan monk. The wheel, often highly ornamented, is seen and described in page 2828

Photo, Underwood Press Service

monasteries with rich lands and organizing a regular priesthood.

From this time down to the beginning of the thirteenth century the history of Tibet is merely a record of incessant struggles against the Chinese. The latter eventually succeeded in imposing a tribute upon them, in 983, but could not prevent the indomitable Tibetans from seizing every opportunity of throwing off the hated yoke.

At the beginning of the eleventh century an Indian monk named Atisa united Tibet and founded a new reformed sect of Lamaism called Kadam-Pa. It is not certain whether the redoubtable Jenghiz Khan actually invaded Tibet, but his grandson, Kublai Khan, the first emperor of the Mongol dynasty, which overthrew the Sung dynasty in the thirteenth century, certainly exercised full authority over the country.

As an ardent Buddhist he treated the Tibetans kindly, and under his rule the old hatred was mollified, abuses were abolished, and the administration was reorganized. He divided the country into provinces and districts of which the chiefs, native or Chinese, were placed under the supreme direction of a learned lama named Pags-Pa. This lama was endowed with a temporal and spiritual power so extended that, but for the name, one might perhaps trace back to him the first institution of the Supreme Magistrature of the Dalai Lama.

Kublai's successors continued this paternal and liberal policy with equal success, for during their reigns one hears no more of Tibetan insurrections. On the downfall of the Mongols in China this spiritual headship became a temporal power, and the head lama, Tsong-Kha-Pa, who belonged to the old royal house, at the end of the fourteenth century made himself ruler of the whole of Tibet, including Ladak. It was he who changed the name of the most prominent sect founded by Atisa from Kadampa into Ge-lug-pa, by which it is known to-day. He was the last reformer of Lamaism and organizer of the Church as it at present exists.

The policy of the Mongols, firm and conciliatory, was continued by the Ming dynasty, which, in order to assure still further the peace of the country, heaped honours and titles on the native chiefs. Above all were the clergy thus honoured, for their interest was the most to be desired owing to its enormous influence over a people highly devout and equally superstitious.

The Ming emperors knew well how to gratify the business instincts of the Tibetans by developing their commerce, and by adding to the honours and titles already bestowed more substantial privileges. Thus the Tibetan history is rather silent during this period of peace and prosperity. Insensibly the country was transformed into a Chinese province.

With the appearance on the scene of the Manchu dynasty the face of things was changed, and Tibet from being a tributary state gradually sank to the status of a conquered province. The monastery of Tashi Lunpo was founded in the middle of the fifteenth century, its founder, Geden-Dub, being the first Tashi Lama. The first Dalai Lama, who founded Lhasa, dates from the middle of the seventeenth century.

It was the famous emperor Kang-Hsi who, in 1723, finally established China's suzerainty over Tibet, and officially recognized the temporal power of the Dalai Lama. Thirty years later, as the outcome of a revolt on the part of a Tibetan chief, the Chinese abolished the royal house in Tibet, and bestowed the prerogative on the Dalai Lama, providing him with advisers, ministers, and troops. All the acts of the administrative hierarchy in Lhasa were scrutinised by two resident Chinese ambassadors.

It was from this time, namely the middle of the eighteenth century, that Tibet was closed to all outsiders save the Chinese, and became the Forbidden Country to Europeans. In 1772 the Raja of Bhutan, claiming rights over the district of Cooch Behar, neighbouring on Bengal, seized without further excuse the coveted territory. Challenged by the English, who also coveted the province, the Raja called upon his suzerain, the Dalai Lama, for protection. This brought about diplomatic intervention, and the government of Tibet recognized the rights of her vassal and obtained a peace.

Tibetan Relations with India

In 1774, on receipt of a letter from the Tashi Lama in Shigatze, Warren Hastings sent a mission under Bogle, who, though well received, was not permitted to visit Lhasa. In 1783 a second mission under Turner was despatched, the result of which was an agreement that any natives of India recommended by the Governor-General might be allowed to trade with Tibet via Bhutan.

In 1792 the Nepal Gurkhas invaded Bhutan and Tsang and advanced into Tibet, but hearing of the approach of a Chinese force, they retired into the mountains with their booty, whither they were pursued, and the Chinese lost no time in imposing conditions of peace—a recognition of their suzerainty and payment of an annual tribute.

The Chinese, believing that the Gurkhas had been incited by the Indian authorities, now established a post at Phari, and forbade natives of India to enter Tibet. In 1834 Goulab-Singh, King of Kashmir, invaded the province of Ladak and advanced as far as Ngari. The arrival of the Chinese army forced him to retrace his steps; he managed, however, to retain Ladak and certain positions in the Himalayas—recognized by the treaties of 1842 and 1856.

British Mission to Lhasa

Almost simultaneously war again broke out with Nepal, this time to the advantage of the latter country; she, in her turn, imposed a tribute on Tibet and claimed certain commercial privileges and the right to send a Nepalese Minister to Lhasa. Not until 1873 was any fresh attempt made to open up trade between India and Tibet, but in that year a road was built through Sikkim (which had been annexed by the British in 1856) to the frontier at Jalep-La.

During the next three decades various abortive agreements were made with the Chinese and Tibetans, and at last in 1903 Colonel (now Sir Francis) Younghusband, who had been appointed British Commissioner, proceeded to Khamba Jong, which had been fixed as the place for negotiations by the Chinese with the consent of the Dalai Lama.

The Tibetans were foolish enough to bar the passage of this peaceful mission, and to prevent a meeting with the Chinese delegate. The mission was subsequently attacked in force by the Tibetans, and the British having received reinforcements captured the fort of Gyantse and finally reached Lhasa after slight opposition in August, 1904.

Here at last they met the Chinese envoy and a treaty in settlement of frontier and other questions was signed, which was finally ratified by the Chinese in April, 1906. As a result of this settlement certain markets and trade routes are no longer closed to the foreigner.

TIBET : FACTS AND FIGURES

The Country

Semi-independent state of Central Asia. On the south the boundary marches with Assam, Bhutan, Sikkim, and Nepal; on the west with United Provinces, Punjab, and Kashmir; on the north-west with Sin-Kiang; on the north-east and east with China. Tibet contains the world's highest mountains, a considerable part of it having a mean altitude of 16,500 feet. The ground is frozen here for eight months in the year. In the south the soil is more fertile and crops can be raised at altitudes of 11,000 feet. A number of large rivers rise in Eastern Tibet, including the Mekong, flowing through Cambodia, and the Yang-tse-Kiang and Hwang-ho, entering the sea through China. Total area about 463,200 square miles ; estimated population, 2,000,000.

Commerce and Industries

Agriculture is pursued in some parts, cereals, barley, and vegetables being grown. Domestic animals include the yak, sheep, camel, buffalo, and pig. Weaving and wool-spinning and the manufacture of decorations and implements for monasteries and temples are the chief industries. Gold, salt, and borax are the principal minerals worked. Exports to India, mainly raw wool, were valued 1921-22 at £231,100, while imports from India, chiefly cotton goods, totalled £551,300 for same year. Commerce with China is considerable. The trade routes traverse passes more than 14,000 feet high, sheep and yaks being the means of transport. The main route is from Yatung and Gyantse in Tibet, through Sikkim, to Siliguri in Northern Bengal.

SNAKE-CHARMER IN TUNIS EXHIBITING HIS INFLUENCE OVER THE IMMEMORIAL ENEMY OF MANKIND

All over the East the snake-charmer is to be found, with his pipe and basket and serpents, whose venomous powers he insistently proclaims, although, in fact, these are destroyed by removal of the fangs. Squatting on the ground, the charmer breathes softly on his pipe until the snake raises itself in the basket and sways in rhythm with the notes, and performs other gyrations in obedience to its master's behest. In Tunis the snake-charmers, whose power over the reptiles, though unexplained, is undeniable, usually give performances in the Souk el Aassar, and always draw an interested audience

Photo, H. Perrin

Tunis

I. Medley of Races Under the French Flag

By A. MacCallum Scott

Author of "Barbary," "Through Finland," etc.

IN the youth of the world, before the dawn of history, before Homer sang the fall of Troy, the earliest navigators groped their way cautiously westwards along the northern shores of Africa. We do not know who these first Argonauts were, whether they were of Tyre and Sidon, or of the Minoan kingdom of Crete, or of some earlier race of merchant adventurers, who have left their rude stone monuments scattered from the shores of the Persian Gulf to those of the English Channel and even the Baltic. Some record of their adventures survives in Greek legend, and formed the basis of the story of Ulysses. They sailed past the delta of the Nile, and along the parched shores of the Libyan desert, broken by occasional oases of palms. They visited the Lotos Island of Djerba in the Syrtes, and then they steered northward along the lagoons of the rich and fertile lowlands of Tunis. A mountainous promontory projected north-east towards Sicily. They rounded it, and the glorious prospect of the Gulf of Tunis was unfolded before their eyes. The gulf stretched south in a long regular curve, the

emerald waters being separated from the golden sand by a delicate edging of white surf. At the southernmost point, almost from the water's edge, as it seemed, there rose the cone of a volcanic mountain, terminating in a double peak which recalled the crescent-shaped horns of their god. On either side of this mountain, Bou Kornein, Father of Two Horns, as it is still called, two rivers descended into the gulf through the fruitful alluvial plains of Grombalia and Mornag.

From the western side of the gulf there extended inland a large shallow lagoon, and beyond it again another lagoon. A series of small heights terminating in a high cliff formed the tip of the western horn of the crescent, beyond which again was the estuary of the Medjerda, one of the largest rivers in North Africa. The panorama was surrounded by a distant wall of savage mountains with precipitous cliffs and jagged peaks.

About twelve centuries before Christ the Phoenicians, attracted by the wealth of the country, began establishing trading stations along this coast. The country was occupied by a people of

TYPICAL BEDUIN WOMANHOOD

Beduin women do not veil themselves. Their usual garment is blue, woven in one piece, secured on the shoulders with fibula brooches, and festooned with silver chains and charms

WIELDING THE FLY-WHISK AT A BAKER'S SHOP

Shops in the native quarter of Tunis are merely square windowless apertures in the walls of the foetid, swelteringly hot souks, or market places. Each souk has its particular trade, and in every shop, especially those where bread or meat or fruit is sold, the merchant squats or, with a long-tailed fly-whisk, vainly tries to keep off the flies that are the horrible plague of Tunis

Photo, Donald McLeish

the Berber race who still form the main North African stock from the town of Tunis to Morocco, and from the Mediterranean to the Sahara. From the native chiefs the Phoenicians acquired sites which gradually, as their commerce extended developed into flourishing towns. Of these towns, Tunis was founded on the narrow neck of land between he outer and inner lagoons on the west side of the gulf ; Utica grew up at the mouth of the Medjerda ; and a little farther along the coast, in a sheltered bay, was Bizerta. Last of all at the tip of the western horn of the Gulf of Tunis, where the cliffs of Sid Bou Said descend abruptly into the sea, a fugitive princess from Tyre landed with her retainers and founded Carthage. She was the original of Virgil's immortal story of Aeneas and Dido.

Carthage grew and flourished and became the capital of the great maritime empire of the Phoenicians in the western Mediterranean. While Persia and Greece disputed the mastery of the Eastern world, Carthage and Rome disputed the dominion of the West.

The three great Punic Wars decided that the civilization of Europe was to be Roman rather than Asiatic.

After a stern siege, which was resisted by the energy of desperation, in the year 146 B.C. Scipio, the Roman general, captured Carthage, the proudest and richest city in the Western world, and razed it to its foundations as a farmer destroys a nest of vipers. " Delenda est Carthago" (Carthage must be destroyed) said Cato. Rome was determined that the rival who had menaced her for centuries should never again raise her head.

For a generation Carthage lay vacant, a mouldering heap of ruins. Then Rome established a small colony, and almost before she realized what was happening, found herself involved in a career of conquest and development in Africa. Carthage rose again from the ashes, a mighty city, the capital of a Roman province which soon began to outshine Italy itself in wealth, in luxury, in art, and in the magnificence of its palaces, temples, and public buildings.

Africa became not merely the granary of Rome, but a breeding-ground for Roman citizens, a school of art and letters, and the cradle of Western Christianity. Several of the Roman Emperors, including Septimius Severus, one of the greatest, were African born. It was the African bishops, Tertullian

in the first century, Cyprian in the second, and Augustine in the third, who built up the Church which later became the official religion of Rome.

Nor was Carthage a mere isolated foothold. The frontier was pushed far south to the Sahara. Roads, bridges, aqueducts, and irrigation works led to a marvellous development of the resources of the country, and numerous splendid cities reproduced the institutions of Rome. For five centuries the new province was as Roman as Italy. And yet, after all this effort and all these centuries of success, something was

TUNISIAN GREENGROCER AT HIS PAVEMENT STALL

Shop fittings are reduced to the minimum in the souks of Tunis, often comprising no more than a pair of scales on an upturned box. The most respectable old greengrocer derogates not a whit from his dignity by spreading his meagre stock on a bit of sacking on the pavement and squatting on his hams beside it, while chaffering over the price of his dates and figs and greenstuff

Photo, Donald McLeish

CENTAUR-LIKE SPAHI ON THE TUNISIAN SANDS

His immense desert hat is the most striking article of the Spahi's costume—a vast confection, three times the size of a Mexican cowboy's hat, a yard across, two feet high, and decorated with huge leather leaves. So crowned, and wrapped in a flowing white burnous, he sits erect, high-throned on a saddle glowing with gilt and crimson, and with his feet thrust into barbaric stirrups

FRANCE'S IRON HAND CONCEALED WITHIN A VELVET GLOVE

French authority is exercised in Tunis with remarkable consideration for native susceptibilities. To all outward seeming the native life pursues its long accustomed way free from foreign interference ; but under the very shadow of the mosque that rises just within the gateway dividing the French from the Arab city, sentries in French service guard the approaches to the seat of the regency

Photo, Donald McLeish

SUBSTANTIAL REPRESENTATIVES OF SHADOWY AUTHORITY: HORSE, FOOT, AND ARTILLERY OF THE BEY OF TUNIS

France maintains an army of occupation in Tunis and keeps absolute control of everything affecting the defence of her protectorate. The French, however, recognize the wisdom of allowing the natives at large to believe in the survival of the administrative authority of their Bey, and in pursuance of this policy the Bey is permitted to maintain a certain number of troops—infantry, cavalry, and artillery—whose services, nevertheless, are almost exclusively spectacular. They are quartered in barracks at the Bardo, the old-time winter palace of the Beys of Tunis

Photo, Donald McLeish.

NATIVE TROOPER OF THE BEY'S CAVALRY AT THE BARDO

Arabs like soldiering, and volunteer readily for service in the Tirailleurs, Spahis, and Gendarmerie, who form part of the French garrison in Tunis. Others enter the Beylical army, whose uniform is modelled closely on that of the French Zouaves and Chasseurs d'Afrique. Half of the Bey's military force is quartered in the Bardo, outside which this well-mounted cavalryman is awaiting orders

Photo, Donald McLeish

wrong with Roman civilization in Africa. The plant bourgeoned and blossomed, but it struck no deep roots. Fierce religious schisms racked the state with civil strife. A handful of Vandals found it an easy conquest; and then, just when it was recovering from that blow, the name, the language, the religion, the civilization of Rome were utterly obliterated by the Arab conquerors from the East. The religion of Mahomet held universal sway, and it has since held the land in a grip which has not been relaxed for thirteen centuries.

It is only a hundred years ago since France occupied Algiers and set out once more upon the great adventure of Europeanising Africa in which Rome had failed. In 1881 she advanced another stage by the occupation of Tunis, and only after the first decade of the twentieth century has she commenced the occupation of Morocco. The tricolour now flies from the Gulf of Gabes to the Atlantic.

The town of Tunis, built on a low neck of land between two lagoons, offers a remarkable contrast to Algiers, which climbs up a steep hillside embowered in orange, lemon, and palm groves. It is a much larger city and the process of Europeanisation has made less headway. In Algiers

SQUADRON OF SPAHIS, THE FAMOUS NORTH AFRICAN CAVALRY OFFICERED BY FRENCHMEN

Synonymous with the word "sepoy," spahi from the Persian "sipahi" simply means soldier. Originally the Spahis were mounted troops supplied to the Sultan of Turkey by his feudal lords and had a great military reputation. When the French occupied Algiers and Tunis these troops were made a unit of the French army. Their uniform consists of blue breeches, red jacket, and two burnouses or cloaks, a red one flowing behind and a white one covering the shoulders. Round the head is bound, besides the turban, a length of cord made of camel hair

PRODUCE FROM THE HINTERLAND AND ITS VENDERS IN THE MARKET BY THE MOSQUE

Bundles of merchandise, carpets, pottery, woolstuffs, that are being unloaded from the grunting camels, olives and dates being stacked for sale, and everywhere a babel of voices and a flutter of white burnouses, all under the blazing heat and glare, give the observer an impression of confusion in which, nevertheless, much business is done. In the background the weary beasts, camels and horses, are being unsaddled, while in the right-hand corner of the photograph is a rich carpet that glows with colour, and upon which the proprietor proudly squats.

MENDICANT STREET ARABS OUTSIDE A MOSQUE IN TUNIS

Absolutely no shame attaches to the practice of mendicity in Tunis, and many of the natives take to
it almost in infancy. Impudence is often more effective than necessity in extracting money from the
pockets of the prosperous, and these children are only samples of a juvenile crowd that pesters travellers
in the streets of Tunis, and does pretty well out of the occupation

Photo, Donald McLeish

WARES THAT ATTRACT THE SWEET-TOOTHED—AND THE FLIES

Sweetmeats of many kinds have a large sale in Tunis. Nougat, a delicious confection of sweet paste filled with chopped almonds or pistachio-nuts, is heaped in the forefront of the sweet-stalls in the bazaars, and exposed for sale on trestles by venders in the streets. Beignets are another very popular sweet-meat, a kind of fritter, not unlike a doughnut fried in oil

WHERE THE BEARERS OF MERCHANDISE MAKE THEIR EXITS AND THEIR ENTRANCES: THE OLD "NEW GATE"

Many of the houses in Tunis are built from fragments of old war-smitten Carthage, whose skeleton, partly unearthed, lies two miles away. But the buildings in the souks, or bazaars, are of humbler and more rough-and-ready appearance. This photograph shows a portion of the outskirts of the bazaar quarter and the Moorish arch of the Bab Djedid or "New Gate" that here pierces the old town wall. In the foreground to the right a bread seller chaffers with a customer

Photo, J. Dearden Holmes

VENDERS OF VIANDS AND VEGETABLES IN THE SOUK EL AASSAR

Traffic is constant in the Souk el Aassar, an open square in the native quarter of Tunis, for not only are bread and meat and vegetables sold here, but it is also the rendezvous of the minstrels and story-tellers. The dome in the background marks the marabout or grave of "My Lord Bel Khir," much frequented by Moslem women, who may not enter the mosques to pray

Photo, J. Dearden Holmes

everyone can speak French; in Tunis only the younger generation can. An Arab interpreter is necessary if one wishes to have much conversation with the natives. In Algiers the stranger may visit any mosque; in Tunis Europeans are strictly excluded from all the mosques. In Algiers the Orient is hidden away behind a French front; in Tunis the Orient is everywhere.

The souks of Tunis, the native shopping quarter of the city, are a world in themselves. From the spacious Avenue Jules Ferry, which might be a section of the Champs Elysées, one passes through the massive Roman-like arch of the Porte de France, into an intricate maze of narrow lanes. Each craft has its own street, or souk, which has been vaulted or roofed over like an arcade to afford a welcome shade from the glare of the African sun.

The country of Tunis is famous for its scents, the southern territories producing a multitude of aromatic and balsamic herbs and perfumed flowers. To find the perfume souk in the city it is literally true that one has only to follow one's nose, though one has to run the gauntlet of many other distracting Oriental smells. The slipper makers' souk, the tailors' souk, the fez cap makers' souk, the saddle makers' souk, the jewellers' souk, the carpet and rug souk, and the ladies' souk, where exquisite silks and embroideries are hidden away in the recesses of the most unpromising, dark, little caves, offer endless scope for exploration and bargain hunting.

In the centre of the souks is a small quadrangle arcaded round by rows of pillars painted with barbaric colours and patterns. This was the slave

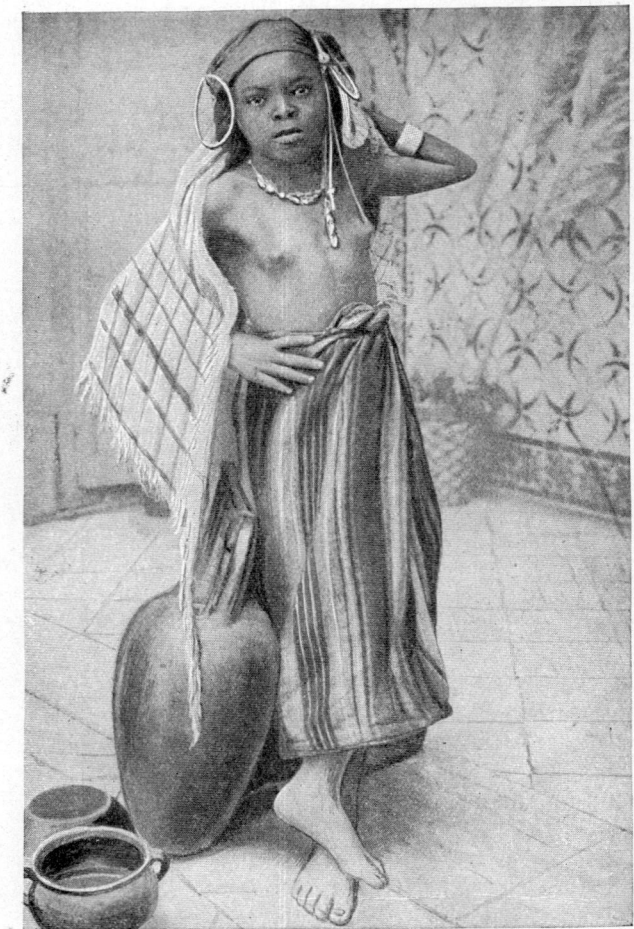

TUNISIAN DAUGHTER OF ISHMAEL

Beduin girls and women often go about extremely scantily clad and are far from particular about personal cleanliness. Their graceful figures are shown to advantage when they are carrying on their heads their large Oriental water-pots

types, the temperament have changed but little.

A dozen auctions are proceeding of articles of dress and jewelry. The runners bear the articles through the dense crowd shouting out the latest bids. Here comes an eagle-beaked Phoenician, his fingers laden with rings. They are his stock-in-trade. Stop him and he will let you examine them all. The Arab burnous has all the appearance of a Roman toga. Grinning negroes shoulder their way through the throng. Jews with heavy eye-lids watch like falcons for bargains. Shock-haired and ragged marabouts, or holy men, and fierce-eyed dervishes, like John the Baptist, from the desert gather alms. Bearded and turbaned Arabs, true sons of the Prophet, sit crosslegged on the café benches and gaze meditatively upon the turmoil.

The changeless East! Said the Prophet Ezekiel in his lamentation for Tyre (xxvii, 12): "Tarshish was thy merchant by reason of the multitude of all kind of riches; with silver, iron, tin, and lead they traded in thy fairs." Tarshish was the ancient name for the district which includes Carthage and Tunis, and "Tarshish and the isles" referred to in the seventy-second Psalm, is an apt description of the Phoenician metropolis of the West which dominated the islands of the Mediterranean.

It was to Tarshish that the ship was bound on which Jonah sailed before his adventure with the whale. Both S. Augustine and S. Jerome believed Tarshish to be identical with Carthage,

market of old, and here, up to the beginning of the nineteenth century, after a successful pirate raid, the corsairs displayed their captives. The arches were the gateways to shame and misery for many a Christian man and woman.

An Arab café flanks one side of the square, and here, on a bench outside the door, one may sit sipping a cup of sweet, thick, Turkish coffee and looking upon a scene as strange as may be seen in any bazaar from Cairo to Samarkand. Even such was the market place of Phoenician Carthage twenty-five centuries ago. The methods, the

TUNISIANS TO-DAY
Dwellers in Town & Tent

*Like the lawgiver and seer of ancient Jewry this Tunisian Rabbi
is dedicated to the study of the civil and canonical law of his people*

The sun-kissed comeliness of young Beduin mothers and their plump
brown babies is seen to full advantage in the favoured Tunisian clime

The Beduin woman's fondness for richly coloured clothing and fantastic trinkets detracts nothing from her devotion to her offspring

*The Beduins, or desert dwellers, are a handsome people, tanned
to the colour of the soil over which it is their lot to wander*

The blind beggar and his child guide are a too familiar sight of the " souks " of Tunis and the market-places of any Tunisian town

*Laughter has little place in the eyes of the town Arabs of Tunis,
but the children are as care free as their parents are poverty-stricken*

A kindly humour plays about his eyes, denoting a momentary relaxation of the venerable dignity of this Jewish Rabbi of Tunis city

Like their hardy beasts, these Arab cameleers are tough and sinewy with long tracking about the Tunisian wastes; by day crawling drowsily over the sun-baked sands, by night resting under the limitless African sky

and the scene of Jonah being disgorged by the whale is a favourite subject for pictorial representation in mosaic or terra-cotta in the early Christian Roman remains which are constantly being unearthed by the excavator.

The Mahomedan women of Tunis are even more closely veiled than those of Algiers. Upper class women are practically never seen in the streets of the city, their few journeys being made in carefully screened carriages. The women of the middle class, when they go out, in addition to being veiled, hold in front of them, hanging from their heads, like a curtain, a richly-patterned piece of silk which enables them to see only a few yards of pavement in front of them.

In Algiers the veil affected by the women of the tradesman class is white, crossing the face in two bands, leaving a narrow slit through which the eyes peer. In Tunis a startling effect is produced by the veils being of jet black crape. At the first encounter with one of these black-visaged spectres in the street one starts with a shudder as if one had been suddenly confronted by a ghoul. It takes several days before one can see them without a shock.

The Arab and all his kin squat cross-legged or sit on their heels. The custom seems ineradicable. He does it as instinctively and automatically as a dog turns round several times before going to rest. He squats beside his work when he should be working. He squats at the door of his shop. He

SATIN-BREECHED DAUGHTER OF ISRAEL

Tunisian Jewesses' favourite costume includes a short white muslin dressing-jacket, white satin knee breeches, often richly embroidered, gay socks, small slippers, and on the head a kind of fool's cap of gilt brocade, covered with a veil

squats on a bench at the café sipping coffee or playing chess. He squats on the pavement waiting for the car. If he is provided with a chair he squats on it cross-legged. He has no use for European furniture in his house. The only piece of furniture he understands and appreciates is a mat or a rug. The squatting instinct has been inbred for thousands of years. It was thus that Job and his three friends squatted as they sat among the ashes.

Beggar's assistant is one of the recognized professions in Tunis. As

OBSTINATE CONSERVATISM OF SAWYERS IN TUNIS

Despite their congenital dislike of hard work Orientals display unanimous reluctance to save themselves labour by adopting mechanical appliances not employed by their forefathers. These Arabs on the Tunisian littoral put themselves to the same trouble of readjusting the tree-trunk they are sawing after the severance of each section, as is incurred by the Indian sawyers illustrated in page 2803

TUNISIAN ARTISTS HAND-PAINTING POTTERY

Tunis has enjoyed a merited reputation for its pottery for a hundred years and more, and a considerable number of men are still employed in the industry. Even in the cheapest Tunisian ware the decoration of each piece shows the variation and irregularity that so charmingly distinguish the handiwork of individual craftsmen from the monotony of stereotyped designs mechanically reproduced

WHILING A QUIET HOUR AWAY WITH A GAME OF CARDS

By some authorities the invention of playing cards is assigned to the Arabs. While their origin remains obscure it is probable that they were introduced into Europe either from Arabia in crusading days, or by the Moors when they entered Spain. Naib, or cards, was a widespread amusement among the Arabs, and in Tunis to-day Arabs often enjoy a game of cards over their coffee and pipe

PREHENSILE TOES THAT SUPPLY THE POWER FOR A SIMPLE LATHE

There is no noise of whirring shaft and wheel in this sunlit workshop, for the workman's foot does the work of an "endless band" in turning this crude lathe. Yet the results are sufficiently accurate and symmetrical, as may be gauged from a glance at the chair-leg upon which the Arab boy is working. He braces his heel against a block of wood and holds the tool with his left hand

SUNSHINE AND SHADOW ON BRIGHT COLOURS IN A COBBLED STREET OF TUNIS

From early light to sundown the traders of Tunis, Arabs and Jews, sit at their shops in the various bazaars. On all sides arise the bustle and chatter of bargain and counter-bargain, and the advent of a European is the signal for a sort of general post. Swarms of eager figures in flowing draperies throng round and offer to show the visitor all the sights, though the real object of these touts is to get the supposedly wealthy foreigner into some particular shop and pester him to buy

DESERT SCHOOL IN ITS TEMPORARY QUARTERS BY A SHADY OASIS

Each with his copy of the Koran in his hands, the young pupils squat in a dutiful half-circle about their master. The books consist of a number of leaves, fastened together at the top by a string passed through them. As a rule, these desert wanderers are less strict about the formalities of their faith than the sedentary population of the towns; nor do the women trouble much about being veiled. It is a free life, bounded only by the borders of the desert

STREET LIFE IN THE SOUK EL AASSAR, UNCHANGED SINCE TUNIS WAS RULED BY ITS CWN BEYS

Under French control the native city of Tunis has lost hardly anything of its Arab character. Though cleaner, less malodorous, and much healthier than of yore, there are still winding streets, narrow blind alleys, and open squares that are almost exactly what they were under the jurisdiction of the Beys. Notable among these survivals of the old time is the Souk el Aassar, with its tiny shops packed into the arcaded walls, its cobbled pavement trodden by the slippered feet of turbaned, shrouded Moslems, its flat-roofed, whitewashed cubes of houses, and its unviolated mosque

HOLIDAY TRAFFIC ON THE BYRSA: TRAGIC SITE OF THE ACROPOLIS OF ANCIENT CARTHAGE

History records no more savage atrocity than the obliteration of ancient Carthage by the treachery of her jealous rival, Rome. Of the Punic city that held 700,000 inhabitants, not one stone now stands upon another. On this sun-bathed hill, the Byrsa, stood its principal temples and its citadel, where fifty thousand Carthaginians were crowded on the last day of their agony. Now the site is occupied by the cathedral and monastery of the White Fathers of the Desert, and curious tourists wander through the garden and museums that have replaced the mighty fortress of antiquity

CAMEL-BORNE PALANQUINS FOR ARAB WOMEN IN THE DESERT

Arab women of the better class travel in palanquins resembling square tents erected on the humps of camels. Gaudy striped cloth is stretched round the framework of the tent, giving an odd cage-like effect to the contrivance viewed from a little distance. When on the move over the desert, the servant women walk beside the camels, and men on horseback guard the caravan

you pause at the door of a mosque a stout fellow will run up with some unsightly and shapeless cripple on his back craving alms. As you sit at one of the little tables in front of a café a well-grown lad who in England would be apprenticed to a trade, will lead up a pitiful object whose livid face is scarred with smallpox, will point to his eyes and his dumb outstretched hand, and refuse to move away until a coin has been produced. Next day, or even the same day, he will beset you again if you chance to occupy the same place. If any other beggar ventures to poach upon this hunting-ground he will drive him off with blows and objurgations: his is the first claim to any possible generosity the stranger may be induced to display.

Another man who could earn a good living as a navvy leads an aged dwarf along the pavement appealing to passers-by to notice his misfortunes. It is not always easy to distinguish which is exploiter and which exploited. Each in his way is necessary to the livelihood of the other and can thus demand his rights; nevertheless, I rather fancied that the cripple who was carried up to the door of the mosque was a regular Old Man of the Sea to his assistant.

Tunis is a city of many nationalities, the main elements of which have changed little in thousands of years. The Arabs retain the characteristics of their patriarchal ancestors of the days of Abraham. The " Jews " are to a large extent the survivors of the Phoenicians, a kindred Semitic race.

They are in many respects different from the Jews of other countries. Jezebel, of unhappy memory, was a " Jewess " of this stock. These modern Phoenicians are not only keen traders but excellent craftsmen, and they are very tenacious of their ancient customs, costumes, and social habits.

The Italians and Maltese are a very numerous colony, greatly outnumbering

Jules Ferry, with their shops, their cafés, and their tree-shaded promenades, the Frenchman finds again the Paris that he loves.

The country of Tunis is divided geographically into three well-marked belts. The north is mountainous, enclosing some well-watered and fertile plains like those round the Gulf of Tunis and the valley of the Medjerda.

WITHIN THE COURTYARD OF A TUNISIAN DROVERS' INN

Arab Tunis has a number of old fondouks—inns where the accommodation for man is vastly inferior to that for beast. An entrance passage, with watchmen's benches on either side, leads into a court-yard where the camels can rest, and low arches, set upon antique columns, form a sort of surrounding cloister affording shelter from rain and sun. Doors in the back wall lead into separate stables

Photo, J. Dearden Holmes

the French and keeping to their own quarter, which has all the appearance of an Italian town. These are the modern Romans. They have never forgiven the French for forestalling them in the occupation of Tunis, which Italy had long coveted as her special heritage from the past. In the spacious Avenue de France and Avenue de

The south is desert, diversified by numerous oases in which the date palm yields a golden harvest. Tunis dates are famous all over the world for their excellence. Between the mountains and the desert lies a broad belt of rolling steppes, which in its lower levels, along the coast, is known as the Sahel (coast belt), and is of extraordinary

ARAB DANCING GIRLS PERFORMING IN A PRIVATE HOUSE

Physical undulation is the essential feature of the dance as performed in Tunis by professional dancers.
On a stretched carpet the dancer takes her stand, and, to the thin music of flute and strummed strings,
waves rhythmically on scarcely moving feet, supple fingers, wrists, and arms curving in serpentine
lines, hips swaying. In the Oriental setting the performance is strangely intoxicating to the senses

HUMAN LINK WITH TUNISIA'S IMMEMORIAL PAST

For an indefinite number of hundreds of years serving women like this have been familiar figures in Tunis, patient creatures preserving good humour in joyless conditions. The fashion of the scanty striped skirt is as unchanged as the shape of the fibula brooch, huge ear-rings, and solid silver armlets and bracelets, and the amphora in which water is drawn is of immemorial antiquity in ware and design

YOUTHFUL DONKEY DRIVER RECEIVES HIS HIRE: A WAYSIDE EPISODE

Patient as ever, but under an unusually light load, the donkey stands while his young driver collects his fare. The elder child, in charge of her little sister, carefully watches the transaction that the little one has begged to be allowed to make. Soon she will have other cares, for at thirteen most Tunis girls take the veil, the sign of womanhood, and may be mothers a year later. But now, in the last few years of childhood, she may go about unveiled and free among the teeming, vivid ways of this city of shadow and fierce hatreds, of sunshine and easy laughter

fertility. This central belt of Sahel and steppe was known to the Romans as Byzacium. It is thickly studded, even where now the desert reigns, with the ruins of Roman cities, villages, and villas, showing that at one time it must have been much more densely populated than it is to-day. The soil only requires irrigation to be as fruitful again. Under French rule the Roman prosperity is returning.

In Algeria the French method of colonisation has been by sales and free grants of land to small farmers. The agricultural development of Tunis has been undertaken by great joint-stock companies which have applied their capital to irrigation works and to scientific organization with most gratifying success. Examples of these great estates may be seen at Mateur and Beja, in the Medjerda valley, and at Enfidaville, in the Sahel.

BEDUIN WOMAN OF TUNIS

A Beduin woman who has any pretensions to dress is seldom without a display of her native ornaments. Heavy silver ear-rings, brooches, and necklaces of varied design are much in vogue; this jewelry often representing a good part of the husband's capital

Wheat, olives, grapes, oranges, almonds, figs, and tobacco are produced in abundance. No sight could be more grateful to the eye than the little French town of Enfidaville, with its red roofs and white walls, which has grown up amid the palms and the orange and olive groves. But France has still far to go before the country as a whole reaches the standard of Roman prosperity.

In sharp contrast to the French townships which have sprung up in these favoured areas is the purely Mahomedan town of Kairwan. It lies high up on the steppes in the midst of a plain on which are reared herds of camels, dromedaries, horses, donkeys, sheep,

and goats. Kairwan was founded by the Arab conqueror Sidi Okba thirty-eight years after the death of the Prophet, and it soon became the capital of the Arab Empire in Africa and the most holy of all the Mahomedan cities. Seven pilgrimages to Kairwan are regarded as equal to one to Mecca itself.

At certain seasons Kairwan (or Kairouan) is crowded with pilgrims. Its numerous mosques are full of archæological and architectural interest, and, strangely enough, this most holy city is the only one in which the French have insisted that the mosques should be open to European visitors. The city is still surrounded by the ancient wall, and it

QUIETUDE OF THE MOSQUE AMID THE BABEL OF THE MART

Encased in tiles, illumined to peacock radiance by the brilliant Eastern sunshine, this small mosque is one of many that rise above the welter of little shops huddled around their base in the native quarter of Tunis. Much more punctilious in their religious observances than the average Christian, some Moslems may invariably be found at prayer within these mosques, wherein no infidel may enter

Photo, Donald McLeish

bears few marks of European influence, the small French quarter being situated outside the wall.

Tunis offers a rich field of study for the historian. The ruins of Carthage, buried forty feet underground, are being excavated by the White Fathers, whose museum, beside the modern cathedral on the summit of the Byrsa, or ancient Acropolis, is full of treasure trove. When the Romans laid waste the city of their dreaded rivals, and built another city above the ruins,

they unconsciously preserved for our time the most interesting relics of Phoenician Carthage.

The excavators dug down through the cornland, through the Arab rubbish accumulated for twelve centuries, through the mosaic pavements and broken marble pillars of the early Christian basilica, through the litter of Roman bricks, tiles, pottery, and mutilated statues, and, at the foundation of all, resting on the original soil bed, they came upon all that is left

TUNISIAN WOMANHOOD'S ORNAMENTAL CHARM

Gold coins inherited from ancestresses deck the headdress of young Tunisian women, while a wealth
of barbaric ornaments is suspended over the bosom.   Tattooed marks disfigure their otherwise pleasing
faces; often a tattooed cross may be seen, which some aver, though the meaning no longer exists, was
the sign whereby the converts, when Christianity swept across North Africa, proclaimed their faith

PLUCKING RIPE FRUIT FROM BRANCHES OF DATE-PALM

Grown from the very earliest times, as Assyrian wall-paintings show, the date-palm, which is found near the same latitude between India and the Canary Islands, is still one of the chief objects of cultivation in Tunis and throughout northern Africa. When the fruit has been stripped from the branches these are used for thatching, while a certain quantity is used for religious purposes

MASTERPIECES OF CRAFTSMANSHIP IN COPPER AND BRASS

Some very beautiful Moorish work in copper, brass, and white metal is produced by Tunisian copper-smiths. Lamps, trays, bowls, flagons, and daggers crowd this shop in the souk of the copper-workers, and very noticeable are the beautiful brass jugs for holding potable essences—tall, slim vessels, suggesting coffee-pots, with delicately carved handles and long snaky spouts

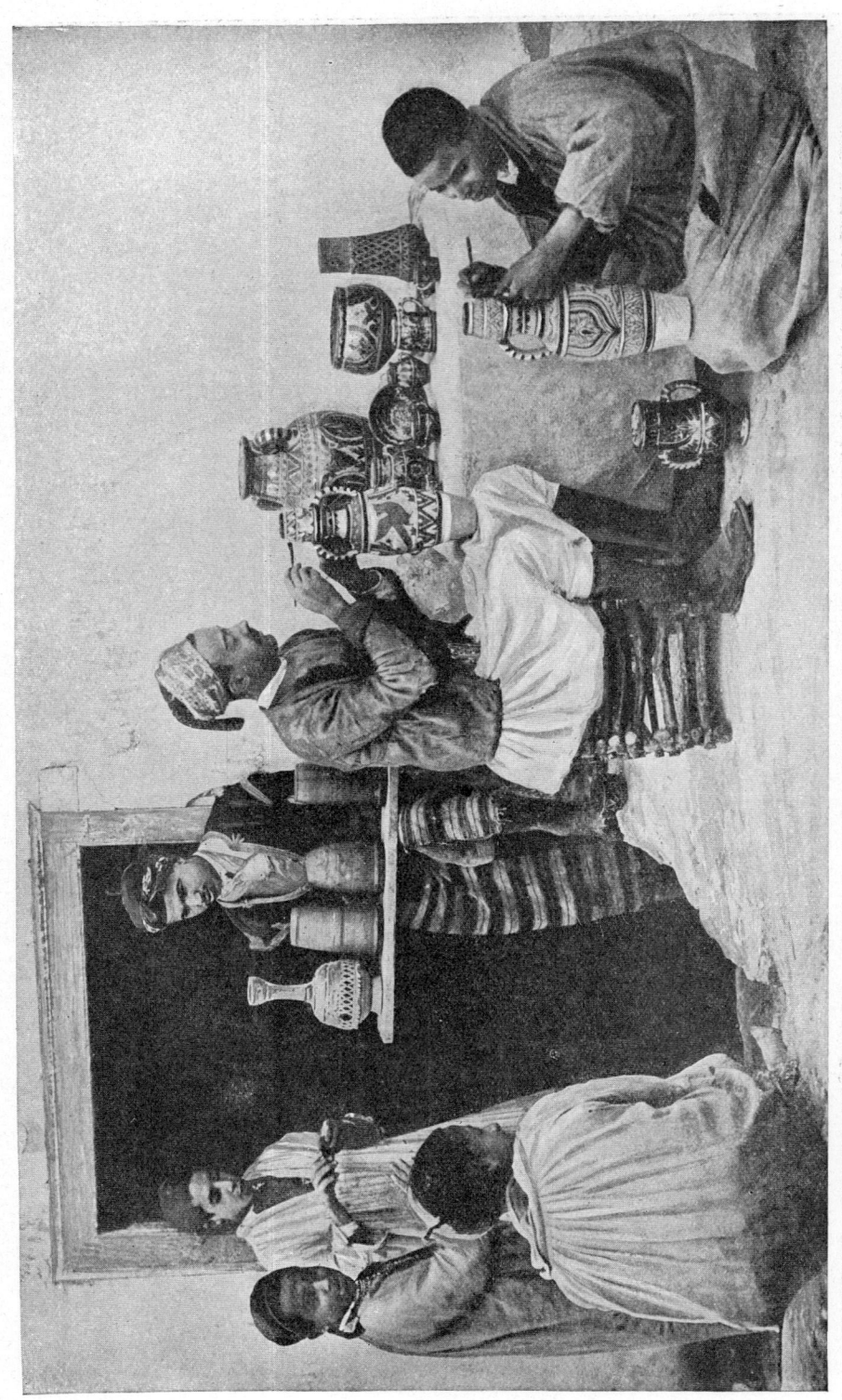

TUNISIAN ARTISTS DECORATING POTTERY WITH DESIGNS FAMILIAR IN THE WORK OF THE ANCIENT GREEKS

Manufacture of pottery has long been a native industry in Tunis, and in the Bab-Souika suburb some beautiful pieces are sold. A principal line of goods is a kind of majolica, mostly green and yellow, fashioned into pitchers of noble size and fine simplicity and into water-bottles of fantastic shape. Another characteristic ware is a pale, reddish-streaked, sun-baked pottery decorated with geometrical or conventional figures in black, both design and shape being almost exact reproductions of prehistoric Greek pottery of the Mycenaean age

TUNIS, "THE WHITE CITY," BASKING IN ITS GLORIOUS SUNSHINE

Tunis is the purest Oriental city in Africa west of Egypt. Viewed from an altitude, as by this cloaked and turbaned Arab, it stretches a dazzling white expanse of rectangular, flat-roofed, stone and plaster houses. The monotony of line and colour is broken by numerous low green-tiled domes of marabouts, and the square towers, encased in variegated tiles, of some five hundred mosques

Photo, G. Long

of Phoenician civilization. The Phoenician tombs, protected for two thousand years by these accumulated ruins, have yielded a vast store of gold and silver trinkets, jewels, amulets, images, carvings, vases, and other articles which throw a flood of light upon the history and social and religious customs of a civilization which was contemporary with King Solomon.

But Carthage does not stand alone. The whole of Tunis, from the sea to the farthest frontiers, deep in the recesses of the mountains and in the oases of the desert, is one vast monument of the splendour of Roman civilization. The gigantic aqueduct which brought the waters of Zaghwan eighty miles to Carthage, the stupendous amphitheatre of El-Djemm rising from the side of a squalid Arab village, the numerous roads and bridges, and

the ruined cities of Dougga, Maetaris Admedera, Sufetula, Cillium, Thelepte, Gigthis, and a dozen others, all bear witness to the previous existence of a prosperity which France exhibits a determination to recreate.

Algeria is governed as an incorporate part of France, represented directly in the Senate and Chamber of Deputies in Paris. Tunis, on the other hand, is a protectorate. The Bey is a member of the Royal Family which has occupied the throne since 1705. The government is controlled by the French Foreign Office much as the Egyptian Government has been controlled by the British Foreign Office in recent years. The form of government is native, but it is a European civilization which they are trying to create. And always they keep before their eyes the example of their great precursor, Rome.

NEED WAITING ON CHARITY AT THE PORTAL OF THE MOSQUE

Beggars are ubiquitous in Tunis, and many of them are repulsive objects. Any physical deformity or affliction is employed to move the compassion of the charitable, and dwarfs and cripples, blind and deaf and dumb, dog the stranger and even employ sturdy assistants to lead or carry them to wherever alms may be forthcoming. The doors of the mosques are always beset by piteous mendicants

Photo, Donald McLeish

Tunis

II. From Carthaginian Empire to French Protectorate

By Edward Wright

Author of "France: Her Colonial Empire," etc.

OF all the oversea possessions of France, Tunis is most deeply coloured with the romance of history. From the legend of Dido and the Trojans to the last tale of the Tunis corsairs, her harbours, fields, and desert tracks glow with glories and adventures of great races.

Probably three and a half thousand years are gone since the merchant seamen of Sidon landed on the coast by old Utica, some twenty miles north-west of Carthage, and dazzled the fair-haired Berbers with bales of purple linen and beads of coloured glass, and obtained so much gold, ivory, and ostrich feathers that they set up trading stations. Then, perhaps in the ninth century B.C., a strong, fierce syndicate of Tyrians, seeing that the best harbour was not being used, took the Bay of Tunis and built a citadel a little north of it, which was known as New Town, or Carthage.

They dug out an extraordinary combination of war port and trading port by their high citadel, and from these great ponds, that still exist, near the still more extraordinary rain-water cisterns which they made in order to withstand sieges, their fleets went out for copper to Spain and for tin to England.

They traded south beyond the Sahara, and explored the coast of Africa at least as far as the Congo. In league with the Persians, they fought the Greeks, and like their successors, the Saracens of Tunis, they made a strong attempt to hold and enslave the old cornland of Sicily.

They conquered Sardinia and Corsica, and established the first connexion between Gaul and Tunis by occupying, some time before 500 B.C., a considerable part of the Gulf of Lyons.

Then, from 264 to 201 B.C., ancient Tunis rose to her supreme and terrible height of power. Her son, Hannibal, rocked civilization to its foundations by his victories over the armies of Rome. It was only through party dissensions in Carthage itself, destroyed by the Romans in 146 B.C., that the world was saved from all the ghastly and licentious rites now buried under the ruins of its former greatness.

In the early Christian period the mingled Carthaginian and Berber stock of Tunis exercised a religious influence upon the world by the school of thought of S. Augustine. Every modern Protestant, with a Calvinist strain of belief, has his spiritual home in Carthage. Thus strangely yet directly has the old capital of Tunis become the sacred city of Scotland, Wales, and a large part of Canada and the U.S.A.

Some centuries after the fall of the Roman Empire Tunis again became a scene of picturesque splendour and far-reaching intellectual influence. The German and Slav mixture of Vandals of the fifth century A.D. concentrated

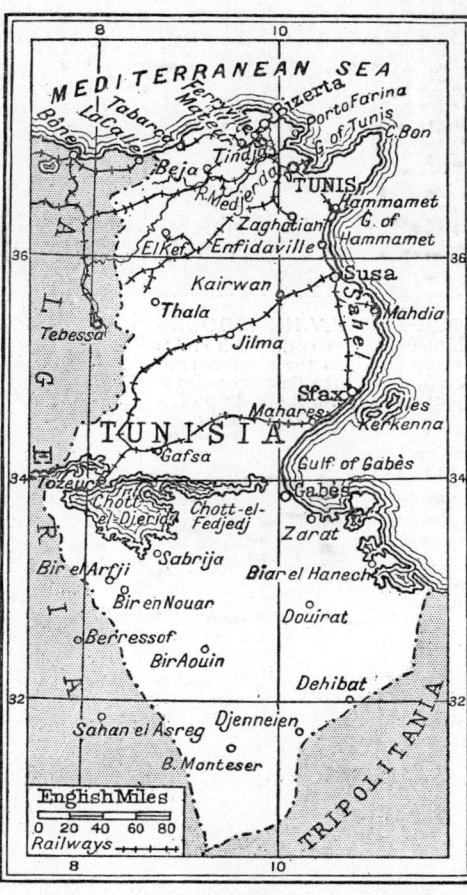

FRENCH PROTECTORATE OF TUNIS

WHERE "SOUL-DISSOLVING ODOURS INVITE TO MYSTERY"

Heavy with the blend of many aromas is the Souk el Attarine, or Street of Perfumes, in the Arab quarter of Tunis. Here every shop sells the essence of sweet flowers—jasmine, musk favoured of the Prophet, lilac, iris, ambergris, sandal tree, dainty orange flower, refreshing vervain, heliotrope, citron and bergamot, and sensuous carnation, a single drop of any of which suffices to enchant the senses

Photo, Underwood Press Service

in Tunis, and, using Carthage as their fortress, won a considerable part of Hannibal's old empire, including Corsica, and starved and pillaged Rome. When the Vandals fell, and the Byzantines weakened, the Saracens came in the seventh century, and, after some fighting, settled below Carthage, and there built the romantic, mysterious, forbidden city of Kairwan.

Then it was that Tunis once more became a centre of radiant culture. The thinkers and artists of Kairwan spread the influence of Moslem liberalism through the conquered territory of Sicily to the European mainland.

In the next period of their own subjection to invading Normans they increased their influence rather than diminished it, by bringing about an amalgamation of Christian and Mahomedan arts and ideas in the eleventh and twelfth

centuries. The end of this movement of enlightenment, to which was largely due the greatest awakening of the European spirit since the Greek renaissance of the seventh century B.C., was followed by the disastrous crusade of S. Louis of France, who died by Carthage in 1270.

Meanwhile, the Arabs of Kairwan had been overcome by the reactionary movement of thought in Islam itself. Liberalism of mind was repressed by a new school of narrow puritans, and the Arab intellect began to sink into the bog of ignorance from which it has not yet re-emerged, leaving to the European mind the task of building the modern temple of knowledge. Menaced by united Christendom the Tunisians, while fighting the nomad Berbers for the gold and ostrich trade of the Central Sudan, built piratic fleets to prey on Mediterranean commerce. At

TUNIS & ITS STORY

the end of the fifteenth century they were reinforced by many fugitive Moors from Spain, raging with a passion for revenge and possessing means to fit out pirate ships. Spaniards, Genoese, and Knights of S. John closed round Tunis. As the sea rovers were in danger, help arrived in the person of the renegade Greek Horuk Barbarossa, who made Tunis Harbour the centre of his predatory expeditions. His large robber state was placed under the overlordship of the Ottoman Empire in the first part of the sixteenth century, and with Turkish crews and garrisons of Turkish Janissaries, the natives were oppressed while the Mediterranean trade was being broken.

Charles V. of Germany conquered Tunis in 1535, in the hope of freeing Christian commerce, but the city was recovered by the Janissaries, who parted from Turkey, and set up their own monarchs, known as Deys. Amid incessant wars and assassinations of their puppet kings, the Tunisians continued to prey upon the merchantmen of Europe. Among their celebrated captives were Cervantes, whom they sold in Algiers in 1575, and S. Vincent de Paul, whom they brought to Tunis slave-market in 1605.

The moneys obtained as ransom for Christians were an important source of income for the Dey, who was more often than not an old corsair, selected for the throne by the Janissaries by reason of his wealth.

In 1705, at the end of a civil war, a soldier of fortune, Hussein-ben-Ali, won the throne, took the title of Bey of Tunis, made the country practically independent of Turkey, and founded the dynasty still reigning under the protection of France. In 1811 his descendant, Bey Hamouda, made himself absolute monarch by the ruthless slaughter of all the Janissaries who used to control him.

For some time piracy continued in a mild form. England had, from the age of Cromwell onward, sent fleets to Tunis to enforce treaties on Dey and Bey for the protection of her merchant ships. France had taken the same course, and by several bombardments, ending with a threat from Napoleon, had won the position of the most favoured nation. In 1816 the British Fleet, under Lord Exmouth, imposed upon the Bey a treaty for the abolition of slavery and the suppression of piracy.

This, however, had no more effect than any of the past treaties, and was observed only so long as the hostile fleet was off the shore. The Bey needed piratic revenue to maintain his state and pomp. It had become the general custom of great maritime Powers to pay him a subsidy for free passage for their merchant ships. Usually it was only when the subsidy was in arrear that the vessels of a great Power were attacked. This subsidy system was finally ended in 1830 by the French Government, after the capture of Algiers. Seized with panic and fearful of giving an occasion for attack, the Bey of Tunis agreed to abolish the enslavement of Christians and also to abandon piracy.

A succession of Beys then tried to reform their country, but the lack of the old subsidies made each attempted reform a step to national bankruptcy. As the end grew nearer Italy contended against France for possession of the little African State, which was falling sadly in population as well as in money power. Italy wanted Tunis as a balance against French Algeria, but she was forestalled, the Bey, on May 12, 1881, signing a treaty which placed himself and his country under the protection of France, a liberty which was consummated by the agreement with Ali-Bey, June 8, 1883.

TUNIS : FACTS AND FIGURES

The Country

Extends for about 550 miles along the Mediterranean coastline between Algeria and Tripolitania, which form the boundaries on the west and south-east respectively. North and east is the Mediterranean. The north coast district and the north central regions are hilly and fertile, and there are a number of almost perennial streams. Farther into the interior the hills become desert steppes and merge into the Sahara. There are a number of salt lakes, many of which dry up in summer. Total area about 50,000 square miles, with a European population of about 156,000 and an estimated native population of 1,938,000.

Government and Constitution

Country is ruled by a native Bey, who holds the sovereignty under French protectorate. Government is in hands of French Foreign Office represented by a French Resident-General, who is assisted by a ministry of eight French and three Tunisian members. Territory is divided into nineteen districts for administrative purposes, the chief official in each district being French, and assisted by native subordinates.

Commerce and Industries

Main industry is agriculture. Chief crops are barley, wheat, and oats. Vines, olives, and dates are cultivated, as well as almonds, pistachios, oranges, lemons, alfa grass, cork-trees, and henna. Among minerals are phosphates, lead-ore, iron, and zinc-ore. Native industries include carpet and wool weaving, saddlery, leather embroidery, and pottery. Fisheries are developed and yield anchovies, tunny, and sardines. Imports, valued at £28,868,008 in 1921, include textiles, manufactured metals, and mealy foods. Among main exports are marble, stone and minerals, crude metals, and grain. Total exports for same year valued at £26,915,756. French coinage is in use.

Chief Towns

Tunis, capital (estimated population 171,600), Bizerta (20,700), Ferryville (4,600), Tindja (1,500).

CONSTANTINOPLE'S MOST FAMOUS EDIFICE: ONCE A CHRISTIAN BASILICA AND NOW A MOSLEM MOSQUE

The glory of the Aya Sophia Mosque is within : in the majestic sweep of its mighty dome, its columns of porphyry and verd antique, its splendid mosaics. At the apex of the dome is the intricate tracery in Arabic of the passage from the Koran beginning, " God is the Light of Heaven and Earth," a thought symbolised by thousands of tiny lamps. Dedicated to Christian worship in 537 on the site of a basilica founded by Constantine in 326, it became a Moslem mosque in 1453, and was restored by an Italian architect in 1847

Photo, H. C. Woods

Turkey

I. Sombre Life of the Turkish Peasantry

By H. A. Milton

Author and Traveller

WHATEVER may be said concerning the government or the ruling class in Turkey, no one who has lived in the country long enough to understand the character of the peasants who form the bulk of the true Turkish population speaks of it with anything but respect. In them the savagery of the Turanian strain, that strain which gave the original Turkish invaders of Europe so bad a reputation, has been softened by Arabic influence and Moslem teaching.

The Turk on the soil is hard-working, faithful to his word, sober, straight in his dealings, honourable according to his lights. His existence is very simple, monotonous, comfortless. He lives, if he is a dweller on the plain, in a mud hut ; only the hill people build their houses of stone.

His possessions are limited. He may be the owner of a small piece of land ; in this case he is better off than the peasants who farm the lands of large proprietors. The latter work on partnership lines. The proprietor finds the land and the seed for growing — wheat, barley, maize, rye, oats, and sesame, which are the chief grain crops. The tiller of the soil contributes his labour and that of his oxen or buffaloes.

The theory of the system is that they divide the result of the harvest between them. In practice it often happens that the cultivator, ignorant, accustomed to being robbed, unable to stand out for his rights, gets a share of the crops far smaller than that which ought to come to him. The only method of keeping accounts which is generally understood by him is cutting notches on a stick. He can easily be cheated, and he has no remedy. A bad landlord can always win an action by bribing the judge, which the peasant has not the means to do. The landlord's agent too frequently trades upon the peasants' helplessness, even if the landlord himself is of a fair-dealing disposition.

In addition to being thus deprived of their just earnings, the cultivators are also kept in bondage to the landowners by the debts which burden them growing heavier year by year. In their cottages they have seldom anything beyond the bare necessaries of life. Bedding, rugs, stools, perhaps a rough divan, a few pots for cooking and storing, a few dishes, a shelf or two, maybe an

PRAYER FROM THE MINARET

From the minarets of all Moslem mosques, five times a day, rises the call to universal prayer, which the muezzin repeats at each of the four points of the compass

Photo, Kadel & Herbert

METHODS OF CEREMONIAL LUSTRATION AS PRACTISED BY MOSLEMS

In Islam are enjoined two degrees of ablution—the Ghost, or immersion in water of the whole body, and the Wodhu, or Abtest, the washing, after a prescribed manner and to the accompaniment of appropriate prayer, of the parts of the body usually exposed—hands, arms, face (including mouth and nostrils), head and feet. Where water is unprocurable, the use of clean sand is permissible

ancient walnut-wood press. Their time is divided between work and sleep. Their food is of the simplest. They smoke a little, using the long-stemmed pipe which stands on the ground, and draw the smoke through water. They drink thick coffee, very much sweetened, out of tiny cups. By their religion they are forbidden to touch wine or any drink containing alcohol.

In the Christian villages of Turkey, among the Greek, Bulgarian, Armenian populations, you hear music, you see the young men and women dancing; there are gatherings on Sunday and on occasions of religious festival outside the church. The true Turks, who are Mahomedans, do not feel the need of social distractions. Their idea is that when a man leaves off work, he should spend his time at home and find his recreation with his family.

They are a grave, dignified, rather melancholy race. Whatever befalls them is " the will of Allah." They are contented because they are convinced that resignation is the only wisdom, and because they have never known, or even imagined, any other mode of existence than that which they follow. Ages of mechanical toil and relentless oppression have turned them into beings more like automata than men naturally endowed with intelligence and power of initiative.

Turkish peasants cannot read or write; they have not among their folk-lore a wealth of stories, told by one generation to another, filling the minds of the young with notions of history, with illuminating fable and moral apologue, with national tradition.

The peasant may play, perhaps, upon a little pipe cut by himself, or upon a very simple form of bagpipes, the bag being of sheepskin, and the notes being blown through a reed. But music brings into his life no gaiety, no joy. His tunes are melancholy and monotonous, nearly all in a minor key. They seem to be an expression of his fatalist attitude towards existence.

The stories that are told among the countryfolk are mostly about genii or jinns, fables in which animals endowed with speech and reasoning power play a part, or broadly comic anecdotes illustrating the greed of priests and the hireling injustice of judges. Sometimes they poke fun at women, as in the tale of the man who wanted to make a present to a warrior chieftain in order to curry favour with him. He asked his wife whether she would advise him to offer figs or quinces. His wife advised quinces. " Then," said her husband, " I shall take figs! "

When the figs were presented, the warrior frowned, seized the basket, and began to throw the fruit at the unlucky giver. As he did this he heard the man say: " Thanks be to Allah that I did not take my wife's advice," and inquired what this meant. The man explained. " If I had done as she wished," he said, " I should have had my head broken

WRAPPED IN QUIET CONTEMPLATION OF HOLY WRIT

Having performed the necessary ablutions—for no good Moslem dare repeat the name of God with unclean lips—this aged inhabitant of Constantinople is reading and repeating the sacred words of the Koran. He is seated in quietude in a shady corner of the courtyard of the Mosque of Mohammed II., place of prayer and worship regarded as second in holiness only to that of Eyúb

Photo, Special Press

READING THE KORAN IN THE MOSQUE OF AHMED

This Constantinople mosque was built by Ahmed I. in 1608-14, and is the only one, apart from the Kaaba at Mecca, that has six minarets. These Moslem houses of prayer consist usually of a large open court with fountain, arcades, niche indicating the direction of Mecca, pulpit, and platform or platforms raised on columns from which the Koran is read and the congregation is led in prayer

Photo, Sébah & Joaillier

COFFEE AND CIGARETTES AT A MODEST CARAVANSERAI
Turkish workers are accustomed to resort, in the early morning, to some convenient " kafené "
there to enjoy the solace and stimulus afforded by coffee and tobacco before beginning their daily
toil, and to return later in the day as opportunity may offer for similar refreshment. To all
classes in Turkey the coffee-cup and the pipe or cigarette have become everyday necessaries
Photo, Georg Haeckel

by the hard quinces. How fortunate for
me that I brought figs. How wise I
was not to take a woman's advice ! "

Turkish methods of agriculture are
pretty much those of Old Testament
times. A wooden plough is used, it has
one handle, and is generally drawn by
buffaloes. Threshing is done with a
great log of wood studded with flints.
This is drawn by ponies, the driver,
usually a girl, standing upon it. Round
and round, over the grain stalks laid
upon the earth, go the ponies, and when
the grain is ready for winnowing, it is
thrown up into the air from big wooden
shovels and so separated from the husks.

No regular manuring is done save by
the few who have studied Western
ways ; the benefits of a scientific
rotation of crops are unknown to the
small farmers. It is only because
the soil is naturally rich, and has not
been made poor by having heavy crops
taken off it, that they can make a living.

The climate helps them, too. The
winters are cold, but the sun is powerful
early in the year, and turns spring into
summer very quickly, so quickly, indeed,
that there is scarcely any spring at all.
The crops are soon ripe, therefore, and
yield bountifully except when they are
destroyed by a long drought. When

that happens, the consequences are disastrous. Not only is the harvest ruined; the cattle die for want of water, or else have to be sold at pitifully small prices to anyone who can take them out of the dry area.

Even when the peasants have no hindrance thrown in their way by nature, they cannot count upon enjoying the full fruit of their labour. They have to pay tithes for the benefit of the Moslem priesthood. Over and above these demands, they have to satisfy the private claims of the tax-collectors, who pay so much for the privilege of making the collection and expect to get rich by fleecing the wretched peasants of whatever sums can be extorted from them in addition to the amounts for which as taxpayers they are legally liable.

There is no just and formal plan of assessment. The tax-collector demands from each locality as much as he reckons it can pay. The local council has to find the money, and by it the share of each individual is apportioned. The members meet to debate the financial position of each other and of all the heads of families in the district. Often the men whose burdens they are adjusting stand anxiously round, listening to what is said about them, and putting in their word every now and then in the hope of convincing the council that they are poorer than is generally believed.

Being so ignorant and superstitious, with a fanatical belief in the truth of what his rulers tell him, the Turk is unhappily persuaded, without much difficulty, to commit atrocious crimes

EAST AND WEST IN A CONSTANTINOPLE THOROUGHFARE
Western influence is seen in the tall buildings rising in the background of the photograph; East meets West in the shops seen in the foreground. Kindred contrasts offer themselves in the varied dress and callings of the passers-by, and the camera has caught a characteristic feature of town life everywhere by including pert-eyed, apron-wearing youth and black-coated official dignity

LITTLE WAYFARERS IN A STREET OF STAMBOUL
Turkish children, boys especially, are allowed much more liberty than is usual in Western countries, and kindness to children is so universal that it is seldom one hears a child cry unless it be in pain

Photo, Merl La Voy

made no complaint) are to be accounted for by the incitements of those in authority who carried out these horrors.

If the Turks had been civilized, they would have to bear their full share of the shame; they would rightly be thought of as fiends rather than normal human beings. But when they are inflamed by fanatical hatred and fear, when they are told that the killing or the torture of Christians will ensure them places of honour in Paradise, they cease to be responsible for their acts. They are intoxicated, obsessed. The whole guilt must be borne by those who incited them, deceived them, used them as instruments for the perpetration of atrocities almost passing belief.

In the big towns or their suburbs rich Armenians have very fine houses and delightful gardens, in which they take a special pleasure. They are Oriental in many of their habits, although they are Christians, and inclined to adopt Western ideas. Women who appear in public dressed in the European style according to the latest fashions, will wear at home and in the gardens, where they spend a good deal of their time, the costume of the Turkish lady, billowy trousers and tunic with loose slippers and a coquettish little cap on the head. In more remote parts the women even cover their faces when they go out, just as Mahomedan women do.

In these parts many old customs are still maintained, such as keeping the

when the savage and intolerant side of his nature is deliberately aroused. Left to himself he is ready to " live and let live "; he is kindly and hospitable to strangers; he lives on good terms with his Christian neighbours. The massacres of the Armenians, for which both Abdul Hamid and the Young Turks will for ever be execrated, and the brutalities practised upon British prisoners of war in certain camps (though the greater number

cattle close to the rooms in which the family live, sitting on divans or on a floor strewn with rugs, taking meals off a tray on a stand instead of sitting down to table, sleeping on the flat roofs in the hot weather, and dwelling in patriarchal groups. When sons marry, they do not set up for themselves in their own houses; they bring their wives to live with their parents. This leads often to a great deal of quarrelling and discomfort.

There is an Armenian proverb which says: "In the happy home only one woman rules." In order to arrive at this consummation, so devoutly to be wished by all who love a quiet life, many Armenian households try to keep up the ancient practice which deprived a daughter-in-law of the right even to speak to any of her seniors in the house. In the presence of his parents she was forbidden even to say anything to her husband. But the emancipation of women from their disabilities and restrictive bonds is reaching even into the valleys and hillsides of the Caucasus. This old law of the household will soon be a memory and no more. Even among the Turks, whose religion

ACQUIRING "LEGAL PURITY" IN THE SHADOW OF THE MOSQUE

Provided that his face be turned towards Mecca, the devout Moslem may pray in a public thoroughfare as properly as in the privacy of his home, but before entering the house of prayer he must perform the "Abtest," in other words become "legally pure" by washing hands and forearms, face and feet in running water, which is provided by the fountains attached to every mosque

sets women in an inferior state, there have been noticeable changes in the life of the harem during the last twenty or thirty years. Up to the latter period of the nineteenth century very few of the harem ladies could read or write. They did not miss the solace of books, they had no curiosity about events in the world beyond their own

the outlook of Turkish women belonging to the higher rank of society.

Turkish men of this class are usually well-informed and sharp-witted, especially if they are in public life, though they may on occasion take some pains not to let their intelligence be noticed. Many of them are sent to foreign universities, generally French or German.

ONE OF THE TWO BRIDGES CROSSING THE GOLDEN HORN

Here we see part of the famous Galata, or New Bridge, connecting Stamboul with Galata and Pera, and ever presenting a moving panorama full of colour and variety as the busy tide of traffic flows between the Place Emin Onu and Karakoï Street, or goes to and from the steamers that use the side pontoon as a pier. About 500 yards in length, its roadway is 35 feet wide

walls, it was not considered necessary that a woman should be educated in the modern sense.

Now, all girls of the comfortable class go to school. They read novels and memoirs. They study history. Many of them write, some of them have published books. There was, as long as thirteen years ago, a newspaper for women published in Constantinople. The French novelist, Pierre Loti, wrote a good many years back a novel ("Désenchantées") describing, after a visit to Turkey, the complete change that had been made by education in

The higher officials can discuss their own and other countries with knowledge and sense, and they often appear to take the Western point of view. They admit that there are plenty of defects and absurdities in the mode of government, but they steadily oppose any proposals for change which would bring the Turkish nearer to the European system.

They used to make fun of the attempts made to keep out of Turkey books which the authorities feared as likely to disturb the minds of those who read them—books in which the Sultan was mentioned, even favourably mentioned :

STEEP SHOP-LINED THOROUGHFARE LEADING TO PERA

Beyond the quays between the bridges on the north bank of the Golden Horn, which divides Stamboul, the Turkish quarter of Constantinople, from the European parts of Galata and Pera, rises steeply a succession of narrow streets, some little more than stone stairways, with houses closely built on either side. The photograph shows one of these streets, with shops kept by Greek and other traders

Photo, Georg Haecke.

VISITING A FRUIT-SELLING MART IN OLD STAMBOUL

The European here seen making his way between the stalls of the fruit-venders is attracting much native curiosity. Throughout Turkey, while fruits are plentiful, they are consumed chiefly in candied form, or in syrups. The chief ingredients of the normal Turkish menu are vegetables, particularly tomatoes, onions, and garlic, the seasoning including pepper, lemon, sugar, and honey. Pilaf is a dish of rice or macaroni cooked with butter or fat, with gravy or tomatoes; but in one form it includes chopped chicken mixed with rice and seasoned with mutton grease, saffron, pepper, tomatoes, and honey

Photo, S. E. Towers

books which contained references to their religion ; books which the Censor considered "immoral," such as the works of Shakespeare, Victor Hugo, La Fontaine, and most modern authors of note. There was a censorship of plays not less annoying and ridiculous. Even the amusements of the foreign colony in Constantinople were sometimes interfered with. The rule of the Sultans, like the rule of the Tsars in Russia, was based on fear ; both knew that they could only hold their positions by force. Both were trying to keep a nation under by antiquated devices.

There was this difference, however ; while in Russia there was a large and constantly increasing number of people eager for a more enlightened system, in Turkey the nation endured the vagaries of its rulers without desiring to get rid of them. They shrugged their shoulders and put up with them as they put up with bad weather—because they could not do otherwise. The most that can be hoped is that they may be governed by men more honest and conscientious than those who have been their rulers hitherto.

What the Turks have left Undone

The founders of the Turkish Empire were a tribe which wandered out of Central Asia, overturned the authority of the Emperors of the East, captured Byzantium (Constantinople) in 1275, next conquered the Balkan countries, and established a vast dominion in Europe, in addition to their Asiatic possessions. Never from their first appearance until this day have the Turks advanced in civilization, founded any tradition of good government, or showed any wish to march forward with the European nations to the conquest of ignorance, superstition, disease.

They have made no contributions to science or the arts. They have shown nothing of the ingenuity and enthusiasm for learning and for the application of ideas to life which characterised the Arabs during their stay in Spain. If the Turkish race were to be exterminated, as its rulers tried to exterminate the Armenians, it would leave no trace of useful activity behind it. It would be remembered merely as a race which, wherever it governed, governed badly ; which pusillanimously allowed itself to be robbed and kept in submission ; which supported its rulers in their age-long fight against progress, and added nothing to the sum of human happiness.

Bustling Life of Bridge and Bazaar

No one who has been in the East can fail to recall many scenes like that which impressed its dreary barren aspect upon Kinglake's imagination and was transferred to the pages of his " Eothen." Even in the capital one has sometimes the same feeling of deadness and desolation. Not certainly in the bazaars or on the bustling Galata Bridge which joins fascinating ancient Stamboul, the city of the Turks, to the dull and pretentious European quarter, Pera, which lies across the Golden Horn.

On this broad thoroughfare there is always a throng. Here you may see men of every race that the Turks have ruled. Greeks abound, as they do in all Turkish towns. Jews and Armenians of reverend appearance hurry over with business in their wary eyes. Circassians, Georgians, Kurds from beyond the Caucasus, Bulgarians, Syrians, jostle the true Osmanli Turks, descendants of the warriors who laid the foundations of the empire upon massacre and robbery and barbarism. These true Turks are employed for the most part as beasts of burden. On their backs they carry all kinds of merchandise.

The Great Turkish Illusion

Yet they do not conceal their contemptuous glances at foreigners, and even at their fellow-subjects who are not Osmanlis.

For the Turk is proud. He holds his head high, remembering that he belongs to the conquering race and deeming

CITY WITHIN A CITY: ONE OF THE THREE THOUSAND SHOPS IN STAMBOUL'S GRAND BAZAAR

Enclosed within high walls, pierced with innumerable lanes and alleys, and covered by a roof decked with cupolas, the famous Grand Bazaar in Stamboul has a circumference of about a mile. Goods of Orient and Occident are massed in amazing diversity, and the place is nearly always crowded. Reminders of a time when all the shopkeepers sat sphinx-like and cross-legged upon a bit of matting, smoking, and outwardly indifferent to custom, still linger, but most of the shops, erected since the earthquake of 1894, are glass-fronted and supplied with chairs. Purchases, however, are still the result of more or less animated bargaining

Photo, Sebah & Joaillier

OFFERINGS IN KIND FROM THE FAITHFUL ON THE STEPS OF THE YENI VALIDEH JAMI MOSQUE AT STAMBOUL

When the traveller crosses from Galata to Stamboul by the New Bridge over the Golden Horn, among the first things to arrest his attention are the fine lines of the Yedi Valideh Jami, the mosque built for the mother of Ahmed I. One of the more notable of the 379 mosques in Constantinople, this building was begun in 1615, but, owing to damage by fire in 1660, was not completed until 1663. During the month of Ramadan, when the faithful fast from sunrise to sunset, and the well-to-do turn the night into day, this mosque is brilliantly illuminated

4981

himself superior to the conquered. This has always been a Turkish illusion. They are entirely self-satisfied, mainly for the reason that they are taught to believe themselves the chosen of Allah. They have learned nothing from the nations which came under their sway. They could not suppose that the "infidels" had anything to teach them. Their dignity would have been wounded if they were told that they had missed great opportunities. Dignity is most often a cloak for stupidity, a bluff which is put up to hide vacuity of mind.

In the bazaars the selling is mainly done by the despised "infidels." With tempting skill the wares are set out. Nothing could be more agreeable than the stalls of the dried-fruit merchants, with their pyramids of sultanas, currants, figs, dates, apricots, and other fruits beyond count. Sweetmeats are arranged, too, with a profusion and daintiness which make one's mouth water. In the metal-workers' bazaars the din of the smiths is deafening, but it is well worth enduring in order to see how cleverly they make and mend. In the street of the carpet and rug sellers all who love colour and exquisite design can spend many profitable hours.

All goods must be bought by the process of bargaining. There are no fixed prices. The seller usually asks twice as much as he expects to get. The purchaser offers half of what he is prepared to give. Many visits will probably be paid by the customer before agreement is reached.

It is this habit of perpetual bargaining which has helped to make the Turks as a nation so fluent in speech. They are never at a loss for words. They are equally fertile in flattery and in abuse. They have always been accustomed also to plead their own causes

LEISURED LABOUR ON THE BANKS OF THE BUSY BOSPORUS

Many pens have described the grandeur of the scenery along the tortuous waterway dividing Europe from Asia and linking the Euxine or Black Sea with the Propontis or Sea of Marmora. Here is a vivid photographic glimpse of the kaleidoscopic life that ebbs and flows about its landing-stages— burly boatmen and hefty porters as notable for their physique as for the diversity of their dress

IN A MOMENT OF EMERGENCY: HOME FLITTING BY WATER

If one is amazed by the ease with which colossal burdens are borne by the Turkish hamal or porter, no less surprise is experienced by all who for the first time come into contact with the dexterity and skill of the Turkish boatman. Topheavy as appear many of the loaded boats seen in this photograph, they can be navigated with combined ease and safety to their destination

Photo, Underwood Press Service

before courts of law. They have acquired, apparently from this, the knack not merely of talking well, but of making speeches. Listen to a dispute among them, and you will hear orations. Notice the bargaining that goes on over a piece of meat or a cauliflower. It is not carried on in crisp sentences, but in long, complicated arguments.

Their style of speech is roundabout and flowery. Instead of saying to a visitor " I am glad to see you," a Turk declares that " most blessed among hours is this the hour of your coming." And at the end of a visit his form of words for " Pleasant journey to you," is something like this : " Proud are the sires and blessed are the dams of the steeds that shall carry your excellency to the end of your prosperous journey. May the saddle beneath you glide down to your destination like a boat swimming on the third river of Paradise. May you sleep the sleep of a child who knows

MOSLEM FUNERAL PROCESSION ON ITS WAY THROUGH THE STREETS OF STAMBOUL

In Turkey the dead are borne to the burial-place on the shoulders of the living, the bearers being continually relieved by others from the following procession of male mourners. The coffin, if it be that of a man, bears upon it the turban or fez of the deceased; if of a woman, her coif. The first part of the burial service is read at a mosque, where an imam remains awhile after the mourners have departed to prompt the deceased in answering the questions believed to be put to his soul concerning his faith by the angels Mounkir and Nekir

Photo, Meri La Voy

WHIRLING DERVISHES IN CONSTANTINOPLE: A FORM OF WORSHIP THAT HAS EXISTED FOR SEVEN HUNDRED YEARS

Distinguished for their real piety among the thirty orders of dervishes are the Mevlavi, or whirling dervishes, whose headquarters are at Konieh. Their performances, dating from the early part of the thirteenth century, are marked throughout with austere solemnity. While an imam reads from the Koran, some of the dervishes play the pipes, and others again form part of the congregation; a number stand with eyes fixed on the ground. Then the leader of this group begins a solemn dance which gradually turns to a whirl in which his companions join, and which is slow or incredibly rapid, according to the rhythm of the music

Photo, Sébah & Joaillier

4985

TOILERS BY THE SEA: HOW TURKISH DOCK PORTERS TRANSPORT CUMBERSOME LOADS FROM SHORE TO SHIP

If not a tiller of the soil or an official, the able-bodied Turk often becomes a porter. He is frequently seen alone carrying a colossal load through streets where wheeled traffic is impossible. Here we see a group of hamals working at Constantinople docks, the weight of the loads being distributed by means of stout poles. Labour is cheap in the Turkish capital, and the worker's dream of happiness is expressed in the wish that one day he may be able to say : "Soul, take thine ease, for thou hast much goods laid up for many years"

Photo, Sébah & Joaillier

that friends are around him. And if enemies should come in your way, may your eyes flame through the darkness at them, redder than the eyes of ten tigers, to frighten them off."

People who have time to talk in that redundant fashion are, it is quite clear, never likely to be in a hurry. Business in Turkey is done at a very leisurely pace, if it ever gets done at all. By business must be understood official business, for the true Turk very seldom occupies himself with any other. Educated Turks, with scarcely any exceptions, become either officers or officials, that is, if they take up any active pursuit.

There is no hereditary rich and noble class. Property must be divided on the death of its owner among all his children, daughters as well as sons. That breaks up wealth almost as fast as it is accumulated. There are no hereditary titles. Indeed, the only Turkish title of honour is Pasha, which is not passed on from father to son.

Credit Side of the Osmanlis

The pride of the Osmanlis has been a bar to the growth of privileged and moneyed families. They are all supposed to be on the same level. The Caliph is the one man who stands above the rest, and that more in virtue of his responsibility as Commander of the Faithful than of his temporal position. Thus, although their government is despotic, the Turks are democratic in their social organization. Any Osmanli, however, meanly born, may climb the official ladder and become the chief minister or grand vizier as the holder of this post is still called, reminding us of the adventures of Haroun-al-Raschid and the " Arabian Nights Entertainments."

Absence of snobbery is therefore one of the more attractive qualities which arise out of the Turkish refusal to make changes. Another is the absence of destitution as all Western cities have known it, and the rarity of crime.

There is no criminal class. Miss Lucy Garnett, who spent many years in Turkey and described it as it was towards the end of the nineteenth century, in a very interesting little book " Turkish Life in Town and Country," could not recall a single burglary during her long residence in the country. Acts of violence are uncommon. There are in certain regions brigands who kidnap persons for whom large ransom can be demanded, but they are looked upon almost as professional men, engaged in an ancient and not discreditable calling.

The Lure of a Little Brigandage

Several English travellers have been captured by them during quite recent years. The brigands are mostly bad characters who have been obliged to fly from justice, or discontented peasants with a passion for adventure. But it sometimes happens that respectable young men take to brigandage for a time, in order to make a little money or for the sake of a change. From time to time forces of soldiers are sent into the mountains to clear out these pests, but as often as not it has happened that the soldiers have been satisfied to exact from the brigands a share of their booty as the price of leaving them alone.

Fatalism and Agreeable Apathy

Apart from this war against society, which is carried on sometimes as a form of political agitation, crimes against the person are infrequent. The sober habits which are imposed upon Moslems by their religion are partly the cause of this, as partly also is the fatalist nature of the Turk, which makes him lethargic and long-suffering, disinclined to pick quarrels or to brood over injuries real or supposed.

They are an orderly folk. In the streets they move about quietly and with a subdued air. There is among them little of the laughter and chatter which go on among Western crowds. When

"NOT MADE TO RULE, BUT TO SUBSERVE": THE TURKISH PORTER

Cabs, trams, and motor-cars are now familiar features of the street life of Constantinople, while the favourite public conveyances are the boats plying on the water surrounding the main divisions of the city. Meanwhile, here, as elsewhere in the Turkish dominions, the hefty hamal or porter continues to perform prodigious feats of physical strength in the transport of goods of all kinds

ORIENTAL AUTOLYCUS HAWKING HIS WARES IN THE MARKET PLACE

His type is to be found in the market places of most large cities of the East and the West, but the infinite variety of this Eastern pedlar's stock-in-trade could only be rivalled with difficulty. Watches, chains, pipes, cigarette-holders, pocket-books, purses, necklaces, walking-sticks, and much besides, suggest a large outlay as well as an enterprise not usually associated with Oriental lands

Photo, A. W. Cutler

PRIVATE HOUSE IN THE TURKISH QUARTER OF CONSTANTINOPLE

Turkish houses are mostly of two storeys, those of the middle class being usually surrounded on three sides by a garden and courtyard, the fourth side abutting on the street. The rooms on the ground floor include reception-rooms, kitchen, and offices; those above, with latticed windows, are the private apartments, to which no male visitors, except near relatives, are admitted

SNAPSHOTTING UNDER DIFFICULTIES IN A TURKISH MARKET

One of the busiest of the markets in Stamboul is the vegetable market, a corner of which is here shown. A juvenile assistant is seen expostulating, at the bidding of an elder, against the attentions of the camera-man. While the average Turk is much more tolerant than he used to be, his religion still keeps active his rooted prejudice against being made the subject of a photograph

Photo, Special Press

BEARERS OF THE BURDEN IN OLD-WORLD SMYRNA

One of the oldest of the old Greek cities of western Asia Minor, Smyrna still pulsates to the rhythm of the Orient, especially in the street leading from the Turkish quarter to the famous Caravan Bridge which, before the city had its railways, witnessed daily the passage of some thousand camels over the River Meles. The camel caravan is often, as here, led by a diminutive donkey carrying the driver

A DISH OF PILAF ENJOYED IN THE OPEN AIR

Adjoining the Yeni Valideh Jami mosque in Stamboul is a general market next in importance to the Grand Bazaar of which a photograph is given in page 4980. Here, in addition to the open shops, are stalls such as that shown above, where passers-by have paused to regale themselves on pilaf (boiled rice or macaroni), which is served on plates and forms a popular item in the Turkish menu

Photo, Special Press

order is disturbed, the disturbance is usually found to have been started by a foreigner of less phlegmatic disposition. Narrow as the streets are and awkward as it is to move through them, the Turks never lose their patience or their politeness. As they allow each other to pass, they murmur the phrases of courtesy which come so readily to their lips. That is the more agreeable side of their apathy. They do not think it worth while to lose their temper any more than they think it worth while to be curious or to exert themselves more than they need.

Poor the Turks are in the mean quarters of their cities, as in their mud hovels on the land. But there is no wretched want and misery such as have disgraced the West ever since the factory system firmly established itself. There is some kind of work for all who are capable of working ; ill-paid, perhaps, but bringing in sufficient to support existence in its simplest form. For those who cannot support themselves, and even for those who prefer to live on charity there are alms to be obtained from religious foundations and from private givers.

Liberality to the needy is one of the articles of the Moslem faith. When a Turkish effendi (the designation which corresponds to our esquire and denotes a member of the comfortable class) sits down in his office or study to start his day's business, there will very likely be waiting for him one or more dependents on his bounty who know they will not be sent empty away.

If the effendi is at home, he will be in his own part of the house, the selamlik. This is shut off from the women's part, which is called the haremlik. The women have the bigger space, but it includes all the sleeping apartments and the living-room which is common to husband and wife. In the haremlik the servants are women, except in establishments of great wealth belonging to owners who cling to old tradition and employ eunuchs. The selamlik servants are all men, and only men are admitted as visitors.

In the harem there is seldom nowadays more than one wife. Moslem law allows four wives and as many concubines, usually slaves, as a man cares to and can afford to keep; but the custom and the law have drifted apart.

Among those Turks who work for their daily bread monogamy is as firmly established as it is in England or France. In general they do not want more than one wife. Nor do the Turks who are well-off usually take advantage of the Prophet's wide allowance in the matter of wives. They, too, find that the expense of more than one is beyond their means, and they also have in

BEGGARS AT THE GATE OF THE MOSQUE OF SULEIMAN

Islam makes charity obligatory and binding upon all who accept the Moslem faith, but alms are voluntary as well as legal, hence the number of more or less professional beggars. The mosque of Suleiman the Great, erected in Stamboul in 1550-66, is one of the two masterpieces of the most famous of Turkish architects, Mimar Sinán Agha, the other being the Selim mosque at Adrianople

mind the many households which were torn by jealousies and made uncomfortable by harem intrigues in the past.

If a second wife is taken, the motive is almost sure to be a desire for children, which the first wife cannot satisfy. Divorce can be obtained for this reason, but very likely it would be repugnant to the husband to put away his wife, or it might not be convenient to him to return the dowry that he received with her, and the amount of caution-money which he settled upon her when they were married. Every husband is supposed to set aside a sum which he undertakes to pay over to his wife if he should divorce her. That is one of the provisions of Moslem law, which gives women, even though they were allotted so low a place in the Prophet's scheme, rights which are more liberal than those that women can claim, or at all events could until recently claim in the majority of Christian countries.

It required a Married Women's Property Act in England during the later years of the nineteenth century to give English wives power to dispose of their own money or possessions. Mahomedan wives have always had control over their own property. They have always been able to insist also that their husbands shall keep up establishments for them suited to their position. The " degraded " position of women under the Moslem law was therefore a myth. If there was degradation, it was social rather than legal.

It was not even ecclesiastical, for it is not the rule of Islam that women shall live apart or that they shall veil their faces when they leave their houses. This veiling has, indeed, long been less honoured in the observance than the breach. Faces have not been really covered, except by very modest or timid women, and often the who'e face was allowed to be seen for a little

"ALMS, FOR THE LOVE OF ALLAH!"

Beggars, conspicuous in all parts of Constantinople, are especially so at the doors of the mosques. They often beg in couples, one perhaps with a withered arm and a companion to attract the attention of passers-by. They are of all races, but while the Greek whines, the Turk will demand baksheesh as a right. It is believed that their sores and wounds are frequently self-inflicted

Photo, Special Press

VENDER OF FÊTE DAY CONFECTIONERY ON THE STEPS OF A MOSQUE

The sturdy old street trader, seated with his wares in front of him in the full glare of the Eastern sun, is offering for sale a variety of cakes for which there is a great demand in Constantinople on fête days. They are compounded of simple ingredients and offer a pleasant change from the generality of Turkish confectionery, which is excessively sweet

Photo, Special Press

while. The dropping of the veil certainly added to the attractiveness of pretty women and lent even to those who were not pretty a momentary charm.

Plenty of Turkish wives, and maids, too, were well aware of this. Parties of them enjoying themselves over picnics in the pleasant spots which lie near Constantinople and other cities would think it a good joke to lift their veils and let foreigners of evidently good manners see their faces. Their pleasure in this was quite harmless and their laughter very pleasant to hear. Such excursions fill them with delight, probably because they are so much indoors and confined to their own apartments.

If the mistress of a haremlik is a woman of taste who understands the beauty of Oriental colours and designs, her rooms will be restful and pleasant to the eye. There will be low and comfortable divans running round two or three sides of them, coffee-tables of inlaid walnut-wood, chests and cabinets of old workmanship, rich hangings and

rugs. If the idea prevails that Western furniture and decoration and upholstery are superior, then the effect is more than likely to be hideous and grotesque. Cheap German or Austrian productions are placed beside really good pieces, colours are mixed in the most disagreeable disharmonies, the arrangement of the rooms is stiff and depressing.

When you go into a Turkish sleeping apartment, you see none of the bed-room furniture to which we are accustomed. There is no bed, no washhand-stand, no dressing-table. When bed-time comes, mattresses and coverings are brought out of a cupboard and laid on the floor. Washing is done in a little room specially built for the purpose. In this the whole body can be bathed, for there is a plug in the floor which can be pulled up to let water run away. But the Turks do not wash a great deal in their houses. They take baths which have the effect of leaving the skin perfectly clean. All dirt is steamed out of it.

Turkish baths are cheap or dear according to the degree of comfort

WHERE TURKISH CHILDREN ARE INTRODUCED TO THE MYSTERIES OF THE KORAN AND THE THREE "R'S"

Education may be at a low ebb in Turkey, but in no European country, perhaps, was primary instruction provided at so early a date. To-day, apart from foreign foundations, two systems are in existence—that including the old Moslem parish school and the mosque college, and that including the modern preparatory and secondary schools supported by the state. In the parish schools, while the instruction given is chiefly religious, knowledge of the "three R's" is now inculcated. The curriculum of the colleges, which, to some extent, resemble the old universities of Western Europe, is confined mainly to training in theology and language

"TURNING TO MIRTH ALL THINGS OF EARTH, AS ONLY BOYHOOD CAN"

Schoolboys in the courtyard of one of the great mosques of Stamboul returning to their lessons after devotions. Turkish boys are just as full of life as any in the world, and the presence of the photographer made the shepherding on the part of their masters rather more difficult than usual. The first day of a boy's school career in Turkey is made memorable by a ceremony for which he is dressed in holiday garb and made to figure on horseback in a procession through the streets, his masters walking backwards in front of him while his fellow-pupils follow, chanting verses in praise of knowledge

Photo, Special Press

POPULAR LOVE OF THE OPEN AIR: OLD AND YOUNG IN THE STREET OF A SMALL TURKISH TOWN

Life in small Turkish towns is exceedingly monotonous, the sole relief from the dull, daily round being provided by weddings, funerals, or other family ceremonies and the occurrence of religious festivals. The streets are narrow and crooked, deep in dust in summer, muddy, or forming the beds of torrents in winter. The houses themselves may be light, airy, and clean; outside of them conditions are often insanitary and evil-smelling. In the large towns the populations are cosmopolitan, but in the interior Turkish influences predominate, and the manners and customs of the alien elements are considerably affected by the ruling race

Photo, Georg Haeckel

4998

required. First, there is a hot chamber, then a very hot one, then a cold douche is taken, and after that one drinks a cup of coffee and enjoys a few pulls at a pipe. Both men's and women's baths are places where people go to meet one another and exchange gossip. It is only the wealthy, with private baths of their own built on to their houses, who are not to be found one day or one evening a week at the least, undergoing massage and steam cleansing along with their acquaintances and friends.

Coffee in Turkey is not at all like coffee in France, or indeed in any other country except Egypt. It is thick and sweet, served in tiny cups, and followed

EX-SULTAN'S EUNUCH
In the older Turkish families of position eunuchs still act as guardians of the ladies of the harem

TURKISH LADY IN INDOOR COSTUME
In Turkey, as in Europe, feminine dress fashions vary, and generalisation is made difficult by the variety of races. Among members of Moslem families indoor costumes are usually less conservative than those adopted when taking the air

by a glass of water. One has to drink a great many of these little cups in the course of a day spent in visiting, or doing business in public offices or bargaining in the bazaars. Everywhere coffee will be ordered as soon as the visitor enters. Sometimes sweetmeats, "Turkish delight," or dabs of rose-jam on a plate are offered with it. To drink so much Western coffee would be to banish sleep and probably to upset the digestion, but Turkish coffee is wholesome and

PASSING FASHIONS IN THE CHANGING EAST

While old customs, especially in regard to costume, change slowly among Turkish ladies of position, many of their sisters have abandoned the once universal yashmak, or spotless white veil, which disclosed only their eyes, and the brightly-coloured feriji or cloak, once so distinguishing a feature of their outdoor dress, has given way to a garment of sombre black

can be taken in immense quantity without inconvenience.

There is a coffee-maker as well as a cook in all the houses of the well-to-do. For those who want coffee away from home there are street coffee-sellers who make it fresh and serve it hot and fragrant in a few moments. Cool drinks are sold in the streets, too, and fruit, and sweets, all very temptingly displayed, not at all like the wares on barrows in London.

Pedlars are common in Turkey, most of them Greeks or Wallachians, whose homes are in the mountains of Macedonia perhaps, or in some other far hill-country, where the mixture of races makes it impossible to say that any particular district is more Greek than Bulgarian, more Wallachian (or Vlach) than Serbian. Even when a family proclaims itself one or the other, it often has a motive for doing so, probably fear, and in a short time it will change its nationality to ensure its safety, as the Vicar of Bray changed his party. They are good peasants, no matter what they may call themselves. They work hard and they make the earth yield a rich increase of corn and wine, and fruit and vegetables. A great deal of the cultivation and harvesting in the Christian lands which have so long been misgoverned by Turkey is done by women, whereas among the Turks it is rare to see women in the fields. In their homes these Greek, Bulgarian, Serbian, and Wallachian women spin and weave from the wool of their own sheep, they knit and embroider very prettily, and on Sundays they turn out looking smart and handsome in their national dresses.

Although their mode of life is in many aspects like that of the Turks, they are a proof of the vivifying power of Christianity. Both it and Islam came from the East, but while the Moslem religion has remained unaltered in any important particular, Christianity has developed and been imbued with the spirit of the West, the spirit of progress. It is the dead hand of the prophet Mahomet that has kept

Turkey backward, and has brought disaster upon her. Change is the law of life. Any organism, whether it be a plant, an individual, or a nation, which does not change has ceased to be alive.

If the Turks could cast off the dead hand, not necessarily abandoning Islam, but allowing it to develop in harmony with the ideas of the modern world, they would no doubt play a worthy part, as a race, in the coming age. If

A STUDY IN BLACK AND WHITE
Simplicity and charm are combined in dress and person of this lady of Constantinople, who is wearing the now popular walking costume of some black material falling into graceful folds

WOMAN OF THE PEOPLE
In some districts of the Ottoman dominions peasant women will not only cover their faces but will turn sideways when a man approaches, and so remain until he has passed

they cling to ancient formulae, they will die out, as a race, "and the place thereof shall know it no more."

This, however, will be a long process. Nations, like King Charles II. of England, are "an unconscionable time a-dying." Whatever may happen to Constantinople and to that part of

TAKING THEIR EASE AT THEIR "INN": GROUP OF WAYFARERS OUTSIDE A TURKISH COFFEE-HOUSE

In Turkey the coffee-house takes the place of the inn and the club of Western peoples. Its appearance and appointments are often crude and plain. Sometimes it is little more than a wooden shanty with an awning or vine-covered trellis, in front of which its patrons contemplatively take their refreshment. Sometimes it resembles the old English tea-garden. A stove, some copper coffee-pots, a number of cups, a few narghilehs, and a collection of wooden benches or stools usually comprise its stock-in-trade. The best of the coffee-houses are furnished with mats, rugs, and cushions on a kind of platform surrounding the interior

Photo, Mrs. Gabriel

5002

the Turkish Empire which was in Europe, there will be Turks ruling for many tens of years to come over wide regions of Asia. Nor would they have any cause to regret the change from Constantinople as the seat of government to Brusa. That city was the ancient capital of the Osmanlis and has always kept a foremost place in their affections. It is livelier and in every way more attractive than most Eastern towns. It is superbly sited; indeed, it may be called without exaggeration one of the most beautiful places in the world.

Its port on the Sea of Marmora is Mudania. Thence a single line of railway winds up and around a delicious wooded valley sloping to the water. Then a vast plain spreads itself before your gaze, with the city on the farther side, glittering in the sunshine on a lower spur of Mount Olympus the "other Mount Olympus," not the home of Olympian Jove, which

LADY OF ANATOLIA

It is in Anatolia that one meets the purer Turkish type, with narrow, almost almond-shaped eyes, brown complexion, placid expression, and high cheekbones. Elsewhere inter-marriage has mixed Semitic and Aryan with Mongol blood

is in Greece. Nowhere do I know a city which is so literally in the mountains as Brusa. Looking upwards from the market place, you see the rounded bluffs towering above, wreathed in a mysterious mist, and where a bridge carries the street over a ravine, you may look into the very heart of the rocky peaks and saddles, or downwards follow with your eye a torrent plashing and foaming, leaping from rock to pool, from pool to gravelly beach, until it finds its tumultuous way to the valley. Across the valley is another rampart of mountains, clear in the morning and the evening,

half hidden by the golden haze of noon. I recollect the streets of Brusa as a jumble of bullock-wagons, buffalo carts, flocks of turkeys, donkeys laden with charcoal, ponies with curious long grape-tubs balanced on either flank, Turks sitting their prancing, curvetting Arab blood-horses like statues, beggars motionless by the roadside chanting their monotonous appeals. There are a fair number of women to be seen here, many of them unveiled, and almost every one in trousers. That fashion sits awkwardly upon ladies of mature years, for maturity in the East brings with it amplitude of bulk. But it lends the small lithe girls an adorably graceful air.

The men's costume most in vogue consists of turban as headgear, striped shirt, wide cummerbund of some vivid colour, and baggy trousers tight at the ankles. They wear this with an indescribably rakish effect. If their clothes were a shade fresher, they might be mistaken for operatic stage peasants or brigands. But really, they are a simple, A'lah-fearing folk, and in the great ligh mosques, after they have washed hands and feet at the fountain-basin in the centre, obedient to the letter of the Prophet's injunction, they can be seen sitting in throngs for hours around some old mullah, expounding in a high up-and-down tone the lessons of the Koran.

Brusa is famous for its mosques as well as for its scenery. It is celebrated too for its silk, which is made in pleasant, airy factories, filled with sunshine, save when the mists come down and swathe the city in their ghostly folds. Other industries besides silk-weaving flourish. Workers at almost every handicraft sit in their open shop-fronts, using their tools cheerfully and with affectionate skill, as those who know not the degradation of labour which machinery has wrought in more sophisticated lands.

The impression left on the mind by Constantinople is neither so delightful nor so clear as that of the ancient capital. Its history gives its stones an interest which those of Brusa cannot claim, the thoughts which crowd into the memory when its name falls on the ear are so vivid and so varied that to walk its streets is like the realization of some strange dream.

Dreamlike, too, is the beauty of Constantinople. Never shall I forget my first sight of it. As our vessel steamed up the Sea of Marmora, the earliest pale yellow of an October dawn was streaking a cold sky behind masses of blue-grey mountain on the Asian shore. Stamboul was still in deepest

COURTYARD OF THE MOSQUE OF SELIM I., ADRIANOPLE

Dating from the sixteenth century, and the dominating architectural feature of the city, this splendid mosque has outer and inner courts paved with white marble, furnished with white marble fountains, and is surrounded with domed cloisters adorned with coloured marble pillars. The body of the structure is one huge dome, and the building is flanked with high towers

Photo, H. C. Woods

FRAGRANT FESTOONS OF THE WORLD'S FAVOURITE WEED

Something like sixteen million acres in Asiatic Turkey are devoted to the cultivation of the tobacco plant, and, despite the exactions of the Regie, or monopoly, the industry has increased in recent years. As regards the best qualities, the leaves are picked as they ripen ; they are then air-dried as shown here, and afterwards subjected to a lengthy treatment of mild fermentation

Photo, H. C. Woods

shadow. A filmy veil of darkness shrouded from view its mosques and minarets, its ancient walls, its irregular masses of close-lying grey-tiled roofs, piled carelessly on the city's seven hills.

Minute by minute, as we shivered in the bitter Black Sea breeze, the yellow streaks lightened and spread. Soon a point of light gleamed coldly on shore. Then another, then a third. Quickly the filmy veil was pierced by innumerable fires, as window after window caught the glow. Higher and higher rose the orange hue of sunrise. At last, in a sudden burst of glory, the sun swam over the summits. Then the city

stood revealed, a forest of slim towers, a vast range of majestic domes, set amidst a welter of whitened house-fronts, all clear and vivid in the golden air.

A dream-city it seemed, too lovely to be true. No element of beauty was missing as the sun gained power and the sky turned from a stone-grey to a deliciously light-hearted blue, while the rippling waters of Bosporus and Golden Horn laughed in the light of a new day.

Now we could see what a green city it was. The meadows of Seraglio Point stretched their brilliant emerald towards the water's edge. Everywhere the eye rested on the tree-tops, pushing

CHILDREN AT PLAY IN THE DILAPIDATED SQUARE OF ANCIENT MARMARAS

For the moment the young people are interested chiefly in the photographer. Some of the boys have a typically Turkish appearance, but one little girl on the left might have stepped out from a scene in Puritan England. Two of their elders are engaged in ablutions by a gulley of running water, where a dog is slaking its thirst and a cat sits quietly watching. Marmaras, or Marmarice, is a little town at the head of a fine bay of the same name, in the Caria division of Anatolia, and was once a landing-place for travellers coming from Rhodes

up among the serried roofs. Until we rounded the Point and had our senses offended by a steamer belching filthy smoke as most of the shipping in the port does, there was nothing to mar the perfection of our panorama, nothing to check the illusion that we were dreaming a delicious dream.

Alas, how differently one regards Constantinople after making its better acquaintance! It no longer seems a

before the great gulf fixed between the European and the Asiatic outlook upon life, I no longer found it hard to believe that only a short while back the streets of Constantinople were running with the blood of murdered Armenians, I felt convinced that if the Sultan who was then in power should see fit to plan an attack of the same sinister savagery upon Greeks or English or French, his orders would be as faithfully obeyed.

RISEN FROM THE ASHES OF A BURNT-OUT HOMESTEAD

The old home of this Adana family had been destroyed during one of the periodical massacres of Armenians by Turks who had been spurred on to their deadly work by political agitators, and the photograph was taken soon after the house had been rebuilt. The massacre took place about the time of the counter-revolution in Constantinople, with its sequel, the deposition of Abdul Hamid II.

Photo, H. C. Woods

dream. It has become more like a nightmare.

One thinks of its crowded narrow streets, where at one moment you are wading in mud, and the next bruising your feet against the rough stones; where, if you drive, you are bumped painfully over their uneven switchback surface.

One recalls the dirt and disorder of all the public services, the brooding atmosphere of decay which afflicts the spiritual and often too the material nostril. I recollect how after a short stay I understood as I had never done

At that time the scavenging of the city was left for the most part to the troops of ownerless dogs which swarmed in every street. How they established their right to be there no one clearly knew. It would have been against the law of Islam to kill them, and they certainly saved a good deal of expense on dustmen and refuse destructors. So they were tolerated then and for many years after that. Gentle creatures they were to those who spoke them fair. Pretty creatures, too, with their fawny, rough-haired coats, their pointed ears and lustrous eyes. Many a time my

CURIOSITY OF ANATOLIAN CHILDREN AROUSED BY THE VISIT OF A PHOTOGRAPHER TO MARMARAS

Marmaras, in the south-west of Anatolia, has a story linking it with the distant past. To-day it is little heard of. But this photograph, and that given in page 5006, suggest that, despite the character it bears for insalubrity, the child-life of the port is both virile and conspicuous. The young people gathered together in a semicircle, the boys on one side and the girls on the other, afford a notable study in variety of facial expression as well as in dress, and the man in uniform on the left seems as anxious to be in the photograph as any of his juvenile companions

heart has been touched by the sight of a mother suckling her puppies, tiny balls of soft yellow down. Many a time did I marvel, as I saw how they organized themselves into districts, that men can speak slightingly of animal intelligence.

If a stranger dog appeared out of his own district, there was immediately a showing of teeth, a growling, and generally a scuffle. Sometimes the stranger would make known his peaceable intentions and would ask for safe conduct across alien territory. Then two dogs of the district would escort him through, and no notice would be taken of him by the rest. I did not find the dogs a plague and an offence, as many did. I thought they lent almost a charm to the streets, though there were rather too many of them.

At last their increase became so prolific and the nuisance of their number so great that an edict went forth for their banishment. The kindest plan would have been to kill them painlessly. That, however, would have transgressed the Prophet's commands. So the poor dogs were driven down to the quay and on board a ship, which turned them loose on an island in the Sea of Marmora, that same Prinkipo Island which was proposed, in 1919, as the meeting-place of men of all parties in Russia. There most of them died miserably. No Society for the Protection of Animals exists in Turkey. Their wretched end aroused no indignation. It is only the shepherds in Eastern countries who look upon the dog as we do, and consider him the friend of man.

TURKISH WOMAN OF SMYRNA

Turkish women have, as a rule, beautiful complexions, fine heads of hair, and, generally, large black eyes, the darkness of which is often enhanced by artificial means. Their costume, especially in the well-to-do classes, is usually most becoming

What is the predominant impression among the images that Constantinople leaves upon the mind of the reflective traveller? An image of disintegration, of melancholy. The few busy quarters are thronged, they are as full of colour and movement as any in the world. There you see Moslems of every nationality. Fat, sensual Ottoman Turks; tall, lean dignified Bokharans in flowing robes; merchants from the cities of Central Asia in furred cloaks and costly turbans set with precious stones; flock-masters from the steppes, their features hard and wrinkled from exposure, wearing sheep-skin coats; strings of pilgrims for Mecca, their nondescript baggage piled untidily on

LADEN WITH RICHES FROM THE FERTILE PLAINS AND SUNNY SLOPES OF THE VALLEY OF THE MAEANDER

This donkey caravan, with panniers heavily laden with the figs for which the country around Smyrna has been celebrated since early times, is approaching the outskirts of the historic port. The pulling and packing of figs form one of the chief industries of Smyrna, whence huge quantities are exported. The Greeks, who developed fig cultivation extensively, are said to have first received the tree from Caria, whence was derived the designation of Ficus carica. According to some authorities there is no farm or garden product of Europe or America which could not be successfully cultivated in the naturally fertile valley of the Maeander

long strings of camels which pick their path with swaying, methodical footsteps.

Among all of these one seldom sees a cheerful face. It is to the elements which are not Moslem that one must look for smiles and chatter and pleasantry. The followers of Islam for the most part wear an expression of dreary resignation. That seems to be the best the Mahomedan faith can do for them.

Leave the few busy spots and you plunge into what appears to be a dead city. The quiet streets are uncannily deserted and still. The closely-shuttered lattice windows of the houses permit no sign of the life within to appear to the passer-by. Occasionally there may pass a figure swathed in black, with opaque veil hanging from brow to breast, followed by two or more soft-stepping Circassian harem slaves. Now and then the echoes will be wakened by the click-clack of the hoofs of a donkey laden with grapes or vegetables.

Islamism and Human Progress

These are rare interludes. The rest is silence and solitude, to the European temperament depressing, though it does not seem to affect the younger Turkish ladies, who twitter like pretty birds to each other when they happen to be taking the air. They are unaffected by the gloom which has settled upon the male part of the nation.

Watch the Mussulman at his prayers, whether in the great Mosque of Santa Sophia (the Holy Wisdom) in Constantinople, or in some small country mosque, or in the desert, or on board ship—you will understand then why Islam has never won a footing in go-ahead Europe and never will.

There is devotion in those swaying figures, now on their feet, now sitting on their heels, now bending low to bring their foreheads to the ground in abasement at the sound of the wonderful names of God. Their evident sincerity, their readiness to perform their religious duties before all the world, even before

unbelievers, as happens on Nile steamboats, for example—these compel respect. But there is nothing soul-stirring in their mechanical exercises. It is a devotion which cannot help on the progress of humanity.

And what chance in this age of Woman has a faith which denies her the possession of a soul ?

Women's Absence from Shops and Streets

The depression of spirit occasioned by the unsmiling faces of the men is heightened by the scarcity of women. None serves in shops or does any work in public. None enters the mosques save in strict privacy. It is not that their absence robs the streets of colour. The red tarbush or fez which is worn by all classes and the variety of men's costume to be seen at every turn, supply as much colour as could be wished for. It is the women's faces that you miss, not their gay dresses ; their kind eyes and dainty contours, their lips curling with quick sympathy or humour, their delicate, soft skins.

There are many corners of Constantinople where the calming influence of quiet, hard-working, affectionate domestic lives spreads itself, where one may feel that all men of goodwill and simple character have much in common, to whatever race they may belong and to whatever faith they may profess allegiance.

Constantinople's Natural Charm

It was not the Turk as he is by nature who made his country a byword and its place among the nations shameful. It was those who traded on his simplicity, those who drew their profit of money or power from his ignorance and loyalty. It is the thought of them and the evil they did which weighs upon the mind in Constantinople.

Only when nature casts a spell of fairy loveliness over the city so stained with blood and sinister intrigue does the nightmare vanish and the dream come back. In the sunset hour the

ISRAEL UNDER THE CRESCENT

Despite the fact that they have suffered relatively little persecution, the Jews in Turkey are not among the best of their race.
Many are descendants of those Jews called the Sephardim who
came from Spain in the fifteenth century

more. Scarcely any of the smaller towns of Turkey are attractive. The pleasant feature of them is that they are rich in gardens and groves of fruit trees. On the coast .they are apt to be feverish. In the interior they are not much more than collections of hovels, with a fine house or two for the high officials, a mosque perhaps of some interest, possibly a public building of some size. Adrianople was a city once that impressed the traveller with its impor-tance, but it has long been on the down-grade. Here the inhabitants include a large number of Jews, not far short of ten thousand. Spanish Jews they are, who have kept up their language and the " courtly Spanish grace " of their demeanour.

Jews were always tolerated in Turkey, even when they were being harried in England. The Prophet taught that both they and Christians must be treated well, and the Turks as a race obeyed that precept until their rulers inflamed them against Bulgarians first and then Armenians, not because they were Christians, but because they were politically troublesome.

The result has been to create an artificial and deplorable " religious question " which makes it exceedingly difficult for the country to settle down. Politics and religion are intertwined. " What is your faith ? " the visitor to Turkey is asked constantly, and if a prominent man of some other nation is mentioned, " Of what faith is he ? " will pretty certainly be inquired.

first impression may be daily recaptured. Against the crimson flush, slowly paling to pink and opal, the domes and minarets stand out sharp and purpley-blue. The waters which give the capital its incomparable situation turn slowly from silver to black. The lamps on the mosque towers gleam bright against the already darkened northern sky. A young moon casts its tremulous smile upon the twilit sea. All up the hills on every side lights are twinkling. Everything but the beauty of the scene is forgotten. The city of the Golden Horn is as you first saw it, a dream once

Turks are affectionate husbands and parents. It is their domestic virtues, added to their straight dealing with all men, that win for this race the good word of all who have become really acquainted with them.

More than any European race do they value men for their good qualities, not for their wealth or their birth. They do not ask, when they want information about anybody, " Does he belong to a good family ? " or " How much is he worth ? " They ask whether he is a man of education and ideals, whether he is faithful in friendship, generous, hospitable, one who remembers benefits. They are not, and never will be, a progressive people.

PROPHET AND PROTAGONIST OF TURKISH INDEPENDENCE

Mustapha Kemal Pasha, here seen addressing the Turkish Nationalist Parliament at Angora, was the man who, without German help, prevented the British from conquering Gallipoli. A Moslem with one idea, the liberation of Turkey from European control, his government is said to have owed much success to the influence of Halid Edib Hanoum, an army officer, later Minister of Education

ANCIENT CLOAKS OF TURKISH CARRIERS STILL TO BE SEEN ON THE TRADE ROUTES IN ANATOLIA

These elaborate cloaks, made to serve as a protection for their wearers in all sorts of weather, and apparently adaptable even as tents at night-time, were seen on the old military and mountainous highway of the Byzantines which runs between Eskisher, or Old Town, and Angora, two important cities of Anatolia now linked by a railway that takes an easier grade down the valley of the Pursak Chai. Cloaks of the kind are made of embroidered felt, and, according to tradition, have been made and worn in this part of the world for a period of something like three thousand years

Turkey

II. The Rise & Fall of the Ottoman Empire

By Sir E. Denison Ross, C.I.E.

Director, School of Oriental Studies, London Institution

THE precise origin of the Ottoman Turks, who captured Constantinople in 1453, is difficult to determine, but there can be no doubt that they were a mixed race containing elements of many other Turkish tribes whom they had encountered on their wanderings from the East. For the original home of all Turkish-speaking peoples is to be found in Northern Mongolia, and the story of their migration from that home is most easily to be traced by following the various dialects of the Turkish language, which, in their stages of modification of the old Turkish, enable us to discover the path followed by the race in its wanderings from the shores of Lake Baikal to the Bosporus.

The Turkish-speaking peoples extend roughly from the Great Wall of China on the east to the limits of Turkey in Europe in the west, to northern Persia in the south, and to the Volga on the northwest. Between Chinese Turkistan and Constantinople a large number of dialects are spoken, and the Turki of Turkistan is the nearest in structure to the oldest remains of the language which have come down to us in inscriptions of the seventh century, while Ottoman Turkish is farthest removed.

We cannot enter here upon the early history of the Turks prior to their becoming masters of the Moslem East, but it may be mentioned that by the middle of the sixth century one branch of them had gained possession of all the Oxus country, had formed an alliance with the Sassanian king of Persia, and in the sixth century A.D. embassies were exchanged between the Turkish Khan and the Byzantine Emperor.

With the rapid spread of the victorious arms of Islam in the seventh century, the Sassanian Empire came to an end, and although in the following century the Caliphs of Bagdad extended their conquests into the Oxus country, the Turks still retained their independence farther east. The rise of powerful local dynasties in northern and north-eastern Persia in the ninth and tenth centuries reduced the authority of the Caliphs to something purely nominal.

The first great Turkish clan to rise to power on the ruins of the old Caliphate

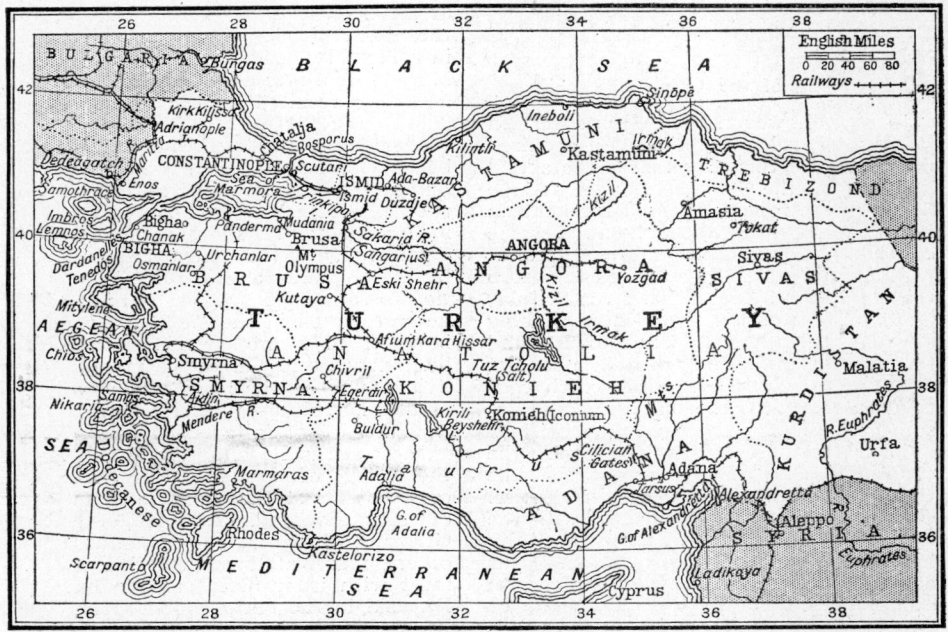

AREA CONTROLLED BY THE GRAND NATIONAL ASSEMBLY OF TURKEY

was that of the Seljuks. Their chieftain, Seljuk, was a Turcoman in the service of the Khans of Turkistan, who had migrated with his people to Bokhara where they embraced Islam. It was his grandson, Toghrul Bey, who in A.D. 1037 set himself up in Nishapur and finally, in 1055, entered Bagdad and proclaimed himself Sultan of the city of the Caliph. The Seljuk Empire, founded by Toghrul, eventually split up into a number of separate Seljuk kingdoms in Iraq, Kerman and Asia Minor. The last-named endured the longest, ruling from 1077 to 1300.

Power of the Mamelukes and Seljuks

The middle of the thirteenth century witnessed the devastating invasion of Persia by the Mongols under Jenghiz Khan, culminating in the fall of Bagdad in 1258. Two branches of the Turks, however, were able to withstand the Mongol invader, namely, the Turkish Mamelukes of Egypt and the Seljuks of Asia Minor. The Ottoman Turks were at this time represented by a small clan in the service of these Seljuks, who, in recognition of help, permitted them to pasture their flocks in the land of Bithynia, which bordered on the Byzantine Empire.

It was there that Othman, or Osman, the founder of the Ottoman dynasty, was born in the year in which Hulagu captured Bagdad. On the death of his father, Ertogrul, in 1288, Othman became head of the clan, which still remained in the service of the Seljuks of Asia Minor.

Beginning of the Ottoman Empire

In 1295, however, the Seljuk sovereign made him ruler of a newly acquired territory, and this date marks the actual beginning of the Ottoman Empire, for the Seljuks were rapidly losing their hold on the country, whereas Othman became daily more powerful and more ambitious. Although he gradually managed to absorb the dominions abandoned by the Seljuks, Othman's attention was more closely devoted to his Christian neighbours, and the Ottomans now embarked on a conflict with the Byzantine Empire, which continued down to the capture of Constantinople in 1453.

Their first great triumph was the capture in 1326 of Brusa, which became the first capital of the Ottoman Empire. Othman, whose death coincided with the capture of this city, was succeeded by his son Orkhan, who continued his aggressive policy against the Greeks with such success that by 1338 only one or two towns in Asia remained in the hands of the Byzantines.

Orkhan spent the next twenty years in the peaceful consolidation of his territories and in the organization of his civil administration and his army. It was during his reign that the famous corps of janissaries (yeni cheri—new troops) was founded. Having thus consolidated his power, and being firmly established on the Asiatic side of the Bosporus, he was in a position to demand concessions and favours from the Byzantine emperor, and although Constantinople remained secure, Turkish forces penetrated into the Balkans, and in 1355 the fortress of Gallipoli was captured by Orkhan's son. Orkhan, moreover, obtained the emperor's daughter in marriage and concluded a treaty which has been characterised as the first act in the drama of the downfall of the Byzantine Empire.

In 1359 Murad I. succeeded his father, whose policy of expansion beyond Constantinople he continued. In 1361 Adrianople was taken, and in 1367 the seat of Ottoman rule was changed from Brusa to that town, the Turks thus becoming a European power. In 1373 they conquered Macedonia and demanded tribute from the King of Serbia.

Military Triumphs of Bayazid

During these expeditions the youth of the Balkan countries was constantly being requisitioned to swell the ranks of the janissaries. At last the Christian princes formed an alliance with the object of driving the Turks out of Europe, but the great battle of Kossovo in 1382, in which Bayazid " the Thunderbolt," Murad's son, first distinguished himself as a leader, resulted in the defeat of the allies.

Murad was murdered in his tent on the battlefield, and Bayazid was proclaimed Sultan by the victorious army. Having reduced Serbia and Wallachia to vassalage in Europe, and having secured all the dominions in Asia Minor formerly held by the Seljuks, Bayazid turned his attention to the religious aspect of the position he had gained in the Moslem world, and in order to please the orthodox Sunnis he induced the Caliph—a mere puppet living under the protection of the Mameluke Sultan—to invest him formally with the title of Sultan.

In 1394 the Pope, at the instigation of the King of Hungary, proclaimed a crusade against the Turks, and an army of sixty thousand, composed of French, Germans, Bavarians, Hungarians and others, marched through Serbia, only to meet with utter defeat at the hands of Bayazid in the battle of Nicopolis, 1396. After this victory, which was marred by his cruel butchery of the many thousand prisoners taken in the battle, Bayazid resumed the siege of Constantinople, which he had already attempted some years before.

He would no doubt have achieved the capture of that city had he not been suddenly called away to defend his Asiatic dominions against the world-conquering Tamerlane, who was devastating Western Asia and India with yet another horde of invaders from Central Asia. He swept all before him as did the Mongols in the thirteenth century, and his passage was only stopped, as was that of the Mongols in Egypt, by the Turkish Mamelukes of Egypt.

Whether Tamerlane would have attacked Bayazid in the ordinary course of events it is hard to say, for there were those who represented to him that it was contrary to Islam for one Moslem monarch to attack another who was engaged in war against infidels. Tamerlane, however, held that this circumstance was outweighed by the fact that Bayazid was granting asylum to certain Moslem rulers whom he had deposed.

Tamerlane and Bayazid

There ensued an acrimonious correspondence between the two great Turkish conquerors, in which Bayazid, underrating the power of his enemy, assumed such a haughty tone that Tamerlane declared war on him, the final issue of which was decided in the great battle of Angora, 1402. In this battle Bayazid was supported by Serbian troops, led by their Christian king.

The well-known story of Bayazid being carried about in an iron cage by Tamerlane after this battle is probably without foundation, as Tamerlane, according to the best authorities, dealt kindly with his captive.

From 1402 to 1413 the Ottoman Empire was in a state of disruption; Asia Minor was lost, and four sons of Bayazid were fighting each other for supremacy in Europe. In 1413, however, Sultan Mohammed I. became sole ruler, and in his short reign of eight years he managed to revive the Ottoman power by friendly treaties in Europe and a firm hand in Asia. On his death in 1421 he was succeeded by his son, Murad II., who, like his father, began to lay siege to Constantinople, only to be called away to defend his dominions in Asia. In 1428 he became possessed of many ports on the Black Sea and conquered Salonica. In 1427 another Christian confederacy of Balkan princes was formed with the object of releasing Serbia from her allegiance to the Turks, and in the wars which followed the leading figure is the great Hungarian hero, Janos Hunyadi. The Ottomans were twice defeated by the confederacy, and by the Treaty of Szeged, concluded in 1444, Serbia regained her independence. This treaty was broken a few months later, and hostilities having been reopened, a desperate struggle ensued, which terminated with the total defeat of the Christians at the battle of Varna, 1444.

The Fall of Constantinople

Murad II. died in 1451, and was succeeded by Mohammed II., who is chiefly famous for having accomplished the capture of Constantinople (1453), which had been unsuccessfully attempted by two Caliphs and three previous Turkish Sultans. The siege lasted forty-three days.

The fall of Constantinople is the most important event in the history of the Turks. Although the Ottomans had already established themselves in Europe, and although the Greek emperors, by the middle of the fifteenth century, had been shorn of most of their power and influence, Constantinople was looked upon, at any rate by the Turks, as the capital of the Christian world, and as such its occupation by a Moslem power constituted a supreme triumph for Islam, and it followed naturally that the Sultan, in possession of Constantinople, should regard himself as the King of Kings in Islam. At this period, however, there was no talk of the Sultan being also the successor to the Caliphate.

Turkish Suzerainty over Egypt

Mohammed II., in his reign of thirty years, apart from this outstanding triumph, did much to enhance the prestige of the Turks in regard to both military exploits and internal administration. Though his northerly progress was effectually checked by the heroism of Hunyadi, he added many islands and seaports to his empire and secured the command of the Mediterranean and Euxine seas.

He was succeeded in 1481 by his son, Bayazid II., who, after an uneventful reign of thirty-one years, was succeeded in 1512 by his son the famous Selim I., who, during a short reign of eight years, nearly doubled the extent of the Ottoman dominions in Asia. Selim proceeded at once to root out the Shiite heretics, of whom he is said to have massacred forty thousand. His first campaign, undertaken against the great Shiite monarch, Shah Ismail of Persia, ended in a complete victory for the Turks at the battle of Chaldiran, 1514, after which he turned his attention to the dominions of the

Mameluke Sultans of Cairo, and in 1516 set out for Egypt by way of Palestine.

The aged Mameluke king, Kansau Ghauri, advanced to meet him, and a battle was engaged at Marj-Dabiq, in which Kansau, deserted by many of his troops, was defeated and slain. Selim in the following year entered Cairo in triumph, and established that Turkish suzerainty over Egypt which endured down to November, 1914.

Selim and the Headship of Islam

We have seen how in the reign of Bayazid there was a puppet Caliph in Cairo enjoying the protection of the Mameluke sovereign. In 1517 the last descendant of the Abbasid Caliphs, by name Mutawakkil, was a virtual prisoner in Egypt, and when Selim had established order in that country and returned to Constantinople he carried away with him the Caliph.

It does not appear that Selim while in Egypt had contemplated adopting the title of Caliph, and it was only after his return to his capital that it occurred to him to receive from Mutawakkil what the last of the true Caliphs was not in a position to bestow, namely, the headship of Islam, which really was reserved for an Arab of the tribe of Quraish.

No very great importance was attached to this transference of the Caliphate until, during the reign of Abdul Hamid, this circumstance was made the centre and pivot of an attempted Pan-Islamic movement. Before he died, in 1520, Selim had further added to his empire the province of Algiers, which he had received in return for a promise of protection from the famous Corsair Khair ud-Din Barbarossa.

Most Brilliant of the Sultans

Selim was succeeded by his illustrious son, Solyman the Magnificent, whose reign of forty-six years is the most brilliant in the annals of the house of Othman. His chief military achievements were the capture of Rhodes in 1522, the victory at Mohacs, 1526, when he utterly routed the Hungarians, the unsuccessful siege of Vienna in 1529, the capture of Bagdad in 1534, the defeat of Andrea Doria in the Adriatic in 1538, the capture of Aden in the same year, which secured the command of the Red Sea, and the conquest of Armenia and Georgia in 1555. It may be mentioned that in 1534 the first French ambassador came to the Sublime Porte.

Solyman died in 1566 and was succeeded by his son, Selim II., whose mother was a Russian and is known to history as Roxelana. The chief incident of his short reign was the naval battle at Lepanto in 1571, when the Turks were defeated by an allied fleet of Christian princes under Don John of Austria. In 1589, during the reign of his successor, Murad III., who came to the throne in 1574, the first British Embassy was sent to Constantinople in order to seek an alliance with the Turks against Philip II. of Spain.

The two hundred years from the close of the sixteenth century to the beginning of the nineteenth century produced no Sultan of outstanding distinction or importance, though during this period Turkey frequently figures, usually to her disadvantage, in the pages of European history—as witness the defeat of the Turks by John Sobieski, King of Poland, at Lemberg, 1675 ; the second Turkish siege of Vienna in 1683, which, after the most heroic resistance against great odds, was at length relieved by John Sobieski, with the result that the Turks were driven back, never again to approach within sight of Vienna's walls ; and by the end of the century her dominions in Europe were reduced to half their former extent.

Turkey in the Nineteenth Century

At this juncture Russia appears upon the scene of European politics and usurps Turkey's rôle of standing menace to the Central Powers. In 1699 Peter the Great occupied Azov and thus gained a footing in the Black Sea.

Ottoman history during the following century is chiefly occupied with alternate wars and treaties with the Russians, resulting in the aggrandisement of Russia and the humiliation of Turkey. At the beginning of the nineteenth century, while England was allied to Russia, she had been nominally at war with Turkey, but with the Treaty of Tilsit this alliance came to an end, and in 1809 England made peace with Turkey.

Napoleon's policy was to encourage hostility between Turkey and Russia in order to weaken the latter, against whom he was meditating his attack. It was Stratford Canning who, by his diplomatic genius, defeated the aims of Napoleon and brought about the Treaty of Bukarest, 1812, by which the Porte made peace with the Tsar, so that the Russian army of the Danube, being released, was able to administer the coup de grâce to the French army on its retreat from Moscow.

From 1812 down to the present day Turkey in Europe is merely one of the protagonists in the long-drawn-out drama of European diplomatic disputation over the fate of European Turkey and of Constantinople in particular. It is a

MODERN GIRLISH GRACE IN OLD WORLD SMYRNA

Standing barefoot in her flowing garb by an old doorway in a corner of the ancient city, this Smyrna girl has a somewhat pensive expression. While the Greek and Jewish women are usually distinguished by their crimson dresses, the Turkish women adopt a costume of solemn black, those employed in domestic service wearing only a simple garment of cotton and being always unshod when indoors

story of treaties and pacts interspersed with occasional campaigns.

At Navarino in 1827 the English, French, and Russian fleets destroyed the Turkish fleet. In 1832 Mehemet Ali, Viceroy of Egypt, marched through Syria and threatened the Bosporus ; Russia interposed, and, having saved Constantinople, gained in return the exclusive right of way through the Dardanelles. France was on the side of Mehemet Ali, and England, after a long period of hesitancy, sided with the Sultan and an English fleet was sent to Palestine.

Events Preceding the Crimean War

In 1841 a treaty was concluded which placed Turkey on an entirely new footing. Mehemet Ali was confined to Egypt, which was to continue under the suzerainty of the Sultan, who, in his turn, accepted the protection of the Great Powers as a guarantee for the independence and integrity of his empire. This treaty was followed by fourteen years of peace, which were devoted to internal reforms within the Ottoman Empire, due mainly to the initiative of Stratford Canning.

In 1852 began the international disputes regarding the protection of the adherents of the various Christian Churches living under Ottoman rule, which, owing to the imperious demands and aggressive action of the Russians, led eventually to the declaration of war by England, France, and Turkey against Russia in 1854.

Before the allied forces of England and France reached the fighting area, the Turks under British generals had practically gained the object of the campaign—of driving the Russians across the Danube. Had the allies been content with this result, England would have been spared the mistakes and misfortunes of the Crimean War.

Deposition of Abdul Aziz

It was, however, the opinion of the English and French that the Russian menace could only be removed by the destruction of her great stronghold Sevastopol, in the Crimea; but they had no idea of the difficulty of the self-imposed task. They knew nothing of the enemy's strength and less than nothing of the country they were to attack.

Every Englishman recalls with shame the failure of the authorities to provide proper stores and equipment. Alma, Balaklava, and Inkerman are indeed proud names in the story of British valour, but it took a whole year to reduce the fortress of Sevastopol, which fell to an assault of the French in September, 1855. No further action was taken to reduce the power of the Russians, and the neutrality of the Black Sea agreed to by the Treaty of Paris in 1856 was repudiated by the Tsar in 1870 when he saw the French too busy in the field to support England should she protest.

By the Treaty of Paris Turkey lost practically no territory in Europe, and the Great Powers undertook to safeguard the integrity of her dominions, as they had previously done in 1841.

Sultan Abdul Mejid, who in his reign of twenty-two years had done nothing for his empire, was succeeded in 1861 by Abdul Aziz. The latter by his extravagance brought his country to the verge of bankruptcy. In 1876 he was deposed by a " fetwa " issued by the religious head of the Islamic congregation, to be succeeded by a nephew who, after three months, was in turn deposed, and in August, 1876, there came to the throne another nephew, known to history as Sultan Abdul Hamid II., who reigned until 1909.

The Famous Treaty of Berlin

The political history of Turkey during the reigns of Abdul Mejid, Abdul Aziz, and Abdul Hamid II. (1839-1909) all turns on two main topics : (1) the status of the non-Moslem subjects of the Sultan, and (2) the European boundaries of the Ottoman Empire.

It was the revolt of various Slav provinces, notably Bulgaria, and the condign punishment meted out to them by the Turks, including the notorious " Bulgarian Atrocities " (1876), that led to the declaration of war by Russia in January, 1877. The most notable feature of this war, which lasted a year, was the heroic defence of Plevna by Othman Pasha. The Treaty of San Stefano, which was concluded by the two combatants in March, 1878, was considered by the other Powers too harsh for Turkey, and, what was perhaps more important, too favourable for Russia.

Lord Beaconsfield intervened, and in June of the same year the famous Congress of Berlin signed a treaty by which Europe went back to her pledges of 1856 and consented to the partial dismemberment of Turkey, whereby she lost Serbia, Montenegro, Rumania, half Bulgaria, Thessaly, Kars, and Batum. England, in return for her support of this " Peace with Honour," obtained Cyprus in fee, in payment of an annual tribute to the Sultan. Thus ended the dominion of Turkey in Europe, which at the height of its prosperity had embraced nearly 230,000 square miles and a population of about twenty millions.

The Treaty of Berlin was followed by twenty years of comparative peacefulness, during which Abdul Hamid, had he so desired, might have inaugurated some much needed internal reforms, including the granting of a Constitution, which had been actually promulgated in 1876 under pressure from the reforming party led by the famous Midhat Pasha, then grand vizier. By the Treaty of Berlin, moreover, England had taken upon herself certain obligations by which it was hoped she might be able to continue the policy of internal Turkish reform which Stratford Canning had so ably initiated.

In 1897 Greece went to war with Turkey on account of Turkish misrule in Crete. Europe again intervened and Crete, though nominally Turkish, was placed under Prince George of Greece, as high commissioner approved by the Powers. Macedonia, seeing so many neighbouring states freed from the Ottoman yoke, now began to revolt. Meanwhile, Abdul Hamid was using every effort to gain acceptance for the Pan-Islamic idea—which implied the union of all Moslems under the Sultan in his position of Caliph.

The origin of the movement was no doubt the waning power and prestige of the Sultans in Europe, and it also implied the revocation of the privileges hitherto granted to non-Moslem subjects and to foreigners. The chief victims of this policy were the Armenians.

In 1898 Germany began her policy of ingratiating herself with Turkey, thus utilising the opportunities which had been missed by England. Valuable railway concessions were obtained, but the Sultan was reluctant to join the Triple Alliance. In 1908 the movement set on foot by Midhat Pasha took form in the establishment of the Young Turk Party (Yeni Turan), and a Committee of Union and Progress in Salonica proclaimed a new Constitution. But, however much the Powers might wish to see a reformed Turkey, Austria, fearing that as a result she might have to renounce some of the territory she had acquired by the Treaty of Berlin, managed to secure at a price Bosnia and Herzegovina.

In 1909 Enver Bey, commander-in-chief of the Young Turks, entered Constantinople, deposed Abdul Hamid, and appointed in his place Mohammed V., who had been a state prisoner and possessed neither the training nor the experience to fit him for public life. The idea underlying the Young Turk movement was quite contrary to that which inspired Pan Islam.

The new movement was patriotic, just as the Pan-Islamic idea had been religious. Nationality and liberty were the watchwords of the new party, while the old Turks clung to their pride in Islam. A government was set up at Angora in 1920, under the name of the Government of the Grand National Assembly of Turkey ; and in November, 1922, the Sultan having fled from Constantinople, his cousin, Prince Abdul Medjid, eldest prince in male descent of the House of Othman, was elected Caliph.

TURKEY: FACTS AND FIGURES

The Country

Occupies greater portion of Anatolia (Asia Minor) and small part of Balkan peninsula. Asiatic Turkey is largely composed of plateaux from 2,500 to 4,500 feet in altitude, with a downward easterly slope. In the south are the Taurus mountains. Among rivers are the Kizil Irmak, Euphrates, and Sakaria Irmak, and there are a number of fresh and salt lakes, including Tuz Tcholu, forty-five miles long. Climate on the plateaux is severe in summer and winter. On the Black Sea coast malaria is common, but in the south and west winters are milder and summers influenced by cool winds from Mediterranean. Under Treaty of Sèvres, total area of Turkey was about 175,000 square miles, with an estimated population of 8,000,000.

Government and Constitution

In 1921 the Grand National Assembly of Angora proclaimed a Fundamental Law, declaring legislative and executive power in the hands of this Assembly. The term "Ottoman Empire" was abolished and the country officially designated Turkey. Republic declared October, 1923, with Kemal Pasha as President.

Commerce and Industries

Population engaged principally in agriculture and stock-raising. Soil generally fertile and produces cereals, cotton, tobacco, almonds, nuts, olives, vines, and figs. Opium is produced at Konieh, silk at Constantinople and Brusa, and there is a considerable output of mohair and wool. There are some 21,000,000 acres of forest. Minerals include silver, chrome, zinc, borax, emery, asphalt, copper-ore and coal. Main industries include brass-turning, copper-beating, and cotton-spinning. Fisheries are important sources of wealth, and sponge fishing is carried on. In 1921, Turkish imports totalled £T121,329,542, and included metals, wool and cereals, while exports for same year were valued at £T30,379,812, among the chief being dried fruits, carpets, opium and tobacco. Nominally £T11=£10.

Communications

Length of railway line estimated as about 2,800 miles, and of telegraph lines about 28,900 miles. Roads for the most part indifferent or bad.

Religion and Education

State religion is Mahomedanism, with a Caliph as head. There are considerable numbers of Armenians, Orthodox Greeks, Roman Catholics, and Jews. Primary education nominally compulsory for both sexes between ages of seven and sixteen. State schools are in hands of a Ministry of Public Instruction. Total number of schools about 36,200, with some 1,331,000 scholars. A university is established at Constantinople.

Chief Towns

Angora, capital (estimated population, 30,000), Constantinople (1,000,000), Brusa (110,000), Sivas (65,000), Konieh (45,000).

MEMBER OF THE PRINCELY HOUSE OF HUNZA WITH HUNZA FOLLOWERS

As brother of the Thum of Hunza, a small hill kingdom nominally tributary to Kashmir, and situated along the Hunza river, this tall, personable magnate enjoys considerable prestige among his fellow-hillmen. Hunza commands an important route from Turkistan across the Pamirs—a plateau region of lofty plains and high mountains, designated locally as the " Roof of the World "

Photo, Sir Percy Sykes

Turkistan

Peoples of the Central Asian Plains

By Sirdar Ikbal Ali Shah, F.R.G.S., F.R.A.S.

Writer and Lecturer on India and Central Asia

This chapter deals with that portion of Turkistan which was emancipated from Russian rule as a result of the Great War. Supplementing the earlier chapters on Bokhara, Khiva, and Sin-Kiang, it completes our survey of the peoples in this region of Asia whose political associations are somewhat unstable

THE Central Asian area known somewhat locally to-day as Turkistan, and forming an autonomous republic, is bounded on the north and north-east by the Steppes, on the north-west by the Sea of Aral, on the south-west by Khiva, on the south by Bokhara, and on the east by Sin-Kiang.

For the most part it is a level and well-watered plain, wild and uncultivated in places, but towards the south-east, in which the only cities of importance are situated, the habits of the people are agricultural and commercial.

Roughly speaking the inhabitants of Turkistan may be divided into those of Persian origin and those of Turkish race. The original inhabitants, the Tajiks, seem to have peopled the country between the Syr-Daria and the Amu-Daria.

The Turkish races were comparatively late immigrants into this region, and when they did enter it they seem to have driven its Iranian inhabitants into the mountain country or the towns. Thus in the cities of Bokhara, Samarkand, and Khojend, the Tajiks form the main element of the population, while on the

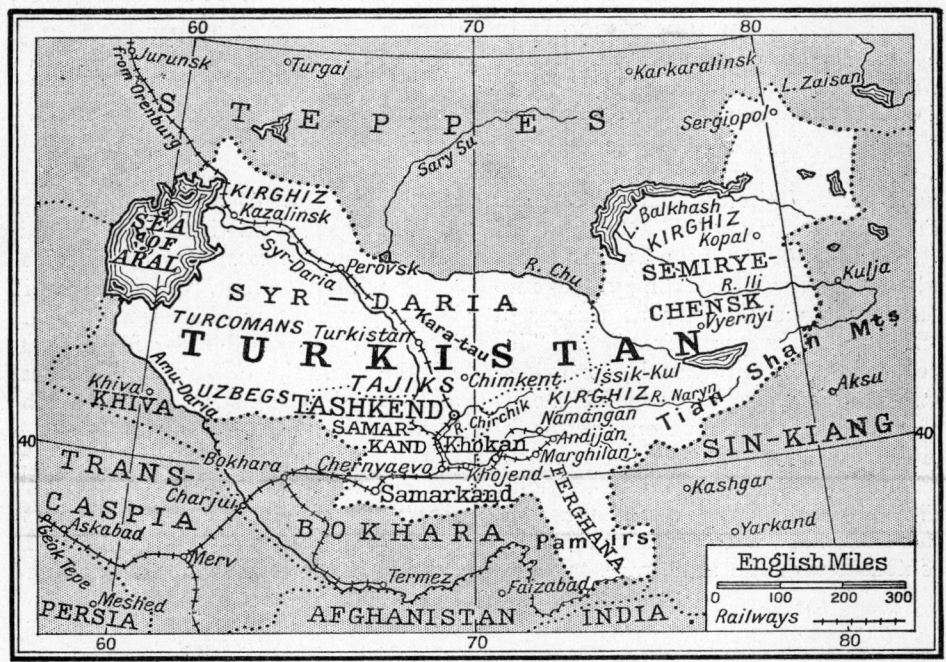

TURKISTAN AND ITS PEOPLES

DOUGHTY TURCOMAN WARRIORS OF GEOK TEPE

A stalwart people and a brave one, with no grain of servility in their character, the Turcomans are renowned for their fiery pride of race. Their martial tastes are strongly developed, and often lead them to seek military service outside their country. They make formidable soldiers, and the Cross of S. George, for valour, adorns the breast of many who served with the Russian legions

Photo, Maynard Owen Williams

right bank of the Syr-Daria, people of Turkish race prevail.

The descendants of the Turkish tribes who at various times migrated into Central Asia are known as Uzbegs, a term which means "free" or "independent." They are said to be divided into ninety-two clans or families, each of which has its divisions and subdivisions. Most of these still pursue a nomad life under certain restrictions. The Kirghiz are also of Uzbeg stock, and the Turcomans were certainly a similar confederacy of the same race.

The Tajik is, as a rule, a taller and heavier man, by no means active in his habits, and with a tendency towards mendacity. The Uzbeg is thinner and more wiry, with a long, strongly-marked face, and is simple in his manners and dress. He regards the Tajik with contempt, while the Tajik looks upon him as a child of nature who is scarcely responsible for his actions. All the same the Uzbeg has a national and racial consciousness which the Tajik lacks.

The Tajik speaks a dialect of Persian which has been influenced by the Turki dialect, but nevertheless it retains many ancient words and expressions of Aryan origin which are not used in modern Persian. The Uzbegs speak Turki or a certain dialect of that tongue. Tajaki is, however, the language of culture and literature.

The population of this region has been estimated at nearly two million souls, one half of whom are nomads. Besides the two races named there are traces of others in the country, especially Persians, Arabs, Hebrews, and Hindus. The Jews have indeed been in the country for centuries and carrying on a trade as moneylenders. The Hindus are usually merchants who visit the country temporarily from the neighbourhood of Shikarpur. The Lurs, who are probably the ancestors of the European gypsies, trade in horses, tell fortunes, and lead a nomadic life.

Agriculture is carried on in a manner quite archaic, tools and implements are of the most primitive character, but, this notwithstanding, the art of irrigation is thoroughly understood and practised.

Cotton is extensively planted, and large and valuable crops have been forthcoming. But of late years the mulberry plantations have suffered sadly. On the other hand valuable deposits of coal and oil have been discovered in the neighbourhood of Samarkand, and in such abundance as to justify the belief that when these resources have been fully exploited Turkistan will be in a position to take its place among the rising commercial communities of the East.

In the mountains of Kara-tau appears the upper strata of carboniferous limestone which may indicate a true coal-producing strata at a lower level. Coal is also found at Khojend and elsewhere, but it is of the variety known as " brown " coal, useful enough for fuel and for smith-work, but of no avail for such metallurgical operations as the reduction of iron ore.

Such coal as I saw in Turkistan appeared to be too friable and too much mixed with stone, and the difficulty of its transport through the mountains

SIGHTLESS EYES THAT CLAIM TO FORESEE THE FUTURE

Divination as a lucrative business is firmly established throughout the Orient. Crystal-gazing is one well-known method, and sand-diviners ply a good trade in many Eastern bazaars. A variant of sand divination is practised by this blind fortune-teller in Khokan, capital of the Ferghana province of Turkistan ; he predicts the future of his clients by the disposition of little heaps of pebbles

Photo, Maynard Owen Williams

BEFORE THE MADRASAH ULUG BEG IN THE SQUARE OF SAMARKAND

Samarkand, an oasis city, has been described as a " jewel set in sand." Its luxuriant gardens, architectural splendours, and the fact that it was the scene of the Arabian Nights' story-telling, explain the glamour that glorifies it in the Eastern eye. The Righistan, the beautiful public square, is fringed by three fine madrasahs, or colleges, one of which is named after the astronomer, Ulug Beg

Photo, Miss Hunter

RHYTHMIC DANCE OF SARIKOLIS IN THEIR CHARACTERISTIC GARB

Dressed in long, dressing-gown coats, quilted, and usually tied round the waist by a narrow band, the Sarikolis present a comical spectacle as they perform the ungainly steps which they call dancing. While the slow shuffling of their feet is in progress their arms, cased in ludicrously long sleeves, are brought into play, the whole accompanied by the " orchestra " in the background

Photo, Sir Percy Sykes

BURLY MEMBERS OF AN EASTERN PASTORAL TRIBE

The grassy stretches of land lying near Lake Aral form the pasture-ground of various communities, chief among which are the Kirghiz of Uzbeg stock. They are nomads, and, possessing extensive flocks and herds, pass from pasture zone to pasture zone according to the season. Their homes are but a collection of movable tents, and their livestock often represents the whole of their worldly wealth

NOMADS FROM THE STEPPE-LAND OF WESTERN TURKISTAN

Far from prepossessing are these Kirghiz with their high cheek-bones, narrow eyes, and broad, flat faces; but they are singularly wiry of constitution, and well-fitted for the roving life they lead about the wide plains and the mountain slopes of Turkistan. Their clothing is chiefly made from the wool and skins of their livestock which comprises horses, sheep, goats, and sometimes oxen and camels

Photos, Florence Farmborough

AGED EASTERN ECCLESIASTIC

He is a priest of Sarikol, and dwells with his blood-brothers, the Sarikolis, below the famous Tagdumbash Pamir. The Sarikolis are followers of the Aga Khan of Bombay
Photo, Sir Percy Sykes

magnificence in an atmosphere of mysterious impenetrability. In the time of Alexander the Great it was a large and flourishing city, and the world-conqueror made it his headquarters in his expeditions against the Scythians.

Alexander's exploits are still preserved by legend and are known to every inhabitant. The ruins of the mosque of Shah Zindeh still retain their appearance of ancient splendour, and are among the finest in Central Asia, the enamelled bricks and inlay of alabaster being in the best style of Persian art. The madrasah, or college, of Bibi Khanym, the favourite wife of Timur or Tamerlane, and the daughter of the Emperor of China, possesses a marvellous double dome, but now does duty as a horse market.

One of the chief centres of the town is the Righistan, or market square, where are three of the principal colleges. On the top of some rising ground to the south of the fortress is the tomb of Timur, gorgeously decorated with alabaster and transparent gypsum. The tombstone occupies the exact centre of the mosque, and is composed of a slab of greenish-black stone six feet long, and fifteen inches wide.

The citadel is an imposing building, and contains several mosques as well as the former place of the Ameer, and the Kok-tash, or sacred stone which served as the foundation for the throne of Timur. There are other remains of the flourishing period of Samarkand in the city. The bazaars of the place are, however, much less imposing and interesting than those at Tashkend and Khojend. The chief portion of the old bazaar is the Timi, a large, octagonal, covered building where smaller articles are sold, and there are separate buildings for silk and cotton goods.

In Tashkend, the administrative centre, the streets are rambling and shaded by trees overtopping the walls on either side. Many of the prospects of the place recall rural conditions, so suddenly does one come upon old mills turning sleepily by the verge of half-

is a serious drawback. Lead ore is plentiful, especially in the Kara-tau mountains, but already these mines have been pretty well worked, and the quantities which remain are difficult to smelt. Iron and copper are also found, but such gold as remains is extremely difficult to win.

Samarkand, famous in poetry and legend, is surrounded by a halo of romance. For centuries it has preserved the traditions of a past

WAITING FOR CHANCE CUSTOM AT A CORNER OF ASKHABAD

Settled industries are still comparatively few and small in the Transcaspian regions bordering on the south-west of Turkistan, but wherever men go shod the shoemaker is sure of a livelihood. This grey-haired cobbler, with so meagre an outfit, is a Persian in business at Askhabad, a town of growing commercial importance on the Transcaspian railway that runs from Krasnovodsk to Samarkand

Photo, Maynard Owen Williams

HORSE MARKET AT SAMARKAND, BY THE COLLEGE THAT COMMEMORATES TAMERLANE'S FAVOURITE WIFE

Glamour of romance invests the very name of Samarkand. As Maracanda it was a mighty city when conquered by Alexander the Great in 329 B.C. A thousand years later it was conquered by the Arabs, and became a centre of the intellectual and religious life of Mahomedan Asia. Tamerlane's capital, it still contains his tomb, the famous shrine of his companion Shah Zindeh, and some architecturally wondrous madrasahs or colleges. Among these is the domed college of Bibi Khanym, Tamerlane's Chinese wife, now used as the market for Samarkand's great trade in horses and asses

Photo, Miss Hunter

KIRGHIZ OF TURKISTAN'S HIGHLANDS LOADING UP THEIR YAKS PREPARATORY TO MOVING CAMP

In its purely wild state the yak lives only in the central plateau of Tibet, where it attains a height of six feet at the shoulder. Very little inferior to this animal, however, is the domesticated "grunting ox," in use among the natives of the Pamirs. Immensely strong and hardy, this yak is black, with long, shaggy hair on the belly and flanks, and with a bushy tail that makes an excellent fly-whisk. In the hands of the Kirghiz the yak is a docile beast, but it is apt to attack Europeans. It is intolerant of heat, and can only live at high elevations, where it is invaluable as a beast of burden

Photo, Sir Percy Sykes

PLAYING A POPULAR GAME IN THE PAMIRS: THE SCRIMMAGE

The game is known as " baigu," and the " ball " is a decapitated goat. The players, men long past the prime of life and sturdy young lads, are splendid riders who, almost cradled on horseback, can perform astonishing feats astride their wiry, little unshod horses. No spurs are used, and the stirrups are short and wide, enabling the riders to spring easily to the ground

Photo, Sir Percy Sykes

dried water courses, and ruined mosques surrounded by tall poplars. Small madrasahs or colleges are everywhere, and it is said that in the more retired quarters of the city old Mussulmans reside who pass their lives in prayer and contemplation, never leaving their houses.

But there is a modern Tashkend as there is a modern Samarkand, and the old buildings are slowly but surely being swept away to make room for new edifices built by Russian or Indian architects, which contrast rather sadly with the more sombre relics of the past which surround them.

The prosperity of the place is entirely dependent on its water supply. All the water is brought from the river Chirchik by a canal nearly sixteen miles in length. The city is divided into four quarters which were originally four separate villages or tribal cantonments, and each of these

has, or rather had, its separate elders and chief of police. The inhabitants are chiefly of the Uzbeg race, but most of the merchants are Hindus and Tajiks.

Khojend is perhaps the most pleasant of any of the cities of Turkistan, and this is due to its situation on the river bank. It is mostly inhabited by Tajiks. Towards the end of the summer the river Khojend frequently dries up, and the city then suffers from want of water, and these conditions are greatly aggravated by the heat, which at that season of the year is intense.

In the corner of the town, not far from the river, is the old citadel, built on an artificial square mound, one hundred feet or more in height. Access to this fortalice is gained by a steep path and from the summit a magnificent view of the surrounding country may be had. From the hollow sound of one's footsteps on this mound, I rather suspect

PICKING UP THE "BALL" IN THE HAZARDOUS GAME OF BAIGU

Here a player is seen bending from his saddle in the act of picking up the "ball," with which he has to gallop round a post and return to the starting-point. He is hotly pursued by the other players on their shaggy, tousled horses, and strenuous efforts are made to overtake him, to surround him, and to snatch the "ball" away before he can proclaim himself victor

Photo, Sir Percy Sykes

that it has been built on a wooden framework, only half filled in with earth; indeed, there is a legend that several soldiers once fell through the floor of the citadel and were never heard of again.

Khojend, which is on the direct road from Khokan to Bokhara, was at one time a place of considerable commercial importance, but since it was occupied by the Russians its trade has languished. For centuries it was an apple of discord between Khokan and Bokhara, and was an appanage of one or the other.

Turkistan was conquered by Alexander of Macedon, one of whose generals, after his death, made it part of the territory of the Graeco-Bactrian dynasty, which lasted until about 130 B.C. This was succeeded by the Yuetchji, apparently a nomad tribe living in the Steppes. While still under their rule it was attacked by the Arabs, who in A.D. 710 introduced Islam. Persian and Turkish princes in their

turn took the place of the Arab dynasty, and at last Jenghiz Khan overran the country in 1221, almost destroying Samarkand. The dynasty of Jenghiz was overthrown by Timur, who made Samarkand his capital, and spared no pains in embellishing and beautifying it.

The country seems to have been under Turkish rule until, in 1868, it was captured by the Russians, who were then at war with the Bokharans, the suzerains of Turkistan. In 1866 the Ameer of Bokhara arranged a treaty with the Russian General Kaufmann by which the boundaries of Turkistan were agreed upon, but this led to hostilities and the subsequent annexation of the country. Samarkand was occupied and the whole region gradually came under Muscovite rule.

Russian rule in Turkistan was for the most part a mere military bureaucracy dictated in a hard and fast manner from Petrograd, and its prime object was to make of Turkistan a centre whence the other Central Asian khanates might be attacked and annexed. The inhabitants were at once subjected to a taxation of the most onerous description, but every year showed a deficit in the budget.

Still, the primary objects which led to the occupation of Turkistan were rather military than financial. Turkistan was a link in the ever-growing chain between Petrograd and India, and as such, it was necessary to maintain it in a fitting manner—a policy the Slavonic race has by no means lost sight of.

Russian rule in Turkistan did not assist the prestige of the European races in Central Asia. The loose social life of the governing classes, and especially of the Russian officer corps, the introduction of paper money and the ineptitude of the Muscovite officials brought European credit into contempt among the sober and well-behaved Moslem population. But within recent years a national consciousness has sprung up in Turkistan which must sooner or later have developments of the utmost importance for all the Central Asian states.

AFTER THE FRAY: THE SMILING VICTOR AND HIS PRIZE

Having successfully repulsed the onslaughts of the attacking parties, the triumphant rider has gained the starting-point with the " ball " in his possession. Here he pauses, his hands clutching the trophy, his short-handled whip—a valued article, no whit less formidable than the Cossack nagaika —between his teeth, while he is vociferously acclaimed victor, and is rewarded with a silk handkerchief

Photo, Sir Percy Sykes

LOVELY PRODUCT OF A TURKISTAN LOOM TO TEMPT THE CONNOISSEUR

Specimen carpets from the looms of Merv and Bokhara are commonly exhibited for sale in the markets of Turkistan spread over the shoulder of some Turcoman vender, contrasting finely with his coloured coat and sheep-skin busby. It is the habit of these salesmen to affect indifference as they display these beautiful fabrics, but in reality they have a keen eye for a customer

Photo, Maynard Owen Williams

CHARMING STUDY OF A UKRAINIAN MAIDEN

She is wearing the festal costume of her district—skirt, apron, blouse and jacket of native-woven material and embroidered by her own nimble fingers. Even the garments of the poorest peasants display work of lovely design, and the artistic stitching in coloured silks and cottons noticeable in the attire of fashionable London or Paris is often an imitation of the needlework of the Ukrainian women

Photo, Underwood Press Service

The Ukraine

Peasant Life in a Fertile Land

By Florence Farmborough

Traveller and Writer on Modern History

THE name Malo Russia, or Little Russia, also known by the Russians as the Ukraine, or the Borderland, is said to have originated many centuries ago, and to have distinguished the southern region of European Russia from Greater Russia, which lay to the north.

Until after the conclusion of the Great War very few people in Western Europe had heard of the Ukraine. As a Slav publicist deprecatingly puts it : "Caesar knew Gaul better than the Western nations know Eastern Europe." Those, however, who studied movements of opinion and disruptive tendencies in the Russian Empire were aware that in the south an agitation was being carried on below the surface, with the aim of securing self-government for the race calling itself Ukrainian, and claiming to be an entirely different people from the White Russians and the Great Russians of the north and east, as well as the possessors of a language and a national culture distinct from those of the Russians and the Poles.

One could not spend any time in the various regions of the Tsar's Empire without being forced to admit these distinctions. Little Russia differed in almost every respect from Great Russia.

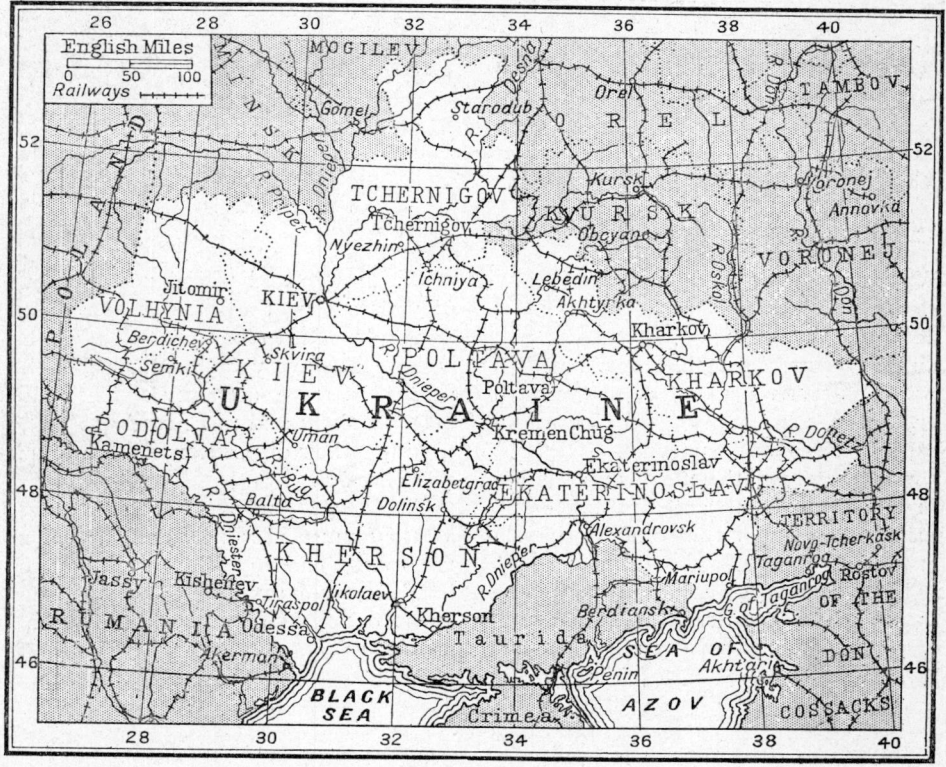

THE SOVIET REPUBLIC OF THE UKRAINE

WHEAT FOR EXPORT IN A BUSY COMMERCIAL CORNER OF ODESSA
Odessa is an ice-free winter seaport of the Ukraine, and the chief business centre in the south of the country. Parks and public gardens impart a pleasant appearance to the city, which is picturesquely poised on an eminence considerably above the sea-level. The wealth of Odessa comes chiefly from the handling and export of grain, here seen on the docks fringing the harbour
Photo, Underwood Press Service

While the latter was characterised by gloomy landscapes and grey, cheerless days, in the former both nature and human nature seemed endowed with a bright attractiveness and all the warmth and gaiety usually in evidence in a land of blue skies and sunshine. The two zones, therefore, the bleak and sombre region of the north and the fertile and brilliant region of the south, formed a striking contrast.

Little Russia is accounted one of the most fertile countries in the world. The richness of the soil and the facility with which it yields its magnificent crops have been undoubtedly among the chief factors in promoting the prosperity of the peasantry; for seldom

is the intense and pitiful poverty that prevails among the rural population of north Russia to be met with in the south. The very appearance of the people is more attractive. They are better-looking and more ready to make friends; their disposition is more genial and cheerful.

The Little Russians, or Ukrainians, as they must now be called, have, in the past, endured the bitterness of bondage for a very long period. Prior even to the two centuries and a half passed under the Russian yoke, they had been subjected to Polish rulers. The first Ukrainian State was established, it is claimed, in the ninth century in Kiev. In the fourteenth century the eastern portion of this state passed over to Lithuania, while Poland conquered the western portion. Finally, however, the whole of the Ukraine came under Polish suzerainty. But in 1648 the Polish yoke was thrown off, and six years later a treaty was concluded with the Muscovite Tsars, by which the territory east of the Dnieper was united with Muscovy ; Galicia being ceded in 1795 to Austria.

In asserting their right to autonomy the Ukrainians declared that the ties existing between them and Russia were purely dynastic, since the Tsar was protector of their state by treaty. When, therefore, Russia ceased to be an empire, they refused to acknowledge the right of the Russian people to arrogate to themselves privileges that had belonged to the deposed emperor. Intent on re-establishing their long dormant independence, they formed a provisional government, stedfastly refusing to recognize the Bolshevist regime. Accordingly, on Nov. 21, 1917, the independence of the Russian Ukraine was proclaimed. In 1920 a Soviet government was set up,

SCENE ON THE FROZEN DNIEPER AT A GREAT ANNUAL FESTIVAL

As the centre of ecclesiastical Russia, " Holy Kiev " was no inappropriate designation. It was in 988, in the Dnieper, that the Russians were first baptized, by Prince Vladimir, into the Christian faith. Annually the " Blessing of the Waters " commemorated this event—an occasion when vast crowds gathered about the Dnieper, many preserving some of the " sacred " water in bottles

Photo, Florence Farmborough

and the present Constitution is similar to that of Russia. In the Treaty of Riga, March, 1921, Soviet Russia and Poland agreed to recognize the independence of the Ukrainian State, which now comprises the following provinces of the former Russian Empire : Kharkov, Poltava, Tchernigov, Kiev, Volhynia, Ekaterinoslav, Kherson, and Podolia, an area estimated at some 174,000 square miles.

About 3,000,000 of the approximately 30,000,000 persons who compose the Ukrainian race live in Galicia, formerly Austrian territory, chiefly in the eastern portion recently made over to the Polish Republic. They are known as Ruthenians, or Ruthenes, and it is a bitter disappointment to them that a frontier still separates their land from that of their blood brothers. Not only, however, does a political barrier separate them, but a difference in creed also ; for, whereas the Little Russians of the Ukraine belong to the Ukrainian Orthodox Church, closely akin to the Russian Orthodox, the Little Russians of East Galicia, Bukovina, and some of the sub-Carpathians districts are Uniats— Catholics, who acknowledge the Pope as

MILKMAIDS OF KIEV MAKING THEIR MORNING ROUND

Every morning similar processions may be seen entering Kiev by all its winding ways. The country-women transact much brisk business in their dairy produce with the townsfolk, and through the streets they carry straight to the doors of their customers milk, eggs, cheese, curds and whey in innumerable earthenware jars, strapped on to the yokes which they bear on their sturdy shoulders

Photo, Underwood Press Service

IN A SILVER BIRCH GLADE OF THE UKRAINIAN COUNTRYSIDE

The womenfolk of the Ukraine are thrifty and industrious; all the work of the house and much
of that on the land is done by them, and in leisure moments they occupy themselves with their
needlework. A love of pretty garments and bright colours prevails, and many village girls may
be seen adorned with flowers, beads, and ribbons, even when performing the humblest duties

Photo, Florence Farmborough

their head but retain their Slavonic
liturgy and many of the rites of the
Greek Church.

The Ukrainians are pure Slavs, and
have none of the Finnish or Teutonic
intermixture which is so notable in the
north. They are, they say, the true
descendants of the founders of Russia,
who began by founding Kiev (attributed
to the year 864 A.D., but according to
some records to the fifth century).
While under Polish domination the
Poles made the peasants serfs. Nevertheless, the Little Russian serf never
became quite the same as the serf of
the north. He served unwillingly; he

had no "little father" feeling towards
his owner; and the family relation
which did much to soften the barbarity
of serfdom among the Great Russians
was scarcely known in the south.

The country fared no better under
the Tsars. Towards the end of the
eighteenth century severe measures of
Russification were introduced into the
Ukraine. A Ukrainian movement of a
nationalistic tendency, which first made
its appearance in the nineteenth century,
was immediately suppressed; the suppression being obviously based on a
determination not to recognize the
Little Russians as a separate entity.

As the Russian Minister of the Interior, Count Valuyev, vehemently asserted in 1863 : " There never has existed, there does not exist, and there never can exist, a Little Russian language and nationality."

Russia certainly did her utmost to make this pronouncement good, and to compress the two branches into one nation, or into what the world would regard as one nation. For many years no books were allowed to be published or imported ; no plays produced ; no lectures delivered ; and no sermons preached in the Little Russian tongue. Every grade of education from primary school to university was conducted in Russian. How slight the education was may be inferred from a Ukrainian Nationalist Professor of Lemberg, who stated in his " Geography of the Ukraine " (1916) that the illiteracy in the Ukrainian provinces of Russia must be estimated at fully 80 per cent. of the entire population.

Whether Ukrainian is a distinct Slavonic language or merely a dialect of Russian is still a problem for philologists. It is certain, however, that whatever claim the language had as a dialect, has been more or less effaced during the last few years. The Nationalists have initiated many alterations, discarding several letters of the alphabet and introducing three not included in Russian, thus purposely making the orthography as distinct as possible from Russian. They have further created a Neo-Ukrainian literary language, dispensing with many of the technical terms of Great Russia. Among the peasantry certain dialects are found,

SELLERS OF DAIRY PRODUCE IN THE UKRAINE'S CAPITAL CITY

The milk-sellers are familiar figures in Kiev's streets, and very picturesque are some of the costumes which they are in the habit of wearing. There are girls and women in top-boots, long quilted petticoats, or in gay printed cottons, broidered aprons, and coloured head kerchiefs—all country folk, for whom the long morning tramp is not the most arduous of the day's duties

Photo, Florence Farmborough

PRIEST AND MONKS IN AN ECCLESIASTICAL QUARTER OF KIEV

Much interest is attached to Kiev as the oldest capital of Russia, and as the metropolis of the Mother Church of the Russian orthodox religion. The Petchersk is a district of the city especially venerated on account of the famous monastery and numerous churches—in rich, decorative Byzantine style—and the catacombs which enclose the embalmed remains of innumerable saints

Photo, Florence Farmborough

while in the Western Ukraine a peculiar mixture of Polish, Slovak, and Russian is usually spoken.

Across the country there stretches a wide belt of rich black soil called the Black Earth Zone. It is of the same dark, immensely fertile soil from which sprang the prosperity of Canada. Here is the granary of Eastern Europe, the great grain-growing district which enabled Russia to export wheat in such large quantities. Everything in this land of promise grows as if by magic ; all kinds of grain are abundant, on every side fruits and vegetables are to be found ; verdure of wonderful richness, flora of lovely variety, grow to perfection.

Nothing is dull in the Ukraine. Even the loneliest steppes are not without animal life, and some parts teem with fur and feather. Wild flowers grow in profusion ; one enthusiast, for instance, collecting nearly two hundred different species from the open steppe alone.

Given peace and reasonably good government, the Ukraine—the richest of all the countries that went to make up the old Russia—should recover from the damage caused by the war-madness of Europe more quickly than any other region. Its wealth lies in the soil ; all that has to be done is to work and to draw it out. It suffers from none of the disadvantages which the long winter inflicts on Russia proper. It has towns of considerable importance ; Kharkov, one of the leading intellectual centres, with a fine university, before the Great War ranked as one of the largest commercial centres in Russia. It has ports on the Black Sea, with Odessa, which is never frozen up, as their head.

Viewed from the sea, Odessa has an imposing appearance. It stands on an eminence, some 150 feet above sea-level, and a fine flight of 200 granite steps, rising from the harbour, gives access to the town. Always the chief port for

NEIGHBOURLY GREETINGS ON THE WAY TO THE FIELDS IN THE GOLDEN DAYS OF THE UKRAINIAN HARVEST

The beauty and the magic of the country districts of the Ukraine make quick appeal to the stranger's eye, and the picturesque little villages scattered about the varying landscape are rife with colour and charm. Harvest-time, when a luxuriance of foliage, a wealth of flora, and a profusion of fruit fill the air with mellow richness, is perhaps the favourite season of the peasants, who throughout the day may be seen gathering in the precious grain from the burnished fields of ripened corn, none is idle, and even the small children take a share in garnering nature's generous gifts to man

the export of agricultural produce from the southern provinces of the Russian Empire, it will undoubtedly play an important rôle in the economic future of the Ukraine.

Kiev, the capital of the Ukraine, extending for a distance of several miles along the right bank of the river Dnieper, with some 500,000 inhabitants, is an ancient city, which, even before Moscow came into being—in the shape of a settlement of scattered log huts— was already in a state of flourishing existence. Kiev was the first Muscovite capital, the most ancient city of the former Russian Empire. This proud distinction, has, however, in no wise debarred it from sharing in the amenities of modern life and civilization. Its imposing structures and broad thorough- fares are up to date, and present the prosperous, business-like aspect of a Western city. There is little here that is Oriental ; no influence of Russian fatalism, no Russian melancholy as the mental environment.

In Russia, Kiev held the ascendancy as a Holy City. To every Russian " Holy Kiev " was the mother city and the Mecca of his Christian faith. It was in this town that Christianity won its first foothold in Russia ; it was here, in the tenth century, that Prince Vladimir converted the people to the religion of the Christ by baptising them in the waters of the Dnieper. Since that time, to its myriad churches, monasteries, and convents, a host of pilgrims of the Greek Orthodox faith resorted annually from all parts of Russia, and even from Siberia, intent on prayer and fasting, or filled with the hope of a recovery of health that had been lost. In so far as cures of disease are concerned, Kiev had a reputation that vied with that of Lourdes in France.

The Petcherskaya Lavra, or Cave Monastery, the most revered quarter, contains catacombs, much used in days gone by as places of refuge. At certain of the church's festivals, vast crowds visit these catacombs, where the embalmed

UKRAINIAN VILLAGE CHARM

Flower - crowned, with bright garments broidered in many flashing hues, the Ukrainian peasant women are still faithful to their attractive national costumes, and in some districts feminine fashions have remained unchanged for generations

remains of many saints are still looked upon as objects of pious memory. The Cathedral of S. Sophia, a spacious handsome building of the eleventh century, with many additions of later years, and a considerable group of golden domes, and the University of S. Vladimir are among the most notable structures.

Of the older buildings of the town a great number were destroyed centuries ago. For Kiev has had a chequered past, not marked indeed by crime and calamity as in the case of Moscow, but subjected nevertheless, since its occupation by the Tartars in 1240, to invasion and pillage. Its history is inseparably associated with that of Mazeppa (the hero of Byron's poem), who, as Hetman of the Ukrainian Cossacks, rebelled against the Russian rule, but was routed, together with the Swedes, at the Battle of Poltava in 1709.

Promising Industrial Conditions

The industries of Kiev are mainly agricultural; there is an extensive trade in grain, timber, and cattle; but the commercial prosperity of the town is largely due to the fact that it is the centre of the beet-sugar industry. Here, in Lipki, the aristocratic suburb, the Russian sugar kings of pre-war fame dwelt in peace and plenty, amassing fabulous fortunes from their enormous country estates which were given over solely to the cultivation of beetroot.

The Ukrainians have now fair-sized holdings of their own and live comfortably; they are clever at poultry-farming and cattle-breeding, and practise that thrift which seems everywhere to distinguish the peasant proprietor. Provided they make a proper use of the cooperative principle, both as regards the disposal of their produce and the provision of farm machinery for themselves, they should become as flourishing a community of cultivators as could be found anywhere.

Drawbacks to Peasant Prosperity

The old allotment of land, twelve or fifteen acres, was not enough, and schemes are under consideration for breaking up the large properties so as to allow for larger allotments. The promoters of these schemes hope to abolish the mud cabins in which the poorer Ukrainians have had to live, as well as to maintain the harvests of wheat and beetroot such as were taken off the big estates.

The Malo Russian was not infrequently charged with indolence by his northern neighbours, and in truth he does not put overmuch energy into his work, but then his land does not require it from him. Still, there are hostile elements against which he has to struggle, and the chief of these is drought. This misfortune is happily but of rare occurrence; but when it does appear, its severity soon turns a rich, crop-laden region into a parched and stricken land, cut across with gaping fissures like great wounds, and there is no water either for man or beast. Care-free, improvident, making no attempt to cope with the evil, the Malo Russian suffers to the full. Another formidable enemy is the locust; the crops are ravaged, vegetation is destroyed, and the labour of months undone in almost less time than it would take to recount the tale; while some districts watered by the river Dnieper are inundated by the spring floods and laid waste.

Simple Charm of the Countryside

The Ukrainian summer is a beautiful season, but the time to see the country in its freshest and loveliest aspect is in spring. With a suddenness and a precision as astonishing as delightful, nature awakens from her winter sleep, and, in a day or two, the countryside is teeming with life, the whole rolling plain becomes one vast expanse of vivid green, while woods, meadow-lands, and orchards are ablaze with colour and heavy with scents from spring foliage and spring flowers.

In many country districts the houses are built mainly of wicker-work, plastered with clay and washed over with blue, pink, or green colouring. The cheerful, homely aspect of the dwellings is enhanced by the trim gardens, and the tiniest, humblest cottage can boast of an orchard, which in spring is gay with pear, plum, and apple blossom, and in autumn is full of ripe, sweet-smelling fruit, destined for the market of the nearest town or even for Kiev, where excellent jams

WINTRY WEATHER IN THE VICINITY OF A BEAUTIFUL MONASTERY

Winter is shorter and less severe in the Ukraine than in Great Russia, and April, which does little to relax the grip of snow and ice in the north, discloses to view the brilliant green of the young crops in the south. Making his way over the wintry road, this peasant sees to his right the famous Petcherskaya Lavra, or Cave Monastery, of Kiev, ancient of origin and exceedingly striking in appearance

DROSHKI FOR HIRE IN A COBBLED STREET OF OLD KIEV

Kiev, " the Mother of Russian Towns," has many quaint characteristics, and in the old parts of the city the picturesque presents itself in great variety at almost every turn. This low, open four-wheeler, without a back, is the prevailing type of light carriage which plies the streets, manned by burly drivers, invariably possessed of the verbosity and the genial disposition of the Ukrainians

Photos, Florence Farmborough

and preserves are made. There are also numerous flower borders, where, invariably, the sunflower rears its majestic golden head.

This flower predominates in the gardens of Little Russia, for the dried seeds are in high favour, especially among the lower classes in rural and urban districts. In some parts of the country entire fields are given over to

sprinkled over many of the breads, cakes, and pastries that are found so abundantly in the pastrycook establishments of the Ukraine.

Dreariness and monotony seem almost unknown words in the vocabulary of the Ukrainian. Even the steppe is not flat. At intervals there are interruptions caused by ravines, not very steep, not very deep, but big enough to enclose

AGED JEWRY FINDS COMFORTABLE QUARTERS IN A HOUSE OF REST
Prominent parts were played by Jews in the commercial life of the Ukraine. The moneyed magnates of Jewish nationality, despite sumptuous surroundings in the fashionable suburb of Kiev, were not unmindful of their poorer brethren housed in the squalid tenements of the Podol quarter, and provided many a home in which the aged and infirm could spend their declining years sheltered from distress
Photo, Florence Farmborough

the cultivation of the sunflower. Wondrous scenes of beauty are these plots, glaringly audacious with their vivid gold, accentuated by the dusky, deep-toned centre of the flower head, and by the fresh, leafy luxuriance that adorns the tall, slender stems.

Another strangely beautiful flowering plant, transforming many a dull corner of some peasant holding into a sea of animated colouring, is the poppy. The little black seeds of this plant are

villages or even small towns, and sheltered enough to allow the slopes to cover themselves with fruit trees and flowering shrubs. These snug little villages, scattered about the softly undulating landscape, or surrounded by fields of grain and rich pasture-lands, alternating with belts of dark forest or woodland trees of silver birch, oak, and chestnut, make pleasing pictures.

All natives of the Ukraine show a partiality for bright colours and pretty surroundings. Their national costumes vary in different villages, but all are colourful and attractive, some very fantastic, with a plentiful display of multi-hued embroidery. Even in the thoroughfares of Kiev many old peasant costumes are visible, put on, not for show, but as everyday wear. The decorative talent of the Ukrainian is conspicuous in the weaving of carpets, and these, in consequence of their beauty and the moderate sum for which their owner is induced to sell them, find their way into distant parts.

In needlework of large design and striking effect, as well as in the finer and more exquisite kinds ; in woodwork and all manner of village crafts, the same talent declares itself.

Influence of Music on Everyday Life

As becomes a fertile country where nature is bountiful and assists the people with generous hand, the Ukraine is full of beautiful old rural customs and ancient traditions. This land, too, is the home of music and song. The delicious melodies which Tschaikovski constantly introduces into his music have in them the spirit of the gracious, smiling landscapes of the south, full of colour, charm, and surprise. Many of the workers on the land, men and women alike, are fine singers, and the still hours of a summer evening resound with distant voices, singing plaintive old songs—and none so sweet or so inexpressibly sad as the folk-songs of Little Russia.

The peasant travelling companies of the Ukraine were well known all over Russia. Their musical plays, in particular, were finely melodious, and, with respect to variety of incident, full of resource. The folk-songs have some-times been divided into Doumki, or "little thoughts," and Shoumki, or "little noises." The former of these usually fall into a minor key, while the latter have a lively lilt about them not unsuitable to dancing. Many songs emphasise a didactic or moral tone, and

it was this class of song that chiefly comprised the repertoire of the popular bards, known as "Kobzars" or "ban-dourists," who were wont to sing them to the accompaniment of the lyre. It must not be overlooked that these hymn-like songs contributed in no small measure to the religious and moral development of the Ukrainian people.

Folk-Song, Dance, and Legend

Some of the Christmas carols, or "Koliadki," delightful songs, full of primitive naïveté, are of pagan origin, having drifted down to our time from the days when the ancestors of the Ukrainians still worshipped the sun god. With singing goes dancing. It is from this country that most of those dances came that have so delighted the world in the performance of the Russian ballet. And it is the fairy-tale country. Folk-lore in all its branches flourishes in the Ukraine as nowhere else. Legends, local traditions, stories of saints and of wonder-workers, all seem to cluster thickly here, and certainly influence the nature of the people.

Active Reconstruction of the State

As it is the most fertile country towards the East in soil, so it is in imagination, excelling in skill of hand and eye, in the spiritual as well as in the material sphere. One finds on review-ing "Russian" specialities, as they were known to the rest of Europe, that it is from the south that most of them came. The complaint that the Ukraine has hitherto been swallowed up in the Empire of the Tsars, or that its national characteristics have not been recognized, can be made no longer. The Ukrainians are now one of the great peoples of Europe, and with every-thing in their favour. The tides of war and of revolution that have swept over the countries of the Near East brought suffering and wrought injury upon this nation, but they possess ample means for recovery and are making use of them with energy. Their future seems assured

NEW YORK'S COMMERCIAL MASTERPIECE: THE WOOLWORTH BUILDING

Originating in the topographical necessity of vertical expansion of buildings in large cities, the American skyscraper is a marvellous product of architectural and engineering genius stimulated by a native inclination towards the spectacularly grandiose. A common height for these edifices is three hundred feet. Most remarkable of them all is the Woolworth Building which has no fewer than fifty-five storeys

Photo, Major Hamilton Maxwell

The United States

I. Contrasts of American Life & Character

By Hamilton Fyfe

1.

Problems of Racial Fusion and Mass Sentiment

THE American nation has been made upon a novel plan. Its members have flocked from all parts of the earth in order to join a society which offered them benefits unattainable in the lands where they were born, abundant work, and the chance for every man to draw the full profits of his industry and enterprise.

A nation thus formed offers a specially fruitful field for study. Into what Mr. Zangwill named the Melting-Pot have gone all the strains of the Old World to be added to the aboriginal North American Indian strain. What is the result of the mixture to be ? Perhaps it is too early even to guess.

Until the drawing together of the population which the Great War effected there scarcely existed an American nation. By far the larger number of the citizens of New York were foreign-born. In a city like Cleveland the foreign-born accounted for eighty per cent. of the population. Milwaukee was reckoned the third largest German city in the world. There were districts in many cities where only foreign languages could be heard. Hundreds of newspapers were published in German, Italian, Russian, Hungarian, Yiddish, and other alien tongues.

Peril of Unrestricted Immigration

For many years the flood of immigrants had poured in without check. The prevalent feeling was that the country needed population before anything else. Nothing was thought of but filling up the empty spaces. The inflow of new citizens brought profit to many interests. No heed was paid to the few voices which were lifted up to suggest that the United States were swallowing more people than they could digest.

The upheaval in Europe gave these few a hearing. The danger of vast blocks of population remaining more attached to their first than to their second Fatherland was acutely impressed on the public mind. The necessity of teaching many recruits the Army words of command before they could obey their drill-sergeants proved how faulty the process of digestion had been. It was not so much a nation which had been brought together as the materials for a nation.

Anglo-Saxons now in a Minority

The war did more to fuse these materials and to breathe a national spirit into the heterogeneous masses inhabiting the United States than twenty years of peace could have done.

Although the Dutch settlers in New York State and Pennsylvania, the French in Louisiana, and the Spaniards in California left traces which still endure, the basis of the North American population was for more than two centuries British. The founders of the colony which became an independent Republic carried with them across the ocean the spirit of British law, the British ideals of liberty and justice. These were embodied in the constitutions of the Republic and of the states which composed it. A common language and literature, a common familiarity with the English Bible, a common ancestry and tradition, kept the American people Anglo-Saxons for a long period.

LEARNED AND UPRIGHT INTERPRETERS OF THE CONSTITUTION

At the head of the Federal judicial system in the United States is the supreme Court of Justice which sits at Washington from October to July every year. Created by the Constitution, it is now composed of nine judges nominated by the President with the concurrence of the Senate and irremovable except by impeachment. Above political strife, its impartiality has never been questioned

Photo, Brown Brothers

Up to the middle of the nineteenth century those who were not of British blood were an inconsiderable minority. Even up to the eighties the British element predominated. After that date the stream of immigration gathered force. In a generation the population nearly doubled. Now it is the Americans of British stock who are a minority.

The geography of the continent and the manner in which it has been colonised seem to split it up into separate regions, each with its own interests and each inhabited by people with characteristics of their own. In the east manufactures and shipping are the wealth-producing industries. The south makes its money out of cotton. The middle west grows grain ; its prosperity has been built up on golden crops of wheat and maize (which the Americans call " corn "). Farther west cattle-raising, mining and timber have made

many men millionaires and spread a high level of general comfort. The Pacific Coast supplies itself with almost all that it needs.

Already there are one hundred millions of people inhabiting these different regions, distinct not only by reason of natural features and resources, not only by varying racial tendencies and economic interests, but also by reason of climates as far opposed as those of Norway and of Spain. Travelling in fast trains you find that the journey from one end of the country to the other consumes between four and five of your nights and days. To attempt to establish and maintain a sovereign state as large as this is an experiment. The only state that has been comparable with the American in size and population was Russia under the Tsars. That came to grief because it refused to move with the movement of the human mind. Whether democracy, the rule of the people, can accomplish what could not be done by autocracy, or rather by bureaucracy, the rule of officials knit together in a closely-guarded and powerful caste, is the most interesting problem of our age for those who agree with Pope's precept that "the proper study of mankind is Man."

Man has tried many methods of government, but none which in complexity was comparable with this.

What makes possible the application of democratic federal authority to so huge an area is that this authority only concerns itself with such matters as are truly national. If the United States had been unlucky enough to adopt the same system (or want of system) of parliamentary government which still exists in the British Isles, it would long ago have broken down. It is only the management of local affairs by local bodies which permits the national legislature and executive to deal with truly national affairs. The forty-eight states in the Union have their own legislatures, their own executives, and these are, within limits, sovereign bodies which can say " Yes " or " No " to measures which touch most intimately the social life and conditions of the people within their borders.

This system of differing laws in forty-eight districts varying in size from the sixty square miles of Columbia to the 260,000 square miles of Texas (omitting the 590,000 square miles of

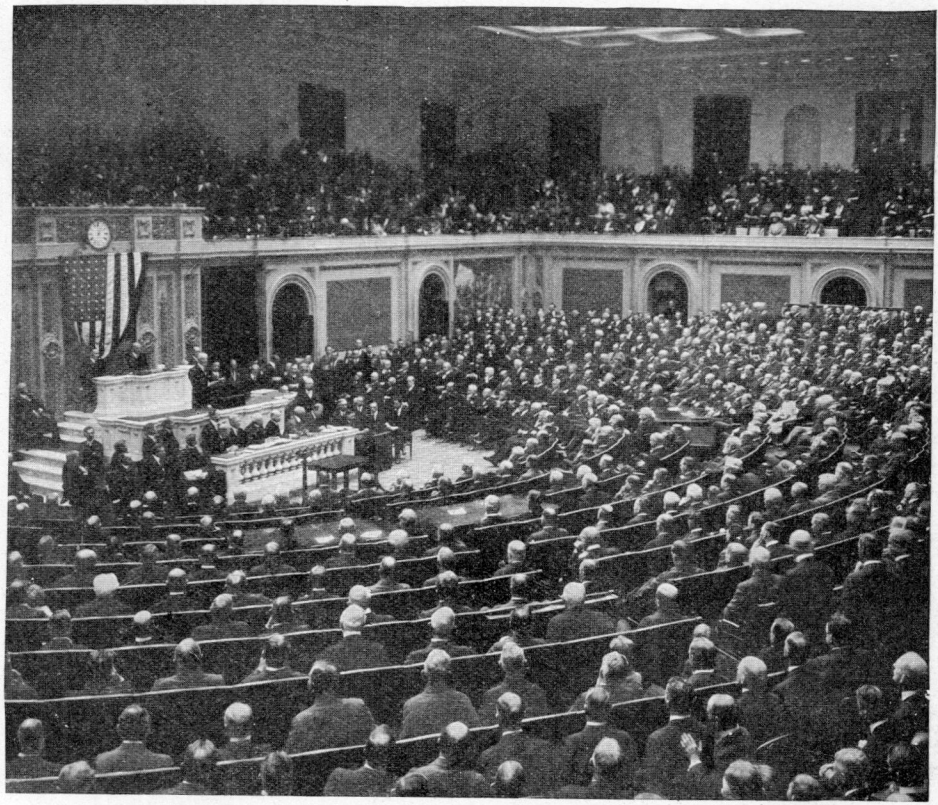

PRESIDENTIAL ADDRESS TO CONGRESS AT WASHINGTON

Crowds flock to the Capitol when the President delivers an address to Congress. While not permitted to initiate legislation, he can emphasise its necessity in any direction, and as supreme controller of foreign affairs and official head of the administration, his pronouncements are of weighty importance. Ninety-six Senators and 435 Members of the House of Representatives compose the Congress

Photo, Brown Brothers

WHEN PARTY SPIRIT BURNS WITH BRIGHTEST FLAME: NIGHT SESSION OF A POLITICAL CONVENTION

American political organizers have an accurate understanding of the psychology of crowds and in the stage management of political meetings omit nothing likely to contribute to the unanimity of large audiences when the time comes for them to pass resolutions and to vote. An impressive spectacle is afforded by the conventions held in great centres, in enormous halls gaudy with bunting and brilliant with arc lamps and packed with serried rows of voters with all eyes turned on the flag-swathed platform whence practised orators work the spell that shall charm the audience to acquiescence in their party policy

Photo, Brown Brothers

NEW YORK PLEASURE SEEKERS FLOCKING TO THE PLAY

Theatre follows theatre in the section of Broadway between Madison Square and 42nd Street, and this stretch comprises the theatreland of New York. The fine Metropolitan Opera House stands between 39th and 40th Streets and a little higher up is the Broadway Theatre, a home of comedy and light opera, outside which this great crowd is waiting for admission to a matinée

Alaska) seems at first glance to be likely to prove in practice inconvenient and irritating. It does not in fact work out thus, save in rare instances. It might suggest also to a hasty critic that there would be great difficulty in reconciling these different laws running in so many " water-tight compartments " and that friction would be frequent between the state and the national powers.

It must be remembered, however, that the states in the Union are not " water-tight compartments." They are not bound to the federal system by merely legal or political ties. The real tie which keeps the United States together is the citizen, who is at the same time a citizen of his state and also a citizen of the Republic as a whole.

He votes for the state governor and for members of the state legislature ; he also votes for a President of the United States and for a member of Congress. Thus he is constantly reminded that there are matters which concern a wider orbit than that of his state. He cannot think only of local interests. He is compelled at regular intervals to give his attention to the national point of view. In theory he chooses for state affairs the men best fitted to handle them, and for national affairs those who are capable of taking a wider survey.

Actually, until the last few years, he has been in the habit of accepting without reflection the candidates selected by party leaders and of voting both in state and national contests upon narrow party lines.

Politics — municipal, state a n d national alike—form a far more insistent part of American life than of life in the British Isles. To begin with, there are more elections, and there are a greater number of people to be elected. Almost every official must present himself to the electors and ask them to choose him. Even judges are under this necessity.

Politicians and the Popular Will

In one election at Philadelphia the voters had lists presented to them containing four hundred names. They were supposed to pick out the men whom they considered most worthy. What they did was to vote a solid " party ticket "; that is, a list drawn up by a party, not with a view to good administration, but to reward persons who had done useful party work.

Until lately the same party lines prevailed at all elections ; or perhaps it would be more correct to write, the same appearances of party lines. For in truth there is so little real difference between the principles of the Republican and the Democratic parties that they have hard work to make their programmes look unlike each other. Politicians in the United States are not leaders of the people, but followers of what they believe to be the popular will.

Big Business and Public Opinion

Besides following the popular wishes, American politicians as a rule pay deferential attention to the voices of the big interests. In some states railway interests were known to be the real force behind the administration and the legislature. In California this position was occupied by the Southern Pacific ; in New Hampshire by the Boston and Maine Railway. The revolt against the predominance of business men intent solely upon increasing riches and cynically contemptuous of the public was brought to a head by the formation of the Progressive party and has made a good deal of way since then.

But the history of the prohibition of alcohol in the United States as a national measure proves that the captains of finance and industry are able to guide American opinion in what appear the most unlikely directions.

The advocates of Prohibition would never have persuaded the representatives of the people to agree—on July 1, 1919—to the suppression of all drinks containing alcohol if the big interests had not come to the conclusion that more work could be got out of the men and women who worked for them if they were deprived, or persuaded to deprive themselves, of alcoholic stimulants.

The Power behind Prohibition

That Prohibition was hypocritically advocated by employers for their own ends was admitted even by Mr. Samuel Gompers, President of the American Federation of Labour. In a report which he wrote for the judicial committee of the Senate he pointed out that wealthy employers who advocated compulsory abstinence for the working class had spent huge sums in stocking their own wine-cellars.

It was by the efforts of women that the Prohibition issue was in the course of forty-five years made a live issue in American politics. During the year 1873 seventy women met in a chapel at a small town called Hillsboro in Ohio, and after prayers marched through the town to the drug-store of a certain William Smith, who sold whisky. They begged him to give up selling it. They prayed aloud for William Smith. Then they went to other drug-stores and made the same appeal. Two of the whisky-sellers promised to sell it no more. That was the beginning of the campaign against alcohol. Thus arose the Women's Christian Temperance

Tribal Types of
North American Indians

All the potent physical characteristics of his people appear concentrated in this magnificent old representative of the Siouan family

Photo, Smithsonian Institute

Manly fortitude is their most characteristic virtue ; vain yet valiant, the bravest of the Indian braves delights in bibs, beads, and baubles

Photo, Brown Brothers

*His fine face is full of the repose unknown to his Kiowa forebears,
so zealous in defending their hunting-grounds from white trespassers*

Photo, Smithsonian Institute

*Pride of race is writ in the stern features and regal bearing of this
Sioux chief and his squaw, seen in the ceremonial dress of their tribe*

Photo, Kadel & Herbert

5060

She is an Ojibwa maiden, of the great Algonquian stock, gentle and soft-eyed as the lovely Laughing Water of Longfellow's famous poem

Photo, Brown Brothers

The Hopi Indians, of Shoshonian blood, hardy hunters of plain and prairie, are some of the most skilled craftsmen of aboriginal America

Photo, Ewing Galloway

Native Justice of the Peace in the Blackfeet Reservation, he teaches his Indian brothers to bury the hatchet and smoke the pipe of peace

Photo, Leslie Clark

The Blackfeet girls, trained to the saddle from infancy, know well the divers paths of their habitat ; by waterways, and through the great forests they ride, the bristling peaks of the Rockies, bathed in mystery, ever in the background

Photo, Ewing Galloway

Union, which remained all through the chief moving force of the " crusade."

If the sellers of drink had not followed their own selfish interests, caring nothing for the harm they did and the wretchedness they caused, the flame of enthusiasm for the Prohibition movement would have died away. If they had taken warning when it started and had put their houses in order, selling good beer instead of bad whisky, they could have smothered it.

One result of the suppression of drink in 1919 was an enormous increase in the sale of ice-cream. This had been consumed in very large quantities for many years. Two gallons of it a head was the national consumption even before the country " went dry." This was about doubled within twelve months. In one city which had been accustomed to drink 300,000 barrels of beer yearly at a cost of £600,000 the quantity of ice-cream sold went up to 3,000,000 gallons, for which the public paid £800,000. The sale of sweets or, as the Americans call them, " candies," became also very much larger.

American Desire for Uniformity

Lord Northcliffe once chaffed the Americans upon their readiness to go in a mass in any direction that may be proposed to them. He playfully called them " white Chinese." It is this characteristic in them which accounts for such phenomena as Prohibition. They are more susceptible to what the hypnotists call " suggestion " than any other of the great nations, and when once they have become possessed by an idea, they are ready to carry it out fully, nor are they at all afraid of impinging upon personal liberty in doing so. They demand uniformity in regard to small matters as well as in the acceptance of the more important standards of conduct.

What can one make of a nation, many people asked with Mr. H. G. Wells, which tolerates so many iniquities, which has made divorce a farcical

process, which continues to look up to many persons, Benjamin Franklin for example, whose morals were of the worst, and yet, as in the case of Maxim Gorky a few years ago, falls upon a Russian ferociously because his domestic arrangements were—Russian ?

Public Prejudice and the Press

The explanation I offer is that the great mass of the American people are very ignorant of foreign manners and customs, know very little about what goes on even in their own country, and imagine that the standards to which they are accustomed must be universal in their application. To this ignorance the American Press attunes its note. It believes that its readers expect moral indignation from them, and they take care to supply it, " good and plenty," as the American phrase goes. They, like the politicians, do not set up as leaders ; they make it their rule to follow as nearly as they can what they believe to be the public desire.

The city populations are credulous beyond belief. They are hungry for sensation. They want some fresh thrill every day. The newspapers are, with of course some honourable exceptions, read for amusement, to pass the time, to get the stirring of interest or passion or emotion which the daily life in factory, office, store, subway or lift does not provide. Thus anything that is capable of exciting attention is written up with small regard for truth. " Sob-stories " are much in demand to draw the ready tear. Indignation of the frothiest kind is aroused by playing skilfully upon public prejudice.

Oratory and the Mass Instinct

There may be insignificant differences of opinion within certain well-defined and narrow limits, such as the difference between Republicans and Democrats. There may even at moments in the life of the nation spring up divisions which seem to waken fierce animosities ; an example of this was the Free Silver

CHOIR PRACTICE IN S. PATRICK'S CATHEDRAL, NEW YORK

New York became a Roman Catholic episcopal see in 1808, and an archdiocese in 1850. In that year the beautiful cathedral dedicated to S. Patrick was begun, to be completed in 1879, save for the Lady Chapel added in 1903. A large choir supplies the music for the services in this church, which in every respect is worthy of the high place it occupies in the Roman Catholic world

Photo, Brown Brothers

issue. But it died away as quickly as it came into being. No one took it seriously. It was an election cry. There are no perennial political plants in the American garden. All are annuals, torn up when they have served their purpose and thrown upon the rubbish heap.

As one travels over the United States one finds the mass of people in all the cities talking about the same things, using the same phrases, making the same jokes. Business has the foremost place in their conversation ; after that the topics which the newspapers put prominently forward. Even the same slang is heard from one end of the continent to the other. Vast as are the distances, the people in all the cities of the Union are more alike than those of, say, Sheffield and Bristol, or of Marseilles and Lille.

It is to the mass instinct that appeal is made by the proceedings which attend the election of a President. There is little argument, but a great deal of oratory. Not the reason but the senses of the voters are aimed at by the clever electioneers. Processions are marshalled many miles in length,

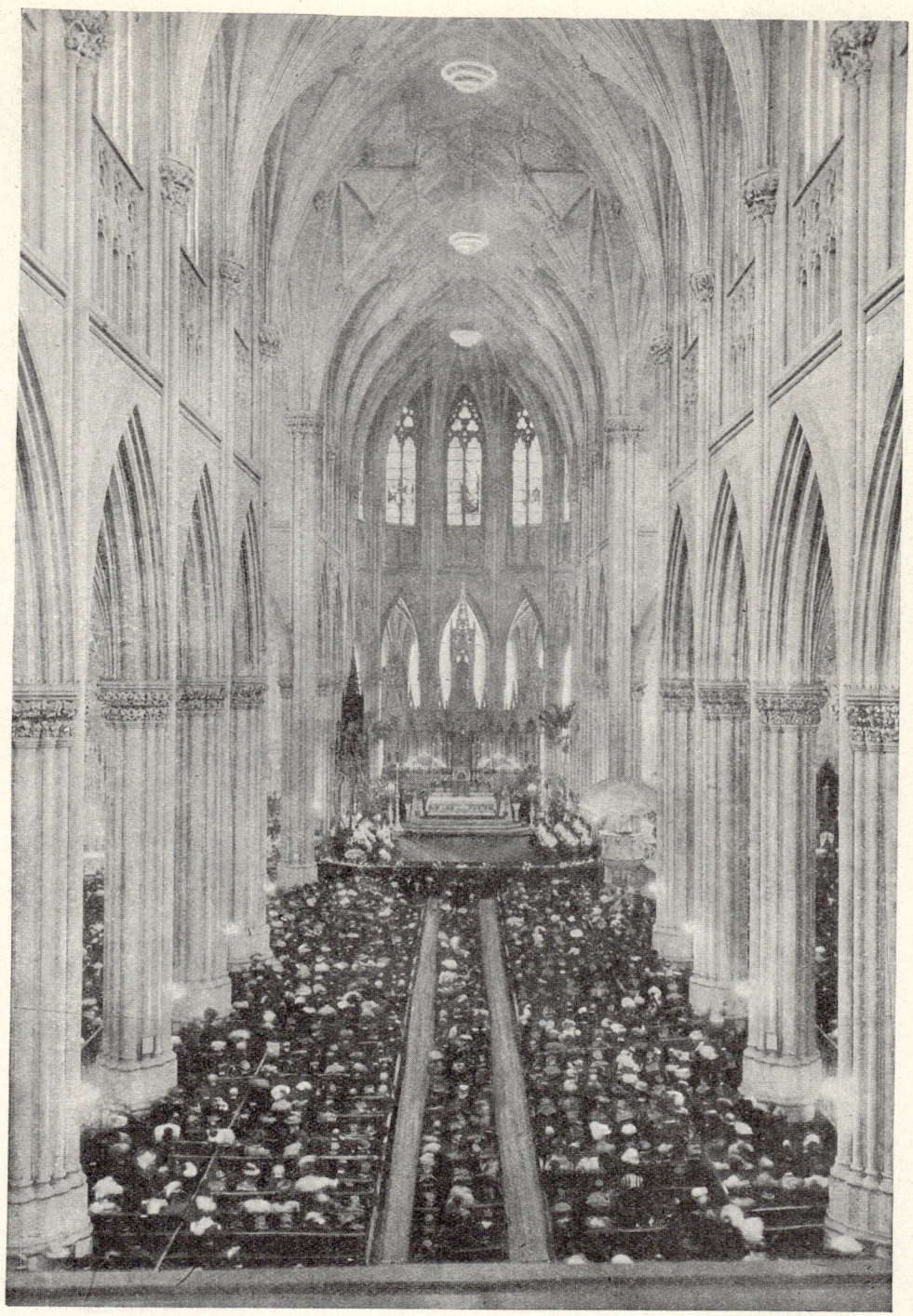

EASTER SUNDAY CONGREGATION IN S. PATRICK'S CATHEDRAL

In S. Patrick's Cathedral, the Roman Catholics possess the finest ecclesiastical building in the United States. It stands in Fifth Avenue, between 50th and 51st Streets, a cruciform building of white marble in the decorated Gothic style, 400 feet long and 180 feet across the transepts, with beautiful spires and much good modern stained glass. Sitting and standing, 8,000 people can find place within it

CHURCH PARADE IN FIFTH AVENUE ANY SUNDAY MORNING

Six miles in length over all from Washington Square to the Harlem River, Fifth Avenue is famous especially for the long section known as Millionaires' Row, where the world's greatest plutocrats have their mansions fronting Central Park. Wide and well paved, and lined with palatial buildings, the Avenue is a parade ground for the wealth and fashion of the city, particularly on Sunday in the season

Photo, Brown Brothers

NEW YORK'S DAILY STREAMS OVER MANHATTAN BRIDGE

Hundreds of thousands of people daily cross the East river separating Brooklyn, "the dormitory of New York," from Manhattan, the business borough, by ferry, by tunnel, and by the Brooklyn, Manhattan, and Williamsburg Bridges. These cars are passing under Manhattan Arch to the track on the lower deck of Manhattan Bridge, which has a footway and railway tracks on an upper deck

Photo, Underwood & Underwood

NIGHT SHINES LIKE NOONDAY ALONG THE GREAT WHITE WAY OF ELECTRICITY-LOVING NEW YORK

New York is a city of late hours where with the aid of dazzling electricity night shines like the day. Broadway, when night falls, becomes the Great White Way, illumined by the names of theatres and restaurants spelled out in steady lamps, and lit to brighter splendour by leaping rainbows, crawling snakes, dancing figures, and zigzag lightning flashes all turning blazing publicity on to all manner of wares. Under this electric phantasmagoria an endless stream of motor vehicles moves up and down among swarming crowds of pleasure-seeking pedestrians

Photo, Brown Brothers

BUSIEST CORNER IN THE HEART OF THE BUSINESS METROPOLIS OF THE UNITED STATES

There is continual turmoil and ceaseless movement in the streets of New York, and no brief description can convey a correct idea of the noise, the rush, and the press which are part and parcel of the outdoor life of the great city. Fifth Avenue is the chief thoroughfare; here a variety of architecture meets the eye, pure and crossbred styles including Rococo, Gothic, and a flavour of Byzantine and Mauresque. The wide, well-paved avenue is beset with an endless moving throng of vehicles and pedestrians, and our photograph shows the new signal tower, installed near 42nd Street, whence street traffic is directed by New York policemen

Photo, Brown Brothers

with brass bands and gaudy banners, with men in uniform, men in sashes, men in coloured capes or hats of unusual hue, men carrying scarlet or yellow umbrellas, floats (or platforms) on wheels bearing groups of allegorical figures. Trades send detachments in costume—bakers in white, broom-makers shouldering gilt brooms, glass-blowers carrying glass swords. As many as a hundred thousand have been known to march in such demonstrations.

Propaganda by Processions

George Steevens, the famous corre-spondent of the " Daily Mail," who watched one take five hours and ten minutes to pass the window where he sat in Chicago, wrote of it : " The eye was blinded with colour, the ear deaf with music, the head dazed with the effort to get it all into focus. There was more colour and more noise and more men than you could conceive were in the whole world—a world of brilliant bunting and brass and horses, and moving men, men, men, till you gave up and let it sweep over you and conquer you and absorb you, annihilated into its titanic self."

Influence of the Pilgrim Fathers

It is the demonstrative character of the Americans which distinguishes them from the race which sent out their ancestors to colonise Virginia and Massachusetts. By some the origin of it is sought in the admixture with the primal stock of Latin and Slav, of German Scandinavian elements. But it appeared before this admixture became considerable. Probably the Puritans who made New England, no less than the earliest Virginians, had a liking for outward show and spectacle. The Pilgrims even could not go to meeting on Sunday without a little ceremony. Their descendants have the same taste.

From Elizabethan and Jacobean colonists the Americans derived other of their still noticeable traits. In that age the English were of a material habit of mind. It was only in his old age that Shakespeare indulged in fancy. His feet all through maturity walked the solid earth. Ben Jonson never left the concrete for the fanciful. All the dramatists who made England a nest of singing-birds, whether they supped on horrors or held up their mirrors at the angle of comedy, put all their ideas into material form.

Materialism goes with the demonstra-tive character. It means believing in nothing that cannot be apprehended by the senses. Tell a citizen of Chicago that there is a strong feeling in favour of some candidate among his fellow-citizens. " Is that so ? " he says, and gives your assurance no further thought. Show him one hundred thousand men who are prepared to show their favour by walking in procession and dressing up : that makes an impression.

Meaning of " The Almighty Dollar "

The Americans have the reputation of being worshippers of money. They are supposed to care for business because they can make money by it. The truth is that they respect money simply because they respect the qualities by which it is earned. In itself they do not value it. No nation spends it more freely or more generously. I never met or even heard of an American miser. I cannot remember ever reading of one in fiction. The dollar is " almighty " in one way : it can purchase anything : or it may be more correct to say that there was a time when it could purchase anything. But it was never worshipped. Men who inherit large fortunes in the United States are not respected for their riches. They are despised, made fun of.

Dollars are the material proof of success. That is why they are valued. By the same token devotion to business is the one and only method by which most Americans can hope to show what stuff is in them. They long to prove their worth before the world. Success in business is their easiest road to the

AFTER THE UNVEILING OF THE NEW TRAFFIC TOWER IN NEW YORK

In the place of the old tower, considered an eyesore, this solid bronze traffic tower now rears its head in Fifth Avenue, in New York City. It is of handsome construction, being made entirely of ornamental bronze. The designer was awarded first prize for this admirable work of art, which undoubtedly helps to beautify the city's most famous thoroughfare—the centre of wealth and fashion

Photo, Kadel & Herbert

NEW YORKERS GATHERED IN BROADWAY AT NIGHT TO LEARN THE LATEST ELECTION RESULTS

One of the unforgettable sights of New York is Broadway at night, with the names of its theatres and restaurants picked out in brilliant points of electric light. Always animated, the great thoroughfare is never so packed with humanity as at election-time, when dense crowds gather about the offices of the "New York Times," near 42nd Street, to read the bulletins issued throughout the night of the results of the elections all over the country. Similar night scenes are enacted in every large city of the Union, so intense and universal is the political excitement

Photo, Brown Brothers

MAMMOTH PARADE OF THE GREAT BROTHERHOOD OF THE ELKS THROUGH THE STREETS OF LOS ANGELES

Americans seem to have an instinctive passion for demonstrations, and from the purely spectacular point of view the processions organized by propagandists to popularise their various movements leave nothing to be desired. Los Angeles, the beautiful city of California, is a favourite venue for conventions of all kinds, which put enormous sums of money into the pockets of the citizens. Here is shown a single section of a gigantic parade by the Elks, one of the leading friendly societies in the U.S.A., founded in New York City by an English actor and now numbering more than 1,500,000 members

Photo, Brown Brothers

CLAMOUR IN "PADDY'S MARKET" ON SATURDAY AFTERNOON

Its noise is the characteristic that most painfully affects visitors to New York.   Electric railways borne overhead upon iron pillars and trams roaring their rapid way over streets paved with granite blocks keep up an incessant din which in the congested districts on the east side is intensified by the polyglot clamour of hucksters in the street markets, especially on Saturday afternoon

Photo, Brown Brothers

attainment of their ambition. That is why so many of them give up to business the best of their lives. To them commerce is not merely a means to earn a living. It is through commerce that they express themselves, as the sculptor does in marble or the poet in verse. Their horizon is bounded by material achievement.

Is it unfair to trace something of this back to the Puritan stock? Were they not materialists in their way? They would not consent to any institution for which they could not find warrant in the Bible. What was written was

written. Unless it was down in black and white between the covers of Holy Scripture, they would have no part or lot in it. That was why they left England for Holland, and why later they sailed from Holland for America. They were determined to read the Word of God literally; they shunned all contact with those who would not do as they did. They could not be content even to live in the same country with "those that walked in darkness." Is it fantastic to trace back to the Pilgrims the American desire for uniformity, for a world in which all

MARKETING IN THE TENEMENT DISTRICT "WAY DOWN EAST"

Almost incredible overcrowding still persists in the tenement quarter of New York, perhaps the most densely populated spot in the world. In the small portion of Manhattan Island, south of 14th Street, and east of the Bowery, more than half a million people are herded together. Aliens from every land gather here, and their street markets ring with a bewildering confusion of tongues

Photo, Underwood & Underwood

accept the same standards of life, use the same expressions, and wear the same clothes?

Nowhere is fashion so powerful a slave-master as in the Land of the Free. At one time everybody will have their boots narrowed to a sharp point in front of the toes; at another all boots must carry a hideous large bump above the toes. The style of hat for each season, the cut of men's suits and women's "shirt-waists" (as they call blouses), even the shape of collars and the patterns of neckties are decreed. In summer all Americans up to fifty wear identical costume, consisting of trousers supported by a narrow belt of leather, coat, no waistcoat, tie neatly secured to a print shirt by an unobtrusive "stick-pin." Very sensible, this dress, and worn with a pleasant regard for appearances. But sometimes one cannot help feeling that a shade more expression of individuality might be refreshing.

Nowhere has advertisement been more studied than in the United States, nowhere is it more effective. The two main lines of recommendation are these: (1) If everyone has it, can you be

without it ? (2) " There's a difference."
The first appeals to the mass instinct,
the anxiety to look and act and think
and talk like everyone else. The
second bases itself upon the hopeful,
enterprising side of the American
nature. When once an Englishman has
settled down to some brand of tooth-
paste, some make of bread, some kind
of breakfast food, he sticks to it. No
amount of advertising will tempt him
away from it. The American is more
open-minded. He is ready to believe
that there may be something better,
something " with a difference." He is
inclined for adventure, for experiment.

That open-mindedness distinguishes
American life in all its material aspects.
Thought and sentiment must be fenced

round, they are fixed and immovable.
Social behaviour must conform to
certain standards. But against all that
must be set the magnificent American
refusal to be bound by what is usual in
mechanics, in methods of business, in
industrial organization, in all the
material activities of existence. The
Englishman's placid willingness to go on
doing a certain thing in a certain way
" because it has always been done that
way " finds no counterpart in the
United States, save in the region of the
spirit and the mind.

Men who have heaped together vast
riches by striking out with daring
disregard of tradition into new and
uncharted waters of trade, men even
who in their business have employed

JUST TWO LITTLE PICKANINNIES

The little " black nigger chilluns " of the South are happy enough in their native haunts, tumbling
about the log-cabins in careless infantile play, and stuffing themselves with corn-cake and sundry
scraps of food. But the bigger " chilluns " in the mill and field work like grown-ups—little
stunted specimens of humanity, with hardship writ large on their pinched features

Photo, Brown Brothers

AMONG THE BLACK POPULATION OF THE SOUTHERN STATES

The Republic is doing much to ameliorate the condition of her nine million negroes—that vast alien body of African origin which presents so many difficulties to the state legislation. The negro, though in the United States, is certainly not of it ; nevertheless, he is responding eagerly to educational influences, is growing more thrifty and reliable, and developing into a property owner

Photo, Brown Brothers

methods which are scarcely distinguishable from crime, continue to attend the church or chapel to which their parents took them as children, continue to profess the same attachments as their parents felt to the code of morality, the explanation of the universe, the meaning of life which that church or chapel taught in their childhood. In this direction " What was good enough for our fathers is good enough for us " remains the creed of the mass of American business men.

But if you asked them to apply that motto to their business concerns, you would be considered insane !

Together with the ingenuity of the Americans in devising new machinery, new arrangements for getting more quickly and more cheaply at what they want, there has been supposed to go a

" lack of thoroughness." This is a peculiarly English reproach. They certainly do not aim at the same high finish which is the mark of English workmanship. They decide what will serve for the purpose immediately in view ; beyond that they do not go. Instances of this could be quoted without number. Methods of cultivation are not as elaborate as on older soil. Factory methods are more rough-and-ready. The aim of American business men is to " get the business," and in order to get it, they have created organizations which are thorough for their purpose down to the most meticulous details.

Consider the department store, the shop covering acres of ground where everything that man, and more important, everything that woman needs can be bought under one roof. This has been elaborated in America to an extent unknown before, at once to the public advantage, and as a money-making machine of the most ruthless and efficient design.

Prices are "cut" in order that certain "lines" may be got rid of with complete disregard of anything but the momentary gain. For example, one of the biggest of the department stores bought up some years ago a stock of bicycles which had been made to sell at £20 apiece. The manufacturers were in difficulties. They were glad to let the machines go cheap. A slight alteration was made in the gearing ; the bicycles were then named after the proprietor of the store, and were offered at £13. As

they did not go off quickly enough at that price, it was dropped to £6 10s., and they were promptly got rid of. Even if no profit had been made, the advertisement was of immense value.

"Deals" of this character win universal admiration, except from small competitors in the lines which are exploited. They help to explain why business is the career which attracts most American young men and employs the best brains in the country. It is not staid and dull. It is an adventure. It gives scope for imagination, even for humour. It holds out possibilities of making a fortune by a single lucky stroke. It sifts out the capable and the quick-witted from the merely plodding and industrious. "Give the

"WHEN I WAS PLAYING WITH MY BROTHER, HAPPY WAS I"

This photograph, snapped a short distance from the banks of the Suwannee river, makes an excellent illustration for the second verse of the best-loved of all plantation songs : "The Old Folks at Home"—that famous classic of American balladry in which Stephen Foster, born nearly a hundred years ago, immortalised the river flowing through the states of Georgia and Florida

Photo, Underwood & Underwood

world something it wants and no matter how young you are, it will give you in return whatever material reward you like to name."

Half the novels that won wide circulation a dozen years ago used to be about the successes of young business men. The stories in the "Saturday Evening Post," a periodical which prints millions of copies and indicates the taste of the average American, are often upon these lines still. There has come a reaction from the purely material view of life, and books which have in them what is called "uplift" have won popularity. But business remains, and is bound to remain for a very long while yet, the most prominent interest in American life.

Unlike English business, it makes men adaptable. They pass from one occupation to another with ease. Failure in one does not leave any mark, does not suggest incompetence. There are proprietors of widespread businesses who tried many times before they found their feet. Many a highly-paid manager will relate his experiences in half a dozen different trades.

The same qualities, if they are applied pertinaciously, may win success in any walk of life, but the American will not be content with the first opening that he sees. He will make the best of it while he looks round for something else. He goes on looking round until he feels he has got something to which he can apply himself heart and soul.

A change has been coming over this feature of American life. As the country has filled up, as in the east

IN "MAMMIE'S" SHELTERING ARMS

The "mammie," or coloured nurse of the South, exists only for the babies committed to her care, and cherishes them with all the fervour of her motherly nature. Often she remains with her "youngsters" until they marry and then nurses their babies

Photo, Brown Brothers

especially, conditions have become fixed, opportunities have become fewer. The feeling so common in England that a man who has a good job had better stick to it and be satisfied, now finds expression in America also. In the west there still abound golden chances, existence is still fluid. In the east, where it has crystallised, the probability is about equal that a man will stay in whatever line he has chosen to begin with. Those who are conscious of more than usual capacity push out into some other line. The others are afraid to take any risk.

As the country settles down, there is also a shortening of the rope which used to be allowed to business adventurers. During the early years of this century the cry against the rich men who were supposed to be aiming at the enslavement of the people by means of colossal " rings " which would control the supply and therefore fix the prices of all necessities of life, was very loud and fierce. The novel in which Upton Sinclair described, with some exaggeration, the process of " packing " meat aroused a storm of indignation. The source of this indignation was not so much the inhuman treatment of the workers in " The Jungle," which it was the author's desire to expose and extirpate, as the nausea produced by his revelations of the manner in which tinned meat was prepared and packed.

A public inquiry was ordered into the state of Packing-town, as the stockyard and canning factory district of Chicago was called. The packers

ABILITY REWARDED
High school graduate and college student, his all-round ability won for him nomination to the U.S. Naval Academy, Annapolis

themselves hastily put their houses in order. Shortly after the scare I went through several of the yards and factories and found prevailing a state of cleanliness which seemed almost as exaggerated as Upton Sinclair's picture of filth and carelessness. The girls engaged in putting the meats in tins had a " manicure parlour " attached to their department and were obliged to submit their nails for frequent treatment.

The tinned meat trade was damaged by " The Jungle " and the outcry against trusts became more insistent. President Roosevelt took it up. The courts were asked under an anti-Trust Law to

AFTER LIFE'S DUTIES LIFE'S PLEASURES
This is no " Broadway Stuff," but a real hardworking cotton-picker, whose year's work is completed and who is now taking life easy in his own particular way. For the moment he has not even a dim recollection of those toilsome plantation days
Photos, Underwood & Underwood

made clear that business which dealt in articles or systems of " public utility " could not be a private matter any longer, and could not be allowed to follow the old practices of free competition. It was established as a principle that regulation of such business in the public interest was necessary ; that the advantage of the community outweighed the profit of powerful " corporations " or trusts.

About the same time began another manifestation of the cleansing fire which burned in the spirits of American reformers. This was the campaign against corruption in municipal government. Here also the magazines proved themselves forcible engines for the awakening of the public conscience. The writers who attacked mayors and

UNFAILING COMFORT
To this aged " mammie " enjoying a quiet smoke beside her log cabin, the pipe is an old friend, not a concession to the mode

dissolve certain combinations whose operations, it was said, were to the disadvantage of the community.

The attacks died away after a short time. Public interest, more fickle in the United States than in any other democracy, was attracted by other more exciting topics. Yet the violence of the shortlived tempest had accomplished in a brief time what an agitation upon sober, unsensational lines would have taken years to bring about. The trusts were frightened into less cynically piratical behaviour. Their claws were cut by legal enactment and decision. Most valuable result of all, it was

CELEBRATING HIS 115TH BIRTHDAY
As the keeper of the grounds, " Uncle Tom " Cotton was known to every person who had ever visited the resort at Pinehurst, North Carolina. His mottoes : " Love everybody," " Keep busy," " Never worry," have helped him, he declares, to reach 115
Photos, Underwood & Underwood

PRESIDENT HARDING WITH A GROUP OF INDIANS IN THE WHITE HOUSE GROUNDS AT WASHINGTON

The White House, the corner-stone of which was laid by General Washington, is the official residence of the President of the United States and was first occupied in 1800 by John Adams. President Harding is here seen with some Indians who have come from all parts of the States to request the appointment of one of their race as Commissioner of Indian Affairs. On another occasion, full of moment for the American Indians, Chief Buffalo Bear of the Sioux tribe, whose photograph appears in page 5060, petitioned the President to set aside a holiday to commemorate the 2,000 Indians killed in the Great War

Photo, Underwood & Underwood

APPLYING THE BRANDING IRON TO A YOUNG STEER WHILE LASSOS CHECK RESISTANCE

Periodical "round-ups" take place on the ranches for the purpose of branding the young cattle. Parties of horsemen, well practised in the art, single out the young, unbranded steers from the rest by skilful riding, and a deft throw of the lasso brings the animal to the ground. Then, while the captive animal writhes like a fish on a line perhaps a second noose will descend and secure one of its wildly-kicking legs and the brander applies his red-hot iron with a sizzle and a puff of smoke. The animal is, however, a good deal more frightened than hurt and, a few minutes later, forgets all about it

Photo, Underwood & Underwood

OKLAHOMA COW-PUNCHERS WATCH AN EXHIBITION OF LASSOING

Oklahoma State lies between Texas and Kansas and its undulating plains support much cattle. These are tended by men who, in their dress, still show traces of the " wild and woolly West," popularised by schoolboy fiction and the cinematograph. The cowboys know their own reputation, and are sometimes inclined to give the stranger a little of what he expects

Photo, Underwood & Underwood

boards of aldermen and city councillors for mismanaging the affairs entrusted to them and for taking bribes, knew that they could get the ear of the nation for a little while.

They must therefore, they saw, exaggerate the evil ; they must write in a style that would cause sensation and set everyone talking. They must denounce individuals, describe in detail particular instances of corrupt practice, give the impression that guilt was widespread, if not universal.

That is how American agitations have to be conducted. It is no use telling people the truth quietly. They must be shaken by it, roused to fury, induced to demand instant remedy. In other lands the belief grew that American municipal government was more corrupt than any other. " Graft " was looked upon as something that was customary in local affairs of American cities, something that was peculiar to the American Continent. It was not understood that over-statement is required in order to induce the nation to pay heed.

In all countries there is municipal corruption. In some it is certainly more flagrant than it ever was in the United States. It is often accepted as a necessary part of the order of things and nothing is said about it. The very attacks upon it which were made by American reformers proved that it was not inherent in the system, not tolerated by the mass of the people, nothing more than a cancerous growth which could be cut away. What the agitation brought into most striking relief was the readiness of the American people to try experiments in municipal government that aimed at making corruption impossible and at improving their cities for the benefit of all classes of their inhabitants.

The form which has been taken by the new city governments is in most cases that which was first employed at Galveston after the city had been ruined by a tidal wave. The citizens entrusted the whole business of clearing up the mess and rebuilding to a small commission. They saw that the usual number of officials all of them elected by the voters was a hindrance to getting things done with rapidity and vigour. This plan spread and was in most places which tried it found to work well, though there were some failures.

Another change which was supposed to be a further step towards managing the affairs of a city as those of private

FIVE HUNDRED ACRES OF HOOF AND HORN: THE UNION STOCKYARDS

Chicago's stockyards are among the wonders of the world. Every year over sixteen million animals are assembled there. The yards cover five hundred acres and supply the great canned meat industry located in the same huge city. The animals are slaughtered wholesale by various ingenious devices, so that, of a pig, it is claimed that nothing is lost for export but the grunt

Photo, Underwood & Underwood

MOUNT VERNON, HOME OF AMERICA'S FIRST PRESIDENT

George Washington inherited this pleasant Virginia home from his brother Lawrence in 1752. The house is built of wood and overlooks the River Potomac from a hill two hundred feet high. The estate was purchased by an association of ladies and is open for visitors who may see there the room in which the great man died, and on the balcony tiles brought from the Isle of Wight

Photo, Underwood & Underwood

persons are managed was to make the mayor the one responsible manager : this was at one time warmly advocated, but the commission plan held the field more strongly.

The one-man system, however, found favour in another shape. At Dayton, Ohio, in a time of crisis caused by the overflowing of the Mississippi, there was sore need of energy and initiative. The citizens decided to appoint a " city manager " and to make him responsible, giving him the same power that the manager of a private concern would exercise. This worked well and was copied by many other cities.

There are in the American character two main features. One is absorption in business, not so much, as I have suggested, for the purpose of making money for money's sake, as with the aim of showing superior qualities of will and brain. The other is idealism. No one who knows the American people well can overlook their desire to be better than they are. It is a desire often overlaid for a while, often forgotten in some sudden rush of anger or excitement ; but it is permanent, while the other feelings pass quickly. If it had not existed, if the greed and callousness of business competition had been

FATHER ASKS A BLESSING ERE THE FAMILY FALL TO

For Sunday dinner there is a special spread in this New England farmstead and everyone is in clothes that are felt to be suitable to the occasion. Round the walls will be noticed a collection of ancient flint instruments, scrapers, arrow and spear-heads and harpoons, all dug up from the farm. In contrast to this archaeological exhibition is the telephone on the left

ROUGH PLENTY AT THE END OF A FARMING DAY

Many a farmer pioneer has left Europe for the U.S.A., and after years of risk and work at length found himself in his own house on his own land and with sons round the family table at meal-times. A glance at the peaked, rough face of the father, heading the table, and another at his broad-shouldered sons will show the strides that an American country population may make in a generation

Photo, Brown Brothers

unchecked by it, anarchy would have supervened.

The wish to improve can be traced in the smallest matters of daily life. Every American uses various toilet preparations designed to keep the hair, the skin, the teeth, in good order. Time and thought are devoted to methods of improving appearance as well as health. Nowhere is more attention paid to diet, nowhere is so much money spent on food advertisements. And alongside puffs of this and that breakfast cereal, warranted to convert itself into fierce energy, or of preparations which the weakest digestions can assimilate, are seen offers of teaching by correspondence; of instruction through the post in any trade, profession or occupation; of assistance in strengthening will-power, in cultivating concentration, and in the enlargement of individual earning capacity.

From their earliest school years American children are filled with the conviction that no limit can be set to the development of their faculties and their fortunes. They start life believing that all careers are open to them if they choose to work hard and to improve themselves by every means in their power. Some say the climate is responsible—dry, invigorating, energy-producing; others attribute the cause to heredity, to the restless anxiety of the Puritan settlers in New England (who sent their descendants into every part of the Union) about their souls' health and their relations with God. Whatever the cause may be, there is no doubt that in the American mind there is a strong eagerness for betterment and firm faith in its possibility.

If you see American life as a struggle between these two forces, material competition which accepts conditions

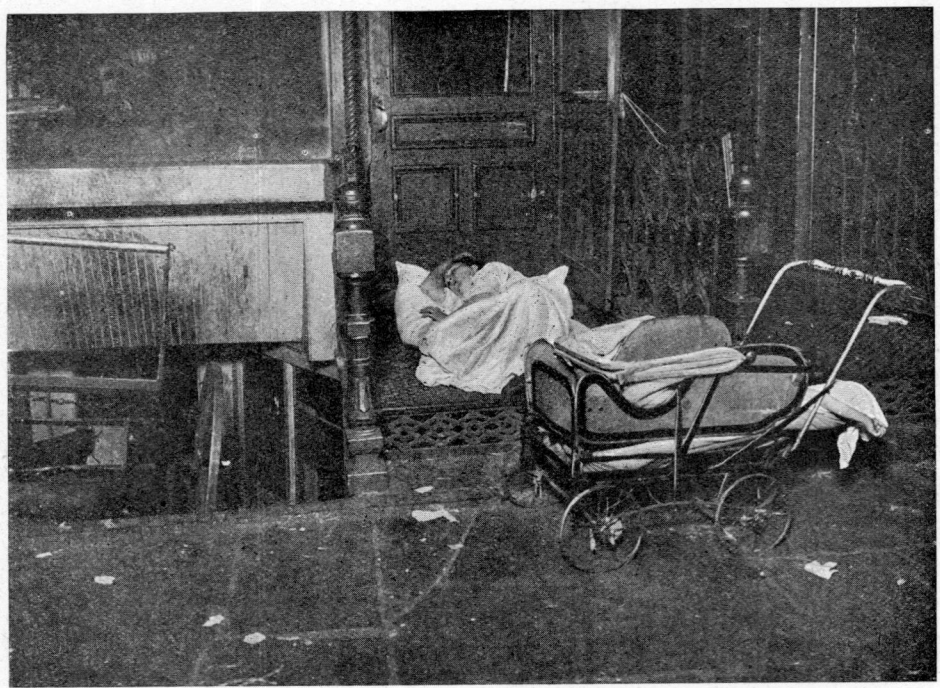

WHEN THE NIGHT BRINGS NO SOLACE FOR THE DAY'S HEAT

If Chicago is one of America's most flourishing and live business centres it is also the place above all others to which attention has been drawn as a city of mean streets and evil conditions. In the hot season the night brings little relief. Here a weary mother has made her bed on the front doorstep, and from the " pram " a baby arm is thrust as if in exhaustion

Photo, Brown Brothers

PRACTICAL COOKERY IN AN AMERICAN UNIVERSITY

Cookery, as a branch of domestic science, is carried out on ideal lines in American universities, as may be seen by an examination of the apparatus used by these students. Indeed, there is as much of the laboratory as of the kitchen about the class-room, for the student of cooking is required also to be a chemist and an expert on dietetics. Further, she must eat what she cooks

Photo, Brown Brothers

as it finds them and is impatient of the suggestion that any motive other than selfish interest should be given play, and idealism which is incessantly aiming at the elimination of selfish interest, then you will be able to explain to yourself many things that would otherwise remain a puzzle.

Very often a man who profits by flagrant abuses of public right and callous trampling on others will be found eagerly supporting movements to purge some kindred sphere of activity from similar evils. He is not insincere, he is mentally short-sighted.

It was very hard for the American of the last generation to persuade himself that any course which was profitable could be really wrong. The present generation has a better-developed social sense. The change has come about partly because the pendulum of feeling

was bound to swing away from unrestricted competition with its waste and cruelty ; partly by the danger that the land, public utilities, means of production, government, everything might fall into the clutches of a few groups of industrial and financial organizers, heedless of any aspect of their activities save that of private gain and power, and dangerously ignorant of the catastrophe they were certain to cause.

Here we have the key to the strange contrasts and extremes which we discover as soon as we look beneath the surface of American life. In no country, for example, has the study of child welfare been carried further than in the United States. Nowhere are experiments in the training and teaching of children more readily made. Yet there is no country where child labour is so pitilessly exploited. Conditions which

IN A NEW ENGLAND FARMHOUSE: AN OLD-FASHIONED COUPLE

With whitened hair in the winter of their life the husbandman and his wife look back on many plough-
ings and many a harvest. There is a sentimental tradition of agriculture about New England though
the rocky soil is little suited to farming compared with the lands of the West. Each year more farms
stand empty and the young generation goes citywards, leaving its parents behind

Photo, Brown Brothers

were abolished in England three-quarters of a century ago still exist in the collieries of Pennsylvania, in the Southern cotton-mills, in factories widely scattered over the Union.

Even in New England child labour is used to swell the profits of the wealthy

Reaction soon came, and once it had begun, it went ahead quickly.

That all abuses, all cruelties, could be excused by the money advantage drawn from them was never a doctrine approved by the American people. When they became aware that the

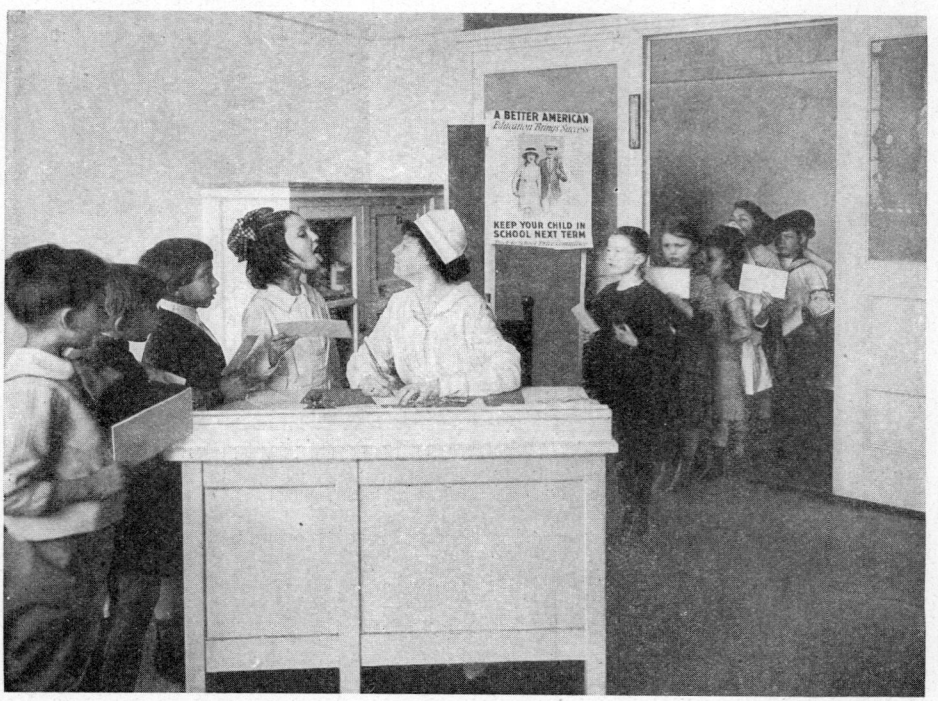

THROAT AND TEETH INSPECTION AT A PUBLIC SCHOOL

Education provided in the American public school is not regarded in any way as a charity, but as a fair return for rates and taxes, like the fire brigade. These schools correspond both to the Council and private school of England, and draw their pupils from the corresponding classes, and the spirit is not only democratic but also co-educational. Each state has its own public school system

Photo, Brown Brothers

manufacturer. In Massachusetts not long ago the Hon. J. F. Carey, member of the House of Representatives, told how small boys packed cloth into chemical bleaching vats, working naked and being bleached themselves until their bodies looked like those of lepers.

The last years of the nineteenth and the early years of this century were the worst years in the United States, the years in which business was worshipped with the most inhuman rites, in which idealism could make little headway against the universal desire to be rich.

practice of Big Business was based upon that anti-Christian, anti-social creed, they revolted from it with a movement of horrified indignation. They set to work to " clean " not only business, but public life also.

A new type arose, the young enthusiast for a saner, kindlier relation between classes. Often it was a young woman who took the lead in reform movements. Many a college graduate of independent means, instead of taking to mercantile pursuits or to a profession, threw himself into the battle against

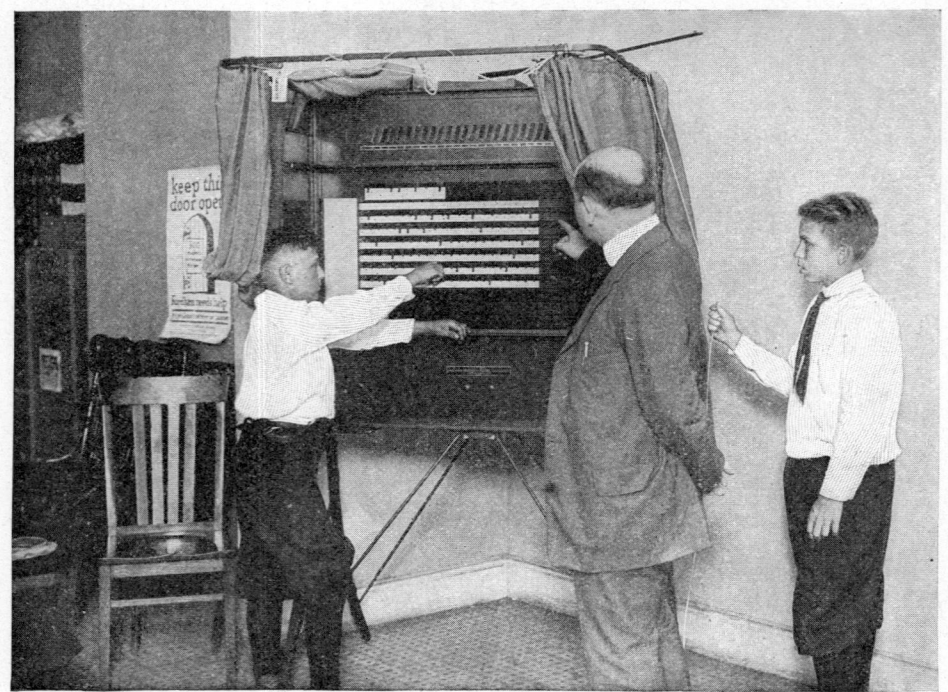

YOUNG AMERICA LEARNS THE USE OF THE VOTING MACHINE

Election voting has raised so many complications and caused so much time to be wasted in re-counts in America, that various kinds of vote-recording machines have been permitted as constitutional in various states. A machine which has had widespread use provides a separate key for each candidate, the keys being numbered and lettered in rows according to party and office

Photo, Brown Brothers

privilege and corruption. The idealists who had been flouted and despised by the " bosses " and other party managers had now to be taken into account.

When Mr. Roosevelt wanted a new party to make him President for the third time, having failed to induce the Republicans to give him their nomination, it was to the idealists that he appealed. Those who gathered round him were not strong enough to carry him to the White House, but the result of their intervention between the two old parties was nevertheless to put an idealist there. The split Republican vote gave the Democrats victory, and their candidate was Woodrow Wilson.

Those who hold that " there's a divinity that shapes our ends, rough-hew them how we will," can point to the election of President Wilson as proof of their contention. If Mr. Roosevelt had never been President, it is most unlikely that Mr. Wilson would have got the

Democratic nomination. If President McKinley had not been assassinated there would have been no President Roosevelt, who succeeded in accordance with the provision that when a President dies in office, the Vice-President automatically succeeds him.

Mr. Roosevelt appealed over the heads of the " bosses " to the people, and the people gave him a second term. He did not break with his party, but he was strong enough to lead it instead of letting the party organization lead him. He did not take sides decisively against Big Business, but he let business men see that if they did not keep within the law, the law would, in his own familiar phrase, " get after them." He shook his Big Stick in a manner which pleased the Progressives more often than it gave satisfaction to those who were all for " leaving things alone."

The Presidency of Mr. Taft, wittily described as " a man of the very best intentions, surrounded by a number of people who know exactly what they want," swelled the ranks of the idealists. The Progressive Party which they formed received support in every part of the country. It was clear to the Democratic managers that they could not rely upon a candidate of the usual type. They must have a man who understood and supported the new order in public life, the new standard set up for private business. They neither liked nor trusted idealists, but they saw that they must have as their candidate for the Presidency a man with ideals.

In Mr. Woodrow Wilson, then governor of the state of New Jersey, they found what they were looking for. He had been only a short time in politics, but in that short time he had proved that his face was towards the rising, not towards the setting, sun. Historian

and professor, he had been elected principal of Princeton University on account of his courage and executive force. In that post he had not been entirely successful. There was a time when he contemplated applying for a pension and retiring to write more history.

It was not until he entered public life that he found his true sphere of action. He showed unexpected mastery of political weapons. He even turned them against the " bosses " who had made him governor and expected him to show gratitude in the usual way.

Thus he drew upon himself the eyes of a wider range of spectators than that which, in the ordinary course of events, takes interest in the doings of a state governor, and, when the time came to nominate a Democratic candidate for the highest position in the land, the choice fell upon him. He was not the

NEW AMERICANS LEARNING THE OATH OF ALLEGIANCE

Immigration is America's greatest problem, and the legislative authorities have been at pains to deal with the task of turning peoples of every nation into good citizens of one. In the photograph a class of aliens has been assembled for the purpose of assimilating the nature of the oath of allegiance. These classes, held in the evening, are an important part of the system of alien absorption

Photo, Brown Brothers

CITIZENS IN THE MAKING UNDER IDEAL CONDITIONS IN A STATE SCHOOL

It is usual for all classes to send their sons to the same State schools up to the age of ten or thereabouts, and the son of the President and of the man who delivers his groceries learn side by side as a matter of course. There are eight grades and the ordinary age of entry is six or seven, while special kindergartens cater for children from four years old. Foreign languages and the classics are left in the hands of the high schools, which the more fortunate pupils may enter at sixteen

Photo, Brown Brothers

first choice of the wire-pullers. They intended to propose Mr. Gaynor, who had been mayor of New York, and had become known to all his fellow-countrymen by being the victim of an attempt to murder. A candidate for the Presidency must be widely known. In the Democratic Party there was no man whose name was sufficiently familiar to make him a really good candidate. The attempt on Mr. Gaynor's life put him in the running, but his uncertain temper threw the chance away. He wrote an injudicious letter to a newspaper editor in Texas, declining an invitation to appear as possible candidate. That letter, written under the influence of un-reasonable annoyance or some other excitant, made him impossible. Then it was that Mr. Woodrow Wilson's name suggested itself. That piece of secret history illustrates the working of the American electoral system.

Mr. Wilson's course of action as President proved how strong the idealists had become. He leaned to their side from the beginning, though he did not, any more than Mr. Roosevelt, cut himself loose either from party ties or from the Big Business supporters of the party fund. The idealist attitude towards war was one of abhorrence. They considered it wrong for a country to send its young men to be killed and maimed for the protection of industrial or financial interests. They even protested against the notion that a country was

HOBOES "HITTING THE GRIT"

American tramps are distinguished from the vagrants of other lands by their habit of using the railways, "jumping trains" to travel free of expense. Tramps are numerous in New York which is said to be "the best town for bums in the U.S.A."

Photo, Brown Brothers

bound to avenge outrages upon the lives or property of its subjects abroad.

Very soon after Mr. Wilson was elected a demand was raised that the United States should call Mexico to account for the murder of some two hundred American citizens in that country, and much material damage suffered by others. Against this it was argued that those who went to Mexico knew the risk they were running, and went because they hoped to make money. Why, it was asked, should other

Americans, who had no concern with Mexico, be taxed heavily and send their sons into battle for so remote a cause? With this view Mr. Wilson showed himself to be in agreement. He declared that the government would refuse to exert itself for the benefit of concession-hunters. Those who engaged in business with contempt when the German Chancellor warned him of its gravity.

"Remember," said Herr Bethmann Hollweg, "that there are twenty million citizens of German descent in the United States."

"In the United States," replied the Ambassador, "there are twenty million

MOONSHINERS' SECRET STILL, FORFEIT TO THE STATE

Despite the heavy penalties provided by the Prohibition Act of 1919, "boot-leggers" and "moonshiners" continue to try to supply alcohol to recalcitrants who resent compulsory total abstinence as an infringement on personal liberty. Chance sometimes helps the Federal authorities in their efforts to enforce the law, as here, where secret service agents, searching for a plant for making counterfeit coins, have uncovered an illicit still

Photo, Brown Brothers

in a state like Mexico must do so, he warned them, at their own peril. He was the first ruler to say openly: "We renounce the practice of making war, whether to vindicate national honour or for the support of business men."

It was far more the strength of this feeling against war among a very large section of the American people than the fear of difficulties with German-Americans that forced President Wilson to walk so warily during the European conflict. The German-American danger was not taken very seriously. Mr. James W. Gerard, the United States Ambassador in Berlin, treated it almost

lamp-posts, and if the German-American gave trouble there would soon be one hanging from each lamp-post."

The detestation of war in millions of American hearts was the real reason why the United States did not decide to join the Powers allied against Germany until the spring of 1917. Mr. Wilson had to lead the idealists step by step, to prove to them by repeated experiments that no reliance could be placed in Germany's promises, to convince them that no course save war was open to a self-respecting nation.

When he at last managed to unite the mass of people and had put in hand

GOVERNMENT OFFICIALS POURING LIQUOR DOWN THE DRAINS

It was the "Big Business" interest, contending that total abstinence from alcoholic liquor made for clear thinking and productive power, that succeeded in the attempt begun by other agencies to persuade the Federal legislature to pass the Prohibition Act of 1919. The Act is being steadily enforced, and government officials search for illicit stores of liquor and pour it into the public sewers

Photo, Brown Brothers

CUSTOMERS IN A NEW YORK "NEAR BEER" SALOON IMBIBING DRINKS THAT CANNOT INEBRIATE

Immense stocks of beer, wines, and whisky were in the hands of the distillers and "the trade" generally when Prohibition came into force on July 1, 1919. After that date their sale was absolutely forbidden throughout the U.S.A., and the stocks were taken over by the government and retained for medicinal or mechanical use. Many saloons closed down altogether, and the rest adapted themselves to the new conditions and supply non-alcoholic beverages, such as "near beer"—a herbal substitute—mineral waters, and refreshment from soda fountains, while ice-cream has attained an enormous sale

Photo, Brown Brothers

IDLERS IN AN OLD-TIME BOWERY SALOON—SWEPT AWAY BY THE PROHIBITION ACT

Peter Stuyvesant, the despotic governor of New York from 1647 to 1664, spent the evening of his turbulent life on his farm called the Bouwerie, on Manhattan Island. Ironical fate decreed that, as the Bowery, the quiet place of his dignified retreat should become notorious as the noisiest and most lawless section of New York. a hotbed of crime and vice, where saloons of the lowest class supplied poisonous liquor to roughs whose generic name, Bowery Boys, was a synonym for ruffians. Now the Bowery is being purged, and the Prohibition Act closed the last of its drinking dens

Photo, Brown Brothers

intensive preparations for sending an army to Europe, public opinion went through one of those rapid changes which are so disconcerting to observers from afar. For two years and a half the greater part of the nation had been pacifist in sentiment. A few months after the declaration of war the utterance of pacifist sentiments was punished by long terms of imprisonment. The United States were making " war against war." They were, in the President's phrase, making the world safe for democracy.

Thus idealism refused to disavow its principles, even while it shifted its view-point, and when Mr. Wilson became the foremost advocate of a League of Nations that should prevent all wars between civilized peoples, he seemed to have the solid support of idealist sentiment. Elections to Congress showed that with a great many party bonds still prevailed over personal attachment, but in the long fight that followed between those who honestly desired the new order and those who sought to damage the President in order to benefit the Republican Party, Mr. Wilson claimed, and appeared, to have the idealists on his side. His defeat at the Peace Conference was seen to be due, not to any weakening of his faith, but to his failure in tactful diplomacy and to the numerical superiority of the adherents to the old order.

The whole march of events in the United States during the war proved what a change had come over the American spirit in less than a generation. From being a people devoted, as it seemed, to the pursuit of material aims, they became a community which

MERCY AND JUSTICE IN AN AMERICAN JUVENILE COURT

Juvenile courts, aiming at the salvation and redemption instead of at the punishment of juvenile delinquents, are philanthropy's most beneficent product. Regarding the state as the over-parent and children as its wards, the Juvenile Court Acts define delinquency and dependency and can deal with all cases affecting children under eighteen years of age. These humane courts, controlled by sympathetic judges and officers, exist in many large cities of the U.S.A.

Photo, Brown Brothers

appeared to be ready to go any lengths in the direction of moral improvement.

Europe had not been well served by those who offered it enlightenment upon the American character. Because American life was utterly different in so many aspects from European life, travellers brought back for the most part unfavourable and usually sneering accounts of it. English travellers especially were inclined to moralise and to make fun in equally offensive veins. They did not allow for the difference of climate, for the effects of settling in a new country, or for the natural rancour generated by the behaviour of the English, first in attempting to dominate over the colonists and later in pretending to patronise them.

It was particularly unfortunate that Charles Dickens lent to the unworthy task of detraction his powerful and picturesque pen.

CHEERFUL OBEDIENCE TO SCOUT LAW

Many a lad in ordinary civilian clothes might be reluctant thus to carry home greenstuff from the garden, but the Boy Scout in the U.S.A. as elsewhere does it cheerfully, obeying the Scout Law to do " one good turn a day "

Photo, Brown Brothers

He was not a man of balanced judgement. Often he was over-generous in his estimates, often hastily censorious. From the moment he arrived on board the ship which was to take him across the Atlantic he grumbled. The welcome he received checked for a time the flow of his dissatisfaction, but soon came his unfortunate speech about copyright, which was at that time denied to British authors in the United States.

This speech raised one of those storms of nervous excitement to which, as we have seen, the American people are still subject. The spirit in which Dickens's " American Notes " was written, leaves the impression of ill-humour and dis-

like. While the more enlightened and intelligent on both sides of the Atlantic deplored the mutual misunderstandings, the mass of people in England accepted Dickens's caricature in " Martin Chuzzlewit " as being, in its main lines at all events, a portrait from life, while the mass of people in the United States only sank deeper into the conviction that the English were proud, domineering, and " effete."

American school history books predisposed children from their early years to contempt for the English, and the general tendency in the country was to speak disdainfully, not of England only, but of Europe. It was supposed that

BOY SCOUTS OF THE UNITED STATES GATHERED ROUND THEIR CAMP FIRE IN THE WOODS

Initiated in England in 1908 by General Sir Robert Baden-Powell, the Boy Scout organization captivated the imagination of the world, with the result that something like a million lads between the ages of twelve and eighteen are now pledged to carry out the Scout Law and wear the distinctive uniform. Two similar organizations, known as the Woodcraft Indians and the Sons of Daniel Boone, were already in existence in the U.S.A., and these were combined and incorporated as Boy Scouts in 1910 and in 1916 were chartered by Act of Congress

Photo, Brown Brothers

the European peoples were still in a condition little removed from serfdom. The diplomatic squabbles and monarchical ambitions which made up European politics were ridiculed.

An American satirist could have found in England, however, persons just as crudely ill-informed about his so busily occupied in building up their material civilization that they had too little time and energy to spare for the finer issues. If they were inclined to worship the Big instead of the Great, there was excuse for them in the bigness of the territory they were trying to develop and to bring under one rule.

GOAL PRACTICE AT BASKET-BALL, A POPULAR AMERICAN GAME

Basket-ball is said to have been invented by an ingenious American to whom someone proposed that a new game be found suitable for both sexes and for indoor as well as outdoor play. The ball, which resembles that used in Association football, may not be kicked or punched, but is thrown, or hit flat-handed, the object being to get it into the net

Photo, Brown Brothers

country as the characters invented by Dickens were about the countries of Europe. To base upon these inventions a judgement of a nation was as foolish as it would have been in a foreigner to suppose that England was peopled by Pecksniffs and Chadbands. The harm done by Dickens is incalculable.

A sympathetic study of them at that epoch would have given to the relations between the peoples a more harmonious, more friendly turn. It would have shown the Americans sensitive to outside opinion, impatient of criticism, uneasily conscious of their youth as a nation, and of defects in their system,

" But why not have been content to let the country develop slowly, to let it take the same course as the older countries ? Why have attempted to do so much in so short a space of time ? "

These questions could only be put by persons who have no experience of the American climate. Its bracing, stimulating effect makes slow development impossible. The energy which it produces must be worked off in violent action, mental rather than physical. The nerves are strung by it to so high a pitch that patient, gradual methods seem sluggish. Whatever Americans do, they do it with their might, with so much might that they sometimes leave it unfinished by reason of having exhausted their energy and their interest before they are " through with it."

Even yet there are many signs of the haste with which the country was populated and its prosperity assured. The people allowed their cities to grow up as the greed of speculators and the pressure of momentary material necessities dictated. They grew like mushrooms on a rich dark soil.

Retarded Growth of Civic Spirit

Everyone in these new " cities " was occupied in making a living, and, when a living was secure, in getting rich. No one had time to think for the community. What did it matter how the " city " looked so long as it could boast of so many millionaires, a volume of business that was " phenomenal," a growth of population that ran ahead of all estimates, a general level of prosperity which kept the citizens busy and content ? The consequence of this neglect of communal thinking was the haphazard, insanitary, squalid style in which most American cities grew up. It is only in the last twenty-five years or so that their defects have been remedied.

Middle-Class America at Home

Idealism has been manifested notably in building. There is an American domestic architecture which, not less in appearance than in convenience, is far ahead of anything to be seen in Europe. Around every city have been laid out suburbs of the pleasantest character. Wide roads planted with trees and with the gardens and lawns of the houses coming down to the sidewalk, not shut off by hedge or fence or ugly railing, make an impression of spaciousness, green beauty, and neighbourly feeling. The houses stand apart, each seems to have a character of its own. Possibly that is sometimes more " seeming " than truth, for houses can be ordered by reference to a number in an illustrated catalogue. These would probably not be seen, though, in the suburbs of a city of any size.

In the construction of the American house wood is employed freely. There is always a " porch " or veranda, and very often a " sleeping porch " for the hot weather. This is built outside an upper floor. The rooms are large, but there are not many of them. The distinctions observed in England between the dining-room and drawing-room, the boudoir and the library, are swept away. There is a living-room as a rule, with a small dining-room off it, connected with the kitchen. The houses described are not those of the wealthy, who live as much as possible in the style of wealthy English or French families, but the homes of the comfortable class which has money enough, but none to throw away upon display or luxury.

Use of Labour-Saving Devices

Everything that can be done to save labour in these homes is ingeniously thought out and installed. The woodwork is dark, not painted white or enamelled, but left its natural colour. Cleaning, cooking, and even washing are done by electricity. Vacuum cleaners are attached to a plug, and the floors are swept in no time. The week's wash can be put into an electric washer, which leaves it ready for rinsing. Then it is wrung dry in another electric machine.

Such appliances and the readiness of men and boys to take their share in the housework enable many families to do without servants, or to keep one only. The sons of the house are brought up like the girls to tidy their rooms, make their own beds, and, if necessary, lend a hand with the washing-up. Men either clean their own boots or get them cleaned at a " shoe-shine parlour," where for ten or fifteen cents (5d.—7½d.) they are made to glisten and so raise the wearer's self-respect.

The " servant difficulty " is greater in the United States than anywhere.

AMERICAN GIRL SCOUTS' SALUTE TO "OLD GLORY"

Girl Scouts of America have the same rules and law as the Girl Guides' organization founded in England by Sir Robert Baden-Powell and his sister. An important and most popular part of their physical training is provided in camps, where daily a bugle rings out and all hands are raised to the salute as the Stars and Stripes is run up to the head of the flagstaff

Photo, Brown Brothers

LIBERTY GREETS THE IMMIGRANT IN THE FIRST FLUSH OF DAWN

Sculptor's allegorical work never found more proper situation than did Bartholdi's great figure of Liberty, presented by the French nation to the U.S.A. to commemorate the centenary of American independence. The familiar figure, 111 feet in height, with electric torch upraised 40 feet higher still, stands on Bedloe's Island in New York Harbour, welcoming newcomers to the New World

Photo, Brown Brothers

Irish and Scandinavian girls used to follow this occupation in large numbers, but even they are becoming harder to find. One reason is that the servant-keeping class rapidly expanded during the period of sudden prosperity. Now it is shrinking almost as rapidly.

Every device to make housework easier is eagerly adopted. The dining-room has disappeared from many small houses. The drawing-room was never so much of an institution as it was in England. Big living-rooms, with dining tables that can be set up and then moved aside, are found to be more convenient than separate rooms, for the reason that servants have become too expensive for families of moderate income. In many cities there are no servants. There are "home assistants" who come in for a certain number of hours a day and receive from £3 to £3 10s. a week.

This means that girls who look forward to marriage, unless they are likely to marry rich men, must be competent to do their own housework and must be prepared to work hard at it. The only alternative is to take rooms in a building where there is a restaurant and where the proprietor has the rooms cleaned and tidied up.

Those who prefer to live near the centres of cities live in apartment houses, with or without service. The rents are high and become higher every few years. Life in them is only possible if the tenant tips constantly all those upon whom his comfort depends. Family life is next door to impossible, because children cannot be brought up healthily in them, and it is not easy in any case to get children into them.

The tipping nuisance has become as bad in the United States as it is elsewhere ; worse, indeed, for it is carried further there. The tips expected are larger and more frequent. In this direction there has been a slipping-back since the days when the American people were satirised. Then they did pride themselves upon having too much self-respect to accept tips. The change may be due in part to the immense number of poor Europeans who now do so large a proportion of the domestic work in the United States, and who snatch at any chance of supplementing their meagre wages. Chiefly, however, it was the fierce struggle for riches in the later years of the nineteenth and the early years of the present century which caused the growth of the tipping habit, along with many other evils.

Whether Americans live in city apartment houses or in the suburbs, they are sure to be well provided with bath-rooms. In a generation the same change occurred in their habits as was effected in the previous generation in England. The bath-room became a necessity of life

But they have carried the change very much further than it has gone in England. Labourers' houses are fitted with baths, and the baths are regularly used. It is nothing out of the common to see residences advertised with, say, seven bed-rooms and four baths. In big houses every bed-room has its own bath-room attached. The more recent hotels consist entirely of rooms with baths.

It is odd that Americans should tolerate washing arrangements on their long-distance trains which belong to the age when people washed only their faces and their hands. South African trains have shower-baths; so do some of the Canadian trains; so do private cars on American railways. But in the Pullman sleeping cars one is still expected to refresh oneself after a stuffy night by dabbling in one of several small basins which are fitted in the "smoking-room." Smoking in the long Pullman carriages

TESTING MENTAL CAPACITY OF FEMALE IMMIGRANTS

Wide discretion has to be allowed to the officials responsible for the admission of immigrants into the U.S.A., especially in respect of the degree of education possessed by non-English-speaking applicants. The Immigrants' Restriction Bill passed in 1921 limits the annual number of admissions to 355,000, and the tests imposed, especially of mental capacity, tend to become ever more exacting

Photo, Brown Brothers

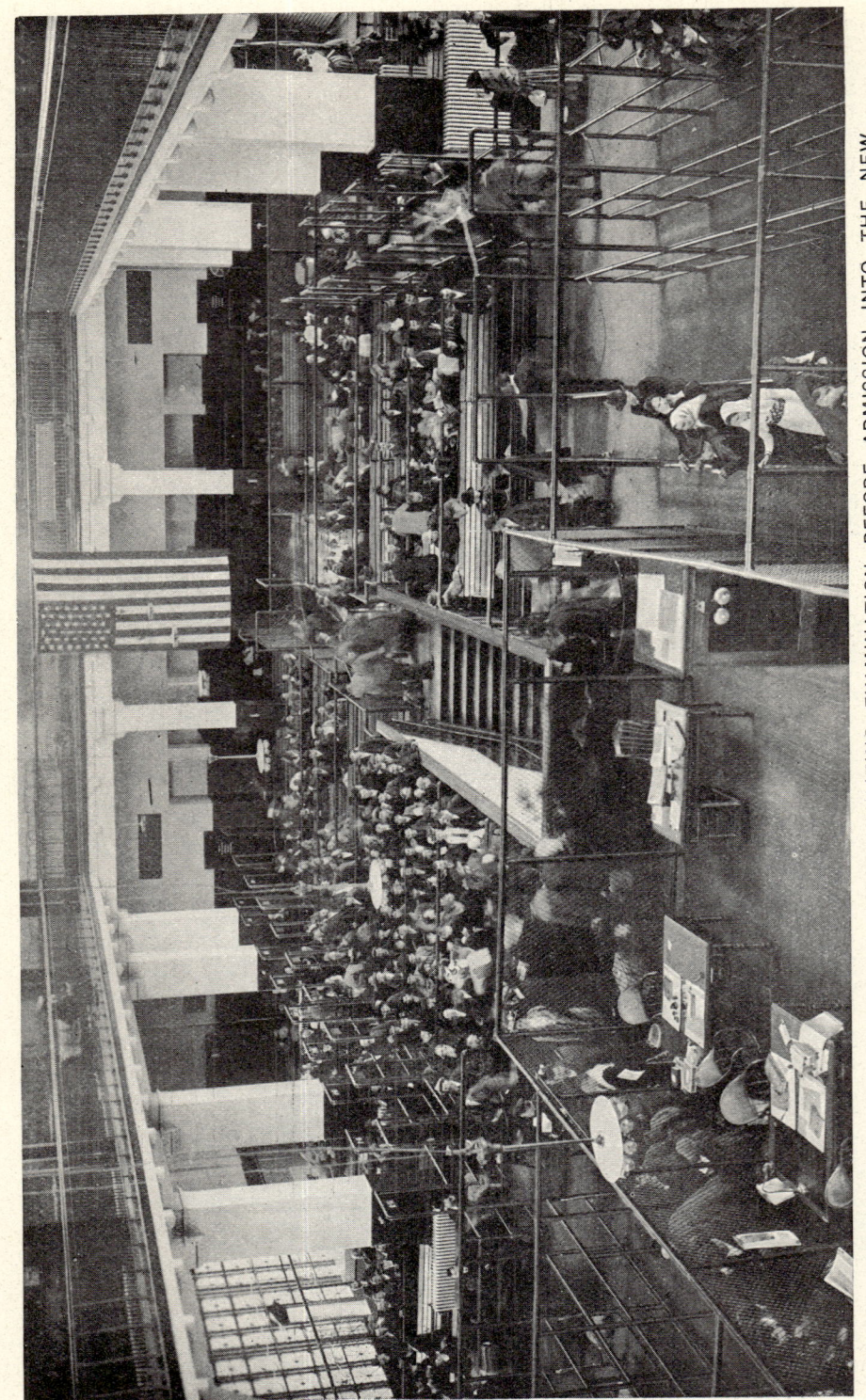

IMMIGRANTS FROM THE OLD WORLD AWAITING EXAMINATION BEFORE ADMISSION INTO THE NEW

Primarily the laws governing immigration into the U.S.A. are sanitary measures intended to protect the commonwealth from the introduction of elements actually injurious to health, such as consumptives and persons afflicted with contagious disease. Inevitably the regulations were extended to exclude "undesirable" elements which might become a public charge, such as the insane and physically and mentally defective persons. "Undesirables" also include criminals and contract labourers. All immigrants are examined and classified by officials of the Federal government at the landing-stage on Ellis Island in New York Harbour

Photo, Kadel & Herbert

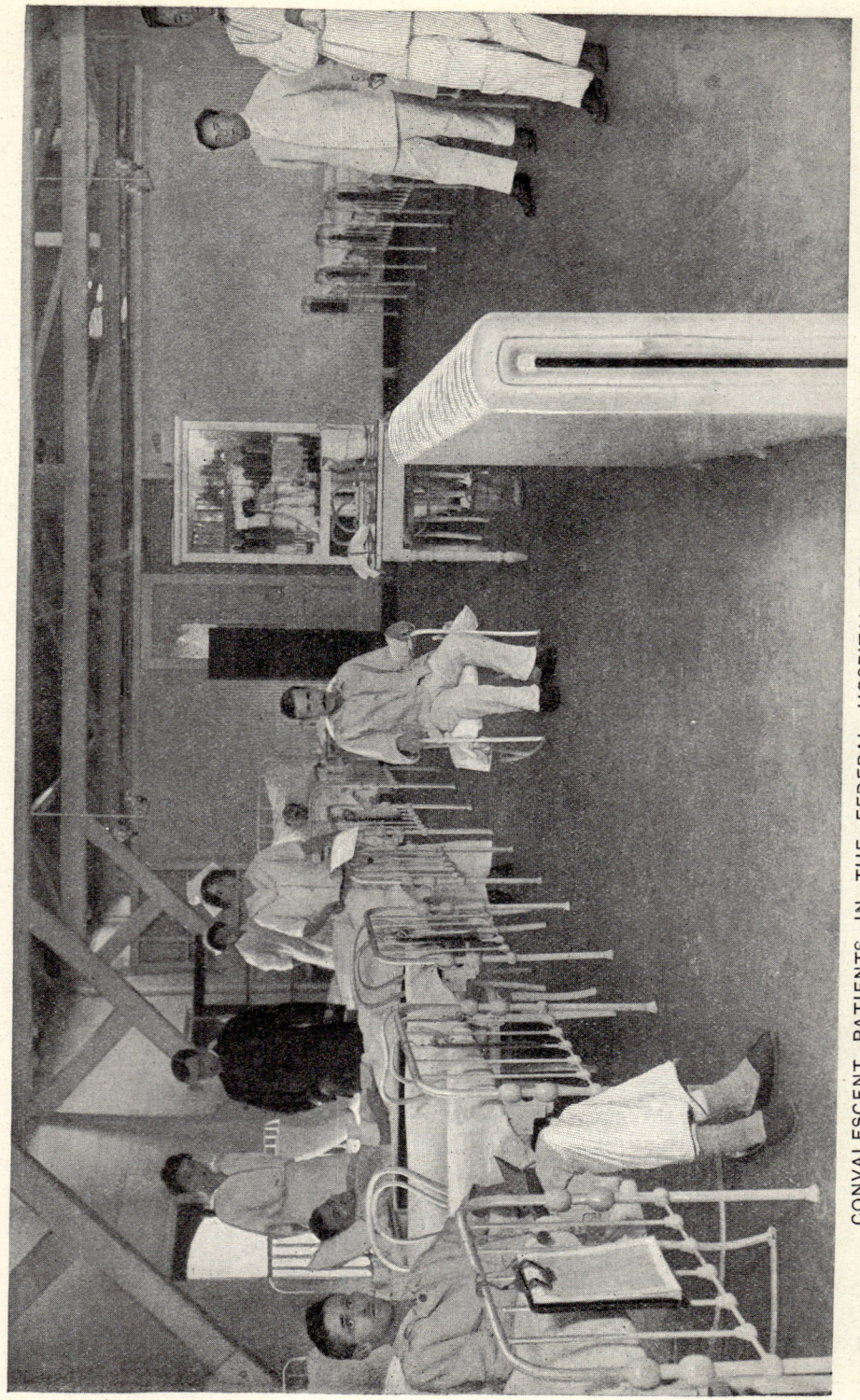

CONVALESCENT PATIENTS IN THE FEDERAL HOSPITAL FOR IMMIGRANTS ON ELLIS ISLAND

Periodically protests are made against the conditions prevailing on Ellis Island, criticism being directed chiefly against the enforced collocation during detention of persons of widely-differing race and social status. Since the Great War came to an end there has been such a vast influx of immigrants lured by the sound conditions and high salaries awaiting the working classes, that some overcrowding and suffering was unavoidable. Criticism, however, erred on the side of exaggeration, and humanity and consideration undoubtedly animate the Federal officials in their execution of a difficult and invidious public duty

Photo, Kadel & Herbert

JAPANESE LABOUR EMPLOYED IN PACKING ORANGES PRODUCED IN THE GROVES OF SOUTHERN CALIFORNIA

California has an established position as the leading fruit-growing district of the United States, and so far back as 1899 it produced more than a fifth of the fruit of the whole Union. Oranges, prunes, olives, figs, lemons, citrons, apricots, almonds, walnuts, and grapes are cultivated with great success. The orange crop is an immense one, and Southern California presents scenes of great beauty; extensive orange groves are spread about the low-lying country— often flourishing at the base of lofty, snow-capped mountains—their serried rows of dark foliage and ripening fruit imparting a lively colour tone to the landscape

Photo, Brown Brothers

is not allowed, but there is at the end of each a little compartment which serves as smoking-room and wash-place combined. However early one dabbles, one is pretty sure to find three or four men sitting there smoking pungent cigars and freely using the spittoon.

Yet the same people who endure this are possessed, when they are not in the train, by an almost morbid passion for cleanliness. In England what might be called the "bath-every-morning" class is small in proportion. In the United States it is very large. In the beginning the habit was copied presumably from England. Then the alert, clear-eyed, clean-shaven American face came into fashion, the polished finger-nails, the athletic poise and tread. Clothes became smart instead of loose and shapeless as they used to be represented in drawings of Americans. The type aimed at became that which could be studied in book and magazine illustrations of young men with hair brushed back to show the firm contour of their brows, with perfect teeth, well-shaped hands, feet in the shapeliest of boots or shoes, a general air of taking pleasure in being clean and vigorous.

The Modern Man and His Dress

The manicure parlour has taken its place among the regular institutions for business men in American cities. They give up half an hour twice a week to the process of having their nails shaped and made shiny. Sometimes the manicure girl may be seen at work on a client's hand while the barber is shaving him. Men have become as uncomfortable about having finger-tips uncared for as they would be with dirty faces or soiled linen. Even young men with small salaries will spend as a matter of course four shillings a week on manicure, and another four at least on special soaps and washes and creams.

Their socks match their suits, their ties strike a colour-note in sympathy. Cuff-links and tie-pins harmonise. Yet they manage to avoid being dandified.

They do not attract attention by being obtrusively well-dressed. They look like men who enjoy harmony and proportion, who take a pleasure in grooming themselves, in being trim and tidy.

In this passion for cleanliness and order is reflected the spirit which rules many larger aspects of American life. Among the fruits of this spirit are the imposing railway stations which have risen up in New York, in Chicago, in Washington, and in other cities to take the place of the muddling labyrinths and shed-like structures of the past. Architects with imagination planned them, every kind of convenience is to be found in them.

Self-expression in Architecture

The grandeur of conception, the hunger for self-expression, the ingenuity of construction which gave us the cathedrals of the Middle Ages have been applied in the United States to these temples of the Goddess of Restlessness.

Each age has its founts of emotion. The religions most prevalent in the United States are not emotional in their appeal. There have been noble churches built even in recent years. There is one on Fifth Avenue, nearly opposite the Roman Catholic cathedral of S. Patrick, a square solid pile of grey stone, and there is the chapel at West Point Military School (where officers of the small regular army are trained), with a beautiful nave. But the devotion which inspired the medieval church builders and the nations for whom they built inspires only scattered individuals to-day.

Building Worthy of Ancient Greece

The feelings to which architects must give expression are feelings of pride in the progress and the institutions of Man. It would be hard to find a finer illustration of this than the Post Office on Eighth Avenue, New York. Raised well above the street level, and approached by perfectly-proportioned steps, is a portico of twenty Ionic columns. Simply that; nothing to lessen the dignity of

STREET GAMES OF NEGRO CHILDREN IN THE COLOURED SECTION OF NEW YORK

Although the negroes' legal rights are secured to them the blacks are not regarded so sympathetically in the northern states of the U.S.A. as they were. In the towns they are collocated in special "coloured sections," and here they occupy comfortable modern dwellings and for the most part lead quiet lives of happy domesticity. As parents negroes set an admirable example, and their children are well fed and well dressed. The cheerful temperament of the race craves expression in music, dancing, and laughter, and a crowd of negro children playing together has always a large and sympathetic audience of adults

Photo, Brown Brothers

their just balance or to mar their beauty, unsmiling yet not austere. Along the architrave runs this glorious inscription, borrowed from Herodotus : " Neither snow, nor rain, nor heat, nor gloom of night, stay these couriers from the swift completion of their appointed rounds."

Nothing could better correct the European misjudgement of the American spirit than this magnificent public building, worthy to be set beside the finest of ancient or modern times.

Close by is the Pennsylvania Railroad Station. Elsewhere it would extort praise. Here it is made to look commonplace beside the unexpected recapture by this Post Office of the Greek idea in architecture. Yet as one passes through its lofty corridors and ample halls one feels that they too enshrine something of the same feeling.

Organization in Perfection

There is, as in the Grand Central Station, a boldness of imagination, a shaking-off of the mean bondage of the " good enough," a soaring towards a great aim. The mind is soothed by the spacious calm, the perfect organization, the spick-and-span convenience of ticket and baggage counters, dining-rooms, buffets, bookstalls, information offices. The spotless white caps of the officials are allegorical. They are emblems of the ideal which is pursued by the planners of the most excellent railway stations the world has seen : stations for supermen, moving, calm and certain, to their desired ends.

The white new City Hall in New York, the cream and gold splendour of the Woolworth Tower (a lofty office-block, close by), the transformation of Washington into a stately and beautiful city, the growth everywhere of suburbs presenting so agreeable a contrast to the hugger-mugger appearance of central districts run up without design or thought for amenity—all reflect the same ideal which drags scandals into light and sweeps out the foul stables of public life.

The Woolworth Tower is one of the " sky-scrapers " which loom through the light sea mist to give the new arrival his first impression of the real capital of the United States. From the sea these buildings affect the imagination like the domes and minarets of some fabled Eastern city. At closer range the charm wears off unless you see them in the early dusk of a winter evening. Then, with their myriad points of light, their dim outlines become beautiful again.

New York's Giant Sky-Scrapers

Walking up Broadway beneath them, one finds a certain magnificence in their immense height. The first of them were ugly, but in the later ones architects have found lines of treatment which entirely redeem their work from this reproach. They are built as a spectacle rather than of necessity. The neck of land between two rivers on which New York is situated is certainly narrow, too narrow for the needs of its immense business population. Since expansion sideways is impossible, it was imperative to expand upwards, and to put up blocks of offices higher than any known elsewhere. But the twenty, thirty, forty-storey buildings are the result of the American eagerness, which has done so much for the national prosperity, to " go one better."

American Sense of the Dramatic

They are a good advertisement. They are a feature which no visitor can ever forget. Nothing like them can be seen anywhere else. Monuments both of business enterprise and engineering skill in hitting upon new methods of construction, they stir American pride and fill all who behold them with wonder.

Americans are gifted with the dramatic sense. They are far readier and more accomplished public speakers— just as they are better actors—than the English. In conversation they employ more racy turns of speech. They enjoy their own performances. They delight in telling stories, in coining or repeating

WORK FOR DARKIES YOUNG AND OLD: PICKING COTTON IN A SOUTHERN PLANTATION

No really satisfactory mechanical method has yet been devised for cotton picking, which is still done by hand and constitutes the most difficult and most expensive operation in cotton production. The work is tedious, but it is not heavy, and provides lucrative employment for old men, women, and children. The picking season begins about July in southern Texas and as late as September in North Carolina, and lasts for about a hundred days. An average hand can pick over 100 pounds a day, and the work is a main part of the livelihood of the negro population of all the southern states

Photo, Brown Brothers

some effective phrase. All this is born of the same self-consciousness which is evident in so apparently small a matter as the manner in which they like to be addressed.

A name to them is something more than a label. It is a trade-mark, a distinction. Very few are content with initials, as the English mostly are. They want something more distinctive. Mr. Hiram K. Dash and Mrs. Ethel Roller Blankson are resolved that their person-alities shall not be overlooked, as they might be if they were known as Mr. H. K. Dash and Mrs. Blankson

Compare American comic writers with English and their humour is seen to be almost entirely subjective, while the English are mostly objective in their attitude. The Americans will nearly all be recognized as professional funny men. Artemus Ward, the funniest of them, the beloved of Abraham Lincoln, was frankly a clown. Mark Twain kept up the comic character even in private life.

Self-Consciousness in Journalism

The two books of his which are most popular in England are " Tom Sawyer " and " Huckleberry Finn." In these he obtrudes himself less than in any other of his works. He lost himself in his creations, in the vivid recollections of boyhood which flowed from his enchant-ing pen. The Dooley books and the stories of O. Henry, vastly as they amused us, were subjective in that they were written according to a formula.

One consequence of this aspect of American self-consciousness is that American newspapers and periodicals are written in a much more entertaining, brisker vein than their counterparts in England. The writers aim at making their personalities felt. They want to be amusing, to make an impression ; they aim at phrasing their ideas in an arrest-ing or an amusing style. This effort and the existence of convenient formulae for impressive writing account for American ephemeral productions, whether in fic-tion or journalism, being so readable.

The American stage is likewise in-debted to the national self-consciousness for its high level of performances. The acting is crisp, emotional, competent. Types of character are represented with truth and completeness. The mirror is held up to nature even in light comedies of the " Potash and Perlmutter " variety. Among American actresses are several who, with opportunities for the regular playing of parts that would call forth their powers, might take rank with the most famous.

Popularity of the Theatre

Unfortunately, the theatre in the United States, while it escaped the Scylla of the actor-manager concerned only with the exploitation of himself, was hurled disastrously against the Charybdis of the theatrical speculator, " handling " plays and performers as if they were parcels of butter or consign-ments of bacon hogs. Some speculators have had a genuine passion for the theatre. Charles Frohman was one such, but his taste was of the crudest. When he produced in London a play which he said was precisely what he thought a play ought to be, it was found to be a clockwork rabbit, oozing with sentimentality of the most treacly brand.

The theatre is a favourite recreation in America. Even the smaller towns or cities (any settlement of twenty thou-sand inhabitants or over is called a city) have their playhouses in which popular plays and players can be seen for one night at a time. Play-writing is taught at Harvard and other univer-sities. " Circles " meet in most cities for the discussion of dramatic themes.

A Moral from the Cinematograph

So far the vogue of the picture theatre does not appear to have harmed the acted drama. The cinematograph was taken up by the Americans as soon as its possibilities were perceived. They formed companies for producing film-plays. They boomed heroines and heroes and comic men into world-wide notoriety. Their scenic arrangements covered large areas, their crowds were numbered by the thousand. The result of so much energy was that they became the chief providers of films to all countries. While others hesitated, the Americans saw that a new industry had come into existence and hastened to take advantage of the opportunity.

There lies the reason of their success in business. Often they are disappointed, their schemes go wrong, their hopes are proved to have been too sanguine. But they are not thereby deterred from further enterprises. They turn with the same enthusiasm to some other opening. Into their sports they fling themselves with the same determination. Football is played by them with a fierceness which compels the players to pad themselves for protection. The summer and autumn game is baseball, an elaboration of " rounders." Every American learns to play baseball and is able to watch the game with an appreciation of its points. The crowds which attend matches are enormous when two famous clubs are engaged ; they are large even for contests of local interest. The spectators are close and unsparing critics. A

DINGY CORNER IN SAN FRANCISCO'S CHINATOWN

After the great earthquake and three days' fire of 1906, active reconstruction soon equipped San Francisco with a fresh supply of modern buildings and monuments. Chinatown, near Nob Hill, was re-raised on lavish lines and, despite certain unsavoury byways swarming with blue-coated Celestials, possesses many points of interest, chief among which are its curiosity shops and theatres

Photo, Brown Brothers

SONS OF THE CHINESE REPUBLIC AT HOME IN AMERICA
San Francisco has a large heterogeneous population. Every European nationality would appear to be represented, and Mexicans, Chinese, Japanese, and other non-European races are numerous. The Chinese alone number many thousands, and their quarter of the city has the appearance of a show-place, with its twelve blocks full of garish temples, bazaars, and restaurants
Photo, Brown Brothers

continuous yelling is kept up, the players are chaffed, encouraged, insulted. Both at baseball and at football matches cries that have been learned and rehearsed are taken up by hundreds, perhaps thousands, of voices at the bidding of an " applause director."

There is more variety in baseball than in cricket. One innings succeeds another far more rapidly. There are no dull passages. Exciting moments occur more frequently. It is a game which exactly suits the American temperament, and every year the number of " fans," as habitual attendants at matches are called, seems to grow larger.

The newspapers print quantities of baseball news. Favourite players are made national heroes, as the most skilful matadors of the bull-ring are idolised in Spain. Public baseball provides the element in the national life which in England is provided by horse-racing, but the betting on baseball is probably very much smaller in volume. Horse-racing in the United States was

never patronised by any but the lower kind of people. There was a great deal of " crooked work " in it, and no great opposition was offered to betting on it being made illegal.

In this, as in the prohibition of alcohol campaign, women took leading parts. They have been active in every movement aiming at better social conditions. The agitation for the suppression of intoxicating drink was, as we have seen, begun by women. It was a woman who founded the first Christian Science Church and so started a new religion which has millions of adherents to-day. Earnest, patient reformers like Miss Jane Addams, and wild, fanatical firebrands of the Carrie Nation type, have each done their share in " holding high the banner of the Ideal "

The position of women in the United States is often misconceived in Europe by those who judge with incomplete knowledge. Most of the American women who travelled in Europe with right of entry into European society, as

IN A NEW YORK FIRE STATION: THE LIGHTER SIDE OF A FIREMAN'S LIFE

For the firemen off duty excellent quarters are provided by the fire department of New York City.
Here, while some have made up a card-party, unperturbed by the song in progress just behind
them, others take their leisure in easy chairs, and the station dog slumbers peacefully. Yet ever
within hearing is the alarm-bell that may at any moment turn ease into action

Photo, Brown Brothers

it existed before the Great War, belonged to the wealthy class. Many left their husbands behind to carry on the toil which provided them with the money for their journeyings and entertainings and sumptuous clothes. They were not often women of intelligence. In a fashion which provoked ridicule they aped the manners of the aristocracies into which their wealth bought them admission. By them too often American women were estimated. No error could have been more complete.

As a recent writer on this theme says : " The two salient points in the position of women in America are these : First, the men and the women are friends ; second, both men and women think of the women collectively as mothers." America is the only country where a Mothers' Day is celebrated yearly. Something of the feeling behind such an observance may be set down to that self-consciousness which we have already discovered. Yet there remains a good deal which is sentiment and not sentimentality. There is among American men more genuine respect for women than is noticeable as a rule in Europe. Women could travel safely and without fear of annoyance in the United States long before this was considered possible in England. In the matter of giving women and girls seats in crowded trains or street cars the Americans are certainly quicker than Europeans.

Among the mass of the population women take their natural place as house managers, sometimes bread-winners as well ; they have the greater or the smaller share in the decision of family matters according as they or their husbands possess the stronger individuality. This is the same

5120

everywhere, in all countries. It is only when we examine the classes which have some leisure, some surplus of comfort over and above the bare needs of day to day, that we discover differences in the status of women.

In America woman was placed by man upon a pedestal, acknowledged to be the " superior " sex. Man did homage to her, professed himself respectful, took upon himself the burden of providing her with luxurious surroundings, spared her as far as possible from contact with " sordid realities."

The effect of this upon many women was deplorable. They flaunted their supposed superiority. They gave themselves up to the pursuit of pleasure and to the devising of means to spend the money which their husbands placed at their disposal. They took up passing

follies with feverish energy. The simple life which had been the pride of Americans gave place to an orgy of extravagance. The millionaires themselves would have been quite content to continue in the old way. Indeed, most of them were unable to eat anything but the plainest food. The strain which they imposed upon their stock of vital force by intense and long-continued brain-work left insufficient for the digestive process. The change in their habits when they climbed out of the humble rank in which they were mostly born was apt to rob them of their most precious possession, health. A quiet home, with frugal meals and a wife to look after and to soothe them, would have been their choice.

Their wives, however, aided by a certain number of men who earned contempt by devoting themselves to

AMERICAN FIREMEN FIGHT FIRE AND ICE SIMULTANEOUSLY

When the fire-bell shrills its sudden insistent clamour with the thermometer well below zero the American fire brigade is seen at its best. A glance at this engine caked in frozen snow and with long icicles pendent from every part gives an idea of the difficulties of fire-fighting in a blizzard. Special arrangements are made on these machines for thawing frozen hydrants with steam

Photo, Brown Brothers

social distractions, created a " smart set " whose members aimed solely at outdoing one another in opulence and ostentation. Their entertainments were spoken of as " Mrs. ——'s ten thousand dollar dinner," and " Mrs. ——'s fifty thousand dollar ball." The " happy thoughts " of Roman emperors were rivalled by the nature of the surprises which awaited guests at these vulgar and sometimes outrageous spectacles.

gramophone playing the latest and most popular tunes of the street.

As the rate of lavish spending went up so did the fierce struggle for the power to pour out money. The standards of living became more elaborate and more costly in other classes. The sharp and painful differences between rich and poor became as noticeable in the larger American cities as in those of Europe, and they brought with them their

RESCUE SQUAD OF A CITY FIRE BRIGADE IN SMOKE HELMETS
To enable firemen to operate in buildings that have been filled with smoke, special helmets have been devised. These are airtight and supplied with a valve through which the wearer breathes exhaled air. This last is freed from the carbon dioxide naturally generated in the breath and mixed with oxygen from a cylinder strapped on the back. A reducing-valve relieves pressure
Photo, Brown Brothers

The purveyors of luxury in Europe soon found that there was a better market for their services in New York. Fashionable dressmakers from Paris and Vienna offered their " most unique creations." An opera was established, with all the most famous singers and conductors, for people who as a rule knew nothing whatever about music, and would have preferred listening to a

invariable accompaniments of social unrest and discontent.

Fortunately for the Americans, they rush through phases very quickly. Flames in their country burn themselves out by reason of their intensity instead of smouldering for long periods, as they do with older nations. Society became a laughing-stock and a byword among all decent and intelligent people. It was

CADETS OF THE MILITARY ACADEMY, WEST POINT, LAUNCH A BOAT

In 1802 an Engineers' Corps was founded at West Point to constitute a military academy. The site was an historic one, for upon it, during the War of Independence, was situated a fort very vital to the patriot cause. The academy buildings overlook the Hudson river from a cliff about 160 feet high and enclose on three sides the parade ground. Officers are trained for all arms of the Service

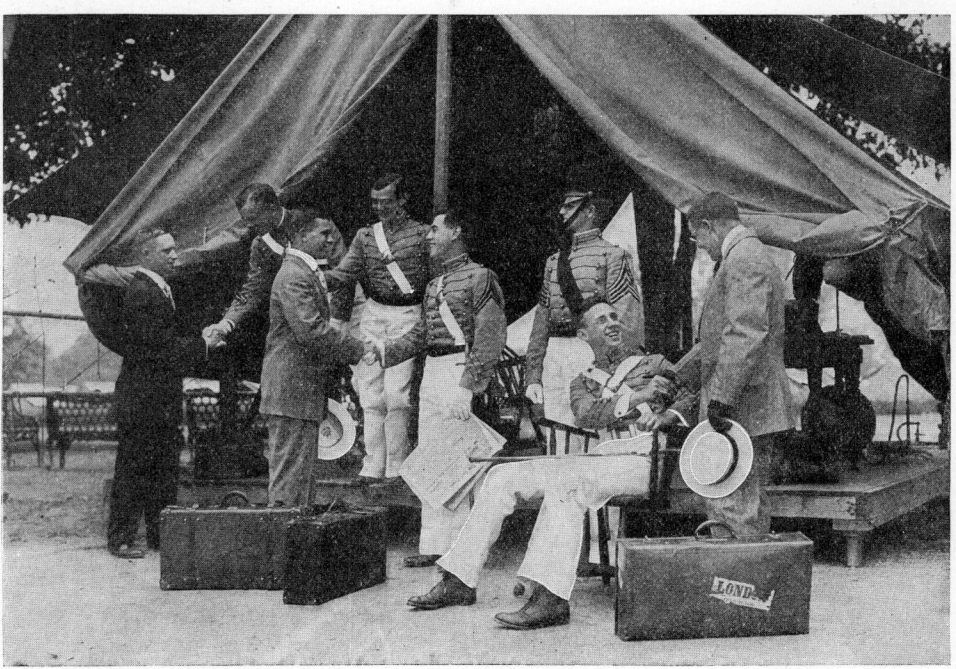

WEST POINT CADETS IN THEIR HISTORIC UNIFORM

As seen in this photograph the cadets of West Point have retained the striking uniform in use about the time of the founding of their academy. A sword-hilt will be noticed at the hip of the cadet with the newspaper in his gloved hand, and he of the double cross-belt who remains seated while he exchanges greetings with a comrade returned from a visit to London has a scabbard across his knee

Photos, Brown Brothers

BUILDERS OF THE FANTASTIC TOWERS THAT SOAR ABOVE THE MARTS AND DOCKS OF NEW YORK

American pride is satisfied and wonder is stirred in every beholder by the skyscrapers that are a unique feature of New York. They represent a wholly new development of architecture, and in their height and line have a real beauty of their own. Built on the ever more crowded neck of land between the East and Hudson rivers, they are the first things to give a new arrival an impression of the largest city of the U.S.A., and viewed from the sea affect the imagination like the minarets of an Eastern city

Photo, Brown Brothers

soon denounced as " bad form " to be ostentatious. The good sense of the mass of the nation reasserted itself and put an end to the more blatant and more banal follies of the rich.

The society woman was, after all, merely a local fungus upon the healthy trunk of American life. The result of the position allotted to women in the United States was manifested in many wholesome activities. They were given the right to equal opportunities with men in education. Professional life— legal, medical, scientific—was thrown open to them. As citizens, they exercised whatever privileges they demanded; until lately, however, these did not include the vote.

The explanation of the delay in adopting Women's Suffrage is worth inquiring into. It is connected with many other disadvantages arising out of the enormous inflow of immigrants from the districts of Europe inhabited by backward and oppressed populations.

Why Women's Suffrage Tarried

The women immigrants had, in general, no conception of the meaning of self-government. They were ignorant and superstitious. They would have been incapable of giving an intelligent vote in any community larger than a village, and even there they would have been liable to let themselves be swayed by personal likes and dislikes, the hope of personal advantage, or some stupid prejudice. To entrust power to such voters who would have been influenced by wild words and fantastic argument was seen to be too perilous.

University education for girls is usual when parents can afford it. If there is not enough money for both boys and girls to attend a university, then it is often the girls who are chosen, while the boys begin at once in business. The level of education and culture among women is certainly higher than among men. The business man seldom has time or mental energy to give to anything beyond his business. He does not regard it merely as a means of making a living. It is his life study, it absorbs the whole of his intellectual activity. There is an enormous market for books in the United States, not only novels, all classes of books; but they are read chiefly by women. This separation of interests, the wide intellectual gulf between husbands and wives, threatens to be a frequent source of domestic unhappiness.

Influence of Women's Clubs and Leagues

The influence of women, however, was brought to bear upon social legislation quite as effectively by means of their clubs and leagues as it could be by the direct vote. Very large numbers of men are content to follow the leads given by these organizations in matters affecting the homes and health of the people. Subscriptions to these societies are small, so that even the poorest can join and feel that they are helping to make the world a better place to live in. The leagues train large numbers of the ignorant immigrant women in the rights and duties of citizenship. They set themselves to enforce cleanliness in public places, markets, and streets, to force shopkeepers to wrap up food in clean paper, and to persuade people to be clean in their homes. They teach mothers how to look after their babies. They arrange for lessons in citizenship to be given in schools; open the schoolhouses in the evening for games and classes; help to find employment for boys and girls as they leave school.

The City as the Home Writ Large

The line taken by the leagues is that a city must be thought of as a big house which belongs to all the people who live in it and that, just as mothers work to keep the single home tidy and fit to live in, so the duty lies upon the women collectively to do the same for the city. To this thought there is usually a very quick response, especially from the poorer women, who suffer more

BALANCING FEATS OF BUILDERS ON THE GIDDY HEIGHTS

Vertigo is absolutely unknown to the men engaged in building the skyscrapers in New York, and
familiarity breeds, if not contempt, at least disregard of the dangers attending their employment.
Here a lad stands erect on the narrow surface of the girder on which his mate sits working, without
any hand-rail to steady him against the wind that must exert appreciable pressure at such an altitude

Photo, Brown Brothers

if the " big house " is neglected. It is a new idea to them that the city belongs to all, and that they can do as much to improve it as the wealthy.

Before the leagues were formed a good deal was done by women's clubs, and still is done, especially in the smaller places. Clubs were established first for educational and cultural aims. The members studied authors in common, listened to accounts of foreign travel, invited strangers to address them and add to their knowledge. Then they broadened out and threw themselves into civic reform movements. The power of the clubs is mighty; as many as two million members are represented in the National Federation, which meets twice a year.

A meeting was being held in the spring of 1918 when the appeal was made to the American people to give up wheat bread until the next harvest was gathered, so that Europe might have it and be saved from famine. The delegates from the two million club members decided unanimously to recommend active cooperation to all clubs. They agreed that they would not only refrain from buying wheat flour, they would send whatever store they had of it to the local food controllers for shipment to France, England, and Italy. In a report to the President Mr. Hoover wrote that " in assessing the credit for the vast export of food which has been saved for our allies by our people no one will deny the dominant part of the American women."

The readiness of men to acknowledge the value of women's work and to follow where they lead proves the cordiality which reigns in the United States between the sexes. There is far more friendship between young men and women than in any of the older countries. Boys and girls are brought up together. No obstacles are thrown in the way of their meeting constantly when they leave school. They take their amusements together. No scandal is caused by their being alone together. They are playmates, comrades, equals.

This equality is reflected by the laws concerning women's property and divorce. Marriages are not dissolved upon easier terms for men than for women. They are treated exactly alike. Wives have control over their own property, their husbands cannot touch it. A wife inherits her husband's "real estate," that is, land or buildings ; she has a legal right to maintenance by him. The suffrage is granted to all women as to all men, and women can be elected to any public office. There is little prejudice against their competing with

men for the choice of the voter. When the first woman returned to Congress took her seat, she was treated with helpful courtesy. Many positions of responsibility under the Federal government, under state governments, and under municipalities are held by women. Women are often found as managers of businesses, with large salaries and large staffs to control.

Lecturing is a most profitable occupation in the United States, and women form the bulk of lecture audiences. They, too, are more numerous than men in the parties which are made up for " seeing Europe " at cheap rates. They feel that their culture cannot be complete without visits to the famous cities of the Old World.

Lately the " See America first " cry has set many more Americans travelling through their own territory, but the distances are so immense that many feel

RIVETING GIRDERS—AND ATTENTION—ON A NEW YORK SKYSCRAPER

Some of these skyscraper builders no doubt take a foolish pride in spectacular deeds, but their ordinary tasks require nerve and daring only developed by long practice. Much of the skeleton framework has to be ascended by iron footholds inserted in the uprights by the man as he goes aloft to work at heights whence people in the streets appear as small as ants

Photo, Brown Brothers

ACTIVITY IN THE OYSTER INDUSTRY: FRESH SUPPLIES FROM THE TEEMING OYSTER BEDS

The oyster is very prolific at points along the Atlantic coast. Cultural methods have attained a high degree of perfection in the United States, an increasing demand constantly compelling the development of beds for planted oysters, apart from the natural beds. The wide geographical distribution of oysters proves their ability to withstand an extensive range of temperature, but they grow and multiply with greater rapidity in the warmer waters. Many oyster farmers transfer some of their crop from the deep water beds to the shallows, where the warmth and abundant food help to fatten them, thus enhancing their flavour and value

Photo, Brown Brothers

SARDINE PACKERS AT A CANNING FACTORY, SAN DIEGO, CALIFORNIA

Much controversy has been held over the kind of fish called sardine. Many varieties of small fish, packed in oil, have been included as being eligible for the name, but it has been maintained that this nomenclature is only permissible in the case of the pilchard, which is confined to European waters. An allied species is found off California, and here workers are seen packing the fish, which are first gutted, washed, and boiled in oil. The name sardine derives from Sardinia, where fish of the kind are abundant. San Diego, on the bay of that name, is a port some 125 miles south of Los Angeles

Photo, Brown Brothers

CHIPPEWA INDIANS FISHING THE RAPIDS IN ST. MARY'S RIVER BETWEEN LAKES SUPERIOR AND HURON

Sault Sainte Marie, the capital of the Chippewa County, Michigan, is situated at the rapids of St. Mary's river, near the outlet of Lake Superior, and on one of the famous ship canals which obviate the impediment to navigation caused by a fall of some 18 feet, and lower or raise vessels from one level to the other. The city is connected with the village Sault Sainte Marie in Canada by the international railroad bridge, thus communicating directly with the Canadian Pacific Railway. Many of the Chippewa tribe, whose habitat is near the Great Lakes, are fine navigators and were expert at shooting the rapids in their frail canoes

Photo, Brown Brothers

WINTER IN THE STATES: BRINGING HOME THE FIREWOOD

Owing to the size of the country the climate varies in different regions. The northern regions are in a zone where winters are long and severe, the southern extremities lie near the tropics. The main land-mass is in the temperate zone, but nevertheless is divided between violent extremes, including intolerable heat waves in summer and blinding blizzards of whirling snow in winter

Photo, Brown Brothers

they might just as well cross the ocean as spend three or four days in a train.

Railway journeys are made infinitely more comfortable than they are in Europe. All rapid, long-distance travelling is done in Pullman cars. In these the seats face one another ; each passenger has one to himself. At night the negro porters fill up the space between the seats and make a bed, while they let down from the roof a shelf upon which another bed is made up. Thus the two passengers sleep. The beds are wide and comfortable. From the roof heavy curtains are hung which shut in both bunks. The aisle then has the appearance of a narrow, enclosed passage, running the whole length of the car.

Attached to each train of Pullman cars is a parlour car, where there are armchairs, a writing-table, and plenty of magazines. Usually this is at the end of the train ; one can then sit outside on the rear platform to take the air and study the country through which one is passing. Some trains on the long trans-continental routes have special observation cars.

In the dining cars excellent meals are provided. There is a bewildering variety of dishes on the bill of fare. For breakfast there is always fruit in season. Ice-cream is never absent from the menu. The cooking, all done in the train kitchen, is, as a rule, good, the service quick, and the charges are not exorbitant.

The differences of scenery, of climate, of cultivation, and of industrial development which are to be found within the borders of the United States make travelling there unusually attractive. If it lacks the charm of historical association, and of the periods of art

AGRICULTURAL INDUSTRY ON AN INDIAN RESERVATION

He is one of the renowned Redskins—a term of no exact somatic significance, seeing that their skin is rather of a coppery brown—a remnant of the aboriginal people of the New World. Before the White Man's coming the North American Indians had attained a considerable degree of industrial and social advancement; now, in the reservations, they are being schooled in modern industry

LAND LABOURERS OF THE FERTILE "EMPIRE STATE"

The surface of New York State, greatly diversified by numerous mountains, lakes, and rivers, is noted for its picturesque scenery; nevertheless, two-thirds of the soil are suitable for agriculture and possess all the conditions favourable to productive farming. Ranking as the second state in value of farms, it has important agricultural products, and industry characterises its rural population

Photos, Brown Brothers

DRYING YARD OF A CALIFORNIAN ALMOND ORCHARD

After some experimenting, enterprising growers in California succeeded in making that state one of the recognized centres for almond production. The fruit of the almond tree is leathery and uneatable, and encloses a nut which when broken reveals the edible kernel. While the tree does well on dry soils in Syria and North Africa, the Californian variety needs well watered land for good production

Photo, Brown Brothers

VARIED MEMBERS OF A FARMER'S FAMILY ON A ROADWAY IN RURAL OHIO

The United States is primarily an agricultural country, despite the fact that its manufactures figure so conspicuously in the markets of the world. Many of the settlers in Ohio are finding farming a remunerative pursuit. The farms are not always large ones, but they are cultivated with a will; their owners realizing that the advice expressed in the well-known couplet: "A little farm well tilled, A little purse well filled," is sound and worthy of practical consideration. Most farms are worked by the owner or tenant and his family, and although labour is employed at certain seasons, farming is usually a family occupation

Photo, Brown Brothers

DARBY AND JOAN ENGROSSED IN AN APPLE-DRYING PURSUIT

Florida and California are the principal states for the production of fruits, but in many districts fruit-growing is a profitable industry. Apples, a hardy fruit, are plentiful, and yearly this old Virginian couple undertake the task of drying their small store—a process involving no little patience on the part of the wife, who slices the apples, strings them, and hangs them near the hearth to dry

Photo, Brown Brothers

which have left their mark upon Europe, there is more to be learned in America, there is a living present to study, an experiment in progress, a melting-pot on the boil which is blending the most varied elements into a new race.

American Life & Character—2

Life in the Great Cities

ONE'S first impression of New York suggests that the city is decidedly more Continental, that is to say European, than English in appearance. One has to remember that it is a southern city. As you look out from a car on the "Elevated," the railway which runs on the level of second-floor windows, you see, if it be summer-time, the streets filled with children playing, people gossiping, women sitting outside the houses, just the sort of street scene you would get in Naples or Seville. There is an enormous number of Italians in New York, and many other southern people; they help towards the making of this first impression.

Featureless, too, the city appears to the fresh arrival, save for the tall buildings in the neighbourhood of Wall Street or Lower Broadway. The streets and avenues all seem very much alike, and so, indeed, with a few exceptions, they are. The two principal exceptions are Broadway and Fifth Avenue. Broadway runs from the sea for many miles up the narrow island on which New York is built. Fifth Avenue begins at

PASSING MOTORISTS INVEST IN A CONSIGNMENT OF APPLES FROM A COUNTRY ORCHARD

Apple growing has one of its chief centres in North America, where the combination of virgin soil and cheap transport have told in the commercial struggle. In certain states the apple is indigenous, but a wide variety has been obtained by cross fertilisation and grafting from imported species. In some localities, however, notably the north-west, the Americans have had to face special difficulties in the way of scorching of fruit by the sun and damage from high winds. These difficulties are combated by planting the trees closely, and so affording mutual protection

Photo, Brown Brothers

GIRLS OF A CITY SCHOOL INCLUDE PRACTICAL GARDENING AMONG THEIR STUDIES

Nowhere has more attention or more encouragement been given to agricultural education than in the United States. This commences in the schools, many of which have their own gardens. Students may then pass on to an agricultural college or take a special course at one of the universities. In connexion with this keenness for advancement in the various branches of husbandry it is instructive to recall the passing of an Act in 1862 granting to each state 30,000 acres of land for every member returned to Congress, for the purpose of instituting colleges where the art could be practised

Photo, Brown Brother.

HARVESTING A CROP ON A TOBACCO PLANTATION UNDER THE SUNNY SKIES OF VIRGINIA

Many southern landowners have found it advantageous to grow the great staples which could be planted and harvested by negroes and by wholesale methods. For long years tobacco was the principal crop of the northern tier of southern states, including Virginia, where its cultivation has been a profound influence in the economic organization of the state. The soil and climate of the United States are, on the whole, well suited to the growing of tobacco, which in many regions has become a prolific source of wealth. The acreage devoted to it has increased enormously, and the weight of the crops amounts to many million pounds

Photo. Brown Brothers

Washington Square, a fascinating relic of old New York, with stately houses of early nineteenth-century architecture and restful green spaces, both telling of a time when Americans still valued leisure and charm. They are now coming back to the just appreciation of those blessings.

Right away to Central Park Fifth Avenue runs, crossing Broadway and gradually becoming "residential." Not long ago the shopping part of it was a long way "down town," but every year the shops crept farther up. Then huge hotels were built, first the Saint Regis, called the Millionaires' Hotel, then the Gotham, then the Plaza at the top. Most of the houses remain which made Fifth Avenue famous as the street of the homes of the richest men in the world, but they are shut for the most part. Commerce has marked this, one of the finest thoroughfares in the world, for its own.

Lofty Office Blocks of Broadway

Broadway cannot be called "fine." Much of it is narrow. There are stretches which are still squalid. Nowhere is it impressive, except, perhaps, in the Money Market section, where the office-blocks are so high that the traffic and the swirling currents of humanity seem to flow like a noisy, hurrying river deep down between very steep and precipitous cliffs. The chief activities of the city are all to be found on Broadway.

At the harbour end are the Custom House and the shipping offices, all the signs of a busy and wealthy port. Then come the banks and the Stock Exchange, and the offices of the firms that deal in money. Here the streets are named instead of being numbered as they are higher up. They date back to an early period of New York history.

No other of the avenues, which run lengthwise, while the streets run across, can be compared with Fifth; indeed, they are undistinguished, uninteresting, mostly filled by the poorer kind of shops, inhabited by the flatter kind of people.

The streets that stand out in one's recollection are also few, but that is equally true of London or Paris streets.

Next after the "Lombard Street" section of Broadway comes the wholesale trade district, then a shopping section, then theatreland, then the motor trade region, and after that miles and miles of nothing in particular. It is still Broadway right out in the country, where trees and bushes take the place of shop-fronts and the blithe "commuter" (as the suburban season-ticket holder is nicknamed, because he "commutes" the daily fare into a fixed quarterly payment) enjoys the scents and stillness after the din and stuffiness of town.

New York's Magnificent Harbour

From one of the business men's lunch clubs on the top floor of one of the high buildings the beauty of New York is seen to lie in her magnificent harbour and the two rivers that flow into it on either side of the tongue of land on which the city clusters. The Riverside Drive, which overlooks the broad Hudson, is a favourite quarter to live in, not so fashionable as the district which lies on the other side of Central Park, but far more attractive.

Contrasting Wealth and Squalor

Over the river is New Jersey, where many New Yorkers live, in such suburbs as East Orange, where you might imagine that the whole state was peopled by comfortable folk living in neatly-constructed spacious houses with gardens round them, and that poverty had been banished—as indeed it has—from the region where the well-to-do dwell. Look the other way and you see Long Island across Long Island Sound.

At one end this shares the grime and turmoil and squalor of toiling New York. In the centre is a pleasant farming district, which reminds one as much as anything I ever saw in the United States of an English countryside. Then the island becomes an uninhabited jungle. On the Atlantic shore, only a

OPERATIVES AT WORK STRIPPING THE "FRAGRANT WEED"

After the wilting and drying process, the tobacco leaves are stripped of their midribs and some varieties are then put under heavy pressure. Great care is taken in the sorting of the leaves, which are placed in heaps according to their quality, as first, second, and inferior grades. Tobacco is brought in bundles to the cigar factories, high-grade leaves for wrappers being kept separate

Photo, Brown Brothers

short trip from the city by train or boat, is Coney Island, the pleasure resort of the millions who inhabit New York, as opposed to the "Four Hundred" who flatter themselves that they give "tone" to its society.

Farther off on the New Jersey coast is one of the favourite holiday-places of the middle class, Atlantic City. In some of its features it recalls Coney Island, though such a suggestion would be indignantly denied by its frequenters. Its long Board Walk by the ocean and its huge summer hotels are its prominent features. A still longer journey must be taken by those who go to Newport, the fashionable seaside "village of palaces," in the state of Rhode Island.

A delightful spot is Newport, in spite of the atmosphere of superfluous riches which is supposed to enwrap it. In truth, the rich cast off here, during the daytime at any rate, the ostentation and luxurious habits which they acquire in cities. They bathe, play lawn-tennis, croquet, polo, ride or drive about the country, make up impromptu lunch and tea parties, wear simple, sensible clothes. Only in the evening does the sway of fashion reassert itself. Dinners are on the sumptuous scale, the most expensive of frocks are worn, bridge is played till early morning for high stakes. Along the coast of Massachusetts are smaller country-home settlements where the wealthy Boston people take their ease amid their carefully-tended gardens and in the bracing Atlantic air. There is a stretch here known as the gold Coast, on account of its millionaire population. Some of them are of the kidney that loves display and that spends lavishly for no other purpose, proclaiming its deplorable lack of taste and education.

But most of them, and particularly those who were born in this part of the United States, are men and women who belong to that really good society which is found in all countries and which demands from its members nothing more than the qualifications of naturally fine instincts, cultivated intelligence, wide interests, and acquaintance with the best that has been thought and imagined since the records of mankind began.

Much ridicule has been thrown at Boston and its people. Possibly they have deserved some of it. They may have set the standard of culture a shade too high. There are Bostonians even to-day who betray their poverty of intellect by being self-consciously "intellectual." But no one who is competent to estimate social values will deny that, as Washington is the administrative and New York the business capital, so Boston is the American metropolis of intelligence and learning, of knowledge and taste, pursued for their own sakes and without any ulterior object of material advantage.

To begin with, Boston has a tradition. Here one's thoughts turn to Emerson and the " Transcendental School," to Oliver Wendell Holmes, to Thoreau and Longfellow and Nathaniel Hawthorne, to James Russell Lowell and Fields, the publisher who earned the right to be included for ever among the authors whom he treated so well. The literary associations thus begun have never been

HAND MANUFACTURE OF THE TOBACCO LEAF INTO THE CIGAR

Throughout the United States there are to be found numberless factories, large and small, for the making of cigars. Very few of them use machinery, for hand-made cigars are still considered the best and are the most expensive. The operative rolls the filler tobacco into the compact shape required, then winds the wrapper leaf round it and fastens it with paste at each end

Photo, Brown Brothers

entirely neglected. It is not by chance that the Boston Public Library is the most famous in the country. Harvard, so close to the city, has fostered, not merely the spirit of learning, but the art of expression, the mastery of language, the study of best models. About the older red-brick and the newer grey stone university buildings there is a mellow air of leisurely yet earnest studentship.

Harvard and its Associations

When you have wandered through the courts and quadrangles, you understand why Harvard men are somehow different from Yale or Princeton men. Their imaginations have been attuned to beauty, their minds to the comprehension of that side of our existence which is not concerned with buying and selling and becoming rich.

The Harvard Club in New York is different from all other clubs there or elsewhere. There is no sham culture at Harvard or in that part of Boston society which appreciates the Harvard spirit. The centre of the city is a tangle of narrow streets and old buildings preserved " for old sake's sake." Outside of this are wide thoroughfares, avenues shaded by fine trees, open spaces which make Boston live in one's memory as a vista of parks and commons. This aspect of their city is highly valued by the people, and they have made plans which will keep it green and airy however monstrous its growth may be.

New Orleans : Old and New

If ever it fulfils the expectations of its town-planners and includes a population of ten millions, these ten millions will nevertheless have an orderly, agreeable dwelling-place. Wide avenues have been planted eighteen miles from the centre, to be ready when they are needed. Stretches of woodland and breezy hillside have been reserved for public use ; so have the shores of lakes and rivers, even the banks of streams.

There is only one other American city which fills the mind of the traveller with pictures from the past as Boston does ;

this is New Orleans. One is disappointed at first that it does not take one aside more often and more insistently to whisper in one's ear of the days when it was a French town and of the later slave-dealing scenes which went on here as openly as if no man believed that there was a God in Heaven. But those who stroll away from the modern part, which is exactly the same as all other modern parts, and look for remains of the old French settlement will still find a good deal to reward them.

There is one street in particular, a street of low houses covered with flowering creepers, a quiet street where it is always afternoon, shut away from the bustle and noise and hurry of new New Orleans, which gave me just the atmosphere I was in search of. Here there is a famous French restaurant, where the waiters have the true French style and where the wine is as good as you might find in Dijon or Bordeaux. The omelettes, too, are quite unlike those of American cooking ; they reminded me of the omelette of the landlady at the Mont Saint Michel.

White and Black in the South

Richmond is a southern Civil War city, Atlanta (Georgia), Savannah and Birmingham (Alabama) represent the New South of industrial expansion and prosperity. But not until you get to New Orleans can you feel that the South has become a reality to your mind.

Strangely you begin then to understand that the negro problem, which is the toughest problem the United States have before them, is not so difficult in the South as it is in those parts where white people and coloured people mix more and meet upon a basis of pretended equality. What the nature of the problem is has been stated succinctly and accurately in these words : " Whether at last the negro shall gain full recognition as a man, or be utterly crushed by prejudice and superior numbers ? "

In the South the negroes accept the position of inferiority assigned to them.

American Indians
of Arizona & New Mexico

Lank hair and solidity of facial contour distinguish this stoutly built and gaily garbed squaw of the Walapai tribe in Arizona

Photo, Underwood & Underwood

In the heart of the sage-brush desert of Arizona Navaho blankets are woven, their beauty and utility attracting many customers

Photo, American Museum of Natural History

Versed in useful arts are the Indian tribes of Arizona, and basketry, skilfully woven and dyed, is a much favoured feminine industry

Photo, Brown Brothers

*Strongly developed is the Pueblo culture in customs, ceremonies,
and dwellings, and, among divers arts, pottery holds a high place*

The portable bed of the papoose is an important article in each Yuma household and the poorest mother lavishes care upon its trappings

Photo, Brown Brothers

If predatory and warlike, the Apache of New Mexico, fastidious and artistic in dress, is a finer man than the so-called Apache of Europe.

Photo, American Museum of Natural History

5150

A Hopi snake-dancer of Arizona, whose ancestors danced in self-same manner and place even before the advent of the Spanish

Photo, Underwood & Underwood

Lovingly this chief handles the gift made to a predecessor by President Lincoln when thanking the Pueblo leaders for aid in the Civil War

surroundings of a good British home, was on a visit to a seaside place in New Jersey. She went into a merry-go-round enclosure and was ordered out by the man in charge.

" Get out of here ! " he said. " We don't allow niggers."

That woman sat by the sea and wished that " the ocean might rise and drown every white person on the face of the earth." She destroyed all the letters she had from her many white friends and made up her mind that she would have no more to say to them. In time her soreness wore off a little, but she never forgets that rough boor's insult or thinks of white people as she had done up to then.

The other incident happened in a street-car. A young American at a college in New York State knew slightly a negro fellow-student from the South.

Growth of Coloured Prosperity

At " commencement," when the students had their relations to visit them, this young man saw the negro come into a crowded car with a girl, who was evidently his sister. " Without a thought I rose, lifted my hat and gave her my seat. Never again shall I see such a look of gratitude as that which lighted up his face when he bowed in acknowledgment of my courtesy. It revealed the race question to me."

In the United States, however well-off the negro may be, he is not contented with his lot any more than the rich Jews, who were tolerated by the Russian government, could be at their ease while massacres were of frequent occurrence among their poor brothers. There is a growing class of prosperous coloured people. Their homes are comfortable in an undistinguished style. Their ambition is to be as much like other people as possible. They live like their white neighbours, have their card-parties and their musical evenings, their dances and " church socials." They go to church regularly, the whole family turning out and all dropping generous gifts into the collection plate.

It is among the black clergy that the demand for full rights and freedom finds loudest voice. They feel more than any other class the sting of the decree which commands the negro " to keep his place."

Education Among the Negroes

The blacks are not tolerated in the North so sympathetically as they were. Their legal rights are still secured to them—on paper—but even places which do not actually refuse service to coloured persons let them see that they are not wanted, and the negro is sensitive enough to shrink from rebuffs. He is a simple, genial, good-natured creature as a rule, and he cannot understand why he should be treated as an outcast. He shrugs his broad shoulders and keeps among his own people. That is in the North. In the South he is compelled to keep among them. He is humiliated, made to feel he is considered inferior to the whites, driven often to crime by his resentment and wounded pride.

Yet in all parts education spreads among the blacks, they rise in larger and larger numbers from the hewer of wood and drawer of water class, they raise a louder and more persistent cry for the dropping of the " colour bar." Yet, so far as can be seen at present, there is a stern and even fierce determination among the whites in the United States for the keeping of that bar severely up.

Results Achieved at Hampton

In the white imagination the dissolute, savage negro represents a terrible danger. That he exists is true enough, but it is true also that he is a rare exception and that he is generally the product of bad conditions created by white people. The negroes are apt to be vain, the men in particular. They appreciate that " dolce far niente " (pleasant idleness) which is foreign to the American of the northern states. They like spending money, they like display.

GLIMPSE INTO THE SORTING DEPARTMENT OF A BEAN CANNERY IN THE UNITED STATES

The kidney bean, or phaseolus vulgaris, was introduced into Europe from South America in 1597, and its culture was first popularised in France, where it is usually known as the haricot. In the United States this bean is plentiful and embraces many varieties, over 150 of which are in cultivation, including both bush and climbing beans. The seeds of many of these varieties, especially the frijole, which is a staple food in the south-western states, are used, either green or dried, as food for man and beast. Large quantities of them are preserved with salt, or by evaporation, or canning

Photo, Brown Brothers

SCENE ON AN ICE FIELD IN THE STATES DURING THE PROCESS OF CUTTING AND CARTING AN ICE CROP

The ice industry is an important one in the United States, where both natural and artificial ice are in enormous demand. The chief fields of operation are in Maine and on the Hudson river. After the snow has been cleared, usually by means of a snow-plough, an ice-plough cuts deep grooves in the ice, first in one direction, then at right angles with the first, thus forming squares. These grooves are deep, and the remaining thickness is cut through with a saw; the blocks are then loosened and floated or carted to the ice-house, there to be held in storage until required

Photo, Brown Brothers

RURAL POSTAL SERVICE SIDE BY SIDE WITH GENERAL STORES IN OLD-FASHIONED AMERICA

Since the year 1775, when their own post office system was introduced, the postal service of the U.S.A. has developed enormously. The free delivery system for cities was introduced in 1863, and the rural free delivery under President McKinley in 1897. Notwithstanding the youth of this last adjunct, it has all the appearance of outgrowing some of the older branches of the service. Numerous receiving boxes and deliveries are provided to meet the convenience of the rural public, and in the remote districts where the more modern modes of transport have not yet penetrated the old-fashioned light buggy is still employed by the post official in his daily rounds

Photo. Brown Brothers

5156

But they can be induced to work hard and steadily. As parents they set a fine example. They are of a cheerful temperament, they delight in music, they love laughter.

Whether their capacity for intellectual development is smaller than that of other races is by no means sure. When it is argued that the American negro population has thrown up many minds of distinction, many possessors of talent in all kinds of directions which can be set beside the talent of white men and women, the reply is that these minds, these talents, belong to persons of mixed blood. Certainly that is often true.

The number of mulattoes is large. Many who are styled black because they are not " white " are really of a brownish hue. But full-blooded negroes have contributed to the world's stock of thought and art. At Hampton, the first industrial training college for black students, founded in 1868, there have been many instances of something more than talent. The standards of intelligence, honesty, accuracy are quite as high as they would be among young white men drawn from the same surroundings.

Climate and Mental Development

Mr. Booker Washington, the first Principal of Tuskegee College, declared that " a country which was not safe with ignorant slaves cannot be safe with ignorant freemen." Certainly the negro has proved that he can profit by education, even of the highest kind, but patient research seems to be necessary over a long period before it can be decided whether the black race is inferior to the white and the yellow in possibilities of mental development.

Climate may have an influence. In the South the damp heat is certainly not conducive to effort of any kind. The southern whites of old family speak with an attractive slowness, and have not until quite recent times displayed any of that fierce unresting energy which is the outstanding trait in the temperament of the northern and western people. They have always reckoned themselves the aristocrats of the country.

While the Puritans were colonising New England and Pennsylvania, Cavalier families were taking up estates in the South, conferred upon them, as was that of the Esmonds in Thackeray's novel, " The Virginians," by Charles I. or by other British sovereigns. Called after Queen Elizabeth, Virginia was made as much like England as possible. The colonists belonged to families of position and long descent. As preservers of the aristocratic tradition they had more in common with English men and women of the ruling caste than had the sturdier, more progressive northern Americans.

Industrial Expansion in the South

They were resolute enemies of change. In the United States the " backward South " was a reproach not undeserved. The North went ahead in manufacture and commerce, as well as in general farming. The South kept on in the old rut ; it has been left for our own time to see its late industrial expansion.

One can see to-day, by comparing the appearances of the southern states with Pennsylvania and Massachusetts, how unlike were the processes of their development. The flood of aliens which has been poured over the land at the rate of a million a year has certainly made a difference to the more English atmosphere of the regions which in soil and climate approach more nearly to the conditions of the British Isles. Even on the land it is common to find the farmers what one is apt to call " foreign."

Lights and Shadows of Pittsburg

Yet even with so largely foreign a population the cities and towns, the cultivation and the culture, both the look of the country and the institutions of the Puritan states are entirely distinct from those of the South, except in those new southern industrial centres which have lately come into being. Much may be said, for example, in

UNITED STATES POST OFFICE SERVANTS SENDING LETTERS BY PNEUMATIC DISPATCH

Pneumatic dispatch, or transport of written communications by means of air pressure, was introduced in London in 1853, and has been adopted for postal and telegraphic purposes in most large cities of the world. In the United States tubes up to 8 inches in diameter are in use, the carriers employed in these being 24 inches long and 7 inches in diameter. They are worked at a pressure of 6 lb. to the square inch, and give a transit speed of 30 m.p.h. Small installations for internal communication in offices, hotels, and shops are in common use

Photo, Brown Brothers

dispraise of Pittsburg. It is smoky, unpleasing, unclean, "almost as bad as your Sheffield," a travelled American said to me with a half smile when I had done abusing it. I had to admit the comparison. Yet with all its unattractiveness, Pittsburg is no mushroom. It is a solid city with a history, though not in all its chapters can that history be described as creditable.

The steel industry of which Pittsburg is the headquarters was built up by ruthless methods, both among competitors and towards employees. Yet the ugliness of much that the Steel Barons practised cannot offset the weight of honest labour and capable management and inventive ingenuity which have made Pittsburg famous.

New England is more English in appearance than any other part of the United States. It has a more settled aspect. One sees lawns which might have been rolled and watered, watered and rolled, for hundreds of years. There are villages which might almost be English. The cities have old buildings in them. They pride themselves upon their history.

Alien Life in the Middle West

Then go up into the hilly districts of New York State and you will find Dutch villages. All the people have Dutch names. They live there cut off from the rest of their fellow-countrymen as effectually as if they were in Holland, whence their ancestors came.

In the middle west, with its vast cultivated plains and its industrial centres of rapid growth, a civilization distinct from that of the east is quickly recognized. Here one begins to understand what the inflow of foreign citizens has done to alter the character of the population. In Cleveland eighty-two out of every hundred inhabitants are foreign-born. There are districts of the city where nobody speaks English.

In the north-western states many of the wheat-farms are held by Germans and Swedes. Here is the country to

which the old-time farmers moved in their "prairie schooners"—as they called their big farm wagons—when they had exhausted the natural fertility of the soil of the middle west. Many of their descendants have gone across the line into Canada. There are districts in Saskatchewan full of them.

Spanish Influence in California

California is another state that bears upon it the marks of an older civilization. Spanish settlements have left their ruins. Spanish names are everywhere. There are traces of Spanish blood in the people. Their speech, soft and musical, is unlike that of any other section of the population. With a climate so kindly, and with sunshine so constant and powerful, it might be expected that a lower degree of energy would be developed here than on the Atlantic seaboard or on the prairie swept by invigorating winds. Yet the Californians are as energetic as any of their fellow-countrymen.

The speed at which they rebuilt San Francisco after the "fire"—no one ever mentions an earthquake in California—was proof of their grit and determination. It was unfortunate that they had not time to consider the claims of beauty. But they felt, no doubt, that nothing mattered for the moment save to get the streets rebuilt and to provide roofs for those who would bring back the prosperity which had received so cruel a check.

Land of Many Opportunities

To see how gigantic have been the strides which America has taken in material wealth within the last forty years you must go to the west. "The wild and woolly west" it was mockingly called not so long ago. Now it counts itself, not without good reasons, the most progressive as well as the most productive part of the United States. Mining camps have grown into well-ordered cities. Public spirit has kept pace with the increase in the population. Street-car systems are swift and

UNCLE SAM'S LETTER CARRIER DELIVERING MAIL

For long the United States had only rudimentary postal services, and the first national post office system was established in 1775. Stamps were introduced by them in 1847; previously only money was collected for the postage, prepayment being optional. Since those early days the public post has assumed gigantic dimensions, and is one of the most effective instruments of civilization

Photo, Brown Brothers

QUICK LUNCH ON THE PENNSYLVANIA RAILROAD

Railway journeys are generally more comfortable in the U.S.A. than they are in Europe. All rapid long distance travelling is done in Pullman cars, of steel construction throughout, with parlour cars and dining cars attached. On the Pennsylvania Railroad luncheon is served in " quick lunch " cars, the menu showing the same dishes at the same prices as supplied in the dining cars

Photo, Brown Brothers

cleanly. Electric light is in universal use ; so is the telephone.

The western people are heartier, more friendly at first sight, more natural than the eastern. From Kansas, with its enormous fields of wheat and oats and its little farmhouses, looking like dolls'-houses, in the middle of them ; through Colorado, where the sage-brush country begins and where you look across to the Rocky Mountains, their snowy summits serene among light clouds ; through Nevada, rich in minerals, and down into California, where the fields are well-tilled and well-fenced, the stacks of hay and straw substantial and the cattle fat, the type of western American is much the same ; it is a type which leaves one with very pleasant memories.

The west is a country of vast spaces, immense vistas, clean, clear air which braces and stimulates. One can understand what makes the westerner imaginative and enterprising. There are so many opportunities to " make good." There is so much wealth scattered about by the careless hand of nature, so much beauty and grandeur, that it would be a shame for mankind not to breed a race worthy of the land. That was

INSIDE THE CAB OF A MIGHTY FREIGHT ENGINE

Seated before the manifold apparatus for controlling the movements of the giant mechanism, the veteran engine driver glances at his watch. To the left and convenient to his hand is the great brake-lever, and above his head dangles the cord of the whistle, while a tea can in a rack adds a somewhat homely touch to this picture of life on one of the great American railroads

Photo, Brown Brothers

OILING THE PISTON-RODS OF A GIANT AMERICAN LOCOMOTIVE

For hauling heavy loads up certain steep inclines that occur on their railroads, the Americans have evolved engines of enormous size and weighing as much as four hundred tons. These are capable of pulling trains, whose total weight may reach three thousand tons, up the most formidable gradients. The dimensions of this colossus may be gauged by comparison with its burly attendant

Photo, Brown Brothers

MONSTER STEAM SHOVEL THAT GROPES IN THE HOLDS OF SHIPS: THE DOCKS AT ASHTABULA

From a huge crane run on wheels is swung the great arm of the shovel. The join of crane and arm is just beyond the upper limits of the photograph. The man seen caged in the arm itself operates the two great claws which, when full, are swung bodily out on to the wharf. The size of the huge mechanism is so great that the freight train seen on the left easily runs under the crane. Ashtabula stands on the river of that name where it enters Lake Erie

Photo, Brown Brothers

the desire of the Mormon community. They aimed at producing a stock which should be perfect, " no physical deformity, no vice, no crime." They believed polygamy would help towards this because it allowed the woman to be treated " as mother, not as wife, during the period when her maternal duties to her offspring are most sacred," and because it could surround her " with scenes of kindness and gentleness, love and holiness."

It was an experiment, and it failed. The stock produced was subject to the same shortcomings as other stocks. Polygamy has for many years ceased in the state of Utah. It could only continue while the state was separated from the rest of the country. When the railway ran through it there came into view the end of Brigham Young's attempt to form a community which should govern itself by means of Church and State in one. The " Gentiles," as the opponents of polygamy were called, gained power ; the old Mormon leaders lost it.

Utah's Debt to the Mormons

Since about 1890 there has not been any Mormon state. It had fulfilled its promise to " make the wilderness blossom like the rose." The Mormons brought water from the mountains, canalised the melting snows, turned the desert into fertile land on which they could produce four crops of lucerne grass a year and three of hay. They established an outpost of civilization at a date when, west of the Missouri river, there was no other settlement until the Rockies were crossed.

When Brigham Young led his followers into Utah, in 1847, he aimed at making his colony independent of supplies from outside. He established industries, wool-weaving, silk-weaving, sugarmaking, shoe-making. He might have succeeded in keeping the Mormons secure from " contamination " (there was an echo in their ideals of the early Pilgrims' anxiety to keep themselves to

themselves) if he had not happened to choose a territory which was rich in minerals.

In Utah there are found all the metals save two. Gold, silver, copper, lead, iron, coal, marble, asbestos, saltpetre, quicksilver, zinc and alum all abound. There is salt in immense quantities. There are very valuable species of mineral rubber. When these riches were discovered there arose the cry among the people of Utah that Mormonism was " bad for business." It kept capital away, and capital had to be attracted if the wealth under the soil was to be realized.

Pleasing Aspects of Salt Lake City

Salt Lake City is built in a pleasant, solid style, with broad, well-paved streets having runnels of water beside them and trees to shade them from the fierceness of the sun. It is probably the best-built city in the United States ; none has a finer situation or a more picturesque setting. Grey-green mountains shelter it from cold winds, the green water of the lake is refreshingly cool to look at and makes for health. While Mormonism was the rule of the state there were no drinking saloons or disorderly houses. Strict Mormons neither smoked nor took stimulants ; even tea and coffee were barred.

Weakening of old Mormon Customs

The Church founded by Brigham Young is still supported by tithes (tenth parts) of all that its members possess. It has a president and two assistants, twelve " apostles " and a council of seventy, modelled after the system of the earliest Christian Church described in the New Testament.

Mormons are not expected to take their disputes before the civil courts. They take them in the first place to an elder of the Church. If he cannot settle them, the parties appeal to a bishop. Should the bishop fail to make peace between the disputants, their quarrel is laid before a council of fifteen. The final decision lies in all cases with the three

ROLLING MILL IN ACTION IN PITTSBURG, ONE OF THE CHIEF MANUFACTURING CITIES OF THE UNITED STATES

Pittsburg is the leading place in the United States for manufactures of iron, steel, copper, and glass, and has numerous large blast furnaces and rolling mills. Among its many sobriquets "the Smoky City" and "the Iron City" best suggest its chief characteristics, while the epithet, "Hell with the lid off" would appear at times not undeserved. Rolling mills are machines used for rolling masses of metal into bars or plates. They comprise a series of rollers in pairs, between which the metal receives successive reductions in thickness, and are driven by powerful horizontal reversing steam-engines, with cog-wheel connexions and axle gearing

Photo, Brown Brothers

TITANIC MOTOR TRACTOR THAT FORMS A BIER FOR FOREST GIANTS

In Washington, the most north-westerly state of the Union, are some of the finest forests in America, and from these, for many years, came the special long timbers for the masts and spars of ships. Most of the logs are conveyed to the saw mill in " drives," or floating groups, but when there is no " driveable " stream at hand, huge motor tractors are employed in the work

Photo, Brown Brothers

presidents. But the hold of the old customs and regulations weakens every year. The people of Utah have come almost into line with the American people at large. Mormons no longer go forth in large numbers as missionaries to spread the faith. These missionaries went forth as the Apostles did, taking neither money nor change of raiment. They were not allowed to beg, but somehow their needs were provided for and somehow their faith was strengthened.

The call for men to set out on these proselytising journeys came suddenly. The authorities of the Church would summon them and they had to leave their occupations at once, whatever they were. There must have been a good side to a system which induced men to serve it so willingly and bend their wills to its orders. There was too violent a prejudice, however, against the Mahomedan practice of the Mormons to allow their doctrines and their theocratic state a fair trial.

Few men among them availed themselves of the liberty to marry more than one wife. For the greater number polygamy was too expensive. But in the popular mind polygamy was the article in the Mormon creed which stood out most prominently and doomed it to extinction. In the white temple of Salt Lake City, with its six spires and its walls nine feet thick, which took forty years to build, the services now are scarcely distinguishable from those of other Christian sects.

Southward from Utah are vast stretches of " dry " land which has not been irrigated, and which presents therefore a painfully barren appearance after the good agricultural land of the Mormon colonisation.

Dust and white heat would be one's principal memories of Arizona, if it were not for the Grand Cañon, one of the most marvellous of the regions of beauty created by the upheavals of nature. Brilliance of colour, magnificence

IN THE GRAND STAND AT A MOTOR RACE MEETING, LOS ANGELES

Only a part of the crowd that fills the huge stand is visible in this and the photograph on the opposite page. The Los Angeles course, or " speedway," is celebrated and both sexes, as may be seen by a glance at the packed benches, find the sport an attractive one. The roof is well designed to allow a cool draught and give shelter from the Californian sun

Photo, Brown Brothers

of outline, the same colossal grandeur which impresses us in the architecture of Egypt, combine to make the Grand Cañon unforgettable.

Texas has nothing to show like this, but the huge state is immensely interesting. It belonged until 1836 to Mexico. In that year the Texans rose and proclaimed their independence. For a number of years there had been a steady infiltration of Americans into the country ; the United States government had made two offers to purchase it from Mexico, but had not been able to agree upon terms.

At first the Texans were beaten, and those who surrendered, instead of being treated as prisoners of war, were cruelly killed. This roused the spirit of the rebels to fury, and in a battle fought by not more than 800 of them, they killed 630 Mexicans, wounded over 200, and captured the rest, including their general, who was also Mexican President. He was obliged to acknowledge the independence of Texas, and was then liberated.

A year later he repudiated his word on the ground that he was a prisoner when he gave it and acted under compulsion. By this time, however, the Republic of Texas had been set up and recognized by the United States, France, England, and Belgium. It lasted until 1845, when it became a state of the American Union, its obvious destiny from the moment of its separation from Mexico.

The Mexican government, however, resolved to fight against the inevitable. They did not like the prospect of having the United States for a neighbour,

RACING CARS LINED UP FOR THE START ON THE SPEEDWAY

All eyes are turned to the track where the eighteen cars with roaring engines wait the starter's signal. On the opposite side of the track and rising from behind the mass of cars parked in the central enclosure is an indicator showing the lap or circuit of the course each car is travelling. Beside the track and on it are a number of " camera men " with their cinematograph machines

Photo, Brown Brothers

and their minister at Washington was instructed to protest, which he did in fiery fashion, declaring the absorption of Texas " the most unjust act which can be found in the annals of modern history."

War followed. The campaign was severe and protracted, owing rather to the nature of the country than to the fighting qualities of the Mexican army. In September, 1847, the Americans entered the City of Mexico, and peace was made soon afterwards. Mexico ceded to the United States Upper California and New Mexico, in addition to agreeing that Texas should become American.

With unexampled generosity the United States determined to pay for the five hundred thousand square miles of territory which were transferred to their sovereignty by the Peace Treaty. In five annual instalments Mexico was paid three millions sterling. The total money cost of the war to the United States was over thirty millions sterling, and 25,000 American soldiers were killed or died of disease. Nearly seventy years later war was again threatened between the United States and their small unruly neighbour. Again in 1919 there was talk of war, but again it died away.

Texas, where it runs beside the Rio Grande (Big River), across which lies Mexican territory, is still almost as Spanish as it was before it became independent. There are many villages where scarcely anyone speaking English can be found. San Antonio still bears many of the marks of its Spanish origin. El Paso is a modern, featureless city, Laredo little more than an overgrown village, but San Antonio has character

NINETY THOUSAND SPECTATORS WATCH A CONTEST FOR THE WORLD'S BOXING CHAMPIONSHIP AT JERSEY CITY

It is seldom indeed that such a multitude as this may be seen at one glance. The octagonal arena, a vast spider's web of seats, was specially built for this fight, and had accommodation for a hundred thousand people. There were seven hundred reporters writing up the fight as it progressed, while a special "crow's nest," seen to the right of the ring, held the cinematograph cameras. The whole thing is an example of American thoroughness, and certainly one of "mass-production" in the way of onlookers who flocked from all parts of the country, and even from Europe, to witness the contest

Photo, Brown Brothers

MIDFIELD PLAY AT AN AMERICAN FOOTBALL MATCH: THE SCRIMMAGE BREAKING UP

Among the colleges where it originated a distinct form of football has developed. There are eleven a side, the goals and ball are similar to those used in the Rugby game, while the field of play, though about the same length, is somewhat narrower. The chief and most striking difference between Rugby and American football lies in the elaborate code of signals used for standardised evolutions. The team in possession of the ball is permitted four attempts to advance it ten yards, and in default must surrender it to the opponents. For this purpose the field is marked out in lines five yards apart

Photo, Brown Brothers

and charm. It possesses one of the most delightful hotels in the world, built on the Spanish plan, around a courtyard, with flowering plants drooping from wide balconies on every floor ; this hotel leaves in the heart of all discriminating travellers a longing to see it again.

The Texans are a race apart. Their chief industry until lately was cattle ranching, and they preserve many of the idiosyncracies of the cowboy as presented in popular fiction. They have produced many men of note and distinction, including Colonel House, who was one of those instrumental in nominating Mr. Woodrow Wilson for the Presidency, and who has been, as confidential agent of the White

BATSMAN AND CATCHER IN A BASEBALL MATCH

"Ball" as they call it, is the Americans' distinctive game. The field of play is diamond-shaped. At one angle is the "home plate," where the batsman stands, while the other three angles are called bases. There are nine players to each team, and the innings closes on the dismissal of three batsmen. Above is seen the special mask that guards the "catcher," who corresponds to wicket-keeper

Photo, Brown Brothers

WHERE AMERICAN SOCIETY TAKES ITS EASE BENEATH THE PALMS

Situated on the east coast of Florida in a sub-tropical region, Palm Beach is an especially popular holiday resort of wealthy Americans, who throng its palatial hotels on the Atlantic shore and on Lake Worth from January to April.   The coconut palms which now are the glory of the place were introduced as recently as 1879, when a Spanish vessel, laden with coconuts, was wrecked off the coast

Photo, Brown Brothers

ENJOYING THE CALIFORNIAN SUMMER WITH A TENT AND A MOTOR TRAILER

With an equipage like this, the holiday-maker can get the best out of a country where the population is relatively scanty and roads and towns are few. When on the move the tent folds up, and is packed on the trailer along with the rest of the luggage while the occupants lounge luxuriously in their car. There is all the advantage of a caravan with ten times its speed. Here the party have stopped near some river pool, where, presently, they will be happily swimming

Photo, Brown Brothers

House, concerned in many great businesses without holding any office in the government.

Between Texan and Mexican there persists an ancient feud. The Mexicans detest the " gringoes," as they call Americans, from the circumstance that the American soldiers in the war of 1846 sang a marching song called " Green grow the rushes O ! " The Texans have a contemptuous dislike for the " Greasers," which is their opprobrious name for Mexicans.

A country of vast spaces, wide, hot sunlight, and invigorating air, Texas brings forth naturally a self-confident, high-spirited people. There is room in it for millions more of them, if ever the United States need elbow-room. Wherever there is water, the soil is fertile and quick to yield its generous increase. One thinks of Texas and the Texans as far more truly American than the half-foreign cities with their polyglot populations which have resulted from the million a year inflow of immigrants.

Philadelphia and the Philadelphians

Even Philadelphia, which kept its old-time appearance and habits longer than any other of the great towns, has been growing more and more cosmopolitan in appearance—and also in spirit. There are still the streets of old stone-built houses, covered with ivy and shaded by oaks and elms. The Philadelphians who live in these and the still older houses of red brick keep up many of the traditions of their sober, righteous, and godly forebears. A Scottish friend of mine who arrived in the city on a Sunday morning, having travelled through from Chicago, saw the streets full of churchgoers in their best clothes and at once said to himself : " I shall be all right in Philadelphia. It is like home." But the city no longer remains a city apart. Its industries needed the immigrants, and the immigrants have made themselves felt.

For some time past the bulk of them have been Italians, Russians, Hungarians, Croatians, Lithuanians, and Eastern Europeans generally, Jew and Christian in almost equal proportions. Few emigrate any longer from the British Isles, France, Germany, or Scandinavia. This change has made a difference to the whole country. The newcomers have now a greater gulf to cross before they can become American in mind as well as by legal formality.

Oath of Allegiance to the Flag

Those who arrive grown-up never do cross it. The children of the immigrants may, however, be indistinguishable from the native-born. In school they are carefully trained in citizenship. They sing patriotic songs, they salute and repeat an oath of allegiance before the Flag. These are the words of the oath : " Flag of our great Republic, inspirer in battle, guardian of our homes, whose stars and stripes stand for bravery, purity, truth and union, we salute thee. We, the natives of distant lands, who find rest under thy folds, do pledge our hearts, our lives, our sacred honour to love and protect thee, our country, and the liberty of the American people for ever."

The grown-up New American may be disappointed when he finds that liberty in the United States is much the same as liberty elsewhere, a comparative rather than an absolute blessing. But the children make no comparisons. They are taught that their country is " God's own country," that there is no European state where the same advantages can be enjoyed, and they believe what they are taught.

A Glimpse of " Packing-Town "

The inhabitants of a Chicago slum may have difficulty in regarding the middle west capital as a model of amenity, but they can always think of the time when, having become rich, they will dwell somewhere " on the boulevards," those pleasant, smooth roads which stretch out away from and around the city among parks and open

HOLIDAY-MAKERS IN THEIR THOUSANDS THRONG THE BEACH OF ATLANTIC CITY.

Atlantic City's prosperity as a seaside resort began in 1852, and since railway communications were perfected it has become the largest and most popular all the year round resort in the United States. It stands on Absecon Beach, a sandy island about ten miles long off the coast of New Jersey. The actual city front is about three miles long, and features of the place are the eight mile "Board Walk" along the beach, a fine carriage drive, and a boulevard for motor-cars. The bathing is excellent, and in a fine season the sands are invisible under the swarming holiday makers

Photo, Brown Brothers

country, and only spend a few working hours amid the dirt, the din, the squalor, and the ugliness of the central district.

The shore of Lake Michigan, an inland sea, with no land visible across it and waves that beat upon the beach in stormy weather, gave the builders of Chicago a chance which they utterly neglected. For many years the shore in the centre remained a wilderness. Lately the movement towards beauty has reached Chicago, with the result that its outer districts are delightful. But the business quarter is a nightmare still, and Packing-Town, where the stockyards receive never-ceasing herds of cattle and hogs for the slaughter-houses to kill and for the packers to put up in tins of beef and bacon, leaves a dead weight of depression upon the sensitive spirit.

Michigan Avenue, Chicago

The nights at Chicago are of a deep and soothing loveliness. The stars burn through a velvety sky. Out on the quiet boulevards the plash of light waves can be heard whenever the road runs near the water. Even in the heart of the city the noise has almost died away, the crude outlines are softened. At dusk Michigan Avenue is brightly lit by clusters of six electric lights in big globes. But the bad reputation which Chicago had as a city unsafe at night has not been altogether outlived yet.

There is a fine public spirit in Chicago and there is corruption on a vast scale ; there is competition carried to its vilest lengths and there is " munificent patronage of Art " ; there is a boast of being " more truly American " than any other city, yet there is a population more mixed than any other and not at all well assimilated.

What would Chicago and its people be like, I wonder, had the city been built where Washington stands ? And what would have been the result of choosing the shore of Lake Michigan for the political capital of the country ?

It is conceivable that a two-fold advantage would have been gained. Three seasons of the year are agreeable in Washington, but the heat and heaviness of summer months wring out the energy from the toughest frame.

The District of Columbia, as the territory marked out for the capital was named, lies on the edge of Maryland. We are in the South here—almost. We are in a region where negroes seem to outnumber whites, where they are evidently on their ancestral soil.

Stately City of Washington

It has taken Washington a long time to claim its place among the world's fine cities. For a great many years it was a jumble of imposing public " edifices " and streets of wooden shacks. Now it has emerged from the undecided state. It has been shot through, this way and that, with avenues of noble proportions. It is full of the homes of cultivated people who take a pride in its seemliness and order. The public buildings, instead of being as they were once, oases of splendour in a desert of muddle, hardly make any impression at all ; the private blocks are just as imposing in character.

What one remembers chiefly of Washington are the green spaces, the broad avenues, the spaciousness, the stateliness, the wide prospects, the trees that gladden the eye everywhere, even in the poorest quarters, and temper the scorching sunshine.

" Abode of the National Spirit "

The plan of the city was made by a French engineer who had a gracious tradition in his mind. Neither a rapid growth of population nor the springing up of factories tempted the authorities to depart from the original lines. Washington has no industries to speak of, no business much beyond real estate and law. It is a city of officials, members of Congress, Senators, diplomatists. Whether it was a good idea to separate them from the life of the country may

SUMMER VISITORS ON THE BOARD WALK, ATLANTIC CITY

About ninety-five miles south-west of New York and fifty-six south-east of Philadelphia, Atlantic City's resident population of under 50,000 is increased in a good season to about 400,000 by holiday-makers. Its famous Board Walk is a steel and concrete promenade with a wooden floor, and upon one side is the ocean pierced by several piers and, on the other, the motley architecture of hotel and store

Photo, Brown Brothers

be doubted, but the result has been a capital of genuine distinction and charm.

The White House, where the Presidents live, might easily escape notice. It is a pleasant, unpretentious residence in a small park of its own. With its pillared front, its rows of large windows, its flat balustraded roof, it is like many American houses, and many English houses, of the late eighteenth century. Inside, there is the same absence of ostentation. The rooms and corridors are of modest size. All that was grandiose in conception went to adorn the Capitol, which is the abode of the national spirit. The White House is merely where the president of the day lives.

Like the city, the Capitol has slowly grown during a century to its present majestic aspect. Like the city also, it has been extended and added to according to a plan. Harmony has been kept between the different parts of it, and though the impression it makes may not be one of beauty, yet there is nothing to offend the eye or detract from the dignity of the whole.

Standing on a low hill, approached by broad flights of stone steps, and girdled by tier upon tier of stone terraces, it lifts a dome that can be seen from almost every part of the city. Some day the inside will be made as dignified and simple as the outside ; at present it is still in the style of European palaces, with heavy gilding, heavy marble, heavy upholstering.

Until lately the nation was too busy making the most of the opportunities offered by its new country to trouble its head very much about politics. There was excitement for a little while over Presidential elections, and some over those which returned members to the House of Representatives (Congress).

The alterations in New York from Tammany government of the city to clean government, and then back to Tammany, prove that the mass of voters pay no more than an intermittent attention to local politics.

The party which stands in the opinion of so many Americans for graft and maladministration took its name from a benevolent society formed in 1789, and called after an Indian chief. The society lent its hall to a party in municipal politics and in course of time became almost identical with it. The power of Tammany Hall lies in its perfect organization. In the less reputable districts of New York one voter in every three is said to be in some way an agent for Tammany. The bartenders who used to serve drinks were active workers, the barbers talked Tammany to their clients while they shaved them or cut their hair, many of the police did what they could to influence votes in favour of the party which looked after them so well.

If a Tammany agent fell on bad times, Tammany helped him. It helped even those who had supported it at the polls if they were vouched for. Very large sums were spent in this way, and on the whole with good effect all round. Tammany was a charitable institution as well as a political machine; it did good by stealth, asked few questions, earned the good word of the poor. There were Tammany picnics for voters and their wives, Tammany entertainments for children. Thus it came about that although from time to time there was

SPRING IN CONEY ISLAND, NEW YORK'S MOST POPULAR BEACH RESORT

Of all the sand spits that fringe Long Island's southern shore Coney Island holds pride of place on account of the immense number of visitors attracted by it. A town has sprung up that is given over to recreation, and the bathing beach is exceptionally fine. West Brighton, about the centre of the island, which is some five miles long and not more than a mile wide, is the most frequented

Photo, Keystone View Co.

HAPPY PICNIC PARTY ATTACK THE LUNCHEON BASKET DURING A MOTOR TRIP TO THE OZARK MOUNTAINS

Once in French territory in the days when France and England were rivals exploiting North America, the Ozark Mountains, which form a wooded plateau between the Arkansas and Missouri rivers, derive their name from "bois aux arcs," or wood suitable for making bows. On a spur of the range is situated the town of Hot Springs, one of the most popular spas in the United States, the waters having been found curative in cases of rheumatic and kindred ailments. The surrounding district is scenically attractive to a degree and may easily be explored thus with motor-car and luncheon-basket

Photo, Brown Brothers

a revolt against Tammany, it always got back after a while.

Here, and in other cities where the same thing happened, the absorption in business affairs accounted as much as in national politics for the lethargy of the electorate. When a special effort was made to rouse it, there was a spurt of energy, but after this the more real interests became predominant again. If this had not been so, the United States would not, within so short a period as a century and a half from their becoming an independent state, have taken the place which is theirs in the world to-day.

American industry and American business have given the country its leading place among the nations. These were created by fierce concentration and lightning enterprise. The motto of Mr. Carnegie, " Scrap old machinery," has been acted upon from the early days of American industries. Men who were throwing all their energy into building these up had none for public affairs.

The Personal Factor in Success

The characteristics of American industry have been rapidity of design and execution, production in vast quantity, foresight, ambition, ingenuity, " drive." The use of machinery was developed in the United States and copied by Europe. Not only did manufacturers offer inducements to their people to suggest devices for improving production; firms existed for the purpose of inventing new methods of saving labour. Industries were carefully studied in order that they might be run on the most economical and profitable lines.

Yet it was not machinery which played the largest part in bringing prosperity to American manufacturers. One of them was asked some years ago what was the most important factor in the success of his business. After a few moments' reflection he replied : " The greatest single factor in our success has been the personal factor." That would probably be the answer of nearly all

men in his position. The constant and acute supervision, the discovering of markets, the encouragement of subordinates, the rapidity of decision, the daring enterprise, and the skill in management shown by her captains of industry have given America the lead in many industrial directions.

Industrial Standardisation

American methods make for the production of business plant and of products for immediate consumption in an almost infinite variety of standardised forms. This process, has been seen in its most spectacular shape at the Ford motor-car factories, but it is very widely practised, and may be called the distinctive note of American industry.

The chief manufacturing region of the United States is situated in the middle Atlantic states, New York, New Jersey, Pennsylvania. The next is found in Ohio, Indiana, Illinois, Michigan, Wisconsin. New England furnishes the third. Here was the original cotton manufacturing district ; in Massachusetts still there are more cotton operatives, mostly of foreign birth, than in any other single state.

But since they began to spin and weave, the southern states, because they had the raw material at hand, have caught up with the North in the production of cotton. Massachusetts is the largest producer of boots and shoes by factory methods. The machine-made boot dates back only to the early 'eighties ; it did away with the hand-worker almost entirely. In no branch of industry has machinery been so elaborately adapted to its purpose or the interest of the worker in his work so completely destroyed.

Automobiles in the Great Cities

The iron and steel works are mostly round the Great Lakes from Buffalo to Chicago. From Michigan, Wisconsin, and Minnesota the ore is shipped to cities which have coal near at hand, principally to Pittsburg, Cleveland, and

HOLIDAY CROWDS THAT ALMOST CONCEAL THE BEACH AT ONE OF THE SEASIDE SUBURBS OF LOS ANGELES

From a slumbrous Mexican provincial town, Los Angeles has grown to the dimensions of a great city. Its natural attractions draw thousands of visitors yearly, so that various sub-towns have grown up along the coast, from which Los Angeles itself is some eighteen miles distant by river. On these fine bathing beaches the long Pacific rollers provide excellent surf-bathing, both for the expert and, in safer spots such as this, for the beginner. A feature of the scene is the mushroom crop of umbrellas that springs up in the morning sun each day of the gay summer season

Photo, Los Angeles Chamber of Commerce

ON THE PROMENADE AT LONG BEACH, A LONG ISLAND RESORT

Long Island is separated from New York city only by a narrow channel at its western extremity, and forms a convenient market garden and holiday ground for the metropolis. Along the south shore of the island are numerous sandbanks, on which are various seaside settlements, owing their existence mainly to the excellence of the bathing facilities. Long Beach is one of the most favoured

Photo, Brown Brothers

Chicago. Of the motor-car industry, in which America far outstrips all other countries, Detroit is the centre, with Cleveland and Toledo large producers also, owing to their situation. They are near the steel mills, and they are well situated for widespread distribution.

The number of motor-cars running in the United States is enormous. Mechanics go to work in their own machines. On Sundays the roads around all the great cities are a moving mass of automobiles. Not to be able to afford one is a sign of poverty. Not to want one is considered a symptom of madness.

To the high wages paid by manufacturers and to the ambition of the wage-earners to enrol themselves in the automobile-owning class may be attributed the steadiness of the Labour market, compared with that of European

lands during the early years of the present century.

For the most part the native-born lived in comfortable conditions, opportunities of enjoying life and saving money were open to them, they suffered under no sense of inferiority or injustice. The immigrants were not so well off. They were ignorant of the language and everything else, they had been accustomed to live in squalor, they took any work that was offered to them, and thought themselves lucky to get it.

As they grew familiar with American life, they grew restive. They wanted to share in the comfort and luxury they saw around them. They resented the notion that " dagoes " and " Bohunks," as they were called, belonged to a low order of mankind. Labour organizers found them easily inflammable. Labour

FROM SHERWOOD FOREST TO LOS ANGELES: ROBIN HOOD SEVEN HUNDRED YEARS AFTER

Robin Hood lived, if ever, about the beginning of the thirteenth century. In the twentieth century he has been recreated in a Los Angeles film studio. Above is a reconstruction, as much as is necessary for the camera's focus, of Nottingham Castle. The romance of Robin, debonair squire of dames, incomparable archer, always turning his enemies to figures of fun, is one of the most precious in all English legend and the most distinctively English. Here in tropic California it lives again, half the world away from "merrie Sherwode" in England's green and pleasant land

Photo, Los Angeles Chamber of Commerce

IN THE CITY OF SKELETON HOUSES: REHEARSAL AT A MOTION PICTURE STUDIO, HOLLYWOOD, LOS ANGELES

Hollywood is the centre of American cinematograph activity, and in the enormous studios of the various companies many different " sets " or groups of scenery may be seen. Only a sufficient area to cover the focus of the camera is used, and portions of architecture, such as are seen in the background, give a curious skeleton effect. The director of the film is inspiring the actress to higher flights of tragedy, while the girl at the table notes every detail of costume lest, in the course of several days, the actors should omit or change some part of it

Photo, Los Angeles Chamber of Commerce

OPEN-AIR SHOP IN SITKA, THE OLD CAPITAL OF ALASKA

Sitka, situated on Baranov Island, was the capital of Alaska until 1906, when it was superseded by Yuneau. The Eskimos, or Innuits, are a short, heavy-set people, displaying a marked willingness for steady work, and have taken up several industries with vigour and enthusiasm. In Sitka this old woman draws a small revenue from selling fancy wares, spread by the wayside to tempt the passers-by

PRESERVING FISH IN THE FAR NORTHERN TERRITORY OF THE U.S.A.

The Indian tribes of Alaska inhabit chiefly the interior and the south-eastern districts of the country, while the Eskimos are found on the north and west coasts. For long years the Redskins have carried on a successful trade in fish and fur-bearing animals. Now that various white companies have killed off so much livestock from land, sea, and river, the Indians are finding their means of livelihood impaired

NATIVE WOMAN OF ARCTIC ALASKA ENGAGED IN A COLD OCCUPATION

She belongs to the Eskimo family which borders the entire Arctic coastal region from Alaska in the extreme north-west to the island of Newfoundland in the north-east. Fisheries are extensive on the ragged Alaskan coast, and provide a regular maintenance for many natives. This Alaskan girl, cosily cased in thick furs, is fishing through a hole in the ice, and her efforts appear successful

DEAD SEALS USED IN THE CAPTURE OF LIVE ONES

This quaint craft is an improvised boat made from four air-inflated sealskins braced with a spear shaft. The ingenious owner is here seen afloat, hunting for seals. The fur-seal, the catching of which is limited by official regulations, is of much moment to many Alaskans, supplying them with food, dress, footgear, tents, and many other useful and necessary articles

Photo, Kadel & Herbert

SNOW HUTS IN A TEMPORARY VILLAGE OF ALASKAN ESKIMOS

If likely to make a more or less prolonged sojourn in one place the Eskimos build extremely neat circular huts of blocks of snow, with a sheet of ice for window. Ventilation is only effected through the entrance passage, and the heat inside the hut, generated by the blubber oil-lamps used for cooking and light, is so great that indoors many of the people strip themselves almost naked

WEIRD IMAGES OF INDIAN TOTEMS AT AN ALASKAN VILLAGE

Along the south-east coast of Alaska, between the northern part of British Columbia and the sea, live a tribe of Indians called Tlingits. Of supposed Polynesian ancestry, they migrated to Alaska, and, borrowing from the Eskimos their bone-tipped spears and their lip ornaments, retained their system of totemism. The strange carven figures in their villages resemble those illustrated in page 1180

WESTERN ESKIMO HUNTING SEAL IN HIS SEALSKIN CANOE

Sealskin stretched over a framework of wood or whalebone makes the light, very seaworthy canoe in which the Eskimo takes the water. He sits in a circular aperture and propels the craft with a double-bladed paddle. In summer he hunts seals in the open water, using a harpoon with a detachable point, often attached to an inflated skin which marks the course of a wounded animal

Photo, American Field Museum, Chicago

UNDER THE STARS AND STRIPES IN A HUNTER'S PARADISE

Housed in a snug log-cabin, with plenty of fuel stacked ready to hand, the hunter can lead a life full of vigorous enjoyment for anyone skilled in the use of rod and gun. Salmon swarm in the rivers, and besides the native moose and caribou and the reindeer imported from Siberia, fur-bearing animals abound for him to trap and afterwards trade the pelts for whatever else he requires

Photo, Keystone View Co.

When he is lucky enough to obtain a knife the Eskimo crams in as much food as possible and cuts off the mouthful

One of the most primitive races, the Eskimos affect ornaments called labrets, of shell and stone fastened by perforating the skin

This woman is of the Chilkat tribe, living round Lynn Canal, a fiord of South Alaska. At puberty the girls' faces are painted

Eskimo women within reach of white influence are quick to take to a pipe. This mouthpiece is of bone and the bowl of metal

STUDIES IN FACIAL EXPRESSION FROM FAR ALASKA

troubles began to be more frequent. Since the Great War the apprehensions of American employers have become more and more gloomy. They feel they can no longer rely upon a vast floating proletariat of low-class immigrants to keep up the supply of cheap labour and to " break strikes." Not only are the immigrants organized, they have been leaving the country at the rate of 300,000 a year in order to return to their own lands now freed from foreign oppression. The supply of many kinds of labour has therefore shortened. Wages have risen to a higher level than had ever been thought of, yet the cost of living has gone up too, so the demand is still for increases of pay.

The body known as the Industrial Workers of the World, commonly called the I.W.W., which federated a mass of the immigrants and taught them how to throw off the harsh conditions imposed upon them by conscienceless employers, has gained in power ; its programme of One Big Union to include all who work with their hands has gained many adherents. Even those who fear it as a fomenter of the class-war have put forward demands not unlike those of the Socialists who control the I.W.W.

Rise of Labour Discontent

Until recent years there was no class antagonism. No privileged and propertied class existed. Social distinctions were slight. That state of things has passed. A propertied class has grown up. Privilege is not unknown. Militarism finds many upholders. Wage-slavery, which could not exist in a country of immense spaces while it was still being developed, has engulfed a great proportion of the manual workers. Discontent has been fanned both by agitation and by the "brutal selfishness" (to quote an expression used by the Washington correspondent of the London "Times") of capitalists. The tendency of the American nature to rush to extremes, and the presence in the country of enormous numbers of new citizens belonging to the most hot-blooded and imperfectly civilized races of Europe, give cause for anxiety among those who for a short while could indulge the fancy that they had established themselves as a Ruling Class.

The experiment which the United States have been making, the experiment of forming a nation out of the most diverse elements without the ties of common origin, tradition, or history, is not completed yet.

Belonging to the U.S.A. since 1867, when it was ceded by Russia for about £1,450,000, is the huge territory of Alaska, with an area of nearly 591,000 square miles, of which one-third is within the Arctic Circle.

Alaska and Its Resources

Here are some of the highest mountains in North America. The natives are of two stocks, the Eskimo or Innuit and the Indian ; the Aleuts, a branch of the Innuits, inhabit the Aleutian islands and the Alaskan peninsula. The country is rich in minerals and timber, and the seal, salmon, and other fisheries are important, but such animals as the moose, fox, beaver, and mink are decreasing in numbers. Reindeer are bred for food and transport purposes. All the chief towns are on the coasts, the capital, Juneau, having a population of about 3,000, that of the whole territory being estimated at about 75,000.

America's Oversea Possessions

In addition to Alaska, and other possessions already described in this work (Hawaii, Samoa, and the Philippines), the government of the U.S.A. administers the Virgin Islands, formerly known as the Danish West Indies, purchased from Denmark in 1917 ; Porto Rico, a West Indian island, and Guam, the largest of the Ladrones or Mariana islands, in the Western Pacific, ceded by Spain after the war of 1898. The Panamá Canal zone is also under its jurisdiction.

INTERIOR OF A WELL-BUILT HUT OF BETTER-CLASS TRADING INDIANS AT YAKUTAT BAY, ALASKA

The interior of this hut displays a certain improvement in Indian architecture, and the unpretentious wigwam has been superseded by a wooden structure of no mean proportions. Nevertheless, the smouldering fire in the centre of the room and the skins drying above it speak of the traditional hole in the roof instead of a chimney. In various ways the Indians of Alaska show a superiority to their southern kinsmen, and many of them have learned trades which they pursue with patience and intelligence. To the right is lying a man who has been wounded in a bear fight, the pelt above him indicating his effective revenge

The United States

II. American Indians of To-day & Yesterday

By H. Spencer Harrison, D.Sc., A.R.C.Sc., F.R.A.I.

THERE is romance in the description of the North American Indian as "the noble savage," but those have done him less than justice who have branded him as inordinately vain, cruel beyond belief, a coward with no taste for open fighting, and a slayer of the weak and defenceless. Within his own circle he had the ordinary virtues without which the most primitive society cannot hold together, and at no period was his character so white, or so black, as it has been depicted from varying points of view. He is not even so red as he has been painted.

Since those far-off seventeenth century days when he was a thorn in the flesh of the early colonists of New England, the Indian has had the power of arresting attention, and even down to fifty years ago, or less, an occasional outbreak of revolt among the imperfectly domesticated Indians of the States assisted readers of Fenimore Cooper to link up present with past, and to realize, with greater clearness than is possible now, at least something of the nature of the original culture and mentality of this interesting people.

Who does not recall with affection "The Last of the Mohicans," and who does not bear in his mind a recollection of scalpings, tomahawks, wigwams, squaws, moccasins, pipes of peace, and birch-bark canoes? Who has not gone — in imagination—in Indian file, in full war-paint and in the rear of a tribe on the war-path, to wind up a perfect day by the capture of the enemy's village and the burning of his wigwams?

Providing the early settler was allowed to take such land as he required, and hunt where the game was thickest, he had no quarrel with the Indian, whom he would only shoot when necessary or convenient. It is the story of colonisation in many parts of the world, though the details differ. The Tasmanians were wiped out. The Australian aborigines are in liquidation, and it is only a question of time for the North American Indians to disappear as a separate people. Owing, however, to their considerable numbers, and to some degree of physical and mental toughness, they will leave behind a fairly marked strain of their blood in certain parts of America, and in some of the backwoods and backwaters they will survive for many years in a state of relative purity. The United States Bureau, and the

"THE STERN MOTHER—EXPERIENCE"
If each strange, deep furrow in her sad face told its story, how thrilling and absorbing would be the recital of this aged squaw's primitive existence on the prairies of the Far West

THE PAPOOSE STANDS FOR HIS PORTRAIT

Scarcely out of the portable cradle which bowed his young mother's back for many a long month, this sturdy papoose is now learning to find his feet. Redskin women are devoted to their offspring, and bestow upon them the utmost love and care

Photo, Underwood Press Service

the loss of a continent. Of late years, although too many of the Indians still hang on to the bedraggled fringes of civilization, there are many who have adopted the white man's mode of life, while ceasing to be objects of charity. In Ontario and Quebec, for example, many of the natives have entered fully into civilized life. As lumbermen, artisans, farmers, teachers, physicians, and the like, there are Indians who have shown they are not unworthy in moral and mental qualities of the great race with which they are allied by descent—the race which produced the ancient civilization of China.

Even the Indians who have not adopted the alien culture which has thrust itself upon them, and destroyed their own, are losing the traits which are characteristic of the childhood of a race. Medical science—that is to say, medical practice—and sanitation are displacing the still cruder experiments of the shaman or medicine-man. Superstition is decreasing, and in a relatively short time it may be that most of the Indians will have forgotten totems, medicine bundles, and ghost dances, just as the English have forgotten what the Druids knew and what the Saxons sang.

When the States could be said to be occupied by descendants of English stock there was little intermixture of white with brown, but since Europe, not to mention Africa, has turned the States into a melting-pot for base as

Canadian Department, of Indian Affairs take care of the poor Indian, whose untutored mind has had so much to occupy it since the days of the Pilgrim Fathers. In parts of the States, and in Canada also, there are Indian Reservations, provided with doctors, nurses, matrons, dentists, hospitals, teachers of farming, and schools ; in some cases the Indians keep to a large extent within their allotted territories, and a few years ago it was said of them that they were the laziest people in America. This was natural, since they were in receipt of the dole, as a recompense for

HEAD MAN OF A MAINE COAST INDIAN TRIBE

As skilful basket-maker, trapper, fisherman, musician, and orator, Chief Neptune was well equipped for the proud position of leader of his tribal brothers. Decoration, always symbolic in origin, plays no large part in his attire, but it will be observed that the swastika, the ancient Aryan symbol of the Wheel of the Law, embellishes his hide tunic and the frontal band of his feathered headdress

Photo, Kadel & Herbert

SENECA INDIANS OF NEW YORK STATE FORSAKE THEIR WAR DANCE IN FAVOUR OF THE MODERN TANGO AND MAXIXE

The Seneca Indians, though a scattered people, have their habitat chiefly in New York State. They are noteworthy as having joined the famous League of the Iroquois, founded in the sixteenth century, and having supported the cause of Great Britain in the American War of Independence. They rank as a highly progressive tribe, well versed in the knowledge of civilization. That they are not backward in assimilating modern ways is exemplified in the above scene, which depicts a group of Seneca Indians engaged in modern dances, into which they entered with as much gusto as if they had been dancing their own war-dance

Photo, Underwood & Underwood

RITUALISM IN THE REMOTE REGIONS OF THE SOUTH-WEST: MYSTIC CEREMONY OF THE HOPI INDIANS

Within the great arid region stretching north of the Mexican border, touching California and embracing several of the south-western states, no less than nine linguistic stocks and some forty-five tribes are represented. For the convenience of distinction these Indians are divided into Pueblo and non-Pueblo peoples. Belonging to the Pueblo group are the Hopi Indians of the Shoshonian family, a virile tribe, about which the influence and mysticism of traditional superstition still cling. Many of their rites, ceremonies, and amusements are very impressive; some are secret, others performed in public, and into most of them the religious motif enters largely

Photo, the Atchison, Tepeka, and Santa Fé Railway Company

PUBLIC PERFORMANCE OF THE UNCANNY TRIBAL DANCE OF THE HOPI INDIANS OF ARIZONA

Of religious character, the snake dance is an ancient tribal dance of the Hopi Indians, which tribe, it is said, performed the dance in the same manner and in the same place when the first white adventurers made their appearance in America in the middle of the sixteenth century. Many of its details are far from attractive, and some spectators have pronounced the whole ceremony to be revolting. It was customary to use as many as a hundred live snakes, which were held in the hands, or the mouths, of the dancers, deposited before a sacred rock, sprinkled with sacred cornmeal to the accompaniment of chants, and finally liberated

Photo Brown Brothers

well as noble metals, there have been found many who do not scorn to take a consort with some excess of pigmentation. Racially speaking, the Indian is less removed from the white man than is the negro, and from his origin is better adapted to absorb, or be absorbed by, the white man's civilization.

But who and what are these Indians, and what did they do in the happy days before the Paleface, urged by the spirit of adventure, first emerged from the sea and extended his octopus-tentacles into the hunting-grounds and the homes of the aborigines?

At a time when land connexion between the extreme north-east of Asia and the extreme north-west of America was less interrupted than it is at present —a time which may perhaps be located somewhere near the end of the Great Ice Age of the Northern Hemisphere, 10,000 years or so ago—wandering hunters began to follow their game from Asia to America. They came as a slow drift of nomadic tribes, discovering new ground where no man had set foot before them.

Problematical Immigrants from Asia

How many years, or hundreds of years, it took for these tribes to spread from the neighbourhood of Alaska to the less strenuous latitudes of the Lakes and Plains no man can guess. But the evidence of physical and cultural characters has led most investigators to the conclusion that the Indians are, in the main at least, derived from primitive Asiatic tribes, whose condition was no higher than the hunting stage.

They were apparently accustomed not only to chip stone into shape for their cutting and piercing tools and weapons, but had advanced to the stage of grinding and polishing it. They twisted fibres, probably sinew, into string, but although they made simple baskets and mats, it is doubtful whether they had got as far as true weaving. Their clothes were of skin,

shaped and sewn. They made fire by twirling an upright stick between the hands while it was in firm contact with a horizontal stick resting on the ground, the friction giving rise to wood-dust as well as to heat which ignited it.

Contrasts in Culture and Habits

They cooked in vessels of wood, bark, or skin, probably by means of stones heated in the fire and dropped into the water placed in the vessels. They painted the body, and perhaps practised tattooing. They used the bow, the harpoon, the throwing-stick, and no doubt traps and snares for hunting; they possessed dogs, but no horses. They perhaps used sledges and snow-shoes in their travelling, but they had no knowledge of the wheel.

As they passed southwards through the new land, some settling down in favourable areas, others ever moving on, they developed diverse characters in material and social culture, in language, and even to some degree in physical type. These changes led to some remarkable contrasts in culture and habits, the highest level being reached by certain tribes of Central and South America.

In various parts of the area with which we are concerned—that now included in Canada and the United States—agriculture, true weaving, and pottery-making were developed, and a little knowledge of copper and iron was acquired. How far these arts were influenced by the higher native cultures farther south, which are themselves believed by some to owe much to problematical immigrants from overseas, is too difficult a problem for discussion here.

Fiction of the " Red " Indian

A few words must be said as to the bodily characteristics which have, in part, led to the conclusion that the Indians are more nearly allied to the Mongoloid peoples of Asia than to any other race. The hair of the natives of

HARVEST FESTIVAL CELEBRATIONS AMONG THE INDIANS

A quaint Indian festival, so old that even the patriarchs of the pueblo know nothing of its origin, is celebrated annually at Taos, New Mexico. Though usually called San Geronimo Day Festival, it is really a thanksgiving to the sun-god for the harvest. Not the least thrilling event is the climbing of a high " sleek " pole to secure the sheep and harvest offerings suspended from the top

Photo, Denver and Rio Grande Railway

FULL DRESS WAR DANCE IN A SCENIC WONDERLAND

The Blackfeet tribe has its large reservation at the eastern border of Glacier National Park, Montana, a beautiful mountainous region the picturesqueness of which is greatly enhanced by the presence of these finely-built, quaintly-clothed Indians. Thrilling tales are told of the once-dreaded Blackfeet, but their war dances are now executed only with a view to friendly entertainment

Photo, Ewing Galloway

the whole of the New World tends to be straight—dead straight, not the absence of curliness sometimes lamented by white women of our own race. Only in Asia is hair of this lank nature to be met with as a widespread characteristic.

Skin-colour varies in some degree, and there are more brown and chocolate tints than any others, though there is often a tendency towards yellow, another Mongoloid trait. The Red Indian is to a large extent a fiction, though sometimes there is a suggestion of a coppery tinge. The face tends towards broadness, as it does in Mongols, and some observers have recorded the " slanting

eye," produced by what is called the " Mongolian fold " of the eyelid. The head is often broad, as in Mongols, but on the other hand there are areas where narrow heads predominate.

As regards languages, it can only be said that, in the U.S.A. and Canada, the speech of the Indians has been classified in some 56 groups, or stock tongues, in which the spoken languages of the tribes may be said to centre. Since the total number of language-stocks of the whole of the American continent has been estimated at over 150, it will be realized that the languages of the original immigrants, who must themselves have been diversified in their speech, have suffered considerable changes.

In connexion with speech, reference may be made to the gesture language, highly developed in parts of this area, by means of which the handicap of Babel was to some extent neutralised. Of equal interest is the picture-writing, especially well developed among the Chippewas and Delawares. Figures of persons, animals, plants, etc., together with a few conventional symbols, were scratched on pieces of bark and slabs of wood, and in this way the chief events in the history of the tribe for many years back could be recorded. Farther south, in Mexico, this picture-writing had passed into a conventional set of signs approximating to an alphabet.

Democratic Social System

The early European colonists of New England spoke of kings, princes, and princesses, and the practice has survived till our own day in the many recent references to the " Princess" Pocahontas. In the main, however, the Indian form of society was a true democracy, and only exceptionally were the chiefs determined by hereditary succession. On the north-west coast there had been a drift in the direction of a plutocracy, though in a milder form than prevails to-day in America and elsewhere.

Spiritual Powers in Natural Bodies

Gitchi Manito, the "Great Spirit" of Indian romances, was probably a child of the missionaries rather than a deity of the Indians ; these were not accustomed to regard the power of the gods as being concentrated in one, or even a few, supernatural beings. The term Manito, adopted and often misinterpreted by the white man, is an Algonquian word which signified the magical power or principle believed to be present not only in every actual being and concrete body, but even in attributes and activities. The sun,

the moon, the stars, the wind, the rivers, the mountains, the trees, and so on indefinitely, were all endowed with this power, and they were in varying degrees personified. The shaman or medicine - man—doctor, juggler, and medium—had especially close relations with these ubiquitous powers, and he was called upon to exercise his influence with them in case of need.

The symbolic signatures used by chiefs in the signing of treaties frequently represented the forms—such as birds, fishes, arrows, and the like—inhabited by their "guardian spirits." Among some tribes, when a youth was approaching manhood, he was sent out into the woods or the mountains to fast and pray, and sometimes to take "medicine." Alone in the wilds, hungry and over-wrought, he would after a time begin to dream dreams, and in one of these there would appear to him some animal or object which was to be for the rest of his life his guardian spirit. It was usually an animal, but in future it was to him a spirit, and in our literature it has often been spoken of as a "totem."

General Belief in a Future Life

True totemism is, however, the relation of a group of people (a clan) to a kind of animal, plant, or other object, all the animals or objects of this kind being regarded as the blood relations of all the people of the totem group. The Iroquois, for example, had as totem-clans the Wolf, Bear, Beaver, Turtle, Deer, Snipe, Heron, and Hawk.

The Eastern Algonquins ascribed the creation and conduct of the world to Michabo, usually conceived as a monstrous rabbit, related to the sun. By magical power he made the earth, provided it with game, taught his favourite people the art of the chase, and, in addition, provided them with maize and beans.

There was a general belief in a future life of similar quality to life on earth, and for this reason the dead were sometimes buried with weapons, tools

PROCESSION OF MASKED RAIN-BRINGERS IN A VILLAGE OF ARIZONA

It is thought by many Indians of Arizona and New Mexico that in time of drought a performance of a certain dance will bring down the much-needed rain. This "rain dance"—in which all participants are grotesquely disguised—is one of their most characteristic ceremonies, and is regarded by them as an important part of their religion and in no sense as a recreation

Photo, Underwood Press Service

HOLIDAY IN NEW MEXICO: SIGHTSEERS GATHERED TO WITNESS THE INDIAN FESTIVITIES AT PUEBLO DE TAOS

The name "pueblo," of Spanish origin, signifying a town or village, is given to a communal or tribal building, or group of buildings, of the aborigines of New Mexico, and was first applied by the early Spanish explorers who made their way northward out of Mexico. Not only is that country referred to as the "pueblo area," and the culture of the natives as the "pueblo culture," but the natives themselves are known as the Pueblo peoples. This large assembly is seen celebrating the San Geronimo Day Festival at Taos, New Mexico; many of the visitors find the housetops a convenient vantage-ground from which to view the Indian races

Photo, Denver & Rio Grande Railway

CELEBRATING A FAR-FAMED FESTIVAL IN HONOUR OF S. JEROME AT PUEBLO DE TAOS, NEW MEXICO

The Festival of San Geronimo Day, held at Taos on September 30, is attended by numerous spectators—Pueblo, Apache, and Navaho Indians, and there are many white visitors from different parts of the States who deem the amusement awaiting them at the end of their journey well worth the twenty-five miles by stage from the nearest railway-station. Devotional exercises, a procession of Indians of both sexes, relay races—one of which is here seen about to start, young braves from two rival houses being the competitors—and dances by hideously-painted clowns are among the varied items of the day's programme

Photo, Denver & Rio Grande Railway

CAMERA STUDY OF INDIAN DOMESTICITY IN THE SOUTH-WEST

The Indians inhabiting the pueblo town of Laguna in New Mexico are industrious and self-supporting. Here Laguna women are seen baking bread in one of the common outdoor ovens; for though each family has its own apartment in the pueblo, the life is to a large extent cooperative, and the bake ovens and many other conveniences belong to the community at large

Photo, Ewing Galloway

of their crafts, and food for the journey to the shades. They were not always buried, however, and the method of their disposal by the Choctaws of the Mississippi Valley was to clean the bones of the dead before depositing them in a box or basket in the bone house; the process of cleaning was carried out by old men who allowed their nails to grow long for the purpose.

In spite of the present position of the American Indians as relics of the dead past, there are still survivals of the old cultural sub-divisions. The Eastern Woodland tribes are those with which the first European colonists came

into contact and conflict. Their area stretched from New England northwards, and comprised much of the region of the Great Lakes. One need only mention the Huron, the Wyandot, and the Mohawks, among the Iroquoian tribes, and the Ojibwa, the Crees, and the Mohicans, among the Algonquian, to be reminded of facts and fiction absorbed in youthful days. These tribes were great hunters of animals, and, when the occasion served, of men.

The killing and eating of prisoners was not uncommon, largely because of the belief that the eating of part of a brave enemy, and especially the eating

COMPACT COMMUNAL VILLAGE STRUCTURE OF NEW MEXICO
This striking photograph is of the Taos pueblo in New Mexico, showing one of the original apartment structures which houses about 200 Indian families. This many-celled, communal building of adobe brick is arranged in terraces, the roofs of the lower houses forming a promenade or yard for the houses next above, access being given by means of a ladder or a hatchway in the roof
Photo, Ewing Galloway

of his heart, was a sure means of adding his share of valour to that of the eater. Maize, beans, and other plants were grown for food, and in some cases large quantities of the seed of the wild rice were collected. The Indians had houses of bark, used snow-shoes, bark canoes and dug-outs, and made their clothing of skin, often deerskin. The men wore sleeved shirts, breech-cloths, leggings, and moccasins, while the women had a skirt and jacket.

In the wars between the English and French, the Iroquois were mainly on the side of the French, while the Algonquins—including the Mohicans—fought for the English. The Last of the Mohicans was by no means the last, though the identity of the tribe has now disappeared, as is the case with many others of this area. In Labrador and the Province of Quebec there still remain, however, some thousands of the Algonquian tribe of the Naskapi, pursuing a life not widely removed in many respects from that of their ancestors, though the nature of the country and climate has forced them to a more exclusively hunting mode of life.

The caribou or American reindeer is their chief source of food and clothing, though fish, birds, hares, and many

PRECOCIOUS INDIAN CHILD VERSED IN THE ART OF THE LOOM

This Navaho child, although only ten years old, can make beautiful rugs, and, like other Indians, has picked up the art of weaving without being trained in a trade school; her talent, of course, being inherited from generations of ancestors. Thanks to their skill at handicrafts such as pottery making, weaving, basket-making, etc., many of the Indian tribes of the south-west are self-supporting

Photo, Ewing Galloway

AMERICAN INDIANS

other animals are made use of. The eggs of wild fowl are eaten in great numbers, and there is no fastidiousness with regard to the age of the contained chicken. Reindeer are speared from canoes while they are swimming a stream ; or they may be snared or shot from ambush in a narrow defile ; or in winter they may be driven into a snow-bank and speared. Pemmican is made from the flesh of the reindeer by drying and pounding, and is stored in baskets and bags for future use. The clothing is similar to that just described, though in the summer the women descend to the use of trade calico, and blankets are purchased from traders in exchange for skins. Polygamy, as in other parts, is common. The dwellings in both winter and summer are tipis—that is to say, skin tents supported by poles.

Indian Dependence on the Bison

If the Eastern Woodland tribes are most important historically, the tribes of the Plains, the great central area of rivers and prairies, are perhaps of more interest from their mode of life. Familiar to many readers will be the names of the Crow, Cheyenne, Blackfeet, Apache, Pawnee, and Dakota. Typically the tribes of this area were dependent on the bison—often miscalled the buffalo—and with the practical extermination of this animal towards the end of the nineteenth century, their means of livelihood was gone. In any case, however, it had been decided by this time that the white man could only spare to the Indian a few small areas of his own country, and he had followed the bison into obscurity, though not without warlike protests which made considerable demands on the United States Army in the sixties and seventies.

The bison provided the Indian with food, clothing, tents, and other necessities, and before the Spanish conquests farther south the hunting was done on foot, with bows and arrows and spears for weapons. The Indian showed his adaptability in his speedy adoption of introduced conveniences, and although it was the white hunters who practically finished off the extermination of the bison by incredibly wasteful slaughter, the use of the horse and gun had already enabled the Indian to make great strides in that favourite blunder of the hunter of all times—the killing of the goose that lays the golden eggs.

Pemmican for Times of Scarcity

In the early days the Indians secured their prey, which swarmed in countless numbers on the plains, by enticing or driving small herds of them into enclosures, where they could be shot down at leisure ; sometimes they were rounded up by firing the grass of the prairie at several points ; when the horse was in use they could be ridden down and shot from horse-back or driven to convenient spots for killing. The Indians showed greater foresight than is the case with many savage peoples, since they were in the habit of laying up a store of food for times of scarcity, the best-known of these storage foods being pemmican. The dried meat of the bison was pounded with stone hammers, and sometimes mixed with wild cherries, also pounded to a finely-divided state. The pemmican thus produced was packed in bags of hide which were sealed with melted fat, and in this condition it would keep for many months.

Difference Between Tipis and Wigwams

It is interesting to note that the Plains Indians made little use of fish, which were, indeed, tabooed, or forbidden in some tribes. Their ordinary dwelling was the movable skin tent, or tipi, which is still in use by the surviving tribes in this area and others. It should be noted that a wigwam is an entirely different form of dwelling, typically made of bark resting on a low oval framework of wood, though the term is also applied to houses covered with mat or thatch ; the wigwam as well as the tipi was used by some of the Plains tribes.

NAVAHO INDIANS WELCOME A SHADY SPOT ON A SUNBURNT, SANDY TABLELAND OF ARIZONA

Among the arid tracks of Arizona, where dusty cactus and dreary sage-brush form the chief vegetation, dwell the Navaho Indians in all their unsophisticated simplicity. Peaceably and quietly they pass their days in their reservations, earning an honest livelihood by their varied handicraft. Most of the native wildness of the North American Indians has already disappeared, and with it much of their primitive delight in life ; they are now reduced to small and thinly-scattered tribes which are slowly wasting with the years, or, to use their own expressive figure, " they are fast travelling to the shades of their fathers, towards the setting sun "

Photo, Atchison, Topeka, & Santa Fé Railway Company

Among other features in the culture of the Plains (though not confined to them) may be mentioned decoration of clothing (deerskin coats, moccasins, etc.), with beads, which were originally of shell, bone, seeds, etc., though at an early date the glass beads of the trader displaced the native products ; wampum consisted of strings of white and purple cylinders of shell, which were used as money and were also made into belts or bands in commemoration of treaties and the like.

The " travois " was the typical means of haulage on the Plains, and was a sort of sliding vehicle made of two cross-connected poles, sometimes tent-poles, which rested on the ground behind, the forward pointed end of the triangular, or V-shaped, structure being attached to the back of a dog, or, later, a horse. Agriculture, pottery, basketry, water-transport, and the working of stone for implements were little developed in this area.

Ceremonial Tests of Stoicism

Ceremonial dances, such as the " sun dance," were characteristic, and each observance would last a number of days, the priests directing the ceremonies, the course of which was determined by strict ritual. Among most of the Indian tribes of North America stoicism was one of the primary virtues, and indeed the torture of prisoners, at the stake or otherwise, was done in order to break down their endurance and extort signs of pain or fear from them.

During the sun dance of the Plains, which was a religious ceremony, not yet entirely given up, designed to influence certain supernatural powers, some of the principal participants would have skewers run through the fleshy parts of their backs, and to these unbreakable thongs were attached; at the other end the thong might be tied to the skull of a bison, and the Indian would drag his burden round the circle of the camp, never touching the skull or thong with his hands, whatever the obstacles that might cause entanglement or strain ; or the other end of the thong was tied to an upright pole and the stoic was raised by the thong and the skewer.

Culture of the Pueblo Indians

Differing in many features of their culture from the groups just considered are the tribes of the south-western area—Arizona and New Mexico—which include the Hopi, Apache, and many others less familiar. They are charac-terised by what is known as the Pueblo culture, and, in the main, they live in fixed villages, or pueblos, consisting of rectangular, small-roomed houses made of adobe (sun-dried bricks), or sometimes of sandstone or lava, with flat roofs supported by beams, the entrance being through an opening in the roof, reached by a ladder. Associated with the pueblos were the cliff dwellings, either caves or stone houses.

There are still pueblos occupied by Indians of this group, and although their mode of life has inevitably been modified by contact with civilization, they are by no means so disastrously tarred with the white man's brush as are most other Indians. They may still be studied in the pursuit of their native occupations, such as pottery-making—by hand, without the wheel— which was one of the best-developed of the aboriginal industries. The pottery was not only admirably shaped, but was beautifully decorated in coloured slips and paints, and, in spite of degeneration, that made at the present day is by no means devoid of grace.

Agriculture and Handicrafts

The Pueblo Indians depend mainly upon maize, of which they grow large quantities, helped by their own methods of irrigation ; they cultivate several other plants, and breed sheep, goats, and some cattle. They use a true loom for the weaving of cloth, and some tribes are famous for their work in wool, which has practically displaced the

NAVAHO BOY LEARNING HOW TO PLAY CAT'S-CRADLE

Indian childhood differs little in its numerous phases from childhood elsewhere, and Redskin boys,
though often obliged to shift for themselves at an early age, are not without their pleasures and
pastimes. Among these is the string game commonly called cat's cradle, played as shown in page 901
by the Kiwai children on the Fly river in New Guinea, and in other remote lands

Photo, Ewing Galloway

cotton of their ancestors; Hopi and Navaho blankets are much sought after for their warmth, durability, and artistic decoration. In their religion, which has the same basis as that outlined above for the Indians in general, the Pueblo Indians have many societies and ceremonies, often associated with agricultural needs—such, for example, as the Rain Ceremony of some tribes. Ritual is very complex, and "priests" numerous.

Lastly, it should not be forgotten that these tribes had domesticated the turkey, and it is to this region that we owe our Christmas bird. There are, indeed, many things, as well as words and notions, that we owe to the North American Indians and their land. Tobacco will never be forgotten, and maize is not to be despised, while animal skins innumerable have enabled our women, and a man here and there, to indulge in the refined barbarism that accompanies the powder-puff and the lip-stick—themselves in reality substitutes for the clay paint and the red ochre of the savage.

Of the other culture areas space will only admit of the bare mention of the Californian tribes, acorn-eaters and great basket-makers; of the tribes of the north-west coast, depending largely on food from the sea, and sometimes on salmon taken in the rivers—where the white man now often employs the Indian to aid in the wholesale slaughter of the king of fishes—living in rectangular houses made of cedar-wood planks, making fine dug-out sea-going canoes, and erecting in front of their houses and elsewhere those great carved wooden posts usually described as totem poles; and finally the still uncivilized hunting tribes of the Déné of north-west Canada, living largely on the caribou, and even yet relatively unknown in the details of their social life.

A brief survey such as the foregoing is perhaps enough to indicate that the North American Indian of to-day is a mere shadow of his former self, and that he has gone down beyond retrieval

OF PROUD IROQUOIAN STOCK
Before their emigration to Canada the Mohawk Indians, said to be the oldest people in the confederacy of the Six Nations, carried terror wherever they went. Their skill as warriors is now less pronounced
Photo, American Museum of Natural History

before the march of events. Civilization has engulfed his continent, and, with it, him. Yet some 15,000 Indians were in the armies of the Great War, most of them by enlistment, and they were highly spoken of by their officers for their courage and efficiency.

BRILLIANT BLANKET COVERING OF A SOUTHERN INDIAN BRAVE

The weaving of native wool has been an important industry among the Pueblo peoples of the south-
western states ever since sheep were introduced by Europeans. It is claimed that the Navahos were
first initiated into the mysteries of blanket-making by a Pueblo woman, and even now many of the
so-called "Navaho blankets" are the product of the looms of the Zuni and Hopi Indians

Photo, Ewing Galloway

The United States

III. Foundation and Development of the Union

By A. D. Innes, M.A.

Associate Editor, " Harmsworth's History of the World "

THREE centuries and a half ago no Europeans save the Spaniards in Mexico had attempted to plant a permanent settlement in North America. Two centuries later the group of thirteen British colonies which, with one exception, had grown up during the seventeenth century were on the verge of the struggle which severed them from the British Empire and converted them into the thirteen United States of North America ; a number which expansion since that date has almost quadrupled. The development of that mighty nation was largely conditioned by the previous history of the colonies which combined to form it.

The two centuries before the War of American Independence broke out fall into three periods : that of the birth of the colonies, finishing with the voyage of the Mayflower ; that of their growth and development, to the close of the struggle with France ; and that of the quarrel with the Mother Country, which made hostilities inevitable.

In the last decade of the fifteenth century Christopher Columbus " discovered America," and British mariners, captained by Sebastian Cabot, came to the North American mainland. But the Spaniards had found a land of promise with store of wealth easily accessible ; the English had found a land which seemed to promise nothing. It was not until the middle of Queen Elizabeth's reign that the visionary Humphrey Gilbert conceived the idea of a vaster England to arise beyond the ocean, and lost his life at sea while seeking to found that realm far to the north. His mantle fell on his half-brother, Walter Raleigh, who year after year sent expeditions to the Chesapeake, where three times settlements were made and three times wiped out. Adventurers were too busy sacking Spanish galleons and raiding islands to settle down to colonising work on land.

Establishment of the Plantations

But with King James came peace. Production and commerce, not robbery, legitimate or illegitimate, were realized as the way to wealth ; and at Jamestown, not far from the spot chosen by Raleigh, a group of money magnates inaugurated anew the colony of Virginia early in 1607, the first of the " Plantation " group. The purpose was commercial ; in the main, the exploitation of products of the soil not procurable in Europe, whereof the most prominent came to be tobacco and cotton.

The system of division was modelled on that of rural estates in England ; the colonists were mostly the younger sons of country gentlemen imbued with the traditions of the English gentry ; the system of government, when the young colony had worked through its first stormy period of struggle with the Red-men, was in rough correspondence with the parliamentary system in England, an assembly of landed proprietors, with a governor and a nominated executive standing on the spot for the Crown and Minister, responsible, however, to the superior authority in England.

Arrival of the Pilgrim Fathers

It was not long before the white men in that climate took example by the Spaniards farther south and imported negro slaves to do the work on the plantations. The first cargo of negroes reached Virginia in 1620.

In the same year the second English colony was planted far to the north at Salem by the group of Puritans known as the Pilgrim Fathers : men and women who were in search not of wealth, but of the freedom of their souls ; essentially a religious community, rigidly bound by their own common conception of the moral law. The voyage of the Mayflower —she came to land in December, 1620— marked the birth of New England.

During the next twenty years new plantation colonies were established in the south, keeping the Virginia type ; and several more New England colonies following the Salem type ; religious communities of Puritans drawn from every class, their social basis being that of the English township which might be called popular rather than democratic, being, in fact, fundamentally oligarchical, but differing essentially from that of the plantations where the oligarchy was not popular, but aristocratic.

Both North and South, however, held by the root idea that the community was and had a right to be in essentials self-governing. Nor had the government at home any disposition to undue intervention, except so far as during the

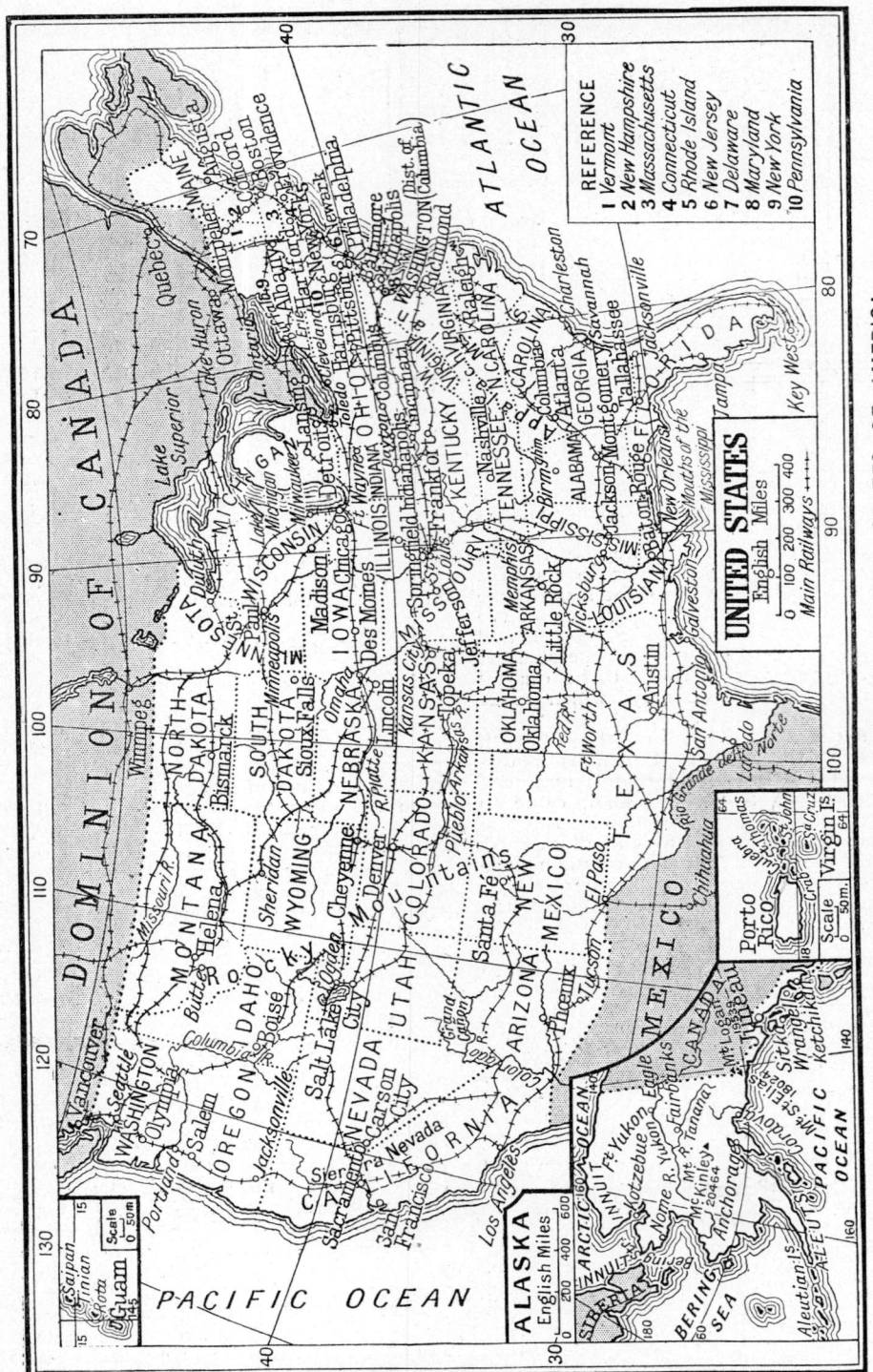

STATES AND DEPENDENCIES OF THE UNITED STATES OF AMERICA

English struggle between King and Parliament, the latter, having command of the fleet, effectively prevented the Cavalier South from succouring the Royalists.

With the Restoration came a new phase. On the one hand expansion was vigorously fostered ; the Carolinas were planted in the south ; the wedge which the Dutch had interposed on the Hudson between the northern and southern groups was ceded by them to England, and New Amsterdam became New York, the strong Dutch or " knickerbocker " element surviving the transfer of sovereignty. The Quaker, William Penn, established the predominantly Quaker but completely tolerant colony of Pennsylvania, where the negro slavery of the South—which had not been reproduced in the North as it offered no economic advantages there—was expressly excluded.

On the other hand, in the Mother Country the doctrine developed that the colonies existed primarily for the benefit of English traders, for whose advantage colonial trade might always be legitimately restricted. The Restoration Navigation Act limited their exports and imports to English bottoms to and from English ports, and accompanying Acts checked or prohibited their manufactures, in order to preserve the market for English goods ; and at the same time the Crown in England exercised an increasing control over governors and executives, while governors and executives themselves became more arbitrary.

Friction with the Mother Country

The Revolution victory of Constitutionalism in England and the subsequent domination of the Whigs reacted, but not to the same extent, on the colonies ; palliating their grievances, which were growing acute, but were, in fact, a part of the price they paid for the security against French aggression from Canada provided by the British Navy. Walpole, who virtually ruled England from 1720 to 1740, was an enemy to all restrictions on trade, but dealt with the colonial trade problem as he did with the Nonconformist problem at home.

He did not attempt to repeal the obnoxious restrictions, but carefully shut his eyes to the organized, systematic, and hardly veiled defiance of the laws which rendered them all but a dead-letter. His policy was continued by his successors, till the Seven Years' War (1756-63) came, and the colonists got their price in the annihilation by British troops and fleets of the French menace, by the conquest and cession of Canada.

The time had come, therefore, for a great readjustment of the relations between the Mother Country and colonies, which were no longer in need of defence by her against the aggression of a great foreign Power.

The fatuity of the British government gave the readjustment a fatal twist in the wrong direction. George Grenville, instead of realizing that the colonies had long suffered from grievances which had only been borne because of the French menace, could only see that the colonies were the principal gainers by a war which had been waged at the cost of Great Britain, and that they ought to contribute to the depleted British treasury.

No Taxation Without Representation

Moreover, his legal soul was vexed by the fact that trade laws had been habitually ignored, with some loss to the revenue. So he set about rigorously enforcing the laws which the most respectable people had been breaking constantly as a matter of course ; and acting upon the letter of the law, he procured an Act of Parliament imposing on the colonies taxation for which there was no precedent, taxation for the avowed purpose not of regulating trade, but of raising revenue from the colonies for the British treasury. He revived and exasperated the old grievances ; he added to them a new one ; and the compensation he had to offer was —an army which the colonies did not want.

It was the old grievances that hurt ; the new one, the Stamp Tax, was in itself utterly trivial, but it contained a menace of more to follow, and it gave resistance something to take hold of. Even if it were technically legal, it had no precedent ; and manifestly it set at naught one of the fundamental principles of the Whig revolution, summed up in the catchword, " No Taxation without Representation."

The War of American Independence

On the one side the legal sovereignty of " the King in Parliament " was indisputable ; on the other, the action of the sovereign was a breach of fundamental principles. The wrath of the colonists blazed out in open breaches of admitted law. Both sides lost their tempers thoroughly. The obnoxious Act was indeed repealed, but the repeal was followed by new Acts in England, equally trivial but equally irritating, and by new deeds of lawlessness in the colonies which public opinion there more than condoned.

Burke and Chatham raised their voices against the insanity ; sober colonials, stubbornly resolved not to yield on the vital point, strove vainly to find some way by which to meet what was just, in the English demand for a contribution to the cost of the war, through self-taxation. Hotheads on both sides fanned the flames ;

the moderates were completely over-ridden; defiance of the law begot threats of force; force begot fresh defiance; Government troops raiding colonial depots of arms were fired upon by local volunteers; and the initial skirmish at Lexington (1775) opened the War of American Independence.

Even then separation was not the avowed aim of the American leaders, though fifteen months after the first hostilities they had nailed the Declaration of Independence to the mast. King George would have nothing short of unconditional surrender; the fact stiffened the colonies into a determination to have nothing short of sovereign independence.

George Washington and Victory

On the face of things, a military victory for the Mother Country ought to have been a certainty, though its effects could have been but temporary. She had regular troops, experienced officers, un-qualified command of the sea, a govern-ment exercising unqualified control and supported by an irresistible majority in Parliament. The colonists had no fleet, a volunteer army without training called up from its civil avocations, officers whose experience was limited to warfare with the Red Indians, and an improvised central government for thirteen several com-munities which hitherto had never, with-out the utmost difficulty, been induced even to cooperate.

But three factors turned the scale, and the military victory went to the colonists. The British were half-hearted in the war, more than doubtful whether right was on their side, and the half-heartedness was reflected in the conduct of their leaders. They lost the command of the sea in the critical period of the struggle owing to the intervention of France. And finally, the colonists had placed George Washing-ton at the head of the army. He was not a military genius of the first order, but his opponents were much less so, and his own subordinates were occasionally brilliant.

Sovereignty of the United States

It was not, however, military talent that won the day, but the inexhaustible patience, serenity, tact, and self-devotion of this rare example of a type which is commonly ejected from control before the work is completed, by the impatience which clamours for more popular qualities and more showy activities. Happily for American Independence, Washington re-tained his ascendancy, and won the war—to be justly enshrined as a hero for ever in the heart of a great nation.

The victory was won when Cornwallis was forced to surrender at Yorktown, the French having successfully cut him off from relief by the British fleet (October, 1781). A year later the peace was signed between Great Britain and the victors, which recognized the independence of the United States of America. After another year the peace was finally ratified (October, 1783) by the Treaty of Versailles.

The new nation still had before it the task of shaping itself, whether as a league of sovereign states or as a unity, but in any case as a union. A common authority could only be established by consent of all, since the existing central authority was only provisional. Not till 1787 was the scheme of union formulated; in 1788 it was adopted by a convention of dele-gates appointed by the several states; and in 1789 George Washington by unanimous choice became the first Pre-sident of the great Republic.

The constitution was no a priori structure; it was based on the precedents provided by the British constitution and the constitutions of the several existing states, while rejecting the hereditary principle and substituting for it election. The place of the Crown was taken by a President elected for a term of years; that of the Commons by an elected Chamber; that of the Lords by a Chamber —the Senate—elected on a different basis.

State and Federal Government

The several states retained their own governments; their powers and those assigned to the central government were strictly but incompletely defined, and a judicial authority was set up with absolute power to decide whether acts of the central government were or were not "unconstitutional," and therefore ipso facto invalid.

Still, the most careful definition left a wide margin of ground debatable between the central and the state authori-ties, and one crucial question was left without a definite answer. Was the union a confederation from which each state was free to sever itself if so minded, or was it a federation from which none could part without consent of the rest? And the Republic had before it another problem which no constitution-making could solve; should America isolate her-self politically from the international relations of the Old World?

For the next six and twenty years, Europe was in the throes of the Revolu-tionary and Napoleonic wars. During that period one aspect of expansion was settled by the "Louisiana purchase" from Napoleon, which left the British in Canada and the Spaniards in Mexico, the only European Powers with a footing in North America. The new Republic, after some hesitation, declined to be drawn into the European struggle; but before that struggle was over it became involved in an unhappy contest with the British, born of the British war-claim to the right of search on the high seas.

In the course of it, the States learnt once for all that Canada was and would remain loyal to the British Empire. The contest was futile and inconclusive; it intensified the feeling of bitterness—more in America than in England—between the sister-peoples of one race, which had been engendered in the last struggle, but it was not till more than eighty years had passed that the States again came into armed collision with a European Power.

During the next decade (1815-25) the struggle of the peoples of South America for independence led to the assertion of the principle which ever since has dominated American foreign policy, the "Monroe doctrine," enunciated by President Monroe, that the States as the premier Power on the American continent would resist any attempt of European Powers to set up a control over states on that continent or to intervene in American affairs, a doctrine of which the corollary was that so long as American and European affairs were separable America should hold herself aloof from European complications.

Assertion of the Monroe Doctrine

Thus for half a century after the war with Great Britain, the foreign relations of the States were mainly confined to frontier disputes with Great Britain on the north and Spain on the south. The delimitations in the treaty of 1783 had been indefinite and ambiguous. These were partly settled by the Ashburnham Treaty of 1842, the awards conceding virtually the whole of the American claims, to the detriment of Canada.

But a contingent question, the "Oregon boundary" dispute, arising out of the expansion westwards both on the north and the south of the Canadian boundary, in regions which lay out of the ken of the first treaty, led to much beating of drums and shouting of war, which, however, subsided peacefully enough in 1846; though there was still an aftermath, when the "Vancouver line" was referred to the arbitration of the German Emperor William I.

In every case the settlement arrived at was heavily in favour of the Americans. The Mexican questions were less peacefully settled. Florida was acquired from Spain on easy terms before that Power had disappeared from the American mainland. But when Texas, largely populated by immigrants from the States, revolted from Mexico and sought admission to the northern union, acute differences arose, which brought about the short and immediately decisive campaign of 1847, and the cession of the ex-Spanish western territories, with California.

The problem not of secession but of state rights as against Federal rights was ever present, for two closely associated reasons, which antagonised the northern and the southern states. The latter, the some-time plantation colonies, lived by, not on, the produce of the plantations, purchasing with them the necessaries as well as the luxuries of life from abroad; and the economic basis of the plantation system was slavery.

Differences Between North and South

The North was agricultural and industrial, living upon its own produce, but hampered industrially by foreign competition; and having no use for slave labour, it was alive, as the South was not, to the moral degradation of slavery. The South depended on slavery and cheap imports, the North upon protective tariffs and free labour. But the North was stronger than the South in voting power, in the central government; it was able to impose Protection on the whole Union; if its predominance increased, it might threaten the South with the abolition of slavery.

Thus interest made the North insistent upon the Federal authority, and the South insistent upon state rights, including the right of each state to repudiate for itself the ordinances of the Federal authority; insistent also that in the westward expansion, bringing new areas as new states into the Union, the balance between slave-owning and non-slave-owning should not be further weighed down in favour of the latter.

In the background hovered always the spectre of secession, the consciousness that in the last resort a minority whose interests were over-ridden at the dictation of the Federal majority would claim the right to sever themselves from the Union and assert themselves as an independent nation.

Federals and Confederates

At the middle of the century the question had come to be whether new states which were taking shape should be captured for the free group or the slave group. By that time the North had come unequivocally to the conclusion that though the existing slave states might have a right to retain that institution, no more slave states should be permitted.

When in 1860 Abraham Lincoln was elected President, the South concluded that under the Federal government, slavery was doomed. The southern states asserted their right of secession and joined in a Confederation with Jefferson Davis as President. The North denied the right of secession, and declared resistance to the Federal decrees to be rebellion. And so in 1861 began the fratricidal war, on the grand issue— should the United States remain united or become two separate nations with hostile interests?

Fratricidal Civil War

Each side, with entire conviction, believed itself to be in the right. The South flung itself into the struggle with its whole forces from the very beginning; the North, with infinitely larger resources to draw upon, did so only by slow degrees, always making good from its reserves whatever its losses might be. The South had no reserves from which to make good, but for long it more than held its own against the growing odds.

Then, at a stroke, Lincoln changed the character of the war by proclaiming the emancipation of the slaves, an issue which had not hitherto been presented. The superiority of the North by sea had enabled the Federals to blockade the Southern ports, cutting off the imports on which the Confederation was dependent for supplies as the North was not.

The Northern armies grew while the Southern armies dwindled; the emancipation of the slaves had raised for the South an enemy within its own gates. When the war had become one of exhaustion, the end was certain, but the complete victory of the North was won only when Lee, the most brilliant of the Confederate commanders was compelled to surrender to overwhelmingly superior forces at Appomattox in April, 1865, just four years after the first hostilities.

Five days later Lincoln, in the eyes of many the grandest figure that the century produced in the new world or the old, was assassinated, the stupidest murder among all the great crimes history has recorded.

Reconstruction After Emancipation

Lincoln, the rough-hewn man of the people, idealist, prophet, and incarnation of level-headed common sense, as tender of heart as immovable in resolve, was the one man capable of controlling the situation which had arisen, in the spirit of the Divine Justice which understands all, above every kind of party rancour. His death gave the control to men who meant to be just, but understood only their own point of view. The North had won; the Southerners were in their eyes rebels who had justly forfeited the political rights to which those who had been down-trodden slaves were entitled.

The work of reconstruction passed into their hands, after a vain effort on the part of Lincoln's successor to over-ride public opinion on behalf of the South. Practically in the South the negroes were enfranchised, their former masters were disfranchised, the enfranchised were incapable of governing, and the disfranchised took the law into their own hands.

It was not till many years had passed that the much-changed South recovered equilibrium on the new economic basis which the abolition of slavery had imposed but with the political predominance of whites over blacks restored.

The great Civil War had for the moment suspended the operation of the Monroe Doctrine, enabling the French Emperor, Napoleon III., to embark on his Mexican venture, already doomed to disaster, before the threat of American intervention following on the peace hastened its close.

A notable advance in another direction was made when London and Washington agreed to refer to impartial arbitration the disputes which had arisen out of the activities of the Alabama and other British-built cruisers in the service of the South during the war. Towards the close of the century, the States began to find themselves involved with European Powers in the problems presented by the Pacific and by China and Japan.

The Principle of Isolation

Curiously enough, however, a dispute between Great Britain and Venezuela, and the somewhat vociferous threats of American intervention, resulted in a novel cordiality between Great Britain and the States; which, before long, bore fruits that once would have seemed impossible.

The States became involved in a quarrel with Spain over the island of Cuba, which issued (1898) in the only armed conflict between the Republic and a European Power which had taken place since that with the British in 1812-14. The friendly attitude of the great Naval Power was an important factor in preventing other European intervention; and the rapid and decisive victory of the Republic, adding the Philippine Islands to its dominions, created a new point of contact or conflict between America and Europe, and a new difficulty in the way of preserving American isolation.

That isolation was broken down in the course of the Great War of the twentieth century, when America, long held back, was at last swept into the struggle and took vigorous part in its final stage. But even that blow to the governing principle of a century and a quarter was not final, and the Republic still holds to the doctrine of aloofness except where her own interests are directly involved.

The Country

Occupies the central and southern part of the North American Continent. Bounded by Canada on the north, Mexico and Gulf of Mexico south, and Atlantic and Pacific Oceans east and west respectively. Main physical features the great ranges of the Rocky Mountains west and Appalachians east, with the great plains between.

Chief among the river systems is that of the Missouri-Mississippi, which drains a basin second only to that of the Amazon. Total mileage of the combined streams exceeds 4,000. Many of the tributaries, such as the Ohio, are navigable for hundreds of miles.

Climate varies according to locality, but is generally temperate. Rainfall generally plentiful on the coasts and diminishes towards the inland regions. Total area about 3,026,000 square miles; estimated population 105,710,000.

On the extreme north-west is the mountainous, and in parts volcanic, territory of Alaska, about one third being within the Arctic Circle. Alaska contains the highest mountain in the Continent, Mt. McKinley (20,300 ft.). Total area of Alaska about 590,800 square miles; estimated population 75,000. Porto Rico, an island in the West Indies, is also a possession of U.S.A. Climate tropical. Total area about 3,400 square miles; estimated population 1,299,000. Guam, area 210 square miles; population 13,000. Virgin Islands, 132 square miles; population 26,000. For information regarding Hawaii, Panamá, the Philippines and Samoan Islands, see chapters under these headings.

Government and Constitution

Administrative power is in hands of a Cabinet of ten, at whose head is a president. These ten are chosen by the President, but must be approved by the Senate, which contains two members from each state elected for a term of six years by popular vote. The Senate and House of Representatives together form what is known as Congress. The House of Representatives consists of members chosen every second year by vote of the citizens of either sex or any race or colour eligible for the suffrage. Eligibility depends on conditions of term of residence, payment of taxes, education and registration that vary in the different states. All voters must exceed twenty-one years of age. A census every ten years determines the number of members each state may return to the House of Representatives. According to the Constitution entire legislative power belongs to Congress.

A body of judges called the Supreme Court has power to declare void and *ultra vires* any act of Congress or state legislatures infringing the Constitution. There are in all forty-eight states in the Union, each having its own republican constitution, with, as legislature, a governor and two Houses which are elective, as is also the governor. Alaska and Hawaii have local legislatures, and Porto Rico is self-governing.

Defence

Army includes, besides regular troops, the National Guard, a volunteer militia recruited from the various states aided by grants from Federal government; the Officers' Reserve Corps, including officers of all grades organized according to the branches of the regular army; the Reserve Officers' Training Corps, for maintaining the strength of the Officers' Reserve Corps; and the Enlisted Reserve Corps, voluntarily enlisted, consisting of men qualified so as to be eligible for enlistment in the Regulars.

Nominal strength of Army authorised by Congress, 144,000 officers and men, all arms. The Navy is administered by a naval secretary, acting under advice of a Naval Department Council. President is Commander-in-Chief of both Army and Navy.

Commerce and Industries

There were, in 1922, 61,230,000 acres under wheat with an average yield per acre of 14·0 bushels. Among chief wheat-growing states are Kansas, which had a yield for same year of 122,887,000 bushels; North Dakota, Illinois, Nebraska, and Oklahoma. For same year the yields of other crops in thousands of bushels were: Corn, 2,890,712; oats, 1,215,496; potatoes, 451,185; barley, 186,118; sweet potatoes, 109,534; rough rice, 41,965; buckwheat, 15,050. Other important crops are cane and beet sugar and hay. In 1922, 33,742,000 acres of cotton were harvested, yielding 9,964,000 bales, each of 500 lb. gross. Among chief cotton-producing states are Texas, Mississippi, Arkansas, North Carolina, Alabama, and Georgia. In 1922 there were 1,725,000 acres under tobacco, yielding 1,324,840,000 lb., some of the main tobacco-growing states being Kentucky, North Carolina, Virginia, Tennessee, and South Carolina.

In 1921 mineral products reached a total value of $4,056,000,000. Gold is mined principally in California, Alaska, Colorado, and Nevada, and silver mainly in Montana, Idaho, Utah, Nevada, and Colorado. In 1921 the production of precious stones was valued at $518,280. Important industries are those connected with food products, including slaughtering and meat-packing, milling, cheese and condensed milk making; textile, including carpets, cottons, silk and woollen goods; metallurgic, including the making of iron and steel bars, ingots and castings; and chemical, including the production of fertilisers, paints and varnishes, dye-stuffs and petroleum refining. In 1921 products of the canned fishery were valued at $46,634,706. In 1922 imports of merchandise reached a total value of $521,601,801, while exports of merchandise for the same year were valued at $754,236,319. Standard coin, the dollar; nominal value 4s. 2d.

Communications

Total railway mileage about 263,800 miles. A number of routes link the Atlantic with the Pacific coast, including the New York Central and Pennsylvania railways, both from New York to Chicago; the Santa Fé, running through Kansas City to San Francisco; the Union Pacific, Chicago, Milwaukee and St. Paul, and Northern Pacific railways. Telegraph lines aggregate about 1,522,000, and telephone wire about 27,819,800 miles.

Religion and Education

Among the many denominations represented the Roman Catholic Church has the greatest aggregate following, the Protestants, though greatly in the majority, being split up among many sects, of whom the more numerous include the Baptists, Methodists, Lutheran bodies, and Presbyterians. There is in every state a system of free elementary schools, and there are numerous private schools and many universities, both public and private. Grants of land have been made from time to time by the government to townships attaining an area six miles square, for purposes of augmenting the funds for local education.

Chief Towns

Washington, D.C. capital (estimated population 437,000), New York, N.Y. (including five boroughs, Manhattan, Bronx, Brooklyn, Queens, and Richmond, 5,620,000), Chicago, Ill. (2,700,000), Philadelphia, Pa. (1,823,000), Detroit, Mich. (993,000), Cleveland, Ohio (796,000), St. Louis, Mi. (773,000), Boston, Mass. (748,000), Baltimore, Md. (733,000), Pittsburg, Pa. (588,000), Los Angeles, Cal. (576,000), Buffalo, N.Y. (506,000), San Francisco, Cal. (506,000), Milwaukee, Wis. (457,000), Newark, N.J. (414,000), Cincinnati, Ohio (401,000).

CITIZENS OF MONTEVIDEO IN THE SPACIOUS AND FLOWERY PLAZA DE LA INDEPENDENCIA

Montevideo has several plazas, or public squares, all occupying high ground in the centre of the city; of these the Plaza de la Independencia is considered one of the most attractive. It is the old central point of the city from which the streets radiate. One of the best constructed cities in the western hemisphere, it is built on a regular plan of cuadrados, or squares; many of its public buildings are very imposing, and include a cathedral, a university, several schools, many theatres, and hospitals, and it has fine views and a general air of openness and cleanliness. Government House, with the Uruguayan flag flying, is seen to the left

Uruguay

I. Progressive "Orientals" of Latin America

By L. E. Elliott

Author of "Brazil, To-day and To-morrow," etc.

LOUNGING upon the platform of the railway that runs clear across the pampas of La Republica Oriental del Uruguay, from the Brazilian border to Montevideo, is a typical Oriental gaucho. His wide hat shades a broad face that shows not only in the peculiar reddish-bronze of the skin, but in the straight, black hair and quick, beady eyes, something more than a trace of the native Charrua folk, the "Indians" found here by the Spaniards four centuries ago.

The South American equivalent of the North American cowboy, and, like the cowboy, fated to disappear in course of time, this gaucho is a strong and bulky type, with big shoulders, thick neck, muscular arms, small hips and the slightly bowed legs of the horseman. He wears the poncho and bombachos: that is to say, the upper part of his body is covered by the heavy folds of a square of thick, striped, woollen cloth, with a slit in the centre to admit the head, while his lower limbs are draped in voluminous cotton or woollen pantalones thickly shirred at waist and ankle.

Dramatic Figure of the Gaucho

Upon a chilly day he will also wear the chiripa, a large woollen shawl folded about his waist, with a corner between the legs, and, beholding him, you will wonder how a man so much encumbered can do a day's work. But this work is performed on the back of a hardy and intelligent horse, strong enough to bear the weight of a high-peaked saddle, sometimes silver-mounted, with huge solid stirrups. This horse is trained to endure the prick of six-inch spurs, and to aid his master actively when the latter throws the lasso or the bolas—that ancient Indian weapon of the wide grasslands. If the gaucho comes from an interior point his equipment is likely to be home-made, from poncho to stirrups.

Modernity in Montevideo

Within a few hours of meeting the gaucho you may dine at a beautifully appointed house in Montevideo, and your hostess is exquisitely dressed in clothes straight from Paris; her jewels are beyond criticism, her hair dressed in the style dictated by the French capital, and she prefers to speak the tongue of France rather than that of Spain when she discusses world affairs. She has, in fact, assimilated with grace and completeness the lesson of Paris, to which very many Latin Americans look as their intellectual foster-mother as well as the arbiter of fashion. The adaptability of the Latin American woman is one of her crowning gifts.

Take, for instance, the case of Madame Blank; she is to-day the gracious châtelaine of a European diplomat, but was born the Señorita Candelaria Gonzales upon a sleepy ranch in Paysandú. Papa Gonzales and his father before him lived through troublous times in Uruguay, and round the fire at night you may hear old tales of the prolonged struggle between the Blancos and the Colorados, the two great political divisions of Uruguay until within recent times, a struggle that became a species of internecine feud, in which the women took an active and ingenious part. The death-blow to the Blanco-Colorado warfare was dealt when the coming of the Uruguayan network of railways, the newspaper, the cinema, and obvious and rapid rewards of

HEALTHY GIRLHOOD OF MONTEVIDEO'S FASHIONABLE COMMUNITY
There are many pleasant streets of Montevideo peopled by prosperous families who, in the healthy and congenial climate, enjoy to the full the amenities of social life. El Prado, a beautiful park lying some three miles from the city, is a favourite rendezvous and frequented by many of the élite from Paso de Molino, a fashionable suburb containing some remarkable varieties of architectural styles
Photo, Publishers' Photo Service

business gave a wider outlet to imagination and energy.

Candelaria ran barefoot as a child, and could ride a horse as soon as she could walk. There was no available school, and at ten she could neither read nor write. Life upon the ranch was simple, for, with cattle worth little more than their hides, there was very slight revenue in cash, and money played a small part in the year's balance-sheet. The house was built of stone, with a wide veranda; peach trees grew in the orchard, and before the door were great willows and acacias, planted for shade near the bright stream that supplied the farm with water. Upon broad, flat stones at the edge all the family clothes were beaten when washing-day came round.

With all the attention of the menfolk of the estancia devoted to stock-raising, the kitchen garden was almost non-existent (Uruguay still imports potatoes from England, although the potato is a South American plant, native of Chile), and although chickens, ducks, and turkeys ran wild, with the prairie for a barnyard, and formed upon occasions of fiesta the basis of succulent, generous dishes well flavoured with pimiento, the mild, red peppers beloved of all Latin America, yet there were only two chief items of the ordinary workaday meal of the estancia—meat and maté.

The gaucho cares nothing whether he has bread and fruit and sweets or not, so long as he has plenty of beef, still frequently cooked in the open in the primitive fashion, " carne con cuero " (with the skin on), and above all if he has his maté cup and bombilla, and hot water for the infusion of the indispensable yerba.

This " herb " is the dried and broken-up leaf of ilex paraguayensis, growing wild in South Brazil and Paraguay, and infused to make a hot drink; it was the only hot drink that the European conquerors of South America could get in a strange land. Having a somewhat bitter taste it is disagreeable to palates unaccustomed to it, but for the last four hundred years it has retained its popularity with the natives, is still credited with almost miraculous recuperating powers, and is sold in thousands of tons in Rio Grande do Sul (South Brazil), Uruguay, Argentina, Paraguay, and, less freely to-day, in the country districts of South Chile. All the cities of the maté-drinking countries have yielded to the stronger and more aromatic tea and coffee; but in more remote regions where trade penetrates slowly yerba maté still retains its place as prime favourite.

SOME MEMBERS OF MONTEVIDEO'S SHOE-SHINE SOCIETY

Street types in Montevideo are very much the same as in other large cosmopolitan cities. Flowers, fruits, and fancy goods may be bought from itinerant pedlars, vociferous newspaper boys elbow their way through the crowds, and the boot-black is on the look-out at the street corner, and for a bronze coin or two will impart a " shine " guaranteed to make well-worn footgear " as good as new "

Photo, Publishers' Photo Service

FASHIONABLE LIFE AT POCITOS BEACH, A SEASIDE PLEASURE RESORT ON THE OUTSKIRTS OF MONTEVIDEO

Montevideo is the capital, emporium, and chief port of the Republic of Uruguay and has nearly one-third of the population. It claims to be one of the most cosmopolitan of South American towns, and almost every language of the civilized world may be heard in its streets. The attractive environs contain many handsome residences, prettily situated in well-kept gardens, while Pocitos and Ramirez on the seashore, connected by trams with the city, are two well-known bathing resorts which yearly attract numerous wealthy and fashionable visitors from Buenos Aires as well as from the Uruguayan towns

When Candelaria was about sixteen Papa Gonzales suddenly found himself beginning to make money. The establishment of great meat canning and freezing plants by strongly-financed foreign firms had the effect of rapidly "valorising" or arbitrarily increasing the market price of Uruguayan cattle. Candelaria and her brother were sent to expensive Catholic schools in France, and it took less than three years to make a flower-like demoiselle of the girl and a trifling young dandy of her brother Ildefonso.

Then came the outbreak of the Great War. Far away in Paysandú, when the Allied armies began calling for huge supplies of food, the meat-product factories were deluged with stupendous orders, and they in turn called upon the stock-raisers. Hides and wool as well as the meat of South America brought prices of a never-expected height, and there rose up a crop of millionaires.

War-time Flood of Prosperity

Papa Gonzales was among them. He bought more land and more livestock, and diamonds for his señora, but he did not change his mode of life; dawn saw him in the saddle, noon in his hammock for the siesta, sundown at the raised hearth in the big room of the estancia which is kitchen and dining and sitting room all in one, while at ten o'clock he was fast asleep.

Candelaria, before 1914 was out, married in Paris the officer brother of a school friend, while Ildefonso exchanged his loitering in studios for life in the French Army. They exemplified in Paris the type to which Paris is accustomed—the fabulously rich South American whose money comes in carloads. Uruguay, strongly upon the side of the Allies, and saying so candidly, was well able to afford the credits that she gave, later on, both to France and to Britain for purchases of foodstuffs.

The pinnacle of Uruguayan golden days came in 1919, when the national peso soared to dizzy heights in international exchange. Uruguay has always been proud of the fact that her gold dollar is worth just a little more than the gold dollar of the United States; but she did not expect to see her paper peso, fixed in pre-war years by the gold backing at $51\frac{1}{2}$ pence, rise to 60, then 70, and at last, in early 1920, to 73 pence.

Patriarchal Life on the Estancias

Following close upon the heels of this dazzling period came the slump, with the international markets too impoverished to buy the raw materials of South America. Uruguayan stock-raisers and meat factories and shippers then had to mark time. Papa Gonzales ceased to buy fine bloodstock at fancy prices, but he is personally unaffected by hard times as by the crest of wealth.

The patriarchal, almost feudal, life of Uruguayan estancias has lingered long, partly because the estates are vast. Even to-day the whole country, of 72,000 square miles, is divided among 600 owners—of whom, by the way, forty are British, chiefly from Scotland, Cornwall, and Wales. The Celt, like the Basque, seems to find Uruguay suited to his special genius.

The country is, roughly, the shape of a squat pear with the stem end upwards; Montevideo, capital and sole city of any considerable size, stands on the rim of the pear's flower-calyx, southward, with little Maldonado on the opposite rim, nearer the Atlantic. Maldonado is the only true seaport of Uruguay, and here is the base of a little seal-hunting fleet, making its catch at Castillos and Lobos Islands.

Natural Charms of Uruguay

Practically all the Uruguayan coast north of Maldonado is rendered useless by swamp and lagoon, the celebrated Merim lagoon connecting by the Jaguarão river with Brazil's Lagôa dos Patos. With all the thick part of the pear bathed by the joining waters of the Atlantic and the Rio de la Plata,

ON AN IMMIGRANT RANCHER'S PROPERTY: WASTE LAND CONVERTED INTO A FLOURISHING FARM

The Uruguayan open country is an extension of the treeless grassy plain of the Argentine pampa, though less flat and uniform, and enjoys an excellent climate in spite of summer heat and the rapid fall in temperature caused by the pampero or furious south-west wind. Large numbers of Europeans have been absorbed in the population, which resembles the kindred people of Argentina, although the Uruguayans are of a simpler and less cosmopolitan type, preserving in a greater degree the old-fashioned ways. The soil is productive, with the exception of that on the east coast, and tillage is on the increase

MEAT-PRESERVING PROCESS IN URUGUAY: WORKERS ON THE DRYING-GROUND OF A JERKED BEEF FACTORY

Jerked beef is the name applied to beef dried in the sun. After the fat has been removed the meat is cut into thin strips and hung in the sun for several days; provided it is kept perfectly dry meat can thus be preserved for an indefinite period. These jerked strips, known as charqui, eaten either cooked or raw, are still prepared by old-fashioned methods in Uruguay for home consumption and for export to Brazil and the West Indies. Similarly preserved buffalo or reindeer meat is prepared by the North American Indians and called pemmican, and the South African variety, made from buffalo or antelope, is known as biltong

TRUSSING FRESH PORK IN A MEAT-PACKING CENTRE

Much of the soil of Uruguay is kept for pastoral purposes, and vast numbers of livestock are raised; meat, wool, and hides constituting the chief products and exports. There are several large establishments for making meat extract, and preserving and tinning meat. The chief centres of the meat trade for export are at Fray Bentos, Paysandú, and Salto

Uruguay's western edge continues to follow the windings of the Uruguay river, with Paysandú and Salto as useful river ports; the north-eastern boundary, sloping from the pear's stalk, looks across to the Brazilian Rio Grande do Sul, very much akin in quality.

There, too, are clean grassy uplands, rich and pleasant cattle country, with a bright and temperate all-the-year-round climate. Deep glades with woodland where the pine lingers afford shelter for the wild deer, and pink and golden and purple flowers carpet the meadow. Well-watered, with no mountain ridge showing peaks of over 2,000 feet, but with plenty of good building stone cropping out from scores of grassy stretches, Uruguay is an ideal pastoral country, and happy in being free from any kind of epidemic disease.

It is well for the Banda that the packing-houses have hastened the creation of a high standard in livestock, for despite the facts that Minas province claims mineral wealth, that there is one small goldmine (British owned) operating in the country, and that talc and manganese exist, and coal, although not of the quality required by the railways, has been discovered, it is plain that she must remain primarily devoted to agriculture and stock-raising. Economic methods are being introduced, and forage planted, and upon her sales of wool, meat products, and hides depends 96 per cent. of Uruguay's exports.

There are many infant industries in Montevideo. Factories turn out excellent shoes, made of native leather upon foreign lasts, and there are well-equipped textile mills from which there was, at one period of the Great War, an export of woollen cloth to France; soap and candles, glass and pottery, tinware made from imported sheet, in fact a long list of domestic needs are supplied from the mills of Montevideo, and the lot of the worker is not hard since he is forbidden by law to work more than forty-eight hours per week.

But the true wealth of Uruguay is not in the city but upon the breeze-swept, healthy pampa, perennially green, where in the transparent air the remote horizon appears as an unbroken ring.

Upon this pampa the population is still so sparse that such native creatures as the little rhea, the South American ostrich, may still be seen running in numbers, unafraid and free. Only one and a half million people inhabit Uruguay, and of these half a million live in Montevideo and its suburbs. There is practically no immigration, for there have never been giant mushroom industries suddenly erected, calling for new masses of labour; and as one result there exists no undigested population to trouble the social structure.

IN A DEPARTMENT OF THE MONTEVIDEO PORTLAND CEMENT FACTORY

Portland cement differs very little in composition all the world over. Its uses are many and varied, and its peculiar property of hardening under water renders it invaluable for harbour, dock, and reservoir construction. At every stage of its manufacture the material is carefully tested, and standard specifications to which cement must conform have been imposed in all countries

SOME OF THE THRILLS AND DANGERS OF GAUCHO LIFE : LASSOING HORSES IN THE WILDS OF URUGUAY

There is little that the gaucho of Uruguay and Argentina does not know about horses. He is essentially a horseman, and so engrained in him is the habit of riding that it is jocularly said that a gaucho will walk a mile to catch a horse in order to ride a quarter of a mile. In some parts of the country wild horses and cattle may be had for the lassoing. Then the skill of these hot-blooded centaur-like men is seen to full advantage, and should they wish to vary their sport there are numerous deer, pumas, and fierce tiger-cats to keep both hand and eye in good training

Photo, Charles Rider Noble

The steady development of a homogeneous type has proceeded without shock, the older Spanish strain, with a certain Charrua admixture, assimilating without difficulty the European newcomer of the last century. Towards the close of the nineteenth century two children out of every three born in Uruguay had foreign blood on one side of their parentage. Traverse the streets of Montevideo, through the shopping and business districts, and the wide streets of stately residences, and saunter through the outlying regions of modest little houses where, in contrast with the humbler dwellings of many Latin American towns, every window is glazed, and you will agree that there is a homogeneous quality about the Orientales. The type is a distinct one, and one that is noticeably of a high physical standard.

It is common to find a large proportion of pretty women in any Latin American centre ; but in Uruguay they are not only lovely, but tall and strong, while their male relatives are notably handsome and athletic.

Life's Amenities in the Capital

The influence of environment is no doubt powerful ; the indigenous races were sturdy folk, children of the pampa, and the climate and soil have their ancient effect. There are no sweltering tropics here to enervate white races, and, although Montevideo experiences a hot season—at its most trying in December noons—the force of the sun is tempered by cool breezes from the water. Buenos Aires, placed farther up the river on the opposite (right) bank, is less fortunate, and pays tribute to Montevideo's climate by sending a yearly shoal of visitors, who swell the numbers of Orientales to be seen daily upon the pleasant beach, where crowds of gay, striped bathing tents, airy hotels, and sedulously-kept promenades create a lively scene of which any European watering-place might well be proud.

Montevideo is a bright, well-equipped city ; the atmosphere is friendly, the bearing of the passers-by dignified and pleasant. No very poor, shoeless class is to be seen here, there is no marked contrast between poverty and silken extravagance ; and to find a trace of that international sore, labour unrest, you must go to the docks, where " Red " trouble-makers have done their best to stir up strife, as they have done at Buenos Aires with more success.

Restrictions Upon Immigration

Before the early years of the present century it was almost if not quite true to say that there had never been a strike in South America ; but during the Great War a host of professional agitators, some from Barcelona, some from Russia, and some from the training-school of the I.W.W. in California, found in patriarchal regions below the Rio Grande a wide and untilled field. There were no organizations able to combat their work—the well-managed and level-headed trades union was practically non-existent— and the open invitation maintained by Latin America to induce immigration smoothed the path of the entrant.

To-day Uruguay, in common with the majority of her sister states, has raised hastily contrived barriers. You must have a passport, you must be newly vaccinated, and you must prove that you are neither insane nor a criminal, before you can enter Uruguay nowadays ; what is more, if you are over sixty years of age you cannot come in at all unless you have a son in the country who is able to maintain you. The negro and the Hindu are excluded altogether.

Wise Foresight and Prudent Patience

The Uruguayan is, in fact, quite frank in saying that he wants as incomers none but folk like the best that have already formed the population ; he wants only hardy white Europeans with enterprise, and trained to serious ideals ; and, since this is

D 30

1T7

GROUP OF HALF-BREED GAUCHOS NEAR FRAY BENTOS, A "CENTRE OF BUTCHERY FOR FAR-OFF CONSUMPTION".

Cattle and sheep raising has long been the chief industry of the Uruguay Republic. The nomad cattlemen, easily distinguishable from the pampas Indians, though their dexterity as horsemen is no less remarkable, are experts in all branches of their calling, and it has been described how a seven-year-old gaucho on horseback successfully lassoed a sheep, cut its throat, and skinned it in most masterly fashion. Fray Bentos, a pleasant port on the Uruguay river, and the centre of a stock-raising district, has a large export trade in meat and animal products, and contains the chief factory for the preparation of meat extract

Photo, Charles Rider Noble

FEAST-DAY CELEBRATIONS AMONG THE NOMADIC HYBRID INHABITANTS OF URUGUAY

The gauchos of Uruguay and the Argentine pampas are for the most part half-breeds of Spanish origin on the paternal side and Indian on the maternal. Chiefly cattle-raisers of nomadic habits, they lead a strenuous, out-of-door life, subsisting almost entirely on meat, and enjoying a far-reaching reputation for hardiness and courage. Their free mode of existence and extensive practice of butchering cattle are said to have been instrumental in promoting the sanguinary violence of their politics, and they are regarded by many as an unregenerate breed, quick to display their rebellious and unmanageable spirit

Photo, Charles Rider Noble

REMNANTS OF A PRIMITIVE PEOPLE AMONG THE WHITE POPULATION OF URUGUAY

The Republic of Uruguay is the smallest in size and smallest but one in population of all the independent states of South America. Notwithstanding a slight Indian admixture, and also some negro blood, the Uruguayan population is mainly European in character. There are now only a few Indians remaining, for the state has been cleared of much of its wild blood, and is growing ever more careful in the choice of its citizens, so that "undesirables," such as negroes and some Asiatics, are being excluded. The country is well adapted for white labour, and there has been a considerable immigration from Italy and Spain

Photo, Brown Brothers

exactly the type of settler eagerly desired by the whole of the three Americas, it is well that the Banda Oriental can afford to wait.

Her biggest groups of labour are clustered far away from the capital, at Fray Bentos, where famous meat-extract and meat-canning establishments employ four or five thousand people, and at Paysandú, where the bulk of the twenty-five thousand population are likewise engaged in the meat business. The network of Uruguayan railways, and the street-car system of the capital, employ thousands of men, but as the operators of the lines are British, and a recent law compels such foreign companies to pension their employees, causes for discontent among the transport workers happily are not momentous.

European Influences in Uruguay

During golden days of prosperity and easy money the worker was prone to listen to the voice of the trained agitator ; but depression since 1920 tends to keep the labourer at his job if he is lucky enough to have one, and Uruguay is in social questions of this kind a faithful reflex of the regions from which she draws her most progressive elements. The liquid speech that strikes the ear so agreeably in any main street of Montevideo is Spanish ; the handsome church at the corner is that of the Roman form of the Christian faith, for although Uruguay has no state religion and all forms of worship are permitted, the majority of the population follows the Spanish custom ; the excellently-cut serges and tweeds of the citizens are modelled upon—if they do not actually come from—London itself.

The street-car system, rolling-stock, rails and all, arrived from Great Britain by steamer ; the docks, public services, the very streets, pavements, and the fine houses with their brilliant gardens, are repetitions in a clearer air of the economic and social suavities of Europe. The horse is here because Europe tamed the horse ; cattle and sheep because, four hundred years ago, the Spaniard was accustomed to breed cattle and sheep.

Distinctive Flavour of the Country

The first importations of livestock, brought ashore by Hernando Arias de Saavedra, in 1586, and turned loose when he failed to conquer the intrepid native and sailed away, multiplied with such extraordinary rapidity that wild herds darkened the pampas and impeded the path of explorers in the next century.

But if the modern life of Uruguay has European bases, it is nevertheless true that the country has a distinct flavour of its own that sets it apart from other countries of South America, equally in debt to Europe.

Throughout the length and breadth of the green Atlantic slope of South America there are no architectural remains of the indigenous folk found by the Spaniards ; not a single temple to whatever ancient gods were revered by the native tribes. That is the rule ; and Uruguay presents no exception. The Charrua, a semi-nomadic hunting race, built frail huts of skin and branches, wore garments of untanned hide, adorned their dark faces with the lip-plug ; smoked tobacco, probably used the bolas to chase the little wild ostrich, deer, and other game, and were fish-eaters ; they made good pottery, chipped their stone arrowheads and spearheads beautifully, and buried their dead in the earth, simply piling stones upon the graves. A typical prairie folk, they needed no permanent chiefs save in wartime, each family being ruled by its patriarch.

Montevideo, Focus of National Life

When Hernando Arias turned loose his hundred head of horned cattle, his mares and stallions, he was putting a new and splendid weapon into the hands of the " Indians " ; for the Charrua

COUNTRY FERRY CONVEYING A HEAVY CARGO ACROSS ONE OF THE NUMEROUS URUGUAYAN STREAMS

The Uruguayan country is remarkable for its grasslands. These are usually treeless, except for occasional plantations, and they sweep in long undulations or ridges, sloping down to watery hollows which mostly feed the affluents of the Uruguay river. Many of these streams, owing to the frequent torrential thunderstorms, which occur during the hot weather almost every week, swell so rapidly that in a few hours a brooklet can be transformed into a river many yards in width, the waters, however, abating as rapidly as they increase. There is little internal navigable water, and bridges are as rare as well-kept roads

SUMMER MORNING ON A BATHING BEACH OF MONTEVIDEO

Despite a high summer temperature Montevideo, situated partly on a promontory, is constantly refreshed by wholesome sea-breezes, and Pocitos and Ramirez, its seaside suburbs, are very popular resorts for visitors from far and near. Uruguay has a well-trained, armed police force; nevertheless, in the more remote districts, the traveller still finds it advisable to carry weapons

Photo, Publishers' Photo Service

speedily learned to ride the horse, and with that the whole of their tribal life was transformed. They ranged afield, beat their enemies, and were ready to wage war on more equal terms with the next shipload of Spaniards.

Against the Portuguese to the north, in Brazil, the Charrua, mounted, organized, and audacious, waged continuous and ferocious war; between 1725 and 1800 they are said to have killed four thousand Portuguese, chiefly Paulistas of the famous banderías, which began as slave-hunting expeditions against the native tribes and developed into a series of gold and diamond rushes.

Small and compact, the country is fortunate in possessing a capital that not only controls the single great mass of the population, but is the one chief channel through which flows the commerce of the country. Montevideo is the only first-class port, looking out to the broad River Plata (76 miles wide at this point); it is the head and front of all trading and financial movements; the seat of government, the fashionable watering-place for Porteños (people of Buenos Aires) as well as Orientales

FIESTA AMONG THE GAUCHOS: HIGH DAY ON THE GRASSY PLAINS OF URUGUAY

The gala days of the gauchos, marked by riotous celebrations, display nevertheless a certain deference to the Muse; tradition demanding that those of their number endowed with poetic power shall declaim at length in extravagant rhythmical language their deeds of daring. Here, in picturesque attitude and attire, the poet laureate of the moment is reciting with bombastic vigour his improvised poem, in which intrepid horsemen with lasso and bolas defy the world at large. The bolas, seen hanging from the belts of the men to the left, is a missile weapon, consisting of balls fastened to cords, and used in hunting cattle and large game

Photo, A. Carbone

themselves, and from it, like a fan, radiate all the railway lines of Uruguay.

This concentration has helped to make possible the social experiments placing Uruguay in the van of South American nations. For example, this is the only Latin American country where women have the right to vote. Laws relating to marriage and divorce are also unusually liberal as regards the woman's position. Capital punishment was abolished in 1907, but it must be noted that the duel still exists.

There is no lack of candidates for political office or for any form of governmental service, for the commercial world is only gradually gaining recruits from the old landed class ; but nowadays you will meet serious young Orientales in London and New York, studying at architectural, commercial, and engineering schools, with a view to returning to Montevideo to take up posts with established firms, or to set up for themselves.

Daily Life in the Bright Capital

The city has definite customs as regards the working hours of the day. One rises early, taking a cup of magnificent (dripped) coffee, toasted rolls, and perhaps a couple of eggs, in one's room before having a bath. The trams are busy, the pavements full of well-dressed, spruce citizens, hurrying to offices. But at noon the scene changes as if a magician had waved a wand.

All the fine shops, displaying pretty shoes, lovely dresses and jewels and quantities of imported delicacies, close their shutters and doors ; the banks and business houses follow suit, and for two or even three hours the sun-flooded streets are practically empty while the Oriental is taking his mid-day siesta after a long and elaborate lunch. During the afternoon all the shutters are opened again, but the effect of the siesta is to postpone the rush of business and shopping until six or seven o'clock.

The evening meal is postponed likewise, and you may be invited to a Montevideo house to dinner at nine, and will be lucky if you sit down to the table before ten o'clock. When it does come, the food is delicious ; it is likely to include big prawns from the bay, pickled partridges from your host's estate, huge home-grown peaches, and South American wine. The mineral water comes, too, from a Uruguayan spring. Table talk will be lively, for while every Uruguayan countryman is an extemporary poet, a clever strummer upon the guitar, this gift is translated in the capital into ready conversational wit, and, in the politician, into an astonishing talent for magniloquent oratory.

Honour Paid to Literature

I believe that it is still true in South America that poets have more power than the politicians ; this tendency to exalt the author of the brilliant written word was never more clearly exemplified than at the funeral of the Uruguayan writer, Enrique Rodó. Rodó died in Italy, and his body was brought back to Montevideo with regal honours. No less than kingly, too, were the funeral ceremonies.

Dense crowds crammed the streets from wall to wall, and not only did the President and the Ministers and all the eminent Orientales walk bareheaded behind Rodó's coffin, but all foreign diplomats added their homage. Eloquent speeches flowed from every gifted Uruguayan tongue, and all the newspapers—and Uruguay has a considerable press—were filled with portraits of the dead literato and excerpts from his work.

Two Aspects of the Banda Oriental

Nothing could have brought home more forcibly the fact that there are two main aspects of the Banda Oriental. There is the new, lively, intellectual life of the capital, and there is, its permanent strength and shield, the widespread, fertile, sun- and dew-drenched prairie, creator of the basic Uruguayan type to-day as it was four hundred years ago.

SURVIVORS OF THE OLD CHARRUA RACE OF SOUTH AMERICAN INDIANS

Charrua strains still exist in Uruguay and South Brazil. Of Guaycuru stock, these Indians formerly occupied Entre Rios, whence they raided Uruguay. They have abandoned bows and arrows for fire-arms and the horse, but still wear their typical head-band and raw-hide shoes. The shawl draped round the man's waist, from which is suspended the bolas, a hunting weapon, is woven on native looms

Photo, A. Carbone

Uruguay

II. The Story of "La Banda Oriental"

By W. H. Koebel

Author of "Uruguay," "The South Americans," etc.

WHEN the intrepid explorer-adventurer, Juan Diaz de Solis, effected his first landing (in 1512) upon Uruguayan soil, he found it inhabited, and himself bitterly opposed, by the warlike tribe of Charrua Indians, who slew him and a number of his men. In 1527, Cabot's lieutenant Ramon was worsted by the Charrua, who in 1603 cut to pieces a little army led by Saavedra. So strenuous was the resistance offered by the Indians that it was not until the middle of the seventeenth century that the Spaniards began to make headway in Uruguay.

For some time thereafter Spaniards and Portuguese strove for the mastery, until in 1726 the Viceroy Zavala, of Buenos Aires, founded and established his headquarters at Montevideo. In 1750 the province was declared independent of Buenos Aires, and in 1777 Portuguese rivalry was crushed by the destruction of their settlement of Colombia, and by the treaty of Ildefonso (October 1, 1777).

Great Britain having been at war with the Spanish for some time, a British force under General Auchmuty attacked Montevideo in 1806-7, the plan being for a general onslaught upon Spain's possessions in South America. The British naval force cooperating with Auchmuty was commanded by Admiral Sir C. Stirling. The troops were landed in the neighbourhood of Montevideo on January 18, 1807. Six thousand Spanish troops defended the place, which was, however, brilliantly carried by assault on February 2, and the British remained in possession until May, when General Whitelocke superseded Auchmuty. Whitelocke, now in command of 12,000 troops, squandered them in the attempt to take Buenos Aires. By a treaty of July 7, 1807, the remnant of Whitelocke's force was transported back to Montevideo, which it evacuated a few weeks later.

Through Revolt to Independence

Argentina's declaration of independence from Spanish rule (May 23, 1810) involved Uruguay's incorporation in the "United Provinces of Rio de la Plata." The Spaniards still retained Montevideo, though defeated by José de Artigas in 1811; but the city fell in 1814, when General Alvear assailed it from the landward side, while the Irish adventurer, Admiral Brown, destroyed the Spanish fleet.

Brazil attacked Uruguay two years later, and in 1821 succeeded in annexing it as the "Provincia Cisplatina." But in 1825 thirty-three Uruguayan exiles from Buenos Aires, led by Lavajella, inaugurated a successful revolt. While Brown made short work of the Brazilian fleet, her army was routed at Ituzaingo, and Brazil and Argentina recognized Uruguayan independence in a treaty signed at Montevideo (August 27, 1828). José Rondeau was appointed Governor and a constitution promulgated. General Rivera was chosen President, and he exterminated the Charrua Indians in 1832. But civil war prevailed from 1835. Manuel Oribe rebelled, and invoked the cooperation of Juan Manuel Rosas, the Dictator of Buenos Aires.

Revolution and Counter-Revolution

In 1843, Rosas and Oribe proclaimed a rigid closure of the Uruguay and Paraná rivers to all foreigners. This high-handed procedure proved entirely inacceptable to Great Britain and France, who determined to reopen the waterway by force. The British Admiral Inglefield was placed in command of a Franco-British squadron. Rosas' inadequate naval forces were led by Admiral Brown, whose squadron was destroyed by the allies (August, 1845), and the San Martin added to the French navy.

Admiral Inglefield's fleet then ascended to Uruguay, to find that at Obligado the Dictator had blocked the fairway by means of a huge boom, supported by formidable batteries on the banks. The allies attacked and conquered these defences, November 20, 1845. Boats' crews succeeded in destroying the boom, landing-parties destroyed the forts, and the Uruguayan ship Republicano was blown up.

Nevertheless, the blockade of Montevideo endured from 1843 to 1852, when the northern boundary of Uruguay was settled by treaty with Brazil. The struggle between the two factions of the "Blancos" (Whites), of whom Oribe was the leader, and the "Colorados" (Reds) went on for years. From 1864 to 1870 President Flores, who then ruled Uruguay, was engaged, in alliance with Brazil and

Argentina, in a war of extermination against Lopez, the Dictator of Paraguay.

All this time the Republic was on the verge of insolvency. President Ellauri was overthrown in 1875 by General Latorre. The latter proclaimed Dr. Varela as Dictator, but was tempted to nominate himself President in 1876. Four years later Latorre was compelled to resign, and for two years (1880-82) Dr. Vidal officiated as head of the state. The Colorado General Santos now assumed power, but proved so tyrannical in his methods that an army was organized for his overthrow. This force was defeated on the banks of the Rio Negro. But eventually his own partisans un-seated Santos. His immediate successor was another soldier, General Tages. In 1890 Tages retired in favour of the civilian Herrera y Obes, who proved utterly unscrupulous, suspended the public debt, and staffed all the public departments with adherents of his own. Idiarte Borda became President (1894) on the nomination of the Colorado party, but turned out almost as unscrupulous as his predecessor. Aparicio Saraiva, a Blanco, placed himself at the head of a movement for his overthrow in 1896-97, and on August 25, 1897, President Borda was assassinated at Montevideo by one Arrendo. After the delay of a couple

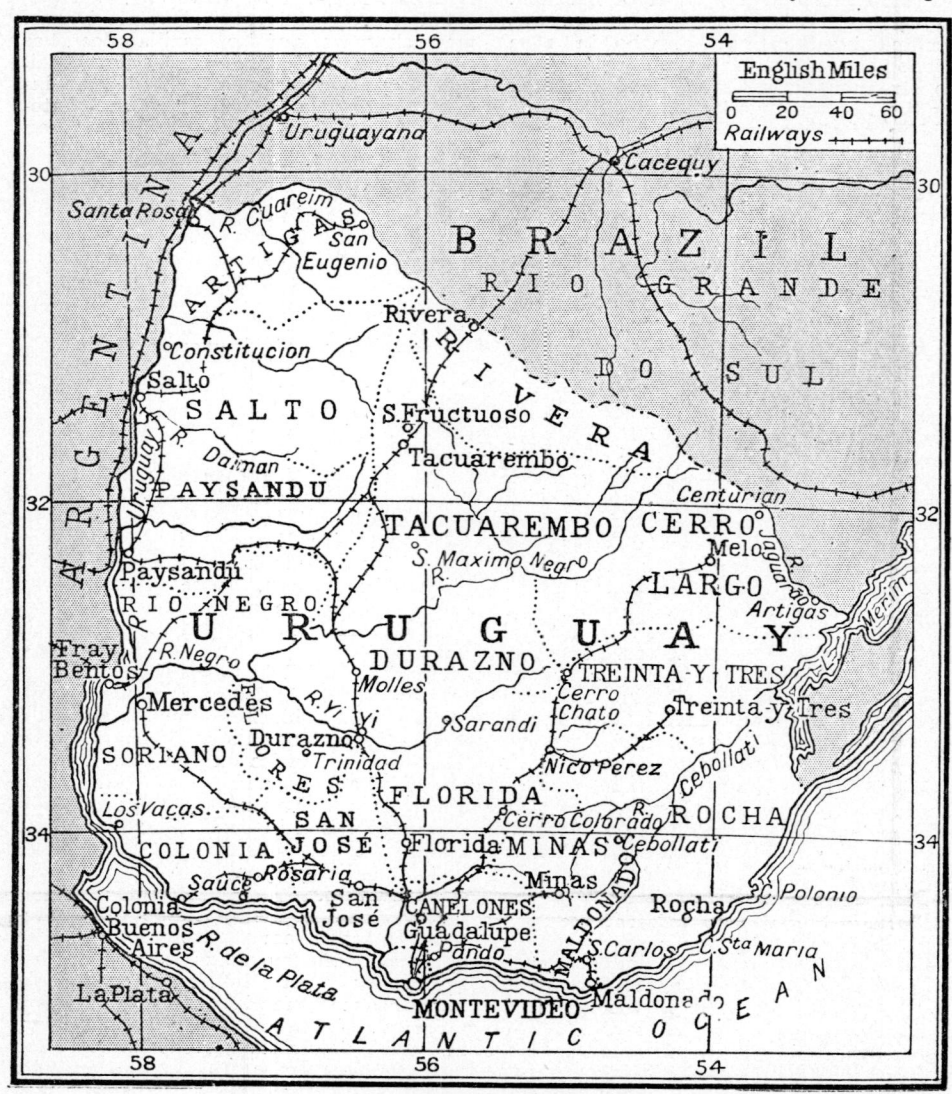

THE REPUBLIC OF URUGUAY

CATTLE ON THE WAY TO THE STOCKYARDS AT MONTEVIDEO

Apart from the enormous meat-preserving industries, the exportation of live animals has greatly increased the foreign trade of Uruguay in recent years, and many by-products of the meat business, such as hides, tallow, and wool, are numbered among the exports. Even the horses are turned to account after death ; the hoofs yield glue, the bones bone-ash, and the skins are sent abroad

of years in bringing him to trial, the murderer was sentenced to two years' imprisonment on the ground that it was a political crime.

Juan Cuestas, as President of the Senate, then assumed presidential powers. He adopted a policy of conciliation, including an amnesty for all engaged in the late revolt, and even a monetary allowance to cover the insurgents' " expenses." He also took measures for placing the distracted country upon an improved commercial and financial basis.

In February, 1898, however, Cuestas proclaimed himself dictator and dissolved the Chambers. He resigned office in the following year, to be re-elected president on March 1, 1899. A murder-plot against him failed in 1903, when a fresh civil war was inaugurated. It continued for some months, until the mortal wounding of the revolutionary leader, Saraiva, after which peace was proclaimed.

Dr. Claudio Williman's term of office (1907-11) was comparatively uneventful. On his resignation, the Colorado party brought about the election of José Battle, and the rival factions had resort to arms once more. It was understood that President Battle favoured a Constitution for Uruguay on lines approximating those on which that of the federal Republic of Switzerland is based.

He was still in office when, in August, 1914, the Great War commenced. President Battle's attitude was consistently anti-German from the outset, and his policy was confirmed by his successor, Dr. Feliciano Viera, 1915. In 1919, Dr. Baltasar Brum was elected president.

URUGUAY : FACTS AND FIGURES

The Country

A continuation of the great grass-covered, treeless plain of the Argentine pampa occupies all Uruguayan territory. The surface is undulating and well watered. Climate is subject to sudden drops in temperature owing to cold and violent wind from the south-west, but is otherwise well suited to Europeans. Main rivers are the Uruguay and its tributaries, the Negro and Daiman, but save on the first navigation is little developed. Total area about 72,150 square miles ; estimated population 1,495,000.

Government and Constitution

Legislative authority in hands of a Senate and Chamber of Representatives, which together form the Parliament and meet annually. Senators, one for each department and elected for six years, are chosen by the members of an Electoral College who are themselves elected by popular vote. Members of the Chamber are elected for three years by male suffrage, ability to read and write being an essential of the right to the franchise. During intervals in the sessions a committee of five representatives and two senators form the executive. Ordinarily, executive power is exercised by the President, elected for four years by popular vote, and a National Administrative Council of nine members.

Commerce and Industries

Stock-raising carried on over 60 per cent. of the total area. Wheat, corn, and oats are produced, while grapes, tobacco, and olives are cultivated. Gold is worked, and deposits of lignite coal, magnesium, silver, and copper have been found. In 1922 imports reached a value of £8,169,645 and exports £14,298,831. Foodstuffs, hardware, and fuel are important imports, while meat and extracts, wool, hides, live animals, and agricultural products are the chief exports. Standard coin, the peso ; nominal value 4·70 pesos = £1.

PACK-DONKEYS LADEN WITH COUNTRY MERCHANDISE PASSING THROUGH A STREET OF CARÁCAS

Carácas, the capital of Venezuela, lies in a beautiful mountain-girt valley watered by the river Guaire and nearly 3,000 feet above sea-level. Sugar and coffee plantations surround the city which, owing to its altitude, enjoys a moderate temperature, and claims to be the most perfectly and salubriously situated of all the South American capitals. The narrow streets are paved with cobbles in the centre part of the city, in the centre with cement, and lined by one-storeyed houses which usually turn their blind side to the street, the barred windows and stuccoed walls suggesting little of the comfortable and even luxurious quarters behind them

Venezuela

I. The "Little Venice" of the Caribbean

By L. E. Elliott

Author of "Brazil, To-day and To-morrow," etc.

THE front door of the Republic of Venezuela is the Caribbean port of La Guayra. There are such side doors as Puerto Cabello, from which you can connect by train with the capital, pretty Carácas, in its upland valley, and there are isolated out-buildings, as it were, such as the new and enormously developing Maracaibo region, and there is the huge back door of the Orinoco's mouth, leading to the up-river town of Ciudad Bolivar and the vast little-known llanos (plains) of Apure and the huge southward-bending area of Amazonas.

La Guayra (a "guaira," by the way, is a beacon fire set upon a hilltop) presents an unchanging face in every season. The steamer manœuvres close to the wall of dark-red, sweltering rock, upon whose feet the narrow streets of the port run, steep and precarious and dirty. The sea is deep and blue against this mountain barrier, and the sun, all the year round, beats down upon the winding town and is reflected back from the crimson rock. Everybody of consequence wears white clothes, and the poorer folk tread, barefoot, the cobblestones of the tilted ways, jostling the mules.

La Guayra Gay with Flowers

The well-to-do, and certainly all the foreigners engaged in business pursuits, dwell in airy houses, with the living rooms often placed upon the second floor, the first being devoted to offices. These houses are built of wood, with heavy red-tiled roofs; the rooms are enormously large and rendered cool by wide balconies, numbers of unglazed windows, and a series of connecting doors which guarantee the utilisation of every faint breeze. Gay flowers, the pretty pink coralillo vine and the viuda alegre's delicate mauve, the daring patchwork of the crotons and the scarlet blaze of hibiscus, the long trail of bougainvillea, adorn every balcony.

When Drake Fought the Spanish Don

A mile or so to the eastward, along the slender strip of shore, lies the pretty watering-place, Macuto. A motor-car, driven by a Venezolano with a bush of black hair and the usual Latin-American passion for rapid transit, carries you along the uneven coast road to a cool hotel and a bathing beach; on the way you pass the four-square white house, inside high walls draped with brilliant flowering vines, where in Kingsley's "Westward Ho!" the Spanish don held the "Rose of Torridge" a prisoner.

From La Guayra runs the railway up to Carácas. There are two other ways; first, the splendid motor road that winds more steeply down the sides of the mountains, skirting precipices and ravines; and, second, the most dizzy route of all, that is nothing but a clambering footpath. According to a very likely tradition, it was up this goat-path that Drake climbed with his band of sailors in Elizabeth's day; it was a Spaniard of Carácas who acted as guide and betrayed his town into the hands of the English invaders. Drake hanged him for his trouble.

The railroad is a fine piece of mountain engineering, and as the train ascends and the fresher air of the hills is reached, you look out of the window and down upon bare purple-red rocky shoulders, with sparse verdure in clefts, and an emerald strip on the shore

DARK-EYED DAUGHTER OF LATIN AMERICA

The houses of the Spanish population of Carácas are usually built in similar fashion to those in their Mother Country. The windows are barred, and a private patio, or court, affords a delightful rendezvous for family gatherings

Photo, Publishers' Photo Service

thickets of bamboo, splendid mahogany and ceiba trees hung with a score of tillandsias and lianes, and beds of roses and lilies.

A string of houses edges the slope of the hills, their private gardens running up at a sharp angle. Many are sumptuously adorned, in a land where gay pictures may be painted on the exterior wall and suffer no damage. For one of these, standing a little back from the road behind tropical foliage, the visitor will spare a curious glance, for this is the palacio built for his pleasure by Cipriano Castro, that dictator of Venezuela who once upon a time defied the Powers, and upon another occasion got together an army to march upon the United States by land. All the flooring of this palacio was specially made of fine tiles with the entwined initials " C.C."

As a result of the modern policy of highway construction, in the dry season the traveller may go right across the huge territory of Venezuela from La Guayra to Ciudad Bolivar by motor-car, in less than four days. From the beginning of the rains, about the middle of May, until December, interior Venezuela is no place for the visitor; water descends in a solid sheet, the plains are blotted out, the roads are roaring cataracts. But in the dry season the fertile country teems with wild life, and the Venezuelan reaps his harvest without the slightest fear of a troubled sky.

No better example of the fine high-roads built of late years and their effect

where a patch of soil gives foothold to a grove of coconuts.

There is not so much as a village perched in the hills between the port and the capital, but Carácas itself is placed in a narrow and lovely vale with a delicious perennial-spring climate. The whole strip is a garden of flowers and birds, with white and pink and blue houses set in this blossomy frame. Every afternoon, when the sun is sinking behind the hills, it is the custom for the citizens to drive, ride, or even walk, along the beautiful stretch of gardens that border the valley, the Paraiso, which is covered with great

upon the enterprising farmer, can be seen than that between Carácas and Maracay. It plunges out into the green, hilly country westward from Carácas, rising to an altitude of 4,000 feet at one breezy spot, Los Teques, frequently skirting the precipitous sides of mountains and dipping to delicious green valleys. All this road is dotted with rich sugar estates, the red-tiled houses nestled among a sea of waving emerald.

It is an all-day run between Carácas and Maracay, and the warm, scented dusk of the little town is illuminated by a blaze of electric lights in the flowery plaza. All the houses are painted with pink or blue or some other delicate colour, the pavements are of stone mosaic, the roads asphalted, and although the residence here of the President is but one storey in height, it is equipped with such modern conveniences as electric fans and telephones.

On the model farm of General Gomez at Maracay, splendid cattle of British breeding fill the beautifully planned and kept stables; at the aerodrome a score of French planes form the nucleus of the military aviation schools. There

STREET IN CARÁCAS SHOWING PREVALENT STYLE OF ARCHITECTURE

Earthquakes are frequent in Carácas, and a terrible shock practically destroyed the city in 1812. The houses, therefore, are low, with strong adobe walls, and there being little or no need of fires for warmth, chimneys are seldom seen. Though alike in style, the houses are relieved of monotony by their colouring, and the red-tile roofs are singularly effective against the mountain background

COMMON MODE OF TRAVEL IN THE MOUNTAINS OF VENEZUELA

The roads of Venezuela are rarely worthy of the name; with the exception of a few high-roads, only bridle-paths are available to the traveller, and these are often of very indifferent quality and some are scarcely passable for mud. The donkey is the chief pack-animal, and is often seen carrying not only country produce and its own provender, but its master as well

Photo, Publishers' Photo Service

is a big wireless installation, which enables Venezuela to speak with points all over the Caribbean. The military hospital is a perfect copy of a European model. A paper factory makes pulp from the rushes growing thickly about the margin of Lake Valencia, a large and lovely sheet of water, dotted with islands, ringed with villages, that lies a stone's throw from Maracay. From a highway running northward to the Caribbean, upon a mountain crest three thousand feet above sea-level, shaded with enormous tropical trees festooned with orchids and climbing ferns, you look down a sweeping declivity to the blue, sparkling bay of Ocumare.

All this Maracay region is a centre of efficiency, typical of the ease with which modern equipment and up-to-date public services can create a new atmosphere in South American towns. Water-power is plentiful, and since the coal-beds of South America have only in a few instances served for public utilities, and the making of gas for illuminating purposes is limited, upon the whole continent, to towns whose number can be counted upon one hand, the installation of electric systems is simplicity itself. The house built of adobe—dried mud brick—with a tiled or thatched roof, the home-made dip candle, the cooking fire of charcoal or sticks, is readily scrapped in exchange for reinforced cement, electric lamps and electric cookers, just as human labour is exchanged for the Diesel engine, or long line transmission.

Before Ronald Ross discovered the guilt of the mosquito as a fever carrier, all the Caribbean margin was a hot-bed of such virulent diseases as yellow and blackwater fevers ; La Guayra was a pest-hole and the sister ports only less dangerous in proportion to their diminished size. But to-day, with the vigorous operation of sanitary services, the worst of the fever plagues have been banished, and careful measures are being taken to reduce infant mortality, to check contagious diseases by vaccination and inoculation, and to raise the standard of public health by

VENEZUELAN WATER-CARRIER STARTS HIS ROUNDS

In the streets of Venezuelan cities cooling " refrescos " are seldom lacking, and inviting drinks concocted from delicious fruits are refreshing, though not always effective thirst-quenchers. On his patient beast—almost every burden is borne by donkeys in Venezuela—the water-carrier makes his rounds, and has many customers, for in the torrid climate a glass of cold water is a boon

Photo, Publishers' Photo Service

regular inspection of foodstuffs and milk. Too much credit cannot be given to the Venezuelan, Dr. Chacin Itriago, trained in England and formerly the head of a department in St. Bartholomew's Hospital in London, for the creation of these nation-wide services in Venezuela. In so far as it is possible to counteract the result of an insouciant negro element in the coastal towns, and

House, and there is also a yield to official pockets, for any flaw which can be detected in the invoice of goods brought into the country results in such goods being impounded without redress, and the hawk-eyed individual who discovers the error receives a half-share of the value.

The bolivar, the national unit of currency in Venezuela, takes its name

BASKETS IN THE MAKING AMONG THE WAIOMGOMO INDIANS

Only in two regions of Venezuela are the aboriginal inhabitants still living in conformity with their traditional habits and racial customs ; these are along the north-eastern frontier and in the Guayana forests ; elsewhere, the Indian element has been almost absorbed into the Spanish-speaking Venezuelan nation. The forest provides food, clothing, and utensils

of a persistently hot climate, Venezuela has benefited enormously from the last few years of trained attention to civic sanitation.

Work such as this, and the construction of the far-reaching network of roads, demands a good deal of money, and in Venezuela the government revenues are mainly obtained from indirect taxation—that is, from export and import dues and from internal dues upon sugar, tobacco and alcoholic liquors.

Nearly two-thirds of the national revenues have their origin in the Custom

from that Venezuelan-born soldier of fortune, the Libertador of the Independence struggle, Simon Bolivar, who, having seen Napoleon enter Paris on one occasion during the Corsican's heyday, became imbued with the same grandiose schemes ; you will see in Carácas the house where he was brought up, with some delightful colonial period furniture, and you may see upon the walls of a government hall some rather excruciating paintings of the glorious victories obtained over the Mother Country ; and, seeing these, you may

BALLING COTTON IN A SETTLEMENT OF VENEZUELAN ABORIGINES

The settlements of the Waiomgomo Indians, scattered about the vast dense forests of Guayana, are sometimes little more than a collection of miserable huts consisting chiefly of thatched roofs on supports, but providing, nevertheless, shelters for numbers of primitive creatures to whom they stand for home. Hand-made hammocks, earthenware pots, and calabashes lie promiscuously about the earth floor

MAKING ARROWS: PRIMITIVE PASTIME OF A PRIMITIVE PEOPLE

The Waiomgomo Indians, a branch of the Caribs, still inhabit their original haunts around the river Caura. In the more fertile regions they cultivate miniature plantations, while in some of the higher forest land the collecting of the odoriferous tonka bean constitutes their chief industry. They generally shun civilization, caring nothing for its comforts and conveniences

with, imported commodities ; it is cheap for those who make the country provide them with all they need. The contrast between Venezuelan houses, built, for example, in the airy upland capital and upon the margin of Lake Maracaibo, displays a difference that is one of kind rather than of degree.

The Carácas residence lies not within the city, but a mile or so outside in a garden suburb developed during the last few years, approached by a charming flower-hung road. A broad motor-car drive runs up to the open front door, giving access to a wide, awning-shaded veranda and the cool rooms of the lower floor. Everybody has a car. Much of the population is of pure Spanish blood.

Here, on such an occasion as a children's party, you appreciate the constancy with which Latin America

A LAKE DWELLER
Dull, heavy faces are common among the women of the Indian races who live in pile dwellings around Lake Maracaibo

remember, if you happen to have seen it, the old farmhouse among the banana groves of Santa Marta in Colombia, where the disillusioned Libertador ended an embittered life, exiled and overthrown by the very people for whom he had done so much, and among whom he had posed as a semi-divine hero.

Speaking generally, life is expensive in Venezuela for those who eat and drink, wear, and furnish their dwellings

WOMEN OF THE MAQUIRITARE TRIBE
Near relatives of, if not identical with, the Waiomgomo, the Maquiritare occupy remote parts of the hinterland of Guayana. Convention makes little or no demand upon them and a practical absence of dress is one of their tribal characteristics

looks across the seas to Western Europe, for all the little guests are dressed like delightful bisque-china dolls in French clothes ; their manners are quite beautiful, and they dance gaily among the pink silk chairs. The parents, arriving in the glowing dusk to take away their offspring, are not the formal folk of Spanish tradition, by which the women are still all but secluded. There is an atmosphere of freedom and comradeship and a frank interchange of thoughts and ideas between the sexes that speak eloquently of new ways.

It is true that you must drink liqueur with your tea, and that there are more extravagant sweets than you are accustomed to see, that the crystal-clear Spanish idiom is in your ears ; but there is nothing " foreign " here ; this

IN WORKADAY GARB

Short lengths of coarse material, or aprons of palm fibre, are the everyday garb worn by the aboriginal Indians of Venezuela

is society that conforms to the pleasant international standard. The parents of your hosts live in the city, in an " old " (i.e. 50 to 100 years old) house upon one floor; the heavily grilled windows open on to a main street, the enormous saguan door leads, through a wide opening, to the inside patio—a courtyard full of flowering shrubs with a pila playing in the middle; a veranda runs all about this patio, with

CONSERVATISM IN THE BACKWOODS

In his forest-clad habitat, surrounded by the solitudes of the Guayana jungle, the Waiomgomo fosters the beliefs and customs of his pagan ancestors, finding their inefficient ways of life more comfortable than those prescribed by white civilization

every room of the four-square house opening on it.

Beyond, a second patio is surrounded by the kitchen and the servants' quarters. With the saguan door barred, this is a fort, or rather, it follows the mode of Oriental houses constructed for the seclusion of women, the mode that the Moors carried to Spain, and that Spain carried to South America four hundred years ago.

No climate could be sweeter than that of Carácas. But for white races none could be more pernicious than that of Maracaibo. Here, along a green, mosquito-haunted, heavily-hot coast, is an enormous lagoon, entered by none but small vessels because the sand-bar across its mouth prohibits ships of any considerable draught. Early Spanish explorers, discovering this bay, saw the same oddly built native houses that you may still find, perched above the margins of the water upon thin, shaky wooden legs, and constructed of wood and palm-thatch.

A primitive ladder, consisting sometimes of nothing more than a stout, notched bamboo pole, leads to this crow's nest, and it was the sight of these lake-dwellings that gave the region the ironical name of Venezuela—" Little Venice." Cassava root, plantains, beans and fish form the staple foods, the hammock is the chief article of furniture, and the villagers inherit much of the blood of the real natives of the country, those implacable " Indians " whose immense bows and poisoned arrows are still feared by the traveller who ventures into the deep interior.

To-day these lake dwellers look down upon scenes of activity that bid fair to affect the life of all Venezuela. For it has been discovered that the great oil belt that lies all across the north of South America, from exterior islands such as Barbados to promontories in Ecuador, has formed huge deposits in the Maracaibo region. For years a keen competition between rival great companies has been fought upon

SULTRY AFTERNOON IN THE MAIN STREET OF PUERTO CABELLO
Puerto Cabello, lying to the west of La Guayra, the port of Carácas, is practically at sea-level and is extremely hot. It has a considerable export trade and its harbour is one of the best in Venezuela; even the name, meaning Hair Port, was bestowed by the Spaniards to signify that a ship could be held with a hair in its tranquil waters

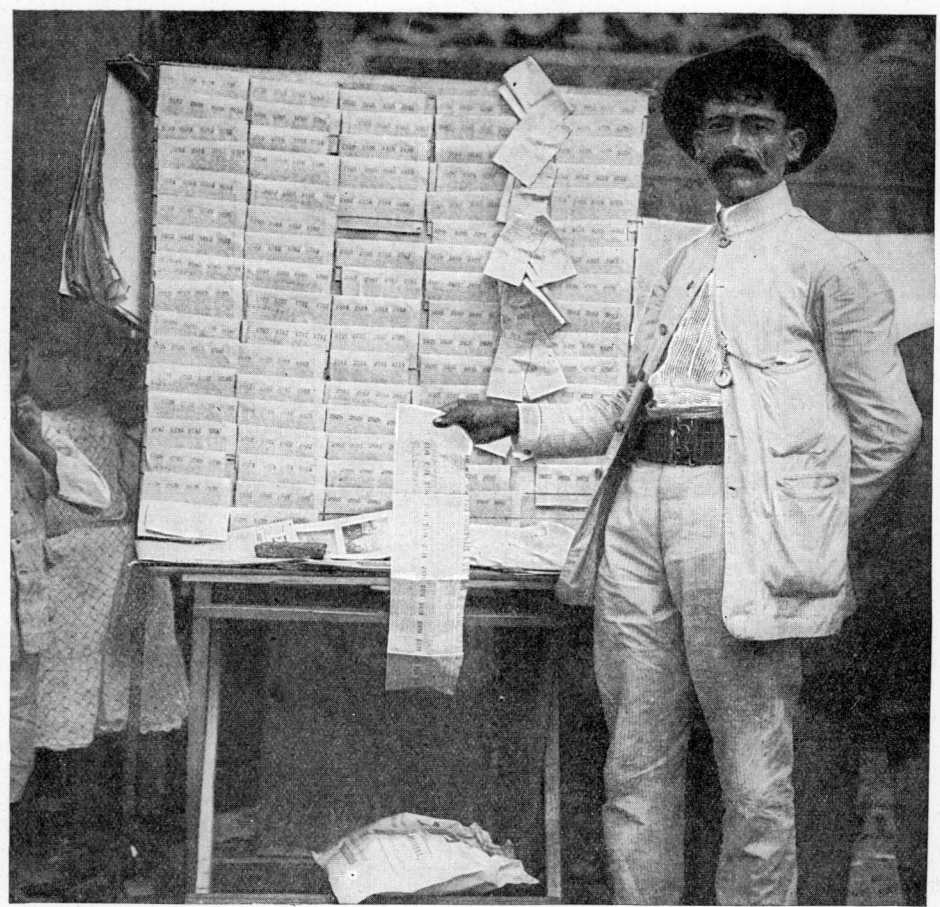

LOTTERY TICKETS FOR THE MANY, LUCKY TICKETS FOR THE FEW

Large public gambling schemes are in vogue in many of the cities of South America. Some governments have suppressed them as being injurious to the public good, while other legislatures authorise
lotteries in order to devote their proceeds to public improvements. In Venezuela these games of chance
are very popular and at La Guayra there is a church which was built by the sale of lottery tickets
Photo, Publishers' Photo Service

this sweltering soil. All over the heat-
hazed swamps near the lagoon, armies of
geologists and engineers and road-makers
have been brought in; thousands of tons
of machinery, endless loads of construction material, carried into the bush and
brought into service. Huge territories
as big as Balkan kingdoms have been
surveyed, probed, made to yield their
underground stores of oil. Ten years
of preparatory work and four or five
millions of pounds sterling have paved
the way for the stream of petroleum
just commencing.

One thousand Venezuelans are
labourers in this field, and the native-

born, dark-skinned, dark-eyed, part
Indian, part negro, with a dash of
Spanish, has accustomed himself to
regular hours and sustained toil.
Wherever, in the colonial period, land
was found suitable for sugar-cane crops,
African slaves were imported, and the
gregarious negro is still clustered in the
same spots. He works as readily in
the oil-fields as upon agricultural lands,
and when you see him engaged in half a
score of other occupations in Veneuzela
you cannot deny his versatility.

In the miasmic swamp of Lake
Bermudez the men work up to their
waists in water, digging out the oozy

asphalt ; just across a strip of sea from the port of Cumaná is the pretty island of Margarita, where pearl-divers fetch up gems to the value of half a million bolivares annually ; in the dry zones the collectors of the divi-divi pods, for tanning, fill thousands of sacks ; the cocoa and coffee plantations call for another class of skill. Near Carúpano is a copra and coir factory ; in the deep forest near Ciudad Bolivar on the Orinoco are the gatherers of balata (rubber), and of the chicle used for chewing-gum.

Profitable Egret Plumes

The fearless riders of the llanos, those wide plains which are only equalled by the pampas of Argentina, are expert cattlemen ; there is the nucleus of a mercantile marine in the Venezuelan owned and operated steamship line which has the monopoly of navigation of the river Orinoco, and there is a unique occupation of certain interior regions near water—that of the men who tend the garzeros.

The garza is a bird of the heron family yielding the dainty white feathers known as egrets, grown and shed in the breeding season. These birds come annually to well-known open, watered areas in such numbers that the ground is white as snow when they settle, and the locality, the garzero, is defined by law and patrolled by armed watchers for the birds' protection. The same authorised guards collect the dropped feathers at the end of the season ; any man found selling the feathers without a licence is sent to gaol.

Religion and Strong Family Ties

The Venezuelan, apart from the civic centres, is a tough, open-air, individual, temperate, inclined to piety, accustomed to the lack of many comforts which are necessities in other climes. The part that women play in Venezuelan affairs, whether in a beautiful house in Carácas or a hut on a river bank, is purely domestic ; the woman worker is practically unknown, and the feminist movement in Venezuela is not perceptible.

The hold of the Roman Catholic church is strong upon the womenfolk and they are as a rule perfectly contented with the interests of their large families. Here, as in many other parts of South America, relatives have a close call upon each other, and there is no out-of-work member of a family who cannot transfer his hammock and his wife and offspring to the house of a cousin or uncle, sure of receiving a welcome until he gets another job, when he will probably receive in like manner half a dozen relatives of his spouse.

With two chief exceptions, the centres of population of Venezuela are clustered close to the Caribbean. They are ports, with their backs to the vast national territory. Here is the asphalt port, Cristobal Colon ; Guanta, shipping coal from the state-owned mines ; Puerto Cabello, with its British-owned frozen-meat factory, drawing supplies from the cattle plains ; Maracaibo, sending out sugar and oil, and Colombia's coffee from the Bucaramanga region ; La Guayra, doing the chief business of the country ; La Vela, Cumanà, Carùpano, shipping coconut fibre and copra and pearls and the famous rum, the ron anciado sold in every cantina.

Damp and Deadly Hinterland

Behind lies a huge region, with great areas of water-threaded forest that are almost as they were in the Stone Age, where the trader seeking supplies of serrapia (tonka beans) and balata rubber takes to the river roads, in native piragua or curial (dug-out), his life in his hands. He fears the ubiquitous biting insects of the sweltering, encompassing forest as much as he fears the blow-gun and the curare poison of the wild Ventuari Indians ; he risks death in the many cataracts of the Orinoco's tributaries, or in an encounter with the caiman (alligator) that infests these banks. The headquarters of this trading is the odd river-port of Ciudad Bolivar, situate three hundred miles from the Orinoco's mouth and fifty miles above the junction of the Caroni, that runs from the south and the legend-haunted mountains of Pacaraima; wood-built, cobble-paved, electric-lit, the town lies steeply on the river bank, a precarious, jungle-surrounded stronghold, where gambling runs high and lives are cheap.

The llanos, the cattle plains where the gauchos are bred, and the fine hilly country from which the rivers run, form another world. The trading centre for the stock-breeder of the plains is San Fernando de Apure, far removed from gracious, bedecked, Europeanised Carácas by more than mileage.

With a population of about seven persons to each square mile Venezuela will be for many generations a "new" country, with plenty of room to grow; so new, indeed is she, that only now are her boundaries being definitely inscribed. With Brazil and with British Guiana a definite conclusion was reached last century; but the question with Colombia has only recently been settled two commissions of Swiss experts.

The country is divided into three separate zones: the mountainous, the plain, and the forest region. Of these, the first is formed by an arm of the Andes range which passes through Trujillo and Tachira, and along the sea-line to the Paria peninsula; the region of the plains extends to the margin of the giant Orinoco river; and the forest area from the right bank of that river to the frontier of Brazil. In the first the climate is very variable, from cold to salubrious; in the second it is for the most part warm and healthy; and in the forests, tropical and unhealthy. The chief mountain peaks are the Sierra Nevada (16,437 feet), Naiguata and Maraguata. Volcanoes are absent, but thermal springs exist.

CLEANING ORCHIDS IN A FOREST OF TROPICAL VENEZUELA
Venezuela lies wholly within the tropics, and fully one half of the country is forest, penetrable only with considerable difficulty. These dense forests, much choked with undergrowth, abound in wild life, and among the exuberant tangled greenery orchids flourish abundantly. Here the orchid-lover can find numerous fantastic flowers in glowing and exquisite colours

Venezuela

II. Chequered Story of a Latin Republic

By W. H. Koebel

Author of "The South Americans," "Central America," etc.

THE Venezuelan coast was discovered by Columbus on August 1, 1498, and explored in the following year by Alonso de Ojeda, who gave the country the name of "Little Venice," from the fact that on one of the inlets he discovered a village built on piles.

Venezuela became the Captaincy-general of Carácas, and the Spanish conquest was complete by A.D. 1600. The country was administered by a succession of viceroys for about two centuries, ending with Vicente Emparan. On April 19, 1810, this official was deposed by Simon Bolivar, himself a native of Carácas. The Declaration of Independence was issued in that city on July 5, 1811, and a decade of warfare with the Spanish power ensued. This was ended by Bolivar's great victory of Carabobo (June 24, 1821), though

Spain did not formally acknowledge Venezuela's independence until 1845. A Republican Constitution was enacted on June 13, 1814.

For some years Venezuela constituted, with Colombia and Ecuador, the Republic of Colombia; but, largely owing to the influence of General José Paez, the Venezuelans broke away from the union in 1829 to become a separate Republic. Paez was practically dictator from 1830 to 1849, in which year he was expelled by General José Tadeo Monagas. The latter, with his brother José Gregorio, ruled the country until 1858, one of their decrees enacting the abolition of native slavery (1854).

Their overthrow was the signal for civil war, and General Juan Falcón established himself as dictator (1863-68). His regime

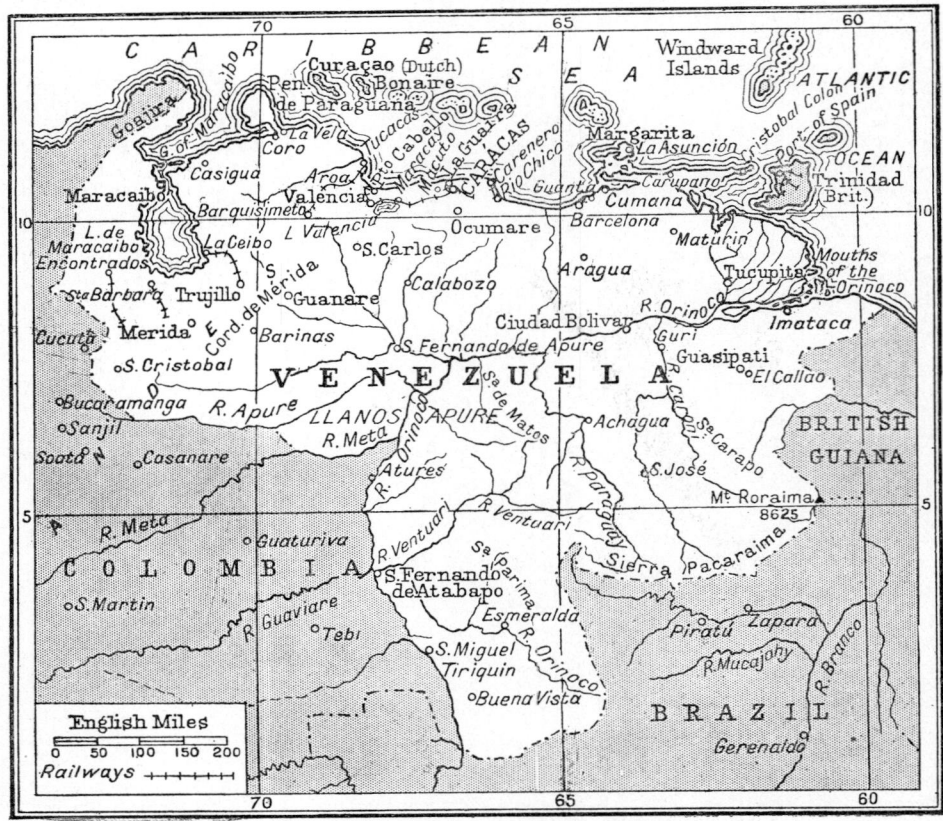

THE REPUBLIC OF VENEZUELA

was one of misgovernment and bloodshed until his expulsion. In 1869 Antonio Guzman Blanco established himself as dictator, and his rule lasted for twenty years. He contrived that a partisan of his own should always be returned to the presidential chair, until in 1889 a counter-revolution broke out. Blanco and his own nominee, Rojas Paul, were driven out, and a popular election returned Andueza Palacio as president.

A partial reform of the constitution included the extension of the presidential term from two to four years. In an attempt to apply this extension to himself, Palacio came into conflict with a faction headed by General Crespo as president for four years. His term of office was chiefly memorable for a serious dispute with Great Britain.

For many years the frontiers of British Guiana and Venezuela had been in dispute, and in 1895 matters culminated in the arrest by Venezuelan officials of two British Guiana police officers. Following this, President Crespo invoked the assistance of the United States in any possible quarrel with Great Britain, and the American President (Grover Cleveland) informed Congress, in a message of December 18, 1895, that any attempt by England to settle the boundary problem without arbitration would be regarded seriously by the U.S. government.

This declaration was the cause of intense excitement in Venezuela, where a boycott of British goods was declared and diplomatic relations were broken off. Relations were resumed in 1897, and two years later the boundary question was settled by arbitration and an indemnity paid by Venezuela to the arrested British Guiana officials. Meanwhile, an attempt to overthrow Crespo, instigated by Blanco's old partisan, Rojas Paul, was frustrated

in 1895 after considerable bloodshed. Crespo resigned office in 1898, to meet with a tragic fate. His successor, Señor Andrade, proved unpopular, and Crespo, while leading the government forces in an attempt to restore order, was killed. In 1900 Andrade was deposed, and a dictatorship was reimposed by General Castro (1900-8). A reversion to the former state of chaos took place, speculation was rife, and in 1903 Great Britain, Germany, and Italy found it necessary to take joint naval action against Venezuela in the interest of bondholders belonging to their respective nationalities.

The Venezuelan seaboard was blockaded, but eventually the Hague Tribunal decided that about £700,000 should be paid in settlement of the British, Italian, and German claims. Castro now refused the United States request for a revision of the so-called "Olcott Award" for the Orinoco Steamship Company, and in 1906 forbade the French Minister to land, claiming that he had broken the guarantee laws ; France thereupon severed relations.

In 1908, a peremptory demand by Castro to the Netherlands government, on the ground that Venezuelan refugees had found asylum in the island of Curacoa, was answered by a Dutch naval demonstration. This destroyed Castro's so-called fleet and blockaded the ports. At the close of 1908, the dictator quitted Carácas for Europe on the plea of ill-health, and a revolution which broke out in the capital resulted, in 1910, in the election as president of General Juan Vicente Gómez. Under his administration tranquillity was restored to Venezuela, and far better economic and other conditions prevailed. The troubles incidental to the Great War of 1914-18 were surmounted, and the Republic preserved a correct attitude throughout the struggle.

VENEZUELA : FACTS AND FIGURES

The Country

Venezuela is bounded north by the Caribbean Sea, south by Brazil, east by British Guiana, and west by Colombia. In the west are the Andes and their extension eastwards along the Caribbean coast, which is fringed by some 70 islands. Running across the country from the south-west is the Orinoco with more than 400 affluents. To the north of this river are great open plains, while to the south of it is a great tropical forest. Climate varies considerably owing to the differing altitudes of the land configuration. Total area estimated at about 600,000 square miles ; estimated population 2,400,000.

Government and Constitution

Congress holds legislative authority and comprises a Senate and Chamber of Deputies, the Senate having forty members, two for every state, chosen for three years, while there is a deputy for every 35,000 inhabitants in each state, chosen for three years, a surplus of 15,000 entitling a state

to a second deputy. Executive power is in the hands of the President, elected for seven years, in cooperation with a Cabinet.

Commerce and Industries

Of the three districts into which the country is geographically divided the first is agricultural, and produces cocoa, coffee, cotton, maize, and sugar-cane, giving employment to about one-fifth of the population ; the second provides land suitable for stock-raising ; while the third, a forest region, yields balata, a rubber-like gum, vanilla, and rubber. Gold is mined south-east of Ciudad Bolivar, and coal, salt, and asphalt are worked. Pearl-fishing is carried on round the island of Margarita. The most important industries are the manufacture of cotton, fibre sacks, glass, and matches. Among the chief exports are coffee, cocoa, hides, and gold, the total exports for 1920-21 being valued at £4,708,961, while imports for same year reached a total of £7,560,080. Standard coin, the silver bolivar ; nominal value 9½d.

CULTURE AND RELIGION IN INDUSTRIAL CARDIFF: THE PUBLIC LIBRARY AND S. JOHN'S CHURCH

Intelligence and forethought on the part of the municipal authorities have been of great benefit to Cardiff in its rapid modern expansion. All the industrial works are grouped about the docks below the town, which is made attractive by open spaces, many trees, and good architecture. Here in the Hayes are shown the public library built in 1894, and on the left the tower of the church of S. John Baptist, the most notable monument of medieval Cardiff with the exception of the castle. This tower was erected in 1473 by Lady Ann Nevill, daughter of Warwick the King-maker

Photo, Charles Reid

Wales

I. Cambrian Life & Character

By Hamilton Fyfe

Author and Traveller

OF all the peoples who call themselves British none has a clearer right to that name than the Welsh. The first inhabitants of Britain about whom we know anything definite were Celts, and the Welsh belonged, with the Cornish folk and also with the Bretons of Brittany, to one of the two main groups into which the Celtic race in the British Islands and in France was then divided.

Not that the Welsh are all alike. Many local differences are to be noticed in the physical and even the mental characteristics of the people. An Anglesea man is unlike one who comes from the Merionethshire mountains; in Carmarthenshire one remarks a decided change from, say, Montgomeryshire. The southern Welsh have not either the same dialect or the same political enthusiasm as the northern.

There is, however, all over this little country, which is more distinct from England than Scotland or Ireland, a recognizable Welsh appearance and manner. Seven-tenths of the nation speak Welsh, in spite of the attempt to supplant that language by English, and only use English when they are obliged. There are still a good many Welsh people who cannot speak English at all.

The Welsh have the same love of music, the same natural gift of eloquence, the same religious fervour, the same restless desire to assert themselves as the Irish and the Highland Scots. Their impetuous temperament, dislike of authority, assertive patriotism, fondness for flattery are all what we are accustomed to call Celtic traits. It has been suggested that Welsh patriotism is due to the Welsh mountains. The vigour of Welsh patriotism is to be attributed rather to the endeavours made to suppress it. English visitors to Wales are often astonished at the warmth of the expressions they hear against England, especially against the Church of England. They do not know how bitterly the effort to Anglicise Wales and to force an alien Church upon the people was resented, and what passions were stirred by the attempt. All that has been changed.

ONE OF CAMBRIA'S DAUGHTERS

Wide-brimmed, steeple-crowned felt hats worn over white caps are the salient feature of Welsh national costume. Tilted backwards they give a rather coquettish air to the girl wearers

Even before the Church of Wales was disestablished by the Act of 1914 it had become the practice to appoint to Welsh bishoprics only Welsh-speaking clergymen ; the habit of using the incomes of those bishoprics as pensions for English ecclesiastics had been dropped. But such things left behind a deep resentment.

Hostility to the Anglican Church

For a great many years the history of the Welsh was the history of their struggle to throw off the burden of an alien religious establishment. Every chapel became a political centre and rallying point. Nationality was identified with Methodism or some other form of dissent from the Anglican Church. This brought with it a social conflict as well. The nobility and gentry, the owners of land on a large scale, were supporters of the Church. The mass of the people were Dissenters. The more the Church tried to coerce them into paying its dues, the more devoted they became to their chapels and their ministers. The ministers envied the rectors and vicars their incomes and their parsonages and their social position. If a Welshman was ordained an Anglican clergyman, he was received by the upper class as an equal, whereas the Methodist clergy were looked down on as inferiors.

Movement for Welsh Home Rule

Gradually, under these influences, all who belonged to the Church were regarded as English, and the feeling grew up that all English were intruders. It began to be asked why the land should be in the possession of English landlords. A Welsh Home Rule movement was set on foot. The desire for independence was a popular theme at political meetings, the flame of national pride burned with an ever-increasing intensity.

Since the chief grievance was removed by the Church Disestablishment Act less has been heard of "Wales for the Welsh." The chapels have not resounded to the same denunciations of the English as used to be heard Sunday after Sunday. The national unity is not so compact and solid as it was. Other lines of cleavage have appeared than that which divided Anglicans and Dissenters.

In South Wales, for example, the miners are the most revolutionary element in Great Britain. The doctrine known as Communism spread among them rapidly and was embraced with the enthusiasm formerly applied to religious beliefs. By their countrymen in general it was feared and detested, for the Welsh have a very keen sense of property. The hunger for land among the small farming class may be compared with that of the Russian peasants.

Keen Eye to the Main Chance

Mystical though they may be in their chapels and at their prayer meetings, the Welsh attend closely to business; they are hard bargainers, they are strong individualists, and they understand the secret of getting on in the world. In the drapery and dairy businesses of London and other cities they have for a number of years held foremost places. Big fortunes have been made by their assiduity and talent for retail commerce.

Beneath their excitability and their restlessness under discipline the Welsh have a great sense of reality and personal profit. They are not idealists, they see no use in anyone sacrificing himself for an idea. Indeed, they have nothing but pitying contempt for the man who disregards his own interests while he is intent upon some public end. They respect the impulse to serve the public, they have a high appreciation of political work, but they consider that these should be combined with personal reward.

There is no conscious cynicism in this attitude. They cannot look at the matter from any other point of view. Welsh congregations are deeply moved

WALES OF TO-DAY
Cambrian Character & Costume

*Many pretty modern maids donned brave old Welsh garb to participate
in the Eisteddfod ceremonial at the little Flintshire town of Mold*

*Modern laundry methods make little headway in North Wales, and
many a thrifty housewife resorts to the nearest stream on washing-day*

Photo, Harry Cox

*Older than Carnarvon's hoary medieval stronghold is the ancient cere-
mony in progress within its grounds—the National Eisteddfod of Wales*

*Man's labour is not wasted in vain in Llanberis, near Snowdon's base;
yearly the verdant valley stands thick with crops and yields rich reward*

Photo, Charles Reid

*Cymric is their one and only tongue, for, imbued with a strong
sense of nationality, the Welsh carefully foster native institutions*

Photo, Charles Reid

In the mountains of North Wales near Beddgelert nestles this ivy-crowned, one-storeyed cottage, beloved by its old owner for the homely shelter afforded to her and to four generations of the family before her

Photo, A. W. Cutler

The procession of ardent Welsh folk in traditional Druidical habit and national dress, comprising vari-coloured garments and high-crowned black hats, was not the least attractive item of the Eisteddfod at Ammanford

*In their glib Welsh patter they are discussing the markets of the day,
for the fishwives of Llangwm have usually a keen eye for business*

Photo, A. W. Cutler

Like grandmother like granddaughter !   A glimpse into the heart of rural Wales, where quaint old-time costumes are still seen occasionally

Photo, A. W. Cutler

Work must surely go hand in hand with pleasure in this fragrant hayfield, where the wide open world of nature greets the eye, and in the blue distance Snowdon, king of Welsh mountains, rises in rugged majesty

Photo, A. W. Cutler

Snug cottages of varied style and undeniable charm adorn the lovely landscapes of South Wales; no whit less pleasing are the contrasting costumes of ancient and modern mode in vogue among the Welsh rustics

Photo, A. W. Cutler

5275

Little Miss Wales, of winsome face and trim figure, still joys in the tall black hat and red cloak of the traditional country costume

Photo, Charles Reid

A stately old Welsh dame, staunch to national costume and possessing all the lively, romantic, and fiery attributes of her Celtic race

5277

This young shepherd signalling to his dog is standing on a peak of Snowdon, whence "Wild Wales," with its lofty mountains, rushing rivers, limpid lakes, and fertile valleys, is seen in its most poetic grandeur

Photo, Charles Reid

Though but a simple shepherd this hardy citizen of the Welsh highlands is thoroughly acquainted with all popular lore relating to the natural beauties and historical associations of the land of the Cymry

Photo, Charles Reid

Wayside fiddler though he be, his talent is no mean one, for the spirit of the music-loving bards of old still lives in the Welsh people

by sermons; they join with fervour in the singing of hymns; they can scarcely refrain from applauding the prayers which meet with their particular approval; but they hold firmly to the law of supply and demand. If ministers can be got for very small remuneration, they can see no reason why they should pay more than the market price. They are committing no injustice, they say, for there are others who would be glad to take on the job for the same money. That is, as a rule, unfortunately true. Many men of learning and intellect are to be found in the chapel pulpits, but they are a small minority.

Severity of Early Methodism

That explains why Young Wales is beginning to drift away from the doctrines and formulae which have satisfied the last four or five generations. Young Wales is not content with hymns which seem to it to have no relation to experience, nor with sermons which do not bear upon the actual problems of everyday existence. No one has ever claimed that there was much connexion in Wales between the Sunday exercises and the activities of the other days of the week, though doubtless in the early years of Methodism there was a closer relation between faith and life than there is to-day. The leaders of the people in those years are revered as saints.

No newspapers circulated then among the scattered population; the people were densely ignorant, they were out of touch with the world outside their own borders. The Methodists appealed to their dramatic sense, undeveloped but very strong; the preachers terrified them and then offered them the healing balm of hope. They were stung out of their lethargy.

It was for the most part materialist theology of the medieval variety, and with it went a severe and uncompromising discipline. The Sabbath was observed more strictly than in Scotland even. The conception of Man as a depraved and worthless creature, corrupt in grain, and only to be saved from eternal punishment by the favour of the Almighty, which favour would only be extended to a small proportion of the human race, made all who really accepted it profoundly melancholy.

Lethargy Dispelled by Religion

The most innocent amusements were denounced as Satan's traps for the unwary. Games were "sinfully carnal." The dances in which the Welsh had been used to find recreation and exercise were forbidden. It was with difficulty that football made its way among the young men, who were told by their pastors that they did wrong to play it.

Lately the Methodism which once threw a gloomy pall over the spirits of a naturally cheerful and sociable people has approached more nearly to the milder forms which prevail in England. Yet the religious revival which stirred the emotional life of the Welsh and awakened them from the lethargy into which they had been cast by the loss of their independence left a very strong impress upon them. It will be counted as the chief factor in making them what they are now becoming—one of the most vigorous and talented of the small nations of the world.

Repressive Policy of the English

When it began they were sunk in sullen servitude. For centuries they had been subjected by the English kings and bishops to a policy of deliberate repression. There were scarcely any schools among them. No Welshman was permitted to own land in England or to hold any municipal office or to exercise the rights of citizenship. An Englishman charged with an offence in Wales could only be tried by English justices. No authority could be entrusted even to an Englishman in Wales if he had so far forgotten himself as to marry a Welshwoman.

The vigour of the national consciousness is proved by its surviving at

MELLOW AGE AT COMFORTABLE EASE

Energy, industry, shrewdness, and thriftiness amounting to penuriousness characterise Welsh women. These, and their other qualities of quick intelligence and friendliness, are manifest in this old Carmarthenshire lady

Photo, F. R. P. Stringer

The fear of Hell, the hope of a Paradise hardly less Oriental than that of Islam, might have roused the Welsh to material achievements; they could not have stirred into activity the intellectual and artistic powers of the nation, could not have renewed their pre-eminence in speech and song. It was the little leaven of mysticism which wrought this seeming miracle.

Respect for the law took the place of turbulence, a high standard of education was reached, a literature came into being, journalism grew so rapidly that Wales a generation ago was said to support more journals in proportion to its population than any other part of the civilized world.

Thus the country rose to prominence, the contributions of the race to the arts, to learning, to philosophy were everywhere acknowledged, while for politics it showed a remarkable aptitude, developing its highest degree in the career of Mr. Lloyd George.

It would be pleasant if one were able to say that the Welsh had won, along with the admiration and respect of the world, popularity and general liking. Those who have the opportunity to know them well in their own country are well aware of their likeable qualities. They are friendly, quick in intelligence, amusing to talk to, eager to learn. How is it, then, that the opinion entertained about them by so many people should be so unfavourable?

all under these repressive conditions. It had certainly fallen very low when the influence of that fierce and alarming Calvinism came to stab it back to energetic life. The remedy was desperate, but so was the disease. Happily there was amid the prevailing materialism of the system which the Welsh embraced with so much violent excitement a tincture of spirituality.

A great deal is due to slight acquaintance and to prejudice. Many childish minds must have been influenced by the slanderous nursery rhyme—

Taffy was a Welshman, Taffy was a thief,
Taffy came to my house and stole a piece of beef.
I went to Taffy's house, Taffy wasn't at home,
Taffy came to my house and stole a mutton bone.

Shakespeare reflected the ridicule which was poured on the Welsh in his time by making Fluellen, in " Henry the Fifth," a figure of fun, though he was careful to represent him as a good fighter. Scots and Irish were ridiculed, too, by the English for their accents, their poverty, their mannerisms, but they have lived down all dislike resulting from ill-humoured witticisms. Not so the Welsh ; they still suffer from an unkind prejudice.

The belief that they are not over-scrupulous has been strengthened, it must be said, by Welsh writers who have exhibited their countrymen in a very uncomplimentary light.

What the casual observer notices is the contrast between the impetuous and exuberant expressions of sympathy in which the Welshman abounds, and his

NATIVE DRESS AND NATIVE HUMOUR TO THE FORE IN WALES
Wales and the Highlands of Scotland are the only parts of Great Britain where national dress—for women and for men respectively—is still preserved. Skirts and aprons in Wales show many combinations of checks and colours, checkered black and white, and vivid reds and greens predominating. Many of the shawls are of great beauty, and the costume is pleasing and quaint

SALMON FISHERMEN AT BANGOR ON THE DEE COMING ASHORE AFTER AN EXPEDITION

Salmon abound in all the large rivers of the Principality, where many of the native anglers go out for them in coracles, the most notable example in the British Isles of a prehistoric vessel in practical use unchanged through the course of ages. They consist of a framework of ash sticks covered with a stout canvas saturated with tar. Although they look clumsy and crude they prove exceedingly serviceable craft in skilled hands. A strong strap fastened to the seat is hooked over the shoulders when the craft is being carried to and from the water. A coracle weighs about 30 lb. and lasts two or three years, according to usage

Photo, A. W. Cutler

ON A WELSH ESTUARY: THE SHRIMPER EMPTIES HIS NET

Into the sea-arm, known as Milford Haven, that pierces the coast of Pembroke run two rivers, the east and west Cleddy. Along the shores of their common estuary, part of which is seen above, quantities of shrimps are found, and, at low tide, the shrimper with his wide net on its T-shaped frame can obtain a basketful without too much trouble

Photo, A. W. Cutler

disinclination to do anything practical to prove them sincere. But it is unfair not to bear in mind that along with his impetuosity and exuberance goes a strong element of caution. He feels the sympathy which he expresses—it is far from being hypocritical; but he does not as a rule feel any impulse to act on it. The open-handed generosity which marks both the Irish and the Celtic Scots is not commonly found in Wales.

The Welsh would be more hospitable if they did not practise so often a rigid economy in their housekeeping. This does not apply to the townspeople, but to the farming population. Good as

their houses are, and well-dressed though they may be, their manner of living is frequently such as would be found only among the very poorest of English labourers. White bread and tea have taken the place of the sour barley bread and buttermilk which used to be the customary farm-house fare, but fresh meat is still a luxury.

Bacon is substituted for it by those who are fairly well-to-do, or the salt meat which in certain parts, especially Cardiganshire, is known as "cowl." This is cow beef salted and kept for some time before it is eaten. A piece of this boiled with potatoes, greens, carrots and turnips, oatmeal, or anything else that may be handy, produces a thick stew which may not be appetising to strangers, but which satisfies effectually the hunger of the home-bred.

Porridge and oatmeal flummery (oatmeal with the bran squeezed out of it and then boiled until it becomes something like an opaque jelly) were commonly consumed in Wales until oatmeal began to go out of fashion. They are not so often found now. Bread and cheese, potatoes, salt meat, tea, and herrings form the staple diet of a large number of the Welsh who work on the land. Excellent butter is made, but mostly sent away to market. Welsh mutton is famous, but the small farmer seldom eats it himself.

It is not so much poverty as thrift which impels him to deny himself the good things which he enjoys as much as anybody can when they come in his way. He is first and foremost a careful man. He does not care to hold much land. Two-thirds of the farms in Wales are of less than fifty acres ; one of two hundred acres is considered large.

IN THE UPLAND PASTURES OF THE SNOWDON RANGE

Welsh farms are commonly much smaller than English, two-thirds of them being of less than fifty acres. Stock-raising is generally preferred to growing cereals, but the stock is bred for the most part on haphazard lines. In the valleys the land is fertile, but among the mountains, as here in Nant Peris in the Snowdon range, hard work is needed to make a living

Photo, Charles Reid

Nor does the Welsh farmer look with favour on what he is inclined to call with some disdain "experiments." Radical though he may be in his political views, he is, like most of the farmers in the world, conservative in his everyday habits and occupations. He stood out against agricultural machinery, he set his face against artificial fertilisers, he would not take the trouble to keep his land clear of weeds. Nor would he understand the importance of careful selection in the breeding of cattle.

This was sneered at as a fad which was all very well for gentlemen farmers or for those who bred on a very large scale, but which the small man could not afford to indulge in. Cattle, pigs, and poultry are all bred anyhow on far too many small farms still, though more advantage is being taken every year of the application of science to agriculture and the raising of stock.

BACK FROM THE FISHING IN SWANSEA BAY

Built between steep weather-broken cliffs of limestone and the shore of Swansea Bay, Mumbles village derives no small profit from the oyster-beds in the vicinity. This old longshoreman can evidently answer "yes" to the query "any luck?"

Photo, Charles Reid

It is their inferior methods and their unreadiness to cooperate that burden the Welsh smallholders with poverty rather than the land system which they are always denouncing. Certainly that system does here and there inflict hardships. Landlords there have been who aimed simply at squeezing all they could out of their tenants. It is partly the memory of these exceptions which makes the people generally speak disparagingly of the land agents who manage the big properties ; partly also the fact (mentioned by Rhys and Brynmor Jones, in "The Welsh People") that "on the most typical estates in Wales the landlord and his family (and his agent) belong to the Established Church, while the bulk of the tenants belong to one or other of the Nonconformist organizations."

In general, however, Welsh landlords are no better and no worse than landlords elsewhere. On the whole they cannot be blamed for the backward condition of agriculture in so many quarters. Defective education is to blame for it.

The Welsh very much prefer ownership to paying rent for their acres. But the peasant proprietors are in no better case than the tenant farmers ; many of them are worse off. This is frequently due to their being at too great a distance

SAWING SLATE IN THE FAMOUS PENBRYN SLATE QUARRIES

Slate quarries employ thousands of hands in Wales, the finest quality of slate being produced at the Penbryn and Bethesda quarries in South Wales. The blocks of rock obtained by channelling machines or by blasting are sent up to huts where large pieces are sawn for use as billiard-tables, chimney-pieces, cisterns, tombstones, and so forth, and smaller pieces are split and dressed for slates

Photo, Underwood Press Service

from a town. Middlemen fleece them, railway companies cannot afford to give them cheap transport because they are so scattered and so irregular in their consignments.

What they need is a cooperative system on the Danish or the Irish creamery model. This would speedily make a difference to their prospects, and that in turn would give them an inducement to work harder and farm more carefully. As soon as a Welshman sees that there is a good profit to be picked up, he will exert himself to secure it, but he must have it well in view. He is apt to be easily discouraged, his temperament is lymphatic, he is not the man to carve out a fortune for himself in face of rude obstacles. In the lonelier spots, among the mountains, there are

QUARRYMEN IN THE DINORWIC SLATE QUARRY ON SNOWDON

Most slates are clays consolidated by heat and pressure into cleavage planes along which the slate splits readily. Where the slates lie near the surface, as here at the Dinorwic quarry on Snowdon, they are worked in terraces or galleries formed along the strike of the beds. Underground beds are worked in chambers reached by shafts, or by levels driven through the overlying earth

many families bound to the soil, just getting a living off their sheep runs, off the young stock they fatten, and off the butter they make in their dairies. They have a hard life, but they do not mind this, for they know of no other. No son or daughter who goes to a town is likely to return to the ancestral vale or mountain side, but there are generally one or two left at home to carry on the

their tenants. All they want as a rule is enough to keep the roof of their old family house over their heads and to let them live in rough comfort, fishing and shooting and riding their sure-footed ponies along the mountain sides.

Their sons and daughters go out into the world, like those of the farmers; they have done much to carry forward British colonisation in the waste places

MOUNTAINEERING ON SNOWDON: NEARING THE TOP OF A GULLY

Snowdon offers some attractive climbs for the mountaineer and, in places, the surface is sufficiently difficult to add the spice of danger and call upon skill and experience. The highest peak south of the Tweed, Snowdon lifts its summit three thousand five hundred and sixty feet amid the scenery of lake and fell. On a clear day the Wicklow mountains in Ireland may be seen

farm when the old folks die. They are of a different stock from the mass of the smallholders, more rugged in character, asking less from life, untouched by the restless spirit of the age.

In the mountain districts the land is owned mostly by Welsh squires, a small class distinct from the English or Anglicised landlords. These squires often have a pretty hard struggle themselves, but they are considerate to

of the earth. They can be found on the Canadian prairies, on the South African veld, ranching in Rhodesia, knocking about from one hemisphere to the other, and sometimes returning in the end to look after the family estate and try to put into practice what they have learned in the course of their rolling-stone lives.

The disinclination of the sons and daughters of the soil to stick to their

HERALD BARD FROM MONTGOMERYSHIRE AND HIS BARDIC WIFE

High honours once belonged to the bards of Wales, whose function it was to celebrate the victories of the people and to sing hymns of praise to God. They formed an organized society, with hereditary rights and privileges, and were exempt from taxes and from military service. To-day the title is conferred upon Welsh poets, of either sex, whose vocation has been recognized at an Eisteddfod

MEMBERS OF GORSEDD IN CEREMONIAL ATTIRE AT AN EISTEDDFOD AT MOLD IN FLINTSHIRE

Eisteddfodau, or sessions of the national bardic congress of Wales, originated in the once politically important Gorsedd, or assembly. They were given their present character in the fourth century, since when many Eisteddfodau have been held under princely and royal patronage. Now held annually, the national Eisteddfod is proclaimed a year and a day beforehand by a graduated bard of a congress and lasts for three or four days. A president and a conductor are appointed for each day, and ancient ceremonies are performed by Druids, bards, and ovates robed in ancient vestments

parents' occupation and style of living is as marked in Wales as in England. Many of them seek employment in the towns, preferring a clerk's or shopman's job, with its fixed hours and regular pay, to the never-ending toil of a farm worker. Many of them emigrate to the Dominions or the United States. For a longish period there was a steady stream of some 6,000 emigrants a year.

Probably the large number of farms in the hands of Welsh women is accounted for by the departure of eldest sons and other sons to seek their fortunes in some wider and more promising sphere. Women occupiers of farms are only about one in twelve in England ; in Wales they are one in every five. They are energetic farmers, up early, with their eyes in every corner, keeping their families and their labourers up to the mark ; but they have more idea of saving money penuriously here and there than of spending wisely so as to bring in a good return.

Hysteria at Religious Revivals

The Welsh have been described as an "abnormally sociable" race ; they certainly seize every opportunity of getting together, they are always great talkers ; they do not drink heavily, but a little is apt to set them talking more than usual. They know they will get no chance of enjoying themselves until next market day. For, beyond chapel-going and Sunday-school, there is little, in the remoter districts, to break the dullness of farm life.

This grey monotony is suggested as the explanation of the extraordinary success of religious revivals in Wales. These have been of fairly regular occurrence, and form very interesting features of the national history. They provoke scenes of emotional excitement which seem to non-Welsh observers to be the result of ungovernable hysteria. Preachers work themselves up into a condition of frenzy. Their hearers groan and cry aloud. They are now wrapped in the beatific vision, now they tremble

at the thought of hell. They cast self-control aside, they abase themselves, they promise amendment in their lives. Many have been reclaimed permanently from habits of drunkenness or loose living by the change wrought in them by their attendance at revivalist meetings.

Truth Sacrificed to Politeness

On the other hand, these orgies of emotional intoxication have led some natures to kick over the traces of convention, even to " overleap the restraints of morality," as a Welsh writer has put it. That consequence of a sudden stirring to the depths of imaginative and not very stable temperaments is, however, known elsewhere.

It is their power of imagination which makes the Welsh over-anxious to say what they believe will be pleasing.

For example, if on the mountains you ask a native how far it is to some place, he will be almost sure to reply that it is not far at all, even though he may be well aware that you have a very long way to go. He thinks you will be pleased to hear that it is not far. He imagines himself in your place—at the moment ; he is not capable of projecting his imagination farther and realizing what will be your disappointment and irritation when you discover that you have been misled.

Timidity in Presence of Strangers

There is often a good deal of nervousness in their manner towards strangers which may have the effect of causing them to speak the thing that is not. They have neither the proud bearing of the Highlander, who considers himself the equal of any man on earth, nor the easy comradeship of the Irish. There is apt to be something furtive in their demeanour, an almost resentful timidity expressed in hurried speech, and eyes which do not look you in the face. That is more noticeable in some districts than in others ; there are parts of the country where you do not find it. Very likely it is due to centuries of

NATIONAL DRESS THE ONLY WEAR FOR WOMEN AT AN EISTEDDFOD

Cultivation of a patriotic spirit among the people by the encouragement of Welsh bardism, music, and general literature, and maintenance of the language and customs of the country are the objects for which Eisteddfodau are held in various parts of the Principality. Thus an Eisteddfod offers an especial opportunity for the native women to wear their distinctive dress

repression, to the lack of sympathy with Welsh aspirations and ideals which they attribute to the English, to the feeling that they are regarded as foreigners in their own land because they speak their own language and have preserved a national type so distinct from that of their neighbours. But this attitude towards strangers may also be partly accounted for by the Welsh " keeping themselves to themselves " so pertinaciously. They are, to put it plainly, too inbred. They are a small race, and they have aimed at reproducing exclusively one particular national type.

How careful they are to marry within their own racial limits may be illustrated by the clear-cut boundaries which mark off the regions occupied in Pembrokeshire by the Welsh and those which were colonised in the eleventh and twelfth centuries by Flemings, brought over from Flanders as mercenaries by Norman kings of England and then used to keep in check the troublesome Welsh and Scottish clans.

In seven hundred years there has been so little intermarriage between these elements that they have well-defined frontiers to this day. They have each kept to their own language, for the Flemings soon learned to speak English, which is closely akin to their own tongue. They have in all respects

CELTIC GENIUS IN THE MYSTIC CIRCLE: PRELIMINARY ASSEMBLY OF THE EISTEDDFOD AT CARNARVON CASTLE

A most impressive and interesting sight was the Gorsedd, the inaugural meeting of the Eisteddfod, held in the grounds of Carnarvon Castle. The Welsh word, Eisteddfod, signifies "a sitting of learned men," and the first mention of the ceremony under that name is recorded in the seventh century—on which occasion King Cadwaladr is said to have presided—and is believed to have originated in the triennial assembly of Welsh bards, which dates back to a very early period. This ancient ceremony is now revived, not only in Wales, but wherever Welshmen are found in sufficient numbers, to encourage Welsh music and literature

ASPIRANTS FOR BARDIC HONOURS: MODERN OBSERVANCE OF AN ARCHAIC FESTIVAL IN MEDIEVAL SURROUNDINGS

The Gorsedd, an open-air solemnity, is very dear to the heart of the Welsh people and arouses deep interest throughout their country. It is invariably attended by numerous spectators, some from curiosity, but the most part from enthusiasm, and not a few who are entirely ignorant of the Welsh language. The robe of white, "emblem of holiness and peculiarly of truth," was the distinguishing dress of the Druids, to which hierarchy the ancient Celtic bards belonged; and here a group of present-day bards is seen in the historical grounds of Carnarvon's famous castle, one of the finest surviving strongholds of the Middle Ages in the United Kingdom

WALES: LAND LASSIES IN A COUNTRY LANE

The quaint Welsh costume still lingers in old-fashioned corners of Wales, and along the country lanes
close to Llangwm comely young faces, under high black hats, may smilingly greet the traveller

remained apart. The " Flemings " look better fed, they wear a more cheerful and contented expression, they have become thoroughly English, they are not worried by social and religious problems, they are inclined to laugh at the Welsh for their clannishness, their obstinate sticking to their language, their preoccupation with abstract ideas.

Racial Purity and Racial Weakness

This cleavage of races enduring for so long a time is not due to any reluctance of the settlers to mix their blood. Elsewhere they have done so. They would, we may assume, have become Welsh long since if it had not been for Welsh exclusiveness. There is nothing in the nature of the country to keep them apart. The frontiers which divide their territories are artificial— a small stream in one place serves as "an impassable barrier." At other points one can drive from a Welsh district into an English over a line of separation which is not apparent, but which is carefully kept up.

Such determination to maintain racial purity has always resulted in racial weakness. It is because the English are composed of so many different national elements that they have made so big a noise in the world. It is because the French intermarry so seldom with other peoples that their vigour has declined.

Preservation of the Welsh Language

The Welsh are afraid that if they do not take great care of the national type, it will be swallowed up. But that has not happened to the Scottish national type, although the Scots have gone far and wide in their choice of wives. When Welshmen go overseas and get into a less limited environment, when they marry women of other nationalities, they do not cease to be Welsh, but they broaden out and become more enterprising and display talents which seldom appear in them at home. Some say this is due to their ceasing to speak Welsh, or at any rate to their being obliged to speak another language besides Welsh, and this brings us to the difficult question : Should the attempt to keep up the language be abandoned ?

That form of the problem, however, is scarcely fair. Welsh is spoken by so large a proportion of Welsh people in everyday life simply because it comes easier to them than English. They use it as the speech which comes naturally to their lips.

The very suggestion that all should speak English is liable to be met with scornful abuse. Yet any Welshman who has anything to write is obliged to write it in English if he wants it to be read by more than a handful of people. Any Welshman who seeks a wider sphere of activity than the village or the small town must make English as much his tongue as Welsh is.

Importance of the Chapel in Wales

Whatever language they speak, it is beyond doubt that the Welsh will remain fond of talking, ready to fall into argument on any theme, lovers of eloquent speaking, whether from pulpit or political platform. Any utterance which is composed of the elements in which they delight, invective, poetic, and especially Biblical illustration, will stir them to enthusiasm. This is principally because they have been trained from their youngest years to listen to preaching and to consider that the finest preacher is he who can make the most successful appeal to their quick emotions.

Much that is admirable and much that is regrettable in the Welsh character can be traced to the importance of the chapel in the nation's life. No other institution had anything like the same prominence. In singing hymns the national genius for music found outlet ; none who have listened on a still evening in some mountain district to a group of peasants or miners or village folk taking parts in some chorale or sacred song are ever likely to forget the beauty of the voices or the perfectly harmonious effect produced by their blending.

A good many Welsh singers have made their mark, Mary Davies, Ben Davies, and Ffrangçon Davies among them. They were unrelated, though they bore the same name. Another reputation in music has been made by Dr. Walford Davies, and he is occupied with a scheme for bringing out more fully Welsh musical taste and ability.

In versifying the Welsh have fatal facility, but they have produced few poets. The only one who is known to a wide audience in modern times is Sir Lewis Morris. The reputation of Dafydd ap Gwilim has survived through some five centuries among those who are learned in Celtic literature, but has made no wider appeal. At the Eisteddfods (more correctly Eisteddfodau), which are gatherings of " bards " and singers, vast quantities of verse are recited, but these exercises are more useful in heightening the national spirit than in assisting the birth of literature.

Burne-Jones, the painter, was a Welshman, so was H. M. Stanley, the explorer (his real name was Rowlands);

GORSEDD CIRCLE IN THE RUINS OF ABERYSTWYTH CASTLE

Many dramatic episodes in the history of Wales have been enacted on the hill above Aberystwyth, on which the Norman, Gilbert de Clare, first Earl of Pembroke, built a mighty fortalice to overawe rebellious Welshmen. The last castle on the site was razed by Parliamentarian troops in 1647, and the chief demonstrations of national spirit now made around its ruins are when an Eisteddfod is held

FORMAL OFFERING OF THE HORN OF PLENTY TO THE ARCH-DRUID

Vested with formidable powers and credited with gifts of magic and divination, the Druids were an awe-inspiring hierarchy in ancient Britain. Revived as representatives of the national spirit, they figure now only in the peaceful ceremonies of the Eisteddfod, whose ritual is attended by much symbolism. Here the Arch-Druid is shown receiving the horn of plenty at an Eisteddfod at Ammanford

so was John Nash, the architect, who designed Regent Street, London; so were Sir Richard Owen, the naturalist, and Sidney Gilchrist Thomas, the inventor of the process which, by separating phosphorus from iron, revolutionised the manufacture of iron and steel. Two Speakers of the House of Commons have been natives of Wales.

Sir George Cornewall Lewis had a well-deserved fame as a Cabinet Minister of a superior stamp in the middle of the nineteenth century. Mr. Lloyd George became the hero of his countrymen when he fought his way into the front rank of politics and took office as the first Welsh Prime Minister. In the theatrical profession Mrs. Siddons and the Kembles both came from the county of Brecon.

The small number of Welsh names on the roll of world-wide fame is to be accounted for partly by the inbreeding already referred to, partly by the absorption in local and especially sectarian interests. It is to be noticed that while no people support more periodicals or appear to be more given to reading than the Welsh, they have, until lately, given their attention to a very small range of subjects. This fault is being repaired now that the colleges which compose the University of Wales put such excellent opportunities in the way of young men and women. Here the narrowing influence of the old-fashioned chapel theology has been opposed by the broadening effect of education in a fresher atmosphere.

The smug Puritanism, the hard-and-fast dogmas of the past, are slowly yielding to the New Spirit. The oppressive belief that amusement was sinful has almost passed away. There still lingers a prejudice against the theatre, dating back to the savage denunciations of the early Methodists. There are still people who hold that gloom should mark the aspect of the true believer, but they are found seldom in the busy haunts of men ; only in lonely farm-houses do the old ideas maintain their hold unmodified.

In bringing about this change the growth of vast industrial and trading communities at Cardiff and Swansea has played a prominent part. Elsewhere towns are small. They are unimportant in their influence on the development of the nation. Carnarvon with its castle, Carmarthen with its fine river, are the most interesting of them. Bangor is picturesquely situated. Denbigh, on market day, provides

RITUALISTIC FLOWERS AT THE GORSEDD SERVICE AT CARNARVON

Floral offerings are made at an Eisteddfod by the children and young people and accepted by the Arch-Druid. In this, as in the other rites of quaffing from the horn of plenty and touching the sword of peace, there is allusion to the ancient ceremonies in which the Druids offered sacrifice and poured libations for a fruitful harvest and used their priestly office to avert war

PRESENTATION OF THE SWORD OF PEACE AT MOLD EISTEDDFOD

An impressive symbolic incident in the ceremonial at an Eisteddfod is the presentation to the Arch-Druid of the sheathed sword of peace. This mighty weapon is borne before him in the processions, enclosed in its scabbard and with the point downwards, and during the service in the Gorsedd circle is laid at his feet upon the Druidical stone on which he stands

ample testimony to the prosperity of the farmers in the Vale of Clwyd. But they are little more than market towns, any of them. Cardiff and Swansea, the ports through which the famous Welsh steam coal passes, the manufacturing cities which have become populated and prosperous because they have coal so near, are the main arteries through which the life blood of Welsh prosperity is pumped; here the currents of all the activities which make up national existence flow with the greatest vigour. In the county of Glamorgan is a tract of the richest land in the Principality. Between the mountains and the sea stretches a strip of sloping country wrongly called a vale, known also as the Garden of Wales. Here a fertile soil and a mild climate make the farmer's task exceptionally easy. But it is not agriculture which puts Glamorgan so far ahead of any other Welsh county in material wealth, so far behind most of them in natural beauty. Coalmines and ironworks scar the face of the land and stain the sky with smoke from tall chimney stacks. Valleys which once charmed the eye are defaced by rows upon rows of mean cottages, cheaply built and of hideous design. These were put up in a hurry to house the workers, who flocked to the newly opened mines and the newly erected ironworks. The cities grew rapidly, too, and for a long time without any attempt to save them from disorderly squalor.

Now Cardiff, at any rate, has done a good deal to redeem itself from this reproach by its park, its municipal and University College buildings, which are pleasing and dignified themselves and are so placed as to gain from their surroundings, making altogether a spacious and agreeable effect. Otherwise, the city is a lamentable emanation of the get-rich-quick spirit, which must be held responsible also to some extent for something uglier in South Wales than Cardiff—the turbulent unrest among large sections of the mining population. The chief antagonist of the colliers for many years was David Alfred Thomas, created Lord Rhondda, whose powerful intellect frequently worsted them,

BARDIC PROCESSION NEAR THE RUINED CASTLE OF ABERYSTWYTH
Here the cornucopia, the horn of plenty, symbolising peace and prosperity, is being borne before white-robed bards to the Eisteddfod—a ceremony which, to quote the words of its promoters, has for its object : " the diffusion of useful knowledge, the eliciting of native talent, and the cherishing of love of home and honourable fame by the cultivation of poetry, music, and art "
Photo, Topical Press Agency

WELSH BARD SINGING PENNILLION WITH THE HARP

Pennillion singing is peculiar to Wales, and is an accomplishment difficult to acquire. A pennill has been described as " part Limerick, part epigram," and is an original topical composition sung to the accompaniment of a harpist, who changes the tune and introduces variations as he pleases. The singer takes up the strain at the second, third, or fourth bar and must end exactly with the music

but left seeds of sullen enmity behind that have since borne many crops of bitter and poisonous fruit.

Next to its coal, the main factor in Welsh prosperity, outside agriculture, is the annual summer flow of visitors to its coast towns and villages. Llandudno, Rhyl, Barmouth, Aberystwyth, Llanfairfechan attract their thousands of seekers after health and pleasure.

Many smaller places reap an ample harvest, and every year large numbers make trips through the mountain districts, staying at such points of vantage as Beddgelert, Bettws-y-Coed, Capel Curig, Festiniog.

They go up Snowdon and, if they are more adventurously inclined, attempt the more difficult Cader Idris. They take the way through the Lleyn, which leads to Pwllheli and Braich-y-pwll, the headland in the Irish Sea, or find in Anglesea delightful out-of-the-way spots and "temperate air enlivened by a benign sun."

If the Welsh had the same talent for hotel-keeping as the Swiss, they would make their mountains a much greater source of profit than they are. They have not, of course, the same majesty as the Alps, there are no snow-covered summits to pierce the blue firmament. Nor is the firmament very often blue in North Wales; that is one of its drawbacks as a holiday place. From the Atlantic there come depressions which

DRUIDICAL SYMBOLISM AT A BARDIC CONGRESS OF WALES

Clothed in emblematic robes of white, these Welsh bards are making their way to the annual musical and poetical contest. The chief bard is wearing an oak-leaf wreath, for oak-woods were the Druids' sacred groves and none of their rites was performed without these leaves. The ornament round his neck is reminiscent of the "breastplate of judgement," part of the judicia habit of the Arch-Druid

seem to have a special fondness for the Welsh mountains. These are too often wreathed in mist. Rain is frequent at all seasons. Yet this lends a charm to the scenery which a lover of beauty can appreciate even when he is wet through. The fresh greenness of the vales, the luxuriance of the undergrowth and the ferns, the waterfalls that are so plentiful, make up in the estimation of a great many for the absence of great heights.

If you look upward in the Alps, you certainly do get a more inspiring prospect than any that Wales can offer. But the foregrounds in the Alps seldom bear comparison with those of the Lledr and the Llugwy glens, the Barmouth Estuary, the Vale of Gwynant, to name only the first which come into mind.

The people have done little enough to supplement the gifts of nature. Calvinism gripped their hearts and imaginations so fiercely that it seemed not worth while to make the best of this world, seeing that life here would soon be over, while the life to come was to last eternally. Whether the Welsh have always been morbidly introspective, whether melancholy has always been preferred to merriment among them, no one can determine. All that is certainly known is that since Puritanism placed its impress upon them their sense of beauty has been deadened, their joy in the graces and the arts of life damped down.

They are not great lovers of nature. Gardens of any charm or character are rare in North Wales. It may reasonably be doubted whether they would care very much for their own scenery if they were not convinced that everything Welsh must be better than anything of its kind to be found elsewhere. That is a Celtic failing. The French suffer from it, the Highlander still cherishes it secretly. The Welsh have not yet acquired the Highlander's discretion. The Welsh Member of Parliament who told the House of

CROWN FOR THE BARD

With gravity befitting the responsibility, a young Welsh girl brings forward the crown to be placed on the head of him who shall be proclaimed the master bard of the Eisteddfod

Commons that his country was the most religious in the world only said what everyone thinks in Wales. As with religion, so with everything. Not a word must be said against anything Welsh.

It is this lack of perspective which makes their politics so narrowly nationalist. Here also we discover one reason why so few of them have made their names in the world. Their self-satisfaction springs from several causes—their deliberate isolation, their in-breeding, their spiritual pride in being numbered among the elect, their habit of looking inwards instead of outwards, and, perhaps as much responsible as any, the foolish attempts made by the English monarchy and Church over so long a period to crush their consciousness of nationality.

They have defeated that attempt. They have conquered their external foes. Now they have to conquer those within their own household. Thanks to their desire for education this process is going on rapidly to-day.

CROWDS OF SEAMEN AND SHIPPING IN THE SOUTH DOCK BASIN AT SWANSEA

Swansea is second only to Cardiff as an industrial city of Wales. Situated in the heart of the anthracite coal district and in the centre of Swansea Bay, it has become a great mineral port. The South Dock, shown in this photograph, was opened in 1859, and is now mainly used for shipping coal and for discharging timber and fish. With the earlier Salthouse and North Docks, and the later Prince of Wales's and King's Docks, Swansea now has a dock area of nearly 150 acres, with six miles of quays and immense warehouse accommodation

defeated him, as they had defeated Rufus, when Owen of Gwynedd and Rhys of Debenbarth stood together. His campaigns ended in a stalemate ; in fact, the Welshmen rather recovered ground, capturing Cardigan in the south and Rhuddlan in the north.

After Owen's death (1172) the hegemony passed for a time to Rhys. The policy of both may be regarded as the consolidation of Wales—at least a Welsh Wales—in actual independence which, for the sake of peace, recognized a technical overlord in the King of England.

This was the policy bequeathed to "the Great" Llewelyn ap Jorwerth, the grandson of Owen of Gwynedd. The marcher barons of England enjoyed the privilege of waging private war, which was denied to the rest of the English baronage.

Virtually, Llewelyn's claim was to rule over Gwynedd and as much of the rest of Wales as would acknowledge him as

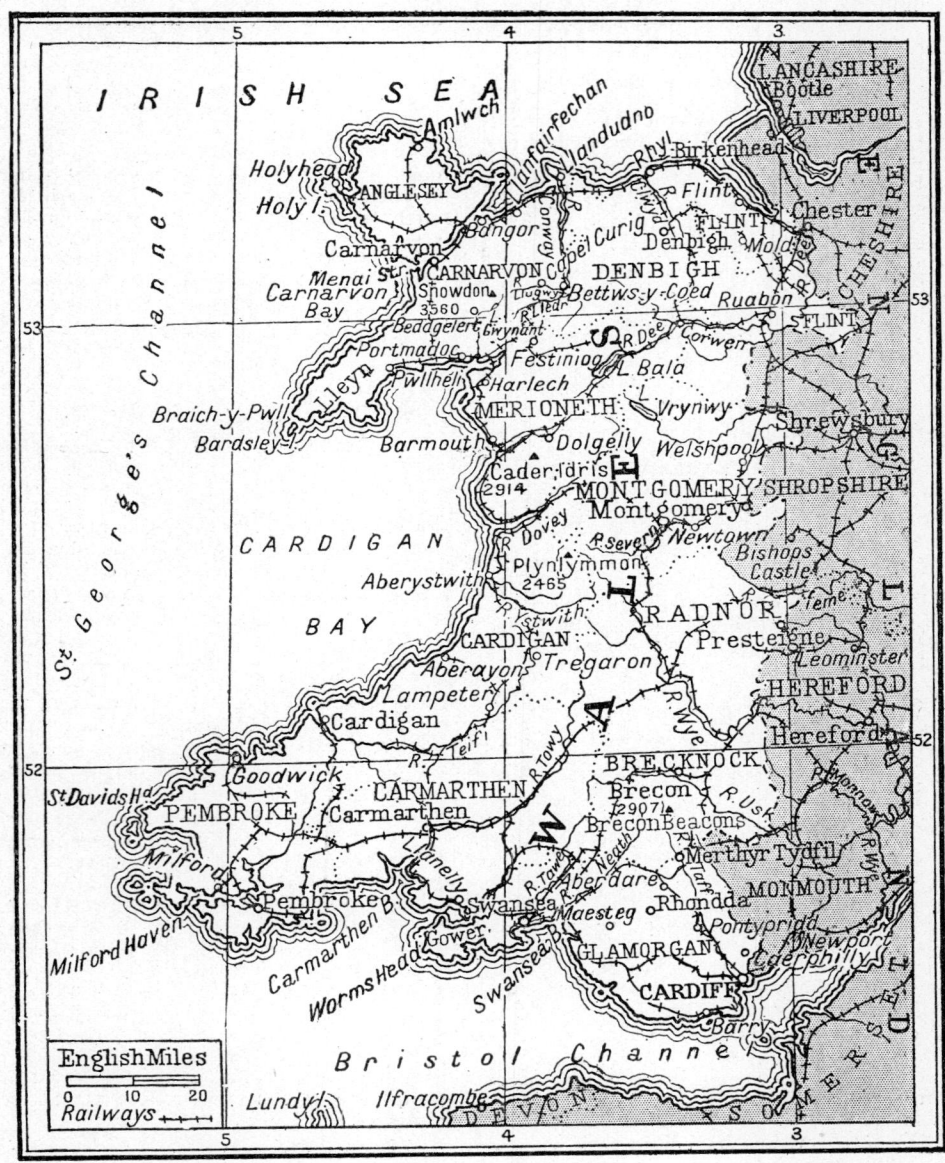

THE PRINCIPALITY OF WALES

overlord, by Welsh law, not English law, while acting personally as a feudatory of the English king, John or Henry III. Consequently, he was in effect an ally of the barons of England in their contests with those two kings in the first forty years of the thirteenth century—except when it suited him to ally himself with the Crown by reason of his rivalry with the marcher barons, among whom the Mortimers of Wigmore were becoming prominent.

Welsh Unification Under Llewelyn

A necessary condition was Welsh unification through the ascendancy of Gwynedd. That purpose he was largely successful in accomplishing. The Welsh princes, at first hostile to any supreme authority, presently found that it was only under Llewelyn's leadership that they could escape subjection to the marchers, with whom he alone as a soldier or diplomatist was able to cope.

Most remarkable of his achievements was the establishment of a Council of Princes ; the difficulty was to imbue them with loyalty to the idea of unity—particularism was as rampant among them as in the city-states of ancient Hellas, and for the time this was overcome by the personal ascendancy which his character and abilities established.

Before Llewelyn died all Welsh Wales—that is, so much of the country as was not dominated by the marchers' castles—owned him as overlord, and it included a good deal which at the beginning of his career seemed to be passing under the marchers' dominion.

Once more, with his death in 1240, dissensions and rivalries revived ; once more, under his grandson Llewelyn, the great antagonist of Edward I., there was to be a brief restoration of unity with the same conception at the back of it—an independently governed Welsh Principality acknowledging the formal suzerainty of the King of England. But that idea was incompatible with Edward I.'s conceptions—as John Baliol was to find in Scotland. The Crown was to be actively supreme.

The First Prince of Wales

Llewelyn had aided Montfort ; Edward distrusted him ; he distrusted Edward. The manifest distrust on each side intensified it on the other side. In 1277 Edward resolved that Llewelyn must be forced decisively to submission, and his campaign of that year imposed on the Welsh prince the treaty of Rhuddlan, which left him " Prince of Wales " in name, but in fact of Gwynedd only. Everywhere else princes and people found themselves at the mercy

either of marcher lords or of royal officers. In 1282 an insurrection broke out. Not Llewelyn himself but his brother David had started it, but Llewelyn placed himself at its head. Edward was now resolved to crush resistance once for all, but conquest was still incomplete when at the end of the year Llewelyn himself was slain in a chance encounter.

There was no one to take his place, the resistance collapsed, and Welsh independence, as the great Llewelyn had conceived it, was wiped out for ever by the Statute of Wales or Rhuddlan (1284), which made the Principality an appanage of the English Crown. Nearly twenty years later Edward handed it over to his heir-apparent, and that practice has been continued down to our own day.

All that had ever owned Llewelyn's overlordship was included in the new Principality, which was reckoned as an estate of the king's. The minor princes were ejected by king's officers, the whole was divided English fashion into shires under the king's sheriffs. New castles, masterpieces of military art, garrisoned by the king's troops, held the country in subjection and became the centres of industrial colonies ; it was long before the new rule ceased to have the character of a military occupation.

How Union with England Came

Though English laws were introduced, much of the Welsh customary law was allowed to survive. The Principality was encircled on east and south by the marcher lordships. Although at the outset in Wales, as in Scotland at the same period, not a little brutality was displayed by the officers of the new government and the English soldiery, the risings which took place were overwhelmed as Wallace was overwhelmed, and there was no Bruce to time a fortunate insurrection at the moment of the great Edward's death.

The tyranny of English conquest gave place to the normal English instinct for ordered justice. Welsh archers (as well as other light-armed troops), from whom the English learnt the military value of the longbow, served valiantly at Crecy and Poitiers, and the Black Prince inspired a personal loyalty. Wales, in short, during the fourteenth century, became reconciled to the loss of her independence, and, in fact, enjoyed a substantial increase of material prosperity ; and though the system of government was imposed from outside, the officers appointed were for the most part Welshmen.

But the feuds with the marchers remained, and it was a feud between Lord Grey of Ruthin and his Welsh neighbour Owen Glendower, in whose veins ran the blood of Maelgwn, that in Henry IV.'s reign led the latter to raise once more the standard of Welsh independence, ally himself with the Percy revolt, and maintain a struggle which was only slowly and painfully subdued. By the end of the reign he was only a fugitive outlaw among his native hills ; and about the time of his death Welsh troops were sharing in the glories of Agincourt.

Then, by a curious turn of fortune, a Welsh gentleman, Owen Tudor, became the husband of Henry V.'s widow, and through his son's marriage to Margaret Beaufort became the grandfather of the man whom the Lancastrians chose to regard as the representative of their claims, so that a Welshman founded the Tudor Dynasty as Henry VII., and was the ancestor of every monarch who has since worn the crown of England or of Scotland.

It was not until the reign of Henry VIII., however, that Wales was actually incorporated with England (1536). Even then Wales, like the north of England, had its executive vested in the arbitrary " Council of Wales " ; both Councils, however, were abolished a century later by the Long Parliament (1641).

Welsh loyalty to the Crown never failed ; it had become ingrained under the Welsh dynasty of the Tudors, and it was consistently displayed in the civil wars of the seventeenth century. Cromwell, himself the great-grandson of a Welshman, was engaged in suppressing a Royalist rising in Wales in 1648, just before he marched to rout the Scots army of invasion at Preston. But the Welsh nationality and the Welsh character remained always distinctive and separate.

The Welsh did not become English ; the English who settled among them became Welsh, and Welsh not English continued to be the everyday language of the people, though the separate political history of Wales closed in the sixteenth century.

The earliest surviving fragments of written Welsh belong to the period of the ninth and tenth centuries, but it was not till somewhat later that " The Four Ancient Books of Wales," which may be described as the beginnings of Welsh literature, made their appearance. Some portions of these deal with topical events and there is a wealth of elemental poetry and powerful prose.

Wales is still unmistakably distinct from England, one—though the smallest—of the units of which the United Kingdom is composed.

WALES : FACTS AND FIGURES

The Country

Forms a peninsula on the west coast of England, being bounded on the east by the English counties of Monmouth, Hereford, Shropshire, and Cheshire, and on the north, south, and west by the Irish Sea. Most of Wales is mountainous, except for the Vales of Glamorgan and Carmarthen and the Pembroke lowlands. On the north-west coast and separated by the Menai Strait is the island of Anglesey.

The main rivers are the Dee, about 70 miles long and falling 530 feet during its course from Lake Bala to its mouth near Chester ; the Conway ; the Teifi and Dovey, flowing to Cardigan Bay, and the Severn, Wye, and Usk, rising near Plynlymmon. Total area, comprising twelve counties, about 7,468 square miles ; estimated population 2,207,000.

Government

For purposes of government Wales is associated with England and is subject in local administration to similar conditions, with the exception that there are separate organizations to deal with health, education, etc.

Commerce and Industries

Commercial and industrial activity is located chiefly in South Wales and the district round Wrexham. The great shipping industry of Cardiff and Swansea, and the South Wales coalfields, one of the world's largest deposits of anthracite, are the chief sources of wealth. In addition there are many works dealing with galvanizing, patent fuel, tinplate, steel, weldless tubes, spelter, and oil refining. There is also an important output of coke and the coal-tar by-products which include pitch, tar, sulphate of ammonia, naphtha, anthracene and creosote oils, sulphuric acid, and naphthalene salts. Slate quarrying is extensive in North Wales.

One of the principal imports is timber, used largely for pit-props and other coal-mining purposes. Imports of timber in 1922 were valued at £2,313,262 and of iron ore for same year aggregated 825,847 tons. Total imports into South Wales ports for 1922 aggregated 2,779,630 tons, and exports of coal and coke 28,258,225 tons.

Communications

Under the Railways Act 1921 the important docks at Cardiff, Barry, Port Talbot, and Penarth and the railway companies associated with them were incorporated with the Great Western Railway.

Religion and Education

The Church in Wales and Monmouthshire was disestablished in 1920 under the Welsh Church Acts of 1914 and 1919, and Wales was created a separate Archbishopric. The property formerly in the hands of the Church in Wales together with £1,000,000 subscribed by Parliament were to be distributed, by a body known as the Welsh Commissioners, among parties representing the Church, and also to the University of Wales and to certain other authorities. The province of Wales contains five dioceses, Monmouth, Llandaff, Bangor, St. Asaph, and St. Davids. Baptists, Wesleyans, and Congregationalists form a large part of the population. The University of Wales, dating from 1903, comprises colleges at Cardiff, Bangor, Aberystwyth, and Swansea, and affiliated theological colleges at Bala, Aberystwyth, Carmarthen, Cardiff, Brecon, and Bangor.

Chief Towns

Cardiff (estimated population 200,000), Swansea (157,000), Merthyr Tydfil (80,000), Pontypridd (47,000), Barry (33,000), Wrexham (19,000), Pembroke (15,000), Bangor (11,000), Carmarthen (10,000), Carnarvon (9,000), Aberystwyth (8,000), Abergavenny (8,000).

DIFFERENT RACES BUT A SINGLE NATION IN THE TRIUNE KINGDOM OF YUGO-SLAVIA

Preëminently Yugo-Slavia is an illustration of a state resulting from the idea of common nationality. The polyglot crowds that gather in its marts, as here in the water-melon market of Köprülü, are composed of men of different races and different religions and speaking different languages, but all animated by a collective conscience, a collective will to live, which is the essence of nationality. It is this that differentiates the cosmopolitan crowds of Yugo-Slavia and of the new Poland from those, animated only by desire for material profit, that throng the markets of other great industrial centres

Photo, L. G. Popoff

THE NATIONAL SPIRIT
in The Modern World
By J. A. R. MARRIOTT, M.A., M.P.

Author of " The Remaking of Modern Europe (1789-1872)," " The European Commonwealth," etc.

This penetrating and illuminating essay by Mr. J. A. R. Marriott is complementary to those contributed to our first volume by Sir Arthur Keith and Mr. Romaine Paterson. The one gave an outline of racial origins and explained how man emerged from the horde at the call of the tribal spirit ; the other showed how the successive industrial agglomerations of mankind that constituted the great States of the ancient world flourished and decayed under the pressure of conflict and cooperation. In the accompanying chapter Mr. Marriott completes the survey by analysing the spirit of nationality, the most potent and the most elusive of the forces that have moulded our modern polity

THE Nation-State is the typical political product of the modern world. To the ancient world, Nations were by no means unknown ; nor were States. But the State rarely corresponded with the Nation. The characteristic political entity was something either much larger or much smaller than the typical modern State : either an empire or a city ; the City-States of Hellas, for example ; the Empires of Assyria, Macedon, or Rome. The idea that a State should be, even roughly, coextensive and coincident with a Nation did not enter the political consciousness of mankind until towards the end of the eighteenth century. Some authorities would date the new conception specifically from the annihilation of Poland. The partition of Poland among its three powerful neighbours wiped out a State which had filled an imposing place in the European polity ; it served to revivify a nation. That nation has now achieved its ambition in a resuscitated Poland.

Elusive Nature of Nationality

Among the forces which have gone to the moulding of our modern polity, that of nationality is certainly the most elusive. It has almost defied definition. Vico defined a nationality as " a natural society of men who by unity of territory, of origin, of custom, and of language, are drawn into a community of life and of social conscience." Is " unity of territory " essential to the idea of nationality ?

Or even " community of life " ? If so, we must deny specific nationality to the Jews in dispersion or to the Poles after the partition of their State. Is identity of language essential, or of religion ? If so, we must deny the existence of a Swiss nationality, for the " Swiss " embrace two, if not three, creeds, and speak three, if not four, distinct languages. And what of the " Americans " ?

Nationality a Collective Conscience

Plainly, we shall involve ourselves in difficulties if we lay over-much emphasis either on religion or on language as essential elements. Yet in the absence of these it would seem difficult to preserve nationality when it is divorced from statehood. Swiss nationality and American nationality are respectively the resultant of the evolution of a Swiss State and of an American State. In other cases the State may be a resultant of the idea of common nationality. The Triune Kingdom, commonly designated Yugo-Slavia, and the new Poland are apposite illustrations of the latter process. We seem, therefore, to be almost driven by exclusions and inclusions to acceptance of the definition proposed by Professor Henri Hauser of Dijon : " Nationality is a matter of collective conscience, of collective will to live. . . Race, religion, language, all these elements either are or are not factors in nationality according to whether they do or do not enter into the collective conscience by virtue thereof." (" The Principle of Nationalities," page 7.)

A " collective conscience." But the doubt obtrudes itself whether such a conscience could have been generated without a sentimental or traditional attachment to a territorial home. Jewish nationality has been sustained during two thousand years of exile, mainly, no doubt, by devotion to a particular creed, by wonderful persistency of blood, but not least by collective affection for the common home of the race : " When I forget thee, O Jerusalem." But for Zionism the modern Palestine would never have been called into being by the Paris Conference. Similarly the Poles in dispersion have drawn their inspiration from the fact that many of their brethren have lived on, though under alien rule, on the plains of the Vistula.

Professor Zimmern's Definition

Professor Zimmern, then, would seem to get near to the heart of the matter when he writes : " Nationality is more than a creed or a doctrine, or a code of conduct, it is an instinctive attachment ; it recalls an atmosphere of precious memories, of vanished parents and friends, of old customs, of reverence, of home, and a sense of the brief span of human life as a link between immemorial generations spreading backwards and forwards. . . It implies a particular kind of corporate self-consciousness, peculiarly intimate, yet invested at the same time with a peculiar dignity. . . and it implies, secondly, a country, an actual strip of land associated with the nationality, a territorial centre where the flame of nationality is kept alight at the hearth fire of home." (" Nationality and Government," pages 78, 84.)

Beginnings of the States System

Yet if the idea of nationality be elusive, it is plainly among the most potent of the formative forces of to-day. For the evolution of the modern States system we must, however, go farther back than the genesis of the idea of nationality. Among the great States of the modern world England was three hundred years ahead of the rest in the realization of its unity and identity. The sense of nationality in England was due, however, to causes, geographical and political, which were unique in their operation. Hardly was there a king of the English before he put forward a claim to be " alterius orbis Imperator " —outside the jurisdiction of the Holy Roman Empire, and, indeed, of the Roman Papacy. Continental Europe was, during the thousand years which intervened between the fall of the Roman Empire and the disruption of Christendom, a quasi-unity dominated in theory by the conjoint authority of pope and emperor, and, in fact, unified by common subjection in ecclesiastical affairs to the Roman Primacy, by common acceptance in the civil sphere of Roman law, and by an all-pervading and all-powerful social system which provided at once a system of land tenure, a nexus for society and a method of government. The Empire, the Papacy, and the feudal system dominated the life of the Middle Ages, and so long as that domination persisted there was no room for the idea of nationality, nor could the modern States system emerge.

Evolution of the Nation-State

The intellectual, political, geographical and ecclesiastical upheaval which is compendiously described as " The Renaissance and the Reformation," opened the door to the emergence of national Churches and the evolution of the Nation-State. Hungary, Poland, and Bohemia had long enjoyed the dignity of statehood. Among the great States of Western Europe, France was (after England) the first to achieve unity and self-conscious identity. The remarkable astuteness of a long succession of kings of the Capet and Valois dynasties ; the absorption by conquest or marriage of the great feudal duchies and counties ; frontiers well defined on two sides though highly debatable on a third ; an administrative system ever increasing in efficiency as it increased in centralisation ; the Hundred Years War against the Angevin kings of England and the dukes of Burgundy—all these played their part in the making of modern France, and by the end of the fifteenth century France had arrived.

Spain reached a similar stage of national evolution early in the sixteenth century. The secular crusade against the Saracens was the central fact in the making of Spain, but King Charles I., otherwise known as the Emperor Charles V., was the first Spanish sovereign to rule over a united Spain. The bitter contest between Spain and the provinces of the Low Countries gave to the seven northern provinces sufficient cohesion and self-consciousness to entitle them to be regarded as a Nation-State from the end of the sixteenth century onwards, albeit a State of a federal rather than a unitary type. Differences of creed between the Dutch and their former rulers at once fortified them during the struggle for independence and accentuated the sense of unity when independence was at last achieved.

European Politics and Antagonisms

Ecclesiastical antagonisms contributed once more to the many disruptive forces which during the Thirty Years War (1618-48) dissipated whatever of unity Germany had derived from the coincidence of the German kingship and the Holy Roman Empire. From the chaos there emerged more than one powerful State. First " Austria," conglomerate in itself and dynastically connected with the Czech Kingdom of Bohemia and the Magyar Kingdom of Hungary ; then Prussia ; but neither could be described with accuracy as a Nation-State ; still less could the lesser German States, such as Saxony, Bavaria, Baden, Württemberg, or the Palatinate, though all were virtually independent sovereignties.

Portugal had meanwhile (1640) regained its independence, and thenceforth must be counted as a Nation-State, while the dissolution of the Union of Calmar (1523) permitted Sweden to take its place as an independent " Power," and for a brief period (roughly 1600-1721) to play a conspicuous and influential part in European politics. Thanks, indeed, partly to the vigour of her kings and the skill and discipline of her soldiers, in part to the friendship which so long subsisted between Stockholm and Paris, Sweden occupied in the European polity a place far more than commensurate with her permanent strength and resources.

Growth of Powers in Modern Times

The rapid rise of the Hohenzollern power in Prussia and North Germany, still more the irruption of Russia into European politics at the close of the seventeenth century, brought to an end the brief ascendancy of Sweden. Russia, though loosely compacted, took her place as a Nation-State in the first years of the eighteenth century, and before the century closed the American continent had brought to the birth the first of the Nation-States in the New World.

How far had the idea of nationality contributed to the establishment of these Powers of the modern world ? The instinctive avoidance of the word " nations," the substitution of the term " Powers " would seem to suggest a partial answer to the question.

Monarchical Factor in State Making

The motive force which was on every side operating to produce a new States system, which found its manifestation in the creation of strong, compact, homogeneous kingdoms, was primarily dynastic, or at least monarchical. France was made by a succession of great kings and great ministers, the apotheosis of the absolute monarchy being reached in the brilliant period which culminated in the reign of "Le Roi Soleil" (Louis XIV.). By the end of the seventeenth century France was, however, indisputably a Nation-State. Richelieu had completed the work of political unification, Colbert had made her one commercially and economically, yet the social fissures were still deep. Not until the Revolution did France become a social unity. In two ways Richelieu left his work incomplete. The destruction of political feudalism served only to accentuate the social cleavage between class and class. Nor did he achieve his ambition in regard to the rectification of the frontiers of France.

Expansion of the Kingdom of France

According to his political testament his aim was to identify modern France with ancient Gaul. His intervention in the Thirty Years War wrung from the Empire a formal acknowledgment of the cession of the three Lorraine bishoprics, Metz, Toul, and Verdun, annexed in 1552, and, in addition, the greater part of the province of Alsace. For the first time modern France touched the Rhine. The acquisition of Franche Comté in 1674 rendered still more isolated the remaining portions of Lorraine, but these did not actually fall into France until 1766. Meanwhile, Henri IV. had brought to the Crown of France the Kingdom of Béarn, or the northern half of Navarre, and Louis XIV. finally rounded off the Pyrenean frontier by the acquisition of Roussillon and Cerdagne in 1659.

Result of Territorial Acquisitions

By a curious legal subterfuge—the Chambre des Réunions—Strasburg was assigned to France in 1683. Later in the same reign the north-eastern frontier was immensely strengthened by the acquisition of Western Flanders, and of a number of strong fortresses like Lille, Cambrai, and Valenciennes, which virtually gave France the command of Artois and Hainault. Louis XIV never dreamt of invoking the principle of nationality to cover these territorial acquisitions. The motive was frankly strategical, to render France secure against attack by her neighbours ; to give France a military advantage should she desire to take the offensive. Of the doctrine of " nationality " there is not a hint ; yet the fact remains that before the process of territorial unification began the French were not a nation ; when it was complete they unquestionably were. Bretons and Burgundians, Normans, Angevins and Acquitainians alike acknowledged themselves to be " Frenchmen," and found satisfaction and pride not merely in common citizenship but in common nationality.

We pass from modern France to modern Spain. The two outstanding characteristics of the Spaniard—his intense nationalism and his persistent provincialism—are both attributable to his prolonged contest with the Moors.

Nationalism Forged by Patriotism

No people in the world have developed a deeper sense of national individuality than the Spanish, yet between province and province—notably between Castile Aragon, and Catalonia—there are differences of tradition and outlook which political unification has not availed to eradicate. Probably nothing less than a secular crusade against an intruding enemy, alien in race and alien in creed would have sufficed to weld Catalans and Castilians, Aragonese and Andalusians into a united nation.

Dutch nationalism is the product of a struggle not less fierce than that in which Spanish nationalism was conceived—on the one hand a prolonged contest waged with the elemental forces of nature ; on the other a brief, but terrible struggle against the tyranny ecclesiastical, economic, administrative and political, of the Spanish rulers of the Netherlands.

Dutch nationalism was forged in the furnace of persecution ; it has been sustained by the necessity for ceaseless

Napoleon and Moreau brought Austria once more to her knees at Marengo and Hohenlinden respectively, 1800; and by the Treaty of Lunéville (1801) Austria confirmed the cession of the Rhineland to France. There then ensued a ludicrous and humiliating rush of German princelings to Paris, where, in order to secure the largest possible slice of the booty, each for each, all paid assiduous court to Talleyrand and his minions.

Napoleon's principles of redistribution were few and simple—to penalise Austria; to cajole Prussia; and, by enlarging and consolidating the territories of the secondary States, to bind them by ties of interest and gratitude more closely to France. Under the Act of Mediatisation, the States were reduced from three hundred and sixty to less than half that number. Of the fifty-one Imperial cities only six were permitted to survive. The old Circles of the Empire disappeared and all the ecclesiastical States, except one, were suppressed. Prussia got a large share of the spoils; so did Bavaria, Baden, Württemberg and Hesse-Kassel.

Sovereignty of the German Princes

The Act of Mediatisation marked only a stage in Napoleon's journey. Austria was not yet completely crushed, the Holy Roman Empire still survived. Before Napoleon gave the final push to the tottering ruin, he prudently laid the foundations of the new edifice. In the autumn of 1805 he concluded treaties with the client States—Bavaria, Baden, and Württemburg—by which they agreed to furnish, in the forthcoming campaign, contingents to the army of France. The Treaty of Pressburg (January 1, 1806) provided that the German princes should enjoy " complete and undivided sovereignty over their own States," and thus were finally shattered the last links which bound the princes to the old Empire. On July 17, 1806, the Treaty of the Confederation of the Rhine was signed in Paris. Charles of Dalberg,

Archbishop of Regensburg (Ratisbon) and Arch-Chancellor of the Empire, the Kings of Bavaria and Württemberg, the Elector of Baden, the Duke of Berg and the Landgrave of Hesse-Darmstadt, together with nine minor princes, definitely renounced their allegiance to the Empire, accepted the protection of Napoleon and pledged themselves to support him with arms.

End of the Holy Roman Empire

On August 1 Napoleon—" the new Charlemagne " and in verity Emperor of the West—announced that he no longer recognized the existence of the " Germanic Confederation," and on August 6 the Emperor Francis, who two years earlier had assumed the entirely new title of Emperor of Austria, renounced the title of Holy Roman Emperor. Thus, after an existence of just one thousand years, that hoary anachronism came to an end. But for Napoleon it might still be cumbering the earth.

The birth of the new German State, perhaps the most conspicuous illustration of the working of the national spirit in the modern world, was rendered possible only by the destruction of that Roman Empire which had for centuries strangled the incipient national life of Germany and had arrested the evolution of a Nation-State.

Colliding Forces Spread Confusion

Events now moved rapidly. The annihilation of the Prussian power at Jena; her humiliation and dismemberment at Tilsit; the remaking of Prussia by Stein and Hardenberg, Scharnhorst and Humboldt; Napoleon's call to the Poles and the setting up of the Duchy of Warsaw; the attack upon Spain and the consequent reaction against the tyranny of Napoleon on nationalist lines; the addresses of Fichte to the German nation and their response in the War of Liberation; the overthrow of Napoleon's military power in the mighty battles of 1813-14—these things seemed to presage the early triumph of Nationalism in Germany. The hopes of the patriots were doomed to disappointment at Vienna, but they were triumphantly realized in 1870.

Napoleonic Reforms Sweep Italy

The policy of Napoleon in Italy was parallel to a great extent with his policy in Germany. To Italy, as to Germany, he went at once as conqueror and as liberator. Italy at the close of the eighteenth century was even more devoid of the national spirit than Germany. Consisting of some fifteen separate States, dominated by the Hapsburgs in the north, by the Papacy and its " Legations " in the centre, by the Spanish Bourbons in Naples and Sicily, Italy had since the sixteenth century been little more than the cockpit of Europe. Deprived of civic independence, ignorant alike of political and social life, her people lay for the most part under alien rule—hopeless, emotionless and benumbed. Napoleon aroused them from their apathy. He reduced the political divisions of the country from fifteen to three ; he introduced the Code Napoléon and unified the administration ; he expelled the Jesuits and initiated educational reforms ; he built bridges and made roads ; above all, he taught the Italians to fight, and to fight not as Venetians, Lombards, or Neapolitans, but as Italians.

European Reaction and Unrest

In Italy, as in Germany, the diplomatists at Vienna attempted to wipe out all traces of Napoleon's work and to set back the hands of the political clock. It could not be done. There was indeed a temporary reaction towards separatism and autocracy. Dynastic influences were in the ascendant at Vienna ; the principle of legitimacy enjoyed a temporary triumph ; the idea of nationality was ignored. The reaction, however, was not of long duration. Within a very few years there were on every hand manifestations of impatience with the policy of simple restoration and the naked reassertion of the principle of legitimacy.

In 1830 France gave the signal for a revolutionary outburst which, in one form or another, was reproduced in almost every country of continental Europe. But these movements, though they achieved something for constitutional liberty, did little to promote, except, perhaps, in Belgium, the principle of nationality. Far otherwise was it with the revolutions of 1848. In most countries, if not in all, a demand was put forward for an extension of popular liberties, but the predominant motive was unquestionably national. It was the alien character of Austrian rule which inspired Italians and Magyars and Czechs to raise the flag of insurrection against the Hapsburgs. It was a desire for national unity which brought to Frankfort representatives of every State in Germany, and led them to offer an Imperial Crown to Frederick William IV. of Prussia. The offer was declined.

Bismarck and Prussian Supremacy

The Hohenzollern sovereign was so distrustful of the democratic temper of the Frankfort parliament as to postpone the realization of German unity. Moreover, he did not want to see Prussia merged in Germany. Ten years of reaction followed upon his refusal. Then Bismarck got his chance. He mistrusted parliamentary methods at least as much as Frederick William IV. ; he believed that Germany must be welded together not by " parchments, votes, and speeches," but by blood and iron ; above all, he was resolved that Prussia should not be merged in Germany, but that, on the contrary, Germany should be absorbed by Prussia.

The first step was to exclude the Hapsburgs with their conglomerate Empire from the Germanic body. The disputes about Schleswig-Holstein and the ensuing war with Denmark enabled him to fix a quarrel upon Austria which led to the Seven Weeks War, to the Prussian victory at Sadowa, to the exclusion of Austria from Germany, and to the break-up of the Bund which ever since 1815 had been powerless for everything but mischief. The dissolution of the Bund was followed by the formation (1867) of a North German Confederation under the presidency of the King of Prussia. Only the States north of the Main were originally members of the new Confederation, which was far more closely knit—more genuinely federal in character—than the old, but provision was made for the admission of the southern States, if and when they should desire it.

Establishment of the German Empire

How long they might have held aloof from union with North Germany it is impossible to say, had not Napoleon III. played straight into Bismarck's hands. The ineptitude of his diplomacy after 1867 not only broke the traditional tie between France, particularly Bonapartist France, and the South German States, but, in 1870, flung them into the arms of Prussia. When France was manoeuvred by Bismarck into a declaration of war upon Prussia the Hohenzollerns found themselves, for the first time, at the head of a united Germany. After the crushing defeat of the French armies and the humiliating surrender at Sedan, Bismarck had little difficulty in converting the North German Confederation of 1867 into the Germanic Empire of 1871, an Empire which included every State of the Fatherland save only the German part of Austria.

If the unification of Germany affords the most imposing manifestation of the national spirit, the unification of Italy is the most romantic. Nothing did so much as the success of that movement to give popularity to the doctrine of the rights of nationalities. Many factors contributed to that success: the administrative uniformity of the Napoleonic regime, the pure-hearted enthusiasm of Mazzini, the high statesmanship and brilliant diplomacy of Cavour, the steadfastness of the House of Savoy, the romantic knight-errantry of Garibaldi.

France Furthers the Italian Cause

Nor was the cause of Italy unfavoured by external circumstances : the outbreak of the Crimean War, the intervention of Sardinia on the side of the allies, an intervention apparently fortuitous, but in reality inspired by high and far-sighted statesmanship, and the opportunity thus given to and seized by Cavour to put the whole Italian case before the diplomatists assembled at Paris. At Paris Cavour met Napoleon III., and of that meeting the pact of Plombières was the result. Napoleon had a real apprehension of the principle of nationality, and his sympathy for the Italian cause was, perhaps, as nearly genuine and altruistic as any of the emotions which stirred that complex personality. The intervention of France in the Austro-Sardinian War of 1859 was of incomparable service to Italy at a most critical juncture of her history. Hardly less important to Italy, though wholly self-regarding, was the diplomacy of Bismarck. His anxiety to isolate Austria induced him to offer Venetia to Victor Emmanuel, and Austria was compelled by Sadowa to give it up.

Mazzini Sows the Seed of Unity

The actual stages on the road towards unity may be rapidly indicated. The stage between the insurrections of 1820 and the revolutions of 1848 was merely preliminary, though far from unimportant. During that period Mazzini sowed the seed, but he did little to help in reaping the subsequent harvest. The first definite advance was registered in 1860, when the States of Central Italy—Modena, Parma, Tuscany, and the Romagna—united themselves by plebiscite with the new Kingdom of North Italy. The credit of that achievement was due almost wholly to Victor Emmanuel and Cavour, though Napoleon's help was timely and substantial.

It involved, however, the painful sacrifice of Nice and Savoy. But the significant transference of the Italian capital from Turin to Florence (1865) brought Italy a step nearer Rome.

Garibaldi and His "Thousand"

The next stage—the union of North and South Italy—was accomplished less by diplomacy than by knight-errantry. In 1860 the Sicilians were encouraged by Mazzini to revolt against the tyranny of Bombino (Francis II.). Garibaldi and his "Thousand" flew to their assistance from Genoa, and within a few weeks had made themselves masters of the island and, under the unavowed protection of English guns, had crossed the narrow straits to Naples.

The Bourbon power crumbled almost as quickly in Naples as in Sicily, but after the conquest of Naples a critical moment occurred when Garibaldi declared that he would annex the southern kingdoms to the Kingdom of North Italy only when he could confer the gift upon Victor Emmanuel in Rome.

Diplomacy and Knight-Errantry

Cavour knew that an advance upon Rome at this moment might have jeopardised all that had been achieved in the recent past as well as the promise of the immediate future. An army was hurriedly dispatched from Florence with the two-fold object of defending the Romagna against the Papal troops and of obstructing the advance of the Garibaldians upon Rome. Both purposes were achieved. On September 18, 1860, the Sardinian army met and routed the Papal troops at Castelfidardo, and ten days later compelled General Lamoricière to surrender at Ancona. Their next task was to deal with the Garibaldians. Garibaldi, flushed with victory, was in obstinate mood, but good sense prevailed. Garibaldi abandoned his march upon Rome, laid the crown of the two Sicilies at the feet of his Sovereign, and on November 7 Victor Emmanuel and Garibaldi entered Naples in triumph and in amity. Unity was almost achieved ; but in the two sides of Italy there were still two gaping wounds. Austria, as we have already seen, was compelled by Bismarck to surrender Venetia to Italy in 1867, but the Trentino, with its Italian population, was left in Austrian hands, and there was bequeathed to the future an Adriatic problem the persistence of which cost Austria and Germany dear in 1915. From 1867 down to the Treaty of Rapallo in 1920 the claim to *Italia Irredenta*, the passionate desire to unite to United Italy these lands upon the shores of the Adriatic which are either predominantly Italian in population or, owing to their sometime inclusion in the domains of Venetia, are culturally Italian, was the most potent force in the external politics of Italy.

Conflict Between Vatican and Quirinal

Of problems which may be regarded as domestic, undoubtedly the most difficult has been the relations of the new Italian Kingdom and the Papacy. Both disputants command sympathy and respect. The House of Savoy accurately interpreted a feeling well-nigh universal among the Italians of the Risorgimento in its resolution to make Rome the capital of United Italy. No other capital was indeed conceivable. On the other hand it is impossible to ignore the strength of the Papal case. For nearly two thousand years the Pope had administered his world-empire from the unassailed security of the Petrine rock. Was not a base of territorial independence, the possession of a temporal sovereignty, essential to the international or super-national position of his spiritual kingdom ? The House of Savoy had, however, no choice. The Prussian attack upon France in 1870 compelled Napoleon to withdraw the French garrison from Rome, and after a feint of resistance from the Papal troops, Victor Emmanuel occupied Rome, and the Pope became henceforward the "prisoner of the Vatican." The occupation of Rome was the crown of the Italian Risorgimento; it marked the final triumph of the most romantic among the national movements of the nineteenth century.

Not that romance was by any means absent from the national movements in the Near East. For four hundred years the Ottoman Turks had been encamped upon European soil. Alien in creed, in race, in social custom and political tradition from the peoples of the Balkan peninsula, they had never absorbed nor even attempted to absorb the indigenous inhabitants; still less were they absorbed by them. But for the fact that they were the votaries of a religion inferior only to Christianity they would probably, like the Teutonic conquerors of Gaul, have yielded to the claims of a higher civilization and a purer creed. As it was they superimposed themselves (much as the English have done in India) upon Serbs, Greeks, Bulgars, and Rumanians, neither absorbing them nor wiping them out. The subjugated peoples disappeared from sight, almost from memory, for four hundred years; but as the tide of Turkish conquest receded, as the government of the Porte sank into greater and greater decrepitude, the submerged peoples re-emerged.

Portent of the Greek Insurrection

Of the principal nations in the Balkans, three—the Serbs, the Bulgars, and the Greeks—could nourish and sustain the sentiment of nationality by an appeal to the memories of the past. The fourth, the Rumanians, proudly claimed descent from the Roman colony planted by Trajan in Dacia.

The insurrection of the Greeks in 1821 was a portent in the history of the modern world. Not only did it challenge the Turkish sovereignty in the heart of the Empire, but it challenged it definitely in the name of a new doctrine, the doctrine that nationalities, like individuals, possess " rights."

If the Greeks had become tardily conscious of this principle, the fact was due partly to the large measure of local autonomy conceded by the Ottomans to the conquered races, partly to the classical revival of the eighteenth century. partly to the stirring of stagnant waters by the French Revolution and the Napoleonic wars, but most of all to the devoted and patriotic labours of the parish priests. Never did any movement display a more confused and perplexing medley of brutality and nobility, of conspicuous heroism and consummate cowardice, of pure-minded patriotism and sordid individualism, of self-sacrificing loyalty and time-serving treachery.

Victory for Freedom and Justice

Yet who, as Mr. Gladstone once asked, can doubt that it was on the whole a " noble stroke struck for freedom and for justice "? But for the opportune outbreak of war between Russia and Turkey, but for the cordial sympathy of England and France, but for the " untoward accident " of Navarino, the Greeks might have been compelled to yield; their success added to the polity of Europe the first of the new Nation-States.

The Danubian Principalities owed their emancipation to the Crimean War, and their union to the ardour with which Napoleon had espoused the doctrine of nationality. The official acceptance of Serbia and Bulgaria as virtually independent Nation-States may be dated from the insurrection movement of 1875-76, and from the Treaty of Berlin, in which the results of that movement were registered.

Nationality in the Balkans

The enduring significance of that treaty consists not, as contemporaries imagined, as indeed its authors supposed, in the new definition of the relations between Russia and Turkey; not in the remnant of the European domains of the Ottoman Empire snatched from the brink of destruction by Lord Beaconsfield, but in the new Nation-States that arose on the ruins of that Empire. The nationality principle may be as elusive as you will, but whatever its essential ingredients none can doubt that it is in the Balkan peninsula that it has manifested its existence most clearly and most unmistakably demonstrated its force.

Nationality in the New World

Not least in virtue of negation. The Balkan Settlement left Crete, the "Great Greek Island" under the heel of the Turk; it left the Rumanians of Bessarabia in the hands of Russia, those of Transylvania and the Bukovina in the hands of Austria, and by Bismarck's encouragement of the *Drang nach Osten* of his Hapsburg allies, it added the southern Slavs of Bosnia and the Herzegovina to the medley of peoples who sulkily acknowledged the rule of the Emperor Francis Joseph. The Great War of 1914-18 was implicit in the " settlement " of 1878.

The nationality principle has demonstrated its potency in the New World no less conclusively than in the old. How far it has been responsible for moulding the destinies of the States which have arisen in South America upon the ruins of the empires of Portugal and Spain it is difficult to decide, but the Republics of Brazil, Argentina, Bolivia, Chile and Mexico, to mention no other, exhibit many if not all the attributes of genuine Nation-States.

Evolution of the United States

As to the United States of America there is no ambiguity. The great Republic absorbs with astonishing ease and rapidity men of all nations, creeds and tongues, all peoples in fact, save those who are descended from the African negroes who first served the economic needs of the planters of the southern states. But for the prolonged and heroic efforts put forth by the northern states in the Civil War there would now be at least two Nation-States, if not more, within the area occupied by the forty-eight states of the American Union ; as it is, there has evolved one great Nation-State, extending geographically from the Atlantic to the Pacific, from the shores of the St. Lawrence to those of the Gulf of Mexico.

To the north of the United States there is rapidly evolving another nation, whose position becomes day by day less ambiguous. If there is any lack of definition in the status of Canada, Australia, New Zealand, and the Union of South Africa, it arises from the fact that as constituent states in the British Commonwealth they present to the political analyst a wholly new type of polity. The British Commonwealth is at present something less than a *Bundesstaat*, it is something more than a *Staatenbund*. To which of the two forms it will ultimately adhere it is premature to predict. On the one hand the Great Dominions are rapidly developing a sense of individual nationalism.

Polity of the British Commonwealth

They have claimed a place in the League of Nations which is hardly consistent with any semblance of imperial connexion ; Canada has asserted her right to separate diplomatic representation at Washington, and the spirit of individualism, stimulated, no doubt, by the heroic part played by the sons of the Empire in the Great War, has so dominated the Dominions that they hesitated to accept the designation of " Imperial Cabinet " for the meeting of the Prime Ministers lest it should commit to common executive action the cabinets of the constituent states, cabinets which are, of course, severally responsible to their own Dominion legislatures. On the other hand, the Dominions are supremely and most reasonably anxious for a voice in the determination of that foreign policy the principles and the success of which are momentously significant to them.

Such a voice could not, however, be claimed by, still less be conceded to, any state which did not share the common burden of imperial defence or failed to realize the responsibilities as well as the privileges incidental to integral partnership in an organic whole. The citizens of the great Dominions may be said, therefore, to possess a dual nationality as they acknowledge a two-fold allegiance. Primarily Canadians, South Africans, Australians and New Zealanders, as the case may be, they are also British subjects, citizens of one Commonwealth, subjects of one King.

The survey attempted in the preceding pages, cursory though it necessarily be, serves at least to illustrate the complexity of the conceptions combined in the term *Nationality* and the difficulties attendant upon precise definition. It should serve also to point a moral to enforce a warning. Phrases are the pitfalls of the half-educated, the despair of scholarship and science. Formulae are the refuge of the politician, but anathema to the statesman.

The Unit of "Self-Determination"

Nationalities may have "rights," and it may be desirable to defer to the principle of "self-determination," but the man who would penetrate from phrases to realities will be curious to ascertain where the sanction of those "rights" may lie, and what is the precise unit which is entitled to invoke the principle of "self-determination." The latter question is crucial. Self-determination for Great Britain might, for example, involve the denial of the privilege to Scotland or Wales, self-determination for Bavaria might mean its denial to Germany. Everything turns upon the selection of the unit. Professor Zimmern goes so far as to affirm that "self-determination is not a principle of Liberalism but of Bolshevism." Without entering upon a discussion so obviously apt to provoke controversy, it may be said that while, in a general sense, the privilege or right or principle will be denied by no reasonable man, the application of it in particular cases will frequently raise difficulties so great as to reduce the practical value of the principle to little more than the realization of an abstract formula.

One question remains. The nation-state is the typical formation of the modern world. Is it likely to be a permanent formation? Is it the final goal of international evolution, or a transitory stage? One thing must be said at once. Nationalism may make for liberty—it affords no security for peace.

The Ideal State Formation

No one who can estimate the debt which mankind owes to the city-states of ancient Hellas or to the republics of medieval Italy will ever seek to depreciate either the political or the cultural value of small political communities. But the conditions under which the Greek experiments were made were peculiar, and the city-states neither promoted peace nor preserved their own existence. To the small nations, too, the world owes a heavy debt. But the small Nation-State is in the modern world a complete anachronism. If it survives it will survive as an exotic in ungenial soil. The ideal formation is, as Lord Acton seems to suggest, the coexistence of several Nations under the same State.

Where Hope for the Future Lies

This, as he points out, affords "a test as well as the best security of its freedom. It is also one of the chief instruments of civilization" ("Freedom," p. 290.). Happy is the State which, with contentment to each, includes many Nations; and well is it for the peace of the world if there be great Commonwealths which comprehend within their ample borders many self-governing States. In the extension of the federal formation, with due provision for variety of detail, lies the best hope for the political future of mankind.

FINE SPECIMENS OF AN ABORIGINAL RACE OF AMERICA

Slight figures with well formed but not muscular limbs, Mongoloid features, long, dark hair evenly
trimmed, and skin of red cinnamon hue are characteristics of the true or " red " Carib Indians.
The heart of South America was the cradle of their race. Aforetime cannibals, they were settled in
Guiana and in the islands of the Caribbean Sea when Columbus discovered the New World

Photo, Sir H. H. Johnston

DICTIONARY OF RACES

By Northcote W. Thomas

Anthropologist and Author of "Natives of Australia," etc.

The accompanying dictionary of races, specially compiled by Mr. Northcote Thomas for PEOPLES OF ALL NATIONS, is unique. No work of reference contains so complete and convenient a list of living peoples. Within its compass is condensed an immense amount of information about the racial origins, geographical distribution, physical types and social customs of the peoples enumerated. But even this is merely supplementary to that embodied in the whole work. It is to be consulted in conjunction with the ethnographical maps and with the General Index, which gives references to the pages wherein individual peoples are described and illustrated

IN presenting this list of the peoples now inhabiting the world it is proper to explain the connotation given to the differentiating words: Race, tribe, family of languages, language and dialect. Absolute scientific classification is virtually impossible, so closely interrelated are many of the groups of both men and tongues, but for practical purposes the following definitions hold good.

Race properly indicates a biological group distinguished by its physical characteristics, colour, hair, features, etc., and is of pure blood. But it is also used (1) of modern groups of mixed descent which by convergence have come to present a certain physical type, and (2) of groups whose bond of union is mainly cultural and linguistic and whose unity is therefore largely due to historical and political grounds.

Tribe is a word of very varied meanings. Two types may be distinguished in India— (1) a collection of families who claim descent from a common ancestor, which may be an animal, and are also to some extent united by the obligation of the blood feud; they generally use a common language and own a definite tract of country; the Pathans of the north-west border are an example. (2) The group that is united by blood feud only and admits strangers, as it does not claim descent from an eponymous ancestor; the Baluchi are an example. Generally speaking in India the tribe tends to pass into the caste, being divided up into an infinity of divisions according to occupation, etc. In Africa the tribe is a group of peoples speaking the same language but often having no common ruler and no feeling of unity; it does not act together and its members are under no constraint not to make war upon each other.

Language. With regard to speech, individual languages are ordinarily composed of groups of related dialects, which are semi-independent units with a certain vocabulary common to them and to the language of which they form a part, but with other words either peculiar to themselves or used in common with a restricted group of dialects. The area over which a given word is used is rarely coincident with the area covered by a given dialect, but is either smaller or larger. A rough test of whether a form of speech is a language or a dialect is given by ascertaining whether speakers of one dialect readily acquire the allied form, or understand it when spoken. Where this is not so, it is really a question of distinct languages. Thus English is a group of languages, each made up of related dialects, speakers of all dialects having in common a language more or less distinct from all the dialects, viz., standard English.

Families of Languages are major groups into which fall the thousands of individual languages spoken on the earth. They include the following among others: Australian, Austric=Indonesian, Melanesian, Polynesian, Mon-Khmer, etc., with perhaps, Indo-Chinese, Dravidian, Finno-Ugrian, Indo-European or Aryan, Nigritic, including Bantu and Sudanic, Papuan, etc. The aboriginal languages of America have not yet been finally classified into families, and there are many forms of speech, like Basque, which are isolated and perhaps represent the remnants of previously existing families. A language is said to belong to one of these families when historical proof is given that it is descended from the remote ancestral form from which the whole family is believed to come.

Ababua or **Babua.** Bantu-speaking people of the Welle-Bomo-Kandi area, Belgian Congo. The Ababua seem to include a number of distinct tribes, such as the Bakete, Mobalia, Mobati, Bakango, etc. At least two types are intermingled, one short headed, the other long headed. The Ababua are of moderate height and had a great reputation for ferocity, spread by the Azande chiefs, who purchased ivory from them at low prices; but they do not seem to be courageous, though the men are skilful hunters, killing elephants with poisoned spears. They are a merry people, and very hospitable.

Abarambo. Rather short-headed people of the Welle area, related to the Madi.

Abchases. Section of the so-called Circassians of the Caucasus, whose language, however, is only distantly related to Circassian. They are much shorter headed than the other Circassians and, generally speaking, brunette; a short but strong folk with irregular features and an uncivilized aspect.

Abor. Small hill tribe of the north-east of the Brahmaputra valley, in Assam, closely connected with the Miri. They speak a language of the north Assam branch of Tibeto-Burman.

Abyssinians or **Abessinians.** People of Abyssinia, a term without racial significance and a corruption of the word "habeshi," used by Arabs of the mixed peoples who

Dictionary of Races

united to form a Christian state. The two chief languages are Amharic and Tigré, both of Semitic origin; the other languages are Hamitic. Among the tribes are the Abyssinians in a more restricted sense, the Beja or Bishârîn, the Hadendoa, the Beni Amer, Galla, Hallenga, etc. Two main types seem to be represented among the population, one negroid with broad nose, the other Hamitic with a skull of somewhat the same type but a narrow nose. But among the Galla, and still more the Hadendoa, is an element, found in ancient Egypt and therefore presumably ancient, with a skull much lower in proportion to its length. Although the south of Arabia is now occupied by a short-headed type it seems probable that the Hamitic stock had its origin there and that from Abyssinia it penetrated into Upper Egypt, where it existed in pre-dynastic times.

Acawoy. Tribe of Guiana Indians speaking a Carib tongue. Somewhat shorter than the Carib properly so-called, they are forest dwellers and, perhaps for that reason, feared for their slyness. They build wall-less houses, and usually limit themselves to one wife. The dead are buried in a standing position.

Achinese. People of Sumatra who are great fighters, depend on agriculture for their subsistence, and are darker and taller than the Malays.

Adighe. Indigenous name of the Circassians.

Aeta. Negrito inhabitants of the Philippine Islands, who live mainly in mountainous districts. The name is often used to mean Philippine negritos in general. The hair is woolly and black, but, as among the negroes, it is sometimes bleached on the top to a reddish tinge; the skin is dark chocolate, sometimes with a reddish tinge. There is a considerable range of stature, but the average seems to be about three inches short of five feet; the head is longer than that of the Andamanese, but not so long as that of the Semang, their nearest negrito neighbours. The nose is very broad compared with its length, and there is virtually no bridge to it. The lips are thick but not protruding. Long after the arrival of the dominant Malay races, the Aeta were recognized as masters of the soil. They live mainly on game, fish and forest products. In temperament they are indolent and timid, but become violent under provocation; they are described as truthful, honest, and virtuous.

Afghans. People mainly of Iranian stock, including the Afghans proper, Pathans, Ghilzais, Duranis, Hazaras, Uzbegs, Tajiks, Aimaks, etc., some with Mongolian elements. Their language is called Pukhtun in the north, Pushtun in the south. They prefer to call themselves Pushtun, which means mountaineers; the meaning of Afghan is uncertain. Pathan is the same word as Pushtun; both may be identical with Paktues, a tribe mentioned by Herodotus.

Afridi. Pathan tribe of the Peshawar border of India, who are divided into eight principal clans. They are tall, spare and exceptionally well built, and brave, but thoroughly treacherous, active but intolerant of heat; nominally Mahomedan, but ignorant

and superstitious. A clan once suffered under the reproach of having no shrine at which to worship; they induced a sainted man of another clan to come among them, and then murdered him to acquire in his burial-place a sanctuary of their own.

Ainu. People of Japan and south Sakhalien, notable for the profusion of their black wavy hair. Short but strongly built, with broad face and nose and rather long head, they differ from all surrounding types. They have been referred to both the Alpine and the Mediterranean races, and supposed to be allied to Russians, Todas and Australian aborigines; they are said to have occupied the whole of Japan for nine centuries, after expelling a dwarfish race, who are known as the Koro-pok-guru. They hold great festivals in honour of the bear.

Akamba. Bantu-speaking people of East Africa, on the eastern slopes of the high lands south of the Upper Tana. They are of medium height with a head somewhat shorter than usual; two types of head occur, one negroid, the other, common among the chiefs, with a wider forehead and narrower jaw; the eyes are sometimes oblique. They chip the upper incisors and knock out the middle lower incisors. Proud, disinclined to work for Europeans, cheerful, hospitable, fond of children, whom they spoil by indulgence, they are attached to their homes and honest, according to their lights; cattle stealing was, however, meritorious. To-day they are peaceful and harmless, but this is due to fear of consequences. In addition to the ordinary negro type, there is a very strong, short-headed element, amounting perhaps to nearly one third, which seems to go back to an earlier pygmy population.

Akha. Tribe of Burma, with coarse, heavy features and only a vague general resemblance to the more effeminate Annamites. They have noses with higher bridges than the Mongoloid people, and the jaw is pointed and somewhat projecting. All villages have large gateways, usually two, to keep out evil spirits. Even ancestors are regarded as malignant, and the west door of the house is reserved for them, no stranger and no male being allowed to pass, and women only with reverence and not as a regular practice. They are also called Kaw, and speak a language of the Lolo group.

Ala. Tribe of Achin, believed to be allied to the Batta.

Albanians. Inhabitants of Albania, descendants of the Illyrians, of whose language they speak the sole surviving form. The Albanians are divided into Gheg (north) and Tosk (south).

Aleut. Branch of the Eskimo. They inhabit the Aleutian Islands and part of Alaska. The name seems to mean " island "; they call themselves Unungun. They are intelligent compared with the Eskimo, but less independent. They were originally warlike, but the treatment meted out by the Russians reduced them to a tenth of their original numbers and broke their spirit.

Alfures. Generic name given to tribes of very different types in the Malay Archipelago. In some cases—e.g. in the Moluccas—

they are light coloured non-Malay people, with black straight hair, oval eyes, and good physique, and of rather small stature; but the Banda people apply the name to the frizzly-haired people of Ceram, the Kei Islands, Tenimber, etc., who are presumably of dark complexion and have some negrito blood. The name does not really mean more than non-Mahomedan.

Algonquins. Linguistic family of North America which at present falls into three sections—Blackfeet of the west, Cree-Ojibwa of the middle-west, and Wabanaki of the north-east.

Alpine Race. Short-headed, pale or swarthy stock composed of French, South Germans, Russians, some Albanians, Armenians, Tajiks, etc., and supposed to have originated in the Asiatic plateaux.

Alunda. Bantu-speaking people of Angola, who were ruled by the Mwata Yamvo from the seventeenth century onwards.

Amambwe. Bantu tribe of the Nyasa-Tanganyika plateau; they knock out the two middle teeth of the lower jaw, it is said, with an axe.

Amazon - Orinoco Tribes. Group covering quite half the South American continent at one time, comprising four main language stocks, Arawak and Carib in the north-west, Tupi and Tapuya in the south and east. The lower tribes live by hunting, fishing, and agriculture, dwell in " long " houses, wear little clothing, signal with drums, and initiate young men by whipping. In Guiana is a rather higher culture with weaving of cotton; on the coast stone work was prominent among the Tupi. The Tapuya, on the other hand, are cannibals, and stand low in the scale of culture.

Ambundu. Bantu-speaking people in the hinterland of San Paul de Loanda.

Amerindians or **American Indians.** The general designation of all pre-Columbian inhabitants of America, including sometimes the Eskimo. Many tribes in North America are concentrated on reservations, where much of the old life is impossible. Census records for this area give an Indian population of under 400,000, a decrease probably of two-thirds since the discovery of America. The most important language groups are : Athapascan, Algonquian, Iroquois, Siouan, Salishan, and Shoshone-Nahuatlan (N. and C. America) ; Arawak, Carib, Tupi, Tapuya, Puelche, and Tsoneka (S. America), the total numbers being 56 (6 extinct) in N. America, 29 in C. America, and 84 in S. America. Culturally they fall, or fell, into a number of groups : Plains, Plateau, Pacific Coast, Eskimo, Mackenzie, Eastern Woods, South-West, South-East, Nahua (N. and C. America), Inca, Guanaco, Chibcha, Amazon, and Antilles (S. America and islands).

Anatolic Languages. Indo-European group, including Armenian and the extinct Phrygian and Scythian.

Andamanese. Negrito natives of the Andaman Islands, also called Mincopies. They range in colour from bronze to " sooty black," and the hair, which is very frizzly, seems, like that of the Bushman, to grow in tufts. They stand about 4 ft. 10 in., and are

well proportioned ; the nose is straight but small and deeply depressed at the root ; the head is small and short in proportion to its length. They depend mainly on fish for food, have no domestic animals, and do not till the soil. They can hardly be said to wear clothing, though they adorn themselves with many ornaments. They dwell in small huts which are little more than roofed spaces, but large communal huts are also found in which each family has its own quarters. There are separate quarters for boys and for girls. Their language is remarkable for the number of vowels—twenty-four, according to one authority ; they classify their nouns, and there are sixteen forms of each personal pronoun, according to the class of noun on which it depends.

Andi. Caucasian people, said to be of Jewish type. They speak an Avar language.

Angoni. Bantu-speaking people of Zulu origin on the west side of Lake Nyasa, and separated from the lake by the Nyanja. They are dwellers in the highlands, 4,000 feet above sea-level, in an open, undulating country, comparatively treeless ; they are not located in permanent villages, but move every two or three years. They broke away from the Zulus in the time of Tshaka (1820), and in their migrations absorbed elements from many tribes ; they are known in places as Mavitu, Maviti, Magwangwara, Wamakonde, and Ruga-Ruga. The name is also applied to the Anyanja, conquered by the Angoni and subject to their chiefs. They are cattle-keepers, and work in the fields is usually left to the junior wives ; the men's place is in the cattle-fold. As conquerors they used to send to the Nyanja for additional wives, and chiefs used to have harems of over a hundred.

Annamese. People of Annam, who speak a language of the Tai group of Siamese-Chinese which has, however, been influenced by some alien speech ; it was formerly attributed to the Mon-Khmer family. The Annamese have a broad, high forehead, high cheek-bones, and small flat nose, rather thick lips, black hair, a scanty beard, and a coppery complexion. The head is round and the features are coarse, with a sly expression. They are tricky, arrogant, and dishonest, hard-hearted, unsympathetic, and grasping. The word Annam is comparatively modern ; the Giao-shi (cross-toed) are mentioned in the legendary Chinese annals of four thousand years back. Some two thousand years ago many Chinese emigrants settled, and merging with the Giao-shi, formed the people now known as Annamese. The name of the Giao-shi is given them owing to the great distance that separates the big toe from the others.

Antaimoro. Tribe of the extreme south of Madagascar. They are of negroid or negro type, with frizzly hair.

Antankarana. Tribe living at the northern extremity of Madagascar, and speaking a dialect with some marked differences.

Antanosy. Tribe of the south-central part of Madagascar.

Anti. Arawakan tribe, also known as Campa, who live in the forests of the Upper Ucayali. They are noted for their cannibalism.

Antilles Area. West India islands, originally populated by Arawaks, later overrun by Caribs, whose culture was closely allied to the canoe culture of the Amazon area.

Antimerina. Commonly known as Hova. The dominant type in Madagascar in the last century; they are descendants of sixteenth century immigrants.

Aoulias. People of Nepal, possibly descendants of lower caste Hindus.

Apache. North American Indian tribe of the south-western group, speaking an Athapascan language, so named probably from a Zuñi word meaning enemy, in allusion to their warlike character. They were originally hunters, rather above medium height, good talkers, and honest according to their lights.

Arabs. People of Arabia, also found in north Africa and in other parts of Asia as a result of movements in historic times. In Iberia, Central Asia, Malaysia, etc., the immigrant Arabs have lost their native speech or their racial individuality, or both. The modern Arabians fall into two groups, the mainly settled agricultural people of Yemen, Hadramaut and Oman, who count themselves descended from Shem, and the northern (Beduin) peoples, who look to Ishmael as their father. But it must be remembered that large parts of Arabia are wholly unknown. The Beduins (dwellers in the desert) have long heads with a short, fairly broad nose, seldom of the " Jewish " type; the southern Arabs are shorter and more variable in skull form, but predominantly short headed. The Himyarites, who were found in Arabia two thousand years ago, are no longer distinguishable in their own land, but they are still dominant in Abyssinia.

Araucan. Aborigines of Chile, the Puelche who moved down the Rio Negro and came into contact with the Pampas Indians. Their culture is that of the Guanaco area, and resembles that of the Plains Indians of North America. They are now mainly occupied with agriculture and stock breeding. They are of small stature but robust, with a short broad nose. In character they are proud, independent, brave, inconstant, secretive, and taciturn.

Arawak. Group of South American tribes, formerly found in the Antilles also. On the continent of South America they range from the Upper Paraguay river to the north of Venezuela. Among the Arawak tribes are the Arawak proper, the Maypure, Mojo, or Moxo, Wapisiana, and Ipurina. They seem to have had their origin in East Bolivia, whence they spread along the basins of the Amazon and Orinoco. In physical type they do not seem to differ much from the Carib, who, in the Lesser Antilles, had killed off the Arawak men and taken the women to wife at the time of Columbus; in the Greater Antilles the population was still Arawak. They are a typical inland race, however, and as they early cultivated the tapioca-plant (manioc), their first home cannot have been in an area subject to periodical floods.

Arawak. Guiana tribe speaking an Arawakan language. They are short of stature and light coloured. Descent is reckoned in the female line, and a man goes to live with his father-in-law at marriage. They are a cleanly people and have taken over much European culture; they make a special kind of fibre hammock and much pottery. They have a remarkable custom of whipping each other as a diversion.

Arecuna. Carib-speaking tribe of Guiana. They are a dark-skinned, strongly-built people of warlike character, much dreaded by the Macusi; as savannah people they build clay huts; they use the blow-gun, which they manufacture for other tribes from the stems of a palm.

Armenians. People of Asia Minor speaking an Indo-European tongue. The head is short but the stature varies considerably, and the name Anatolian has been given to the taller type. The skin is swarthy white, and a peculiarity of the head is that it is very high and much flattened at the back, so that it seems to fall almost vertically; the nose is high and narrow. Representatives of this type are to be found in Persia, and among Greeks and Turks; it has been suggested that they are descendants of tribes who formed the great Hittite Empire.

Armenoid. The type represented by Armenians.

Arunta or Aranda. Tribe of Central Australia, ranging from the Macumba river to the Macdonnell Ranges, which rise to a height of 5,000 ft. They have a complicated social organization with eight intermarrying classes.

Aryan. The same as Indo-European. It is often used erroneously in the form " Aryan race" of the peoples who speak Aryan tongues.

Aryo-Dravidian. Group, also termed Hindustani, of people in the United Provinces of India, Bihar, Ceylon, etc., with a longish head and a nose which varies in shape according to social station, the upper ranks having narrow, the lower broad noses in proportion to length. The complexion varies from light brown to black.

Ashango. A Bantu-speaking tribe of the Gabun on the Ogowe and behind the Nkomi-Galoa, French Equatorial Africa.

Ashanti or Asanti. Warlike people of the Gold Coast, near kin of the Fanti, to the north of whom they live. The " customs " of the king of Ashanti, involving many human sacrifices, were formerly notorious; one of his chief possessions was the golden stool or throne. Gold dust was in use among them when the first European voyagers reached the coast in the fifteenth century; it is probable that the Carthaginians and Egyptians had dealings with the coast. Beliefs closely resembling those of the Egyptians are held by the Twi (Fanti-Ashanti tribes) with regard to reincarnation.

Assamese-Burmese. Stock of Tibeto-Burman family.

Assiniboin. North American Indian tribe of the Plains group, speaking a Siouan language and now on reservations in Montana. They separated from the Yankton more than three hundred years ago near the head waters of the Mississippi, and were thenceforth constantly at war with the Dakota, their kinsmen. They

Dictionary of Races

seldom cut their hair and add false hair at times till the twist reaches the ground.

Atayal. Group of savage tribes inhabiting the north of the island of Formosa. They are active and aggressive head-hunters, and their trophies are put on a platform in the open air. They are certainly not of Mongoloid type and may be primitive Indonesians. They live on millet, rice, taro, and other vegetables, together with the meat of deer and wild pig; some of them do not use salt. A curious feature of the marriage customs of one section is that a newly-married couple for a few days occupy a habitation raised twenty feet above the ground on piles. Their religion is mainly ancestor worship.

Atyo. The Bateke to the north of Stanley Pool, in Belgian Congo. Atyo is their own native name; Bateke means pygmy.

Australians. Aboriginal population of Australia, always very small in numbers and to-day almost or quite extinct in many places. Linguistically, they fall into two main groups, one, with an older and a younger section, called the Australian languages, occupying the southern part of the continent; the other, perhaps related to the Papuan family, in the north; the languages of the second group are very much split up and not necessarily related to each other. There is a considerable difference in skull shape that corresponds in distribution only in part to that of languages. There may have been a negrito element present in small numbers before the Australian type arrived, when Torres Strait was still dry land. A wave of immigrants of negroid type seems to have followed, which has left some traces in the hair, almost frizzly in some cases, almost straight in others; the stature varies from 5 ft. 2 in. to 6 ft. 3 in. in men. The ridges over the eyes are strongly marked, and the forehead has a backward slope; the nose is broad and deep-set at the root. The Australian seems to be quick at learning, at any rate in youth; but he is unreflective in the main and tires quickly when he is called upon to undertake tasks in which he has no interest. He is on the other hand tireless in carrying out ceremonies, which may continue for days, associated in his mind with the multiplication of food stuffs or the initiation of youths. In their natural state the Australians are found to be gentle and good-natured, indulgent to children, and kind even to their dogs.

Avars. Most important Lesghian people of the Caucasus. An Avar people migrated in the sixth century to the Danube, but there is no evidence that this Sarmatian people is the same as the modern one. They are a warlike folk.

Awatwa or **Batwa.** Negro tribe living in the swamps on the Luapula river, south of Lake Bangweolo, Central Africa.

Awemba or **Babemba.** Bantu tribe of Rhodesia, who mummify the corpses of their chiefs by rubbing them all over with boiled maize till the skin becomes dry and shrivelled.

Aymara. People of Bolivia. The name was early applied to the Colla and other Titicacan tribes, but it seems to belong properly to non-Quichua peoples, also short-headed but entirely distinct from the Quichua, though some authorities assert that the tribes are physically indistinguishable, save that the Aymara no longer deform the skull. In burial customs they differed widely, the Aymara using a square edifice, the Quichua an underground chamber. The Aymara Indian of to-day is a dweller in the highlands, strong and muscular, of bronzed complexion; according to some observers, the eyes have a slant reminiscent of Mongoloid ancestry. They are a reticent people, sober and industrious, except when religious rites occupy attention. Like the Quichua they have a primitive kind of weaving in which the loom consists of four stakes driven into the ground. Their most important domesticated animal is the llama, which serves as a beast of burden. Though they profess Christianity, they still hold to their old gods, who are believed to dwell in ice and snow.

Azande. Important tribe or collection of tribes of the Nile-Welle watershed, Central Africa, formerly known as the Niam-Niam from their addiction to cannibalism. The skull is of a medium type inclining to long, and though they have been described as tall they appear to be in general shorter than the Nilotes and also somewhat lighter skinned, inclining to a reddish colour. They were formerly a warlike people and belonged to the group of tribes which made use of the throwing knife, a many-pointed piece of iron which probably had a curved flight.

Aztecs. Mexican tribe representing a mixture of the ancient Aztecs and Tlascalans. Their houses are made in three parts—god house, cooking house, and granary; there is also a vapour bath house of stone. Idols are built into the granary as talismans.

Baba. Term for a Malay of Chinese descent.

Babunda. Bantu-speaking tribe of the Kasai-Kwilu area of Central Africa. Exceedingly black and a fine, stalwart people with abundance of hair in the case of men, they are a warlike race who are great rubber traders. They do not build villages, but live in the middle of their plantations, so that a single settlement may be a couple of miles long.

Babwende. Bantu-speaking people of the Congo, inhabiting the cataract region.

Bachama. Tribe of the northern provinces of Nigeria, allied to the Batta, on the Middle Benue. They speak a language of the Benue-Chad group and are said to be cannibals, but there is no evidence of it.

Badaga. Agricultural tribe of the Nilgiri Hills of the Deccan, India. They speak a Dravidian language, said to be allied to old Kanarese, and are a long-headed people who dwell in extensive villages situated as a rule on a low hill, in which all the houses on one side of a street are under one continuous roof. The milk house is very sacred and no woman may enter it. The women do most of the work in the fields, and as a reward get worse food than the male members of the family.

Badakshi. Round-headed people of the Upper Oxus.

Badjok. Bantu-speaking people of the Kasai, Central Africa, who came originally

5331

from the south. They are undersized and dirty, but have a great reputation as warriors, have no sense of fear, are great elephant hunters, and do a large trade in rubber.

Baggara. Arab tribe of Darfur, Sudan, whose name means " cattle keepers." Some are as dark as negroes but their features are fine and regular.

Bagesu. Cannibal Bantu-speaking tribe of the eastern slopes of Mount Elgon, East Africa. They are of medium height, with broad noses that show no bridge. The skull is short. There is nothing repulsive about their faces, which can even be termed pleasing. They are now agricultural, but were probably originally a cattle-keeping people.

Baghirmi. Sudanic-speaking tribe on the south-east of Lake Chad, North Central Africa. They are tall and healthy, but the women are over-stout. They hunt elephants on horseback with poisoned spears.

Bahurutse. Section of the Bechuana, of South Africa, also called Bakwena. They followed a chief known as Mohurutse and took their name from him.

Bahutu. Subject people of Urundi, East Africa, governed by the Batussi. They are of small stature, with legs disproportionately short, but the body muscular. They differ from the Batussi in the projection of the lower part of the face. In colour they are of a dark coffee tint with a violet sheen, but some show the reddish clay colour of a South American Indian.

Ba-ila. Bantu-speaking people of northern Rhodesia. Two distinct types seem to be found—one tall and finely made, with a long nose and thin nostrils, generally speaking good-looking ; the other, short, heavily made, bull-necked, with a flat nose. These types are not distributed according to rank. In colour they are chocolate-brown to almost black, but a new-born child is a dirty yellow, and with hair also lighter. They knock out six teeth in the upper jaw.

Bajau. Malayan people of the west coast of Borneo.

Bajabi or **Bajavi.** Bantu-speaking tribe of the Nyanza and other Ogowe tributaries.

Bakango. Welle tribe of Central Africa, allied to the Ababua, who seem to intermarry with Azande. They are short in stature, fifty per cent. not exceeding 5 ft. 4 in. A river people, their diet is largely composed of fish.

Bakhtiari. Inhabitants of Susiana (Khuzistan), Persia, who speak Kurdish dialects and are probably northern Mongols who have taken over an Iranian speech.

Ba-'Eshi-Kongo. People of the old kingdom of Kongo, who occupy a large part of the area south of the Congo river between the Kwango and the sea. There is a second Bakongo tribe between the Kasai and the Lulua, who are probably a branch of the Bushongo.

Bakuba. A branch of the Baluba people of the Belgian Congo.

Bakulia. Bantu-speaking tribe of East Africa, to the east of the Wageia. They were at one time called Wassuba. They are a tall people, over 5 ft. 7 in. on an average, and are probably of mixed origin, with some Hamitic blood.

Bakusu. (1) People of Yakusu, Stanley Falls ; (2) a tribe allied to the Manyema. They are located between the Middle Lomami and the Lualaba and are not to be confused with the Bankutu or Bakuchu of the Kasai.

Balali. Section of the Bateke, on the north bank of the Congo, a little east of the Kenka river.

Balangi, Balengue, or **Balengie.** Bantu-speaking tribe of the coast of Spanish Guinea, between the Campo and Kribi rivers.

Balti. People of Tibet, identified by some with the Dards, by others with the Sacae of Herodotus who invaded India from the north about two thousand years ago. They are now Moslems and speak Tibetan. It is certain that their physical conformation is not Mongolic, for they have ringlety hair, a full beard, and abundant body hair, together with a long head and straight eyes, in striking contrast with the neighbouring people of Ladakh, who are thoroughly Mongoloid in appearance. In their country are remarkable rock carvings attributed by the present inhabitants to a long-vanished people. They are famous horsemen and the original inventors of the game of polo.

Baltic Languages. Small Aryan group, comprising the extinct Old Prussian, Lettish, and Lithuanian.

Baluba. Warrior people of the south-east of the Belgian Congo. The name is also given to mixed peoples of the Kasai. The name appears to mean " wanderers." The western Baluba have been called Bashilange.

Balunda or **Alunda.** Bantu-speaking people south-west of Lake Bangweulu, northern Rhodesia.

Bambala. Bantu-speaking people of the Kwilu river, West Africa, also called Bushongo. They have a curious custom of covering their bodies with a kind of reddish clay. They are a cheery, happy-go-lucky folk, much given to gambling, by which a man will lose, not only his wife and children but even his own liberty. In colour they are a very dark brown, but thick lips and flat noses are exceptional ; the northern Bambala are strongly built, but there is less food in the south ; a lighter colour seems to go with the slighter build of the southern portion of the tribe. Cannibalism is of everyday occurrence among them ; as a rule enemies and criminals are the victims, but slaves may also be slaughtered. This notwithstanding, they are a pleasant, peaceable folk, kind even to their slaves, who are treated more like children than serfs.

Banda. Important group of tribes in French Central African territory north of the Ubangi. Some of them use lip disks of one or more inches in diameter, like the Yao of Nyasaland.

Bangala. Bantu-speaking people of the region between the Ubanghi and the Congo and south of the Congo, including the Boloki, Mbala Bolombo, and others. The name seems to be derived from the fact that there was a large group settled at Mangala ; they do not know the name themselves. The Bangala language has come to be used as a means of inter-communication over a large area. The height varies considerably, with an average of about 5 ft. 7 in.; there is a short-headed element in the tribes mixed with a more important long-headed type; a certain number have thin lips. They file four or more teeth to a point.

Bankutu. Cannibal tribe of the Upper Lukenye, Belgian Congo. They are a small and dirty people, timid, treacherous, ugly, sullen, and of unprepossessing manners. They have, however, an unusually neat and picturesque type of hut.

Bantu. Sub-family of African languages, allied to Sudanic in respect of a large proportion of its word roots and to the semi-Bantu portion of the Sudanic sub-family in respect also of morphology and syntax. The characteristic feature is that all nouns have a pronominal prefix, which is repeated before adjectives or verbs to show the concord. Bantu-speaking peoples of the extreme south differ so little in speech from those of the extreme north, that Zulu is intelligible in Cameroon. The Bantu languages occupy all the southern part of Africa from near the Equator southwards, excepting areas of Hottentot, Bushman and Pygmy (?) speech, or such parts as are now Europeanised. There is no corresponding Bantu race nor yet any physical type of which it can be said that it is specifically Bantu, but the term is applied in a narrower sense to tribes with a strong Hamitic element.

Banyoro. Tall and well-proportioned Bantu-speaking people of Uganda, who extract the four lower incisors. A long-headed people, they are on the whole honest, but have the reputation of being splendid liars, though this seems to be due to past oppression by their chiefs.

Banziri. Trading people of the Ubangi river, Central Africa. They build beehive huts and arrange them in two long lines, sometimes over a mile in length. They are good farmers and expert watermen.

Bapindi or **Bapende.** Bantu-speaking people of the Kwilu-Kasai area, who are expert weavers. They should not be confused with the Bapindji or Babindji.

Bapuko, Naka or **S. Banoha.** Bantu-speaking tribe of Spanish Guinea, between the Kribi and Nyon rivers.

Bara. Tribe of south-central Madagascar, with the reputation of being distrustful and churlish; they are a Plains people and relatively uncivilized.

Barabra. Dark-complexioned tribe of Nubia, with long skulls and woolly hair. The name is the same as that of the Berber; it is derived from Arabic and means "foreigner."

Barotse. Conquering Bantu tribe which founded a great empire in what is now northern Rhodesia.

Barundi. People of East Africa, made up of the subject Bahutu and the dominant Batussi, whose privileged classes include the Waruanda.

Bassa or **Gbasa.** Name of a Kru tribe of Liberia. There are also tribes known as Bassa in the northern provinces of Nigeria (Bassa Komo, Bassa Nge) and in Cameroon.

Bashkirs. Mixed people of Russia, of Mongoloid type. The name is said to be of Turkish origin and to mean " bee keepers."

Basques. People of the western Pyrenees, partly in France, partly in Spain. They speak a language that is by common consent non-Aryan and is generally regarded as a survival of the pre-Aryan languages of two or three thousand years ago, possibly that of the people called Iberians, who occupied the sea-board of Gaul from the Rhône to the Pyrenees, and were originally resident between the Ebro and the Pyrenees. There is a distinct Basque type, characterised by a rather triangular face, broad temples, and long, pointed chin, with dark eyes set rather close, a long thin nose, and dark hair. North of the Pyrenees, however, the skull seems to be noticeably shorter than in the Spanish provinces, though the dividing line is not exactly coincident with the national boundary. The French type has been regarded as the purer. The Basques are assigned to the Mediterranean race, being regarded as a variety evolved by isolation and in-breeding. Many suggestions have been made as to the affinities of the language, e g. that it is akin to Berber, Finno-Ugrian tongues, Kolarian, etc., without any very clear evidence being forthcoming.

Basundi. Bantu-speaking people of the north bank of the Lower Congo, who seem to have come from the Lower Kwango.

Basuto. Bantu-speaking people of south-east Africa, east of the Orange river, where they seem to have arrived about a hundred years ago. They are made up of a great number of different clans or tribes. The traditions of some of them have been interpreted to mean that they crossed the Zambezi in the eleventh or twelfth century. They preserve genealogies of their chiefs going back to the sixteenth century. Less than a century ago some of them were still cannibals; but they took to the practice, it appears, when their flocks and herds had been captured by invading peoples, who also killed much of the game.

Batak. (1) The same as Batta, a tribe of Sumatra; (2) a negrito tribe of Palawan, Philippine Islands. Described as very shy, they have long, kinky hair, and use the blow-gun.

Batetela. Bantu-speaking tribe east of the Sankuru, Belgian Congo, many of them much influenced by Arabs and Europeans. Their country is fertile, and abundance of food has enabled them to develop into a race of great stature. Brave, hospitable and kind-hearted, they are, as a rule, dark in colour, but some are light yellow.

Batta. (1) Tribe of the Middle Benue, West Africa. They are allied to the Bachama and speak a language of the Benue-Chad group. (2) Sumatran tribe of small stature who live mainly north of the Equator, also called Batak. Their stature is about 5 ft. 3 in., and the skull somewhat short; the skin is clear and the face round, but the cheek-bones are not prominent; the nose is straight or concave, the beard thick; the hair is fine, of black colour, with chestnut as a variant. They are cannibals, but eat only enemies killed in battle, prisoners of war, and convicted criminals, never their own relatives.

Batussi. Dominant people of Urundi, East Africa, who rule the Bahutu, numbering about one and a half millions, by superior intelligence. The Batussi are proud, quiet and reserved compared with their subjects, and seldom say what they think. They are reputed to be untruthful, lazy, and cowardly, leaving all work to the subject people. They are tall, some over 6 ft. 6 in., and no grown-up man less than 5 ft. 9 in.; but they are well proportioned, though the body is often slender, yet their hands are smaller than those of the average European. There are two types of face among them, the superior, with narrow nose, thin lips, and small mouth; the other more negroid, but oval, with small but well-developed chin. A singular feature is that the upper teeth often project over the lower; the hair is, however, as woolly as in the ordinary negro.

Batwa. Pygmoid people of Urundi, East Africa, who are, however, considerably taller than the real pygmy. Those who have taken to agriculture reach 5 ft. 3 in., no doubt owing to admixture with the Bahutu, who are themselves but little taller. They are a mixture of pygmy, forest Bantu, and inter-lake Bantu; and some observers have suggested the presence of a long-headed Bushman type. They form not more than one per cent. of the population of Urundi, and as a pariah class are naturally driven to trickery and slyness. They are, however, friendly with the Batussi and are actually the guards of the king in Ruanda.

Bayanzi. Name given to several distinct African tribes. Stanley gave this name to the Bobangi (?); it appears to mean " savage " and is applied also to some of the Kasai tribes.

Bechuana. Number of tribes extending from near the Zambezi to the Orange river, one important section being the Basuto. The name goes back not more than a hundred years, and is not recognized by the natives themselves. They are allied to the Bawenda of the Transvaal.

Beja. Hamitic people of East Africa, including the Ababdeh, Bisharîn, Hadendoa, Halenga, Beni Amer. They are essentially a nomadic and pastoral people though a few have taken to agriculture.

Belgians. *See* Netherlands.

Benga. Group of tribes, including the Banoho, Banoko, or Malimba, of Spanish Guinea, etc. Some of these tribes have penetrated south into French territory. The Benga proper inhabit a narrow coast belt between the Benito river and Corisco Bay.

Bengali. " Mongolo-Dravidian " inhabitants of north-east India. The type varies widely according to social status, and in certain castes, such as the Brahman, the Alpine type is dominant, as it is on the southern slopes of the Himalayas. They are quick-witted and versatile and find scope for their abilities in official work and commerce.

Berber or **Libyan.** North African peoples speaking either Arabic or Berber, but in the main of western Hamitic stock. The Arab is taller than the Berber and has usually a longer head; his face is a regular oval,

while the Berber's is squarer and his nose straight or concave; the Berber has also a transverse depression on the forehead. The Berber is essentially a highlander, non-nomadic, and less dependent upon flocks and herds. Although the Berbers have lived in close contact with Arabs for a thousand years, they do not amalgamate with them to any great extent.

Betsileo. Negro or negroid tribe of Madagascar. They are tall, with an average height of 6 ft. for men, large-boned and muscular, much darker than the Hova, and differing from them also in hair character, which is always crisp and woolly. Apart from negro slaves, however, there is little reason to suspect an African element in Madagascar, and the negro type is probably of Oceanic origin.

Betsimisaraka. Name often given to the people of the east of Madagascar in general. Properly speaking, they are a Plains people of light complexion and straight hair.

Bhil. Tribe of the Central Provinces of India, said to have been at one time the ruling race. They now speak an Indo-Aryan language. It is uncertain whether their original tongue was Munda or Dravidian. The jungle Bhils are described as active and hardy, with high cheek-bones, wide nostrils, and coarse, almost negroid, features; those of the plains are often well built and tall, but are clearly of mixed blood. The Bhil proper averages 5 ft. 6 in. in height, is an excellent woodsman and huntsman, and Sanskrit works call him " lord of the pass " because the approach to his land is through defiles which none could traverse without his leave. The name is said to occur first about A.D. 600, and to be derived from a Dravidian word for bow, the characteristic weapon of the tribe. The Bhil was at one time a professional thief, and became so, perhaps, through oppression by neighbouring governments.

Bhutia. Sanskrit name of the people of Tibet, including the Bod-pa, or Tibetan proper, the Lepcha, the Rong, etc. The Bod-pa are the southern, more or less civilized, section who till the land and have Lhasa as their chief town. The Dru-pa are semi-nomadic but peaceful tribes of the northern plateaux; while the Tangut are predatory tribes of the north-east borderland, so called by the Mongols, who, indeed, use the term for all Tibetans. The typical Tibetan is the Dru-pa, who have for ages been isolated from the alien peoples that surround them; they stand about 5 ft. 5 in., and are round headed, with wavy hair, brown eyes, a thick but prominent nose, depressed at the root. In complexion they vary from white to dark brown, according to exposure, and rosy cheeks are common among the younger women. From this description it is clear that the Indo-Chinese element is not pure.

Bicol. Philippine tribe of mixed type, probably Proto-Malay mingled with Indo-nesian to a slight extent, and with Chinese. They are predominantly round headed, and the back of the skull is curiously flattened. They are a lively and intelligent people with musical gifts.

Bilin. Pastoral and agricultural people of Upper Nubia, who are also called Bogo.

Binbinga. Australian tribe near the south-west shore of the Gulf of Carpentaria. Culturally they belong to the same group as the interior tribes, and differ from the Mara and Anula of the coast region.

Bisaya. (1) A Klemantan people of Borneo. (2) a Philippine tribe on islands of the same name and in Mindanao.

Bisharin. Division of the Beja who live to the south of the Ababdeh, towards the territory of Suakin. They have been modified by some short-headed element that did not affect the tribes to the south of them. They are moderately short, slightly built people with reddish brown skins tinged with black. The hair is usually curly, but is at times wavy. They closely resemble the pre-dynastic Egyptians in skull form and physical characteristics.

Blackfeet (Siksika). Tribe of American Indians of the Plains group, which once held an area from the Missouri to the Saskatchewan; now on reservations. They speak an Algonquian tongue, and migrated from the Red river to the north-west.

Bobangi. Bantu-speaking people of the Congo, between Stanley Pool and Equatorville.

Bogo. Pastoral and agricultural people of Upper Nubia, who call themselves Bilin.

Boloki. One of the constituent tribes of the Bangala group on the Congo and intermingled with the Bomuna. They owned the town of Mangala at one time, whence the name Bangala.

Bongo. Red-brown people of the south-west of the Bahr-el-Ghazal, Sudan. They are of medium height, with considerably wider skulls than the Dinka; both are said to deform the head soon after birth, but in opposite directions. They are essentially an agricultural people with no interest in cattle rearing. Their conical huts are remarkable for the low entrances which compel the visitor to creep in. They are expert iron workers and smelt ore. The women wear a plug quite an inch in diameter in the lower lip. (2) Another tribe in the same area with a wholly different language.

Bre. Tribe of Burma. They speak a dialect of Karen, which is assigned to the Sinitic group of the Siamese-Chinese branch of the Tibeto-Burman family of languages.

Bubi. Group of Bantu-speaking tribes of Fernando Po. They are remarkable as the sole example of an African tribe still in the Stone Age at the time of discovery; they also differed from other African tribes in having no drum.

Buduma. Fisherfolk of Lake Chad. They are tall, with high foreheads and blunt noses. They make canoes or floats of bundles of reeds ten inches thick, which take a month to build, and are propelled by men swimming or wading behind.

Bugi. Maritime people of the south of Celebes, who are reputed to be very honest traders. They have a clear skin, straight black hair, a prominent nose and wide eyes; like the neighbouring Macassar they seem to have a negroid element among them.

Bulgarians. Inhabitants of Bulgaria, of Ugrian origin, with some admixture of Slavs. They speak a Slav tongue. They were driven from the south Russian steppes by the Huns in the sixth century and subsequently crossed the Danube, but long before this they were known to the Armenians as a great people, dwelling to the north far beyond the Caucasus. At the outset they were a coarse and brutal people, but have become assimilated to the Caucasian type and merged in the surrounding Slav populations. They take their name from the Bulga (Volga).

Buriat. Mongol tribe of the region about Lake Baikal. They are yellower than the Kalmucks and have round heads, but the nose is narrower as a rule and they are clearly of mixed origin, as indeed are the Kalmucks, but, unlike them, the Buriats may have a Tungus strain.

Burmese. Mongoloid people of Further India, who have been described as intermediate in type between the Chinese and the Malay. They are of yellowish-brown complexion, with black, lank hair, no beard, a small but straight nose. They are identical with the people of Arakan, also known as Mag. Their ancestors came from the north some time after 600 B.C., according to some authorities from the mountains of the south-east of Tibet, according to others from the head waters of the Yang-tse-Kiang. About a thousand years ago the Burmese were in Upper Burma and the Mon on the lower Irawadi; some five centuries later the Tai invasion forced the Burmese to unite with the Mon. The Burman lives largely on rice and drinks water; he is a Buddhist in religion. His temperament is bright and genial, but he is somewhat indolent. A remarkable feature of Burmese society is its democratic character, due perhaps in part to the fact that the priests have not become a privileged class; for all, at some period of their lives, become priests. The women, partly owing to the freedom they enjoy, are reputed to be virtuous, thrifty and intelligent beyond the common run; they have a great capacity for business.

Bushman or **Sa** (pl. **San**). A Hottentot name. Yellow-skinned, woolly-haired inhabitant of South Africa before the arrival of the Bantu. He is now confined to the Kalahari and less desirable areas. His average height is about 5 ft. and his short and black hair rolls up into little knots so as to present the appearance of being distributed in clumps. The nose is extremely flat. The language is remarkable for its large use of " clicks," sounds produced by drawing the breath in. To the Bushmen are due the remarkable rock paintings in South Africa.

Bushongo. People of the Kasai, whose traditions say they came from the north, possibly the Shari neighbourhood. A fine race, with both dignity and grace of manner, they possess a remarkable culture unlike that of their neighbours, and have great artistic gifts. They are not skilled as hunters, and employ the pygmy Batwa to procure such game as they need.

C. Many tribal names are spelt with a C or K alternatively, in the same way as

Celt and Kelt, and if not found under the initial letter C reference should be made also under the letter K.

Caduveo. Guaycuru tribe of the Gran Chaco who cultivate the ground and are noted as expert weavers and potters.

Cakchiquel. Tribe of Guatemala, to the south of the Quiche.

California Area. District occupied by tribes without canoes or pottery, living largely on acorns and wild seeds. They are often opprobriously termed " diggers."

Canelos or **Quijos.** Important tribe of Ecuador on the head waters of the Napo.

Carib. Group of South American tribes including Acawoy, Bakairi, Galibi, Macusi, Rucuyen, etc. Their first home was perhaps near the sources of the Xingu ; they are to a great extent a fishing people, and in their migrations followed the course of rivers ; at the time of the discovery of America they were ousting the Arawak in the Antilles. They are essentially an upland people ; the custom of eating their male enemies was widespread among them.

Carib. Tribe of Guiana, speaking a language which has given its name to the Carib group. Their proper name is Carinya. They are rather dark in colour, taller than the Arawak and of more powerful make, but coarser in features. They are famous as warriors, and one result of this was that the island Caribs had two distinct languages in use, one used by or to men, the other by women among themselves. The women distort their legs by cotton bands round the ankle and disfigure their lips with pieces of wood with sharp points turned outwards ; men wear crescent-shaped nose pieces. They are skilful pot-makers.

Cashibo. Tribe of Pannoan stock, west of the Ucayali, whose own name for themselves is Carapache, " bat."

Caucasian Languages. Four groups, each with subdivisions, may be distinguished : (1) Lesghian with Avar, Andi, Dido, Lak, Varkun, Akusha, etc. ; Udi, Kurin, etc. (2) Chechen. (3) Cherkess with Kabard and Abchase. (4) Kartwelian (Georgian). In addition to these Osset, an Indo-European language, is spoken there ; it may be a descendant of Scythian ; it is certainly not Iranian.

Caucasic or **Caucasian.** General term embracing Nordic, Alpine and Mediterranean stocks. It includes the peoples of the Old World (with the exception of the Chinese, Japanese, and inhabitants of the Arctic zone) whose normal habitat lies outside the tropics.

Cayuga. American Indian tribe of the Iroquois confederation. Some of them removed to Canada when the American Revolution took place.

Celtic Languages. One section of the Italo-Celtic group now in north-west Europe. It includes the Brythonic tongues with Welsh, Breton and the extinct Cornish, and Gadhelic, with Gaelic, Erse and Manx.

Celt or **Kelt.** Term used in a number of different and contradictory senses ; some Continental writers oppose Celts and Gauls, who also spoke a Celtic tongue, supposing the former to be short headed, the latter long headed ; archaeologists attribute the culture of the earlier and later Iron Ages to the Celts, regardless of physical type and language ; philologists speak of Celts when they mean peoples whose language is a branch of the Italo-Celtic group. What has happened is that, as in the case of England, which takes its name from a single one of the conquering tribes of invading peoples, the word Celt has been applied indiscriminately both to the original Celts and to the peoples whom they subdued and Celticised.

Cham. Remnants of a once powerful people who dominated Cochin-China, Annam and part of Cambodia some two thousand years ago and were still formidable in the days of Marco Polo. They were determined foes of the Khmer of Cambodia and were conquered by the Annamese at the end of the fifteenth century. In physical type they differ widely from the surrounding people and seem to be of Austronesian stock. They are tall, often reaching 5 ft. 8 in., and sturdily built, and they vary in complexion from light brownish red to brown, thus resembling many Indonesians. They have wavy hair of fine texture and black or dark chestnut in colour ; the face is rather broad, but the nose is narrower at the root than is the case with Annamese ; the eye is large and full. A singular feature of their life is that many of them do not build their own houses, but employ Annamese. Their religions are a corrupted Brahmanism and Mahomedanism.

Chantos. People of Turkistan of mixed descent. Their features are European rather than Mongoloid. They are occupied with trade and agriculture.

Chargars. A Mongol tribe in the north of the Chinese provinces of Chih-li and Shansi.

Charruas. Tribe of Uruguay who use the bolas, and hunt on horseback.

Chechen. Caucasus people of the Middle Terek, Assa, etc. Their own name is Nakchi, and their usual name is taken from a town now destroyed, the chief of which subdued most of the people. The language is independent, but has elements in common with some of the Lesghian languages. The Chechen include the Kists, Galgais, Ingush, etc. They are a good-looking people, proud, and very hospitable.

Cheremiss. Finnic people inhabiting the Volga basin. They are divided into mountain and plain sections, of which the former is more Russianised, taller and stronger. The name means " merchants," their own designation is Mori. They are a people characterised by shortish heads, narrow eyes, small beards and flat noses.

Cherokee. Iroquoian tribe of Virginia, etc., afterwards in Indian territory. They are one of the Five Civilized Tribes, probably 30,000 strong.

Chewsures. Georgian people of mixed origin. The type differs considerably, probably owing to the intermarriage of near neighbours. The whole family takes vengeance for the shedding of blood, and thus arise family quarrels that hold different areas apart for generations.

Cheyenne. Tribe of Plains Indians speaking an Algonquian tongue. They were originally agricultural, living in a timber country ; their great rite was the Sun Dance ; some thirty years ago they took up the modern Ghost Dance religion.

Chibcha Arca. District in the north of South America inhabited by tribes using poisoned arrows, hammocks, fish poisons, etc., and living in palisaded villages. This type also extends some distance northwards into Central America. Some of the tribes of high culture exist no longer ; but there are still highly organized groups in the centre of Colombia surrounded by a ring of wilder tribes of the same group.

Chickasaws. Muskogian tribe now in Oklahoma, who seem to have crossed the Mississippi from the west in early times and settled in what is now Mississippi State in pre-Columbian times.

Chilkat. Tlinkit tribe of Alaska, famous for their blankets.

Chin. Southern Mongol people speaking a Tibeto-Burman language of the Meithei sub-group. The Chindwin valley is named from them ; they are related to the Kachin, but should not be confused with them. Their original home seems to have been in Tibet, together with the Kuki-Lushai, if we may judge by customs, technology, and traditions. The term Chin is said to be a Burmese form of Chinese *jin* (men). They have no common name, but call themselves Yo in the north, Lai in the south, and Shu in Lower Burma. They are a fine people, tall and stoutly built, men of nearly 6 ft. being not uncommon ; in some areas, however, goitre and leprosy are common. The Chin is treacherous in warfare, for a man who has killed many enemies goes to the next life with a fine retinue of slaves ; but the killing of a man brings vengeance on the slayer, who himself becomes the slave of the avenger in the next world. The Chin Hills, according to the Chins themselves, are formed of the ruins of a tower they were building in order to induce the moon to give light permanently.

China : non-Chinese Peoples. These include Miao-Yao, Min-chin, Wa-Palaung, Shan-Tai, Lolo, Kachin, and other stocks. The Miao call themselves Mhong, and are alleged to belong to the Mon-Khmer group, the construction of the language being also identical.

Chinese. Mixed people of far from uniform type. There is a considerable Manchu element in the north ; in the south are the tribes known collectively as Miao-tse. The north Chinaman is fairly tall, standing on an average 5 ft. 7 in. in Shantung, and the round-headed Alpine type is dominant, mixed, however, with a type similar in respect of nose and in height of the head, but much longer. In the south-east the average stature is about three inches less and the type is less mixed with long heads, but there is also a broad-nosed element. Very little information of a reliable kind is available. The Chinese proper were some thousands of years ago an agricultural people in the valley of the Wei river, surrounded by barbarians like the Hiung-nu. They conquered and absorbed their neighbours, but the Yang-tse was their southern border for centuries. The Chinese character is complex, and cannot be summed up in a few words.

He is honourable, especially in commerce, and has the reputation of being a liar only because he lies in a way novel to the Westerner ; he is not more dishonest than most people, and is accounted dirty because his ideas of cleanliness differ from ours. When he is well treated he is faithful and grateful ; he is polite according to a traditional code ; he is temperate. But he is undoubtedly cruel ; he is unkind to children, and, judged by European standards, he cannot be termed moral.

Chinook. Pacific Coast tribe north of the Columbia river, now nearly extinct. Their language formed the basis of the Chinook jargon, an Indian trade language used before the discovery of America. They flattened their heads by pressure of a board on a child's head in its cradle.

Chippewa or **Chippeway.** Another form of Ojibwa or Ojibway, an Algonquin tribe, not to be confused with the Chippewyan, an Athapascan tribe.

Chippewyan. Athapascan tribe of Canada, not to be confused with the Chippewa.

Chiquito. Bolivian tribe or group of tribes, belonging to the Tupi linguistic family. They were originally supposed to be dwarfs, because their huts had low doorways and they left them untenanted when the country was first invaded. They are peaceful and industrious, manufacturing sugar in copper boilers of their own making. Their language is said to have no numerals beyond one. They are of olive complexion with an average height of 5 ft. 6 in. ; their heads are round, but the cheek-bones do not project, and the eyes are horizontal. They are good natured, sociable, hospitable, and lazy.

Chiriguano. Bolivian tribe, perhaps the same as Camba, also found in the east of the Gran Chaco, speaking a language of the Guarani group. They are of yellowish-red complexion, of rather small stature, with round heads and small nostrils.

Chitrali. Round-headed people on the south of the Hindu Kush. They are, perhaps, descendants of an Alpine people who occupied the western plateaux in Neolithic and early Bronze times.

Choctaw. Important Muskogian tribe formerly on the Mississippi. The name by which they are known may be from the Spanish " chato," flat, from their custom of flattening their heads. They were noted for agriculture and waged war in the main only for purposes of defence. It was their custom to clean the bones of the dead (old men removing the flesh with their finger-nails) and deposit them in boxes or baskets in their " bone-houses."

Cholo, Chola. Local name of half-breed Indians of Bolivia.

Cholones. South American tribe on the left bank of the Hualaga.

Chontal. Indian tribe of Nicaragua and Mexico, often called Popoluca, a Nahuatl word meaning " stranger."

Chorotegas. Indian tribes of Nicaragua and Mexico, who formerly spoke Mangue, a language allied to Chiapanec.

Chukchi. Palaeo-Siberian tribe occupying the extreme north-east of Siberia. There are two main groups. One possesses numerous herds of reindeer that pasture on the tundra but are neither milked nor used for transport, being bred for food and trade. The other group is dependent on fishing. As the pasturage is poor, herders of reindeer lead a very nomadic life ; in summer the reindeer go up into the hills. The Chukchi are said to have warred with the aboriginal tribe known as Onkilon and gradually mingled with the survivors. It is the custom among them for old people to be killed with much ceremony.

Chuvash. Finnic people of the Kazan area. Of short stature, they have undergone Tartar influence. In character they are hard-working and economical even to parsimony, excellent at agriculture compared with the Cheremiss, but naturally timid and indisposed either to commerce or manual labour.

Circassians or **Cherkess.** Name of uncertain origin and meaning, applied to a Caucasus people who call themselves Adighe. They seem to be of mixed origin, as their heads are of medium length with some twenty per cent. long headed and about the same of round-headed folk. They are a tall, slender people, but well built with broad shoulders, and are noted as horsemen. The women are famous beauties with black eyes ; after marriage they are kept closely confined. The Circassian has been described as warlike, fearless and hospitable, but thievish and treacherous ; they are disinclined to labour. A stranger who comes to a place selects a host, who may be known to him only by name, but is thenceforth responsible for his safety.

Coast Tribes. Indians of the North Pacific coast. They are dependent on the sea for food ;. make large dug-out canoes ; have totem poles ; cook with hot stones in boxes and baskets ; use armour and wooden helmets but no shields. They live in large square houses of wood, which is also worked for many other purposes ; they believe in guardian spirits. The " potlatch " is a complicated system of gifts on a loan and credit system, which have to be returned at a later date, the most valuable articles being blankets and certain copper plates.

Comanche. Plains tribe speaking a Shoshonian tongue. They formerly lived in Wyoming ; they warred for centuries with the Spaniards and were bitter enemies of the Texans, who seized their hunting-grounds.

Cossacks. Disappearing Russian type, formerly falling into two groups, the Zaparog of Little Russia and the Don Cossacks. War was their original occupation, but to-day they are a separate people only in the Caucasus.

Cree. Indians of the Mackenzie group, speaking an Algonquian tongue. They were honest in everything but trade, hospitable, and generous ; they are closely related to the Ojibwa or Chippewa.

Croats. South Slavonic people allied to the Serbs. The name is identical with Khorvat, the form of the name used in Hungary, and means " highlands," being in fact the same word as Carpathians.

Crow. American Indian tribe of the Plains group. They speak a Siouan language and are an offshoot of the Hidatsa.

Cushite. Group of East African tribes. They include the High Cushite (mountain dwellers) or Agao, and the Low Cushite, including the Galla, Somali and Afar-Saho.

Cuyono. Philippine tribe. Of yellow skin, but somewhat negroid head character ; they have deep brown eyes, prominent cheek-bones, and straight black hair with a tendency to wave. The big toe is widely separated from the others and abnormally large.

Czechs. The inhabitants of the north-west part of Czechoslovakia, known as Bohemia before the Great War. In prehistoric times there were considerable changes of type in this area ; at the end of the Old Stone Age the population was influenced by a round-headed element coming probably from the east ; in the Neolithic period, however, this influence cannot be traced ; there are practically no short skulls, so far as has been discovered. When metals were introduced the population remained long headed, but the proportion of skulls high in proportion to the length was greater than before, that is to say there was a Mediterranean element. With the coming of iron the short-headed Alpine type was largely increased. They were the representatives of the Slavs of to-day, it may be ; but there was another swing of the pendulum and fifteen hundred years or more ago the long-headed peoples got the upper hand again and in their graves the objects are of undoubted Slavic origin ; but singularly enough there is a distinct difference of type between males and females, and the latter have shorter heads. At the present day the Czechs are of the Alpine type, short headed and dark, above medium stature, though not so tall as the people of the plains of Germany to the north of them. For earlier periods the facts are of uncertain interpretation.

Dafla. Himalayan tribe, also called Banghin, who subsist by hunting.

Dakota or **Sioux.** Plains tribe which lived south-west of Lake Superior. They now number about 30,000 and represented the best type of Indian.

Danakil or **Afar.** Hamitic tribe of the arid coastlands between Abyssinia and the sea. Physically they resemble the Somali, but are less Arabised.

Danes. Inhabitants of Denmark, whose language may be regarded as the same as Norwegian. There is every reason to suppose that Denmark was not inhabited till Neolithic times. It seems likely that the early short heads are the same people as we find in France and Britain, who must have passed along the North Sea coasts ; in the Iron Age these folk had almost disappeared and the long heads, i.e. Nordics of the German plain, were in force. At a later period great changes occurred which have left little trace in history. We read of the Cimbri leaving Denmark as a result of inundations, and being finally wiped out in north Italy by the Romans after a sanguinary career ; we know that later the Jutes came to the shores of England and formed an element in the present population, while other Baltic peoples streamed in other directions over Europe ; but we do not know what happened in their fatherland. One-third of the children of to-day seem to have light eyes and hair, and it seems that tallness goes with fair coloration, but in parts of the country there is a round-headed, fair type, not very tall, side by side with a taller, dark type.

Dard. People of north-west India. Their language, also called Pisacha, is ranked as a branch of the Indo-European languages.

Dard Group. Languages spoken in Kashmir and the country to the north and east.

Daurians. Tungus tribe of the east and outer Mongolia, at the present day inhabiting the valley of the Nonui.

Delaware or **Lenape.** Formerly the most important Algonquian confederacy, originally in the basin of the Delaware river, U.S.A. Other tribes accorded them the title of " grandfather," in recognition of their position.

Dene or **Tinneh.** North American Indian tribe of the Mackenzie group, speaking an Athapascan language. They are dependent for food on the caribou and use snares and nets made of bark fibre; their baskets of spruce root are food vessels used in cooking with hot stones. They strike fire with iron pyrites. The house characteristic of this area is the lean-to.

Dialect. *See* Language (p. 5327).

Dinka. Arabic form of the name of a collection of independent tribes stretching from about five degrees south of Khartum to less than two degrees north of Gondokoro and extending many miles to the west in Bahr-el-Ghazal. They call themselves Jieng or Jenge; they are independent of each other and have never recognized a supreme chief. They are tall and very long headed, but differ considerably from each other in physique, due in part perhaps to differences in food. The cattle-owning Dinka are far better off than the poorer tribes who have no cattle and hardly cultivate the ground, but depend largely upon fishing and hippopotamus hunting. The last-named tribes live in the marshes near the Sudd, and their villages, dirty and evil-smelling, rise little above the level of the reed-covered surface of the country. The cattle-owning Dinka call them all Tain. Other tribes are Agar, Bor, Shish and Aliab. The Dinka who own cattle look down on the Shilluk.

Diola. Sudanic-speaking people near the mouth of the Gambia. They speak a Semi-Bantu language.

Dravidian Languages. Principal languages of South India, with Brahui, spoken in Baluchistan, Malto in Bengal, etc. Three groups are distinguished: Dravida with Kanarese, Kota, Toda, Tulu, Tamil, and Malayalam; Andhra with Telugu, and intermediate with Kurukh, Malto, Gondi, etc.

Dravidian. General term for the short dark peoples of South India. Physically they are indistinguishable from the inhabitants of northern India in many cases. Two varieties have been distinguished, one with a broad nose, the other with a narrow nose. On the whole the term seems to be used on a linguistic base.

Druses. People of Lebanon and Anti-Lebanon. They are of very mixed origin, speak Arabic, and are officially Mahomedans,

though their creed contains many heterogeneous elements. They are of the non-Semitic type termed Armenoid.

Dualla. Important people of Cameroon who speak a Bantu language.

Durani Afghan. Agricultural population of west and south Afghanistan.

Dusun. Borneo tribe. They are probably of mixed origin, but tending towards the long-headed Indonesian type. They are cultivators of the soil, an amiable people but given to head-hunting.

Dutch. *See* Netherlands.

Dzungars, Dzungans or **Dungans.** Western Mongol or Turko-Tartar people of the Ili valley. They are Mahomedans, but follow a Chinese mode of life.

Edo or **Bini.** People of Benin and the surrounding country, formerly celebrated as the seat of a powerful kingdom, which in the seventeenth century extended its power as far as the Gold Coast. Benin was notorious for its human sacrifices; the king was surrounded by an elaborate hierarchy of functionaries, and traced his descent to a Yoruba who founded the royal line about seven hundred and twenty years ago, taking the place of a native line of kings whose successors still remain in Benin and enjoy certain privileges. The Edo speak a language of the Lower Niger group allied to Ewe, the language of Togoland, and to Kukuruku. In character they are a brave and proud people, and their chiefs regarded themselves as better than Europeans; they are, however, less open and more grasping than some of their neighbours. Their houses have no real roof, each room having an open space in the middle, so that in bad weather there is no refuge from the rain.

Egyptians. Inhabitants of Egypt. From the earliest period, seven thousand years ago, the population has been mixed, Hamitic elements being mingled with two broad-nosed types. Two thousand years later the long-headed Mediterranean type began to take the place of what is regarded as the Hamitic type, and they became supreme in the eighteen centuries before the Roman empire; at the same time the round-headed Alpines assumed a position of importance. The population is still predominantly long headed, but there are differences according to provinces; above Assiut the Mahomedans are mostly long headed and broad nosed, and below it, in the Delta, the Alpine and Mediterranean types found in Europe predominate.

Ekoi. Bantu-speaking people of Nigeria, beyond the Cross river.

Eskimo or **Innuit.** Inhabitants of the extreme north of America. They are of medium stature with high and comparatively long heads and eyes of Mongoloid character. They are peaceful, cheerful and honest. In winter they live in earth or snow huts; the kayak is the man's boat, and is covered with skin except where the occupant sits; the umiak is a woman's open skin boat. In language, culture and physique the Eskimo differ from all other aborigines of America, but it seems likely that they are of Asiatic origin; it is probable that they formerly extended as far south as New England.

English. Name originally applied to the Anglo-Saxon invaders of Britain, then to the compound of Anglo-Saxon and Dane, and finally, not long after the Norman conquest, to the people formed of the Norman and pre-Norman population. Many different types are represented, some of which, as in Tynedale or Cornwall, attain great prominence in certain areas. For pre-Roman times there is little certainty, but at present there is nothing to show that any elements of the population can be referred to races resident in the British Isles before 12000 B.C. The foundation of the English people seems to be the agricultural and pastoral race with long high skulls, known as river-bed people. The Long Barrow people were of much the same type and may or may not have been immigrants from north-west Europe. A broad-headed people, perhaps from east Europe, succeeded them, tall and strongly-built, found more especially in south Britain, whereas, e.g. near Aberdeen, the type is squat and bullet headed.

In the Bronze Age came a dark, broad-headed people, seen especially in Cornwall and Wales, which reached the islands in quest of gold. Then came a long-headed people who introduced bronze axes—they were perhaps leaders of a round-headed peasantry—and are on the whole confined to east England. They perhaps brought with them the Gaelic language, and represent the origin of the original tall, fair, rather long-headed aristocracy. They seem to have come from the Hungarian plain. The long-headed, fair people may have brought the speech of Wales and Cornwall when they introduced iron ; they were followed a few hundred years later by the Belgae, who came two centuries before Caesar from north-east Gaul ; they were tall, fair, and rather broad headed.

When the Roman legionaries came they left the rural parts to the older peoples ; there is no evidence to show that they had much influence on the racial type ; more important may have been the exportation of soldiers and slaves to Rome, and the emigration from south-west Britain to Brittany (Armorica). From Ireland came fair-haired people, whose descendants are still to be seen in mid-Cardigan. After the leaving of the Romans, Germanic peoples descended on the shores of Britain. Jutes, Angles, and Saxons on the east coast ; Norsemen on the Hebrides and down the Irish Sea ; then came the Danes. All these invaders were probably long headed and fair.

The last invasion to introduce a fresh strain was that of the Normans, but craftsmen like the Flemings were introduced—near Norwich and in Pembrokeshire—by Anglo-Norman kings, while in medieval times trade brought to Kent many a broad-headed Frenchman ; Germans from the Hanse towns settled in London ; Jews came from many parts, Huguenots driven out by persecution added to the mixture of peoples ; and in later times have come both Germans and east Europeans to fuse with natives in two or three generations.

A hundred years ago provincial peculiarities were more marked, for men wandered little, save in centres of trade. To-day the Norsemen,

Celts, and earlier types of the north and west are rapidly blending with the more cosmopolitan and Anglo-Saxon types of the south-east. The so-called "Anglo-Saxon race" is not defined by differences of breed or origin, but in the main by differences of culture (language, political institutions, educational ideals, etc.). Even where racial types persist in Britain, they indicate, not the existence of separate breeds, held asunder since a far-distant past, but the handing on, from generation to generation, of groups of associated characters which persist in spite of intermarriage with people of other inheritance.

Esths or **Esthonians.** Finno-Ugrian people of the Baltic. They are now assimilated in type to European peoples.

Ethiopians in the Main. Name given to the eastern Hamites, of whom the Galla are typical representatives. They are rather tall, with long heads and a prominent straight, narrow nose. The hair type is frizzly, intermediate between the woolly hair of the negro and the curly hair of the Arab. They are of slender build, with long, well-developed limbs.

Euscara. Indigenous name of the Basques. They are divided into Guipuscoan, Labourdin, Souletin, and other groups.

Ewe. Tribe of southern Togoland. They speak a language closely akin to that of Benin City, and were suzerains of the coast area in the seventeenth century. There is a short-headed type intermingled with the normal long-headed negroid which probably indicates an earlier pygmy population ; cases of apparently normal persons have also been observed whose height did not exceed that of a pygmy. They believe that each man has an aklama or genius ; in this word there is reproduced the Egyptian ka, which was probably carried to West Africa by wandering traders in the search for gold.

Falasha. Division of the Hamitic peoples of Abyssinia, termed collectively Agao. They claim to be descended from Jews who came from Judea with the Queen of Sheba, and practise Jewish rites ; but there is no reason for regarding them as Jews by descent. They have broad faces, with high cheekbones, straight hair, and yellowish complexions.

Fang, Pangwe, Pahouin. Large group of Bantu-speaking tribes in the area between the Ogowe and the Sanaga. The main mass of the people belongs to an older stock, upon whom another people descended from the north-east, and two types are distinguishable, one with a broader skull, short face, flat nose, and thick lips ; the others with a narrower, higher skull, longer face, high bridge to nose, European-like jaw and lips. The first type, of dark chocolate brown hue, is more numerous ; the colour of the other type is light, almost reddish.

Fanti. Negro tribe of the Gold Coast, nearly related to the Ashanti or Asanti ; it is probable that both have come down from the north. The Fanti language has been swallowing up the Guang language, spoken on the coast less than a century ago. On the coast they are expert canoe men, and employ themselves in fishing ; inland, they cultivate the ground. They are less warlike than the

Ashanti, but probably the most intelligent of all negro peoples ; they are clever traders and often well educated.

Fijians. People on the eastern edge of the Melanesian area. Mainly long headed, they have undergone considerable admixture with Polynesians. They were originally very warlike, but their character is gentle, and even timid, courteous, and anxious to please.

Finnic Tribes. In addition to the Finns properly so-called, there are a number of allied tribes to the east of them. The northern group comprises the Zyrian, Permiak, and Votyak, who range as far north as Archangel ; the southern group, from Kazan southwards on both sides of the Volga, comprise the Cheremiss, Mordvin, and Chuvash. The latter, however, speak a Turko-Tartar tongue.

Finns. People of Finno-Ugrian stock which arrived in Europe from Central Asia comparatively late. The Finns of to-day are allied to the Esthonians, Livonians (now nearly extinct), and Lapps, though the Finns are Europeanised in type. They are divided into two sections geographically, the Karelians and Tavastians.

Finno-Ugrians. Group including from the genetic standpoint Finns, Esthonians, Livlanders, Magyars, all of whom have ceased to be typical in respect of appearance ; Bulgarians, who have also adopted a Slavonic tongue ; and typical Ugrians, like Cheremiss, Samoyed, Votyak, and Lapp. Generally speaking, the typical Ugrian has a yellowish-white skin and straight black or yellow hair ; he is not tall, and may (as in the case of the Lapp) only just exceed 5 ft. in height ; his nose is straight or concave, his head long or medium, but there are exceptions.

Five Civilized Tribes. Term for the American Indian tribes : Cherokee, Chickasaw, Choctaw, Creek, and Seminole. They maintained their own system of government in Indian Territory, now Oklahoma.

Flemings. Population of the north of Belgium. The people of the plain of Flanders are a tall people, and this feature is more noticeable the farther north one goes ; the head is between long and short, a medium type, but becomes longer towards the north and blondness also increases in the same direction. This type is commonly called Nordic, and corresponds to that of the Franks who were in southern Belgium in the sixth or seventh century.

Flemish. Teutonic language of the Low German group. More than one dialect is spoken in the north of Belgium, and is not very different from Dutch. The speakers of it are known as Flemings.

Fon. Ewe-speaking people of Dahomey.

French. Inhabitants of medieval and modern France. They take their name from the invading Franks of the fifth century. In the last fifty years many remains of human beings of a very early type have been found in France, especially the south, where they dwelt in the cold period at the end of the Early Palaeolithic Age. They were followed by men of entirely different types, some of whom may have come from Africa, others across Central Europe, perhaps from south

Russia ; but as long as they subsisted by hunting the population was never very numerous. With the coming of agriculture in the more temperate climate of the New Stone Age man grew in numbers and more waves of invaders, some long headed, some round headed, drifted into Gaul, as the country came to be called in the centuries before the Roman conquest.

Two thousand years ago the inhabitants of Gaul were almost all short headed ; but then long-headed Nordic peoples began to move across the Rhine ; the Cimbri came, it is said, from the north of Denmark, and, after ravaging France, penetrated into Italy, only to be destroyed by the Romans. Roman rule left few traces on the type of the natives, and, as it weakened, more Germanic tribes streamed across the Rhine—Franks, Goths, Burgundians, etc.—and put an end to Roman power. The Teutonic element thus introduced ruled the land for a time, but was then swallowed up in what became the French nation, just as were the Northmen of a later date.

The Frenchman of to-day is, in the main, round headed, but there is a broad band of longer headed people running through Paris, and, as among the upper classes in England, the higher in the social scale a family stands, the greater its tendency to long headedness. It has sometimes been said paradoxically that France is more Teutonic than Germany ; taking it all in all, though the Alpine peoples of central Europe are dominant in France, they are so to a less extent than in Germany and Austria.

With such mixed blood it is not surprising that the French character varies even more than the physical type. The Gascon is proverbially loquacious and boastful, the Norman cautious and slow to act, the Breton fanatically religious and somewhat remote from the population of the rest of France. The Burgundian is quick and enterprising ; the Basque, if he has a special character, pliant and versatile, while the native of Touraine is even-tempered and intelligent. The inhabitant of the south differs in temperament from the men of the colder north.

Fula. Ordinary form of the name of a people who call themselves Fulbe (sing. Pulo). They are also called Filani (Hausa), Peulhs (French), Fellatah, etc. The proper name of the language is Fulfulde. The Fula are found over a wide area from the Gambia to Darfur, usually in the form of scattered communities, without any tribal organization. They fall into two sections : cattle Fula, wandering herdsmen, for the most part non-Mahomedan, who have preserved in many places a purer type ; and house Fula, all Mahomedans, who have intermarried with negro tribes. The pure Fula has straight hair, a swarthy white or light bronze skin, aquiline profile and high cheek-bones and thin lips ; he is unmistakably non-negro, and it seems probable that he is an immigrant from Asia who has adopted and modified a negro language. Historical records show the Fula as migrating from west to east ; but there is little doubt that they originally came from the eastern part of Africa, the reflux beginning when they reached the Atlantic coast. In recent times the Fula penetrated Hausaland, Bornu, and Adamaua, establishing themselves as a ruling class ; their advance was checked by the Yoruba, Sura, Tangale, etc., in different areas. The Fula language has sometimes been attributed to the Hamitic family, but it forms a type by itself, though it has influenced some neighbouring negro tongues. A language of Fula type has been regarded as one of the elements that went to form the Bantu family, but little evidence has been produced to support the theory.

Funj. Nilotic people of Sennar, in the Sudan. They are somewhat lighter than the Shilluk, who have thin legs and a somewhat shorter head than other Nilotes. They are mainly agricultural, but own some cattle. They founded a kingdom about five hundred years ago which disappeared in 1786. Their name is a Shilluk word which probably means " stranger."

Ga or **Accra.** Small negro tribe of the Gold Coast. They speak a language distinct from the neighbouring Fanti and Ewe.

Galego. Language of Galicia in the north-west of Spain. It is more nearly allied to Portuguese than to Spanish.

Galla. Hamitic tribe of Abyssinia and north-east Africa, also known as Oromo. In pre-Mahomedan times they seem to have occupied the southern shore of the Gulf of Aden, and were pushed by the Somali into the Abyssinian highlands. They seem to represent the purest Ethiopian type. Of Galla descent are, perhaps, the pastoral Ba-Hima in the neighbourhood of Victoria Nyanza, who dominated the Bantu tribes of that area.

Garo or **Garrow.** People on the west of the Khasi, in Assam. They are Mongoloid, and speak a Tibeto-Burman language of the Bodo type. A short, wiry people of pleasing character, they are honest and fairly truthful, but not notable for cleanliness. They are not very industrious, but they live in a fertile land where hard work is not necessary. They squander their grain resources in brewing rice beer, but are generally quiet and law-abiding.

Georgians. European name of a people that call themselves Karthli, and live chiefly to the south of the Caucasus. They have been grouped into five sections : Lazes, Mingrelians, Imeretians, Gurians, and Grusinians, or Georgians proper. With the Chewsures, Tush, Pschaw, Swanetes, etc., they are branches of the Karthaline people, which broke up in the fourteenth century. Generally speaking, they have black eyes and hair, long, aquiline noses and rounded faces. They are an open-hearted, cheerful, and sociable people, hospitable, sincere, and of a martial nature, but unpractical and indisposed to regular work. They are not intellectual, though some of their poets were notable.

Germans. (1) Inhabitants of Germany, (2) the German-speaking peoples of Germany and Austria. In the Old Stone Age we find in Germany, first, the extinct Neanderthal type, and at a later period more than one kind of both long and round headed peoples. But when we come to the more immediate ancestors of the population of the early historic period, we find, in the New Stone Age, the long skull was everywhere in the majority and no well marked short types, which were, however, very prominent in France and the Netherlands. These long heads were not, however, of the Nordic type, but rather negroid, with broad noses, and we must not look to them as the important element in the later long heads whose migrations at the decline of the power of Rome had so much influence on the history of Europe.

With the knowledge of metals the type changed, the Mediterranean long head coming to the fore in the south-east, the Alpine type in the south-west. Nothing of note seems to have occurred in the Early Iron Age but in the La Tène, or Later Iron Age, south Germany became almost purely Alpine. Two long-headed types, one coming from the south, the other from the east, seem to have combined at this period to produce the Nordic type, tall, blond, and long headed, which is for Teutonic writers the typical Germanic people. When the historic period began, the long heads (Germanic and Slav) started southwards and south-westwards ; and the end of these migrations did not come till the ninth century. The so-called " Row Graves " (Reihengräber) of this period are regarded as the remains of these wandering tribes, which changed the prevailing type of south Germany from the Alpine to the long-headed Nordic, and still persisted for another five hundred years, though the women remained preponderantly Alpine in type. It does not follow that all the people of Germany were Teutonic ; for a Slav (Wend) element is found as far as Mecklenburg ; indeed, some of the river names of Holstein are Slavonic.

The four hundred years that followed the twelfth century saw an enormous change in the type of south Germany ; the long head was reduced to about one per cent. of the population, and more than eighty per cent. were pure short heads. The same change has taken place in much of north Germany, and the modern Prussian differs little from the Bavarian. The great mass of the population of Germany is not physically distinguishable from the people of Switzerland, or even of northern France ; even in Westphalia the average index of head breadth to length is 80, which is the lower limit of short headedness. On the other hand, the fair types are in a majority, though there is a large dark element in the south.

Only in the north, more especially in the north-west, does the traditional German type survive. The tall, blond Teuton has been almost everywhere submerged by the Alpine types of the mountains of central Europe and the plains of Eastern Europe ; no one has yet given an explanation in detail of how the change came about.

Germanic or **Teutonic Languages.** One of the chief groups of Aryan languages of West Europe. There are three main divisions : High German (Old, Middle, New) ; Low German, with the extinct Gothic, Saxon, Dutch, and Frisian, together with English ; and Scandinavian with Swedish, Norwegian, and Danish, and Icelandic.

Ghilza or **Khilji.** Tribe of the east of Afghanistan, probably of Turki stock.

Gilyaks. Tribe of unknown racial affinities of the north of Sakhalien. They are below middle height, squarely built, broad headed, dark, and short legged. Their chief occupation is fishing.

Gola. Tribe on the borders of Sierra Leone and Liberia, as to which very little is known. They speak a language that appears to belong to the semi-Bantu group, but does not seem to be of the same type as the languages of the Coast group in its immediate neighbourhood.

Greeks. Inhabitants of modern Greece, who speak a language of the Hellenic branch of Aryan. For lack of data the ancient history of Greece is shrouded in almost complete mystery. At the beginning of the historic period came the Dorian invasion, perhaps of an Alpine type, which probably exists in our own day in a very pure form in the middle of the three peninsulas of the Peloponnesus. It seems clear that the historical peoples of Greece, Achaeans, Argives, Dorians, Ionians, etc., arrived as independent, often hostile bands, and we are not entitled to assume from the fact that they all spoke Greek in the historic period that they were of one common stock. It seems probable that at the highest development of Greek civilization the upper classes were long headed, the peasants round headed. Of the modern population not much more can be said than that they are predominantly round headed and dark, with smooth, oval faces, rather narrow and high. On the whole the western area seems to be of a purer type than the eastern.

Grusinians or **Groussians.** Chief people of the Georgian group residing on the east of the Suram Mountains, Caucasus.

Guanaco Area. District stretching from Cape Horn to Bolivia. It is inhabited by tribes in the main non-agricultural and nomadic. Like the Plains tribes of North America, they took to the horse and quickly adapted their life to it, becoming hunters of wild cattle instead of the guanaco, a wild form of the llama.

Guarani. People of Paraguay and South Brazil. They are probably of much the same type as the Guaycuru and speak a Tupi-Guarani tongue.

Guaycuru. Paraguayan tribe of mixed type like the Guarani. They seem to be in the main round headed with high skulls and broad noses, but there is also a long-headed, narrow-nosed type.

Gurians. Georgian people of the Suram Mountains, Caucasus.

Gurkha. Dominant tribe of Nepal. The name is used, as a rule, in a vague sense to include such tribes as Khas, Gurung, and Mangar, from which British-Indian regiments are largely recruited. According to one authority they are of Tibetan origin; but their adopted language, Pahari, shows evidence of affinities in other directions.

Gypsies. Nomadic people scattered throughout the world, but located mainly in the Balkans, where they appeared probably from north-west India, some nine hundred years ago, and spread over the rest of Europe about four hundred years later. Norway and Sweden alone are said to have no gypsies. In India the Banjars and Nats are identified with them; in Persia and Turkistan the Luli and Mazang; in Syria the Chingane, a name clearly cognate with the European Tzigane, Zigeuner. They seem to diverge widely in physical type and approximate to the characters of the surrounding population. The gypsies are probably everywhere more or less of the same pursuits and mental disposition; they mend pots, deal in horses, or steal them, making an honest living when circumstances debar them from an easier mode of life. But their existence is modified by their environment. In England there are only small bands, for there is seldom suitable camping ground for great agglomerations of nomads whose presence, even in small numbers, is not always welcomed by the sedentary inhabitants. But in Russia, before the Great War, this wandering folk would be found moving about the country in battalions, thousands going to form a single group.

Haida. Coast tribe of British Columbia. They are great carvers, and their huts and totem posts are famous, the latter sometimes fifty feet high. The dead were sometimes placed in boxes on carved poles.

Hakka. Chinese people in the hills of Kwantung. They emigrated from Honan in the fourth and ninth centuries, and their language stands somewhat apart.

Hamites. Non-negro inhabitants of north and east Africa, sometimes called Ethiopians. They include Galla, Somali, Masai (eastern or Kushitic), Berbers, Tuareg (western or Libyan), and the extinct Guanches of the Canary Islands. Some authorities add the Hottentots, who are perhaps an Hamitic cross, and the Fula or Fulani. There is a Hamitic aristocracy in some of the Bantu-speaking tribes. If all the peoples mentioned above be included, no definition of the Hamitic type can be given, save in the most general terms, for the hair varies from frizzly (but not woolly) to kinky (but not quite straight), and their complexion from reddish-brown to swarthy white. The languages have not been shown to be related. The Hamites differ from the negro in their thin lips, straight or arched nose, and suggestion of kinship with European races.

Hanak. Czechs who live in the valleys of Bohemia, Moravia, and north Hungary.

Hare. Athapascan tribe of the north-west of Canada.

Hausa. A numerous people of the northern provinces of Nigeria, who have spread, as traders, far beyond their tribal limits. Their language, which seems to have been deeply influenced by Hamitic forms of speech, is a means of intercommunication over a wide area. They are moderately tall and usually very black, but some observers declare that their hair is less woolly and their lips not so thick as in the true negro. It seems probable that there has been a considerable non-negro element, perhaps long before historic Arab movements, which certainly came from the east. The Hausa is an excellent farmer, but seldom herds cattle, as that is the occupation of the Fula or Fulani ; he is also an excellent soldier, while as a carrier he is powerful and shows great endurance. Where there is an admixture of Fula blood, he is less disposed to labour, but gains in enterprise and intelligence ; he also shows administrative gifts and a power of command. The Hausa language has acquired its importance because it is not only simple in grammar, with few difficult sounds, but also because the vocabulary is large, and it readily admits of the introduction of foreign terms ; to the European it presents more resemblance to a European tongue than any other negro language.

Hazara. Turki people of Afghanistan, who claim Mongol descent, though they now speak Persian. They are Mongol Tartars who have lost their Mongol speech, but retain their characteristics ; they are a simple-minded people, poor and hardy and reputed faithful and industrious.

Hidatsa or **Minitaree.** North American tribe of the Siouan stock, at one time closely allied to the Crows. Their great ceremony was the Sun Dance.

Himyarite. Inhabitants of southern Arabia. Some are found in Abyssinia, and it is probable that migrations of this sort have been in progress since prehistoric times.

Hindus. Believers in Hinduism. The term is also used as a general name for the people of Bengal, who fall into seven main sections, beginning with Brahmans and Rajputs and ending with unclean castes like the Dombs.

Hoklo. People resident on the south-east coast of China.

Hopi or **Moqui.** American Indians of the south-west group, speaking a Shoshonian tongue. Agriculture is their principal industry ; they are skilled in weaving, dyeing, etc., devote much time to rain ceremonies, and their villages, known as pueblos, consist of stone or adobe houses.

Horak. Czechs who live in the uplands of Bohemia, Moravia, and north Hungary.

Hottentots. South African people with bodily characteristics resembling those of the Bushmen, but taller. Like the speech of the Bushmen, their language contains clicks, and it is probable that their presence is due to the fact that the Hottentot is a cross between the Bushman and some other type. The Hottentot are often called Nama or Khoikhoin.

Hova. Highest class of the Madagascar tribe whose proper name is Antimerina.

Huichol. Mexican people to the east of the Cora or Nayarit, to whom they are allied. The name is a Spanish corruption of Vishalika, the healers, which is their own name, from the fact that they have a great reputation as doctors. They are a light chocolate brown in colour, quick witted, with much self esteem, but they are confirmed liars, and very cunning, wholly without personal courage and very emotional.

Hungarians (see also **Magyars**). The inhabitants of Hungary, who speak a Finno-Ugrian tongue, but so modified in physical type as to be quite Europeanised. We have very little information as to the early population of the Hungarian plains, and it is certain that the essential period for the understanding of the present conditions is that of the " Völkerwanderungen " from the third century onwards. In 550 the Hunagars advanced from the Urals to the Volga and reached the Danube some two hundred years later ; with the aid of other Turki tribes like the Magyar they dominated the Slavs, who, like the Goths and other Teutonic tribes, had raided and partly settled in the south-east of Europe, while the Huns and Avars had simply swept through, leaving no permanent traces, so far as can be seen. At any rate, with the foundation of the kingdom of Hungary towards the end of the ninth century the remains of these Mongolo-Turki peoples who had come to south-east Europe in the preceding four centuries were absorbed.

At this time the Hunagars were horsemen, skilled from childhood in the use of javelin and bow ; the period of lawless raids, which took them as far west as Burgundy and Alsace, came to an end with the conversion of Stephen to Christianity. When the Hunagars came in contact with the Slavs the latter were, in the main, long headed, though to-day they are of the Alpine type, as were, in all probability, the Hunagars themselves. At the present day the Hungarian seems to be like the Slav of the same short-headed type ; in stature he is tall in the eastern area of the Szeklers, where the average is just under 5 ft. 9 in. The complexion varies, but is, in general, dark ; but blue eyes are more common than one would expect in a region so far to the south.

Huron. French name of an Iroquois tribe allied to the Algonquins against the Iroquois in early times. They formerly numbered about 20,000, but are now almost extinct. They wrapped the dead in furs and packed them in bark before putting them on a platform ; every eight or ten years the remains were collected and buried in a common grave.

Iberian. (1) The prehistoric inhabitants of south-west Europe ; (2) a synonym sometimes used for Georgian.

Ibibio. Negro tribe of south-east Nigeria, of the same stock as the more cultured Efik of Calabar. They represent a comparatively low type. The language appears to be of the Ibo stock, but either of an older type or more influenced by foreign elements.

Ibo. Negro tribe numbering some four million, of whom a small proportion are on the west bank of the Lower Niger, not far above the delta, and the remainder on the east bank as far as the Cross river. They are strongly built and were formerly exported as slaves in large numbers. They speak a language of the Lower Niger group, which was probably imposed on them by a conquering people, perhaps the Nri of Aguku, coming from the north-east. They are almost entirely agricultural, but certain towns are composed of blacksmiths, doctors, etc., and the father hands on his knowledge to his son. They make use of an extraordinary kind of face scarring, the whole of the features being ridged in the case of certain men with parallel lines running obliquely. They are an open-hearted people, of generous disposition, hard-working and naturally peaceful. In many parts they have no tribal chiefs and each quarter of a town is an independent unit.

Icelanders. Scandinavian folk settled in Iceland more than a thousand years ago. They speak an archaic form of language of the Scandinavian branch of the Teutonic family.

Igabo. Sobo tribe on the east of the Niger.

Igara. Tribe of the east bank of the Niger below the Benue. They speak a language allied to Yoruba, but are politically independent of them.

Igorot. Head-hunting tribe of the Philippines. They are excellent agriculturists and irrigate, in places, the whole face of a mountain. They are usually a light yellowish-brown with flat noses, are short in stature, and probably mixed with negritos. Their tradition is that they came from the south, but they are probably of mixed origin, as their head shape varies from very long to almost circular, the nose from broad to narrow, and the skin from light brown to bronze with saffron undertones. Among the tribes are Tinguian or Itneg, Bunayan, Nilapan, Ifugao, or Mayoyet, etc.

Ijo. Tribe of the Niger delta. They are of strong build and differ a good deal in appearance from the surrounding people. They speak a language of the Middle Zone with some affinities to semi-Bantu, and make distinctions in the gender of nouns, quite contrary to the usage of Sudanic languages. They are essentially a river people who formerly made much money as purveyors of slaves to white exporters and are still important as middlemen in the palm oil business.

Ilongote. Philippine tribe. They are of small stature but powerful build, with straight hair but frizzly beard ; their eyes are dark brown and so is the skin, but with a yellowish tinge ; the nose is well shaped, but rather broad at the base. Before a man can marry he must produce a head, which after nine days is buried below the bride's future home.

Imeretians. Georgian people on the Middle and Upper Rion. They are, with the Gurians, the best-looking of all the peoples of the Caucasus. Their faces are described as noble, with large, dark brown eyes, regular eyebrows, fine beards, and thick, dark brown hair. Their hands and feet are remarkable for their small size. In character they do not differ from the Grusinians.

Inca. Tribe of Bolivia near the Rio Apurimac. They are of Quichua stock and speech. The Inca were formerly the dominant tribe of Peru, possibly the descendants of the builders of Tiahuanaco, at the south end of Lake Titicaca, the earliest known centre of culture in that area. There are Inca Indians in the Putumayo valley, probably descended from the ancient Inca, the rulers of Peru at the time of the Spanish conquest. They have long black hair, which is tied, sometimes with the inner bark of a tree, above the ears. Their principal food is maize, which is first scalded in great earthen pots and then chewed by the family ; after being mixed with unchewed maize, the mass is allowed to ferment and used as required. They use blow-guns obtained through middlemen from the River Napo Indians.

Inca Area. District with many culture variations with the Quichua and Aymara, as dominant tribes. The upland tribes are sedentary and agricultural with temples and organized priesthoods. The tribes are largely agricultural and use irrigation ; the llama was domesticated in pre-European times.

Indic Languages (Aryan Group). It comprises two main divisions : the extinct Sanskrit and Vedic ; and Prakrit with, first, Pali ; secondly Bengali, Punjabi, Gujarati, Hindustani, Marathi, Uriya, Sindhi, Kashmiri, Naipali, and Pushtu (Afghan) ; and thirdly, Romani or Gypsy languages.

Indo-Afghan. Race to which are assigned the Afghans, and some higher castes of India.

Indo-Aryan Languages. Branch of the Aryan group of Indo-European languages spoken in India. It includes Outer, Mediate, and Inner Sub-branches, the Outer branch including Assamese, Bengali, Oriya, Bihari, Marathi, Sindhi, and Lahnda ; the Mediate including the Eastern Hindi language ; and the Inner branch two groups—Central, with Western Hindi, Punjabi, Gujarati, Bhili, etc., and Pahari, with Khas-Kura or Nepalese.

Indo-Aryan. Group of peoples in the Punjab. They include Rajputs, Khatri, and Jats, who in all but colour closely resemble Europeans and show little difference between higher and lower classes of the population. Their characteristics are tall stature, fair complexion, plentiful hair on the face, long head, and narrow, prominent nose.

Indo-European Family of Languages. Speech of the greater part of Europe and part of Asia. The main groups are Iranian (Persia), Sanskrit and Prakrit (India) ; Greek ; Italo-Celtic (Latin, etc., and Romance languages ; Gaelic Welsh, etc.); Germanic (Germany, Scandinavia, British Isles, etc.); Baltic (Lithuanian and Lettish) ; and Slavonic (Russian, Polish, Czech, Serb, etc.); Albanian ; Armenian. These languages are also termed Indo-Germanic (in Germany) or Aryan. The term Aryan race has no intelligible meaning at the present day. It is an error to regard Indo-European, the primitive speech which was the mother of the family of languages, as primitive in any other sense than that it preceded the origin of the individual groups. It originated in a form of speech poor in inflexions and may perhaps form a larger unity with Semitic, Caucasic, Finno-Ugrian and some Mediterranean tongues like Basque.

Indonesians. Inhabitants of the East Indian Archipelago and (in a few cases) of Further India. The hair is black and wavy, and the skin yellow or light brown. The skull is medium, but was probably longer at one time before the coming of the short-headed Proto-Malayan stock almost everywhere mingled with them. With the Indonesians are classed the Dyaks, Batta, etc. Physically they are classed with the Oceanic Mongols ; their languages, with Melanesian and Polynesian, make up the Austronesian family, which is again part of a larger unity, formed by the addition of Mon-Khmer and some Central Indian tongues.

Ingush. People of the Caucasus. Belonging to the Chechen group, they have the reputation of being inveterate thieves

Ipurina. South American tribe of warlike character on the Purus river.

Iranian Languages. Branch of Indo-European languages. It includes Persian in one group, and Pushtu (Afghan), Baluchi, and Ghalcha in another.

Irish. Population of Ireland with the exception of the descendants of English and Lowland Scots who began to arrive in the twelfth century. Little is known of the earlier peoples, but it seems probable that the mass of the population is pre-Celtic. The Goidels (or Scots) entered Ireland through the Dublin coastal gap and later there came into Leinster, according to Rhys, some of the Brythons who imposed their tongue upon Wales. At a later period Goidels flowed back into Wales. There is also a Viking element in the population which founded among other towns Dublin, Limerick, and Waterford.

Iroquois. Group of American Indian tribes of the east woodlands. They comprise the Five Nations (Oneida, Mohawk, etc.) and are allied to the Huron, Cherokee, etc. The Iroquois were bitter enemies of the French ; kinship is reckoned through females, who also nominate the chiefs. The Iroquois seem to be increasing in numbers, but are concentrated on reservations.

Irula. Dark-skinned tribe of the Nilgiri Hills of southern India. They speak a corrupt form of Tamil, till the ground very roughly, and depend a good deal on the sale of forest products for the purchase of grain for seed or food.

Italians. Inhabitants of Italy, who speak a language of the Romance sub-group of Italo-Celtic languages. It is not till the coming of metal that we can say that the population was of mixed types, long headed north of the Apennines, round headed in the south. It seems likely that the population at that time, both in the peninsula and in Sicily and Sardinia, was chiefly of Mediterranean type, with survivals of older long-headed elements, and that a round-headed type was filtering down from central Europe or coming by sea from the eastern Mediterranean, leaving colonies behind in their way to Spain and perhaps the British Isles.

In the Bronze Age the same round-headed immigration went on by land, and we find in the Iron Age another type, long headed with a high skull, which was also prominent in the valley of the Danube. At the beginning of the historic period we find the Etruscans with a non-native type predominant ; the early Romans were hardly less mixed than the Etruscans ; in both cases, singularly enough, the sexes differ considerably in type. In the next four centuries the Roman type changed completely, and we find them mainly Alpine, though the women show a characteristic which had been in earlier times that of men, the long high skull. This change was due in the main to the absorption of the subject peoples.

Cis-Alpine Gaul, invaded by Gauls in the fifth century B.C., was conquered two hundred years later, and had in the meantime no doubt become round headed in type. In the later days of Rome came legionaries from Spain

Gaul, the Danube, etc., and then the barbarian invaders—Goths, Lombards, Huns, and so on—who were in the main long headed. A small series of skulls in the eighth century has long types to the extent of forty per cent. but six hundred years later this had fallen to about one-third, and that is about the proportion at the present day. In our own time the Alpine type is dominant, and the Mediterranean negligible in the north of Italy.

From measurements of recruits it is clear that in modern Italy long heads are rare save in the extreme south and in Sardinia. In stature we find tallness associated with short heads, shortness on the other hand with long heads ; dark complexion is found everywhere, but where the head is longest blond or even mixed types are almost wholly absent. Of the immigrant Goths and Lombards barely a trace is found— the tendency towards blondness and tallness in the valley of the Po.

Italic Languages. Southern member of the Italo-Celtic group comprising Latin, Umbrian, Oscan, and other extinct tongues, and the Romance languages of to-day.

Ittu. Galla dialect spoken in Harrar.

Jagatai Languages. Group of Turko-Tartar languages. It includes Uigur, the most classical Turkish speech ; Koman, Jagatai proper, Usbeg, Turcoman, and Kazan. Uigur inscriptions going back to the seventh century are found on the burial mounds of the Yenisei valley. In the time of Edward I. the Mongol Khans of Persia sent letters in the Uigur character, the object of which was to arrange an offensive alliance with England against the Saracens.

Jakun. Mixed people of the Malay Peninsula, especially the southern portion. Probably blended more or less with Semang and Sakai, they are of Malayan type with round heads, dark, coppery skin, straight, smooth hair, thick, flat, short nose, and eyes that show little tendency to obliquity. The Malay divide them into Hill and Sea Jakun, of whom the former practise agriculture.

Jambi. Malayan tribe of Sumatra.

Jambo. People of Abyssinia who live on the Sobat.

Japanese. Main mass of the population of Japan, the Ainu and Gilyak being excluded. The native of Japan is decidedly short, with a fair or yellowish skin and at times a rosy tinge ; wavy or curly hair occurs, though it is usually black. In head shape they appear to be in the main of Alpine type, but in some areas long heads are in a majority. In the north and north-east early Neolithic types are recognized by some observers. There seems to be a considerable Manchu-Korean element, tall and slender, with oblique eyes, aquiline nose, and chin somewhat receding ; the Mongol element, on the other hand, is strongly built, with a broader face and more prominent cheek-bones ; the nose is flat and the mouth wide. A Malayan type has also been distinguished, small of stature, with well-knit frame, short nose and projecting chin and jaws. The language is unclassified.

Jat or **Jut.** People of north-west India who seem to have conquered the Indus Valley in prehistoric times.

Javanese. People of the middle third of Java. They are flanked on the east by the Madurese ; on the west by the Sundanese, from whom they differ but little in type. They have lightish skins and straight or slightly wavy hair ; their stature is greater than that of the Sundanese but they are below middle height. It seems likely that they are round headed, but deformation of the skull is common ; the nose is usually narrow.

Jefe. Variant form of Ewe.

Jekri or **Shekri.** River tribe of Nigeria. They speak a tongue allied to Yoruba.

Jews. Term properly applied to the children of Judah, but long since applied to the whole people of Palestine before the dispersion but after the disappearance of the Ten Tribes of Israel. The Jews are now a people without a country ; the traditional view is that they are a true Semitic people who have preserved their purity of blood, but detailed investigation into physical types has made this extremely doubtful. The majority of European Jews are found in central and eastern Europe, and constitute the Ashkenazim branch; the Sephardim, who are Spanish and Portuguese Jews driven out five hundred years ago to other countries, regard themselves as a sort of aristocracy. In England the Jew has a head of medium type, neither long nor short ; in north Italy he is short headed ; so, too, are the Spanioli of Bosnia, though perhaps twenty per cent. of long heads are mixed with them. The Spanioli of Constantinople and Jerusalem, on the other hand, are mainly long headed, though there is only a small majority. The last-named type is the one that corresponds to the type of the Arab, who is certainly a true Semite.

As a general rule the Jew comes to resemble the type of the surrounding people ; competent authorities consider that the Sephardim were originally long headed, but by intermarriage, partly perhaps in Spain, but as a rule, since their expulsion, have been Alpinised in type. The peculiar nose which is commonly called " Jewish," is found in about one-third of the Sephardim. When we consider the Ashkenazim we find that they are by a great majority short headed, with a narrow nose. In addition to these two groups, there were Jews in the Caucasus, Syria, central Asia, etc., dating as far back as the dispersion of the Jews under the Roman empire and even further. The Grusinian and Mountain Jews of the Caucasus are both short headed, with very few blonds, differing in this respect from the Ashkenazim. There are some grounds for suspecting the presence of a Kirghiz type among them. In Samarkand and Bokhara are Jews of mixed descent, and here " Semitic " noses are rare ; in Damascus the Jew is longer in the head and the " Semitic " nose more frequent.

Generally speaking the western Asiatic Jews agree in type with the Ashkenazim. In south Persia, Arabia, north Africa, etc., are other groups of Jews, many of them of old standing ; those of Persia and Mesopotamia show the long heads and are equal in numbers to the Alpine types, and the " Jewish " nose is found in Mesopotamia in more than half the subjects. At Yemen, where they are more than anywhere else an isolated group, four-fifths have long heads and narrow noses, while the surrounding Araby are now short headed. In north Africa the Jews are again extremely like their neighbours, and what is of more importance, they have among them a type, probably derived from the Berbers, who were at one time converted in numbers, with round heads and broad noses. If, therefore, there are two such diverse types, one long the other broad headed, among the different groups of Jews, which is to be called the true one ?

How is the existence of the other type to be explained ? It seems likely that the great majority of the Jews of to-day had their origin not in the types indigenous in Arabia and ancient Palestine, but in the uplands of Armenia, where are found descendants of short-headed people like the Hittites, who also resemble the modern Jew in type of nose ; the Hebrews may even have undergone a certain amount of mixture with this type in the early days of their occupation of Palestine. Another important element in the type of the Ashkenazim was derived, it is suggested, from the Turki-speaking Khazars, converted to Judaism in the eighth century, and were crushed and scattered two centuries later by the Slavs. They were a cultured, commercial, well-organized people, who made their influence felt in the heart of what is now Russia. They and the Jews metamorphosed by centuries of contact with short-headed peoples are in all probability the origin of the mass of East European Jews.

Jivaro. Tribe of the head waters of the Amazon. They are remarkable for the custom of drying the heads of enemies till the skin, still covered with hair, is reduced to the size of a small orange. They are described as brave, amiable and faithful in character, and great lovers of freedom.

Jukun. Sudanic-speaking tribe south of the Benue. They are also known as Kororofa. Their ancient law was that a king might reign only two years, and even during that period if he fell ill or sneezed or coughed, he was at once put to death.

Ka or **Kha.** Hill tribe of Siam, speaking a Mon-Khmer language. They are long headed and probably akin to the cave dwellers, perhaps of Neolithic age, of Tong-king, and also to the people who left the shell heaps by the Great Lake of Cambodia.

Kababish. Richest and most powerful Arab tribe of the Anglo-Egyptian Sudan.

Kabardians. Mahomedan people of the Caucasus. They form the western section of the Circassians, but differ from them in many respects ; they claim to have come from Arabia, and use Arabic characters in writing their Circassian language. Their faces are oval, with fine features, and they are accounted the most refined of the people of the Caucasus.

Kabiri. People north of the estuary of the Fly river, New Guinea. They are also called Girara. They are head-hunters, and in their ceremonies wooden figures of crocodiles play an important part.

Kabyle. Term often applied without very definite sense to the Berbers of Algeria. Some belong to the Djerba type, some to the Elles type, the latter being longer headed, with broad face. They are Mahomedans. The name seems to mean no more than tribe.

Kachari. Group of Assamese tribes. It includes Mech, Garo, etc. They are of Mongoloid type, with almond-shaped eyes, stand mentally much below their Hindu neighbours, and are very clannish and exceedingly obstinate.

Kachin. South Mongoloid people, speaking an Assamese-Burmese tongue and living on the head waters of the Irawadi. They are also called Kakhyen, but their own name for themselves is Chingpaw, i.e. men. Kachin is an opprobrious Burmese name and Singpho the Annamese form of Chingpaw. They stretch from the eastern Himalayas into Yunnan, and at least two well-marked types exist; firstly, the true Singpho or Chingpaw, with short round head, low forehead, oblique eyes, and broad nose, who has disproportionately short legs; secondly, a people of more Caucasic type, some of whom have fair skins and large, lustrous eyes. In temperament they are pugnacious and vindictive.

Kadayan. Klemantan people of Borneo.

Kafirs. (1) Tribes of north-east Afghanistan who are supposed to be descendants of the old Indian population that refused to embrace Islam in the tenth century; they include the Katirs, the Kam, the Wai, etc. They are of fine physique, but lightly built and usually of only medium height. As a rule they are good-looking, but looks vary with social position. They are fond of intrigue, inquisitive, jealous, grasping, fond of blackmailing, great liars, and great haters; but they are lovers of freedom, dignified, polite, hospitable, brave, loyal to each other and affectionate in family relationships, tolerant in religion and sociable. Their idea of a good man is one who has shown himself a successful murderer, a good hillman, ready to quarrel, and a lover of women. (2) The Bantu tribes of Natal.

Kaitish. Tribe of Central Australia. They are located round Barrow Creek, with customs that closely resemble those of the Arunta.

Kaizak. Turkic people living in the north-east of the Aral-Caspian basin and closely connected with the Kirghiz. Their sub-divisions are complicated and they classify themselves according to "horde," tribe, clan, sub-clan, etc., often distinguished by crests and war cries. They are chiefly nomadic cattle and horse-breeders; as they leave their stock on the pasture for a whole year, they change the ground annually, but of late years they have taken to laying in stores of winter fodder. They have permanent houses and make use of irrigation canals. They bury their dead in substantial structures of wood, clay and brick, and are perhaps to be reckoned as akin to the builders of the burial mounds known as kurgans.

Kalabit. One of the Borneo tribes known collectively as Kalamantan. They practise a kind of irrigation.

Kalamantan. Group of Borneo tribes of a type mainly Indonesian, i.e. long headed. They cultivate the soil, whereas the jungle tribes, such as Bakatan, are nomadic hunters.

Kalkadoon. Australian tribe of east Queensland.

Kamchadal or **Itelmes.** Palaeo-Siberian tribe of the southern part of the Kamchatka peninsula. They have given up their language and taken over a good deal from the Russians.

Kamilaroi. Group of Australian tribes of the north of New South Wales. They speak a Neo-Australian tongue and are divided into four intermarrying classes.

Kanaka. Polynesian word meaning man, applied by French writers to all South Sea islanders. In a restricted sense it refers to the natives of New Caledonia and the Loyalty Group, who are, apart from a few stray Polynesian colonies, typical Melanesians, very long headed, with massive jaws which often contain supplementary molars. Their colour is a rich chocolate, often with a purplish tinge. The average height is about 5 ft. 4 in.

Kanarese. Dravidian language of south India. It is spoken in Mysore and the south-east of Bombay.

Kanembu. Tribe of the northern provinces of Nigeria, south-west of Lake Chad in the old empire of Bornu, allied to the Mobber, Kanuri, etc. The name means "man of Kanem." Speaking a Sudanic language of the Chad group, they are a fine people, and prosper as farmers and traders; they have a monopoly of the salt trade as middlemen to the Buduma, who produce it.

Kanuri. Tribe to the south-west of Lake Chad. They speak a Sudanic language of the Chad group, much influenced by Hamitic forms of speech. They are just over medium height and the skin colour is, as a rule, dark or very dark. The Kanuri is of virtually unmixed negroid type, resembling in this the Nilotes. They are tall and good-looking, courteous to people of their own race, but despising the Hausa as a labourer.

Karagas. Turkic tribe of the eastern (Altaian) group.

Kara-Kalpac (Black Caps). Turkic group of the Amu-Daria district. To the extent of half the population they are settled agriculturists, the others being nomad cattle-breeders. The remnant of the Chuz Turks remained in Russia when the others were driven over the Danube and later returned to Asia. The language of this people is closely related to that of the western Turks, as a result of their belonging to the stream of Turks which moved westwards some ten centuries ago.

Karamundi. Native tribe, now almost extinct, of South Australia.

Karaya. Indian tribe on the Araguaya river of Brazil They are of medium height with long and high skulls, and wavy black hair with a reddish sheen. They speak a language of uncertain affinities. The speech of men and women is different, the latter being perhaps an older form.

Karelians. Eastern Finns, so named from their own term Kariailaset, cowherds. They have come to resemble the surrounding Russians in speech and customs; they are tall and slim, with regular features, grey eyes, and chestnut hair.

Karen. Southern Mongoloid people who compose a large part of the population of Burma, and are also found in the west of Siam It was at one time supposed that their original home was in Turkistan; their own account is that they came from Yunnan in the fifth century, probably forced down by the Tai; it is probable that they were later comers than the Mon. They are related to the Kuki-Naga peoples. There are two types, known as Red and White. They are a short, sturdy race with straight black or brownish hair and light or yellowish-brown complexion They have no name for themselves beyond designations of groups, such as Sgaw or Pwo. They were probably driven from China by the Tai and claim to have settled in Ava ; about fifteen hundred years ago they moved southwards. The White Karen are of squarer, heavier build than the Burmese and more stolid ; they are also dirty and drunken but truthful ; they seem to be of a suspicious disposition and devoid of humour. The Red Karens are small but wiry ; their faces are broad and reddish-brown, and though their heads are long, their eyes are apt to be oblique. Their marriage laws are so strict that old bachelors and spinsters are frequent owing to the lack of suitable matches.

Kashgais. Tribe of southern Persia, of Turkish origin.

Kavirondo. Two tribes of East Africa. One, also called Jaluo, has a Sudanic language ; the other, called Bantu Kavirondo, speaks a language called Lu-Masaba.

Kayan. Member of the dominant group of Borneo tribes. They are rather short in stature, with somewhat broad heads. They are agriculturists, and clear the low hills that flank the tributaries of large rivers, leaving a few scattered trees standing. Their headmen have undisputed sway, but as a people they are rather turbulent.

Kayapo. Tribe of Brazil on the west bank of the Araguaya. They have roundish heads, are light brown in colour, have slightly oblique eyes and black hair, which is wavy only when very long.

Kazikumuk. Lesghian tribe of the Caucasus whose own name is Lak. They are also called Ghazi on account of their having been the first converts to Islam in that area.

Kei Islanders. Population made up of Malay and aboriginal elements, the latter with frizzly hair. They are divided into three classes : Melmel (nobles), Rinrin (subjects), and Iri (slaves), and the latter are the frizzly-haired element.

Kenyah. One of the dominant tribes of Borneo, perhaps the most advanced. They smelt iron and make good steel blades and spear heads, using two bellows in a form widely spread in Malaysia.

Kha. Word, meaning man, applied to many tribes of Indo-China, e.g. the Moi, who are called Penong by the Khmer. There seem to be two types of Kha tribes, the short headed, possibly connected with the Cham, and the primitive tribes, who are long headed, with high, rounded, narrow foreheads, straight eyes and hair, and a clear skin.

Khalkas. Tribe of lower Mongolia, forming part of the eastern Mongol group. They are of yellowish complexion, and somewhat shorter than the allied Buriats.

Khasi. People of the Khasi hills in Assam, who speak a Mon-Khmer language. They are of a brown colour, varying in shade from light to dark according to the elevation ; the head is medium in length and the eyes are black or brown They are short in stature,

but exceedingly muscular ; they will carry a load of 80 lb. by means of a head-band for a distance of thirty miles in a day. They are cheerful in disposition and more industrious than the Assamese ; unlike many primitive peoples, they have an appreciation of nature and will sit in contemplation in the woods. They are given to gambling, and are not remarkable for truthfulness.

Khmer. People speaking a Mon-Khmer tongue and inhabiting Cambodia, parts of Siam and the south of Cochin-China. Before the coming of the Annamese they occupied a still larger area. They are a tall, round-headed people, but their eyes are seldom oblique and their hair is often wavy ; some observers have, therefore, pronounced them to be " Aryan," i e. Caucasian, in every characteristic. Their tradition is that they came from India and both physical type and language lend support to this tradition. In the earlier centuries the Chams were their mortal enemies ; about a thousand years ago a mythical ruler, Yacovarman, who could slay elephants without weapons, built the great city of Angkor, which covered five square miles. The Khmer are well grown and muscular, with large dark eyes ; they seem to represent to-day the lower classes of the population that built the great cities. They are a ceremonious and hospitable people, but never allow a stranger to take up his abode in their houses ; in family life they are gentle and affectionate ; the peasant population is hardworking, but in other parts the Khmer are apt to be apathetic and thoughtless. They prefer to live in the plains, and their houses are built on piles, of one storey only, for native custom forbids them to live under anyone else. Their official religion is Sinhalese Buddhism.

Khond or **Kondh.** Dravidian tribe of the Orissa Hills, India. Known also as Gonds, they are a bold and proud mountain peasantry who, till recently, would engage in no kind of manual labour, except in their own fields. They burn the forest, cultivate rice on the patch for three years, and then move on, leaving it for a period that may be as much as thirty years to lie fallow. They are keen hunters, and a sambar once wounded has little chance of escape, as they follow it as though insensible to fatigue. The men drink palm wine to excess, but the women are abstemious. The Khond were given to human sacrifice at one time in order to secure good crops, but a ram is now substituted for the human victim. They were also given to female infanticide, one reason given being that woman, as a mischief-maker, is better out of the world. A curious feature of the language is that they count by twelves instead of by tens.

Kikuyu or **Akikuyu.** People of East Africa who live in the highlands west of Mount Kenya. The name may perhaps mean " people of the country of figs " ; the language is closely related to Akamba. When they entered the country they found in it the Asi (Akieki), or Wandorobo, and the Agumba, a pygmy people. The men stand about 5 ft. 4 in., the women considerably less. But they are strong and muscular ; they carry loads on the back. They are naturally honest, intelligent and truthful, polite in intercourse and kind to children; but they are hospitable only to clansmen or near relatives, and will stand by and see a man starve to death if nothing is to be gained by saving his life.

Kiowa. Amerindian tribe that once resided on the Missouri and later on the Arkansas. Their language forms a distinct linguistic stock, but they were never very numerous. With the Kiowa proper were associated the Kiowa Apache, an Athapascan tribe identical in culture but with a language of their own.

Kipchaks. Of these people the western group formed the Golden Horde in the thirteenth century; the eastern were the White Horde.

Kirei or **Kerrait.** Turanian Turks of north-west Mongolia, also called Kirei-Kirghiz. They were Nestorian Christians for a few centuries, when Prester John is said to have lived among them, but have now embraced Mahomedanism. They are nomadic hunters.

Kirghiz or **Khirghiz.** Name given to the Turanian Turk people, but often used of the Kaizak, who belong to the Iranian Turkic group. The name seems to be derived from kir, meaning cultivated field, for the Kirghiz originally tilled the earth, at least from the sixth century onwards; but when the Russians came to the Upper Yenisei many of them were forced south, where they became a pastoral people. Even now some hunt and cultivate the ground. Only those who have migrated most often have adopted " horse culture," by which is meant that they use the animal for transport, food, and clothing; for heavy draught work, however, they prefer the dromedary. The Russians call them Eastern (Burut), Black (Kara), or Mountain Kirghiz. They are comparatively isolated from other Turkic tribes. Many sections of them are named from famous Mongol chiefs, and there is probably a strain of Mongol blood, which is indeed evident from the features. The cheek-bones are prominent, the eyes oblique, and the complexion is yellowish-brown, but they are generally supposed to have preserved the original Turki type. Of two sections the Kara Kirghiz live in the uplands and the Kazak in the lowlands. The true name seems to be Kazak (riders), which we know best in the form Cossack, for they were originally freelances. The word Kirghiz is used of the uplanders by the Kazak. They claim descent from a legendary Kirghiz-beg.

Kists. Chechen people of the Caucasus. Mahomedan in religion, they have much in common with the Chewsures, but were at one time their enemies. They practise the blood feud, unknown to other Chechen peoples. They are slenderer than their neighbours, more cleanly and more industrious, but notorious horse thieves.

Kiwai. People of the Lower Fly river, New Guinea. They speak a Papuan tongue and are great cultivators of the sago palm and the banana. The island is all mud, and, as a result perhaps, the Kiwai man is gloomy in the extreme; one observer records having

been there a whole week without hearing a single laugh.

Klemantan. *See* Kalamantan.

Kohistani. People of Kohistan, North-West Frontier of India. They are also called Tajiks. There are other areas with the same name, one north of the Hindu Kush, another in Baluchistan.

Koli. Caste or tribe of west India, formerly notorious thieves.

Kombe or **Ngumbi.** Bantu-speaking tribe on the coast of Spanish Guinea, between the Benito and Campo rivers.

Konde. (1) The same as Wa-Nkonde; (2) the Makonde of the Msalu river, Portuguese East Africa.

Konjara. Tribe of Darfur, Central Africa, of somewhat uncertain position. Some observers have described them as an olive-skinned people of Berber appearance; others declare them to be dark complexioned, of irregular features and middle height.

Kootenay or **Kutenai.** Tribe of British Columbia whose proper name is Kutonaqa. Their language forms a linguistic stock by itself, and they are also remarkable for a bark canoe of unusual type, which has some resemblance to one used on the Amur. They are a river and lake people, but have taken to horses. They are moral, kindly and hospitable, little given to drink, intelligent and artistic. They are, however, great gamblers. One section of the tribe was noted for the watertight baskets which they manufactured.

Korean. People of Korea. They are of uncertain affinities and differ in appearance from both Chinese and Japanese. They have high cheek-bones, a flattish nose, thin lips, and stand about 5 ft. 4 in. There appear to be two well-marked types, one of Mongoloid appearance, with short nose, flat at the root, oblique eyes and yellow skin; the other of a bearded European type.

Korinchi. Tribe of Malay stock. They inhabit the mountainous region near Padang.

Koryak. Palaeo-Siberian tribe living in and near Kamchatka. Most of them are dependent for subsistence on herds of reindeer, but some subsist by fishing.

Kota. Artisan tribe of the Nilgiri Hills of south India.

Kotoko. Tall Sudanic people south of Lake Chad. They use boats made of pieces of wood sewn together.

Khwesi or **Kpwese.** Tribe of Liberia. They speak a language of the Mandingo group.

Kredj or **Kredy.** Broad-headed people of the Bahr-el-Ghazal district. They are somewhat below average height, with thick lips and wide mouths; the upper incisors are filed to a point or cut away. They are coppery-red in colour, clumsily built, and unintelligent.

Krobo. Twi people of the Gold Coast.

Kru. Negro people of the coast and hinterland of Liberia. They speak a language of a type very unlike the ordinary Sudanic tribe. They are famous as canoe men and sailors, and are recognizable by a blue line down the forehead. The name comes from the Krao tribe of this group.

Kubu. Nomadic tribe of Sumatra. They are on an average about 5 ft. 3 in in height, and have longish heads, slightly more elongated than the Batta. They are of a rich olive-brown tint and the hair is inclined to curl. They are possibly of Malay affinities, but pre-Dravidian relationships are on the whole more likely.

Kuanyama. Bantu-speaking tribe of southern Angola and northern Damaraland.

Kubiri. New Guinea tribe of the neighbourhood of Cape Nelson.

Kui. Proper name of the people usually called Khonds.

Kunama. Sudanic-speaking tribe of south-west Eritrea. They are divided into a great number of small tribes.

Kurds. Tall people of Asia Minor and the uplands of Armenia, often with fair hair and blue eyes. They speak an Iranian tongue.

Kurumba. Wild tribe of the Nilgiri Hills of south India. They are identified with the Pallavas, who were a powerful people of south India in the seventh century. The civilized section is known as Uru or Kuruba. The wild people build their huts of mud and wattle and depend largely on jungle produce for subsistence. They are gifted with extraordinary powers of vision in matters that come within their experience, such as the search for honey, but are not keener sighted in ordinary matters than the average European.

Lacandon. Tribe of Central America, allied to the Maya of Guatemala. Their heads are somewhat shorter and the skin colour is lighter; they are also more honest and truthful. They carry loads by means of a band over the forehead, which produces a flattening of the skull. They speak a Maya language and live by agriculture, hunting, and fishing.

Ladakhi. People of Ladakh. Of southern Mongol type, they are, however, decidedly more long headed than the typical southern Mongol. The same type is also found in the south of China.

Lahu. Burma tribe of the Lolo group. They have much more of a nose than most Tibeto-Burmans, and have straight-set eyes. The national arm is the crossbow, and they use aconite as a poison for the bolts. They also have a kind of reed mouth organ, with pipes from 1 ft. to 3 ft. in length, which the men play on their way to and from market.

Lampong. People of Sumatra. They are of mixed origin, with Indonesian, Javanese, and Kubu elements in their blood. They claim descent from the Menangkabau Malays.

Languedoc. Language of south France. It has four main divisions: Gascon, Provençal, Rhodonian, and Catalan. The last-named is found at Roussillon in France, Catalonia and Valencia in Spain, the Balearic Islands, and a point on the west coast of Sardinia.

Languedoil. Language of north France. It embraces both literary French and many provincial dialects, and Walloon, the tongue of south Belgium. The southern boundary runs from the Gironde past Angoulême, Lyons, the Jura, terminating in Fribourg (Switzerland). It includes Malmedy, in the German Republic, and parts of Luxemburg.

Laos. Siamese tribe of the Tai or Thai group. They are round headed and short,

with yellowish skin and straight black hair. The eye usually shows the Mongoloid fold, and the nose is often broad.

Lapps. Finno-Ugrian people of Norway, Sweden, Finland and Russia. In historic times they extended much farther south than they do at the present day, and may at one time have occupied a large part of the area of Scandinavia and north-west Russia. They are predominantly Mongoloid in type, but there are Alpine folk in considerable numbers, who differ from the first-mentioned type in both the height of the skull and the relatively narrow nose. They are on an average about 5 ft. in height. The Russian Lapp shows a considerable amount of variation as regards both the shape of his head and his pigmentation. The Scandinavian Lapp is the purest representative of the Mongoloid type in the world. One of the few nomadic peoples of Europe, the Lapps are not improbably a branch of the Permian Finns who reached north Russia before the Finns took up their station in Finland. They are nominally Christians, but the old pagan deities still subsist. At one time Lapland witches attained fame even in England, but shamanistic rites have long ceased.

Latuka. Nilotic tribe. They are found some sixty miles east of Gondokoro and north of the Bari.

Lazes. Caucasus people of Georgian stock who call themselves Tsan. They are of slender and graceful build and very active; their faces are regular, but somewhat severe in expression they are regarded as the purest type of Georgians.

Lengua. Tribe of the Paraguayan Chaco. They speak a language of the Arawak group, sometimes called Nu-Arawak.

Lepcha. Nickname, meaning "vile speakers," given to a tribe whose real name is Rong. They live in Sikkim and speak a Tibeto-Himalayan language.

Lesghians. Caucasus people of Daghestan, Transcaucasia. They are of mixed origin. The name is a Tartar form of Leki, the term applied to them by the Grusinians. The languages fall into four main groups: Dargwa, Avar, Kurin and Lakic, or Kasi-Kumish.

Lishaw or **Lisu.** Burma tribe of the Lolo group. It is also known as Yawyin.

Lolo. Tribe of south China. They are allied to many other peoples of Indo-China and speak a language of the Tibeto-Burman group. They are of middle height but muscular, with narrow foreheads, square faces, horizontal eyebrows, black eyes and coppery complexion. More than one observer has remarked upon their resemblance to European gypsies. The women are often taller than the men. They live at high altitudes, side by side with Meo tribes and above the Man; but they have a tradition of residence in a valley where they cultivate rice by irrigation. They live in pile huts in which, on account of taboos to be observed by women, there are always two fireplaces. They are pleasant but indolent, and do not differ widely in character from the Meo.

Lur. Mahomedan tribe of Persia. They speak a language allied to Kurd and are divided into clans which bear animal names.

Lusatian. Another name for the Wend.

Macassar. Tribe of the southern peninsula of Celebes. In colour less coppery than the Malays, they are a mixed people with a negroid element, but somewhat taller and lighter in colour than the Toala. They are said to press the noses of their children in order to flatten them.

Mackenzie Area. The north-west portion of Canada, inhabited by Athapascan and Algonquian tribes, dependent on the caribou (American reindeer) for food. They use birch-bark canoes, toboggans, and skin or birch-covered tents, but make no pottery and do no weaving.

Macusi. Guiana tribe of Carib speech, closely allied to Arecuna. They are darker than Caribs, taller, slighter, and better made; they seem to be somewhat timid, and dread their hereditary foes, the Arecuna. They live on the savannahs and build houses with thick mud walls, but also use pile huts. As a weapon they use the blow-gun. They make hammocks and the famous curare poison.

Madurese. Inhabitants of east Java, of much the same type as the Javanese proper.

Mafulu. New Guinea tribe, also called Mambule. They are mixed with pygmy blood, and probably influenced by immigrant Melanesians. They live on the Upper St. Joseph river.

Magyar. Finno-Ugrian tribe which came from the eastern frontier of the south Russian steppes in the tenth century, and, joining the related Hunagar (Hungarians), displaced the Slavs, who till then had probably been the main element of the population of the plains of Hungary.

Mahafaly. Warlike tribe living in the south of Madagascar.

Mahmund or **Mohmand.** Outlying tribe of Afghanistan. They talk Afghan and recognize the Ameer as their spiritual head. They are practically independent, but are in reality much more Afghan than the majority of the peoples of Afghanistan.

Makaraka. Sudanic tribe allied to the Azande. They are of ruddy-brown complexion, of smallish stature, but well proportioned and muscular. The cheek-bones are rather high and the forehead is low, but they are on the whole a pleasant-looking people.

Makololo. Branch of the Basuto. They migrated northwards about a century ago and reduced the Barotse to servitude; the Barotse revolted subsequently and wiped out the Makololo almost to the last man. The Barotse took over the language of their conquerors, and the speech still survives though the tribe has vanished.

Makonde. *See* Konde.

Makua. Bantu tribe of Mozambique. Their language resembles Sechuana in some important particulars. The Anguru or Alolo of British Central Africa are of the same stock. They file the four upper front teeth to a point.

Malay. Oceanic Mongoloid people of late origin, found in the Malay Peninsula, Sumatra, Borneo, etc. The name has been extended to the other Oceanic Mongoloids who preceded them; these, however, do not term themselves Malays. The Malays proper were originally an obscure tribe of Sumatra whose migrations date back less than eight hundred years, a century before they were converted to Mahomedanism, which all Malays now profess. They call themselves Orang-Malayu, and their language is a much simplified form of the Austronesian tongue spoken by the Malayan or Proto-Malayan peoples who preceded them and are now intermingled with them. In character they are easy-going, indolent and taciturn, but wily and unreliable, and great gamblers; they are, however, notable for patriotism, respect for law, and, among the upper classes, for courtesy, and are very ceremonious. Outside the peninsula the most important Malay peoples are the Menangkabau and Lampong of Sumatra. The Malay is essentially a cultivator of the fields.

Malayalam. Dravidian language of south India.

Malayan. Pre-Malay peoples of the East Indies. Of Oceanic Mongol stock, they fall into two groups: (1) the Orang Benua, Men of the Soil, rude aborigines like the Jakun of the Malay Peninsula, numerous also in the interior of the Philippines, Celebes, Borneo, etc., and also forming the population of Madagascar for the most part; (2) the cultured Mahomedan tribes forming large communities with flourishing industries, like the Achinese, Bugi, Tagalog, Javanese and Madurese.

Maltese. Inhabitants of Malta who are cosmopolitan in the coast areas; dwellers in the interior have been regarded as descendants of the Phoenicians; but little is really known.

Malto. Dravidian language spoken by the Maler tribe of the Rajmahal Hills, Bengal.

Man. Word meaning properly " barbarian," applied by the Chinese to the non-Chinese peoples of the southern frontiers. In Tong-king a single tribe is thus designated, which seems to be of Mongoloid type, with oblique eyes; the women are much shorter than the men. They speak a language in which tones are important.

Manchu. People of Manchuria. They speak a Tungusic language related to others in the Amur basin. They seem to be, without exception, short headed; but it is uncertain whether they practise deformation. The skin colour is yellowish, the eyes are dark and usually Mongoloid. They are comparatively short in stature.

Mandan. Tribe of Plains Indians speaking a Siouan tongue, which formerly lived near the Upper Mississippi. Their huts were of logs covered with clay, and the village was defended by a strong palisade.

Mandars. Tribe of west central Celebes, living on the coast; they are of the light Malay type.

Mandaya. Philippine tribe which appears to be of the same round-headed type as the mass of the population of the islands southeast of the Asiatic continent. The women are noted for the fairness of their complexions and are often carried off as wives by Mahomedan tribes.

Mandingo. Large group of tribes of the western Sudan. Numbering several million in all, they are also called Mande. There are several score of tribes who range from near the mouth of the Gambia to the Middle Niger and from the coast of Sierra Leone to the Upper Niger. Many of them are Mahomedans. They include the Susu, Bambara, Vei, Kpelle, Yalunka, Boko or Busa, Khassonke, etc. The original Mandingo came to the Niger about a thousand years ago, probably from the east, and founded a great empire on the Upper Niger. They seem to vary a good deal in type, some being very black, others fairly light ; some have hair that is long and frizzly, others the short, woolly hair of the negro. Their average height has been put at 5 ft. 8 in., and they are more slender in many cases than negro tribes in general. The nose is typically negro.

Mangbettu. Tribe of the Upper Welle, first described by Schweinfurth. They have an aristocracy, probably of Hamitic origin, with pale olive-brown complexion, high-bridged noses, though the nostrils are somewhat broad, and abundant beards. They appear to be intelligent and reliable ; they are brave and skilful warriors, with comparatively highly developed industries. The lower classes are probably of mixed origin ; their skulls are relatively broader than those of the Azande. The skin, where it is not exposed to the sun, is described as of a clear bronze colour, and the hands are almost white. The hair is in some cases brown or reddish. They are said to lengthen the heads of children by bands of bark, but this does not agree with the information as to head shape. The Mangbettu speak a non-Bantu language.

Manjia. Sudanic-speaking group of peoples in French Congo. They are of tall stature with medium or short heads. They sharpen the upper teeth to a point. They cultivate the earth and, though apt to greet a stranger with a shower of arrows, are on the whole quiet and peaceable. They are cannibals and seem to do a good deal of fighting among themselves.

Manobo. Indonesian tribe of the Philippines. There are two distinct types : one tall, with a high forehead, aquiline nose, slightly frizzly hair, and clear skin recalling the Polynesian ; the other brown skinned, shorter, with a straight nose.

Manx. Celtic language of the Isle of Man, allied to Erse and Gaelic.

Maori. Pre-European inhabitants of New Zealand. Traditionally they are made up of two groups : an older aboriginal stratum, identical with the Moriori of the Chatham Islands ; and the immigrants who came to New Zealand a few hundred years before the discovery of the islands by European navigators, probably in the thirteenth or fourteenth centuries. According to the native account, the last-named people came from the Cook and Society Islands, and when white men first saw the islands the later comers formed the great majority of the population, especially in the North Island. It is not clear whether they absorbed the older stratum or exterminated it. Exactly where the aboriginal stratum hailed from cannot be determined at present. It does not seem to have been Melanesian, for not only is the long-headed Melanesian element more prominent in the North Island, especially in the northern peninsula, but the type of native

in the South Island agrees with that of the Moriori, who left New Zealand some time before the coming of the invaders from Polynesia, and in the South Island there is only a very small majority of long-headed people, the rest being of the Alpine type. Even the long-headed people of the South Island are unlike Melanesians, for their noses are not broad ; on the other hand, they seem to resemble an important part of the population of western New Guinea and of western Polynesia. The Alpine type not improbably passed through Micronesia on its way and reached the Marquesas, but hardly affected the Cook and Society Islands. They were, however, more daring navigators, and though there is little evidence that they were at all numerous among the people who fared southward to New Zealand, it is perhaps to their adventurous spirit that the inception of the voyage was due.

Maratha. Fighting caste among the Marathi-speaking people of India. As a rule they are middle-sized and regular featured, and as a class simple, frank, courteous and, when kindly treated, trustful. They are fond of show and proud of their former greatness. They occupy themselves with husbandry and as servants of the state, but never keep shops. The women seldom leave the house and in well-to-do families have much leisure, as they neither cook nor look after the house. It is a costly matter to get a husband for a daughter, and the higher the father's position the more expensive it is, so that girls of high families remain unmarried after they come of age and have to take husbands not of their own social position.

Marathi. Language of the southern branch of Indo-Aryan languages, spoken in Bombay and the Central Provinces of India.

Maronites. Christian sect to the north of Lebanon. By their isolation in the mountains and their refusal to intermarry with Mahomedan or Druse neighbours, they have preserved their Armenoid type with great purity. They have extremely high skulls, so flattened behind as to look as though artificially deformed, which, however, is certainly not the case.

Marquesas Islanders. Polynesian people of an aberrant type whose heads have been broadened, perhaps by admixture with a Proto-Malay stock. It has been supposed that the Polynesian migration reached the islands between A.D. 650 and 700.

Masaba. Language spoken by the Bantu Kavirondo.

Masai. Hamitic people of East Africa. They are of tall, slender build, and their skin colour varies from chocolate to dark brown. The head is long and relatively high, and appears rather small ; occasionally oblique eyes are seen. Thick lips are the exception and earn a special name, Lebeleb, for their possessors. The Masai woman carries on her neck and upper and lower arms many pounds of copper wire. The lobe of the ear is distended to admit the insertion of a large wooden plug. The Masai have been supposed to be descended from the Jews, but there is no evidence of this. The Masai is proud of his race, regards his immediate relatives with affection, and in the days of slavery would offer all his savings to free one of them. He despises all kinds of work, for his true calling is to be a warrior. There are two sections, one of which keeps cattle, while the other depends on agriculture ; the former build low, continuous flat huts, which are plastered with mud, while the tillers of the ground use a round hut with a conical grass roof, and live in their villages permanently, the others being semi-nomadic. Though the Masai is familiar with the use of weapons of war, he is not a great hunter, and kills only such game as he regards as akin to his cattle ; he also abstains from the use of fish.

Mashona. Peaceful tribe of south-east Africa. They are often confused with the Makalaka or Makalanga, with whom they were to some extent mingled. They seem to have crossed the Zambezi in the eighteenth century, but their origin is obscure. The ruins of Zimbabwe are in Mashonaland, but there is no reason for connecting the Mashona with them. The name, given by the Matabele, means " baboons," and refers to their habit of building their villages among the rocks.

Mashukolumbwe. Bantu-speaking people of Rhodesia, north-east of the Barotse, remarkable for a conical style of hairdressing.

Massim. People of the Trobriand Islands, New Guinea. They have been influenced by Melanesians, bury their dead, but dig up the bones after a time and use them as lime pots, spatulas, etc.

Matabele or **Amandebele.** Tribe of Zulu origin, also called Abakwa-Zulu. They originated from the followers of Moselekatse, who fled northwards from the anger of Tshaka. They lost their independence at the end of the nineteenth century.

Maya. Short-headed people of Guatemala, once the possessors of a great culture. They are of short stature with broad shoulders. The lower part of the face is somewhat projecting ; in colour they are a dark golden brown. They are hospitable and generous, but noted for lying.

Mbundu. Name of two distinct languages, one in south Angola (Umbundu), the other in north Angola (Kimbundu).

Mediterranean Race. Most southerly of the three types into which Europeans of the present day have been divided. They are commonly supposed to have originated in Africa, where the Hamites are the modern representatives of the ancestral stock. Outlying members are the Indonesians, Dravidians, and Semites. The skull is long, and the hair dark and curly or ringlety, the beard full ; skin colour varies from white to brown or blackish ; the nose is usually large and narrow. In temperament Mediterranean man is quick-witted, excitable, and impulsive, but not always quite reliable.

Meithei. Dominant people of Manipur. They speak a Tibeto-Burman language of the Kuki-Chin type. Some are described as Mongolian, others as Caucasian in features. It is not uncommon to meet among girls a type with brownish black hair, brown eyes, fair complexions, straight noses, and rosy cheeks. Although the face is described as Mongolian, the Meithei are in some cases

distinctly long headed, while others show a head of medium type. They are mainly agricultural in their pursuits, but also trade, and it is to women that such work is entrusted. They have bazaars at convenient places by the roadside, where cloth, fish, etc., are sold. Women are comparatively uneducated, owing to the circulation of a fiction that there is a scarcity of women in England, whither educated Meitheis would be shipped off.

Melanesian. Oceanic negro of the Western Pacific. The physical type varies considerably, and some non-negro element must be present. The hair is at times curly or merely wavy, and the skin lighter than that of Papuans, chocolate, or even copper-coloured. Stature ranges from less than 5 ft. to nearly 6 ft. The skull is usually long, but is in places very short. The Melanesians include natives of the Solomon Islands, New Caledonia, the New Hebrides, Fiji, etc.

Menangkabau Malays. True Malays resident in the south-west highlands of Sumatra. They are Mahomedans, and probably recent immigrants, rather short in stature, and yellowish brown in colour, with black straight hair and at times the Mongoloid eye. They are physically not unlike the Chinese of Fukien.

Mendi. People of the east of Sierra Leone. They speak an aberrant language of the Mandingo group, and in physique are of medium stature, but strongly built. They make excellent carriers and hammock boys, are of a merry, light-hearted disposition, and are celebrated for their great secret society, Porro. The Mendi are probably the modern representatives of the Mane or Sumba, who invaded Sierra Leone by sea about the beginning of the sixteenth century, after having spent ten years on the way. They probably married women of Mandingo speech, but transmitted to their children a number of words of non-Mandingo origin. It is not known where they came from. They were deadly foes of the Temne tribe who dwelt to the west of them.

Mentawei Islanders. People who live off the coast of the Malay Peninsula. Their affinities are somewhat uncertain, but their own tradition says they came from Sumatra. They are described as yellowish brown with a tinge of red ; one observer attributes to them light eyes.

Meo. Annamese pronunciation of a word pronounced Miao-tse by the Chinese. The Meo call themselves Mung, and say they came to Tong-king from China. They are short, with a relatively long body, have straight black hair, brown eyes, complexion almost white when it is not bronzed by exposure, and a straight nose. They are industrious and intelligent, fond of independence, brave and open. Maize is the chief food, but they eat rice when land suitable for its cultivation is available. Unlike many primitive peoples, they do not live in perpetual dread of evil spirits, and are held by neighbouring tribes to be regardless of dangers because they can turn into wild beasts.

Mexican. Name applied both to the European inhabitants of Mexico and to the descendants of the Aztecs who had dominated the country for some three hundred years when the European conquerors overthrew them.

Micronesian. Population of the Gilbert, Marshall, Caroline, and Marianne Islands. They may be regarded as Polynesians influenced by later migrations from the mainland of Asia and perhaps by an earlier stock of Papuan origin. They appear to be rather shorter than typical Polynesians, but have longer heads.

Mikir. People of Assam who call themselves Arleng, the name Mikir being given by the Assamese. They are not a tall people, though they are taller than the Khasi ; the head is longish and the nose flat. They speak a Tibeto-Burman language intermediate in type between Bodo and Kuki-Chin. They seem to be homogeneous in type, owing, perhaps, to their exogamous customs producing inter-mixture between the different divisions. They differ from other hill tribes in their peaceable character which has earned for them, for at least two centuries, the reputation of being good subjects.

Minahassa. Malayo-Polynesian tribe of Celebes. They are strongly built, of medium height, with light brown skin of reddish tinge. Girls have red cheeks and lips, but in men the lips have a violet sheen. The eyes are brown, the hair is black and coarse, the nose broad, and the eye shows the Mongoloid fold. They were great head-hunters, but are now Christianised.

Mingrelians. Georgian people in the basin of the Rion, who are probably descended from the Colchians mentioned by Greek geographers. They are ignorant, lazy, and unenterprising, but strong and good-humoured. Many of them become porters in the towns.

Mishmi. People of the northern frontier of Assam, divided into Midu, Mithun, Taying, and Miju. They speak a Tibeto-Burman language of the north Assam type.

Mittu. Tribe of the area of the Sudan between the Rohl and Roah rivers, bordering on the Dinka in the north and the Azande in the south. They are dark coloured and physically weak. The women pierce and insert wooden plugs in both upper and lower lips.

Mixes. Tribe of Mexico. They live in the uplands, weave cloth in the pre-Columbian method of long strips, and make suspension bridges of lianas.

Mixtecs. Intellectual and progressive tribe of Mexico. They carry baskets with a head-band.

Mohawk. Most easterly Iroquois tribe of American Indians. They were twice nearly exterminated by the Algonquins, with whom they fought ; then they obtained guns from the Dutch, and for fifty years played a great part in the Iroquois league. Then their numbers declined rapidly.

Mohegan or **Mohican.** Algonquian tribe of New England. Treacherous warriors, they fortified hill-tops with palisades and stockaded their villages, the houses of which were often 180 ft. long by 20 ft. wide.

Moi. Tribe of Indo-China. Of rather small stature, they are mostly long headed

with straight-set eyes, and therefore not Mongoloid in their affinities. Their skin is described as reddish ; the nostrils and mouth are disproportionately large, and they are said to file their teeth ; hence they are or were reputed to be cannibals. Some authorities describe them as timid, others as brave ; they are indolent, simple, and confiding and lead a nomadic life.

Mojo. Indian tribe of Bolivia. They are an agricultural people, quiet, and well-behaved.

Mombutto. Tribe of the Kibali river, Nile-Welle watershed, not to be confused with the Mangbettu. They are strongly-built dwellers in the hills, with broad faces, blunt noses, and thick lips ; they file the upper teeth.

Mongo. Bantu-speaking tribe of the great bend of the Congo, south of the Bangala. Sometimes regarded as a Balolo sub-tribe, they differ a good deal in type, some being described as a fine virile race of a high order of intelligence, while others are termed weakly, lean, and insignificant-looking. They were at one time notable traders and manufactured a kind of black pottery that was in great request.

Mongol. Group of tribes that includes the Kalmuck and Buriat. A wide extension is given to the terms Mongol and Mongoloid, but properly speaking the type is confined to a narrow area along the northern border of the Mongolian plateau. The Mongols leapt into prominence in the Middle Ages for a brief period under Jenghiz Khan, but their part in the racial history of Asia is obscure. The word " mong " means brave. The head is round and low and the nose broad, but even among the Kalmuck there is a type with a narrow nose.

Mongoloid. (1) Stock with two main branches (a) Mongolo-Tartar, or Mongols proper, including Sharra, Kalmuck, and Buriat ; (b) Tibeto-Indo-Chinese, including the bulk of the populations of Further India, Indo-China, Himalayan peoples, Chinese and Tibetans ; a sub-branch of Oceanic Mongols includes the peoples called better Proto-Malay from whom the present Malay are derived. The term Mongol was originally applied to nomads recruited from Turki and other tribes ; it now often means all Asiatics with round heads and straight hair. They have a yellowish skin, and often oblique eyes. They are usually short, and though the cheek-bones are prominent the face generally is flat. The plateau of Central Asia may be regarded as their centre of origin. (2) Group of people in India, Nepal, Assam, and Burma, of which the Kanet, Lepcha, Limbu, Murmi, Bodo, and the Burmese are representatives. They are short, with dark complexions, tinged with yellow ; the hair is scanty, the head broad, with characteristic flat face and oblique eyes.

Mongolo - Dravidian. Group, also termed Bengali, found in Bengal and Orissa. In it are Tibeto-Burman elements mingled with Caucasian. The complexion is dark and the head noticeably broad.

Mon-Khmer Languages. Group of tongues spoken in south-east Asia. They are allied on the one side to the Munda languages of India, on the other to Polynesian, Melanesian, etc., and, more distantly to the Indo-Chinese languages. The group includes the languages of the Mekong ; Mon, also called Talaing or Peguan, Annamese, etc ; Khmer or Cambodian ; Palaung - Wa, Chindwin, etc. ; and Khasi, including Synteng, War, etc.

Montagnais. French name for an Algonquian-speaking tribe of the Mackenzie Group. Roaming from the south of Labrador nearly to the St. Lawrence, they are a timid people, but were inveterate foes of the Iroquois.

Montenegrins. Serbo-Croat people, whose name is derived from the Black Mountain, where they dwell.

Monumbo. Papuan - speaking people. They live in the neighbourhood of Potsdamhafen, in what was formerly German New Guinea.

Mopla or **Mappilla.** Hybrid Mahomedan people of the western coast of south India. Their numbers are increasing by the conversion of the lower caste natives. On the coast they are traders, in the interior cultivators ; prosperous and successful in both. The head is of curious shape like a coconut, with high forehead and pointed crown, made more conspicuous by their custom of shaving the head. They are enterprising and industrious ; some enlist in the army and prove themselves hardy and courageous. They appear to be unusually fertile ; there is a case on record of a Mopla with seven wives, each of whom had presented him with seven sons, not to speak of a large consignment of daughters.

Moqui. Synonym of Hopi, derived from some foreign tongue.

Mordoff. Language of the Mordvins.

Mordvin. Finnic people of the Volga basin who long maintained their pagan religion. They are short headed and of medium stature, with hair that is chestnut or black, but never red ; the eyes are often blue and sometimes oblique, and the face oval. They are a hard-working, thrifty people, among whom the father has comparatively little power over his children.

Moriori. Inhabitants of the Chatham Islands, eastward of New Zealand. They emigrated thither from New Zealand six or seven hundred years ago, and are a people of mixed type with long and short-headed elements in about equal numbers. It is quite likely that the long-headed group represents a Caucasian element, for it is generally agreed that a people of this type was prominent in India some thousands of years ago, and India or Further India is the natural jumping-off place for those who went forth into the watery wastes of Oceania. The short-headed people are of the same type as was prominent in the western part of Polynesia and must have come from there ; passing, probably, through Micronesia on their way from the Asiatic continent to western Polynesia.

Moros. Round-headed Philippine people of Mindanao and the Sulu Archipelago, so called by the Spaniards because of their dark complexion. They are below medium height,

but are taller than the Ifugao, Igorot, etc. ; the type resembles that of the Menankabau Malay of Sumatra. They are said to be the most faithful and intelligent people of the Philippines. Their real name is Magindano.

Mosquito. Properly Miskito, an Indian tribe of the eastern shore of Nicaragua.

Mossi. Tribe of the Volta group in the great bend of the Niger. The language is called Mole.

Mpongwe. Bantu-speaking people of the Gabun area, not to be confused with the Pangwe, the name they apply to the Fang of the same neighbourhood. The language of the Mpongwe is allied to that of the Galoa. Their real name seems to be Abuka.

Mumuye. Fula name of a tribe of the northern provinces of Nigeria, which calls itself Fungun or Zagum. They are allied to the Waka, Yakoko, Zinna, etc., all of them south of the Benue river. They are an agricultural people, whose staple food is yams, but cattle are also kept, though they give no milk. They put a stone over the grave, without filling it in and later remove the skull and carry it in a pot to its resting-place in the village. They speak a language of the Adamaua group.

Munda Languages. Group of languages of Hindustan shown to be related to the Mon-Khmer and Austronesian families. It includes Mundari, Ho, Santal, Kurku, etc., and was at one time called Kolarian.

Mundrucu. South American tribe of the Tapajos.

Munshi. Tribe of the northern provinces of Nigeria, south of the Benue, whose proper name appears to be Tivi. Said to number about 350,000, they speak a semi-Bantu language of the Nigerian group, are of medium stature but muscular, unusually black in colour, and the men grow beards of some length, which they plait into three or more strands. They use hollow wooden drums for sending messages. They are a warlike tribe, hostile to the white man, and excellent hunters and farmers. They are confirmed cannibals, but by no means repulsive in appearance.

Murut. Tribe of the Kalamantan group, Borneo. They live in long communal houses built on the banks of rivers, and are mainly long headed, but there is a considerable brachycephalic element.

Muskogee. Group of tribes in the southeast of the United States, including Choctaw, Creeks, etc., who were transferred to Oklahoma ; they seem to be mostly round-headed, but the nose varies in breadth.

Mwamba. Language of the Bawanda of British Central Africa, nearly related to the Nkonde.

Naga. Number of tribes of the hill country south of the Brahmaputra, including the Angami, Lhota, Ao, Sema Naga, etc. The languages are of the Assamese-Burmese type. The skull is of medium length and the average varies for the different tribes, the Kezami Naga being quite long headed. He is tall, from 5 ft. 9 in. to 6 ft., and has great powers of endurance, carrying a 60 lb. load with ease with a forehead sl.ng. The facial type varies from one with flattened nose and oblique eyes to one with almost Caucasian traits ; the eye is brown, the hair reddish in childhood, but always black in later life, is wavy or even curly. The skin is fair and ruddy cheeks may be seen, accompanied at times by freckles. The people are intelligent and readily assimilate novelties such as vaccination ; but they are in no hurry to adopt new manners from love of novelty. They are independent, frank, honest, hospitable, genial, and very loyal, but given to exaggeration.

Nago. *See* Yoruba.

Nahua Area. District of Central America inhabited by tribes descended from the Maya, Aztec, and other peoples civilized before the discovery of America. They had extensive agriculture (maize, beans, etc.), spun fine cotton, used large canoes, picture writing, etc. Their descendants fall far short of the old standard, for the Maya culture was confined to the priests, and, with the Aztec culture, passed into oblivion at the Spanish conquest.

Nandi. East African people living near Mount Elgon. Of apparently mixed origin and related to the Masai, Turkana, etc., with negro, Masai, and pygmy elements, possibly also Galla, they are said to be nearly related in language to the Bari. They are hardy mountaineers and skilful warriors who refused access to strangers ; but they cannot have resided in their present country for many generations, for before them came an agricultural people who made use of irrigation. They were probably hunters originally, but they have taken to cultivating the ground ; men clear the land and then all the work is done by women. The chief occupation of the men and big boys is cattle herding, and the bulk of the stock live on the pastures away from their owners' homes. The Nandi are classed with the Niloto-Hamitic tribes, but are in physical type much nearer the Baganda.

Napo. Geographical designation for many distinct tribes of the River Napo, such as the Orejones, who take their name from the large wooden studs worn in their ears. There are no individual houses in this area ; one large circular dwelling, ten yards high and sixty yards or more in circumference, lodges the whole group, which moves on to another residence when, after two or three years, the old one becomes ruinous.

Nascopies or **Nascapees.** Algonquian tribe of Labrador, who call themselves Nanenot, " true men." Their accepted name is a term of reproach applied by the Montagnais.

Natchez. Muskogian tribe of the Lower Mississippi who worshipped the sun.

Nayar. Originally a member of a military body, but now of a caste including a number of occupations on the Malabar coast of south India. They are said to have practised polyandry until within recent times, but though marriage is still dissoluble at will and descent is reckoned through the mother, a woman is now restricted to one husband. As a class the Nayars are the best educated and most advanced of all communities in Malabar, and are the equals intellectually of the Brahmans of the east coast.

Negrillo. Woolly-haired pygmy of the equatorial forests of Africa. The skin colour is reddish or yellowish brown and the hair rusty brown, sometimes very dark. In stature they vary from 4 ft. 4 in. to 4 ft. 9 in. ; unlike the typical negro, they have thin lips. They are nomadic hunters without domestic animals and rely on exchange with negro tribes for agricultural products.

Negrito. Term covering the pygmy woolly-haired black peoples outside Africa, such as the Andamanese, Semang, Aetas. In stature they fall short of 5 ft., and the skin colour varies from sooty to dark chocolate brown. The head is medium or round, and it is not uncommon to find the nose much sunken at the root, a feature shared with many Australian aborigines.

Negro. Dark - skinned, woolly - haired inhabitants of west and central Africa, including the negro proper, the Nilote, and Bantu-speaking peoples. The hair is almost invariably black, but red hair is found sporadically ; the skin colour is never quite black, but varies from dark chocolate to yellowish-brown within the same tribe ; the height varies, but probably the average is about 5 ft. 4 in. The head is generally long, but in many tribes there is an admixture of a round-headed type. Some of the Bantu tribes are pastoral, but the West African negro depends on agriculture, though he keeps goats, sheep, fowls, and sometimes cattle ; near important rivers fish is largely used as food. Under European influence the negro is often lazy, but in unsophisticated tribes he does not shirk the laborious tasks of agriculture where the only tool is a hoe.

Neo-Siberians. Tribes of central Asiatic origin that have been resident in Siberia so long and have become so hybridised as to call for a generic name. They include tribes formerly called Ural-Altaian or Turanian as well as Finnic tribes like the Ostyak (in part) and the Vogul, the Samoyeds, Mongolic, and Tungusic tribes, and some Turkic, the most important being the Yakut. There is, however, considerable diversity of physical type.

Netherlands or **Low Countries.** Kingdoms of Holland and Belgium, in which are spoken Frisian, Dutch, Flemish, and Walloon. The population falls into two sections : one, inhabiting the Ardennes plateau and some of the coastal parts of Holland, is markedly short headed and dark ; those of the plains of Flanders and most of Holland, on the other hand, are longer-headed and fair in type ; but even in Friesland there are quite a number of round-headed folk of the same type as we find on the coast of Scotland and southern Norway, who differ from the central European round heads in having a head that is low in proportion to its length. This type seems to have persisted since Neolithic times, more than four thousand years ago. They were, however, probably reinforced at the time of the great tribal migrations of the sixth century by central Europeans of another type. At this period there were quite a number of Frankish long heads in south Belgium as well as in Friesland ; a different type predominated among the women, who were of the type of folk that lived in the Belgian uplands in the Iron Age ; no doubt the invaders did not hesitate to kill off the males and take the females as wives. This Teutonic invasion produced little lasting effect in the south of Belgium ; farther north, in the open lowlands, both the physical type and the language give evidence of the invasion ; in the Dutch coastal regions the type has been less affected, but the language is the same as that of the rest of the country.

Newars. People of Nepal. They are of mixed origin, with possibly Mongol and south Indian relationships. Their language, which resembles Tibetan, is called Gubhaijius.

Ngombe. Bantu-speaking people of the central Congo, with probably some admixture of pygmy blood. The word means, perhaps, " bush people."

Nigerian Semi-Bantu. Group of Sudanic languages, apparently of considerable size, including Kamuku, Kamberi, Yeskwa, Munshi, etc.

Nilotic Languages. Of these there are two groups ; the Niloto-Hamitic and the Niloto-Sudanic, the latter forming a sub-group of the eastern Sudanic languages.

Niloto-Sudanic Languages. Group of the eastern Sudanic languages. It includes Mittu, Madi, Abukaya, Luba, Wira, Lendu, Moru ; the Shilluk stock ; Dinka and Nuer.

Nordic Race. Fair, long-headed race, possibly of comparatively recent origin, whose typical representatives are found in north Europe, e.g. Scandinavians. With this race have also been classed Thracians, Kurds, Afghans, some Persians, Dards, etc. The complexion is ruddy and the eyes are often blue ; in stature Nordic man surpasses the Mediterraneans and Alpines. Temperamentally he differs widely from the other two races ; in Europe he is steadfast, energetic, reliable, and somewhat stolid.

Norwegians. Inhabitants of Norway, who speak a language of the Scandinavian section of Teutonic. We know little of changes in the population of Norway, but history tells of the exploits of the Vikings or Norsemen who raided and sometimes invaded the lands that offered promise of plunder, including the British Isles, France, and more remote shores. Norsemen colonised Iceland and settled colonists on the inhospitable coasts of Greenland, and there is reason to suppose that they sailed south of Labrador and landed in New England not long after without, however, effecting any permanent lodgment. In medieval times and in our own days Norway, the west coast excepted, represents one of the chief centres of the Nordic race, characterised by tall stature, a fair complexion, and a long head. If the Viking was a typical Nordic man, it seems as if the type has changed in the last thousand years, as it has over the greater part of Europe.

Nosu. People of south-west China, probably a Lolo tribe.

Nuaroak. Group of South American tribes usually called Arawak.

Nuba. Mixed people of Kordofan. Three types are readily distinguishable, negro, Hamitic, and Bantoid (i.e., one resembling

in appearance the north-eastern Bantu of Uganda). They lie west of the true Nilotes and have a considerable short-headed element, but the decrease in stature that might accompany this is counter-balanced by the Hamitic element.

Nupe. Tribe of the Middle Niger. Formerly they were notorious slave-raiders. Their language gives its name to a group of negro languages, including Gbari, Jukun, Igbirra.

Nyanja, Anyanja or **Mang'anja.** People of Nyasaland. Related to the Makalanga, they are of medium stature, with long heads. There is much difference between river and hill people, the latter being of poorer physique, while the so-called Angoni of the Upper Shire, really conquered Anyanja, are small, wiry men, usually rather dark.

Nyika or **Wanyika.** Group of tribes in the neighbourhood of the Tana river, including the Wagiriama, the Wadigo, etc. The name is also applied to a quite distinct group north-west of Nyasa. The word "nyika" means wilderness.

Ojibwa or **Chippewa.** Large American-Indian tribe of Algonquian speech. They were formerly located near Lakes Huron and Superior, and still number 30,000. They were expert canoemen and lived largely on fish ; their wigwams were of birch bark or grass mats ; they believed in manito, objects endowed with a mysterious power, and regarded dreams as revelations.

Ona. Branch of the Patagonian Tehuelche, or Chuelche, now resident in the east of Tierra del Fuego.

Oneida. Tribe of the Iroquois confederation, formerly resident in New York, where a few hundred of them are still to be found. In olden times they were reputed to be cruel, cunning, and prone to bloodshed.

Onondaga. Important Iroquois tribe formerly resident in New York, where a few still remain. There are nine clans in Canada on Grand River reserve, which they received in recognition of their support of the British in the war of 1812-14.

Orang Bukit or **Land People.** Generic term for the ruder inland pre-Malayan peoples of the Malay Peninsula, Borneo, etc.

Orang Darat. Aborigines of Billiton, Dutch East Indies. They are, perhaps, akin to the Battas.

Orang Ulu. Malay name of a wild tribe of Sumatra, who live on anything that comes to hand and do not practise agriculture.

Orang Sekah. Malayan boat people of Billiton.

Orejone. *See* Napo.

Oriya. Language of Orissa, allied to Bengali, Bihari, and Assamese.

Ossetes. Foreign name of a people of the Caucasus who call themselves Iroi, Tualt, and Digor, without any common appellation for the whole people. The language is Indo-European, but not Iranian, and is not related to that of any other Caucasus people. Blond hair and blue eyes are common among them, and they salute by removing the hat—a form not practised by any other Caucasus people. The men are tall and strong, but leave all work to the women. The head is shortish, and they seem to be of mixed origin; some have Mongoloid eyes, but they are, as a rule, blond with some blue eyes. They are physically inferior to other Caucasus peoples, but dominated them by force of character. They were at one time notorious for brigandage.

Ostyak. (1) Palaeo-Siberian tribe on the lower Yenisei; (2) Finno-Ugrian tribe of the Obi.

Otomi. People of Mexico. There are two distinct types, one tall, yellow, with oblique eyes; the other small, dark, with straight eyes, which are specially common among women. Men wear pigtails. They use two kinds of granary, one on posts, the other with sticks in cobwork. They are a somewhat stupid people and despised accordingly.

Ottawa. Algonquian tribe noted as traders, whence their name. They were originally a rude people, and went unclothed, but when they took to agriculture they became more civilized.

Ova-Herero. Tribe of south-west Africa, speaking Bantu. They are known to the Hottentot tribes as Damara.

Ovambo or **Ovampo.** Bantu-speaking tribe of Damaraland.

Padaung. People of Burma. They are remarkable for the amount of brass wire worn as ornaments by the women; they begin with five coils, as thick as the little finger, on the neck, and add more as the neck stretches, till as many as twenty-one are reached weighing 80 lb.

Pahari. Language of the lower Himalayas, Indo-Aryan of the Inner sub-Branch. It includes Khas-Kura or Nepalese, etc. The people seem to be descended from the Khasa of Pliny and other ancient writers. The Khasa hailed from central Asia, and were related to the Pisacha or cannibals of Indian writers; the Gurjara joined the Khasa some thirteen hundred years ago and influenced the language, which is allied to Rajasthani.

Paiwan. Group of uncivilized tribes of the extreme south of Formosa. In their ears they wear a circular piece of wood about an inch in diameter; they were once great head-hunters and preserve their trophies in stone boxes specially made for the purpose.

Palaeo-Siberian. Group name of the most ancient Siberian stock. Formerly called Palaeasiatic, they include the Chukchi, Koryak, Kamchadal, Ainu, Gilyak, Eskimo, and other peoples. It was formerly an accepted view that they represent ancient peoples driven back by later comers to the north-east of the continent; but there are grounds for arguing that they are related physically and culturally with the natives of north-west America, probably in respect of language also, and that they represent a recent backwash, not the primitive stock from which the American tribes issued. It must, however, be noted that the group seems to contain elements of very diverse origins, for while the Eskimo are very long headed, the Gilyak and other tribes are round headed. Generally speaking, they are peoples with flat faces, prominent cheek-bones, oblique eyes, yellowish-brown colour, lank hair, and sparse beard.

Palaung. People of Burma. Speaking a Mon-Khmer tongue and allied to the Wa,

they live on the Upper and Middle Mekong. They are a peaceable and industrious but uncouth and hypocritical people, short and sturdily built, with fair skins and eyes, grey or light brown being not uncommon. They have no facial resemblance to the Mon.

Papuans. Inhabitants of New Guinea other than recent Melanesian immigrants and pygmies, together with the Louisiade Islanders, and many Malaysian islands westwards from New Guinea as far as Flores. True Papuans appear to be dominant in the Aru group and perhaps in Flores; a hybrid type in Timor, the Kei group, Ceram, etc. The hair is black, frizzly and mop-like, but the beard is scanty or absent; the skin is deep chocolate-brown. There is a wide range in stature, and the skull is also variable, extremely long or, in areas of mixture, short. In temperament the Papuan is excitable and imaginative; he is not unintelligent. Although he reckons as an Oceanic negro, it must be remembered that his nose is large, straight, and generally aquiline, but blunt and with wide nostrils; it therefore departs considerably from the type of negro nose found in Africa.

Papuasian. General term for Oceanic negroes, including both Papuan and Melanesian, together with negritos and Tasmanians.

Papuo-Melanesian. Name given to the mixed peoples of the eastern peninsula of New Guinea and the islands beyond, who have been influenced by a relatively late Melanesian backwash. They are smaller and lighter-coloured than the true Papuan. The head is not so high, but brow ridges are more prominent, while the forehead is usually rounded and not retreating. Skin colour varies from light yellow to dark bronze, and for some obscure reason the lightest shades are always found among the women. The nose is generally smaller than in the Papuan, who has what is often called the Jewish type— long, stout, and arched.

Parsee. Originally a synonym for Persian but now the name of a religious sect, worshippers of the sun.

Pasuma. Sumatran tribe south of the Korinchi. They have, perhaps, been subjected to Javanese influence.

Pawnee. Tribe of Plains Indians speaking a Caddoan tongue who dressed the scalp-lock with grease and fat so that it stood up like a horn, whence their name. Religious rites, including human sacrifice, were observed in connexion with the cultivation of maize, and the morning and evening star were important in their beliefs.

Pepo or **Pepowan.** Name applied by the Chinese to the uncivilized tribes of the western plains of Formosa.

Permiak. Eastern Finnic tribe in the neighbourhood of Perm. They were originally on the Arctic seaboard, where Samoyed have now replaced them, for King Alfred speaks of Beorma, the Biarmians of the Norsemen. They are now much mixed with Russians.

Pigmies. Alternative spelling of Pygmies (q.v.).

Pisacha. Non-Sanskritic Indo-Aryan languages.

Plains Indians. Group of American tribes, originally dependent largely on the bison for food and clothing. Famous as workers in skins, they lacked basketry and pottery. They had their habitat in the plains west of the Mississippi. They took to the horse in historic times. The typical dwelling was the tipi, a tripod of poles covered with birch-bark or bison skin. Canoes were unknown, and they did not fish. The Sun Dance was a famous ceremony.

Plateau Tribes. Indians living in the interior of British Columbia. They make great use of salmon, deer, roots, and berries as food ; their winter houses are half underground ; highly developed basketry, but no pottery ; clothing usually of deerskin, with skin caps for men, basket caps for women. The dog is used as a pack animal, but canoes are of little importance.

Poles. Inhabitants of Poland, speaking a language of the western sub-group of Slavonic languages. It is a matter of dispute what the original Slav type was. The matter is complicated by the fact that by the fifteenth century Poland was occupied by a people as round headed as that of Russia. In the present day there is in Poland a predominance of round heads with a strong element of people with heads of medium length in the north and north-west, where is found also the darker type ; difference of stature goes in general with difference in social status, the peasant being short. In the Pinsk marshes is found a type with straight, light yellow, or flaxen hair with blue eyes, square cut face, and nose frequently turned up. This has been regarded as a distinct race by some authorities.

Polynesian. Mixed stock speaking Austronesian tongues, often with an underlying Melanesian stratum. It has been supposed that the Proto-Polynesian stock was Indonesian mixed with Proto-Malayan, and, drifting into the western Pacific, it imposed on the Oceanic negroes now known as Melanesians their language and some elements of culture. Later migrations colonised the east Pacific, possibly from Samoa. The typical Polynesian is tall, with a head usually long or medium, black straight or wavy hair, and light brown complexion. They are capable seamen, but the huge canoes of former times are no longer in use. They are on the whole indolent save where, as in the case of the Maori, the climate has favoured a more energetic type. They are dependent in most cases on agriculture. An analysis of their culture shows that more than one stream of migration has gone to make up the population of these scattered islets.

Portuguese. Inhabitants of Portugal who speak, together with the Galego of north-west Spain, a tongue belonging to the Romance sub-group of European languages. In general the population of Portugal is composed of the same elements as that of Spain, but the average skull is considerably longer, as there seem to be no pockets of round heads ; the type is, however, by no means uniform, as a negroid skull is found in mountainous areas.

Prakrit. Non-Sanskritic language of the Indo-Aryan group, including Bengali, Hindi, and Hindustani, Punjabi, Gujarati, Marathi, Oriya, Sindhi, etc.

Pre-Dravidian. Name given to certain jungle tribes of India, the Sakai of Malaysia, the main element in the Australian aborigines, the Toala of Celebes, etc. The hair is wavy or curly and usually black, the skin colour dark brown, the skull very long (Vedda) or rather broad (Toala). As a rule these tribes have not advanced to the point of becoming cultivators of the ground.

Pschaws. Georgian people, taller and slenderer than the Grusinian and darkish in complexion, but often with grey or blue eyes. The face is rather sharp, but they are a dignified people, though lively in gesticulation.

Punan. Mild, unwarlike jungle tribe of Borneo, not unlike the Ukit.

Punjabi. Indo-Aryan tongue, spoken by the Sikhs and others.

Pygmies. Negrillo of central Africa and the negrito of the Malay Peninsula, New Guinea, etc. It seems certain that these people are of mixed origin, for there is great variation in the physical characters of negritos. The negrito element among the Mafulu of New Guinea is dark sooty brown in complexion, while the Tapiro are at times yellow ; the hair of the former is usually brown or black, but sometimes so light that it would not be termed dark in Europe. The negrillo group is imperfectly known and scattered among Central African Bantu-speaking tribes ; they are of very primitive culture, and depend wholly on hunting, but obtain other products by exchange from surrounding tribes, whose languages they usually speak. They are of very short stature, from 4 ft. 3 in. upwards, and differ from the negro in having a reddish-yellow skin and somewhat hairy body. Their noses are flat, but the skull is mainly of non-negroid type, being distinctly short, though in some groups long heads are in a majority, and it seems probable that there are in reality two pygmy types. It is probable that they are pre-negro, but practically nothing is known of a real pygmy language. They do not appear to be related to the Bushman, and differ from him especially in the strong projection of the lower part of the face.

Quiche. Tribe of the centre of Guatemala. They are rather below middle size, of yellow brown to copper in colour, with round full faces of mild expression. The eyes are black and small, with the outer angle turned upwards ; the head is described as slightly conical. They are essentially agricultural.

Quichua. Indian tribe of Bolivia. They were ruled at the time of the discovery of America by the Inca, whose dominion spread over a wide area in Ecuador, Peru, Chile, etc. They are a short thick-set people, with heads of a rather striking shape, due to the custom of deforming them, which is still practised as it was in the days of the Inca. They are sometimes called Charca and are readily distinguished according to some authorities from the Aymara, as their features are less rugged and their character is gentle and more submissive. In Potosí they still dress as they did in the days of the Spanish conquest. They build huts of a distinctive character, grouped by fours, with a wall surrounding each group. They are of a rich olive brown, neither coppery nor yellow, heavily built, with broad shoulders and have large lungs, owing to the altitude at which they live. The head is long, compressed at the side with a bulging but somewhat retreating forehead. The face is large, round rather than oval, the nose long and aquiline and the chin short. Their faces are serious and rather sad ; they are sociable, obedient, industrious and discreet, not to say secretive, of a hospitable nature and good to their children.

Quitu. Older of the two principal tribes of Ecuador, perhaps of Quichua origin.

Rajput. Tribe or caste of north India which claims to represent the Kshatriya of classical tradition. The pure-blooded Rajput delights in endless genealogies and ranks mankind according to descent ; he has an exaggerated idea of the importance of ceremonial purity and a passion for field sports. Although they are supposed to be of one blood, the group seems to include many whose only title is the possession of land. But an infinity of social distinctions limits the choice of a wife ; a man may not give his daughter in marriage to a man of a sept that stands lower than his own, and endeavours to marry her above her own position, but a man of a higher sept may take a wife from a lower one ; the result of this is a superfluity of women in the higher septs which enormously increases the expense of finding a husband and encourages infanticide. In religion they are Hindus and employ Brahmans for religious and ceremonial purposes.

Romansch. Dialect of the Upper Inn and Upper Rhine, spoken in the Engadine.

Romance Languages. Tongues derived from Latin, including Languedoil (north French), Languedoc-Catalan (south French and eastern Spanish), Spanish, Portuguese-Galego, Italian, Romansch-Ladino and Rumanian.

Ronga. Tribe of south-east Africa, sometimes called Tonga.

Ruanda or **Waruanda.** One of the four privileged classes of the Batussi, not to be confused with the Warundi.

Rumanian. Inhabitants of Rumania, who speak a language of the Romance sub-group of Italo-Celtic tongues and claim descent from the Roman colonists of Dacia. If that account of their origin is the true one they have been subject to great vicissitudes, for the Goths and Mongolo-Turki peoples no less than the Slavs swept clean the area now occupied by Rumanian-speaking peoples, who must have been driven southwards and then at the break-up of the Eastern Empire forced northwards again to their former seat. The language has a somewhat composite character. Moreover, they seem to have been at the outset nomadic in their tendencies—a strange life for the descendants of Roman colonists. At present, therefore, their early history is shrouded in mystery. There is little information as to the physical characteristics of this people either for early or later times ; they seem to be of the Alpine type in Moldavia, but this feature diminishes in the mountainous area of Transylvania and in Wallachia.

Rumanian. Language of the Rumanians and of the Armani (Aramani, i.e., Romans) of Macedonia, who are nicknamed Tsintsars and Kutz-Vlachs. It is fundamentally Neo-Latin, but embodies Albanian and Slav elements.

Russians. The great mass of the population of Russia, with the exception of the Finno-Ugrian peoples. The Russian language belongs to the Slavonic group of Aryan speech. Russians fall into three main groups, all of which are of the Alpine type : Great Russians in the north, east, and centre ; Little Russians, also called Ukrainians or Ruthenians, in the south ; and White Russians in the west. The name Ruthenian is chiefly applied to the Slav of Galicia and the Bukovina, of whom the names Gorales, Huzules, etc., are also used. It seems likely that in the north of Russia, at any rate, the Lapp preceded the Finn and the Finn came before the Slav, whose expansion can be dated to the period between the sixth and twelfth centuries.

The people of Russia were, a thousand years ago, in the main dolichocephalic or long headed ; in a few centuries there was a complete transformation and round heads were everywhere in a large majority ; yet no one can say how this revolutionary change came about. It is even a matter of dispute whether the original Slavic type was long or round headed. For two hundred years the Tartar held the land in subjection ; and the Tartar is of Mongoloid type, round headed ; perhaps he may have had something to do with the change ; but, unfortunately for this guess, the Mongoloid type hardly appears at all in the north and central Slavs. The Tartar theory may, however, hold good for the Ukraine, for in Kiev the round-headed type, some time after the sixth century, changed from the Alpine type to the Mongoloid type plus another constant element.

At the present day in Russia the people are mostly round headed ; but in the Volga-Don area the head is of a middle type ; this seems to point to Finnic influence, by intermarriage with Cheremiss, Mordvin, etc. A second similar area is that of the White Russians and most of Poland. Light eyes, especially towards the Baltic, are more numerous than dark ; dark hair, on the other hand, is more frequent and darkness increases towards the south.

Ruthenes or **Ruthenians.** Slav people identical with the Ukrainians or Little Russians.

Sailau. Ruling class of the Lushai, whose name was at first used as that of the whole people.

Sakai or **Senoi.** Jungle people of the Malay Peninsula, assigned to the Pre-Dravidian stock. They stand about 5 ft. and have wavy hair, black with a reddish tinge, a broadish face and head, and a low, broad nose. They are largely nomadic and practise only a very primitive kind of agriculture, with the digging stick as their usual implement. As a refuge from wild beasts they sometimes build their huts in trees, but they also make square huts on the ground. As clothing they had formerly a garment of bark cloth, and, like the Semang, they make fringed girdles of a black thread-like fungus. They use the blow-gun, but have no canoes. Much of their food consists of jungle products. They appear to have only family property.

Sakalava. Tribe of western Madagascar. The name is taken from a small tribe of conquerors that lived on the River Sakalava. The Sakalava of to-day are made up of a number of different tribes and are regarded as falling into only two sub-tribes. They are dark-skinned, with long, frizzly hair, live on the plains in a relatively warm climate, and are more dependent on manioc than on rice.

Salish. Tribe of Plateau Indians in British Columbia. They are often known as Flatheads because, unlike surrounding peoples, they left their heads flat on top. War, slavery and the potlatch (a ceremonial distribution of gifts) were regular institutions among them.

Samaritans. Predominantly long-headed people of Samaria. They are tall of stature and show a large proportion of " Semitic " noses. In the hinterland of Palestine is found a strongly round-headed type, from which it is clear that they are of mixed origin.

Samoyed. Neo-Siberian tribe of the Arctic regions on both sides of the Urals. They and the Lapps, who are akin to them, are the only true nomads to be found in Europe. They are a sociable and laughter-loving people, of short stature and Mongoloid appearance. A Ugrian people, their name is a compound of suoma, a word of doubtful meaning, which enters into the name of the Finns (Suomalaiset). Their centre of origin was on the head waters of the Yenisei, whence they drifted northwards to the Arctic Ocean, and then westwards into Russia. They are a pastoral people with herds of domesticated reindeer on whose milk and flesh they live.

Santali. Dialect of Kherwali, one of the Munda languages which form part of the Austric family and are remotely allied to Mon-Khmer, Polynesian, etc., and still more remotely to the Indo-Chinese languages.

Sara. Important tribe near the Shari in the French Congo territory. They have receding foreheads, long, rather pointed noses and small eyes. They are a timid people who were much raided by Baghirmi, but are good and industrious farmers, men and women working together in the fields. They are called Kurdi by the Baghirmi.

Sarcee or **Sarsi.** American-Indian tribe of the Athapascan stock whose name is said to be derived from Siksika " sa arsi," not good. They were associated with this tribe at a remote period and their culture has been modified accordingly.

Sarts. Mixed people of Turkistan. In them are combined Iranian and Turkic elements, namely, the Tajiks and the Uzbegs ; in physical type they resemble the former. They are successful cultivators of the earth, but their main occupation is commerce. They are Sunnite Mahomedans, and keep their women more strictly secluded than any other Turkic tribe. Their educational standard is not very high, and their idea of the world is that it is a plain surrounded by mountains. The name Sart is sometimes applied to the settled Kirghiz. The Sarts of Kulja are known as Taranchi.

Sasak. Aboriginal inhabitants of Lombok, Sunda Islands, which they call Sasak. They are Mahomedans, and quite distinct from the Hindu Balinese who conquered them early in the nineteenth century.

Scots or **Scotch.** In a general sense, the inhabitants of Scotland, almost Scandinavian in the far north, the Gaelic-speaking but probably pre-Celtic Highlander in the centre, and the Lowland Scot, probably Teutonic in the main. The prehistoric Picts of Galloway were overrun by a people known as Scots, who arrived from Ireland in historic times and established the Gaelic realm of Argyll. Other Picts, possibly different from those of Galloway, as they were red-haired, inhabited Buchan and the country to the south. A portion of the British kingdom of Strathclyde and of the Angle realm of Bernicia passed into the power of Scotland in the time of William Rufus ; but it is by no means clear how the mass of the population was made up at that time. The English language spread gradually into Strathclyde and northward as far as Buchan.

Scythian. Supposed element in the population of India. It has been suggested that they were " Turanians," Iranians, Slavs, Germans, Mongols, etc. ; the name seems to indicate a political unit of very mixed origin.

Scytho-Dravidian. Group of western India, including the Maratha Brahmans, Kunbi, and Coorgs. They are of medium stature, fair complexion, and broad head. It has been objected that the name of the group is ill-chosen, as there is insufficient evidence of Scythian immigration ; moreover, the name Scythian does not bear a strictly defined meaning.

Sea Dyak or **Iban.** Proto-Malay people, originally resident in Sarawak, whence they have spread inland. As the Malays proper must have reached Borneo some five centuries ago, it seems that the Iban migration is earlier than this. They are short and have broader heads than other tribes, and their darker complexion contrasts with the cinnamon shade of the inland tribes, with whom they share their typical long black, slightly wavy hair. They prefer low land, and grow swamp rice, but also cultivate maize, sugarcane, etc. They are essentially agricultural, but as a former coast people devoted to raiding ; they are warlike and addicted to head-hunting, and the Malay pirates gained their assistance by assigning to them as their share of the booty the heads of the slain.

Selung. Sea gypsies of Mergui, on the south coast of Burma, also called Mawken. Their language is supposed to be an archaic type of Indonesian. They spend their whole life upon the sea, living in dug-outs from 18 ft. to 30 ft. long, with a freeboard of 2 ft. or 3 ft. only. They live largely on fish, but exchange some of their produce for rice. During the heavy rains they go ashore and camp in temporary huts, but seldom stay more than a week in one spot.

Semang. Negrito people of the Malay Peninsula, also known as Pangan, Udai, Mandi, etc. The hair is short, black, and woolly, and the skin colour dark chocolate brown approximating to a glossy black, at times with a reddish tinge. They seem to stand about 5 ft. high. The nose is short and flattened, remarkable for its great breadth, which is indeed greater than the length in some cases. The lips are thick and the cheek-bones are broad. They are a nomadic people, living by collecting wild fruits and by hunting ; very often they remain no more than three days in a place, but a few have taken to agriculture. They have no canoes, but drift down stream on rafts in case of need. Their faculties are developed mainly in the direction of the search for food and escape from their enemies ; if they are hard pressed they will, it is said, stretch rattan ropes from branch to branch and pass over them when the distance is too great for a leap.

Semi-Bantu. Section of Sudanic languages which come near to Bantu in respect of syntax, but differ from it in the roots with which its vocabulary is connected. It uses either prefixes or suffixes, where Bantu uses prefixes alone. It includes the following groups : Coast and Senegal, Volta, Togoland, and Nigerian, and the Adamaua group of pre-Semi-Bantu also belongs to it. The Semi-Bantu languages stretch in a broad band, generally speaking, between the West Sudanic and the Central zones.

Semite. Term that is to-day almost synonymous with Arab, but is commonly applied to the Jews, who are, however, a mixed people. The typical Semite has a long head and a narrow, straight nose, with jet-black hair and regular features. From their original home in south-west Asia they have wandered both eastwards and westwards, especially into north Africa, where they found a kindred people, the Hamite.

Seneca. North American tribe whose name means " place of the stone," an anglicised atom from the Dutch of the Mohegan form of the Iroquois name, Oneida. The Iroquois tribes were second to none in statesmanship and military organization ; cruel in war they burnt alive the women and infant prisoners ; they were, however, normally kind and affectionate, full of sympathy for kinsmen in distress ; their wars were primarily to secure their independence, and the Iroquois league was formed to prevent shedding of kindred blood and to promote peace. They were sedentary and agricultural, but built strong wooden castles of logs for defence.

Senufo. Important group of tribes, also known as Siena, south-west of the Volta group in the hinterland of Ivory Coast.

Serbs. South Slavonic people which crossed the Danube from the Carpathian lands some twelve hundred years ago. Included were also some Sorb (Wend) tribes from the Elbe, and on the Lower Danube were the Severenses or seven nations, also Slavs, so that the whole of the area from the Danube to the Mediterranean—some parts of Albania and districts near Constantinople excepted — became Slavonic. The Serbs are allied to the Croats.

Seri. American Indian tribe of the Californian coast, whose own name for themselves is Kun-kaak, or Kmike. They are of splendid physique, the men standing about 6 ft. on an average, and the women 5 ft. 9 in. In colour they are bronze-black, and the hair jet-black

and long, growing tawny towards the tips. They are habitual rovers of incredible fleetness, outstripping a horseman, even when they are laden with looted meat, and are accustomed to chase birds on the wing. They have practically no tools, preferring teeth and nails. They are even more hostile to other Indians than to white men.

Shan. Southern Mongol people of Burma, China, etc. They speak a Siamese-Chinese language of the Tai group ; Tai is, in fact, the Shan name for themselves, and means " noble," or " free." They first appear in history in Yunnan, south-west China, and two thousand years ago they began to enter Burma in small numbers ; some five hundred years later they peopled the Shan States, to be forced westwards in the thirteenth century by the Mongols. They are generally of finer physique than either the Chinese or the Siamese, and lighter in colour than the latter. The head is finer than that of the Chinese, with horizontal, dark eyes and straight nose, with an expression recalling rather a Caucasian than a Mongolic people. They have everywhere kept their language comparatively unchanged ; it contains less than 2,000 monosyllabic words, but each such word is modified by musical tones in such a way that the vocabulary is multiplied by five. They have four different kinds of writing, due to remote Hindu influence by Brahman and Buddhist missionaries, and this, too, has contributed to preserve their language from change. It is possible that there is a considerable Shan element both in the Chinese people and in the language. They are usually fairer than the Siamese and Burmese, and rather taller ; the nose is small, rather than flat. In character they are mild and good-humoured, very abstemious as regards both alcohol and tobacco. Like the Burmese, they tattoo, and probably borrowed the custom from their neighbours. They are generous and hospitable, and if a house door is open, visitors may enter without being considered rude. They are often great gamblers, and will play for houses and children, or even the girl they are to marry ; but it does not follow that she has to marry the other man if she is lost to her original owner.

Shawia. Berber tribe of the Aures highlands. These " Pastors " form numerous sub-tribes, all of which are said to claim Roman descent, and some still call themselves Rumaniya. A few Latin words like kerrush (quercus) still survive in their language. They belong to the Berber sub-group known as Djerba, characterised by short stature and roundish head.

Shawnee. Algonquian tribe that seems to have wandered far but was probably resident near the Ohio in the sixteenth century.

Shilh. Berber people of Morocco, who include the Rifi or Riff.

Shilluk. Tall, very long-headed negroid people. They live on the west bank of the Nile from Kaka, in the north, to Lake No in the south, and also on the east bank and the Sobat. They have, as a rule, coarse features and broad noses, but in the families of chiefs it is possible to find men with shapely features and thin lips, who may represent a conquering Hamitic stock. The Hamitic element in the Shilluk is at a maximum compared with the other Nilotes. Their territory is entirely grass land, and they are a cattle people who often do not grow enough dura to provide for their dense population. Their kings, who were regarded as divine, were killed as soon as they began to show signs of old age or ill health. They are allied to the Acholi or Gang and to the Lango of Uganda ; it seems likely that their cradle land lay to the south of their present habitat. They call themselves Chol, which seems to mean " black." The average height of the men is 5 ft. 10 in., and they have a curious habit of standing on one leg with the sole of the other foot on the knee ; they are lean, rather narrow-shouldered, and excellent runners. The nose is usually flat ; they remove the lower teeth. They are a proud people, who feel dislike and even contempt for foreigners, but they are also frank and openminded, brave in war, by no means idle, with plenty of intelligence.

Shilluk Group. Number of Nilotic tribes speaking languages allied to Shilluk, such as Anywak, Jur, Beri, Gang, or Acholi, Nyifwa, Lango, Alur, and Chopi.

Shoshone. Tribe of American Plateau Indians. Originally hunters, who did not cultivate the soil, they are allied to · the Comanche. Some of this tribe hunted the buffalo, but others depended on fish, roots, and seeds. They formerly occupied Wyoming.

Shuwa. Pastoral people of Arab origin settled to the south-west of Lake Chad. The name is probably from an Abyssinian word sha or shoa, meaning pastoral. They are known to have been in Wadai five hundred years ago, and four sections reached Bornu a hundred years later, but these intermarried with the natives and are now merged with them. The present Shuwa arrived not much more than a hundred years ago. They are slight in figure, of fair complexion and warlike disposition, but intermingled with them are many of more negroid appearance, probably the descendants of slaves, who are born free.

Siak. Malayan tribe of Sumatra.

Siamese. Tai people of Indo-China, who received their culture from India through the Khmers of Cambodia. They are a good deal mixed with neighbouring peoples, but have a distinct type of their own, with narrow foreheads but broad faces and thick lips ; the hair is black and coarse, but not thick. They are reputed to be gentle and charitable, of a happy, timid, thoughtless, and rather childish disposition ; they are uneducated, judged by Western standards, and their daily life is full of irrational rites and beliefs grafted upon the Buddhism in which they profess to believe. They have a great horror of shouting and quarrelling.

Siamese-Chinese Languages. Stock of Tibeto-Burman.

Siberian Tartars. Mass of Turanian-Turkic peoples of different origins. Most of them call themselves Tuba, as do the northern Uriankhai, but the term is a vague one. The Russians give the name Chern or Black Forest Tartars to the people who call themselves Iish Kysi, who are also termed Altaians. They are sedentary in any neighbourhood where they can practise agriculture ; their religion is Shamanism.

Siberian Turks. Two groups of Turanian peoples, the Yakut in the east and a conglomerate known as Siberian Tartars north of the Sayan mountains.

Sihanaka. Tribe of the west of Madagascar. They were conquered by the Hova in the last century, when idols were introduced by the invaders. Living in country which is largely marsh, they are fishers and cattlekeepers, and reputed to be lazy ; some of them in the rains, when the water rose inside the house, would build a raft inside which rose with them as the flood increased.

Sikh. Indian Plains caste, with a religion allied to Hinduism, which has its centre at Amritsar. They are usually Jats, an agricultural folk of fine physique, resolute, obedient, and self-respecting. The Sikhs provide some of the finest native soldiers in India, the profession of arms being hereditary with them, and they are lovers of games and athletics.

Sindhi. Language of the Punjab, allied to Lahnda. It belongs to the north-west branch of the Indo-Aryan languages.

Sinhalese. Natives of Ceylon other than Veddas. They began to come from the mainland in the sixth century B.C.

Siwash. Indian tribe of Vancouver I.

Slavonic Languages. One of the chief groups of Aryan tongues. It comprises three sections ; eastern, including Great Russian, Little Russian (Ukrainian or Ruthenian), and White Russian ; western, with Polabian, Wend, Czech (Bohemian), and Polish ; southern, with Serb, Slovene, and Bulgarian.

Slovaks. Western Slav people. They formerly formed part of the Austrian Empire, but are now an element of Czechoslovakia.

Slovenes. Yugo-Slav people of Carniola, north of the Croats. The name is perhaps derived from slovo, speech, meaning the people who understand each other.

Sobo. Group of Edo tribes formerly subject to Benin. They live in the creek system of the Niger delta, but usually away from the immediate neighbourhood of the water, which is occupied by Shekri or Jekri, a tribe allied to the Yoruba.

Somali. Name given to an Hamitic tribe of the eastern horn of Africa, said to be derived from the words : so mal, fetch milk. They themselves distinguish two peoples in their land, the Asha or true Somali, with two great divisions, both claiming descent from certain noble Arab families, and the Hawiya, who are reckoned as pagans, but this distinction is religious, not racial. Some of the groups are said to be Semitic in type, though it is not clear what is meant ; the type is very variable owing to Arab and negro blood. The hair is ringlety and not so thick as that of the Abyssinian and Galla ; it is at times quite straight ; the forehead is rounded and prominent, the nose straight as a rule, the head fairly long. Intellectually and morally, they stand lower than the Galla, owing to the greater influence of Arabs and Abyssinians.

Sorb. Alternative term for Wend (q.v.).

South - western Tribes. Group of American Indian tribes characterised by dependence on agriculture, the use of masonry, the loom, pottery, etc. They domesticated the turkey, use a grinding-stone instead of a mortar, and men, not women, cultivate the ground and weave cloth. Their pottery is decorated in colour.

Soyot. Turko-Tartar people of the Sayan-Altai border country, probably no more than a sub-tribe of the Uriankhai.

Spaniards. Inhabitants of Spain, who, as a rule, speak Spanish but use Galego, a form of Portuguese in Galicia, and Catalan, allied to Provençal or southern French, in Valencia and Catalonia, while the non-Aryan Basque is spoken in the western Pyrenees. We know but little of the earlier population of the peninsula. In the Neolithic period the skull was everywhere predominantly long. In the Early Bronze Age the population of Granada was very mixed in type. It is probable that a long skulled type had reached southern Spain from Africa. In the early metal ages there came by sea to Huelva and other mines people of an Alpine type, lured by the mineral wealth ; others came in from France at the end of the fourth century B.C., when Celtic speech seems to have been introduced ; their union with the earlier Iberians originated the so-called Celtiberians. Before this time the Carthaginians had settlements, Cadiz being one of the chief, but it does not follow that they affected the racial type.

It is uncertain how far the Roman domination brought about any change, but when, in the fifth century, the flood of invasion from central Europe swept over the peninsula, the Nordic types included under the names Vandals, Goths, Suevi, etc., cannot have left the type unchanged, at any rate in the north and north-west. In the south the eighth century saw the coming of Berbers and related peoples from north Africa, who added other long-headed types. At the present day the Spaniard is, in the main, long headed, except in Huelva on the Gulf of Cadiz and in Cantabria from Corunna eastwards. The Spaniard is prevailingly and strongly brunette in complexion but fairer types occur also, especially in the north-west.

Stoney Indians. Same as Assiniboin.

Subuano or **Subano.** Indonesian tribe of the Philippines (Mindanao).

Sudanic Languages. Tongues of negro Africa other than Bantu. They fall into two main divisions : Semi-Bantu, which classifies its nouns by means of prefixes or suffixes according to no rule clearly defined at the present time, but which must have been originally connected with the meaning, one class being assigned to human beings, another to liquids, etc. The second group, held together by community in word roots, has no well-defined type of syntax ; its members are often far nearer Hamitic forms of speech than to other Sudanic languages ; in its most extreme form the Sudanic language is isolating and almost monosyllabic.

Suk. People of eastern Africa allied to the Nandi and Turkana, but of composite origin with at least two different elements. The name is said to be a Masai word ; they call themselves Pokwut. They fall into two sections, pastoral and agricultural, the former in the Kerio valley, the latter on the Elgeyo escarpment. They have been much influenced by the Nandi. Unlike the Turkana they do not seem to be very fertile, and children are often sickly. They are unintelligent, but honest, vain and exceptionally generous. The men wear no clothing at all and the women very little. In addition to the Hamitic element, they seem to have, like the Akamba, a short-headed type, which must represent the remnants of a pygmy stock.

Sundanese. Inhabitants of West Java, of much the same type as the Javanese proper, but slightly shorter.

Swahili. Bantu-speaking people of east Africa in the neighbourhood of Zanzibar, whose tongue has become the commercial language of much of east Africa. The word properly means " coast people," and connotes descendants of Arab settlers by native women of various tribes, chiefly Bantu. There is no uniform Swahili type ; complexion and features vary indefinitely, even in one and the same family, one having woolly hair, another silky, straight hair. The Bantu groundwork of the language seems to have been Pokomo, but Arabic has largely contributed to its vocabulary ; both sounds and grammar are much simplified compared with ordinary Bantu tongues.

Swanetians. One of the smaller Georgian peoples, whose history goes back thousands of years. There seem to be two types, one blond and light-eyed with a longish face, the other darker with a broader face. They differ from other Georgians in build and character, being less good-looking and appearing rude and sly.

Swazi or **Waswazi.** Section of the south-eastern Bantu-speaking peoples, closely related to the Zulu. They are often termed Kafirs, or Kaffirs, from an Arabic word meaning " unbeliever."

Swedes. Inhabitant of Sweden, speaking a tongue of the Scandinavian section of Teutonic languages. From early Swedish graves we get both long and short skulls, the latter of Alpine type, but the long skulls are some of the Mediterranean type, some, on the other hand, lower in proportion to the height, these being the two elements from which the Nordic race has apparently been compounded. In Neolithic times we find relatively large numbers of Alpine and Mediterranean folk who are, curiously enough, less conspicuous in the Danish islands ; it has been suggested that they came to Sweden by sea from the British Isles. With the coming of the Iron Age these types are displaced by a long-headed people with broad noses, which were at an earlier period prominent in Mecklenburg. As in the case of Denmark we have little information on which to go for the next two thousand years. In our own day the area north and west of Stockholm is one of the great reservoirs of the fair, long-headed, tall Nordic type ; in southern Sweden long headed and round headed folk are about equal in numbers, and a darker complexion and hair usually goes with the shorter head. In the north of Sweden there is a strong Lapp element which no doubt goes back to very early times.

Swiss. Inhabitants of Switzerland, who speak as their mother tongue either German, French, Italian, or Romansch. They are short in stature and usually dark, but there are blonds in the open country between the Jura and the Alps. They are probably everywhere round headed, as they were from the twelfth to the seventeenth centuries.

Tagal. Tall, strong tribe of Borneo of predominantly Indonesian type.

Tagalog. Philippine tribe of the neighbourhood of Manilla.

Tagbanua. Tribe of the Calamianes Islands in the Philippines. They are short, with abnormally long legs, black, frizzly or wavy hair, and short, flat nose. They are a docile and timid people, but excellent workers.

Tai or **Thai.** Large group of tribes of south China and Indo-China, who speak Siamese-Chinese languages. If we except a few unclassed remnants of tribes, and perhaps the Lolo, they seem to be the earliest traceable inhabitants, and began to move down from the Yang-Tse valley four thousand years ago. The largest tribe is known as Tho; they are of moderate height, with about 5 ft. 7 in. as a maximum; their hair is long and coarse, black to rusty in colour, the skin yellow, more or less deeply bronzed according to exposure. Their eyes are somewhat Mongoloid, but in the projection of the jaw and lower part of the face they present a feature incompatible with pure Mongoloid descent and suggestive of negrito influence. In youth the Tho is quick to learn, but in later life he becomes sluggish and lazy, a result due in part to the use of a special kind of tobacco. They live in pile huts.

Tajik. Tall, round-headed people of the east of Persia. They are mainly sedentary and agricultural, and divided into hill and lowland groups; the former are called Persivan (" of Persian speech ") or Dikhan ("peasants"), while the latter are a Persianised people who originally spoke Galchic. The Tajik are probably the Dadicae of Herodotus; it is possible that they are mentioned by Ptolemy. They are tall and brown or white, with ruddy cheeks, black or chestnut hair, fair eyes, long, well-shaped nose, and oval face.

Talamanca. Tribe of Costa Rica, speaking a Chibcha tongue.

Tamil. Language of the Dravidian family, spoken in the south of India and the north of Ceylon. Some Tamil-speaking castes appear to be long headed like the Palli, Parayan, and Vellalla, while in others the round-headed type almost predominates. It is the oldest, richest, and most highly-organized of Dravidian tongues; the literary form is called Shen (perfect) and the colloquial Kodum (rude). Both Tamil and Dravidian are corruptions of Dranida.

Tanala. Madagascar tribe of negroid type who live in dense forests, whence their name. Arab origin has been attributed to their chiefs, but they do not differ in physical type from their subjects.

Tangut. Peoples of south-west China of several different types, some Mongoloid, some non-Mongoloid.

Tapiro. Negrito people of New Guinea, living at the source of the Mimika river. They are lighter in skin colour than the surrounding Papuans, some being almost yellow, and thus differ widely from other negrito peoples. In stature they range from 5 ft. to 5 ft. 4 in., and the skull is very variable in shape, a sign, as a rule, of mixed blood; the nose, too, is very variable in its proportions. Their pile dwellings are copied from those of their neighbours.

Tarahumare. Tribe of Mexico who live in the mountainous area of the north. They are of a light chocolate brown colour, and powerfully built.

Taranchi or **Ili - Tartars.** Turkic people who migrated to Russian Turkistan when Kulja passed under Chinese rule. They are close kinsmen of the Sarts, but give their women more freedom and are chiefly agricultural in pursuits. They are among the least Turkic of all Iranian Turks, and are now strongly Persianised. They are probably descendants of the old Uigur of eastern Turkistan and overlaid an originally Caucasian population with a culture of Perso-Hellenic type.

Tarasco. Tribe of Mechoacan, Mexico, who call themselves Purepecha. They are a brave and upright people in their natural state, but easily offended and unmanageable in their fury. With strangers they are reserved and suspicious, but kind and hospitable to each other. The women delight in ornaments of all sorts; they carry a child slung between their shoulders. The Tarascans make lacquer at Uruapan by cutting out the wood in the required shape and laying the lacquer on with the finger.

Tartar or **Tatar.** Term originally applied to a central Asiatic people now extinct. It has been transferred to the Western people known as Turks, and is applied collectively to the Turkish tribes intermixed with Mongols who have perhaps a strain of the old Tartar blood in them.

Tartar Languages. Group of Turko-Tartar, including Kirghiz, Bashkir, Nogai, Kuman, Karachai, Kara-Kalpak, Meshcherak, and Siberian.

Tasmanian. Extinct natives of Tasmania, related in certain directions to the negrito but not of pygmy stature. Half-breed descendants of the Tasmanians survived the last pure bred native, who died in 1877, and preserve to our own day in their descendants at times an almost pure type of this isolated and primitive people.

Tavastians. Western Finns, who call themselves Hemelaiset (lake people). They have rather broad, heavy frames, small and oblique blue or grey eyes, towy hair, and white complexions, without the ruddiness of the Germanic peoples. In temperament they are honest, but somewhat vindictive and sluggish.

Teda. Negroid people of the Sahara, north of Lake Chad in the Tibesti Range. They are practically the same as the Tibu and are related to the Kanuri, speaking a language of the same group. They are the Garamantes of classical authors. Mixed with the large negro factor is a short-headed element which may represent an earlier pygmy element. Though they are very black, they are non-negroid in respect of hair character, which is wavy or curly ; their noses also are aquiline, and the lower part of the face does not project.

Tehuana. Zapotec tribe of Mexico, dwelling in Tehuantepec.

Tehuelche. Natives of Patagonia, renowned for their great stature, ranging from 5 ft. 8 in. to 6 ft. They subsist mainly on the flesh of the guanaco, but also eat horse flesh ; they cultivate no vegetables. Their dwellings are leather or brushwood, and their characteristic weapons are lasso and bolas. The dead were buried in a sitting posture.

Telugu. Language of south India. It is spoken in the main by Dravidians under middle height with very dark skins and wavy or curly hair. Some appear to be long headed, but there are others with a strong, short-headed element.

Temne. Negro people of Sierra Leone. They speak a language of the coast group which has many words resembling those of Bantu languages geographically remote. They are a fairly tall people, lighter in colour than the Mendi and allied to the Landuman and Baga. They were one of the first tribes with whom Europeans came in contact and a detailed account of their religion has come down to us from the beginning of the sixteenth century. They live mainly on rice ; their villages are exceedingly small, five hundred being a population of unusual size.

Tenggerese. Mountain people of east Java who differ from the Javanese in having long heads and broad noses, with wavy or even curly hair. They are perhaps descended, at least in part, from south Indian immigrants of the seventh and later centuries.

Thonga. Bantu-speaking people of Portuguese East Africa, on the Limpopo river ; they are also called Gwamba.

Tibetan. A feature of the social organization of Tibet is polyandry ; a woman is taken to wife by the eldest brother of a family, but he shares her with a number of other men who may be but are not necessarily brothers. This seems to be a result of the struggle for existence, making it necessary to limit the increase of population ; it must, however, be remembered that the poor pastoral nomads of the northern steppes practise monogamy. The essential element in Tibetan religion is subjection to the priest or lama ; lamaism has been imposed upon a form of Buddhism, and Buddhism itself is only a veneer upon more primitive pagan creeds. Tibetan worship is a mechanical system with the prayer-wheel as its main characteristic, the object of which is to baffle the evil spirits that belay man on every side. The Tibetan had been described as knavish, treacherous and subservient or tyrannous according to circumstances ; but other observers display him as kind-hearted, affectionate and law-abiding. See Bhotia, Balti, Horsok, etc.

Tibeto-Burman Languages. Sub-family with three branches — Tibeto - Himalayan, Assamese-Burmese and Assamese-Chinese.

Tibeto-Himalayan Languages. Stock of Tibeto-Burman. It includes Tibetan, Himalayan, north Assam, Bodo, Naga, Kuki-Chin, Meithei, and Kachin, through which a double line of relationship between Tibetan and Burmese can be traced.

Tiki-Tike. Pygmy tribe of the Upper Ituri, between the Congo and the Nile, the name being probably identical with that of the Atyo, usually known as Ba-Teke. They are nomadic and obtain from the Mangbettu or Momvu fruits, weapons and bark cloth in exchange for game. They live in the shelter of rocks.

Tinguian or **Itneg.** Pagan mountain tribe of north Luzon. They are head-hunters and cultivate rice.

Tlinkit. (1) American-Indian tribe of the west coast of Alaska. They are a tall, round-headed people of a pale-brown or yellowish colour, and, like the Haida, famous for the totem posts erected in front of their huts. (2) Group of tribes, also known as Kalosh or Kolush, on the islands and coast of north-west America. They depend largely on the sea for subsistence, but are also hunters. They are skilled in canoe building, in the working of stone, and in the making of blankets, etc.

Toba. Tribe of Bolivia, between the Pilcomayo and the Bermejo. They are tall and a little darker than the Chiriguano. They depend entirely on hunting and fishing.

Toda. Small tribe of the Nilgiri Hills. They speak a Dravidian language, and are of rather more than medium height, well proportioned and stalwart, with a narrow nose, regular features and an extraordinary amount of hair. The women are somewhat lighter in colour than the men, and are said to be of a warm copper hue. In the case of the great majority the skull is long or very long. The most important element in their life is the buffalo, which is tended by men ; women are excluded from the dairy and even from the paths assigned for certain purposes such as the approach to the dairy for the man who goes to feed or milk the buffaloes. A woman has more than one husband, and they are often brothers ; the one who performs a certain ceremony with a bow and arrow about two months before the child is born becomes the father for all legal and social purposes, of that child. In olden days it was the custom of the Toda tribe to kill female children, and it is to this that their marriage custom is no doubt due.

Tomak. Bulgarians who have embraced Mahomedanism.

Tomutes. Turkish people in the neighbourhood of Khiva.

Tonga. Bantu-speaking people who live to the west of Lake Nyasa. There is another people of the same name near Inhambane on the coast.

Tongkingese. Peoples of Tong-king fall into two groups, Annamese in the south, and a congeries of tribes in the north, including Tai, Man, Meo, Lolo, and the ancient La-tchi.

Topa. Name given to the Portuguese of Pondicherri.

Toraja. Wild tribe of Celebes. They are of varying complexion, some yellow-brown, others brown-black, and the hair is sometimes wavy ; as the nose is broad and flat it is possible that there is a Mongoloid element superimposed on an aboriginal strain. They are described as simple, truthful, honourable and hospitable, patient in suffering, and grateful for kindness.

Tsu. Formosan tribe of the south central mountains. They were formerly head-hunters and still preserve the skulls in the communal house known as Khuva, which serves as a sleeping house for the young men. They are of a non-Mongoloid type, with long, straight hair and straight eyes ; the lips are thin ; they knock out some of their teeth.

Tuareg. Saharan people of Berber stock, known to the Hausa under the name of Asbenawa from the Asben oasis, which they invaded in 1515. Their own name for themselves seems to be Imoshak, and their language is Tamoshak. There is a considerable negroid element in the lower ranks of the population, but the Tuareg, who dominate the western and central Sahara, differ from the northern Berbers chiefly in respect of stature, which is extremely tall ; in this they resemble the Nilotes and some of the Chad tribes.

Tugeri or **Kaia-Kaia.** New Guinea people noted for their head-hunting propensities.

Tukano. Tribe of the Amazon area, who are deadly foes of the Desana. A typical Tukano is round headed, with eyes usually horizontal and a good-humoured expression ; the nose is broad with wide nostrils and the hair wavy and sometimes almost curly. Fishing is the chief occupation of the men, and the women cultivate the fields. They have an assembly house in which men and women take their meals, but at different times. In many places animal food is hardly used, but they are great frog eaters. Their language belongs to the Betoya group.

Tungus. Neo-Siberian tribes allied to the Goldi, Manchu, Orochon, etc. They seem variable in type, being shorter and more predominantly round headed in the south ; the hair is straight ; the eyes are often without the Mongoloid fold. They are probably the same as the Tung-hu, of Chinese annals. The type has been described as essentially Mongolic, with some admixture of Turki characters, but little reliable information is available. They are daring hunters, cheerful even in the deepest misery, of gentle manners, proud and upright, obliging without being servile. They are for the most part Shamanists.

Turanian. Term used linguistically as an equivalent to Ural-Altaic ; but also applied in an ethnological sense. The name Turan is Asiatic ; Tura is mentioned in the Avesta, the sacred book of the Old Persians, where Tuirya is used of the countries now called Turanian, the people of which were enemies of Airya. Turan is one of the names applied to what is also called Tartary, though it is not known to the Asiatic Turks. Some philologists have spoken of a South Turanian group of languages, meaning thereby Tamulic, Malayic, etc.

Turcomans. Turki peoples of Bokhara, Khiva, and Persia together with a small number in the Caucasus. In religion they are all Mahomedans ; linguistically they belong to the Jagatai division. A large number are still nomadic horse breeders ; they are forbidden to marry outside their own people, and, as there are more men than women, there are large numbers of bachelors, in some places they number twenty-seven per cent. of the population. In culture as well as physique they may be reckoned with the Iranians.

Turkana. People of east Africa on the west of Lake Rudolf. They are reputed to be the tallest of the human race. In one district they are said to average 7 ft. in height ; the allied Suk do not exceed 6 ft. 6 in. They depend for sustenance upon fish to some extent, but are mainly a pastoral people. They seem to come near the Nilotic negroes in physical type ; their language is classified as Niloto-Hamitic. They have a smaller non-negro element than the Masai or even the Baganda.

Turki. People of central Asia. Their stature is above the average, and they have a very round head, elongated oval face, eyes non-Mongoloid but with an external fold in the eyelid ; thick lips, somewhat prominent nose. They are essentially nomadic ; the Turk who takes to agriculture has been deeply modified by inter-mixture.

Turki or **Turko-Tartar Languages.** Of these there are three groups : Jagatai, Tatar, Turkish ; the two former are more closely related to each other than to the third.

Turkic Tribes. Group including Yakut, Kirghiz, Uzbeg, Turcoman, etc. They are of medium stature and yellowish-white complexion, with short high head, elongated oval face, straight and rather prominent nose. Probably they are allied to the Ugrian peoples.

Turkish Language. Speech of the western Turks, consisting of the following groups : Derbent, Azerbaijan, Crimean, Anatolian, and Rumelian, the last two constituting Osmanli.

Turko-Iranian. Group including Baluchi, Brahui, and Afghan, a broad-headed people with abundant hair and fair complexion.

Turko-Tartars (Russia). The following tribes come under this head : Kazan Tartars, Tartars of the Crimea and Taurida, Kirghiz, Nogai of Stavropol near the Caspian, Bashkir of Orenburg. It is possible that the Bashkir were originally a Finnic tribe who were later Tartarised.

Turks. This people may probably be identified with the Tu-kiu, whose name is mentioned in the sixth century ; but three thousand years ago the Hiung-nu mentioned by the Chinese as their neighbours on the north-west must have been their ancestors. When the Great Wall of China was built more than two thousand years ago these Hiung-nu had to turn westwards. Soon after this most of the Turkic tribes of central Asia were united under the Hun-nu Empire ; it is probable that Hiung-nu and Hun-nu are the same. They were probably the Huns of some centuries later who were on the Volga in A.D. 275, and ravaged Europe in the fifth century ; another section advanced on India in the following century. The Hun-nu, who moved westwards, had as their chief element the On-Uigur. The Togus Uigur remained in Asia, and were subdued for a time by the Tu-kiu, afterwards assuming the leadership themselves.

Tuscarora (hemp gatherers). Important confederation of Iroquois tribes of North Carolina. The Tuscarora, in New York, are still governed by chiefs, who are, however, no longer responsible to the clan. Like other Iroquois, they traced descent in the female line and had also women chiefs. In olden times they stuck prisoners full of small splinters and set them gradually on fire. They were passionately fond of gaming.

Tush. Georgian people, mainly on the north of the Caucasus.

Twi, Agni-Twi, Tshi or Otyi. Group of tribes of the Gold and Ivory Coasts. They speak allied languages which show some signs of having been taken over by non-negroes It is probable that they came from the east.

Tynjur. Name of a people of Nubia, and also of a section of Shuwa Arabs south-west of Lake Chad, who are, however, possibly not of Arab descent at all, though they speak Arabic. Tradition says that they came from Tunis, and they say that their forefathers were once rulers of Wadai.

Ukit. Tribe of nomadic hunters in Borneo. They are a slender, pale-skinned people, grouped in small communities, who live on what they can find in the jungle, and barter from friendly settled people iron implements, etc., in return for rubber and camphor.

Uled Nail or **Ouled Nail.** Aures tribe of Berbers.

Ural-Altaic Languages. Family the existence of which is not universally accepted, including Mongol, Finno-Ugrian, Turkish, Manchu, and Samoyed.

Urdu. Form of Hindi that uses many Persian words and Persian script.

Uriankhai or **Uriangut.** Turanian Turks near the Sayan mountains. They are sometimes called Soyot, but the northern section call themselves Tuba. They seem to be a mixed people with much Mongol blood, but some authorities have classed them as Samoyed mixed with Turks. They are the most successful reindeer breeders known ; some depend on hunting and fishing. They breed horse, yak, and reindeer for draught purposes in a way that suggests a combination of Mongol, Turk, and Tungus.

Uzbegs. Turkic people of Samarkand, Bokhara, etc., allied to the Kipchak of Ferghana. The Uzbegs are the ruling class of their land, occupying the same position as the Osmanli farther west. They seem to take their name from Uzbeg Khan of the Golden Horde of the fourteenth century, and are a mixture of Turkic, Iranian, and Mongol with some predominance of the former element. They are exchanging nomad life for a sedentary one, and their customary law is being replaced by written law. Though they make use of clay and wood houses, their old felt tents are still to be seen, especially in summer. They seem to have much in common with the Kazaks or Kazak-Kirghiz. They are probably peoples who escaped from Turkic rule in the thirteenth century to go back to a nomadic life ; this drove them to constant war with the Mongols, who possessed

the steppes before them. There is a proverb, " Where the hoof of the Kataghan's horse arrives, there the dead find no grave cloth and the living no home." The Kataghan are a tribe of Uzbegs.

Vai. Tribe of the Mandingo group on the coast of Liberia and Sierra Leone. They possess their own system of writing, invented in the nineteenth century by a native. They are of the usual Mandingo type, but have a rather larger, short-headed element ; in stature they are rather shorter ; it is probable that they are mixed with tribes who previously occupied the coast area.

Vedda. Primitive tribe of Ceylon, classed with the pre-Dravidians. They stand about 5 ft. high, and have wavy, sometimes almost curly hair ; the skin colour varies enormously from yellowish brown to deep brown-black. The head is long and narrow, and the nose only moderately broad, depressed at the root, and never really flattened. All trace of their original language has been lost. They adopted, in the first place, a primitive form of Sinhalese which, by paraphrases, was transformed into a kind of secret language, and now the archaic words are being replaced by modern Sinhalese. They are divided into wild Vedda, living in caves, village Vedda, and coast Vedda, the two latter having undergone considerable foreign influence. The coast Vedda speak of themselves as Verda. In temperament they are grave but happy, honest and hospitable ; their only weapon is the bow and arrow, and the iron-tipped arrow is their only tool. The language is Sinhali, borrowed from their Tamil neighbours, but it is strongly modified ; they have only one word to express number, and do their counting with sticks. Hunting, honey, and the cult of the dead are the three most important things for the Vedda, but the wilder sections put their dead in caves and simply abandon them.

Visayan, or **Bisayan.** Philippine tribe called Pintados by the Spaniards, from their custom of body-painting. They are probably of the prevailing round-headed type.

Vlach, Wallach or **Wallachian.** People of Wallachia. The word has been derived, without much evidence, from the same root as Wales, Walloon, etc., as applied to Celtic peoples by Slavs and Germans. There are also Vlachs in the population of Czechoslovakia.

Voguls. Ostyak name of a people who call themselves Manzi. They are a Ugrian people, closely related to the Ostyaks, of small stature and longish heads, with long, blond hair and grey or blue eyes, flat noses and round faces. They are a hunting people, melancholy, timid, and indolent in disposition.

Volta Languages. Group of languages of the Semi-Bantu zone, spoken in the northern territories of the Gold Coast and French Niger territory, including Mole or Mossi, Grunshi, Dagomba, etc. They fall into a number of sub-groups, and differ from the major type of Semi-Bantu tongues in using a suffix instead of a prefix in the noun classes.

Vonum. Group of uncivilized tribes in the mountains of central Formosa, where they often live at great elevations. They were formerly head-hunters ; women carry burdens on their backs with a band over the head. Mongoloid traits are not conspicuous, and it is possible that they are primitive Indonesians.

Votyak. Eastern Finnic tribe which left the Urals about fifteen hundred years ago for their present home between the rivers Kama and Viatka. They are chiefly heathen, and worship Inmar, god of heaven, to whom they still offer, it is said, human sacrifices. They are of short stature, with blue or grey eyes, a straight nose, and blond or red hair. They are not robust.

Wa or **Vu.** People of Burma, some of whom are head-hunters, speaking a Mon-Khmer language. They are short and broad, with bullet heads, square faces, and heavy jaws. The nose is on the whole prominent and very broad in the nostrils ; the eyes are round and well opened, and the complexion is dark in the case of the wild Wa. They surround their villages with a rampart 6 ft. or 8 ft. high, with a ditch outside and a tunnel entrance. In character they are brave, energetic, and industrious, especially in cultivating the soil ; beans are the staple food.

Wabanaki. North-eastern section of Algonquins, including Passamaquoddy, Penobscot, Abenaki, Micmac, and Delaware or Lenape.

Wadigo. One of the so-called Nyika tribes of the hinterland of Mombasa, related to the Wagiriama, etc., and speaking a Bantu language. They are a shortish people, some men not exceeding 5 ft. 2 in., and it is clear from the variation in head shape that there is a distinct pygmy element among them.

Waganda or **Baganda.** Inhabitants of Uganda. The form Waganda is of Swahili origin. They vary greatly in features and build, some being thoroughly negro in type, others with faces that have been compared to those of Romans ; some stand over 6 ft., others barely 5 ft. ; the upper classes have silkier hair, but it is black and woolly in all ; the complexion varies from copper colour to jet-black. They have been called the most advanced of Bantu-speaking tribes, are careful of their appearance and of their homes, courteous in manner, and hospitable to guests. Unlike other Bantu-speaking peoples of eastern equatorial Africa, they neither knock out teeth nor mutilate their person in any way ; they do not even pierce their ear-lobes. They are divided into a great number of clans, which appear to differ from each other in build or in features, so that it is possible to distinguish at sight members of certain clans, though they have been inter-marrying for ages. The Uganda house differs in type from that of any other people of negro Africa, with its lofty roof and vast framework of palm midribs or sticks extending right down to the ground, with openings cut away to serve the purpose of doors in front and back.

Wageia. Bantu-speaking people of the south-east shore of Victoria Nyanza. They are remarkable for their finely developed figures, and appear to have a Nilotic element in their blood. The men go completely naked, but wear large straw hats with great tufts of feathers in them.

Wahabi or **Wahhabi.** Mahomedan community of Nejd, named after Abd el Wahhab. They have representatives in Mesopotamia, India, and Africa.

Wahehe. Mixed people of Uhehe, East Africa. They are composed of the remnants of tribes conquered in the nineteenth century by the Wahehe proper. Tall, with regular features of non-negroid noses and strikingly light complexion, they are brave and terrible warriors, and take their name from their war-cry, " Hehe, he, he ! " Burton saw a tribe whom he calls Wahehe, but they do not appear to be the same.

Wahima. Negroid people of Uganda. Usually tall and long headed, with small hands and feet, they have sometimes almost European features and differ from the average negro tribe in the length of the neck, but their hair is hardly distinguishable from that of the pure negro. They are the aristocracy of Unyoro, the cattle herdsmen of Uganda. The form Bahima is more correct than Wahima, Wa being the Swahili form of the plural prefix.

Walloon. (1) Number of dialects of north French, spoken in the southern part of Belgium ; (2) the name of the people who speak Walloon. There is a Walloon element in the population of Kent. The people of the Ardennes plateau are just under medium stature, dark complexioned, and on the whole short headed ; the same type, but with a more pronounced shortness of head, is found in some of the coastal provinces of Holland ; even in Friesland the same type is found. The earliest remains, of the Old Stone Age, show a long-headed people, who were replaced in the Neolithic period by a short-headed people which does not seem to have been identical with the Alpine stock of central Europe. Belgium thus formed a notable contrast to both France and the British Isles, and it seems likely that this stock explains the head shape of the people of the Ardennes.

Wambutte. Pygmy tribe of the Ituri Forest, Belgian Congo.

Wandorobo or **Andorobo.** Nomadic people of the Masai country, who have attached themselves to the latter as helots. They speak a dialect of Nandi, but their physical type shows them to be of very mixed descent. They tend towards short stature, and in facial type some seem to resemble Bushmen, whose kinsmen they may be. Their name is Masai, and means " poor." They call themselves Asa.

Wankonde or **Nkonde.** Bantu-speaking people at the north end of Lake Nyasa, whose name seems to mean " people of the plain." They include the Awakukwe, Awawiwa, and other tribes. They assert themselves to be nearly related to the Wamaraba near the coast. They are very dark and usually tall, but there seems to be a tendency to bowleggedness among them. They lead an easy life, and both men and women are said to be comparatively good-looking. They are cheerful, harmless, and intelligent, but superficial and unreliable. They cannot be called lazy, though they are indisposed to exert themselves for gain.

Wanyamwezi. Tribe of Uganda made famous by the travels of Livingstone. The name means " children of the moon."

Wapisiana. Savannah-dwelling tribe of Guiana, speaking an Arawak language. They are taller than most tribes, with refined features. They are great traders, and in their canoes they use a peculiar form of paddle with perfectly circular blades.

Wapokomo. Bantu-speaking tribe of the Tana valley in the north-east of British East Africa. They are cultivators of the soil and also hunters and fishermen ; they seem to be related to the Wasanye, for both tribes bury their dead in the forest instead of following the usual Bantu custom. They seem to be of mixed origin, and even in the same family children vary in colour from black to " red."

Warramunga. Central Australian tribe living in the Murchison Range. Both men and women are considerably taller than in the Arunta tribe to the south. A feature of their customs is the practice of pulling out the hair on the forehead and upper lip.

Warrau or **Warraw.** Coast people of Guiana, forming an independent linguistic group ; they are short and, though thick set, their muscular development is not great. They lived in the mud and were essentially a dirty people. They practise plurality both of wives and husbands. They were the great canoe builders and formerly lived in pile dwellings and even now, after their removal to higher ground, the old custom is kept up.

Wasania or **Wasanye.** Tribe of British East Africa. Though possibly not allied to the Pokomo, they have some customs in common with them. They live on the middle Tana and support themselves by hunting and fishing.

Watuta. Name of the Angoni (q.v.).

Waunga. Negro tribe of the swamps south-east of Lake Bangweolo, Central Africa.

Wayao or **Yao.** Finely built Bantu-speaking tribe of Rhodesia and British Central Africa. Their original home was in the Unango mountains. They are a tall people, with heads that seem round compared with the Anyanja.

Waziba or **Baziba.** Bantu-speaking people of the west shore of Victoria Nyanza. They are industrious, good humoured, and happy, of remarkably good physique, and simple in their requirements. They wear a curious costume of fibre threads and are also remarkable for their method of burying their chiefs, who are placed standing in a deep narrow pit, with the head peeping above ground. The head is watched by sentries for two months and then pushed down into the earth. Unlike most negro peoples, they care little for music and dancing. In olden days no man was allowed to wear a beard.

Wazir or **Waziri.** Mahomedan people on the frontier of Afghanistan. Living in wild and inaccessible country and giving continual trouble, they have plenty of cattle, but cultivate only strips of soil along their mountain streams. They are related to the Afridi, and belong to the Pathan group who talk Pushtu.

Welsh. Inhabitants of Wales descended from Welsh-speaking ancestors. In the moorlands we find dark, long-headed people, of average stature and ruddy complexion. In parts of south Wales is found a powerfully-built stock, with broad heads and faces, square jaws, and dark complexion ; another type, dark, bullet headed, and thick-set is found in the Montgomeryshire valleys. Finally, there is a fairer type found in Pembrokeshire, on the borders much taller than the other types, and a darker variety along the cleft from Bala to Towyn. In general, however, there is not so much racial difference between England and Wales as is commonly supposed. The Welsh language does not date back more than some two thousand five hundred years. *See* English.

Wends. Slav people of the Lausitz in Germany. They have been sometimes confused with the Veneti ; their name has not been explained, but it has been suggested that they inherited it from the Venedi, who were on the Vistula some time before the Christian era. They are also termed Polabs, from po, by ; Labe, Elbe.

Wepsian. Language spoken on Lake Onega, in the government of Olonets and elsewhere. They are called Chuds by the Russians, and further south Chuhars, but these are used of various Finnic peoples. Wepsian is a name taken from the Novgorod people of this language. They leave agriculture to the women and children ; some men occupy themselves with fishing, but they are by preference journeymen masons. Their life is exceedingly primitive ; the whisk is used in the place of the churn, which is unknown ; there are no spinning wheels, and the canoes are dug-outs propelled by a single oar. The word Chud applied by the Slavs to the Finns is said to mean giant as well, and we may perhaps see in them the tall people who in the Norse Eddas are called Jötuns.

Worgaia. Australian tribe of the Central Group, located to the east of the Warramunga.

Wyandot. Synonym for Huron.

Yakut. Turkic tribe of eastern Siberia. They are dependent on the reindeer, but have to supplement this means of subsistence by fishing, etc., as their pasture area is limited.

Yami. Inhabitants of a small island south-east of Formosa. Described as a mixed people with some Malayan elements, they do not stand more than 5 ft. 2 in., and are yellowish-brown in complexion. Some are of Malayan type, others show negrito traits, but the hair is not frizzled. Their boats are said to have a close resemblance to those of the Solomon Islands, and this suggests some strain akin to the people who imposed on the inhabitants of Melanesia the language of Indonesian origin spoken to-day. The head varies from very round to very long.

Yaqui. Important section of the Cahita tribe which dwelt on both banks of the Lower Yaqui, Mexico. They belonged to the Pima family and were allied to the Maya, though the two tribes were not on good terms. They seem to be an industrious people and are employed as farm labourers and sailors ; they are good pearl divers ; on the other hand, they are given to alcohol, gambling, and stealing. In 1903 they numbered about 20,000 ; their present numbers are unknown, as in 1906-7 the Mexican government planned to deal drastically with the hostile Yaqui and deported thousands of them to Yucatan and Tehuantepec, where a changed environment is likely to have affected the deportees.

Yezidi. Short-headed people of western Kurdistan. Often with straight hair, much hair on the face, a very short high head, swarthy white skin and a narrow, generally aquiline nose, they are allied to the Kurds and are noted for their devil worship and their cult of the peacock.

Yao, Wayao or **Ajawa.** People of Nyasa who originally lived nearer the coast but were driven away by tribes coming from the north. They are of better physique than their Anyanja neighbours, but vary considerably in height, some being over 6 ft. They have a great reputation as strong carriers. The women wear a ring in the upper lip, a custom borrowed from the Anyanja, who have now given it up.

Yolof, Jolof or **Wolof.** Sudanic-speaking people of western Africa between the Senegal and the Gambia. They are tall and extremely black, but very good-looking.

Yoruba. Originally the name of a single tribe of an allied group, to all of which the name is now applied ; Egba, Jebu, etc., are sub-divisions. They extend from the sea coast to the Middle Niger and differ from surrounding tribes in their tall stature and comparatively slender build. They number about 2,000,000 and are great traders. The Yoruba country is remarkable for its large towns, some of which are said to have nearly 250,000 inhabitants, and for the absence of dialects in the language. They have tribal heirlooms in the shape of bronzes that can be shown to be two thousand five hundred years old. Secret societies play a very important part in their life. They are also known as Nago or Aku.

Yuracare. South American Indian tribe to the south of the Moxos. Their name means " white " ; they are of light colour with a yellowish tinge, of tall stature with an average of 5 ft. 6 in., oval faces, and small horizontal eyes.

Zapotec. Mexican tribe which, at the time of the Spanish conquest, occupied the present state of Oaxaca on the Pacific side. They are, as a rule, markedly short headed.

Zulu or **Amazulu.** Bantu-speaking people of south-east Africa. Arriving in their present location at a comparatively recent date, coming from the north, they developed some marked peculiarities of language. The Zulu were an exceedingly warlike people of splendid physique. At the end of the eighteenth century they were a small tribe, which was united by a famous chief named Tshaka with the Abatetwa, and soon turned into a people organized for war. Tshaka drove the Basuto into their mountain home.

Zuni. Pueblo tribe of the south-west area of North America.

Zyrians. Finnic people of moderate stature, with round heads, straight noses, and blond or chestnut hair. They are of strong and graceful build and have the reputation of being skilful and unscrupulous traders.

FINE ASIATIC WOMANHOOD

As the Caribs shown in page 5326 may be regarded as perhaps the finest type surviving of the old American strain, so the Bugis of the island of Celebes now represent the Malayan stock at its best

Photo, S. P. Lewis

DISTRIBUTION OF RACES

By Professor G. Elliot Smith, F.R.S.

The ethnographic atlas to which this article serves as an introduction has been edited and revised by Professor G. Elliot Smith, F.R.S., with the assistance of Dr. Charles Hose, to enable the reader to see at a glance the disposition and boundaries of the nations and the distribution of the various branches of the human family. As many ethnographic problems still await solution and many races are mingled, the delimitation cannot be absolute ; but this atlas and Mr. Northcote W. Thomas's Dictionary of the world's races together form the handiest and most comprehensive conspectus of the peoples of all nations ever compiled.

IT is impossible to represent upon a map the exact geographical distribution of the members of the different human races with even an approximation to accuracy. For there has been racial admixture in every region of the world ; and in most regions, especially of Europe, Asia, and America, the mingling of people of different racial origins has been so widespread that, in the case of any individual, only rarely is it possible to state that he belongs wholly to a definite race.

Hence, in the maps that are submitted here, racial boundaries are shown in Africa and some of the outlying areas in Asia and America ; whereas in Europe and the greater part of Asia and America the distributions are based mainly on language, and in some cases on more or less arbitrary political subdivisions.

Racial Distribution and Language

Ireland affords an example of the latter. So far as the racial ingredients of its population are concerned, Ireland should not be differentiated from Britain. Then, again, the vast majority of its people use the English language, so that, if chief importance is assigned to the linguistic factor in plotting out the distributions, only certain very limited areas in the west where Erse is spoken should be distinguished from the English-speaking area which forms the bulk of the island.

In the map, however, neither racial nor linguistic considerations are given chief consideration, but the political subdivision into Northern Ireland and the Free State is roughly indicated. There is a certain measure of justification for this procedure, as it emphasises the essential kinship of the people of Ulster with the southern Scottish population.

The population of Europe, to which the misleading name " Caucasian " is sometimes applied, is composed mainly of three races ; and although it is improbable that any of these three originated in Europe, the distinctive names Nordic, Alpine, and Mediterranean, usually applied to them, refer to their geographical location in Europe.

Ancient Nordic Colonies

The range of each of these races, however, extends far beyond the limits of Europe. The Nordic race is characterised by fair hair and blue eyes, and is found in its purest form in Norway, but it is also the obtrusive ingredient in a large part of the population of the British Isles, Northern Europe, and certain regions of north-western Asia ; but ancient colonies of this race are found in most parts of Europe and the northern and western parts of Asia, as well as in North Africa ; and in modern times a large part of the European populations of North America, Australia, and New Zealand belongs to this race.

The Mediterranean race has occupied the coasts of the Mediterranean Sea, European, Asiatic, and African, since prehistoric times, but it also enters largely into the composition of the population of western Europe and the British Isles and is the main element in the Iberian and Italian peninsulas. But

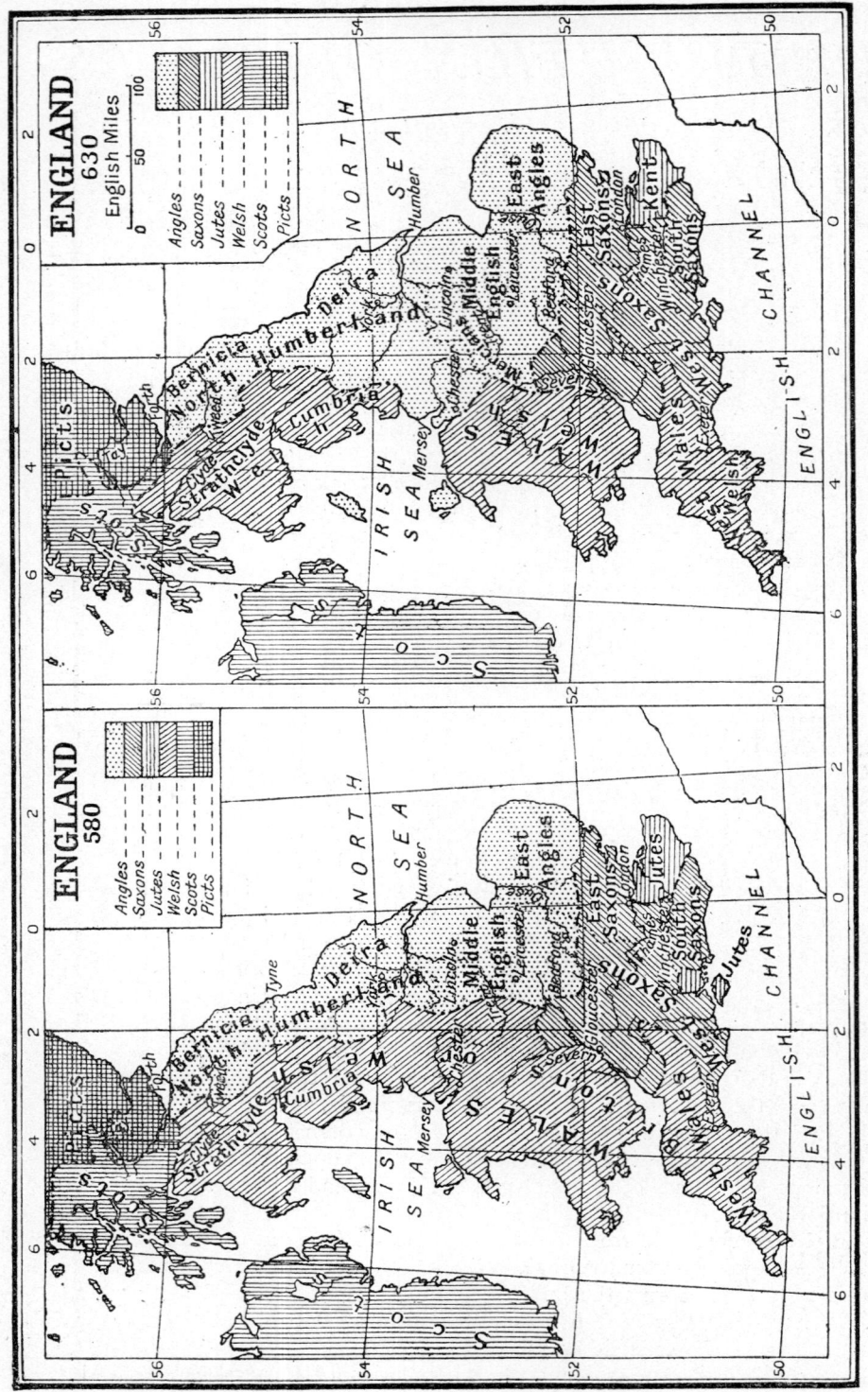

BRITISH RACIAL ORIGINS SHOWN IN HISTORICAL MAPS: THE WESTWARD ADVANCE OF THE ANGLO-SAXONS

On the left, the map of England shows the invading races, Angles, Saxons, and Jutes, with a firm footing in the east of the country, the result of 130 years of conquest. The map on the right shows England at the period when Northumbria, in consequence of Edwin's victories, was the dominant kingdom

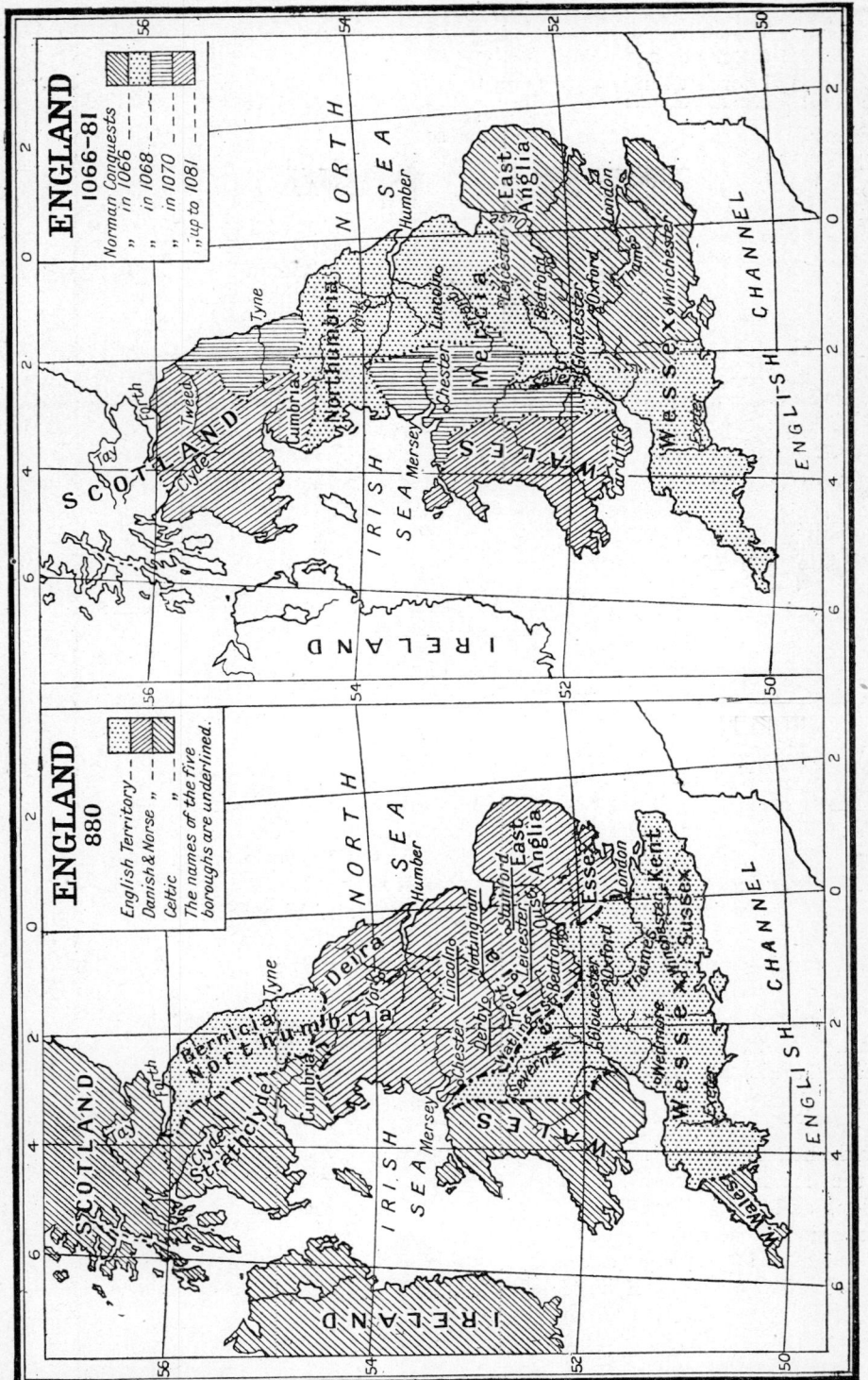

ANGLO-SAXON CESSION OF ENGLAND, TEMPORARILY TO THE DANES, THEN PERMANENTLY TO THE NORMANS

On the left is shown the division of England between the Danes and the Anglo-Saxons, as fixed by the treaty between Alfred the Great and Guthrum; the Danes securing the north-eastern portion of the land. The map on the right shows successive stages in the conquest of England by the Normans under William I.

it is also the chief ingredient in the population of northern and north-eastern Africa, of Arabia, southern Persia, and the so-called Dravidian people of India, while, with considerable admixture, it is also found in Indonesia and Polynesia.

Alpine and Mongol Races

The Alpine race is found not only in the region of the Alps, Switzerland, Savoy, northern Italy, Tyrol, etc., but also in southern Germany, Brittany, the Balkan Peninsula, Russia, Asia Minor, Syria, Turkistan, etc.; and as an element in the mixed population of most parts of Europe, Polynesia, and America (both ancient and modern). The Turkic people, which used to be included in the Mongolian race, really belongs to the Alpine race, and such Mongolian traits as individual members of this people reveal are the result of intermingling with Mongols.

The Mongol race includes the Chinese, Tibetans, Gurkhas, the Burmese, Siamese, Annamese, Malays, the Mongols, Manchus, Koreans, Japanese, and such Siberian tribes as the Tunguses, Kamchadals, Koryaks, Chukchis, and Yukaghirs; but the Yakuts, Ostyaks, Samoyedes, Finns, Lapps, Kirghiz, Uzbegs, Turcomans, Turks, Bulgars, and Magyars, in spite of frequent admixture of Mongolian blood, really belong to the Turki branch of the Alpine race. The American Indians were derived from a primitive branch of the Mongolian race with a not inconsiderable admixture of Alpine (Turkic) blood.

Colour Schemes of the Maps

In the map of Asia the regions occupied by the Tamils in southern India and Ceylon, and the Telugus, Gonds, and Santals in India, are represented as a uniform dark sepia colour called in the key Dravidian. The chief ingredient of the people who speak the Dravidian language in India (and the same tongue is spoken by the Brahuis in Baluchistan) belongs to the so-called Mediterranean race intermingled with a minority of Proto-Australians and negroes. The Proto-Australian element predominates in some of the jungle tribes of southern India, in the Veddas of Ceylon, and in some of the peoples of the Malay Archipelago; but the aboriginal population of Australia includes the vast majority of this most primitive race of the human family.

The black population of southern India, however, probably contains a definite strain of negro blood, of both the pygmy and taller varieties. For the negroid population of Melanesia, New Guinea, the Philippines (Aetas), Malaya (Semangs), and the Andaman Islands perhaps made their way from Equatorial Africa, the probable home of the race, to these eastern centres of colonisation.

Africa, Asia, and America

The distribution of the different tribes of the negro race is shown in the map of Africa. The areas occupied by the pygmies (Akkas, Bambutes, and Batwas) are shown in brown, and by the more specialised pygmy negroids (Bushmen and Hottentots) in a lighter shade of brown. The domain of the taller negroes is shown in green, the Sudanese negroes as a band (coloured light green) from West Africa to the Nile, and the Bantus farther south (from the Welle River north of the Equator to the Transvaal and Natal).

It is not known for certain when America was first colonised, but it is commonly assumed that when Europe was in the Neolithic phase of culture, possibly not more than three thousand years ago, people belonging to a Proto-Mongol strain mixed to some extent with Proto-Alpines, crossed the Bering Strait from the north-eastern extremity of Asia to reach America, and in course of time occupied the whole continent from Alaska to Cape Horn. The Eskimos represent another branch of the Mongol race, who spread throughout the greater part of the fringe of the Arctic, including America.

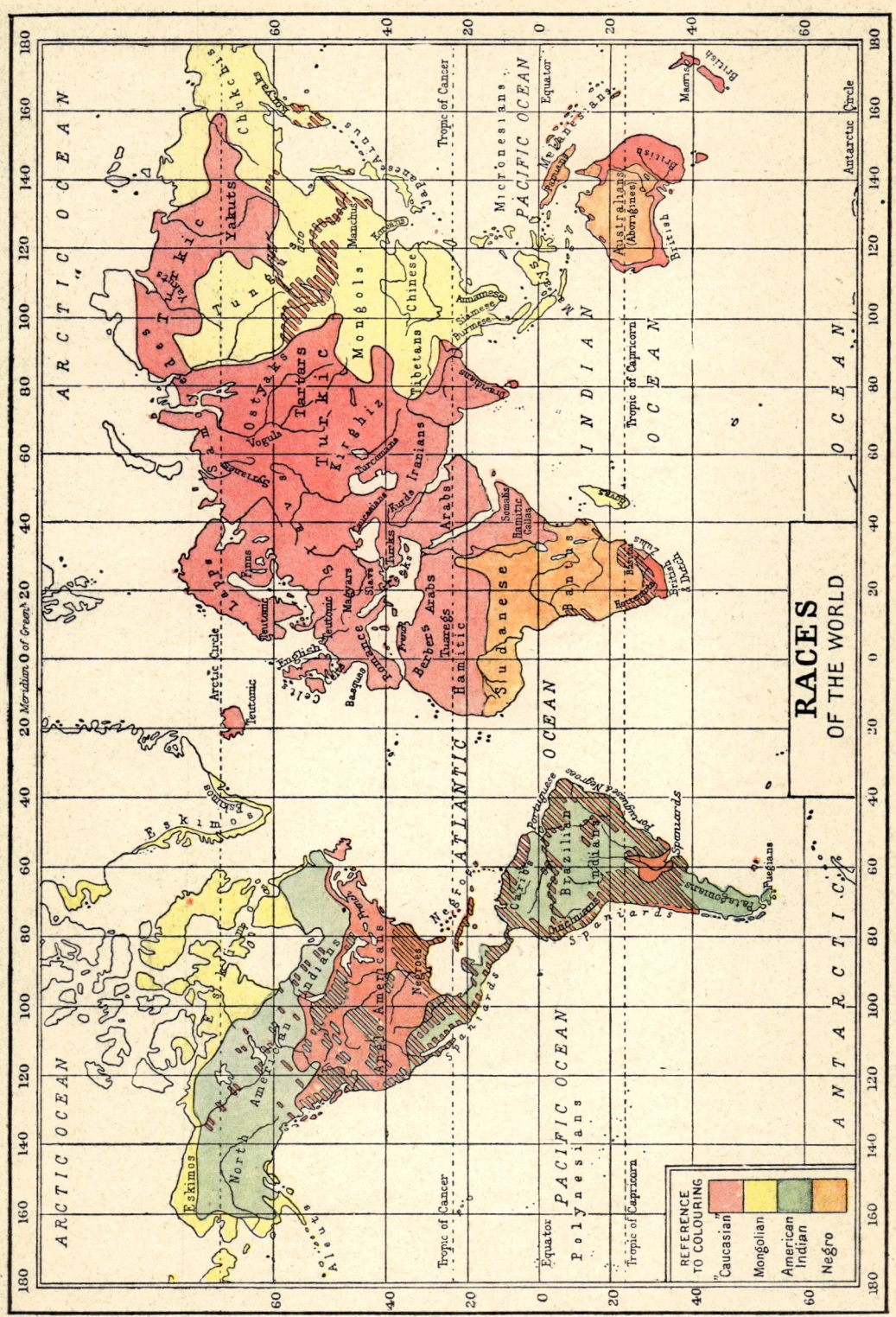

RACES
OF THE WORLD

REFERENCE
TO COLOURING

Caucasian
Mongolian
American Indian
Negro

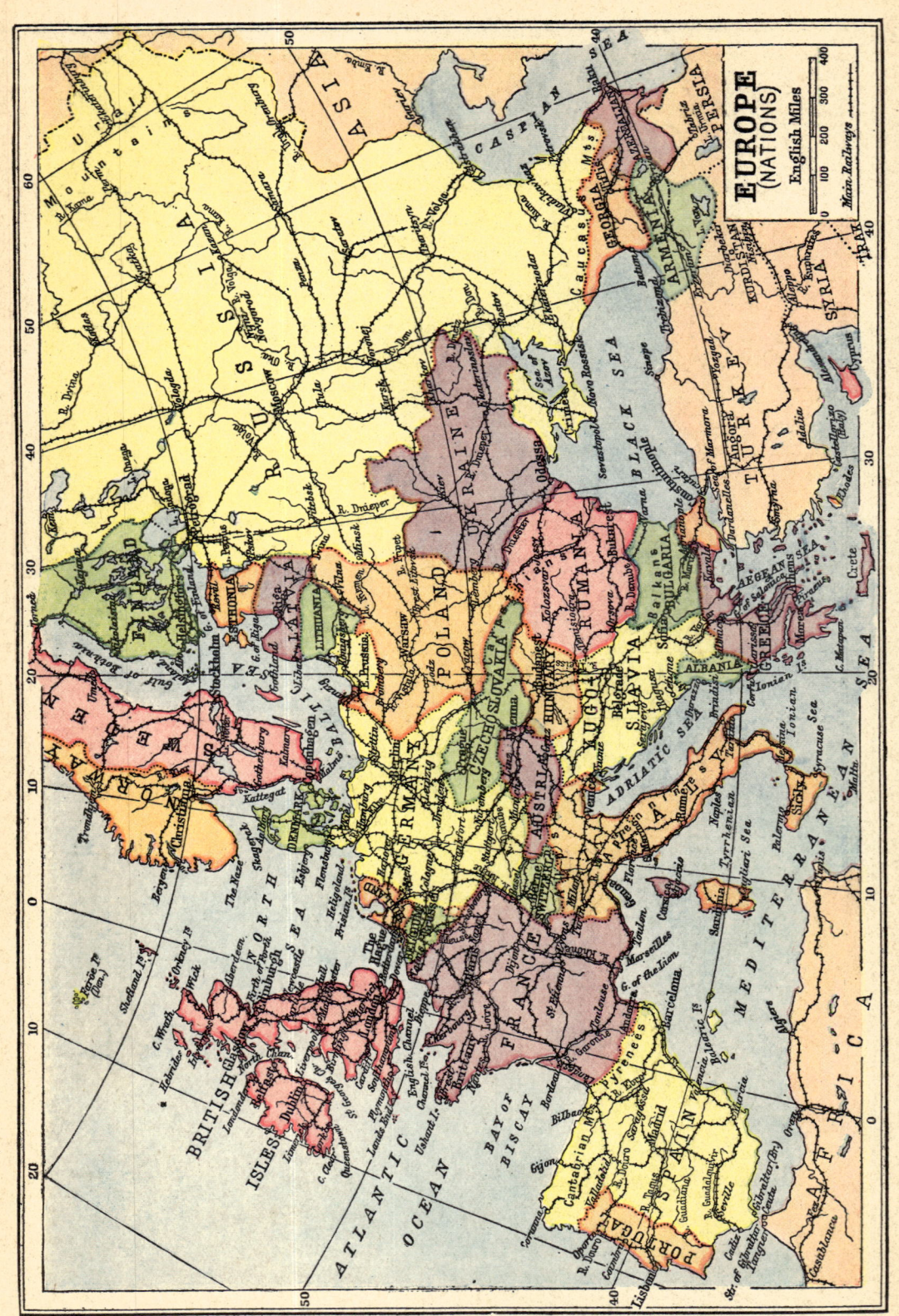

EUROPE
(NATIONS)

English Miles

Main Railways

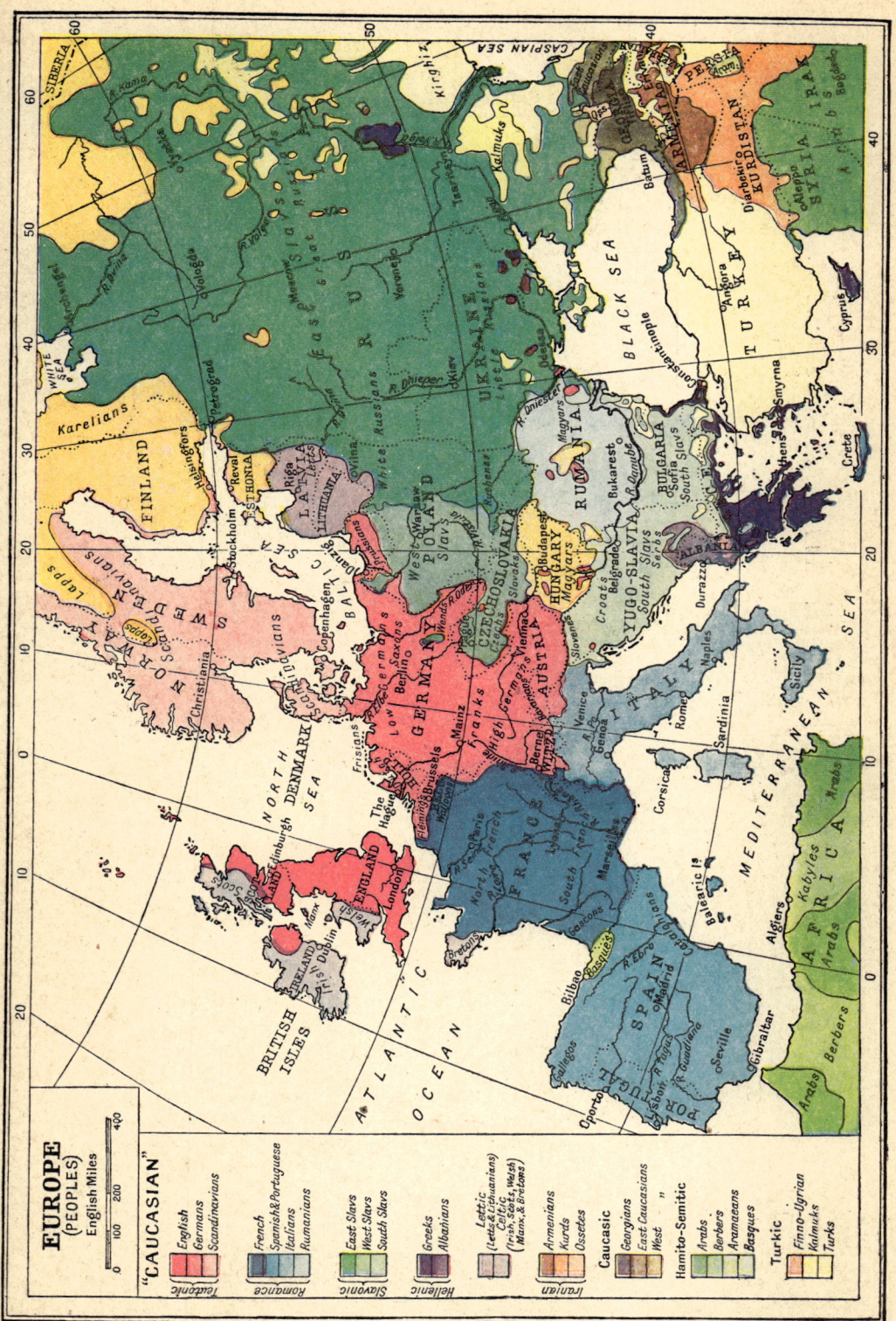

EUROPE
(PEOPLES)
English Miles
0   100 200   400

"CAUCASIAN"

English		
Germans		
Scandinavians		
Teutonic		

French	
Spanish & Portuguese	
Italians	
Rumanians	
Romance	

East Slavs	
West Slavs	
South Slavs	
Slavonic	

Greeks	
Albanians	
Hellenic	

Lettic
(Letts & Lithuanians)
Kelto-Celtic
(Irish, Scots, Welsh
Manx, & Bretons)
Iranian

Armenians	
Kurds	
Ossetes	

Caucasic
Georgians
East Caucasians
West "

Hamito-Semitic
Arabs
Berbers
Aramaeans
Basques

Turkic
Turks

Finno-Ugrian
Kalmuks

5379

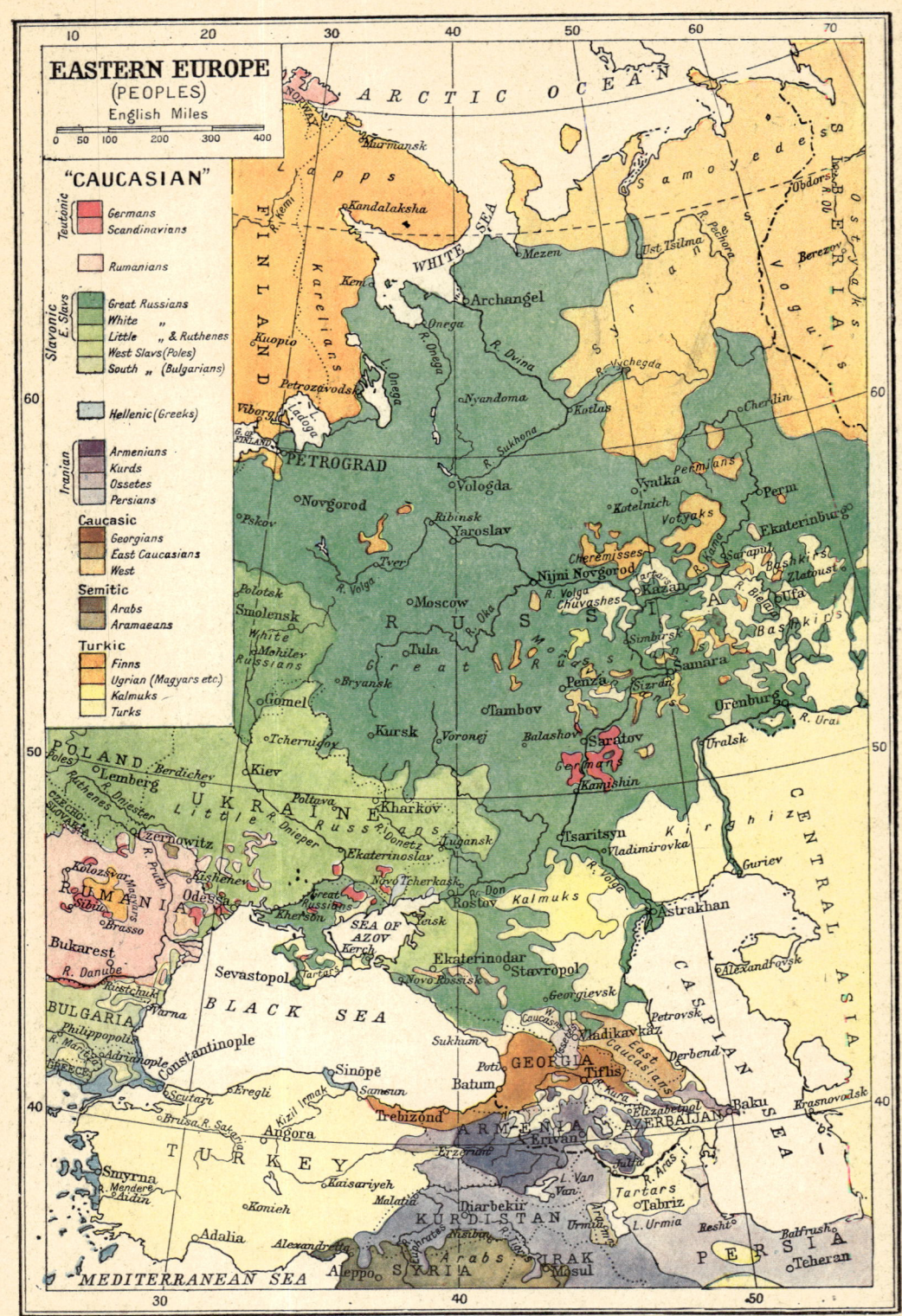

EASTERN EUROPE
(PEOPLES)
English Miles

0 50 100 200 300 400

"CAUCASIAN"

Teutonic
- Germans
- Scandinavians
- Rumanians

Slavonic E. Slavs
- Great Russians
- White ,,
- Little ,, & Ruthenes
- West Slavs (Poles)
- South ,, (Bulgarians)

- Hellenic (Greeks)

Iranian
- Armenians
- Kurds
- Ossetes
- Persians

Caucasic
- Georgians
- East Caucasians
- West

Semitic
- Arabs
- Aramaeans

Turkic
- Finns
- Ugrian (Magyars etc.)
- Kalmuks
- Turks

ARCTIC OCEAN

WHITE SEA

Murmansk
Kandalaksha
Lapps
Karelians
FINLAND
Kuopio
Petrozavodsk
Viborg
Ladoga
G. of FINLAND
PETROGRAD
Pskov
Novgorod
Polotsk
Smolensk
White Russians
Mohilev
Gomel
Tchernigov
POLAND
Berdichev
Poles
Lemberg
Ruthenes
Czernowitz
Kishenev
Kolozsvar
Sibiu
RUMANIA
Brasso
Bukarest
R. Danube
Rustchuk
BULGARIA
Philippopolis
Adrianople
Constantinople
Scutari
GREECE
Smyrna
Aidin
Adalia

Archangel
Mezen
Onega
R. Onega
Nyandoma
R. Dvina
Kotlas
R. Sukhona
Vologda
Ribinsk
Yaroslav
Tver
R. Volga
Moscow
Tula
Great Russians
Bryansk
Kursk
Voronej
Kiev
UKRAINE
Little Russians
Poltava
Kharkov
Ekaterinoslav
Donetz
Lugansk
Odessa
Kherson
Great Russians
Novo Tcherkask
SEA OF AZOV
Kerch
Sevastopol
Tartars
BLACK SEA
Sinope
Eregli
Samsun
Bursa
Angora
TURKEY
Kaisariyeh
Konieh
Alexandretta
Aleppo
SYRIA
MEDITERRANEAN SEA

Murmansk
Ust Tsilma
Pechora
Mezen
R. Vychegda
Tcherdin
Perm
Permians
Vyatka
Votyaks
Ekaterinburg
Cheremisses
Nijni Novgorod
Kazan
Chuvashes
Simbirsk
Samara
Penza
Sizran
Balashov
Saratov
Germans
Kamishin
Tsaritsyn
Vladimirovka
R. Volga
Kalmuks
Don
Rostov
Yeisk
Novo Rossisk
Ekaterinodar
Stavropol
Georgievsk
Petrovsk
Vladikavkaz
Caucasus
East Caucasians
Derbend
GEORGIA
Tiflis
Batum
Sukhum
Poti
Trebizond
ARMENIA
Erivan
Erzerum
Diarbekir
KURDISTAN
L. Van
Van
Malatia
Nisibin
IRAK
Mosul
Arabs

Berezov
Ostyaks
Voguls
SIBERIA
Samoyedes
Obdorsk
Syrianians
Vyatka
Sarapul
Bashkirts
Zlatoust
Ufa
Bashkirs
Orenburg
R. Ural
Uralsk
Kirghiz
Guriev
Astrakhan
CENTRAL ASIA
Alexandrovsk
CASPIAN SEA
Baku
Krasnovodsk
AZERBAIJAN
Elizabethpol
Djulfa
R. Aras
Tartars
Tabriz
L. Urmia
Urmia
Reshi
Balfrush
Teheran
PERSIA

60

50

40

10 20 30 40 50 60 70

30 40 50

5380

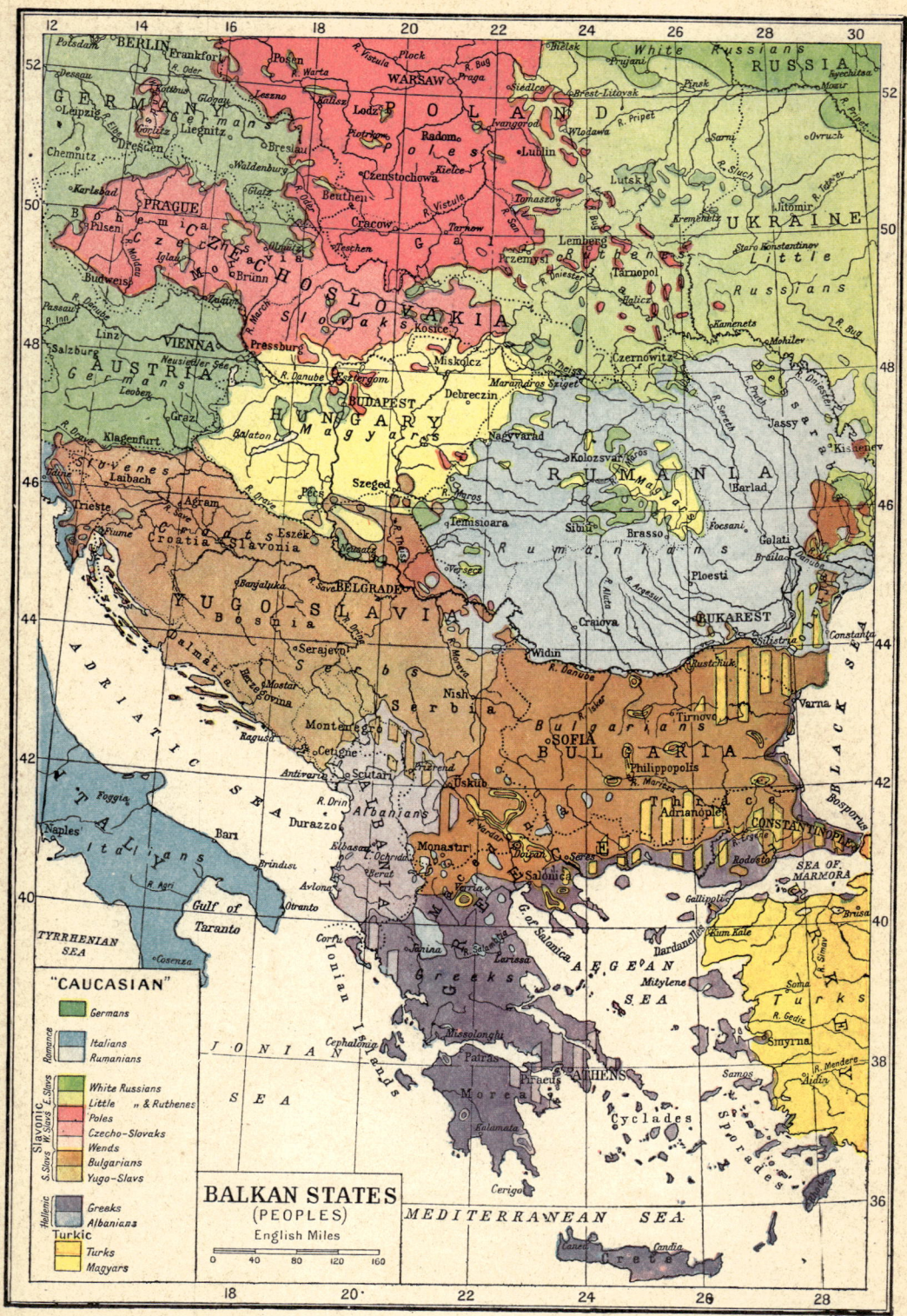

BALKAN STATES
(PEOPLES)
English Miles

"CAUCASIAN"

Germans

Italians
Rumanians

White Russians
Little ,, & Ruthenes
Poles
Czecho-Slovaks
Wends
Bulgarians
Yugo-Slavs

Greeks
Albanians

Turkic

Turks
Magyars

5381

40 20 0 20 40 60

NORTH SEA

BRITISH ISLES LONDON

Queenstown Antwerp Berlin Riga Kazan Omsk

Havre Brussels Warsaw

B. of Biscay Paris EUROPE Odessa

Berne Vienna *Black Sea* Astrakhan Aral Sea

Bordeaux Genoa Trieste Belgrade Bukarest Sevastopol *Caspian Sea*

Bilbao Oporto Rome Durazzo Varna Sinope Tiflis Baku Krasnovodsk

Madrid Naples Salonica Constantinople Batum

40 Lisbon Sardinia Smyrna Konieh Alexandretta Nisibin

Azores Gibraltar Athens Mersina Aleppo Mosul Teheran

OCEAN Str. of Gibraltar Sicily Crete Cyprus Damascus Tekrit ASIA

Madeira Is. Casablanca Oran Tunis MEDITERRANEAN SEA Beirut Jaffa Bagdad

Funchal Fez ALGERIA Tripoli Benghazi Jerusalem Port Said Basra Bushire Bander-Abbas

Mogador Morocco Tougourt LIBYA Matruh Maan Koweit Persian G.

Agadir El Golea Sollum CAIRO Medina

Canary Is. Ifni W. Draa Ghadames Jarabub EGYPT Khargeh Jeddah Mecca

Villa Cisneros RIO DE ORO *Tropic of Cancer* Ahaggar Massif Ghat *Libyan Desert* Shellal

C. Blanco Wadan Sahara or Great Desert Wady Halfa Nubian Desert Port Sudan FRENCH SOMALILD.

20 Bir Asin Tibesti Kerma Berber Suakin Aden Socotra

FRENCH WEST AFRICA Agades ANGLO- Omdurman Khartum Massawa G. of Aden Guardafui

Timbuktu Bamba L. Chad EGYPTIAN El Fasher Gondar Jibuti BRIT. SOMALILD.

SENEGAL Zinder Yao El Obeid SUDAN Addis Abbaba ITAL. SOMALILD.

GAMBIA Sokoto Kano FRENCH ABYSSINIA Obbia

PORT. GUINEA IVORY NIGERIA Calabar CAMEROONS EQUATORIAL UGANDA KENYA COL. Magadoxo

SIERRA LEONE GOLD COAST AFRICA PROT. Nairobi INDIAN

LIBERIA C. Palmas SPAN. GUINEA Libreville BELGIAN L. Victoria Kismayu OCEAN

0 Equator Annobon CONGO Kisumu Mombasa

Leopoldville Stanleyville TANGANYIKA Zanzibar Dar-es-Salaam

Boma TERR. Tabora Pemba

Loanda L. Tanganyika Aldabra Is.

St. Helena PORT. W. AFRICA Lobito B. Benguela Mossamedes Lubango NORTH RHODESIA Broken Hill Farquhar Is.

SOUTH Livingstone SOUTH RHODESIA Salisbury Quilimane MADAGASCAR Tamatave

ATLANTIC SOUTH WEST Bulawayo Beira Antananarivo

20 *Tropic of Capricorn* AFRICA BECHUANAL. PROT. Walvis Bay Swakopmund TRANSVAAL Pretoria Lourenço Marques C. St. Mary

OCEAN Angra Pequena Mafeking Johannesburg NATAL Durban

Orange R. Kimberley ORANGE FREE STATE Bloemfontein Pietermaritzburg

CAPE OF GOOD HOPE East London

CAPE TOWN C. of Good Hope Port Elizabeth

40

AFRICA
(NATIONS)
English Miles
0 200 400 600 800 1000 1200 1400
Railways

20 0 20 40 60

5382

AFRICA
(PEOPLES)
English Miles

0 100   500   1000

"CAUCASIAN"

Hamito-Semitic
- Hamitic
- Semitic

Indo-European
- Teutonic
- Romance
- Hellenic
- Slavonic
- Iranian

- Caucasic
- Turkic

NEGRO
(African)
- Sudanese
- Bantu
- Hottentot & Bushmen
- Negrito

MONGOLIAN
- Malay

AFRICA
Scale 0   300 Miles
(COMMERCIAL LANGUAGES)
- English
- French
- Spanish
- Portugese
- Dutch
- Arabic

NORTH & CENTRAL AMERICA
(PEOPLES)
English Miles

0 100 200 300 400 500 1000

Indian Reservations thus ▬

ARCTIC OCEAN

Eskimos

Arctic Circle

R. Yukon

Athapascans

Tlingit

Juneau

Haida

Kwakiutl

Nootka

Vancouver

Seattle

Salish

Columbia

Hupas

San Francisco

Hares

Gt Bear L.

Mackenzie R.

Gt Slave L.

Eskimos

Eskimos

Eskimos

Eskimos

Eskimos

HUDSON BAY

Crees

Chipewyans

Algonquins

Algonquins

Edmonton

Calgary

Regina

R. Saskatchewan

Crees

R. Church

Blackfeet

L. Winnipeg

Winnipeg

R. Albany

Ojibwas

Ojibwas

L. Superior

Ojibwas

Huron

Mohawks

St John

Micmacs

Halifax

Quebec

Montreal

Ottawa

Toronto

Ontario

Erie

Buffalo

New York

Boston

Philadelphia

R. Missouri

Assiniboins

Minneapolis

Duluth

Chicago

Shoshoni

Shoshonis

Shoshoni

Utes

Salt Lake City

Denver

Pawnees

Omaha

Kansas City

St. Louis

Ohio

Chickasaws

Hurons

Pittsburgh

Washington

Norfolk

R. Arkansas

R. Colorado

Utes

Navahos

Hopis

Zunis

Los Angeles

Santa Fé

Apaches

Apaches

Apaches

Pueblo Indians

Papagos

Opatas

Osages

Cherokees & Natchez

Muskogees

Choctaws

Chickasaws

Cherokees

Memphis

Atlanta

Muskogees

Seminoles

Charleston

Seminoles

Dallas

Comanches

Grande del Norte

Chihuahua

New Orleans

Galveston

R. Mississippi

Monterey

GULF OF MEXICO

Havana

ATLANTIC OCEAN

Bermudas

WEST INDIES

Pimas

Aztecs

Tampico

Tropic of Cancer

PACIFIC OCEAN

Guadalajara

Huichols

Otomis

Mexico

Tarascos

Mixtecs

Zapotecs

Chontals

Vera Cruz

Merida

Mayas

Lacandons

Quiches

Pipils

Guatemala

Managua

Chorotes

Sumo

Mosquitos

S. Juan del Norte

Panama

Santiago

Kingston

Port au Prince

CARIBBEAN SEA

Merida

SOUTH AMERICA

Bogota

Chibchas

Inset map (lower left)

SIBERIA

ALASKA

GREENLAND

PACIFIC OCEAN

CANADA

UNITED STATES

MEXICO

ATLANTIC OCEAN

West Indies

Cuba

Haiti

Jamaica

SOUTH AMERICA

NORTH & CENTRAL AMERICA (POLITICAL)
Scale 0   500 Miles
1 Guatemala 4 Salvador
2 Honduras   5 Panama
3 Nicaragua 6 Costa Rica
7 Brit. Honduras

Legend

AMERICAN INDIAN
- Northern
- Central
- Southern

NEGRO

EUROPEAN

Romance | Teutonic
- English
- Germans
- Scandinavians
- French
- Spanish

MONGOLIAN
- Eskimos

5384

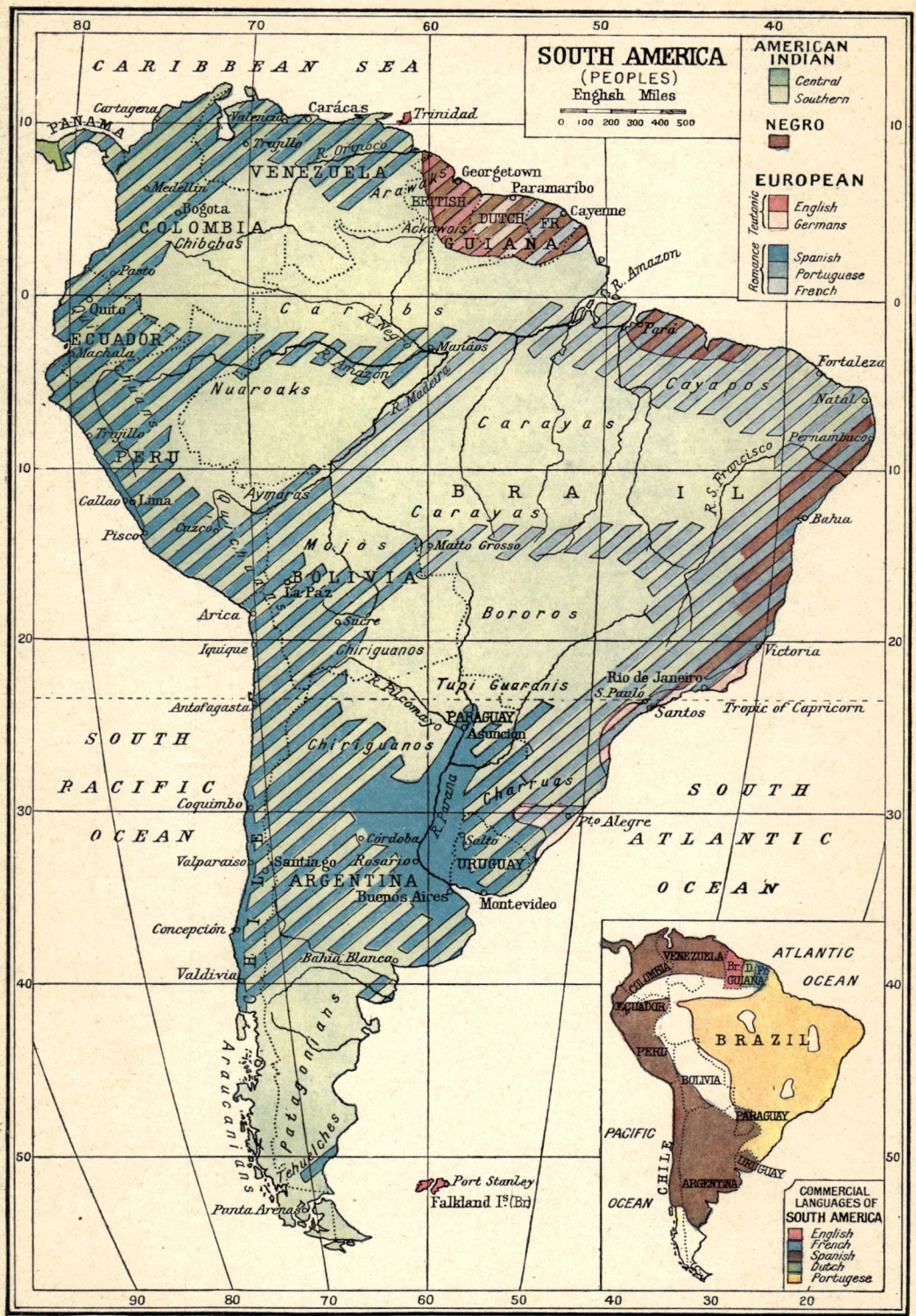

SOUTH AMERICA
(PEOPLES)
English Miles

0 100 200 300 400 500

AMERICAN INDIAN
- Central
- Southern

NEGRO

EUROPEAN

Teutonic
- English
- Germans

Romance
- Spanish
- Portuguese
- French

CARIBBEAN SEA

PANAMA

Cartagena
Carácas
Trinidad
Valencia
Medellin
Trujillo
Bogota
R. Orinoco
VENEZUELA
Arawáks
Georgetown
Paramaribo
Cayenne
COLOMBIA
Chibchas
BRITISH
DUTCH FR.
GUIANA
Pasto
Ackawois
R. Negro
Quito
ECUADOR
Caribs
R. Amazon
Machala
Manáos
Pará
Fortaleza
Nuaroaks
Amazón
Natal
Cayapos
R. Madeira
Carayas
Trujillo
PERU
Pernambuco
R. S. Francisco
Aymarás
Carayas
Callao
Lima
BRAZIL
Cuzco
Quechuas
Pisco
Mojos
Bahia
Matto Grosso
BOLIVIA
La Paz
Arica
Sucre
Bororos
Iquique
Chiriguanos
Victoria
R. Pilcomayo
Tupi Guaranis
Rio de Janeiro
Antofagasta
S. Pavlo
Tropic of Capricorn
PARAGUAY
Santos
Asunción
Chiriguanos
R. Parana
Charruas
SOUTH
Coquimbo
PACIFIC
Córdoba
Salto
Pto Alegre
OCEAN
Valparaiso
Santiago
Rosario
URUGUAY
SOUTH
Concepción
ARGENTINA
Buenos Aires
Montevideo
ATLANTIC
OCEAN
Valdivia
Bahia Blanca
Araucanians
Patagonians
Port Stanley
Falkland Is (Br)
Tehuelches
Punta Arenas

COMMERCIAL LANGUAGES OF SOUTH AMERICA
- English
- French
- Spanish
- Dutch
- Portugese

VENEZUELA
Br. D. Fr.
GUIANA
ATLANTIC
OCEAN
COLOMBIA
ECUADOR
BRAZIL
PERU
CHILE
BOLIVIA
PACIFIC
OCEAN
PARAGUAY
URUGUAY
ARGENTINA

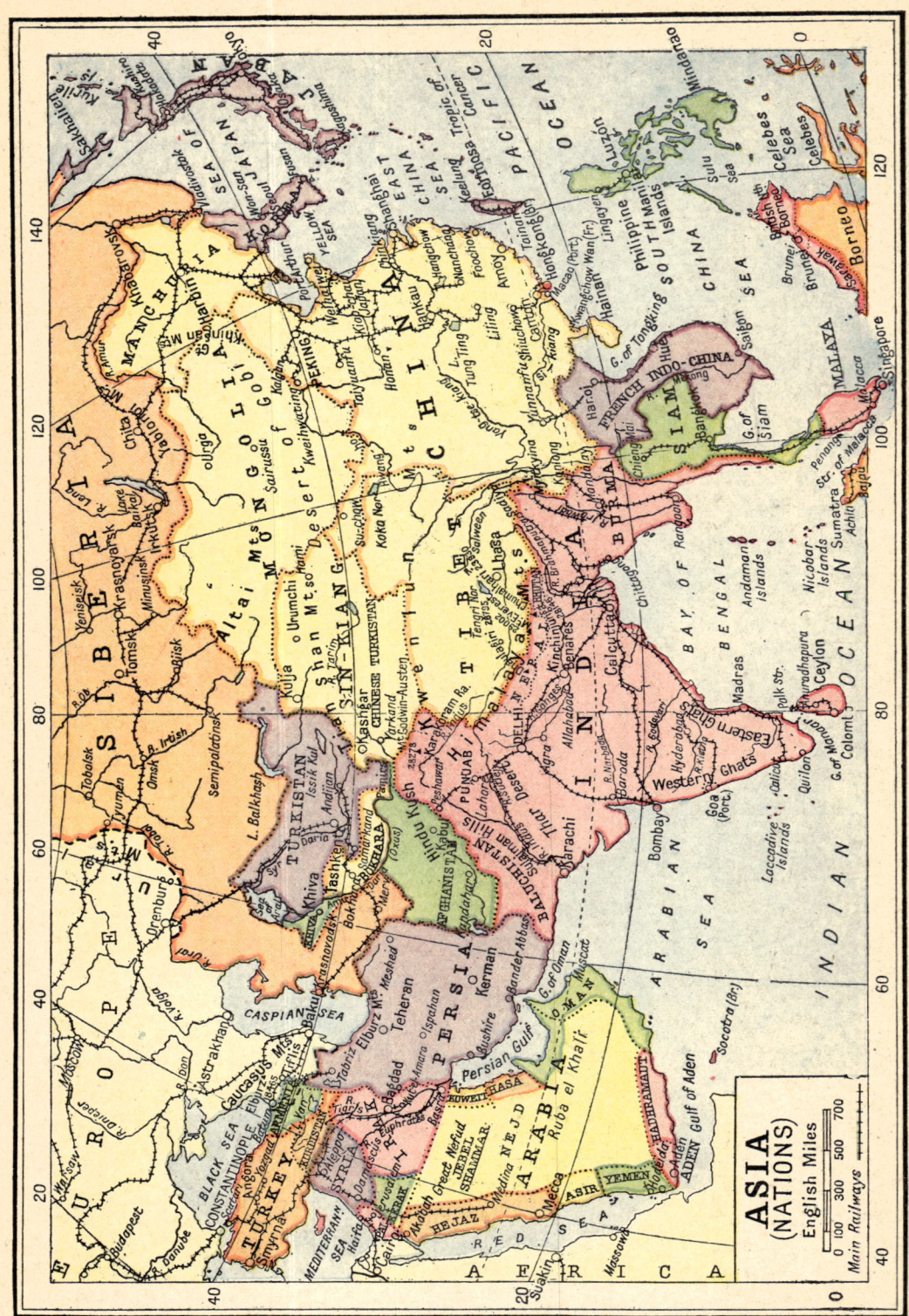

ASIA
(NATIONS)
English Miles

0 100 300 500 700

Main Railways

5386

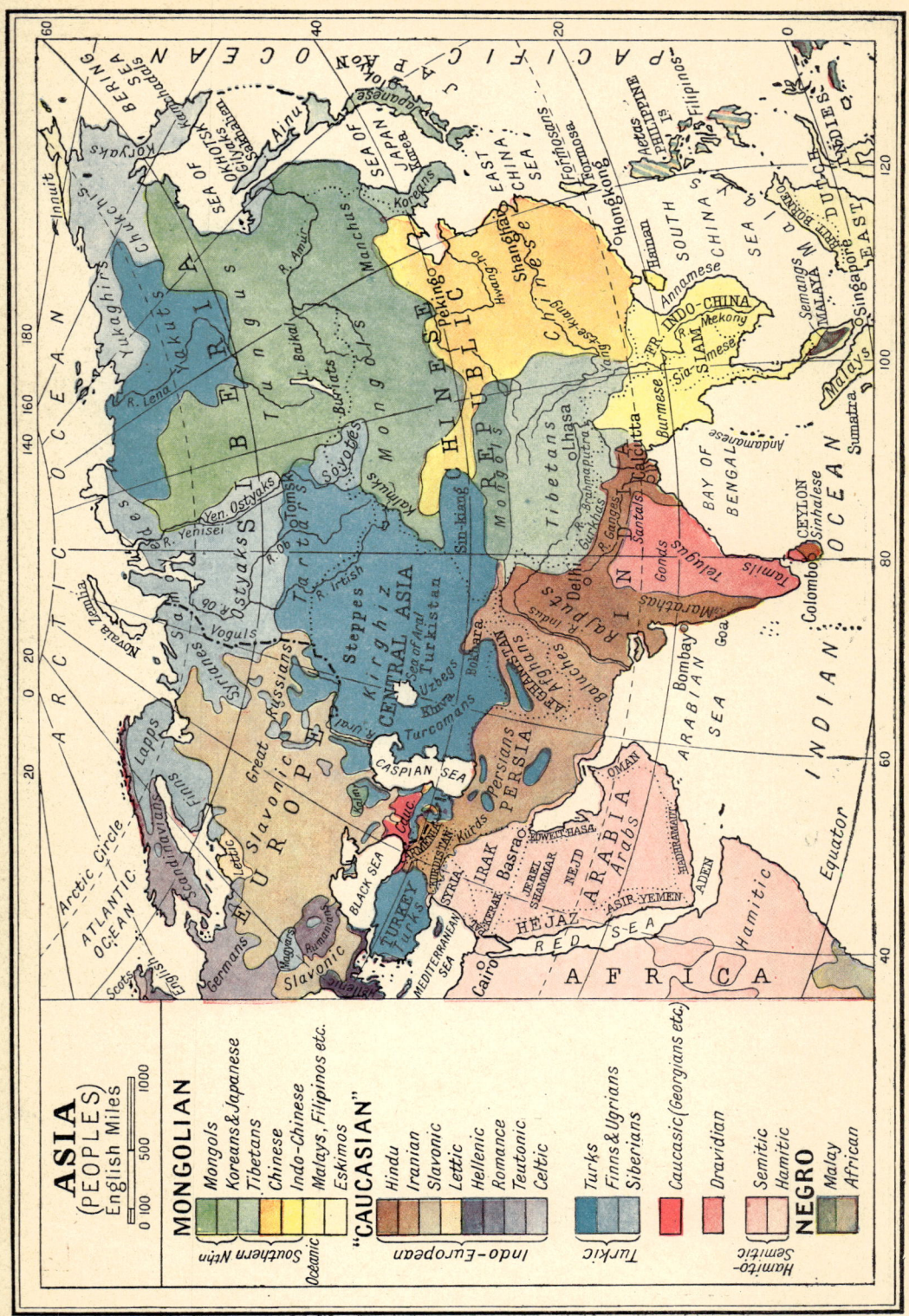

ASIA
(PEOPLES)
English Miles

0 100 500 1000

MONGOLIAN
Mongols
Koreans & Japanese
Tibetans
Chinese
Indo-Chinese
Malays, Filipinos etc.
Eskimos

Northern
Southern
Oceanic

"CAUCASIAN"
Hindu
Iranian
Slavonic
Lettic
Hellenic
Romance
Teutonic
Celtic

Indo-European

Turks
Finns & Ugrians
Siberians

Turkic

Caucasic (Georgians etc.)

Dravidian

Semitic
Hamitic

Hamito-
Semitic

NEGRO
Malay
African

5387

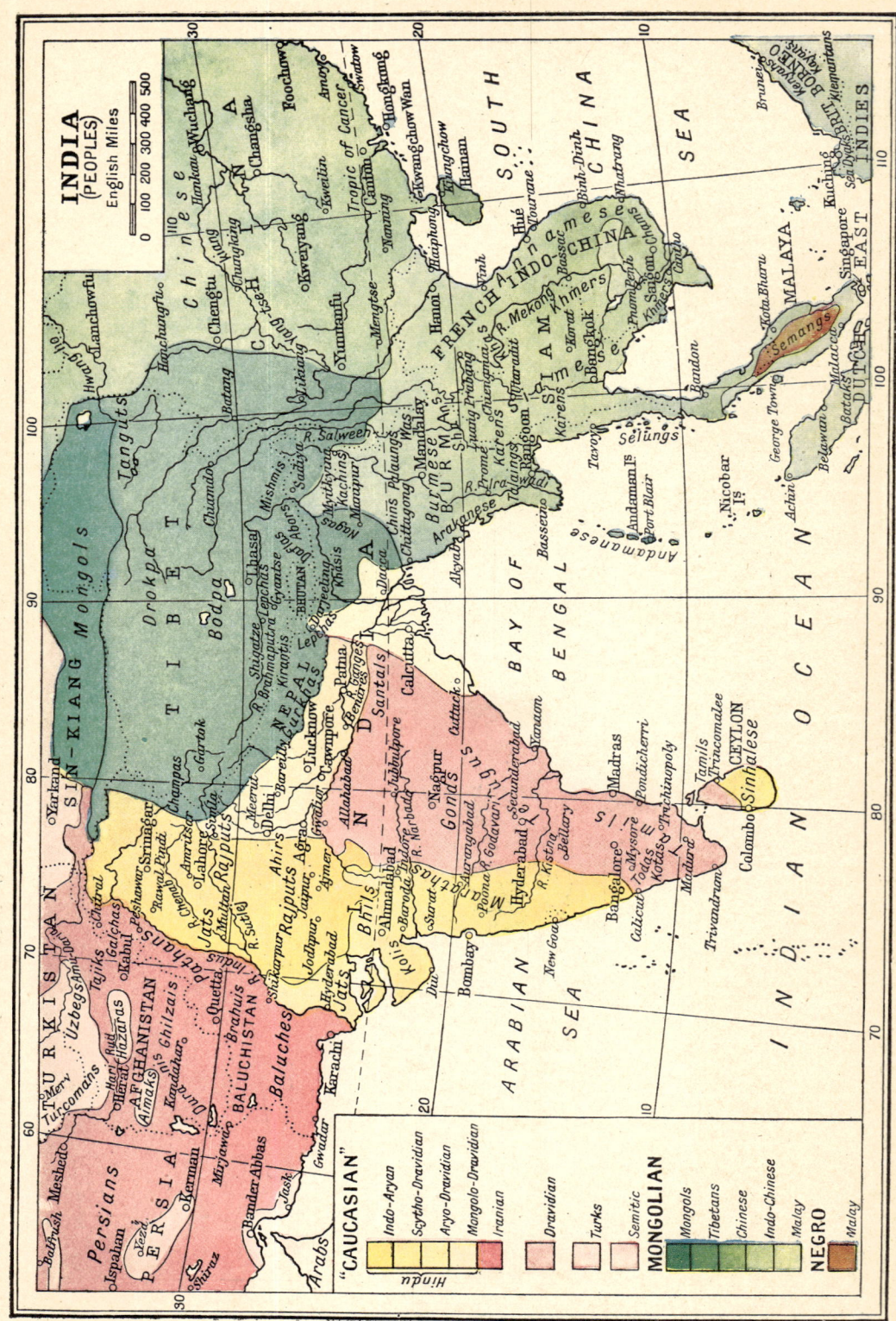

INDIA
(PEOPLES)

English Miles

0 100 200 300 400 500

"CAUCASIAN"

Indo-Aryan
Scytho-Dravidian
Aryo-Dravidian
Mongolo-Dravidian
Iranian

Dravidian

Turks

Semitic

MONGOLIAN

Mongols
Tibetans
Chinese
Indo-Chinese
Malay

NEGRO

Malay

Hindu

GENERAL INDEX

Specially Compiled by Monica Gillies

The appended general index to the seven volumes of PEOPLES OF ALL NATIONS *has been so planned as to afford instant reference to the pages in which every country, tribe, or race is to be found. Every subject is arranged under its specific heading, in alphabetical order. The reader specially interested in ethnography is advised to consult also the " Dictionary of Races," by Mr. Northcote Thomas, in pages 5327–5372.*

A

END OF VOLUME VII.